CONSUMER BEHAVIOUR

CONSUMER BEHAVIOUR

Isabelle Szmigin and Maria Piacentini

OXFORD
UNIVERSITY PRESS

OXFORD
UNIVERSITY PRESS

Great Clarendon Street, Oxford, OX2 6DP,
United Kingdom

Oxford University Press is a department of the University of Oxford.
It furthers the University's objective of excellence in research, scholarship,
and education by publishing worldwide. Oxford is a registered trade mark of
Oxford University Press in the UK and in certain other countries

Published in the United States of America by Oxford University Press
198 Madison Avenue, New York, NY 10016, United States of America

British Library Cataloguing in Publication Data

Data available

Library of Congress Control Number: 2014940869

ISBN 978-0-19-964644-9

Printed in Great Britain by
Bell & Bain Ltd., Glasgow

To Janusz, Alex, and Nick
To Bob, Sandro, and Rosa

CONTENTS IN BRIEF

CONTENTS IN FULL

PREFACE

Why consumer behaviour is important

All over the world people are consuming—every minute of every day, 365 days of the year. Countries as diverse as China, Russia, Brazil, and Sweden rely on consumption for their economic development and progress. In some countries people have little to consume and barely enough to survive from day to day while in other countries people are able to consume much more than they need, so much so that their health can be affected, particularly by the excessive consumption of food and alcohol or the choice of unhealthy or even illegal substances. So, while understanding consumer behaviour is at the heart of economic development and business, and particularly marketing, it also produces some concerns. In this book we hope to give you a broad understanding of consumer behaviour—both its benefits and some of its problems. However, above all we hope to show how consumer behaviour is at the heart of marketing.

For students of business, and especially marketing, consumer behaviour is a critical area that practitioners need to know about. Central to the marketing concept is the need for organizations to understand the factors that shape and influence people's behaviour in different environments. Marketers have to recognize and appreciate how consumers respond to the various aspects of their offerings. This implies that business needs a solid grasp of consumer behaviour in many different settings and contexts, which means thinking about all types of individual consumers, including different age groups and different social and cultural settings. We require a knowledge of how the individual makes decisions and how the market 'makes' decisions. We take a global perspective in this book by ensuring the inclusion of examples and cases from a range of countries, including China, India, Mexico, Japan, Korea, Australia, Germany, Austria, the Netherlands, and the UK. We also play close attention to trends and developments in technology and social media and how organizations use these as they interact with consumers. Current research is also incorporated, including sustained treatment and inclusion of studies from consumer culture theory.

The framework for our book is logical and developmental. Our model (Figure P.1) begins from the inner circle with Part 1, which comprises two chapters that look at the *historical and contemporary context* of consumer behaviour. In Chapter 1 we ask the question: how did we arrive here? We do this in terms of the role that consumer behaviour now plays in business. In particular, we consider the disciplines and changes in marketing that led to the development of consumer behaviour as a discipline that is so important to business and marketing. In Chapter 2 we move on to explore some contemporary trends in consumer behaviour. Part 2 consists of five chapters which we have termed the *micro-view*, and in this part we consider elements of the individual that impact consumption from the nature of

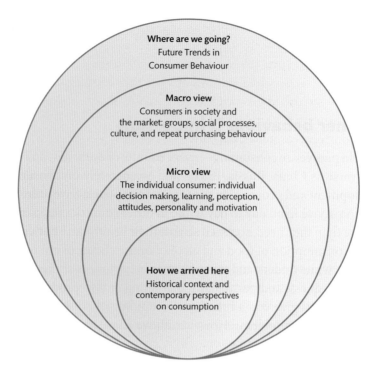

Where are we going?
Future Trends in
Consumer Behaviour

Macro view
Consumers in society and
the market: groups, social processes,
culture, and repeat purchasing behaviour

Micro view
The individual consumer: individual
decision making, learning, perception,
attitudes, personality and motivation

How we arrived here
Historical context and
contemporary perspectives
on consumption

Figure P.1   Organizing framework for how this book approaches consumer behaviour

their decision-making through to how their attitudes are developed and changed. Part 3 is entitled the *macro-view*. Here we look at consumers in a broader context, from how they operate in groups and as part of a culture to how they function as a whole within the marketplace, i.e. the impact of the decisions of thousands of consumers on the market. Part 4 consists of one chapter which considers *future trends* in consumer behaviour. This chapter is entitled 'Where are we going?'. Although this part contains only one chapter, it is a very important conclusion to the book as it looks at some of the current opportunities in terms of how we view consumers and the technologies that will impact on consumer behaviour today and in the near future.

In order to consider further why we study so many elements of consumption, let us consider just one product—coffee. The 1990s TV show *Friends* popularized the idea of the coffee shop as a place to hang out with friends, and many people share this view of coffee shops as a social space, as a place to get together with friends or even to meet new people through organized events. But did you know that coffee houses in the Ottoman Empire in the 1550s served a similar, perhaps more transgressive, function? At that time coffee houses provided an important meeting place for people to engage in a range of transgressive behaviours (such as gambling, taking drugs, discussions against the state) and were often banned by the state. Despite this, coffee houses survived and flourished, and their discourses often challenged the authority of the state and religion and led to changes in society. The first coffee houses in England appeared in the 1650s, and in 1675 Charles II tried to suppress them (unsuccessfully) because they had become such important centres for political discussion. Thus, both the Ottoman and the British coffee house culture could be said to represent an early example of consumer activism, which highlights how powerful one product can be! So here we have insights on coffee consumption, and consumption more generally, that come from historical reflection and understanding of consumers, and this is the kind of issue we explore in Part 1.

If we think of ourselves as individual coffee consumers, we might consider how we buy and prepare coffee ourselves. Companies are interested in the process of individual decision-making, from choosing which coffee shop to go to, to which size and combination of coffee and milk you choose on that day and in that shop. The influences that affect this decision-making (Chapters 3–7) can include many aspects related to the appearance of things, down to what tastes we prefer. So here we might think about the experience of going into coffee shops. The smells and sounds within the coffee shop assault our senses, and help us form an impression of the place and the coffee on sale. The noise of the coffee machines, the aroma of coffee beans roasting, the look and appearance of other consumers, the music being played, the crockery used, the coffee flavour itself—all these are perceived by us and combine to help us develop a preference for particular coffee brands. We learn what sizes and types of coffee are served at different places, and we may form attitudes to different coffee brands. Coffee companies also try to connect with their customers through various initiatives that help to form more personalized relations with them. In 2012, Starbucks brought the policy of writing customers' names on their cups to the UK. By writing your name on a cup, and creating a more customized experience (of what is actually a highly standardized offering), Starbucks aimed to build consumer loyalty by forming relationships with their customers. All these points show the importance of understanding the range of individual influences on consumption.

We have already mentioned some of the social elements of coffee consumption, and the social and cultural aspects of consumption that we deal with in Chapters 8 and 9 often influence our individual consumption choices. Thinking about culture and its impact on consumption, if we asked consumers from different cultures what coffee means to them, we would not only learn how coffee is viewed, but would also would gain some insights into what it is like to live in that culture. While French consumers may talk about espresso machines and smoky brasseries, and American consumers may think more about bookstores and large milky drinks, in Asian countries coffee is more likely to be routinely sold by street vendors and is an entirely different concoction, made with both condensed and evaporated milk, and often chilled in ice bags and drunk through a straw. And do you know where and when the 'flat white' was created? It was in Australia and New Zealand in the 1980s. These different approaches to coffee reflect the geographical and sociocultural aspects of different countries, and the role that consumption occupies within different cultures. But there is another aspect to the macro-view of coffee consumption. All businesses need to know how their consumers are choosing their product rather than the many others available to them. What does the whole market look like? How does the market share of

Caffe Nero compare with that of Costa or Starbucks? What is influencing our loyalty and how often do we switch between brands and why? This aspect of understanding consumers is covered in Chapter 10. You might like to consider for a moment how your own loyalty in buying coffee is influenced. Many of us own loyalty cards that we use in coffee shops, which are used by companies to encourage our repeat business. We might have these loyalty cards because we really do feel a positive emotional connection to the brand, which is great for that company. But at other times we use coffee shops for reasons not really down to our choice, but more through convenience and location—buying a coffee from whichever coffee outlet is available at the station we use to get to work. It makes sense to have a loyalty card for this, since we are repeat buyers, but it is not necessarily our favourite choice of coffee. And what about the future of coffee? Now you can make coffee in many different ways from powdered to filter to instant espresso machines. There are many different apps dedicated to coffee lovers. For example, Coffee Buzz lets you check into your favourite coffee shops and share what you are drinking, and Beanhunter finds the nearest coffee shops to your location.

As we can see from this analysis of coffee consumption, there are very many aspects impacting on what people are doing, and all have something useful and valuable to offer to organizations interested in knowing their consumers better.

In this book, we aim to show and explain the range of ways of thinking about and examining consumers. The latest issues in behavioural, psychological, and sociological approaches are presented alongside important techniques such as neuromarketing, and their application to marketing is discussed. There are many new trends, research, and discoveries occurring in such fields as economics and psychology, and new ways of understanding how and why people behave socially and culturally in a changing world, that are helping us to understand the factors that shape and influence people's behaviour in different environments. Many of these new approaches have been embraced by marketing practitioners, and in this book we provide various examples and illustrations of these theories being used in practice through our practitioner insights where we ask people actually involved with consumer behaviour what they think and do.

This book will take you through the key issues associated with developing a deep understanding of consumers, drawing insights from contemporary theory and marketing practice to ensure that you have a comprehensive appreciation of contemporary consumer behaviour.

How the book is organized

In Part 1, Chapters 1 and 2 provide an overview of the historical context for understanding consumption and also outline the different perspectives on consumption. Chapter 1 is important in providing a *historical perspective* on this subject, showing how our understanding of consumers has evolved and examining some of the debates around how we view consumers. In the second complementary chapter we consider *contemporary perspectives on consumption* that have had an impact on our understanding of how consumers are behaving in the twenty-first century and their importance for the theory and practice of consumer behaviour.

Part 2, comprising five chapters, provides a micro-view of consumption. Chapter 3, which focuses on *consumer decision-making* is the first of five chapters that look at the individual. We continue the focus on the individual in the following four chapters and take a closer look at some of the psychological aspects of consumption. Chapter 4 considers the processes of *learning*, the different approaches to learning theory, and how these impact on consumption decisions. Chapter 5 focuses on *perception* and the processes underpinning the ways that consumers perceive and absorb marketing messages. In Chapter 6 we consider *attitude formation and change*, discussing some of the ways that attitudes are used in practice by both marketers and policy-makers. In Chapter 7 we turn to *personality, self and identity, and motivation* and consider how these impact on consumption, and discuss the sociocultural aspects of identity.

Part 3, which comprises three chapters, provides a macro-view of consumption. In Chapters 8 and 9 we move on to consider important cultural and social influences on aspects of consumption. In Chapter 8, we look at specific *social groups*, and the processes within and across groups that may impact upon how people consume, while in Chapter 9 we consider *culture* and how this shapes consumption. Chapter 10 complements Chapter 3 in terms of considering decision-making, but rather than looking at the individual it considers the macro-aspects of decision making and what all the thousands of decisions made every day mean for companies. We consider actual purchasing behaviour mostly derived from large (often in the thousands) consumer panels and give close consideration to *patterns of repeat buying behaviour* and how this tells us what consumption actually looks like in the marketplace.

Part 4 focuses on where the field is going, and in the final chapter, Chapter 11, we consider the *future for consumer behaviour*, thinking about developments on the horizon and their implications for marketing practice.

How the book works

As discussed above, the book is in four parts and can be used in different ways depending on the structure of your consumer behaviour course (Figure P.2).

While we are suggesting above that one way to use this book is to move from Part One directly through to Part Four starting with the historical context and current perspectives through micro and then macro influences to future trends, reading the book in different ways will not hinder your understanding of consumer behaviour. An alternative approach is to follow the first two chapters, then Part 3 (the macro-view) and Part 2 (the micro-view). This approach will take you from the broadest aspects of understanding consumption to the specifics of individual behaviour and how this is observed in the market.

Each chapter is organized in line with this framework, and at the start of each chapter we show how this topic fits with our overall understanding of consumer behaviour. We have provided learning objectives at the beginning of each chapter to help you follow the material covered, and navigate you through the chapter.

One of the key aims of this book is to bring together leading thinking on consumers, alongside insights and examples from contemporary marketing practice. To do this, we have developed a set of 'insights' from research, marketing practice and consumer situations which run throughout the book.

We bring cutting-edge thinking to your understanding of consumer behaviour in every chapter by featuring *Research Insights*, which provide a flavour of the current big ideas in the field and some of the important historical research findings and hint at where things are going. These Research Insights draw on academic work from around the world, and provide a combination of classic studies and others recently published in major international journals, including those from consumer culture theory. We hope that you will be sufficiently interested and encouraged to go to the original sources to discover the full import of the Research Insight.

One of the best ways of explaining consumer behaviour theory is through examples, and in this book we provide many different types of examples to help you develop your understanding of consumers. Throughout each chapter many examples are integrated into the main text. Each chapter contains a number of *Consumer Insights*, which are mini-case examples, and include topics such as social networking in China, the US launch of Mariah Carey's perfume line aimed at young girls, the use of social media in the 2013 re-opening of the Rijksmuseum in Amsterdam, and attitudes towards breaking the speed limit among drivers in Australia. Additionally, every chapter includes an extended *Case Study* covering topics such as Pinterest, Havaianas, Oreos, lifestyle in India, and repertoire shopping in China, which bring together the themes discussed in the chapter, and help you to connect with the material.

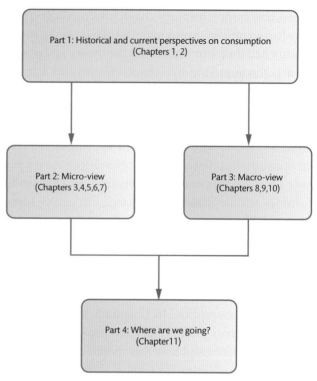

Figure P.2 Pathways for organizing your course using this book

To bring these theoretical approaches and ideas to life, every chapter contains *Practitioner Insights*, which are commentaries from marketing and advertising professionals who discuss consumer behaviour issues for their organization. Companies and organizations such as Renault, Dettol, Milward-Brown, Age UK, Thinkbox, and BrandSense all provide real-world views on the topics being discussed.

This book uses a variety of tools to help you understand consumer behaviour from a range of perspectives. We build on the traditional psychological approach to acknowledge more holistic perspectives of consumer behaviour and incorporate new areas of research, all of which are impacting on our understanding of this fascinating subject.

About this book (for lecturers and tutors)

The format and main features of this book have already been described. It is designed to be worked through systematically, over a period of 10 or 11 weeks. Each chapter is accompanied by PowerPoint presentations covering key aspects and including additional illustrations and animations that bring the concepts to life. As we have already discussed, while we have suggested a structure and approach moving from historical influences on consumer behaviour through the micro- and then macro-view, we do not feel that the book imposes this structure on any course and it will easily accommodate a range of course structures.

Each chapter contains *Review Questions* which students can use to check their base knowledge from the chapter. In addition, we provide a set of challenging *Discussion Questions* at the end of each chapter which can be incorporated into workshops. The Case Studies in each chapter are also intended for use in workshop/seminar settings, and solutions are provided as part of the tutor pack. Finally, there is a blog to accompany the book, where we provide commentary and insights on consumer behaviour issues and news on an ongoing basis.

GUIDED TOUR OF THE BOOK

Identifying and defining

Learning objectives

Clear, concise learning objectives begin each chapter and help to contextualise the chapter's main objectives. These are then revisited in the chapter conclusions. This feature can help you plan your revision to ensure you identify and cover all the key concepts.

Glossary of key terms

Key terms are highlighted in bold where they first appear in the chapter; these terms are then collated into a glossary at the end of the book. This provides an easy and practical way for you to revise and check your understanding of definitions.

Consumer behaviour in practice

Practitioner insights

Learn from the real-life experiences of people in business, advertising, and government to understand how they embrace new developments in marketing. Each practitioner insight focuses on a different aspect of consumer behaviour from neuroimaging and experiential marketing to the regulation of brand ambassadors. This feature helps you understand exactly how the theories and developments play an important role in key organizations.

Case studies

An extended case study, about companies such as Havaianas in Brazil and Pinterest and topics such as repertoire shopping in China and gym culture in the UK, is provided at the end of every chapter. This feature concludes with thought-provoking questions encouraging you to think about how developments in consumer behaviour theory impact organizations in practice.

LEARNING OBJECTIVES

Having read the chapter, you will be able to:

1. Identify key topics from behavioural economics and how they may impact behaviour.
2. Understand the theories and practices of *experiential consumption and culture theory*.
3. Understand *the role of technology* in influencing consumer behaviour.

Absolute threshold is the smallest amount of stimulation that can be picked up by any of our senses.

Acceptance/rejection when the consumer considers existing choice criteria and elaborates the message received to reach a point of acceptance or rejection of the information.

Acculturation relates to the idea of movement between places or cultural contexts.

Attitude object/act is the thing titude is held, and can include br people, and behaviours.

Attributes are the characteristi attitude object/act.

Attributions 'arise when one ev which the initial product perfor to one's level of aspiration vis-à-

---

PRACTITIONER INSIGHT 4

Rachel Hartley, Business Development & Marketing Director, Nutracheck

In 2005, Nutracheck developed the UK's first mobile phone program to track what you ate. Its latest barcode scanning app, together with the interactive food diary website, is designed to track your food intake and empower you with knowledge to make better choices to manage your diet for weight loss or maintenance.

Managing your diet is all about learning. Many people genuinely have no idea about the calorie content of foods and how many calories their body actually needs. Nutracheck has a food database (UK foods) of over 100,000 products. We also have the calorie content of foods that don't have nutritional labelling, such as coffee shops, alcoholic drinks, take-aways, and eating out places.

Nutracheck is an app with a dedicated website designed to help people track their calorie intake by keeping a food diary—either via the barcode scanning app or online. It is an educational tool to make people more aware of how their food choices contribute to their daily calorie allowance—and

---

CASE STUDY 4

Learning Brazilian

Most young people have heard of the Havaianas brand of flipflops. In this case study we consider the history of the brand and how we have learned what the brand stands for. While all consumers learn, this case illustrates that the brand has to ensure how they learn and that they learn the right things to ensure success.

What are the first things you think of when someone says Brazil to you?

Maybe you think of football, but then perhaps sunshine, beautiful bodies, having fun, bright colours and sunlight, beach life. And if you are on the beach you usually need a pair of flipflops. Flipflops are basically a piece of rubber with two straps. They are simple and practical, but one thing we can learn from Brazil is that even the simplest functional item can become a coveted brand. Over the last twenty years the Havaianas brand has been transformed from cheap footwear to the chosen footwear of catwalk models and film actors, as well as consumers all over the world.

The brand was developed in the late 1950s based on the Zori sandals worn by Japanese immigrants in Brazil. These were made from fabric straps and rice straw soles, and Havaianas have main-

Testing and applying understanding

Consumer insights

CONSUMER INSIGHT 4.1

Celebrity endorsers and classical conditioning

Celebrity endorsement is widely used in advertising (see Figure 4.3). The 'match-up' hypothesis (Till and Busler, 2000) suggests that celebrities are most useful when there is commonality between them and the product they are endorsing. So, while Rihanna would be an unlikely endorser of Halford's bikes, the Olympic gold medal winner Victoria Pendleton matches up with the product and brings credibility to the endorsement. Nike makes extensive use of celebrity endorsement across the world, for example the use of Liu Xiang, the Chinese Olympic hurdler, as an endorser of Nike to promote the spirit of Nike—'Nike: Find Your Greatness'.

In experimental studies Till et al. (2008) found support for the use of

Every chapter contains a number of consumer insights which explore issues such as celebrity endorsements, attitudes towards digital marketing, and social media. These mini-case examples are illustrated by well-known companies and organizations such as Lucozade in the UK, Phillips in Taiwan, Uniqlo in Singapore, and Abercrombie & Fitch in the US. They are accompanied by questions which encourage you to think critically about how consumer behaviour theory is applied in a variety of contexts.

Review questions

Review questions

1. Compare and differentiate low and high involvement decision-mak
2. Explain the difference between need and opportunity recognition.
3. Explain the difference between enduring involvement and situationa
4. Which methods would you consider for increasing involvement wi

There is a set of review questions at the end of every chapter, designed to test your knowledge of the key concepts in each chapter. Use them in your revision to ensure you understand the primary issues, theories, and developments.

Take your learning further

Research insights

RESEARCH INSIGHT 2.4

Cayla, J. and Arnould, E. (2013), 'Ethnographic stories for market learning', Jou July, 1-16.

This paper offers insights into the ways that companies use ethnographic appro of consumers' lives into the boardroom. Drawing on data from a consumer go cleaning products and a financial services company, the authors argue that ethn vide an important and valuable way of understanding the complexity of consu explore ethnography as a means to learn about and understand market contex

 Visit the Online Resource Centre to read the abstract and access the ful

A number of research insights are included in every chapter to encourage you to read around the topic discussed and learn more about the current big ideas in consumer behaviour and some of the most important historical research findings. These research insights draw on academic work from around the world, and provide a combination of classic studies and others recently published in major international journals, including those from consumer culture theory.

Discussion questions

Discussion questions

1. If you were producing a matrix of 'reference group influence on brand decisions', what products that are important to you would the four squares that reflect those reference groups. How do you thi vary if your parents or friends were doing this?
2. Identify situations where conformity with the group might affec al's behaviour. How might the situation impact on the product, s brands purchased?

Discussion questions can be found at the end of every chapter and are intended to help you develop your analytical and reasoning skills, encouraging debates.

GUIDED TOUR OF THE ONLINE RESOURCE CENTRE

The Online Resource Centre that accompanies this book provides students and registered adopters of the textbook with ready-to-use teaching and learning materials. These resources are free of charge and designed to maximize the learning experience.

Student resources

Web exercises
Arranged by chapter, the web exercises help you to undertake online research and enhance your understanding of key consumer behaviour concepts with a variety of exercises.

Multiple-choice questions
Interactive multiple-choice questions for every chapter give you instant feedback, as well as page references, to help you focus on the areas that need further study.

Flashcard glossary
Learning all the jargon related to consumer behaviour can be a challenge, so these online flashcards have been designed to help you understand and memorize the key terms used in the book.

Research Insight 1.1

Source: Samuel, L.R. (2010) *Freud on Madison Avenue*, University of Pennsylvania Press, Philadelphia, PA

Insight: By the 1950s, Freudian psychology had become the adman's most powerful new tool, promising to plumb the depths of shoppers' subconscious minds to access the irrational desires beneath their buying decisions. That the unconscious was the key to consumer behavior was a new idea in the field of advertising, and its impact was felt beyond the commercial realm.

Research insights

Follow the links to read the abstract and access the full paper of articles and books covered in the research insights.

Chapter 01

Birdseye:
http://www.birdseye.co.uk/

Hubwear (Flickr page):
https://www.flickr.com/photos/georgeaye/sets/72157594202610332/

Web links

Follow the web links to learn more about the companies and organizations covered in the book.

Lecturer resources

These resources are password protected, but access is available to adopters of the book.

Case 1: Supermarket responses to the recessionary consumer.

General points

The case is focused on shopping behaviour and consumption at a particular time i.e. after a recessionary period. But it may be useful to ask students to consider how they think shopping for groceries has changed generally in their lifetime. Are there different types of shops e.g. express stores, hypermarkets? How do we shop now e.g. self service checkouts, online, mobile and how has what we purchase changed – more or less ready meals, different types of foods etc? How we shop changes depending on the consumer, technology and culture (see Consumer Insight 1.3 Tesco Homeplus in South Korea which can be referred to in this context as well).

1. Consider the four types of recessionary shopper described. What particular needs might each type have?

Instructor's manual

The instructor's manual is a substantial and superior ready-to-use online package of supplementary teaching resources that provides you with:

- notes on the case studies in the book and guidance on how to use them in class;
- additional questions for seminars or for assessment with indicative answers, and;
- additional questions and discussion points on the practitioner insights in the book.

Seminar Activities

Chapter Reference

Chapter 1: A Historical Context for Understanding Consumption

Activity 1: Morning Consumption Choices

This activity introduces students to the prevalence of consumption and decisions around consumption that they make every day.

Learning activities

This feature includes a range of more detailed workshop-based activities, shorter lecture-based in-class exercises, and suggestions for assessment approaches.

Stages in consumption history

- Subsistence level consumption
- Sharing and bartering

PowerPoint slides

Accompanying each chapter is a suite of customizable and illustrated PowerPoint slides for you to use in your lectures.

Author blog

This blog will provide you with ideas and additional cases for discussion in seminars and lectures. Stay up to date with the latest developments, saving you time in searching for new examples to illustrate consumer behaviour theories.

ACKNOWLEDGEMENTS

Authors' acknowledgements

The authors would like to thank the practitioners who took time to talk about their work to illustrate how important the understanding and application of consumer behaviour is to marketing products and services: Lord Mitchell (House of Lords), David Jaime Hernandez (NPD Group), Simon Tunstill (Thinkbox), Rachel Hartley (Nutracheck), Frederique Hull (Dettol), Edward Langley (Ipsos), Graham Staplehurst (Millward Brown), Ian Douthwaite (Dubit Ltd), Roger Clough (Age UK Lancashire), Tom Lloyd (Metametrics), and Simon Harrop (BRANDsense). They also thank Professor Byron Sharp (Director of the Ehrenberg-Bass Institute for Marketing Science University of South Australia) for reading and commenting on Chapter 10, Lee Swinnerton (Lancaster University) for assisting with Case Study 8, and Dr Ahmad Daryanto (Lancaster University) for providing input on perceptual maps (Chapter 5).

The authors would like to thank the team at Oxford University Press for their support and guidance throughout this process. In particular, they thank Helen Cook and Nicola Hartley for their editorial assistance.

Isabelle Szmigin would like to thank students at the University of Birmingham and the Singapore Institute of Management for 'trying out' the text. She would also like to thank Andrea Solomons, Kate Goldrick, and Jane Robertson for their support and advice.

Maria Piacentini would like to thank her students at Lancaster University, who have provided valuable feedback on the exercises and material contained in this book. She also thanks Emma Banister, Katy Mason, and Imogen Tyler for professional support and advice through this process. She also thanks her husband Bob and children Sandro and Rosa for providing a welcome distraction from the book and offering so many thoughts and insights as twenty-first century consumers, and also for their tolerance in putting up with it all!

Publisher's acknowledgements

The publisher would like to thank the practitioners and professionals who gave their time to provide us with an insight into how consumer behaviour theories play an important role in the real world.

The publisher would also like to thank the very long list of people who kindly granted permission and supplied the images to illustrate this textbook: Kirklees Image Archive, George Aye, Bon Marché, Tesco Ltd., Canoe Inc., Waitrose, Bob Cromwell, Marie-Hélène Cingal, LazyTown Entertainment, John Cairns and the Department of Engineering Science at the University of Oxford, AB InBev, FreshMinds, Karina Minteer, Appleby Westward Group, Selfridges & Co., Dollar King, Whitbread PLC, United Biscuits, Boden, Eat Big Fish, Barry Doyon, Havaianas, the NSPCC, Costa Coffee, Zandera, Robert Opie and the Museum of Brands, Audi, Ogilvy & Mather, Nutcase Helmets, Paul Carrington, Honcho PR, Triodos Bank, Chillblast, Reckitt Benckiser, Oase Outdoors, Marks & Spencer, Microsoft, Springer, Jung von Matt, Millward Brown, Cartier, Casio, Zizzi, Nicoletta Reggio, Nike Inc., Volvo Cars, Ecover, Beattie McGuinness Bungay, Emma Poole, Gozogomo, Uniqlo, Argos, Leagas Delaney, Patek Phillipe, PETA, Unilever, Cognation, Atelier Opa, Argos, Sanrino, The Victoria Tea Room, Phillips Taiwan, Bettys & Taylors Group, INTAGE Inc., Nestlé, MyNetDiary Inc., ID&C Ltd, ING Nederland, Pocket-Lint, Buy Nothing Day, Transport for London, Jo Hodge, Martin Thuresson. Nest Labs Inc., and Hiut Denim.

PART 1

HISTORICAL AND CURRENT PERSPECTIVES ON CONSUMPTION

Where are we going?

Future Trends in Consumer Behaviour

Macro-view

Consumers in society and the market: groups, social processes, culture and repeat purchasing behaviour

Micro-view

The individual consumer: Individual decision making, learning, perception, attitudes, personality and motivation

How we arrived here

Historical context and contemporary perspectives on consumption

1

A HISTORICAL CONTEXT FOR UNDERSTANDING CONSUMPTION

Introduction

Consumption is a core part of our everyday lives. From the minute we wake up we are confronted with situations that have some element of consumption to them. Just getting ready to go to a college or university class in the morning, you face many consumer decisions: What to eat for breakfast? Which clothes to wear? What fragrance to put on? Which form of transport to use? What music to listen to (and in what form)? Which books to take, and in which bag? These are just *some* of the consumption-related decisions consumers have to think about, and most of these take place within 30 minutes of getting up!

Marketing practitioners and policy-makers need to understand consumer behaviour. Central to the marketing concept is the need for organizations to recognize the factors that shape and influence people's behaviour in different environments. The cultures of those of us living in affluent societies are influenced by consumption. We shop, consume, and compare ourselves with others through the products and brands we use. What food we eat and how much exercise we take may have a long-term impact on our health and well-being, which is also of importance to government and policy-makers. Businesses want to understand how and why consumers shop and consume in the ways they do both to develop products and to effectively communicate with customers. Arnould et al. (2002: 5) describe consumption as 'individuals or groups acquiring, using and disposing of products, services, ideas or experiences'. But to gain a solid appreciation of consumer behaviour, it is important to look to the past to understand how people thought about and practised consumption, and to think about how this has moulded the ways we consume today.

LEARNING OUTCOMES

Having read this chapter, you will be able to:

1. Understand the **early history of consumption** and the role of economics and philosophy in the development of consumer behaviour.

2. Understand **how consumption became a part of everyday life**, including the rise of conspicuous consumption.

3. Recognize the **key trends in the development of shops and shopping,** as well as the rise of **motivational research**.

4. Understand the role of **consumerism** in the development of consumption.

5. Learn how **consumers can be classified** and identify types of consumers.

6. Explain what a **postmodern consumer** is.

7. Understand the **different approaches to studying consumers**.

An early history of consumers and consumption

Hundreds of years ago most people would have produced their own food and clothing, primarily concerned with sourcing what they needed to survive. They had no opportunity to make choices between alternative products or brands, partly because there was so little to choose from and because few would be living above subsistence level. If surplus was produced, then it may have been exchanged for other goods. This contrasts sharply with contemporary living, and while much of our thinking around consumption is based on consumers living in developed and relatively affluent countries, it is important to remember that in many parts of the world subsistence level consumption still exists. In Tanzania, for example, many people farm small plots of land which provide most of their food and engage in alternative forms of economic exchange to meet their various day-to-day needs (Figure 1.1).

In medieval times there were traditional patterns of exchange through sharing and bartering, often within a fixed geographical location such as a village. Once goods are being made specifically to be bought and consumed by others, we begin to see one of the most important aspects of marketing: the relationship between production and consumption. Companies produce goods and services for people to buy; in order to buy, consumers have to see value in these goods and services, so that they are prepared to exchange money for them. We shall discuss some of the issues that have arisen from the development of the process of exchange later in this chapter when we consider Karl Marx's views on the relationship between production and consumption.

Figure 1.1   Subsistence farming in Tanzania
Source: © iStock.com/nwbob.

Historians and economists debate over when consumption, and hence consumer behaviour, became a feature of society (Benson, 1994; Stearns, 2001). Early accounts prioritized production over consumption, but consumption has clearly been a feature of human society and culture since the earliest times. The growth of trade, and more latterly globalization, has been a key element in the development of consumption beyond subsistence. Spices were one of the earliest traded goods and were highly valuable; for example, nutmeg was worth more by weight than gold (Szczepanski, 2013). This trade dates back to before Roman times, but it became highly significant across Europe and Asia in the medieval period. In the late Middle Ages the wealthy developed a taste for sugar, which led to an increase in production, with sugar plantations established in European colonies.

Products such as sugar were the privilege of the elite, and their widespread consumption did not begin to pick up until the rise of the urban middle classes in western Europe. This idea of a middle class of society purchasing consumer goods only emerged in the late nineteenth century (Loftus, 2011), although the term 'middle class' was first used in the eighteenth century. Those able to afford such goods before this time were primarily members of the aristocracy. In aristocratic circles, consumption was a required and visible part of daily life. For example, in the court of the French King Louis XIV (1638–1715) there was a social code that required discretionary spending on frivolous items such as silverware, jewellery, and handkerchiefs (Kroen, 2004). The Elizabethans also recognized some 'must-have' fashion items. As Neil MacGregor (2012), the Director of the British Museum, notes, the man of fashion needed his rapier and dagger just as today he would want his watch or trainers. Courtiers had to conform to social norms which required spending large amounts of money on fashions dictated by the monarch (see Figure 1.2).

Figure 1.2   Portrait of King Louis XIV
Source: © iStock.com/hrstklnkr.
Original painted by Hyacinthe Rigaud (1701).

Recent historical accounts have challenged the view that most consumption of luxury goods was restricted to the elites. New evidence suggests that the consumption of goods such as tea and coffee (and the utensils required for their consumption) grew rapidly throughout the eighteenth century and was on a scale that suggests widespread consumption (McCants, 2007). Not only was consumption extensive, but it also proved a key stimulant of the Industrial Revolution, and therefore, arguably, the rise of contemporary mass consumerism, as local attempts at producing exotic goods multiplied. Associated with this revision has been an emphasis on the global aspects of consumption, with an increased understanding of the role of trade with Asia, a source of many of the groceries and manufactured goods consumed at this time.

As the rate of consumption grew, so did its critics. Historically, the rise in consumerism has been accompanied by the development of various critiques of consumption attitudes and behaviour, from early Christian and Judaic asceticism through Puritanism to present-day ideas around anti-consumption and voluntary simplicity. Some of these ideas have been enshrined in law. An interesting aspect of early consumption was the development of **sumptuary laws**, which are laws that attempt to '*regulate expenditure, especially with a view to restraining excess in food, dress, equipage, etc.*' (*Oxford English Dictionary*, 2013).

Throughout history, sumptuary laws have played a role in many countries as a way of regulating people's expenditure and curbing conspicuous consumption. For example, sumptuary laws in China can be traced back to the Qin dynasty (221BC), embodying the Confucian virtue of restraint. In medieval England, sumptuary laws were important for distinguishing ranks within society, with an emphasis on the clothing that different social groups could or could not wear, thus reinforcing social hierarchies. For example, knights were not allowed to wear gold or ermine (Berry, 1994). In renaissance Italy, sumptuary laws focused on women's clothing, restricting the wearing of low necklines and jewelled sable furs as accessories (Killerby, 2002). These laws are a manifestation of an important theme found in many studies of consumer behaviour that centre around the idea of the 'right' or 'best' way to consume. Today, while some people are accused of excessive, wasteful, or conspicuous consumption, others are concerned about ethical consumption and the impact that their behaviour has on the environment and on people living in socio-politically oppressive regimes. Throughout the history of consumption we see this juxtaposition of conspicuous or inappropriate consumption against more considered or thoughtful ways to consume. We begin to see some of these concerns expressed in the work of the Scottish economist Adam Smith, which we discuss in the next section.

Economists, philosophers, and consumption

Adam Smith's *Wealth of Nations*, first published in 1776, is credited with first articulating the relationship between consumption, production, and democracy that has been central to the concept of the consumer in the twentieth and twenty-first centuries (Kroen, 2004). Smith lived at a time when the priorities of economists lay largely in issues around production. However, he began to look for the connections between consumption and production, writing that 'Consumption is the sole end and purpose of all production; and the interest of the producer ought to be attended to, only in so far as it may be necessary for promoting that of the consumer' (Smith 1776/1981: 660). Smith was very concerned that justice and some degree of fair distribution of wealth were assured. He was particularly anxious that labourers with little education and many physical needs would always be at a disadvantage in the marketplace as they did not have the resources to better themselves. We shall see concern for the disadvantaged consumer again when we look at 'types' of consumer later in this chapter. In this quotation we also see one of the first discussions of the relationship between production and consumption. In this case Smith made it clear that producers had a responsibility to their consumers.

In the *Wealth of Nations*, Smith recognized that consumption could help to stimulate an economy. While he suggested that consumption be restricted to promoting economic growth, he also believed that luxury consumption could prevent stagnation. Luxury consumption was a concern of another philosopher and economist, John Stuart Mill, who criticized the purchase of luxuries such as gold, lace, pineapples, and champagne as 'unproductive' consumption (Mill, 1848/2004). Such unproductive consumers were placed in opposition to the productive ones whose consumption helped the working man, who in turn would buy necessities which would further assist working people. Today, consumption is more complex. We may recognize that some goods such as branded trainers are not essential for children, but we are also aware that without the appropriate clothing they may be victimized or feel inferior in some way to their peers at school (Elliott and Leonard, 2004).

In the nineteenth century, Karl Marx was concerned that people did not recognize the value of the commodities they consumed (Marx, 1867/2000). For Marx, a commodity was primarily a product of labour. Wood cannot become a table unless it has been turned into a useful object through the process of someone working on the wood. As workers moved into factories, rather than producing goods at home or locally, they had no control of how much they were able to sell their labour for and so were open to exploitation from the rich factory owners who controlled their employment. Consider today the people who make cheap clothes for high street shops; they too have no control over how much their labour is worth to the factory owners or to us, the end consumers.

Value is a hard idea to pin down, so consequently there are a number of different conceptions of it. A common concept of value for a good or service is **exchange value**, which in most circumstances is the same as the market price. Exchange value can be said to represent what the value of a good is to the consumer and therefore what it could be exchanged for, usually its price. Therefore we expect uniform exchanges in shops—we expect the same T-shirt to be priced consistently. In a competitive market, the price balances the maximum consumers will pay against the minimum suppliers will take, so exchange value is critical in how markets function. **Use value** is another notion of value that adds a further dimension. It means the satisfaction we get from a good or service, which is usually thought of as being determined by a set of attributes that define its quality (e.g. for a car this might include fuel economy, performance and boot space). **Use** value can be described as *the value of a good to the consumer in terms of the usefulness it provides.* Use value is necessary for exchange value, but can be above it or below it for an individual buyer or seller. Most home-owners do not have their house on the market; its use value to them is higher than its exchange value. You might decide not to buy a jacket because it is too expensive, meaning that the exchange value is higher than its use value to you. These traditional economic concepts treat the consumer as self-contained, unconcerned about how others view them. Today, however, we also talk about **the sign or symbolic value** which is *the symbolic meaning consumers attach to goods to construct and participate in the social world*; in doing so they consume the idea of the good to signal identity in social relationships. This can turn the traditional categories on their heads, so that a higher price signals that a good is exclusive and may make purchase attractive even if in traditional functional terms its use value may be similar to an alternative that is cheaper or has a lower exchange value. Purchase can be important because it sends a social message about how you want to be seen in society.

Imagine the actual cost of making a handbag compared with the price for which it can be sold in a designer store, such as Prada or Gucci. The *exchange value* of that handbag does not represent its *use value*, because the function could just as easily be provided by a much cheaper alternative. However, the *sign value* of such a handbag is probably higher for those who purchase them than either the exchange value or the use value. Of course, for most of us today these are difficult concepts to grapple with, as many of the objects we consume are defined by their sign or symbolic value more than their use value. Although Marx lived at a time before the proliferation of designer handbags, he recognized that once goods had lost the link with their nature of production and their use value, they took on a mysterious quality that he termed the **fetishism of commodities** (Marx, 1876/1976) which can be described as '*the disguising or masking of commodities whereby the appearance of goods hides the story of those who made them and how they made them*' (Lury, 1999: 42).

During the First World War, rationing of consumption became a reality; consumption was restricted not only by the scarcity of goods but also by government actions such as wage restraints, tariffs, and 'buy national' campaigns (de Grazia, 2005). After the war, the British liberal economist Maynard Keynes began to consider how wages could be increased to aid people's purchasing power. Keynes recommended that the British government find ways to increase consumption as a means to economic recovery and developed the concept of the **consumption function** which *maps the relationship between disposable income and level of wages*. In particular, it showed that the rich saved proportionately more of their income and therefore consumed relatively less than the remainder of the population. Therefore it was necessary to find ways to encourage the rich to spend or invest their savings in the production of goods to be consumed.

These traditional concerns shadowing the relationship between production and consumption still continue today. In the wake of the global financial crisis, there is a concern that reduced buying is holding back world economic recovery. Consumers have been encouraged to spend to ensure continuing production during these recessionary times as a means of aiding fiscal recovery.

Consumption becomes part of everyday life

The first half of the nineteenth century saw a major economic transformation. The Industrial Revolution of the eighteenth century led to the increased production of goods and to forms of manufacture that produced more goods quickly, which meant that prices dropped and more people could purchase them. At the same time, the marketing environment began to develop with improved forms of distribution, retailing, and advertising.

Before the Industrial Revolution much production and consumption had been through cottage industries, small-scale farming, bartering, and buying from neighbours, at fairs, and from hawkers or others who travelled the country selling door to door. Markets were the most formal site for buying and selling. Shops were barely recognizable in the medieval period. They had no glass windows, but were open during the day, often with a simple stall outside, and protected with shutters at night. More recognizable shops began to appear in the seventeenth century, and spread in the eighteenth century with the development of new methods of producing glass. The first shopping mall or gallery, the Royal Exchange Shopping Gallery, appeared in the UK in 1568; the still thriving London store, Fortnum and Mason, was founded in 1707. Accompanying these developments were new approaches to marketing. Goods could now be displayed in shop windows to entice customers into shops to purchase. Advertising began to develop, and the first shopping arcades appeared in the late eighteenth century in Paris.

Figure 1.3   A Victorian grocer's shop

Source: Image courtesy of Kirklees Image Archive (www.kirkleesimages.org.uk.)

The types of products sold also changed. Industrialization and early global trading provided a hugely expanded range of goods. Manufacturers and shop owners realized they could persuade people to buy more than they needed. For example, new fashions in clothing could be introduced to ensure that people bought items regularly. Department stores became the place to shop in urban areas, and mail-order companies emerged as a way to transport a wider range of goods to rural consumers.

The increase in the range and nature of products was influenced by industrial innovations in all aspects of human life. Some of these were in materials such as plastic, which was introduced around the middle of the nineteenth century, and artificial fibres such as rayon, nylon, and viscose. These gave expanded possibilities for the design and manufacture of consumer goods. Transport was the site of successive waves of innovation, from steam to air travel, with the car in particular proving a consumer success on a massive scale. Household appliances multiplied, and food and cooking was revolutionized by inventions such as canning and freezing (see Consumer Insight 1.1). More recently, technological innovations in electronic products have meant that computers have become increasingly small but with more capacity. But perhaps more importantly computers, mobile phones, and the internet have built a new need among consumers to be continually connected with one another—friends, family, and places of work—and in turn this has led to different modes of working, shopping, and keeping in touch with people on a 24 hour, 7 days a week basis.

CONSUMER INSIGHT 1.1

How innovation changed the way we eat and live

Most of us have at least some convenience food in our diets. Innovations such as canned food were introduced to Britain after the First World War, and frozen foods, introduced in the USA in the 1920s by Clarence Birdseye, meant that storing food became much easier. By 1961 over 60 Birds Eye products, including fish fingers, were available to UK consumers (Hardyment, 1995). Such innovations meant that many people had a better and greater variety of food. It also meant that women did not have to spend so much time at home cooking, and working outside the home increased. In 1900 only 21 per cent of American women worked outside the home; by 1999 this had increased to 60 per cent, and so innovations such as the microwave were invaluable but also changed how people ate. Convenience meals could be heated quickly, and different members of the family could easily cook their meals at any time of the day. In 1989 fewer than 20 per cent of the French population had microwaves at home, but by 1995 over half did (Fernandez-Armesto, 2001). In the 1980s India saw the introduction of convenience brands such as Maggi instant noodles which offered mothers convenience and children fun and novelty. However, there are critics of the increase in convenience food; Nestlé (2003: 20) comments: 'Many food products relegate cooking to a low-priority chore and encourage trends toward one-dish meals, fewer side dishes, fewer ingredients, larger portions to create leftovers, almost nothing cooked "from scratch", and home-delivered meals ordered by phone, fax, or internet'.

Questions

1. Outline the main advantages of convenience foods.

2. What do you think have been the main societal impacts of convenience food?

3. Take another product class, such as books or cars, and consider how changes that you have seen have impacted on how we use them.

Sources: Hardyment (1995); Fernandez-Armesto (2001); Nestlé (2003).

 Visit the Online Resource Centre and follow the weblinks to learn more.

While product innovation has meant that consumers have more and better products to choose from, it has also led to what is often termed planned or built-in obsolescence, where a product has a limited life span and is regularly replaced with new versions. Early car-makers were concerned with producing standardized and durable cars, but by the 1920s and 1930s they were introducing regular (often annual) model changes. Often just superficial changes to the appearance of the car, they were designed to encourage people to feel that their car was out of date and needed replacing. This practice is now common in consumer behaviour; we regularly update our wardrobes, mobile phones, computers, and furnishings long before they no longer work or are worn out. So today many of us are not only able to buy more types of goods, but we buy the same item many more times than previous generations.

Conspicuous consumption

American economist Thorstein Veblen introduced the idea of 'conspicuous consumption', where goods represented a way to compete and gain social recognition, in his book *Theory of the Leisure Class*' (Veblen, 1899/2007). Veblen was concerned with the very wealthy and how they consumed and compared themselves with one another through their mansions, furnishings, carriages, and clothes. The possession of goods signified esteem; without them an individual was no-one. An important aspect of Veblen's analysis of this leisure class was their ability to be extravagant and wasteful; they could pay huge amounts of money for clothes that they would rarely wear or food that they would not consume. Today we are encouraged not to be wasteful, and the waste that consumer society produces has itself caused huge problems in landfill sites and impact on the environment. It might be that some people in countries where there is serious poverty and people are malnourished would see western society as a modern day equivalent of Veblen's leisure class. Also, consumers in former Eastern Bloc countries, developing countries, and other former communist countries, are playing catch-up in order to experience the pleasure and novelty of being able to consume in the way that the west has done for so long. It may be difficult for such people to hear others exhort them not to consume excessively when so many of us have been able to do so for so long.

CONSUMER INSIGHT 1.2

Needs versus wants

Alain de Botton, in his book *Status Anxiety* (de Botton, 2005), uses Veblen (1899/2007) as a starting point for considering what material goods are necessary for happiness. Today, many people are concerned not only about the goods they possess but also about whether they are the 'right' products and brands. Trendwatching.com (2010) describes five features of the 'Statusphere', the term used to describe the diverse ways that consumers are finding to express their status in the twenty-first century. These include things such as showing one's green consumption credentials or having knowledge and skills as ways of displaying status. Just as traditional luxury symbols still signify status (as illustrated

by the 112 per cent growth of Mercedes car sales in China in the first quarter of 2010), so too is it important to show that you have relevant consumer knowledge and skills, facilitated greatly by technology and the use of apps by consumers, which puts them 'in the know'. Beck's Gig Finder app helps users to find local music gigs, and its map and GPS interface allow people to see how close they are to the gig. Similarly, the Adidas Urban Art guide is a travel guide for Berlin and Hamburg's best graffiti where users can retrieve images and information about artists. Some goods can provide understated status, such as Hubwear's customized T-shirts that show the airport codes of the wearer's memorable trips. While to those not in the know this may just look like a T-shirt with a series of letters, to the wearer it is truly meaningful. Can you work out the two destinations in Figure 1.4?

Figure 1.4 A Hubwear T-shirt

Source: Image courtesy of George Aye at Hubwear (www.hubwear.com).

Questions

1. Think of ways in which people might use products or services to signify their status. How do you think that this differs by culture and age?

2. Can you think of any items that have been used for status but are no longer perceived in this way?

3. Trendwatching.com talks about 'unconsumption' as being a potential status tool. How do you think people would use this?

Sources: Veblen (1899/2007); de Botton (2005); www.hubwear.com; www.trendwatching.com

 Visit the Online Resource Centre and follow the weblinks to learn more.

Figure 1.5   Le Bon Marché in the nineteenth and twenty-first centuries
Source: Images courtesy of Le Bon Marché. Image to the right is copyright Gabriel de la Chapelle.

Key trends in the development of shopping

To satisfy people's desires for more and different goods, a greater variety of shopping sites began to appear in the nineteenth century. Le Bon Marché in Paris opened its doors in 1838. To begin with, it was just a mix of clothing stores grouped together a bit like a modern shopping mall, but by the 1850s it was recognizable as a modern department store. Gradually, items other than clothes were added—furniture, kitchen goods, and toys. The department store offered the consumer huge choice, with the opportunity to browse and look at items other than those they had intended to buy.

New ways to shop

Department stores developed ways of enticing consumers with sales and special promotions and exciting new window displays built around seasons and festivities such as Easter, Thanksgiving, and Christmas. Other famous department stores, such as Macy's in New York, and Harrods and Selfridges in London, opened soon after, with the department store concept spreading rapidly to other countries, such as El Corte Ingles in Spain, GUM in Russia, Edgars in South Africa, and METRO in Singapore. An important feature of department stores was that the customer became anonymous. Previously, in local shops and markets, the customers were known to the store or stall owner; in department stores they were not, and indeed the shop assistants were not encouraged to develop such relationships. Alongside the development of department stores other new ways of shopping were introduced. With a large rural population unable to get to department stores, catalogue shopping became particularly popular in the USA at the end of the nineteenth century. Through catalogues, department stores could be brought directly into their customers' homes. Today people still shop in department stores or from catalogues alongside new opportunities such as shopping on the web using their computer or mobile phone. What has changed is the variety of opportunities to shop, the variety of items available through such different channels, and that every part of the day is now available for shopping.

From service to self-service

While department stores had increased the personal distance between the customer and the retailer, this found its most extreme form in the development of the supermarket in the USA in the 1930s with the introduction of self-service. Customers were required to find what they wanted in the shop and place their shopping in a trolley which was able to carry more than the traditional basket, thus encouraging more purchasing. In her book *Carried Away*, Rachel Bowlby describes the effect of supermarkets as signalling the difference between 'doing the shopping' and 'going shopping': 'doing the shopping involves definite articles, a necessary task; going shopping is out of the way, open-ended, a diversion' (Bowlby, 2000: 32). This is an important point in the history of consumer behaviour as it signals that even grocery shopping no longer needed to be purely functional but could be something more akin to leisure. Impulse purchasing was encouraged by the supermarket, where a customer would see an item that they had not previously been aware of or thought that they needed and put it into their basket. The presence of goods and their apparent easy availability, such that the shopper could pick them up without having to ask an assistant, was an important feature and a major opportunity for retailers and producers in developing packaging and point-of-sale material. The suburban shopping mall as we recognize it today appeared after the Second World War and was designed to overcome customers' problems with parking and the weather. As more women were in the workforce people became time poor, and daily grocery shopping was replaced by weekly shopping facilitated by the car.

Today most western consumers have access to diverse shopping environments. High street shops, farmers markets, charity shops, shopping malls, express supermarkets, vending machines, and out-of-town supermarkets are all part of the shopping environment. Exam-ples of all these modes of shopping can be found across the world. Dubai, known for its mega-malls and shopping complexes, is beginning to develop a market for more individual and artisan food shops (such as Baker & Spice), and also recently held its first farmer's market, selling organic pro-duce sourced from the UAE region (Hirsch, 2013). Developments in vending machine technology have resulted in a vast range of foodstuffs being sold this way, including a live crab vending machine in China, a vend-ing machine selling bouquets of flowers in Japan (see Figure 1.6), and an egg, milk, and

Figure 1.6   A vending machine in Japan selling bouquets of flowers

Source: Image kindly supplied by Margy N. Javier.

cheese vending machine in Germany (Knutson, 2013). Increasingly technological advances are helping to innovate how we shop as highlighted in Consumer Insight 1.3.

CONSUMER INSIGHT 1.3

Tesco Homeplus in South Korea

Tesco's stores in South Korea are known as Homeplus. The brand was doing well but had fewer stores than its main competitor. Tesco's research found that weekly grocery shopping is an unwelcome task for South Koreans, so they decided to bring the store to the people. They created virtual stores, hoping to blend into people's everyday lives. They began with subway stations and, although virtual, the displays were exactly as you would see the goods in the shops (see Figure 1.7). The difference was that customers used their smartphones to shop. By scanning the QR code with their phone the product automatically appears in the customer's online cart. The goods are delivered rapidly after their arrival back at home. Customers like it because it is like 'real' shopping as you can see the goods you are purchasing and their waiting time at stations is changed to shopping time. Tesco increased its online market by 130 per cent and has now extended the virtual stores to selected bus stops across the country.

Figure 1.7   Shopping in the underground in South Korea
Source: Image courtesy of Tesco Stores Limited.

Tesco prides itself on being at the forefront of experimentation and innovation. Its online grocery store was introduced in the UK 12 years ago; today, customers can also use Mapster, an app allowing online customers to track delivery in real time.

Questions

1. What are the advantages and disadvantage of online grocery shopping for consumers?

2. What does this example tell you about how consumers want to shop in the twenty-first century and how might other retailers you are familiar with respond?

Sources: www.bbc.co.uk www.telegraph.co.uk

 Visit the Online Resource Centre and follow the weblinks to learn more.

One of the most recent phenomena in retailing has been pop-up shops, although 'pop-upping' (see www.Trendwatch.com) has also spread to pop-up food outlets and even pop-up brands. The first pop-up shops appeared in the late 1990s, but recent recessionary pressures have stimulated the pop-upping phenomenon with the increased availability of cheap retail space and the lack of capital to invest in longer-term projects. Pop-up stores offer consumers surprises, novelty, and something different, and because their life span is limited they introduce an element of urgency among consumers and, in the case of food outlets, almost a cult following. Mostly these are small-scale shops or food trucks that offer producers the opportunity to engage with customers without the capital cost of a restaurant or shop, but others are more sophisticated. The Icecreamists, a UK brand of ice cream, first opened as a pop-up shop for a limited period inside the prestigious department store Selfridges. The Icecreamists is positioned as a premium, X-rated, controversial brand with very unusual flavours. Fashion pop-up stores are also very popular, with examples including the Tribe Pop-Up Shop in Kenya, based at the boutique Tribe Hotel and showcasing the work of local designers (Lati, 2012), and the Love Story Pop-Up shop in Sydney, which sells designer clothes, typical of many fashion pop-ups.

In 2011, the first pop-up mall, Boxpark, appeared in London's East End (Figure 1.8). On a site which had been derelict for the previous 40 years, sixty recycled shipping containers form the shops which make up the mall. Boxpark offers small brands what the owner terms 'low-risk retailing' where they can sign up to stay for between one and five years, when the lease on the site will run out. Box Park has already become popular with locals and a tourist destination.

A similar logic underlies the way that big brands have taken to marketing products as limited editions, where they introduce a new product for a limited time to encourage a sense of urgency among their customers. Kit Kat introduced a number of limited edition Chunky bars including Double Choc, peanut, orange, and white chocolate flavours.

Figure 1.8   Pop-up shops in Boxpark, Shoreditch
Source: Image kindly supplied by Canoe Inc.

Consumers were encouraged to vote on Facebook for their favourite as only one of the flavours would survive.

Motivational research—from the rational to the emotional

After the First World War a divide in terms of consumption appeared between the USA and Europe. While in Europe the horse-drawn carriage was still a means of travel, in the USA the car was taking over the roads. The USA had embraced mass production which led to a virtuous circle of investment, production, and wealth creation, while providing more goods to more people at lower prices. As a country at the forefront of production and consumption, it was US companies that first embraced the latest thinking from Europe of Sigmund Freud, the Austrian founder of psychoanalysis, and his followers. They applied Freud's psychoanalytical research to help them understand why consumers did or did not buy their products (see Research Insight 1.1). When goods were scarce and few people had the money to buy more than what was necessary for their survival, there was no need to understand consumer psychology. Once mass production increased what was available, and consumers began to have disposable income, they were able to choose how to spend their money, and so businesses had to compete for buyers.

RESEARCH INSIGHT 1.1

Samuel, L.R. (2010) *Freud on Madison Avenue*, Philadelphia, PA: University of Pennsylvania Press.

In this book Samuel recounts how the work of Sigmund Freud and his followers influenced motivational researchers (particularly Ernst Dichter) and laid the foundations for much of today's current advertising and marketing techniques. He notes how Freud had recognized people's unconscious hidden desires that could be exploited by marketers, referring to Freud as a godsend to Madison Avenue.

 Visit the Online Resource Centre to access this ebook.

An important aspect of Freud's psychoanalytic research was that he suggested that people's behaviour was often determined by irrational and unconscious motives and by socialized inhibitions (Berlin, 2011). Freud believed that unconscious thoughts were as important as conscious ones. A number of researchers put Freud's ideas and influence into action, aiming to understand how and why consumers liked or did not like certain products and brands. If choice was determined by motives other than the purely conscious and rational, asking straightforward questions as to why you liked or did not like a product were unlikely to reveal the real reasons for behaviour.

In his book *The Hidden Persuaders* (Packard, 1957), Vance Packard describes how a brewery was trying to find out what kinds of people drank their two types of beer, a regular brew and a light version. The brewery asked people (whom it knew favoured the brand in general) whether they drank light or regular. They found that those saying they preferred the light beer outnumbered those saying they liked the regular beer by more than three to one. This was despite the fact that the brewery produced nine times more regular than light beer every year to satisfy demand. According to Packard, what appeared to be happening was that the company was effectively asking: 'Do you drink the kind preferred by people of refinement and discriminating taste, or do you just drink the regular stuff?' (Packard, 1957: 38). What marketers needed to do was to find a way of uncovering consumers' more subconscious desires that they were less able or willing to articulate.

The rise of motivational research

A key figure among the researchers who took Freud's ideas into the marketplace was Austrian-American psychologist Ernst Dichter, who in the 1930s developed so-called motivational research to help companies understand some of the more irrational motives for choice (see Research Insight 1.2). Motivational research will be discussed further in Chapter 7. Perhaps the most important characteristic of this period was the recognition of both the role of emotions in our choice decisions and that these decisions could not always be analysed or explained from a rational viewpoint. There are many examples of how

Figure 1.9 An advertisement for Camay showing bathing as an indulgence
Source: Image supplied by Heritage Images.

Dichter applied his theories to consumer behaviour. He often used 'in-depth interviews' to identify people's real motives for using certain products or choosing a particular brand. He found from such in-depth research that bathing could be seen as a ritual which allowed a woman a few moments of indulgence (see Figure 1.9). He also recognized that the choice of brand of soap did not necessarily depend on its price or even its smell, but rather on how the consumer perceived the personality of the soap. This in turn was dependent to some extent on the consumer's personality, such that the brand acted as a mirror or extension of them. As a result he was able to classify the personalities of soaps then on the market. One named Ivory was perceived as representing purity, while another named Camay was perceived as a seductress (Samuel, 2010).

RESEARCH INSIGHT 1.2

Dichter, E. (1947) 'Psychology in market research', *Harvard Business Review*, 432–443

In this paper Dichter was appealing primarily to the business community and explaining how motivational research could help them better understand their consumers. He outlines his approach to motivational research, the techniques he uses, and some of the projects they have been used on.

 Visit the Online Resource Centre to read the abstract and access the full paper.

One of Dichter's most famous uses of motivation research was for the marketing of Chrysler's Plymouth car, which had not been selling well. Dichter talked to potential customers and studied the existing advertising. He concluded that by using a message that the car was different from any other that the customer may have tried before, potential customers were fearful of the unknown in a market where familiarity was equated with safety. He also found that although convertibles were bought by very few customers—in 1939 only 2 per cent of the market was accounted for by convertibles—it was frequently the dream of middle-aged men to own one. Convertibles could be put in dealership windows to lure potential male buyers. Indeed, when they were used in this way more men visited the dealership. Inevitably when they returned with their wives they were more likely to actually buy a sensible saloon car, reflecting the importance of wives in the decision-making process. Dichter interpreted wanting a convertible as symbolizing youthfulness and freedom, even the desire for a mistress, but also not something that they often take seriously and actually buy. In this way Dichter helped Chrysler with their Plymouth in two ways. By putting the convertible version in the windows, it drew the attention of the males and brought them into the dealership to enable further selling. In addition, they started to advertise in women's magazines with a line that presented a reassuring and familiar message for the brand. Their campaign informed the consumer that after 'only a few minutes' they would feel at home with their Plymouth (*Economist*, 2011).

Critiques of motivational research

In the 1950s there was increasing fear that, as the marketing industry grew, consumers were being 'sold' things they neither needed nor really wanted but bought only to fulfil their consumerist lifestyle. Vance Packard's *The Hidden Persuaders* (1957) remains a powerful critique of marketing and advertising at a time when an increasing range of psychological techniques were being tried out. Some thought that such techniques invaded the minds of consumers and persuaded them to buy using inappropriate secret methods such as subconscious advertising. Packard identified four major complaints against the kind of motivational research that Dichter had used for his commercial clients.

1. Motivational research could not be a cure-all for all marketing problems.

2. Taking diagnostic tools from clinical psychiatry and applying them to consumer behaviour was not wholly valid.

3. Motivational research relied too heavily on the person making the interpretation with few standardized or validating testing procedures.

4. The findings of motivational researchers had not been subjected to objective confirmation by conventional methods before they were applied to business situations.

While these are all reasonable criticisms of motivational research, and indeed reflect questions raised by others regarding the validity of such research today, the most significant criticism was presented by Packard in his final chapter, entitled 'The Question of Morality', which dealt with the issue of whether these techniques were not only commercially but also morally appropriate:

> On the other hand, a good many of the people-manipulating activities of persuaders raise profoundly disturbing questions about the kind of society they are seeking to build for us. Their ability to contact millions of us simultaneously through newspapers, TV, etc., gives them the power, as one persuader put it to do good or evil 'on a scale never before possible in a very short time'.
>
> (Packard, 1957: 209)

Although motivational research suffered from the attacks of Packard and others, particularly in light of the difficulty of making valid inferences from the data, it has in one way or another continued to be used by many companies up to the present day, and researchers recognize the contribution motivational research has made to understanding consumer behaviour (Tadajewski, 2006).

From consumers to consumerism: the politics of consumption

The late nineteenth and early twentieth centuries saw an increasing number of people able to purchase goods, and more of them. This period also saw the development of a more active consumer, with increasing concern that governments should protect the rights and safety of other consumers particularly with regard to the safety of the products they bought. Ideological activists had been involved in consumption issues from the late eighteenth century (e.g. the abolition of the slave trade), while in the nineteenth century much activity revolved around issues relating to the welfare relating to those producing the goods to be sold, such as working conditions in factories.

The term 'consumer sovereignty' was first coined in the 1930s (de Grazia, 2005) and came to represent the exercise of freedom that people could have through consumption. Consumer rights organizations also began to increase, and in 1957 Michael Young founded the Consumers' Association (now known as Which?) in the UK. There are now a number of similar organizations operating in many countries, such as the Consumer Federation of Australia, the Consumers' Association of Canada, the Consumer Guidance Society of India, the Uganda Consumer Action Network, and the National Consumer Agency in the Republic of Ireland. All share the goal of ensuring that consumers are protected in their marketplace dealings.

This focus on consumer protection subsequently became an issue of concern to both companies and governments, and many countries introduced legislation to protect consumers. In the UK, the Consumer Credit Act 1974 was introduced to allow consumers paying by credit to have a period of time in which to change their mind regarding the purchase they had made. Other countries have consumer legislation in place to protect the interests and safety of consumers, including the Republic of China's Consumer Protection Law 1994, the Indian Consumer Protection Act 1986, and, in Europe, the European Charter of Fundamental Rights (2000). Today, protection of consumers with regard to credit (and in particular the interest that they have to pay) continues to be a major social and political issue, as is highlighted in Practitioner Insight 1.

One of the most famous consumer activists is American-born Ralph Nader who famously took on the car industry in an article he wrote in 1959 for *The Nation* entitled 'The safe car you can't buy'. Nader continued his campaigns against the US car industry in the 1960s with attacks on General Motors, whose cars had been involved in numerous accidents. Over the years Nader's work produced results at a national level, and to some extent it has been activists like him who have changed the perspective of producers away from the concept of *caveat emptor*, i.e. 'buyer beware', to recognizing that producers and retailers have a responsibility to the consumer not only in producing goods but ensuring that they are safe, fair, and of the value promised. Nader helped to bring about national laws improving vehicle safety and in particular heralding the introduction of additional safety features.

Today, many people are actively involved in campaigning for better, safer products and fairer working environments. In 2000, Naomi Klein's book *No Logo* was published with an overtly anti-corporate and 'alter-globalization' message. Klein discusses the appalling acts of multinational companies, including the use of sweatshops and the rise of short-term contracts and 'McJobs'. Many people also think that the consumer should assume some responsibility, as we consume too much or inappropriately. This has led to boycotting and anti-consumption movements. In 2004, independent film maker Morgan Spurlock's film *Supersize Me* chronicled the impact of his weight gain and psychological well-being from spending 30 days eating only food from McDonald's, as well as documenting the fast-food industry's wider influence on the nutrition of the American public.

Alongside this increased activism, consumers now have access to large amounts of information which allows them to make better and informed choices. A quick search on the internet will reveal not only price comparison websites but also whether the company has been involved in dubious or unethical practices.

Classifying consumers

Early attempts to classify consumers centred on classic variables such as age, gender, occupation, and income, with efforts aimed at facilitating the segmentation and targeting of products and brands to different consumer needs. Increasingly, as consumers have understood that businesses were marketing goods to them in ways that were not always straightforward, they have become more sophisticated in the manner in which they respond to marketing, product innovations, pricing, advertising, promotions, and offers. This, in turn, has led to a range of new attempts to classify types of consumer. Such classifications have generally involved the development of wider-ranging variations, not necessarily mutually exclusive but still often with some categories in opposition to one another. These typologies are examined in more detail in this section. One of the most cited classification of consumers is that of Gabriel and Lang (1995, 2006) who have defined nine types which are detailed in Table 1.1.

If we examine the brief descriptions in Table 1.1, we can see that Gabriel and Lang's typology of consumers is really describing trends and ways of consuming (or not) rather than types of people. We can be hedonistic in our consumption on one day, but that does not preclude us from being an activist on another. Aldridge (2003) criticized the typology

Consumer type	Description
Chooser	The rational problem-solving consumer, requiring genuine options, finance options, and information
Communicator	Uses goods to communicate: this can be functional as in the use of a burglar alarm to convey status or taste
Explorer	Consumers increasingly have places to explore, for example, from car boot sales to the internet: often we explore with little idea of what, or even if, we wish to buy.
Identity-seeker	Creating and maintaining personal and social identity through consumption
Hedonist/artist	Consumption as pleasure: consumption can fulfil needs for emotional aesthetic pleasure and fantasy
Victim	The exploited consumer: the consumer may be uneducated or unaware of choices, or they may have limited choice because of their socio-economic situation
Rebel	Using products in new ways as a conscious rebellion: this can include consuming differently, or less, or boycotting, and can also refer to active rebellion (joyriding, looting, taking over consumption spaces, etc.)
Activist	Presented historically from the co-operative movement, the value-for-money movement, especially fighting against corporate greed and political activism, seeking more ethical consumption
Citizen	Consumers are also citizens with rights and responsibilities: awareness that consumerism encroaches on areas such as housing, healthcare, and education as well as consumer goods

Table 1.1   A typology of consumers   *Source*: Adapted from Gabriel and Lang (1995, 2006).

for being underdeveloped and having overlapping categories—one might see similarities between the consumer as activist and as rebel. However, as an indicator of the roles and positions that consumers may take, this can be a useful typology. Gabriel and Lang's 'consumer as victim' is an interesting category, and resonates with Bauman's (2007) idea of the 'flawed' consumer—someone who is effectively excluded from consumer society because of their economic or social position. We can all feel as though we are consumer victims at times, but certain groups in society are particularly vulnerable, perhaps because they live on a low income or have a disability. Some people are effectively excluded from the opportunity for choice or for exploring or engaging in hedonistic consumption; they may be excluded through their economic position or their inability to engage with the expectations of modern consumer society. Consider how those who do not have access to or cannot use the internet are excluded, not only from shopping opportunities but also from financial deals which might be economically advantageous. Consumers living on low incomes, who have to borrow money at high interest rates, can find themselves in very difficult financial situations which can be particularly damaging, as Lord Mitchell explains in Practitioner Insight 1.

PRACTITIONER INSIGHT 1

Lord Mitchell, House of Lords, UK

Lord Mitchell told us about the work he had been doing with short-term loan companies, often referred to as payday loan companies.

One of my greatest successes since being in the House of Lords was to get an amendment to the Financial Services Act in 2012. This will mean that the Financial Conduct Authority (FCA) will be given powers to cap the total amount charged by short-term loan companies. In addition, borrowers will also be prevented from repeatedly rolling over loans, and lenders who fail to comply with the FCA's rules will not be able to enforce repayment. Non-compliance will have drastic consequences for payday lenders. In addition, in March 2013 the Office for Fair Trading came out with hard-hitting recommendations. They cited most of the industry as acting illegally and gave them 60 days to sort themselves out or risk losing their licences.

Why is this so significant for consumers? Since 2008 the payday loans industry has grown significantly as households have struggled to balance rising bills with falling wages and retail banks have resisted offering unsecured loans. There are some consumers who are more vulnerable than ever before and we need to recognize that this may lead them to make decisions that ultimately do not serve them well. In Rochdale in 2010 the BBC *Panorama* reporter Richard Bilton found it easy to collect nearly £1,000 from money lenders with no security. Also, consider the example I gave in the House of Lords of a friend whose son with mild attention deficit disorder had taken out two payday loans totalling £800, only to find that in just a few months the amount had escalated to £5,000. Yet the Office for Fair Trading (OFT) guidance for creditors on irresponsible lending pointed out that: 'All assessments of affordability should involve a consideration of the potential for the credit commitment to adversely impact on the borrower's financial situation, taking account of information that the creditor is aware of at the time the credit is granted.'

We must remember that payday lenders fill what in today's climate is an important gap, but when we hear stories of lenders charging an APR in excess of 4,000 per cent we have to find ways to protect vulnerable consumers from becoming victims, while providing them with financial services that will allow them to continue a reasonable quality of life.

There have been other attempts to classify consumers. Edwards (2000: 13) differentiates between five 'perceptions' of the consumer, all 'to some extent at least, stereotypes, yet contain a grain of truth'. They are the consumer as king, victim, criminal, anti-consumer, and voyeur. Dagevos (2005) argued that modern consumers defy traditional segmentation by age, gender, or income, and that classical criteria to distinguish homogeneous groups (with corresponding behavioural intentions and patterns) have lost much of their explanatory power. Instead, Dagevos proposed four consumer 'images' which are based on two key dimensions, materialistic/non-materialistic and individualistic/collectivist as shown in Figure 1.10.

These consumer types capture the relations between consumers and products, and Dagevos characterized the types as follows.

- *Calculating* is rational, mainstream, efficient, and effective, 'Keep up with the Joneses', concerned with convenience.

- *Traditional* is conformist, cost-conscious, self-disciplined, fearful of new things, community-oriented.

- *Unique* is described as fun and impulsive, seeks variety, seeks status, distinction, and new things.

- *Responsible* is captured by involvement, altruistic, 'Keep down with the Joneses', informed, environmentally aware.

Overall, consumer typologies are popular in commercial and academic research, and while these typologies are interesting and useful in terms of recognizing differences among consumers, few have been based on empirical research and therefore we must be somewhat circumspect in their application.

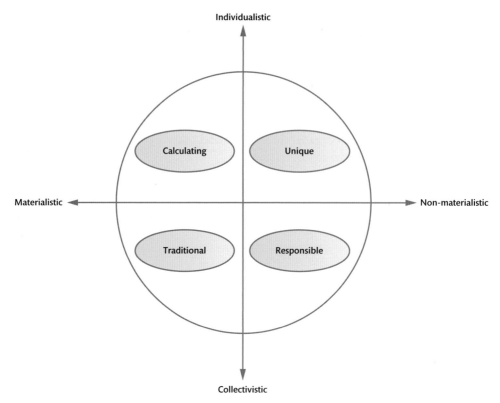

Figure 1.10 Four images of the consumer

Source: Dagevos (2005), 'Consumers as four-faced creatures. Looking at food consumption from the perspective of contemporary consumers', *Appetite* 45, 1, 32–39. Copyright © 2005, Elsevier.

The postmodern consumer

The progressive nature of the consumerist movement could be said to represent modernity and progress, but alongside this arose the concept of the postmodern consumer (Firat and Venkatesh, 1995; Goulding, 2003; Simmons, 2008). An important feature of postmodern consumers is their fragmented nature. Rather than being one 'type', as described in the section on 'Classifying consumers', the postmodern consumer truly crosses many types and it is difficult to tell when he/she will be one or the other. No longer does consumption provide support to a unified idea of a person framed by their work, gender, moral choices, and achievements. Rather, postmodern consumers do not seek a unified theme but want to explore different and separate identities to match the fragmenting markets and the proliferation of products. This suits not only the different segments but also the different moods of the consumer and can take many forms around the world, as demonstrated in the example of the mod-tradi consumer discussed in Consumer Insight 1.4.

Firat and Schultz (1997) represent the fragmentation of postmodern consumers as a result of a loss of a central core of being where multiple selves can address the same product category.

CONSUMER INSIGHT 1.4

Sri Lanka's mod-tradi consumer

Bernard Cova (1999) suggested that we no longer have expectations of what people do and what they buy based on their class or occupation. He illustrates this by saying that a government minister could as easily be driving a Citroen 2CV as an unemployed person could be driving a BMW. Other commentators identify postmodern consumption as deconstructing patterns of old shopping behaviour, erasing the boundaries across price, image brand, and location (Fassnacht, 2007), such that you might eat your lunch at McDonald's and your dinner at a five star restaurant, or buy cheap socks at a discount shop and an expensive iPod at the Apple store.

Different cultures respond in a variety of ways to new sociocultural forces that shape behaviour and consumption. In Sri Lanka the seemingly opposing forces of traditionalization and modernization have in fact been converging to produce a response that Liyanage (2011) refers to as the mod-tradi consumer. Identifying the lines of fusion between the traditional and modern is a challenge to marketing in Sri Lanka in terms of identifying not only disparate sociocultural but also urban–rural groups and how they are impacted. Sometimes different social groups show a preference for the traditional or the modern. For example, higher social groups may choose cement floors and traditional furniture, while lower socio-economic groups prefer the convenience of glossy floor tiles. In some cases old and new become fused. Young people may wear faded branded jeans and a T-shirt while also wearing the **pirith nool**, a string around the right wrist which is believed to ward off evil and is an important traditional religious symbol. Food is also subject to mod-tradi consumption with traditional food being eaten alongside sausages at home and trips to McDonald's.

Questions

1. Can you find examples of mod-tradi consumption in your own lives?

2. How have marketing companies used such preferences for the new and the traditional?

Sources: Cova (1999); Fassnacht (2007); Liyangage (2011).

 Visit the Online Resource Centre and follow the weblinks to learn more.

Baudrillard (1981) suggested that consumers use goods to create and manage identities. We can use brands to make us appear as one thing in the morning and something else later in the day—we have learnt to use the market and what it offers to change who we appear to be. There is no longer any logic to production being important in the Marxist sense; instead, the only thing that matters is the signs that are represented through consumption. A pair of jeans could be considered only in terms of their strength and durability (related to their use value), which was the focus of the original advertisements for Levi jeans. Today, however, use value is of less significance, and instead it is the sign and hedonic value communicated through wearing Levi's (or some other high-fashion brand) that is important for consumers.

Similarly Bourdieu's (1984) thesis, as summarized by Gronow and Warde (2001: 221), presents the consumer as using goods to act 'as signs of inclusion and exclusion: people like me or us, prefer objects like ours whereas the "others" choose, dress or design and use theirs otherwise'. While the postmodern consumer has appeared as a powerful theme in much academic literature, the question raised by some has been how relevant this concept actually is to real people's consumption experiences (Miles, 1999; Goulding, 2003). If anything, it is a concept of use to marketing and advertising in terms of the amount and variety of products and images available to us that encourage consumption in increasingly competitive markets. Some have critiqued the idea of postmodernism as having been appropriated by late modern forms of capitalism for their own managerial purposes (Boje, 2006). Boje uses McDonald's as an example of a company that has used a clever juxtaposition of engaging with children and parents with both cartoons and celebrities to construct the idea of fast food being nutritious, but also using scientific-seeming charts of fat and nutrition content with endorsements from fitness experts. McDonald's uses a range of discourse types (both visual and fun, cognitive and scientific) to 'story themselves to customers and employees' (Boje, 2006: 31). On the other hand, Boje classifies other companies, such as Blackspot Sneakers and No Sweat clothing, as postmodern organizations because they are critical of some of the features of modern capitalism such as global sweatshops. Blackspot began as a consumer co-operative where consumers pooled orders for trainers and found a unionized factory with a long-standing history in the shoe industry employing men and women, young and old. Their marketing and advertisements clearly position Blackspot as anti-Nike; the high-top Hemp boot is called the 'Unswoosher'—a direct reference to the Nike Swoosh—and tagged 'the most Earth-friendly shoe in the world'.

Postmodernism in marketing was seen as breaking down the divide between production and consumption, leading to what is referred to as the co-creation of value whereby the consumer played a constructive and value-creating role not only in consumption but also in production, by creating their own products or taking part in production through connections with the firm. The most extreme version of this is the creation of one's own products with no engagement with a firm. Boje (2006) describes building his own motorcycle using what he describes as 'after-market products'. See also Research Insight 1.3 where you can learn about prosumption.

RESEARCH INSIGHT 1.3

Cova, B. and Cova, V. (2012), 'On the road to prosumption: marketing discourse and the development of consumer competencies', *Consumption Markets and Culture*, 15, 2, 149–168

Cova and Cova (2012) provide an interesting overview of marketing approaches and, in so doing, show how perspectives and views on the consumer have shifted over the last 30 years. They first describe the relationship perspective, with its corresponding emphasis on the individualistic consumer, then the experiential perspective, which emphasizes the hedonistic consumer, and lastly they discuss the collaborative perspective with its emphasis on the creative consumer. The implications of these different perspectives are discussed, as well as the consequence for markets and brands.

 Visit the Online Resource Centre to read the abstract and access the full paper.

Post postmodernism

Some academics now suggest the end of postmodernism as a theme in consumer research (e.g. Cova and Maclaran, 2012). This is partly because it has become subsumed by consumer culture theory (Arnould and Thompson, 2005) and possibly because both researchers and consumers have moved beyond it. Cova and Maclaran see the new fields of interest as being: cultural (consumer culture theory), neuromarketing, and the material turn. Consumer culture theory will be discussed further in Chapter 2, and will be referred to throughout this book where relevant, while neuromarketing will be covered in Chapter 11. The material turn refers to the role of non-human objects (things) in shaping behaviour. For example, we might consider how we use shopping trolleys and the implications of their invention for the size of supermarkets and how much we buy (Cochoy, 2009). What is clear from these and other studies is that theories which describe and aim to understand consumer behaviour will continue to be developed, just as consumers themselves will develop new ways of behaving in the market that will need to be explained.

Approaches to studying consumers and consumption

Interdisciplinary perspectives on consumption

Just as there are different ways of thinking about consumption and how it is classified, it is also useful to think about how different social science perspectives lead to different approaches to studying consumer behaviour. It is clear that many academic disciplines are relevant to the study of consumers, but the main perspectives we see in consumer research relate to anthropology, sociology, psychology, and economics, with history and geography also making a contribution.

Anthropology is concerned with people as they live in their society and culture. When applied to consumer contexts, this perspective tends to focus on consumers' behaviours and practices, looking at how rituals, myths, and symbols all contribute to understanding the meaning and significance of consumption to consumers. The sociological perspective on consumption contributes insights into the social forces that influence individual and group consumption, including the social structural concepts of social class, ethnicity, gender, and lifestyles. Perhaps the most influential social science in understanding consumers is psychology, the scientific study of mental processes and behaviours. We have already seen how aspects of psychology were incorporated in the work of the early motivational researchers. The ideas of personality, the self, and the individual, how we learn and perceive the world around us—ideas essential for the study of the consumer—are derived from psychology. It has also been influential in terms of the research methods used in consumer research. Economics also has a role to play in understanding consumption. Classic microeconomic theory is the source of the utility-maximizing framework used to explain some aspects of how we process information and make decisions. Macroeconomics provides indicators of consumption behaviours which are very useful in understanding global differences in consumption. History and geography help in our understanding of the origins and development of consumer culture, including marketing communications and advertising, and the impact on urban and suburban landscapes of marketing institutions and practices, especially retail spaces.

To see this holistic approach to studying consumption in action, it is useful to look at the issue of excessive alcohol consumption which represents a very real and significant public health problem for many societies. Different perspectives on studying this issue may focus on different things. Anthropologists might focus on the ritualistic practices around socializing. Sociologists might focus on how local community policing influences the behaviour of young people in the night-time economy. Psychologists might examine the links between personality type and alcohol consumption, whereas economists might be interested in how alcohol consumption might change following the introduction of minimum unit pricing. A historical perspective might consider how patterns of alcohol consumption have changed over time, and geographers might undertake an audit of off-license shops (which sell alcohol) in local communities and relate this to consumption levels.

Relating perspectives to methods of studying consumers

While many disciplines may be interested in consumer behaviour, approaches to investigating consumers tend to be divided into two broad research orientations: the positivist approach and the interpretivist approach.

The **positivist approach** to consumer behaviour emphasizes *the objectivity of science and the consumer as a rational decision-maker* (Calder and Tybout, 1989). This approach sees the world as having an external objective reality, and the goal of research using this perspective is to understand consumers in terms of theories that have been rigorously tested and which can explain this external reality. Methods from this perspective often focus on examining relationships between key factors (or variables) that explain some aspect of consumer behaviour, and research tools allow relationships to be observed and quantified in some way. For this reason, most methods involved in this approach to consumer research tend to be quantitative, with qualitative methods being used in a limited supporting role. Many commercial companies use this approach, and typical techniques include structured questionnaires, experiments (laboratory-based and in context), consumer panels, and hall tests.

The **interpretivist perspective** *stresses the subjective meaning of the consumer's individual experience and the idea that any behaviour is subject to multiple interpretations rather than one single explanation.* This approach is driven by a need to develop a deep understanding of people's lives and behaviours, recognizing that the researcher interprets this data in terms of a particular system of ideas and assumptions about the nature of reality. This approach recognizes that reality is socially constructed, and that the researcher is an active participant in the research process (rather than an objective bystander). The unstructured depth interview is a classic method used in interpretivist research, allowing the researcher to adopt a flexible approach to the interview and to probe more deeply areas of particular interest to the consumer being interviewed. Other methods include ethnography, personal introspections, participant observations, and narrative analyses. These approaches are more associated with qualitative methodologies, although it is important to note that not all qualitative research is interpretivist.

Conclusions

This chapter introduced you to some of the key aspects relating to the ***early history of consumption***, examining the historical links between consumption and social class. Our discussion of the sumptuary laws during the period of the Qin dynasty in China, medieval England, and renaissance Italy showed that historically there have been concerns about the moral implications of consumption, something that continues to the modern day.

Examining the ***role of economics and philosophy*** in the development of consumer behaviour, we considered how production and consumption are connected, and the way that value has evolved. Analysing designer handbag consumption, we showed how the different types of value are interrelated, concluding that many objects we consume today are defined by their sign or symbolic value more than their use value.

It is important to ***understand how consumption became a part of everyday life***. As shops appeared, shopping became a pleasurable experience, and this led to increased investment in production as manufacturers recognized that people were prepared to spend more on goods above their needs. Consumer Insight 1.1 mapped how innovations in domestic technology influenced the ways that consumer eat and live. We also introduced the concept of ***conspicuous consumption***, looking at the example of Hubwear's customized T-shirts (Consumer Insight 1.2) as a way for consumers to signal status.

We examined some ***key trends in the development of shops and shopping***, such as global innovations in online shopping (shown in the example of Tesco Homeplus in South Korea in Consumer Insight 1.3) and the trend towards pop-up shopping due to its 'low-risk' nature, particularly in the fashion sector. The twentieth century saw major changes in our understanding of consumers, and in particular this occurred as a result of an interest in the work of Sigmund Freud. ***Motivational research*** has been important for studying consumer behaviour as it recognizes that not all consumer decisions can be explained by rational or economic arguments.

Nowadays, ***consumerism*** is part of everyday life. For a range of reasons, some groups of people have rejected the marketing message and have become active in attacking businesses which they believe are producing inappropriate, dangerous, or simply too many products. Examining consumer protection legislation across the world, we discussed a range of issues associated with consumer activism.

Classifying and identifying 'types' of consumers is important for marketing practice, and this is looked at in more depth in Case Study 1, which examines how different groups of supermarket shoppers use branded and own-label goods during a recession.

As consumers became more familiar with marketing, they became more sophisticated, and some refer to the **postmodern consumer** as encapsulating the uncertainty and playfulness of behaviour, image, and identity in consumption in the twenty-first century. The mod-tradi Sri Lankan consumer was discussed as an example of the postmodern consumer.

Changes in understanding consumption and consumers over time have led to many **different approaches to studying consumers**. Much consumer behaviour is now manifested online. Consumers discuss brands and products, and recommend or complain about the choices they have made on social networking sites and internet communities. As a result much more research uses online ethnography or netnography (Kozinets, 2010) to study such behaviour.

Review questions

1. Explain exchange value, use value, and sign value. Are exchange and use value still helpful in understanding consumption today?

2. What are the main economic and philosophical arguments regarding production and consumption that are relevant to understanding consumer behaviour today?

3. What was the significance of 'wastefulness' in Veblen's *Theory of the Leisure Class?*

4. Outline Packard's four criticisms of motivational research. What do you think of these criticisms in relation to what you understand of marketing today?

5. Using Gabriel and Lang's typology, suggest which you think are the most common consumer types today and why.

Discussion questions

1. Identify some examples of what you would consider to be conspicuous consumption today. In your opinion what are such goods offering to the people who consume them?

2. Do you consider that consumption has a moral dimension today? What are the major moral issues concerning consumption in the twenty-first century?

3. Look at the advertising for three brands of soap. Analyse the messages they use and consider whether they relate to Dichter's utilitarian or indulgent types. What other kinds of messages are used today?

4. Consider how car advertisements are presented in women's magazines today. What messages are used to convince women of the value of the car brand today? How do you think that car advertising differs today?

5. Jeans, cars, and handbags could all be said to encapsulate sign value. Take one of these product categories and choose three brands. Explain which sign value, in your opinion, each brand represents.

 Visit the Online Resource Centre to test your knowledge further and complete the Multiple Choice Questions for Chapter 1.

CASE STUDY 1

Supermarket responses to the recessionary consumer

This case looks at how consumers have changed their approach to supermarket shopping as the result of the recession following the global financial crisis of 2008. It considers how retailers respond to market research on shopping behaviour and highlights how people use branded and own-label goods. The questions ask you to consider the likely preferences and behaviour of different types of shopper. In doing this you should also reflect on what you have learned about consumers and their behaviour in the chapter.

What changes might one expect in consumers' attitudes and behaviours following a recession? A number of organizations have looked at consumer behaviour in times of economic hardship. In 2009, shoppercentric.co.uk undertook a study of over 1,000 individuals in the UK to see how the recession had affected them. They identified four types of reactions to the recession.

- **Unaffecteds**—13 per cent claim to be unaffected but making small changes.

- **Planners**—15 per cent were not affected yet but making changes in case. They had noticed that their household costs had risen. They have a focus on price, avoid temptation, and economize by making meals from scratch.

- **Soft Reactors**—48 per cent have had to make changes to household spending but the changes are small. They may have switched to own-label brands, large shops, and no top-ups. They are price aware, avoiding waste and temptation.

- **Strong Reactors**—24 per cent are making major changes, and are moving between stores for best prices.

By April 2012 this had changed, with Unaffecteds at 12 per cent, Planners at 6 per cent, Soft Reactors at 46 per cent, and Strong Reactors at 35 per cent. Perhaps surprisingly, planners were somewhat lower, but Strong Reactors, i.e. those making major changes, were up by 11 per cent. This may indicate the long-term impact that the recession has had on some consumers, whether they are choosing to be more prudent with their spending or because they have to be.

Post-recession developments included openly looking for bargains, taking time to get the best purchase (i.e. maximizing), looking for free offers, reducing wasteful consumption, seeking transparency in dealings with big companies, and using their mobiles for everything—shopping, communicating, playing. The impact on living standards in the financial crisis, with increases in food and fuel prices, is also thought to have made supermarket shoppers more discerning, searching for lower prices, special deals, and bargains. However, the picture may be somewhat more complex than this.

UK research on grocery shopping by Kantar Media TGI in 2012 reported that low-income families often prefer premium branded goods and services over retailers' own brands. When asked about the importance of price, many people living on lower incomes said price was a conscious factor influencing choice. However, when their actual purchases were inspected, it was seen that consumers with lower incomes preferred more premium brands; brands like Birds Eye, McCain, Kellogg's, and Coca-Cola did well. According to this report, buying premium brands enables low-income consumers to assert their social position when other means—such as surroundings, income, and education—are inaccessible to them. Jo Ruddock, head of consumer and market insight at Kellogg's, also recognizes the status role that branded goods may play for lower-income families: 'This is a hugely complex area with a large number of factors at play but I think there is an element of "what a brand says about us" that determines brand choices'. This, she says, may apply more for public categories that are seen by others. Savvy shoppers choose branded products in categories that matter most to them (Chahal, 2012).

According to Nick Canning, Director for People and Customers at Iceland, the key to understanding this trend is an appreciation of the risks inherent in food shopping when living on a low income. According to Canning, 'They [lower income customers] would rather buy something they know the quality and taste of, as opposed to something they are not 100 per cent sure about'. Research in nutritional science supports this, showing that low-income consumers tend to be more risk averse in their food shopping since the costs associated with foods not being acceptable to their families are high.

So how do businesses respond to such changes in consumer behaviour?

John Lewis is a famous British high street department store with a grocery arm, Waitrose. The profile of Waitrose is of a store catering primarily to the middle classes; as *The Guardian* noted, it is often perceived as 'posh but pricey'. It stocks a full range of grocery items which includes many upmarket brands. It prides itself on quality, but knows that some shoppers will only purchase certain items from Waitrose and go to cheaper stores for commodity shopping. In 2009 it recognized the impact of the recession on its consumers by introducing 'Essential Waitrose', a cheaper own-brand alternative. The aim was to encourage more existing customers to do their full shop with Waitrose and to give a cheaper offering without compromising on their quality reputation. At the same time, they did not want to alienate their loyal customers who might be suspicious of 'down-market' offerings. The Essential Waitrose product range included over 1,000 fresh and everyday staples, and also involved rebranding 1,200 existing own-label products. Waitrose made their Essential Waitrose products more visible and relevant to customers at a time when their competitors had been building their competitive advantage by developing what had been Waitrose's key areas of differentiation. These included improving product quality, sourcing standards, and ethics, but they too had recognized the recessionary trends and had been moving their emphasis back to price and value. So Waitrose's biggest challenge was to ensure that their new Essential Waitrose products offered both quality and value, and that this was evident to customers in the way the products were labelled and the packaging designed. In choosing the name, they avoided the language of 'value' or 'basics' so as to reassure customers of the maintenance of the quality of the products. The *Oxford English Dictionary* defines essential as 'Absolutely necessary, indispensably requisite', and hence Essential Waitrose was seen as appropriate to indicate the everyday staple nature of both food and non-food items.

In 2010, *Management Today* reported on Waitrose's 15 per cent increase in sales, saying that 'The success of its Essentials range suggests that it's done a much better job than M&S [Marks & Spencer] of catering to the new austerity trend'. But alongside Essential Waitrose the company maintained many of its higher-end, own-label, and branded lines such as 'Menu from Waitrose' and Duchy Originals.

Figure 1.11 Essential Waitrose and Tesco Everyday Value product lines

Source: Waitrose and Tesco Stores Ltd.

In the past other supermarkets have launched product lines aimed to offer value to customers affected by recessionary times. Perhaps the best known of these was Tesco's Value range launched following the recession of the early 1990s. In 2012 Tesco announced that they were rebranding as Everyday Value. The supermarket's stark blue and white striped Value range was seen as too basic in comparison with supermarkets such as Waitrose's Essential range, emphasizing affordable quality in the classier packaging and attracting what *Management Today* called 'the increasing volume of cash-strapped yet status-conscious shoppers' (see Figure 1.11). Some customers also questioned the quality of the Tesco brand, and its distinctive blue and white packaging was perhaps more obvious in their shopping basket than they might have liked (Haslett, 2010).

Research with low-income consumers tells us that they have greater trust in brands and believe that there is a difference between national brands and retailer own-label brands. The 2012 Aldi campaign tackled this head on by showing consumers who liked both the national brand and Aldi's own-label version of the product. Aldi's advertising shows people comparing a main-line brand and Aldi's own-label version (see Figure 1.12). The price is always clearly visible in the advert, with Aldi's product usually about half the price of their branded competitor. The adverts are light-hearted and, interestingly, do not suggest that the own-label brand is better than the branded version. In one advert an older lady says that she buys the branded tea (at £3.00) for her husband, and then says that he also likes the Aldi own-label brand (at £1.99). She finishes by saying that she doesn't like tea, she likes gin.

Figure 1.12 Aldi advertisement

Source: Image supplied by The Advertising Archives.

Aldi simply puts across the results of price checks and taste tests. These results show that, despite Aldi's own-label products costing about half the price of their branded competitors, many people 'also like them'. So Aldi presents the parity of the products, but with Aldi's being much cheaper.

In 2012 Waitrose introduced the Waitrose Brand Price Match initiative, which is intended to ensure that customers will pay no more for cupboard staples like washing powder and baked beans than they would at the likes of Tesco, Morrisons, and Sainsbury's. This is expected to apply to over 7,000 products. Other supermarkets have run similar campaigns, such as Asda's Price Guarantee and Sainsbury's Brand Match, which generates coupons at the till if branded goods can be bought cheaper elsewhere. *The Grocer* commented that Waitrose was likely to balance this by charging more for their own-label goods (Leyland, 2012). The big supermarkets have also used the internet to offer price comparisons, with both Asda and Tesco running internet-based price-checking facilities, and increasingly shoppers are using their mobiles and tablets to order their food online. Although many of Britain's supermarkets offer delivery to your house, at the time of writing Waitrose was the only store to offer it free of charge.

Questions

1. Consider the four types of recessionary shopper described. What particular needs might each type have?

2. How might the way they do their supermarket shopping differ for each type? What would be different about their behaviour and how might supermarkets use this information?

3. Consider any of Gabriel and Lang's types of consumer in relation to supermarket shopping. How might they differ from those described in the Case Study and what kind of supermarket consumer behaviour would you think they would exhibit?

Sources: Haslett (2010); Collins (2012); Chahal (2012); Wood (2012); Leyland (2012); Steiner (2012); www.shoppercentric.co.uk

 Visit the Online Resource Centre and follow the link to the authors' blog where you can keep up to date with the latest developments in consumer behaviour and further explore theories through additional articles and real-world examples.

References

Aldridge, A. (2003), *Consumption*, Oxford: Polity Press.

Arnould, E.J. and Thompson, C.J. (2005), 'Consumer culture theory (CCT): twenty years of research', *Journal of Consumer Research*, 31, 4, 868–882.

Arnould, E.J., Price, L., and Zinkhan, G. (2004), *Consumers*, New York: McGraw-Hill.

Baudrillard, J. (1981), *For a critique of the political economy of the sign*, St Louis, MO: Telos.

Bauman, Z. (2007), *Consuming life*, Cambridge: Polity Press.

Benson, J. (1994), *The rise of consumer society in Britain, 1880–1980*, London: Longman.

Berlin, H.A. (2011), 'The neural basis of the dynamic unconscious', *Neurophsychoanalyis*, 13, 1, 5–71.

Berry, C. (1994), *The idea of luxury: a conceptual and historical investigation*, Cambridge: Cambridge University Press.

Boje, D.M. (2006), 'What happened on the way to postmodern?', *Qualitative Research in Organizations and Management*, 1, 1, 22–40.

Bourdieu, P. (1984), *Distinction: a social critique of the judgement of taste* (transl. R. Nice), Cambridge, MA: Harvard University Press.

Bowlby, R. (2000), *Carried away by shopping*, London:Faber & Faber.

Calder, B.J. and Tybout, A.M. (1989), *'Interpretive, qualitative and traditional scientific empirical consumer behaviour research'*., E.C. Hirschman (ed.), *Interpretive consumer research*, Provo, UT: Association for Consumer Research, pp 199–208.

Chahal, M. (2012). 'Lower income consumers snap up big brands', *Marketing Week* 11 October, http://www.marketingweek.co.uk/trends/lower-income-consumers-snap-up-big-brands/4004162.article (accessed 6 December 2012).

Cochoy, F. (2009), 'Driving a shopping cart from STS to business and the other way round: on the introduction of shopping carts in American grocer stores (1936–1959), *Organization*, 16, 1, 31–55.

Collins, D. (2012), 'Honest upfront message is making the brand relevant to the British shopper', *Marketing Magazine*, 4 July, http://www.marketingmagazine.co.uk/article/1139369/adwatch-webwatch-july-4-top-10-recall-aldi (accessed 8 April 2014).

Cova, B. (1999), 'From marketing to societing: when the link is more important than the thing', in D. Brownlie, M. Saren, R. Wensley, and R. Whittington (eds, *Rethinking Marketing*, London: SAGE, pp 64–83.

Cova, B. and Cova, V. (2012) 'On the road to prosumption: marketing discourse and the development of consumer competencies', *Consumption Markets and Culture*, 15, 2, 149–168.

Cova, B. and Maclaran, P. (2012), 'Rethinking consumer culture after postmodernism: in search of a new "turn" ', presented at *McDonald's Consumer Culture Theory Conference*, University of Oxford, August 2012.

Dagevos, H. (2005), 'Consumers as four-faced creatures: looking at food consumption from the perspective of contemporary consumers', *Appetite*, 45, 1, 32–39.

de Botton, A. (2005), *Status anxiety*, Harmondsworth: Penguin.

de Grazia, V. (2005), *Irresistible empire: America's advance through 20th century Europe*, Cambridge, MA: Belknap Press.

Dichter, E. (1947), 'Psychology in Market Research', *Harvard Business Review*, 432–443.

Economist (2011), 'How Ernest Dichter, an acolyte of Sigmund Freud, revolutionised marketing, http://www.economist.com/node/21541706 (accessed 7 December 2011).

Edwards, T. (2000), *Contradictions of consumption: concepts, practices and politics in consumer society*, Maidenhead: Open University Press.

Elliott, R. and Leonard, C. (2004), 'Peer pressure and poverty: exploring fashion brands and consumption symbolism amongst children of the 'British poor'. *Journal of Consumer Behaviour*, 3, 1, 347–360.

Fassnacht, M. (2007), 'Postmodern shopper', *Marketing Geek*, 28 January, http://marketinggeek.blogspot.co.uk/2007/01/postmodern-shopper.html (accessed 4 January 2013).

Fernandez-Armesto, F. (2001), *Food: a history*, London: MacMillan.

Firat, A. and Shultz, C. (1997), 'From segmentation to fragmentation: markets and marketing in the postmodern era', *European Journal of Marketing*, 31, 3/4, 183–207.

Firat, A. and Venkatesh, A. (1995), 'Liberatory postmodernism and the reenchantment of consumption', *Journal of Consumer Research*, 22, 3, 239–267.

Gabriel, Y. and Lang, T. (1995), *The unmanageable consumer*, London: SAGE.

Gabriel, Y. and Lang, T. (2006), *The unmanageable consumer* (2nd edn), London: SAGE.

Goulding, C. (2003), 'Issues in representing the postmodern consumer', *Qualitative Research*, 6, 3, 152–159.

Gronow, J. and Warde, A. (2001), *Ordinary consumption*, London: Routledge.

Hardyment, C. (1995), *A slice of life: the British way of eating since 1945*, Harmondsworth: Penguin.

Haslett, E. (2010), 'Now John Lewis' online customers won't be knowingly undersold (kind of) ', *Management Today*, 27 September, http://www.managementtoday.co.uk/news/1030995/John-Lewis-online-customers-wont-knowingly-undersold-kind-of/ (accessed 8 April 2014).

Hirsch, J. (2013), 'Dubai's first farmers market', *Modern Farmer*, 17 July, http://modernfarmer.com/2013/07/dubai-farmers-market/ (accessed 8 September 2013).

Killerby, C.K. (2002), *Sumptuary Law in Italy 1200–1500*, Oxford: Oxford University Press.

Klein, N. (2000), *No logo*, London: Flamingo.

Knutson, A. (2013), '24 vending machines you won't believe exist', *Buzzfeed Food*, 14 January, http://www.buzzfeed.com/arielknutson/vending-machines-you-wont-believe-exist (accessed 8 September 2013).

Kozinets, R.V. (2010), *Netnography: doing ethnographic research online*, London: SAGE.

Kroen, S. (2004), 'A political history of the consumer', *Historical Journal*, 47, 3, 709–736.

Lati, M. (2012), 'Fashion shop is seeking platform for local designers', *Business Daily Africa*, 28 November, http://www.businessdailyafrica.com/Fashion+shop+is+seeking+platform+for+local+designers/-/539444/1632194/-/9i5adk/-/index.html (accessed 7 April 2014).

Leyland, A. (2012). 'Hot Topic: Waitrose has shifted from high-low pricing to something more knowing', *The Grocer*, 5 May, http://www.thegrocer.co.uk/opinion/the-grocer-says/waitrose-has-shifted-from-high-low-pricing-to-something-more-knowing/228916.article (accessed 8 April 2014).

Liyanage, U. (2011), 'Sri Lanka's new mod-tradi consumer', *Sunday Times*, 30 January, http://www.sundaytimes.lk/110130/BusinessTimes/bt09.html (accessed 23 May 2013).

Loftus, D(2011), 'The rise of the Victorian middle class', *BBC History*, 17 February, http://www.bbc.co.uk/history/british/victorians/middle_classes_01.shtmlC (accessed 2 July 2013).

Lury, C. (1999), *Consumer culture*, Cambridge: Polity Press.

McCants, A.E.C. (2007), 'Exotic goods, popular consumption, andthe standard of living: thinking about globalization in the early modern world', *Journal of World History*, 18, 4, 433–462.

MacGregor, N. (2012), *Shakespeare's restless world*, London: Allen Lane.

Marx, K. (1867/2000), *The culture industry: enlightenment as mass deception*, in J.B. Schor and D.B. Holt (eds), *The Consumer Society Reader*, New York: New York Press.

Marx, K. (1876/1976), *Capital: a critique of political economy*, Vol. 1, Chicago, IL: Charles H. Kerr.

Miles, S. (1999), 'A pluralistic seduction: postmodernism at the crossroads', *Consumption, Culture and Markets*, 3, 145–163.

Mill, J.S. (1848/2004), *The principles of political economy*, New York: Prometheus.

Nestle, M. (2003), *Food politics*, Berkley, CA: University of California Press.

Packard, V. (1957), *The Hidden Persuaders*, London: Penguin.

Samuel, L.R. (2010), *Freud on Madison Avenue*, Philadelphia, *PA*: University of Pennsylvania Press.

Simmons, G. (2008), 'Marketing to postmodern consumers: introducing the internet chameleon', *European Journal of Marketing*, 42, 3/4, 299–310.

Smith, A. (1776/1981), *An inquiry into the nature and causes of the wealth of nations*, Indianapolis, IN: Liberty Press.

Stearns, P.N. (2001), *Consumerism in world history: the global transformation of desire*, London: Routledge.

Steiner, R. (2012), 'Tesco ditch basic range after admitting shoppers are "too embarrassed" to buy the blue and white striped products', *Daily Mail*, 24 September.

Szczepanski, K. (2013), 'Nutmeg: the unsavory history of a tasty spice', *Asian History*, http://asianhistory.about.com/od/colonialisminasia/p/Nutmeg-Unsavory-History.htm (accessed 25 November 2013).

Tadajewski, M. (2006), 'Remembering motivation research: toward an alternative genealogy of interpretive consumer research', *Marketing Theory*, 6, 4, 429–466.

Trendwatching.com (2010), 'Statusphere', http://www.trendwatching.com/trends/statusphere/ (accessed 16 September 2013).

Veblen, T. (1899/2007), *The theory of the leisure class*, Oxford: Oxford University Press.

Wood, Z. (2012), 'Waitrose matches Tesco prices with "never knowingly undersold" pledge', *Guardian*, 2 May, http://www.theguardian.com/business/2012/may/02/waitrose-johnlewis (accessed 7 April 2014).

2

CONTEMPORARY PERSPECTIVES ON CONSUMER BEHAVIOUR

Introduction

In 2010, the UK government set up a Behavioural Insight Team, under the guidance of behavioural economics expert Dr David Halpern, to inform public health reforms (Lawrence, 2010). Similar initiatives have followed in Canada, Australia, and the USA. The use of behavioural economics in this way provides just one example of the new ideas, discoveries, and research studies that are emerging from fields such as economics and psychology which enable us to understand the factors that shape and influence people's consumption behaviour in different environments. These new approaches have been embraced by marketing professionals, and there are many examples of how they are used in practice. At the same time the discipline of consumer behaviour is developing in other ways, and researchers are examining consumers from a range of different perspectives, such as how they experience consumption activities and relate these to their social contexts. In this chapter we shall consider some recent developments that have impacted on our understanding of how consumers are behaving in the twenty-first century and their importance for the theory and practice of consumer behaviour.

LEARNING OBJECTIVES

Having read the chapter, you will be able to:

1. Identify key topics from **behavioural economics** and how they may impact on consumer behaviour.

2. Understand the theories and practices of **experiential consumption and consumer culture theory**.

3. Understand **the role of technology** in influencing consumer behaviour.

4. Explain the difference in the **nature of innovations**, and understand how and why innovations are adopted and rejected.

5. Recognize ways in which **social media** can be used to influence consumer behaviour.

The contribution from behavioural economics

Traditionally, economists have presented consumers as behaving rationally, making logical decisions about their consumption based on factors such as price and quality, but increasingly behavioural economists and psychologists have recognized that human behaviour is more complex in terms of how we assess the cost and benefits of our choices. Behavioural economics focuses on the **contexts of decisions**, placing emphasis on the *environment within which consumption choices take place*. For example, you may be on a diet, but when invited to a dinner party you eat more because of the social nature of the occasion and because you do not want to offend your host. The behavioural economics perspective recognizes different modes (or ways) of behaving, and how these influence our behaviour in different ways.

Automatic and reflective modes

Researchers in behavioural economics refer to two modes of thinking, automatic and reflective. When in the **automatic mode** *you are operating routinely with little effort and no feeling of voluntarily being in control*. You smile when you see a baby, flinch or jump when you hear a sudden loud sound. In the same mode you may pick up a bar of chocolate at the checkout almost without thinking about it, even though you may wish to lose weight. When in **reflective mode**, however, *a person gives effortful attention to a mental activity, and this is often associated with considered choice and concentration*. If you were working out the relative price per gram of two different-sized packs of pasta you would be operating in reflective mode; it would take some effort and concentration. In terms of understanding behaviour we would conclude that the automatic mode is more involved with the context of a situation, whereas the reflective mode represents the cognitive information-processing aspect of

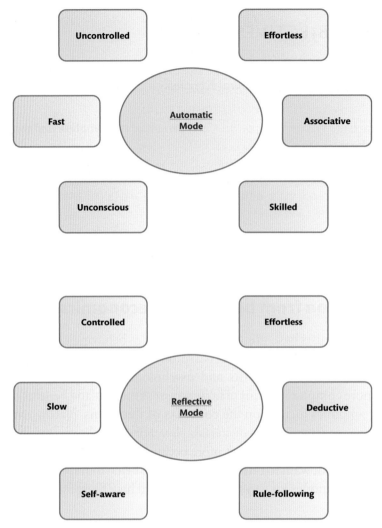

Figure 2.1 The word associations of the two cognitive systems: automatic mode and reflective mode

decision-making, which will be further discussed in Chapter 4. Figure 2.1 highlights some of the differences between the two modes.

An example helps illustrate the two modes. Imagine going to a new supermarket for the first time: you will most likely go around slowly in a controlled manner, identifying the appropriate aisles for the goods you want to purchase. The whole experience may be quite an effort; you are operating in reflective mode. However, after a couple of visits you are familiar with the location of items on the shelves; the whole process takes less effort and you can almost go around unconsciously knowing where things are. You have switched to automatic mode.

Researchers in this field are interested in the context of decision-making and whether we are operating in automatic or reflective mode at any given instant. They have looked to use the context of a decision to nudge people towards a particular behaviour; often this requires only minor changes to the environment or context in which the behaviour takes place. This frequently involves what is called **choice architecture** which describes *how the way a choice is presented influences the choice made.*

One example of the use of choice architecture is the 'house fly target', introduced at Schiphol Airport to help reduce unnecessary spillage in their men's toilets (see Figure 2.2). The image of a black housefly was etched onto the bowls of the airport's urinals. This resulted in an 80 per cent decline in spillage. Houseflies and other targets (e.g. football goals) are now appearing in urinals all over the world. A minor change in the environment, in this case giving men something to aim at, made a significant reduction in mess and probably shifted their response in the toilet from automatic to reflective mode.

Figure 2.2   The black house fly at the base of the Schiphol airport urinal

Source: Image courtesy of Bob Cromwell, http://toilet-guru.com

Such measures have had a significant impact on governments and policy-makers who are concerned to find the most effective ways to change people's behaviour in areas such as saving enough for retirement, or not drinking or eating too much. Similarly, it has been traditional for supermarkets to place sweet products at eye level where they know people will spend most time looking and are likely to just pick up items in automatic mode. Other important aspects of behavioural economics that can affect consumer behaviour include mental accounting, loss aversion, norms, defaults, and priming, which are discussed in the following sections.

Mental accounting

Mental accounting *is when individuals allocate assets into separate, non-transferable groupings to which they may assign different levels of utility.* How people save provides a good example of mental accounting; for instance, parents may have a current account, a savings account, and an account earmarked for medical bills or for their children's education. We use these mental accounts to help us control our lives; parents will think carefully before removing money from a child's account to pay for some immediate household need. Sometimes this results in irrational behaviour, such as putting money into a savings account while continuing to pay a higher rate of interest (than this savings account provides) on outstanding credit card debt. Gross and Souleles (2002) found that a typical US household had around $5,000 in savings accounts earning less than 5 per cent interest, while also holding $3,000 on credit card balances which often carried an interest rate of 18 per cent or more.

Consumers may follow similar processes in how they think about money more generally. For example, you may be willing to spend time waiting in line for a reduction of £10 off a £30 shirt, but be less keen to queue for a £10 reduction off a £500 television. The reason we engage in mental accounting is because it acts as a way to frame and keep things under control within our own cognitive limitations. While it might not always be the most economically sound way to behave, mental accounting can help us feel more secure. If you are on a limited budget, allocating a small amount every week for pleasurable activities, such as going to the cinema, may make your life more worthwhile even if you still have debts to pay.

Incentives and loss aversion

Another important aspect of human behaviour is known as **loss aversion** and refers to *how we generally dislike losses more than we like gains of an equivalent amount.* Often companies and governments will try to change behaviour through the use of incentive schemes offering rewards. However, this may not be the best way of achieving change if an incentive is not perceived to be as important as a loss. Ebhohimhen and Avenell (2008) looked at ways of treating obesity involving financial incentives but found no significant effect on participants' long-term weight loss or maintenance. An alternative might have been to frame the incentives as a charge imposed if people fail to do something. An example of this kind of 'reverse' incentive was used in a study examining another method for trying to help people lose weight (Volpp et al., 2008). Participants were asked to deposit money into an account which was returned to them (with a supplement) if they met weight-loss targets. After a number of months this group showed significant weight loss, while the weight of participants in a control group without this incentive did not change. It appears that this was a classic case of the loss acting as a greater incentive than the gain. Not reaching a goal can also act as a loss. A student might be saving up for a pair of shoes in a sale, but they are sold before she has saved enough money to buy them; this can feel like a loss even though she never actually owned the shoes.

An important aspect of loss aversion is what is known as the endowment effect. Above all, the **endowment effect** *shows that people assign specific values to a thing that is relative to their situation.* In an experiment that has been repeated numerous times (Thaler and Sunstein, 2009), students were given coffee mugs decorated with their university crest. The owners of the mugs were then invited to sell them to students who did not own such mugs. The buyers and sellers had to ask each other: 'At each of the following prices, indicate whether you would be willing to give up your mug/buy a mug'. The results revealed that the owners of the mugs required about twice as much to give up their mug as the mugless students were prepared to pay. As Thaler and Sunstein concluded, once you have a mug you do not want to give it up, but if you do not have one you do not feel compelled to buy one. Similarly, a person might buy a stool very cheaply at a car boot sale, but when someone offers to buy it from them within minutes of their purchase, the value they assign to it is much more than the amount that they originally paid for the item.

Norms

Norms refer to the kinds of behaviour that we see around us and consider to be appropriate. **Norms** *can be defined as informal rules that govern behaviour.* Norms are cultural and social and may be rule-driven—for example, not smoking in a pub, train, or plane. Often they are generally known in a social or cultural group. For example, forms of greeting vary from country to country, based on the social norms of different cultures. In European cultures, such as Italy, Spain, and France, the usual form of greeting is to kiss on the cheeks, which contrasts with the more formal handshake that is customary in the USA and UK, and again with the forms of bowing witnessed in China (a nod or bow), Japan (a bow from the waist), and Korea (a slight bow). Social influence through information or peer pressure can impact norms (see Research Insight 2.1). With regard to information, if we see or hear a number of people doing something, we may use this as information and follow their lead. If we visit a foreign country, we may observe how people operate in train stations or shopping queues and use this information to help us navigate new and strange environments. Peer pressure works when we care what others think about us; you might go along with the crowd to avoid punishment or to stay in their favour. We shall see some of the effects of peer pressure when we consider groups in more detail in Chapter 8. An example of how a social norm can be introduced is recycling towels in hotels. One US study (Goldstein et al., 2008) found that a sign asking clients to recycle towels to help the environment led to 35.1 per cent recycling. But when the sign said that most previous occupants of the room had reused towels during their stay, recycling increased to 44.1 per cent.

Norms can work both positively and negatively. In a study of energy use in 300 US households, Schultz et al. (2007) informed the householders how much energy they had used in recent weeks alongside information about the average consumption in their area. In the following weeks the above-average users decreased their use, but unfortunately the below-average users increased their consumption. This is known as a 'boomerang effect' and reveals the danger of showing people that their behaviour is better than the existing social norm (Thaler and Sunstein, 2009). Interestingly when householders were

---

RESEARCH INSIGHT 2.1

Martin, S. (2012), '98% of HBR readers love this article', *Harvard Business Review*, 23–25 October.

In this paper, Steve Martin outlines a number of UK and US examples of how social norms have been used to shape and change behaviour. In particular he emphasizes the importance of identifying social norms and then drawing attention to this in communications, as in the example of recycling towels.

 Visit the Online Resource Centre to read the abstract and access the full paper.

shown visual representation (in this case, emoticons) as well as being given information there was an even greater impact on their reduction in energy use. Therefore when high users received an unhappy emoticon they decreased energy use even more. However, the boomerang effect was removed for below-average users when they received a happy emoticon.

CONSUMER INSIGHT 2.1

Nudging for better health?

Obesity is a global problem, and many countries are developing various campaigns to help manage this public health issue. Concerns about the 'obesity epidemic' led New York State to pass legislation in 2009 to make restaurants note the calorific content of all regular menu items. However, initial studies found no noticeable change in calories purchased after the introduction of labelling (Elbel et al., 2009). About half of the respondents reported noticing calorie information, and only a quarter of these reported that the information influenced their food choices. One reason might be that the information did not mean much as many people were not aware of what levels of calories were good or bad for them. New York State subsequently introduced an educational campaign inform-ing residents that 2,000 calories a day was the most that adults should eat. The state of California also requires calorie counts on menus. Now McDonald's have announced that they will list the calorie counts on menus in all their US outlets. Dumanovsky et al. (2011) found in their study that although total cal-ories had not reduced following calorie labelling, one in six lunchtime customers were using the cal-orie information and making lower-calorie choices.

Other initiatives have been used to try to encour-age people to eat more healthily. For example, in a pilot study conducted by the New Mexico State University College of Business yellow tape was put on supermarket trolleys and shoppers were asked to put their fruit and vegetables in front of the line of tape. This doubled purchases of fruit and veg-etables (Cabinet Office, 2010). Putting fruit by the lunch checkout in a school increased fruit bought by 70 per cent (Just and Wansink, 2009). Another interesting initiative is the use of musical stairs to encourage people to walk up steps rather than take escalators. Examples of these can be found in Stockholm, San Francisco, and Paris (Figure 2.3).

Figure 2.3   Musical stairs in Montparnasse station in Paris

Source: Image kindly supplied by Marie-Hélène Cingal.

In Iceland, children have been encouraged to exercise and eat health-ier food by Sportacus, the hero of the children's TV show *LazyTown* (see Figure 2.4). In one of their campaigns children and parents can sign an 'Energy Contract' where they are rewarded for their healthy eating and being active. One supermarket labelled its fruit 'Sports Candy'—*Lazy-Town's* name for fruit and vegetables—and increased sales by 22 per cent (www.lazytown.biz). *LazyTown* has seen similar results in other places around the world, including the UK and Mexico. Iceland is one of the few places in the world to have seen levels of child obesity starting to fall (Cabinet Office, 2010).

Questions

1. Imagine that you have been asked to develop a plan to encour-age schoolchildren to eat more fruit at school. How might you use social or cultural norms in this plan?

2. For each of the examples suggested, identify what problems you might have in implementing the measures more widely.

Sources: Elbel et al. (2009); Just and Wansink (2009); Cabinet Office (2010); Dumanovsky et al. (2011); www.lazytown.biz http://www.rolighetsteorin.se

 Visit the Online Resource Centre and follow the weblinks to learn more about how nudge theory has been used in public health campaigns.

Figure 2.4   The character Sportacus from *LazyTown*

Source: Image courtesy of LazyTown Entertainment. All rights reserved, © 2014.

Defaults

Every day we accept default options because our environment is set in a particular way. A **default** is *a preselected option without active choice*. Default behaviour relies on our inertia, i.e. it is more bothersome to have to do something than to remain with the status quo. Yet as consumers we are often the losers because of our inertia while companies gain from an understanding of defaults. For example, *many people do not change their savings accounts even when there are better interest rates elsewhere*. Similarly, many companies offer 'free' magazine subscriptions for a period of time and unless you cancel the subscription after the free period you will continue with it, and of course have to pay for it.

Another important example that helps us to understand default behaviour is 'opting in or opting out'. This is particularly important for government initiatives; if you are auto-matically considered to be in some kind of scheme and have to make an effort to opt out, you are probably likely to remain in it unless you feel very strongly against it. Similarly,

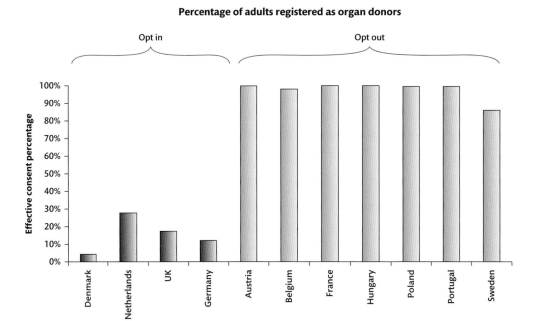

Figure 2.5 Comparison of organ donation registration in opt-in and opt-out systems

Source: Johnson and Goldstein (2003).

if you have to do something to opt in you may just not find the time to complete whatever paperwork is required. In Figure 2.5 we can see one very powerful effect of opt in versus opt out for registered organ donors across countries. There are far fewer registered organ donors in those countries where you are required to opt in than in those where you have to opt out.

Priming

Think about how certain actions may be linked to how you feel or vice versa. Feeling happy makes you smile, and just smiling can make you feel happier. This kind of association is a form of priming. It is a highly useful concept in the understanding of behaviour and has the potential to be used to manipulate our behaviour. **Priming** *is the altering of people's behaviour outside of their conscious awareness as a result of their first being exposed to certain sights, words, sensations or activities.* In other words, behaviour or feelings can be changed by priming people with certain cues without their being conscious of this happening. See Consumer Insight 2.2 for a discussion of some studies which included priming.

One of the most striking things about priming is that people do not appear to be aware of the effect of the different cues on their behaviour (see Research Insight 2.2). This clearly has major implications for the use of subliminal or other manipulative techniques that may

CONSUMER INSIGHT 2.2

How easily are we influenced?

The UK Government's Cabinet Office has produced a report that discusses in detail how behavioural economics can be used to help design various features of choice contexts to prompt people to make choices that are in line with their underlying motivations (Cabinet Office, 2010). A number of stimuli can be used to influence behaviour. Central amongst these relevant to consumer behaviour are words, sights, and smells.

1. Words—studies have revealed how powerful words can be in influencing the way people act. When people were exposed to words relating to the elderly (e.g. 'wrinkles'), it was shown that they subsequently walked more slowly when leaving the room and had a poorer memory of the room (Dijksterhuis and Bargh, 2001). This effect is explained by the fact that these people had been 'primed' with an elderly stereotype and behaved accordingly. In a similar vein, asking participants to make a sentence out of scrambled words such as fit, lean, active, and athletic, made them significantly more likely to use stairs rather than lifts (Wryobeck and Chen, 2003).

2. Sights—what people see can influence their behaviour. For example, we know that the size of food containers primes our subsequent eating. Moviegoers ate 45 per cent more popcorn when it was given to them in a 240g container than in a 120g container. Situational visual cues, such as walking shoes and runners' magazines, may prime a 'healthy lifestyle' in people (Wansink and Kim, 2006).

3. Smells—in a canteen setting, exposure to the scent of an all-purpose cleaner had an effect on the ways that people interacted with the space. A Dutch study showed that people were more prone to keeping their table clean as they ate in the canteen than when not exposed to this scent (Holland et al., 2005).

Questions

1. Consider how you might use what you have learnt about priming to try to increase children's reading.

2. Think of some examples of how manufacturers use priming to encourage us to purchase their products.

Sources: Dijksterhuis and Bargh (2001); Wryobeck and Chen (2003); Holland et al. (2005); Wansink and Kim (2006); Cabinet Office (2010).

 Visit the Online Resource Centre and follow the weblink to learn more.

RESEARCH INSIGHT 2.2

Hastorf, A.H. and Cantril, H. (1954), 'They saw a game: a case study', *Journal of Abnormal Psychology*, 49, 129–134.

This classic study reported how the fans of two American college football teams perceived completely different actions by the team they supported compared with their rivals. The match had been rough, and what was seen as fair by one side was viewed as a foul by the other and vice versa. Clearly, both sides had seen the match only from their perspective.

 Visit the Online Resource Centre to read the abstract and access the full paper.

affect behaviour. As well as marketers, political leaders may use priming to try to control a population or induce a particular kind of behaviour. Figure 2.6 shows a poster of Lord Kitchener which was used in Britain during the First World War to recruit soldiers. The poster's powerful imagery, staring at passers-by, arguably affected young men to join up to fight (Surridge, 2001).

Experiential marketing

Experiential marketing was first proposed by Morris Holbrook and Elizabeth Hirschman in 1982. Their purpose was to shift emphasis from the consumer as rational decision-maker to a model where the consumer was viewed as an

Figure 2.6 Recruitment poster for the First World War

experience-seeker. Their work aimed at offering a way of analysing and explaining how experiential consumption acts in consumer behaviour terms. Considering the consumption of the arts, entertainment, and other leisure activities as forms of consumer experience (rather than consumer behaviour), Holbrook and Hirschman (1982) emphasized the sensory and hedonic aspects of consumers rather than thinking of them as problem solvers seeking to maximize decision-making effectiveness through rational processes. Their work highlighted the multisensorial aspect of consumption. This approach offered insights into consumption not revealed in other models. For example, if you attempt to analyse the purchase of tickets for your favourite band or football team, you will quickly see that a purely rational approach does not do justice to the strong emotional connections you feel. If you consider going to see a band you really love, what are you consuming when you see them? On one level it is the band itself, but the experience of the performance coupled with the sense of being part of that audience sharing an unrepeatable moment are also important aspects of the consumption experience. If you think about the things that you enjoy doing, whether it is going to the gym, to the cinema or to a music festival, or volunteering, you can start to see how central the idea of experience is to these activities. Arnould et al. (2002) divide the consumption experience into four stages:

- the pre-consumption experience—searching for, planning, and imagining the experience;

- the purchase experience, which includes the choice process and the interaction with the service setting;

- The core consumption experience, which involves the sensation of consumption and whether we feel good or not about it;

- The remembered consumption and the nostalgia experience, which are about reliving the past experience and classifying this experience amongst others.

Although these ideas first surfaced in the 1980s, the effect came to the attention of the wider business community through books such as *The Experience Economy* (Pine and Gilmore, 1998), and its impact has been enduring, mainly in shifting companies' emphasis away from consumers as buyers to a focus on consumer experiences with services and goods. Some insights into how companies use the ideas relating to experiential marketing emerged in our discussions with David Hernandez from the NPD Group about his company's work with Renault in Mexico, relating to experiential marketing (Practitioner Insight 2).

PRACTITIONER INSIGHT 2

David Jaime Hernandez, Retail Business Group Manager at the NPD Group

People have to make choices when fulfilling their needs for every-day living, from the simple selection of morning coffee to other more complex purchases such as clothes. But there are some of these choices that are special, that only happen a few times in their lives, such as buying a new house or a new car. In developed countries buying a house tends to be the most important and informed purchase and happens on average up to two or three times during a lifetime. In other parts of the world, like Mexico, buying a house may be a once in a lifetime experience and not everyone has this opportunity. In comparison, buying a car is a purchase people may make more often than buying a house, and in some ways the car purchase process is a more important choice, since this occurs on average about six times during a lifetime. This is very important for car manufacturers as they strive to be selected in one of these limited purchase acts.

We know that when people buy a house they go on to add furniture, a refrigerator, a washing machine, and so on to make it more functional and to adapt it to their lifestyle. The same happens with a car; there are many things that can be added to personalize it, to make it more practical and comfortable, to look faster, to sound better, or to be safer. For some people adding insurance may be very important to secure their investment, or may even be compulsory in some countries. In Mexico, it is all about the exterior look: people want to show off; they want their neighbours to know that they have a new car and to see their style. They may even park the car in the street and not inside the garage to draw attention to their purchase and to 'make' their neighbours notice it. And with Mexican consumers, we see similar scenarios with other consumption patterns; for example, people always have a large flat screen TV in their living rooms, so that visitors notice they have the newest largest model. Smartphone consumption is reaching record sales year after year, with design (look and feel) being one of the main drivers, as opposed to functionality or performance. But Mexican consumers will also want a good balance between what they pay and what they receive, and this is where manufacturers play an important function by downgrading some specifications in a product, while still offering good looks, in order to get a better selling price.

Renault noticed this trend and decided to bring to Mexico cars that have great exterior looks, but with less attention, and therefore lower costs, focused on the interior (which some considered to feel quite cheap in quality). They changed the entire model line-up to fulfil this cost–benefit trend, including rebranding as Renault some models from their Dacia and Samsung subsidiaries, and sourcing from countries other than France. This approach allowed Renault to balance costs and be more competitive against other brands, and was possible because the interior was not a major concern for Mexican consumers (who want to show off their cars, but don't necessarily want others to get inside them). In addition, a strategy to personalize the outside of the car was developed, which made use of various accessories, such as styling kits and decals (car stickers), which would enhance and customize the appearance of the car exterior. A key aspect of the sales strategy was mounting these 'exterior enhancers' in showrooms so that people could touch and feel the products, which led to increasing accessory sales for the franchises that implemented the strategy. Sales did not increase much for those dealers who did not mount the products in their showroom cars, because in the end looking at the product inside a box does not engage the client at all. Direct experience with the accessory was important for sales. An appropriate execution at the point of sale was also important, because salesmen need to make sure that the client understands the options they have and how they can make their recently acquired car unique. Sales workshops had to be implemented nationwide to prepare the sales force for an appropriate implementation. Check this link for one of the suppliers that helped us implement the strategy (www.airdesign.com) where you can see pictures and many examples from the industry.

Alongside this development in thinking about consumers as experience-seekers was a shift in how consumer behaviour was investigated, with a move towards greater use of qualitative methods and a more holistic examination of the factors affecting consumption. This shift is illustrated in important papers by authors such as Belk et al. (1988, 1989), Rook (1988), and O'Guinn and Faber (1989). This early work paved the way for the consumer culture theory approach to consumption (Arnould and Thompson, 2005), which is discussed in the next section.

Consumer culture theory

Consumer culture theory (CCT), a term first proposed by Eric Arnould and Craig Thompson in 2005, aims to capture an approach to the study of consumers which emphasizes the social and cultural aspects of consumption. The CCT approach places consumers in a wider context than previous research. For example, a CCT investigation into consumer food shopping behaviour might focus on the various practices around food shopping, including menu planning, list-making, domestic storage availability and use, family routines and practices around shopping, and cooking arrangements, in order to develop a full and deep account of how these various aspects of food shopping come to influence the acts of purchasing food. Arnould and Thompson (2005) organize key studies from consumer culture research over the last 20 years into four main strands of research (see Table 2.1). Common to the studies that are classified as CCT is an emphasis on the sociocultural processes and structures and how these are linked to consumption (see Research Insight 2.3).

Another important aspect of the CCT approach is that it has developed new ways of thinking about how to approach research with consumers, some of which have been

CCT theme and explanation
1. Consumer identity projects This research has focused on consumers seeking to develop their identity through their consumption behaviour. Identity projects relate to the idea that throughout our life we are engaged in a process of construction of a story (or narrative) of ourselves, and use consumption to mark this story. Jewellery often serves this function for consumers. The Danish jewellery company PANDORA markets its charms and charm bracelets with the promise 'You're certain to find one for each of your special moments in the PANDORA range of charms'.
2. Marketplace cultures This strand focuses on how consumers interact with the marketplace, how their particular consumption needs are served by it, and how consumers become influencers and producers of culture. Nightclubs provide a good illustration of a marketplace culture—the fashions and trends in music, styles of dancing, clothes worn, and drinks and drugs consumed are influenced and shaped by both clubbers and club promoters.
3. The socio-historic patterning of consumption This strand looks at how the institutions and social structures in our lives influence consumption, and draws on more sociological understandings of consumer lives. This approach might typically consider how representations of consumption have evolved over time, and how these are supported in society. Efforts to understand sociocultural influences on men's eating habits, for example, may systematically analyse representations of men, food, eating, and health in various media over a historical period of time to gain a sense of the ways that this has evolved.
4. Mass-mediated marketplace ideologies and consumers' interpretive strategies This research strand is concerned with how consumers make sense of marketing messages and develop responses to them. From this perspective, consumers are active agents, engaged with meaning-creating activities. Examples of this type of activity may focus on the ways that consumers subvert and resist marketing messages that they find offensive in some way, as found in the Canadian anti-consumerist campaigning group Adbusters and its offshoot organizations around the world.

Table 2.1   Themes of consumer culture theory

Method	Explanation
Ethnography	Ethnography is a qualitative research method which aims to understand the cultural phenomena reflecting the knowledge and meaning systems associated with the everyday life of a cultural group. This method aims for deep immersion in the culture of interest. Examples of ethnography include studies of desire in the USA, Turkey, and Denmark (Belk et al., 2003) and studies of domestic use of kitchen cupboards and storage space (Coupland, 2005).
Introspection	Introspection is a form of structured self-reflection, and has been used to examine a range of consumption practices, including music consumption (Shankar, 2000), consumer value (Holbrook, 2006), and more recently a long-term visit to Sweden (Montanari, 2012),
Narrative analysis/ inquiry	Narrative analysis stems from literary criticism, and from this perspective the 'consumer story' is viewed as a repository for emotional, cognitive, and affective responses to brands, advertising, and interpersonal exchange. Examples include narrative analysis of sports shoe purchase experience (Stern et al., 1998), Australian consumers' use of brands to construct their self (Schembri et al., 2010), and Chinese tourists' evaluations of their travel dining experiences (Chang et al., 2011).

Table 2.2   Some research methods favoured in the CCT approach

transferred into commercial marketing practice. Some of the research approaches now being used are detailed in Table 2.2.

Companies using experiential, ethnographic, and CCT approaches

Experiential approaches to and ethnographic methods of understanding consumer behaviour are not only used by academic researchers (see Research Insight 2.4). They have now

RESEARCH INSIGHT 2.3

Bradford, T.W., Grier, S.A., and Henderson, G.R. (2012), 'Gifts and gifting in online communities', in R. W. Belk, S. Askegaard, and L. Scott (eds), *Research in Consumer Behavior*, Vol. 14, Bingley: Emerald Group, pp 29–46.

A paper presented at the 2012 CCT conference reported on a study of online weight-loss communities. This paper looks at how consumers interact in online weight-loss forums from the perspectives of sharing and gifting. Sharing within these communities served to develop relationships, mainly through the sharing of weight-loss experiences, but in addition these relationships were enriched through gifting rituals. Both self-gifts and gifts to others were highlighted, including tangible gifts (e.g. rewards/treats, recipe exchange) and more symbolic gifts (e.g. clothes purchased signifying weight loss, praise, and encouragement for others). This paper adds to recent consumer literature that discusses sharing as a form of consumer behaviour (Belk, 2010), and offers a new and interesting perspective on online community interactions.

 Visit the Online Resource Centre to read the abstract and access the full paper.

RESEARCH INSIGHT 2.4

Cayla, J. and Arnould, E. (2013), 'Ethnographic stories for market learning', *Journal of Marketing*, 77, July, 1–16.

This paper offers insights into the ways that companies use ethnographic approaches to bring stories of consumers' lives into the boardroom. Drawing on data from a consumer goods company selling cleaning products and a financial services company, the authors argue that ethnographic stories provide an important and valuable way of understanding the complexity of consumer culture. They also explore ethnography as a means to learn about and understand market contexts.

 Visit the Online Resource Centre to read the abstract and access the full paper.

become accepted and widely used methods in marketing practice, with companies such BP Ultimate Fuels, Nokia, and Tesco regularly turning to such techniques to understand their consumer markets.

Technology and consumer behaviour

Another important aspect of understanding consumers in context is appreciating the role of technology as an influence and driver of consumption. Technological developments are a key force for social change, and as technology stabilizes, its design begins to influence user's practices and behaviours in relation to it.

Technology in a sociocultural context

Technology is changing the infrastructure of business and markets, but it has also dramatically altered the social fabric of consumer lives. The extent to which technology reflects and responds to consumer needs is a matter for debate. While some technological advances are developed as a direct response to some consumer needs, others appear in some way to create or engender consumer needs.

The development of the climbing harness is a good example of how technological advances develop in response to consumer needs. Harnesses for rock climbing and outdoor pursuits were developed in the 1960s by climbers who realized that the protection achieved by directly tying onto the rope was inadequate for the standards of climbing difficulty being achieved. Climbers began experimenting on an individual basis, and ultimately it was a group of climbers who developed and produced the first commercially available harnesses. In this case the impetus for technological change was a grass-roots development, arising from the demands of the situation and an understanding that the tools currently available were inadequate. This case also shows the interaction between consumer demand and technological development—one feeds the other in the development of new products.

But just as technology can emerge in response to consumer need, often the development of the technology itself drives change and influences consumption in ways hitherto unimaginable. A good illustration of this kind of technological determinism is provided by the smartphone, whose emergence around 2001 fuelled a major shift in practices and behaviour around mobile phones. With consumers now interacting with their phones as mobile computing devices, the result was a new set of consumption behaviours involving the consumption of web-based media and the purchase of dedicated software—apps. These behaviours imply a high level of downloading, and thus have implications for mobile operators in terms of pricing, speed, and access. When interacting with mobile technology and social media, consumers have come to experience a sense of immediacy which impacts on their expectations of consumption experiences; they expect speed and ease of access as the norm, as further discussed in Consumer Insight 2.3. Of course, this is where the situation becomes more complex, and a simple model of technological determinism breaks down as humans start to respond to the technical parameters and constraints that existing technology imposes on the consumer, with their attitudes, views, and buying behaviours feeding back to the manufacturers and their development teams.

CONSUMER INSIGHT 2.3

The power customer replaces consumer power

According to Gartner Research, technology is placing greater power in the hands of the customer. Armed with their smartphones, consumers are becoming more savvy in all aspects of the shopping experience, as they have unparalleled access to the information they need to make more informed consumption decisions. Research for Google conducted by Ipsos OTX (an independent market research company) looked at the ways smartphones are used in everyday consumer lives. One thing that this research found was that consumers used smartphones increasingly to find out about local businesses, where they were, what times they were open, prices, etc. Dealing with empowered consumers makes life more challenging for brands, but presents an opportunity for competitive differentiation to organizations that are prepared to invest in meeting the demands of power customers. But is this true? Nagiah (2013) argues that the idea of consumer power is illusory, and companies are giving consumers the feeling of being in control (facilitated by technology), when actually companies have considerable knowledge about and power over consumers.

Questions

1. Taking the example of shopping locally, how do you think that local businesses could capitalise on consumers' use of smartphones?

2. What disadvantages may there be for businesses as more consumers use their smartphones in the ways described in this consumer insight?

3. Read the article by Nagiah (2013). Do you think that consumers are really empowered?

Sources: Nagiah (2013); http://www.gospelware.co.uk/ http://www.gartner.com/newsroom/id/1984415

 Visit the Online Resource Centre and follow the weblinks to learn more about the concept of consumer power.

Types of technological innovations

Innovations are best classified in this context by a product-oriented classification, where the focus is on the degree of novelty in the product and the effect that this has on consumer behaviour. This perspective helps us consider some of the central issues for consumers responding to technological developments in the marketplace. **Continuous innovations** *are those that tend to create little change in consumption patterns, and generally involve the introduction of a modified product rather than a totally new one.* Examples are the introduction of a new version of software (such as the launch of Windows 8) or minor improvements or modifications to existing equipment, such as an updated version of an iPod. **Dynamically continuous innovations** *create some change in behavioural patterns, but the magnitude of change is not very great.* This might involve the creation of a new technological innovation or the modification of an existing one, but is best thought of as evolutionary rather than revolutionary; the product tends to be used in the same way as its predecessors were used. The introduction of digital cameras is a good example of a dynamically continuous technological innovation; consumers may still take photos in the same way they did with a film camera, but the practices around printing (developing) and sharing photographs are very different, and require different support structures.

The final type of innovation is **discontinuous innovation**, *which has a disruptive effect, and will require the establishment of new behavioural patterns.* Such innovations are very likely to be technology based, and would be characterized as revolutionary—so new that we have never known anything like it before. Examples of discontinuous innovations include the internet and email. Recently, there has been a great deal of interest in the development of the computer-controlled car, commonly known as the 'driverless car' (see Figure 2.7). The driverless car is an auto-driving system that can navigate entirely without human input, and although only at the prototype stage in 2013, it is envisaged that it could be commercialized in the near

Figure 2.7   The Oxford University RobotCar

Source: John Cairns and the Department of Engineering Science at the University of Oxford.

future, radically altering how we approach driving. Benefits associated with this technological advancement include fewer road accidents, more productive commutes, and fewer traffic jams. But there are still questions about the extent to which these driverless cars would be received by consumers, and how the various infrastructural aspects of motoring would assist or hinder the acceptance of this technological innovation (Araujo et al., 2012).

The market for driverless cars depends on more than consumers being persuaded to give up driving and 'buy into' this system. For driverless cars to work, the whole infrastructure around driving needs to be considered and

> …they [driverless cars] have to fit with the current automobility system or the system needs to be reconfigured to accommodate a novel entity. Some of those adaptations will require minor changes in the practices that make use of cars in our everyday lives, whilst others will need major investments in changing or upgrading existing networks (e.g. service and maintenance).

> (Araujo et al., 2012: 7)

It is very important for both marketers and consumers that products and services that support the use of such innovations are available.

Adoption of new technology

When discussing the adoption of new forms of technology, the milestone of reaching 50 million users is often mentioned. To reach 50 million users, the radio took 38 years, TV 13 years, the internet 4 years, and Facebook approximately 3.5 years. In 2012, it took the Angry Birds Space app 35 days (Annan, 2012). Not all new technologies will enjoy quite this type of pattern of adoption and uptake, and these social technologies are closely linked to the overall increased processing power of computers, but it is useful for firms to consider what it is that makes users or consumers adopt innovations and new ideas.

The most influential work on the diffusion of innovations is by Everett Rogers (1995) who argued that an innovation is communicated through certain channels over time among the members of a social system. Within the context of rural farmers, he proposed that an innovation must reach a critical mass in order to sustain itself. Rogers suggested that there are five main categories for adopters based on their readiness and desire to adopt innovations and new ideas: innovators, early adopters, early majority, late majority, and laggards. This model and approach has informed much marketing thinking and analysis of consumer adoption of new technology and is still used today to understand the nature of adoption. Table 2.3 provides an overview of how the main categories of consumer adoption apply in contemporary technological innovation contexts, along with approximate indications of the size of each segment within the market.

A study in the USA by First Direct focused on how consumers use and adopt financial services technology. Along similar lines to Rogers' classification, the research identified six distinct categories of banking consumers based on key demographic, behavioural, and

Category	Characteristics
Innovators (2.5%)	Visionary imaginative individuals, who are technology enthusiasts. They want to be the first to get new technological products.
Early adopters (13.5%)	Genuinely enjoy the process of discovering new technologies and love talking to others about it. They are likely to embrace new social technologies before most people do.
Early majority (34%)	These consumers deliberate a little longer over adoption and take their cues from 'innovators' or 'early adopters' they know personally. They tend to look for innovations offering incremental predictable improvements on existing technology. They do not like risk, care about the reputation of the innovator, are fairly price sensitive, and like to see competitors entering the market so that they can compare features.
Late majority (34%)	Conservative, somewhat sceptical, cautious of new products and progress, preferring and relying on tradition. They fear high-tech products and usually adopt new technologies only when forced.
Laggards (16%)	Exhibit similar characteristics to the late majority (bound in tradition; sceptical) but even more so. Likely to be found among older consumers and consumers with lower socio-economic status.

Source: Based on Rogers (1995); Huh and Kim (2008); Hoyer and MacInnis (2008).

Table 2.3 Characterizing the categories of adoption

attitudinal measures, including their inclination to use banking technology products and services.

- *Fast trackers*—young family types who rely on smartphones and banking apps.
- *Young aspirationals*—singles with varied interests and little banking loyalty.
- *Simplifiers*—middle-aged lower-income wage earners loyal to their local banks.
- *Middle of the roaders*—middle-aged wage earners who wait until technology is proven.
- *Value seekers*—older, well-educated, and financially comfortable customers; little interest in technology.
- *Conventional stalwarts*—fixed-income retirees who prefer paper statements and live tellers.

Factors influencing technological impact on consumption

What are the factors influencing technological impact on consumption? One major issue relates to how disruptive the technological innovation is; the example of the driverless car is a good illustration of the extent of change in the socio-technical context that is needed to support new technology. Technological developments occur within a complex matrix of infrastructural elements and stakeholders or actors, and consumers are just one set of actors in this matrix. Environmental factors can also impact on technological advancements, since many are developed in response to environmental and ecological conditions (see Consumer Insight 2.4). Linked to this is an understanding of the cultural and social systems within which the technology is developed. The Tata Nano car was launched by Tata Motors in 2008, positioned as the world's cheapest motor car, and is produced and sold in India. The stripped-back design has no air conditioning, no electric windows, and no power steering, and in 2013 had a base price of around 150,000 rupees (approximately £1,760). The Tata

CONSUMER INSIGHT 2.4

Wind farms: good or bad?

Wind farms provide a good illustration of technological advances in response to environmental concerns, but also how acceptance is influenced by social and cultural factors. The Eurobarometer Standard Survey (EB), conducted biannually, has shown a positive picture with regard to renewable energies and, in particular, there is support for wind energy in some European countries, notably Denmark, Greece, and Poland (www.windenergythefacts.org). Nevertheless, there is still resistance to wind farms in many countries. The visual impact on the landscape has been considered to be a major influence on attitudes to wind farms and a key motivation to opposition (Warren et al., 2005). One study identified harmony with the environment as the most critical perceptual dimension, with those who viewed turbines has having a high degree of unity with the landscape showing less opposition to them. Studies in the UK, the Netherlands, and Ireland found preferences for smaller-scale turbine installations (Devine-Wright, 2005).

Wind farms are a source of great debate in the UK. Those in favour argue that they provide a clean source of renewable energy, with no pollution and no waste products; they have a small footprint (the base inhabits only a small area and farmers can still cultivate the land around them); they create jobs (manufacturing, installation, and maintenance); and they can be built offshore beyond the horizon line, meaning that they are not visible from the land.

Conservation groups and members of local communities living near proposed sites often argue against wind farms saying that they and their associated infrastructure, such as roads and tracks, are an eyesore, spoiling the natural beauty of the landscape and causing noise pollution; that they are expensive and at current levels not as efficient as fossil fuel or nuclear energy; and that turbines can cause disruption to TV and radio signals, and even the migration of birds, when not positioned correctly. Opponents also claim that turbines are only cost-effective as a result of extensive government subsidies. Clearly, the arguments are not expressed purely in terms of environmental impact, but rather reflect the complexity of issues involved, and the actors affected, when introducing such a disruptive new technology.

Questions

1. From your understanding of the issues, what advice would you give the Department of Energy and Climate Change to convince local people of the benefits of having a wind farm in their community?

2. What other innovations can you think of that have caused major debate and differences of opinion? Consider what the major reasons for people to resist innovations are in each case. Do you find similarities and/or differences?

Sources: Carrington (2012); Kirkup (2012); www.wind-energy-thefacts.org www.energychest.net

 Visit the Online Resource Centre and follow the weblinks to learn more about wind farms in the UK.

Nano was originally launched as a cheap car, aimed at people in India and China who were looking to buy their first car in place of a motorbike or scooter (Chang, 2008). However, environmental critics were concerned that the increase in the car market in India would lead to even more traffic congestion, as well as adding to India's pollution problems. But these fears were premature; as of April 2012, only 175,000 Nanos had been sold in India (which has a population of 1.2 billion) and the most recent sales figures show a steep decline. The car is now being repositioned as a smart car, offering good value for money (BBC, 2013).

Finally, technological innovations often have unanticipated social and economic consequences. The effects of technological innovations are not always positive. As smartphone technology has evolved, often with high-specification digital cameras, many consumers have shunned dedicated cameras in favour of such multipurpose devices (Mintel, 2012). This move towards people using their smartphones for digital photography, and the shift towards people sharing photos online via social media (rather than having them printed), has contributed to the decline in the popularity of film-based photography and the closure of specialist shops and services that support it (e.g. the closure in the UK of Jessops camera stores). To survive and prosper businesses have to keep pace with technological change and see how consumers are responding to it. However, it is difficult for businesses to predict how consumers will react to innovations—they embrace some, and reject others—and recognizing what changes in behaviour mean to business is essential for survival.

Social networks and consumer behaviour

We are all familiar with the power of social networks around the world. The rise of social media use has been incredibly fast, and has changed the ways that we socialize and interact with each other. YouTube is the second-largest search engine in the world (socialmediatoday. com) and over 90 per cent of marketers use social media in some way. From a consumer behaviour perspective, these new forms of communication with millions of people around the world have changed not only the way we communicate with one another, but also how we comment on, complain about, and recommend brands. Companies have little control over this behaviour. However, they can use social networks to listen to what consumers say to one another, and watch what people are doing. Companies can also create platforms for buyers to engage with, either to find out more about their consumers or to offer the opportunity to develop and market products and services to them.

Table 2.4 demonstrates the increasing popularity of Facebook, but other popular sites include VK (Russia), Tuenti (Spain), Badoo.com (Southern Europe, South America, Eastern Europe, and parts of Asia), Arkut (popular in India and Brazil), and Cyworld (South Korea).

Country	SNS 1	SNS 2	SNS 3
Australia	Facebook	Linkedin	Twitter
Austria	Facebook	Badoo	Twitter
Belgium	Facebook	Badoo	Linkedin
Brazil	Facebook	Orkut	Badoo
Canada	Facebook	Linkedin	Twitter
China	Ozone	Tencent Weibo	SinaWeibo
Denmark	Facebook	Linkedin	Badoo
Finland	Facebook	Linkedin	Twitter
France	Facebook	Badoo	Skyrock
Germany	Facebook	Wer-kennt-wen	Xing
India	Facebook	Linkedin	Orkut
Italy	Facebook	Badoo	Twitter
Japan	Facebook	Twitter	Mixi
Netherlands	Facebook	Hyves	Twitter
Norway	Facebook	Linkedin	Twitter
Portugal	Facebook	Badoo	Orkut
Russia	Odnoklassniki	V Kontakte	Facebook
Sweden	Facebook	Twitter	Linkedin
Spain	Facebook	Tuenti	Badoo
UK	Facebook	Twitter	Linkedin
USA	Facebook	Twitter	Linkedin

Source: http://vincos.it/world-map-of-social-networks/

Table 2.4 Preferred social network site (SNS) by country, June 2012

CONSUMER INSIGHT 2.5

Social networking in China

In June 2012 the China Internet Network Information Centre (CNNIC) reported that mobile internet users had reached 388 million. By the end of 2012 regular users of social networking sites (SNSs) were well over 300 million (www.chinanetwatch.com). The top social networks in China are QZone, Tencent Weibo, Sina Weibo Renren, and Kaixin001.com. In China, 80 per cent of SNS users are aged between 20 and 34, with those between 18 and 27 spending an average of five hours a day online. Wolf (2012a) noted that young people in China may be uncomfortable meeting strangers in a face-to-face situation and find that SNSs offer them the opportunity to have low-risk interactions where they are able to craft their profile and persona in advance. Marketing opportunities on China's SNSs are trickier, as Chinese consumers appear to be less sensitive to advertorial content than western consumers. RedTech Advisors (www. RedTechAdvisors.com), a Shanghai-based consultancy, reported that marketing information may not have an advantage unless it is transmitted by friends or peers. Other studies suggest that urban users born after 1990 rarely use traditional media and go directly online for information and entertainment. This means that advertisers may well start their SNS presence in China with low-key branded advertisements.

One brand that has gone for a more interactive approach is InBev's Budweiser. In 2010 they launched the first non-commercial TV advertisement featuring the famous pop star Eason Chan to promote responsible drinking; in 2011, they launched the first jingle (composed and performed by famous pop duo Yu Quan). The 2012 campaign is also supported by offline and PR events, and began with a mini-film premiered in Shanghai called 'True love needs a designated driver' (see Figure 2.8). The film, featuring movie star couple Sha Yi and Hu Ke, was available to view on a number of Chinese sites and achieved six million hits in one day (with a total of 55 million hits in three months).

The brand used Sina Weibo (a Chinese microblogging website, similar to a hybrid of Twitter and Facebook) and the Baidu search engine to engage consumers and gain participation by asking drivers to commit to not drinking and driving in order to win an exclusive 'I do' badge on his/her personal page. The objective was for participants to identify potential designated drivers, willing to drive them home, from among their Sina Weibo friends. In 2012, the 'I Do' campaign moved to a new level. Following the premiere launch of the mini-movie, AB InBev China kicked off an online charity campaign called 'Exchange one commitment for another' on weibo.com. AB InBev committed to building a Hope School in the Jiangsu Province when over half a million 'netizens' posted or forwarded the Budweiser 'I Do' commitment link. They donated 500,000RMB ($78,125).

Questions

1. Do you think that a similar scheme to Budweiser's would work in your country? Why? Why not?

2. Take a look on SNS for other responsible drinking campaigns. How do they use the site to get their message across?

Figure 2.8 Promotion for 'I do' campaign

Source: Image courtesy of AB InBev.

3. Consider your own reaction to advertising on SNS. Do you look at it? Do you go on many commercial pages? What do you like about marketing on SNS? What don't you like?

Sources: Wolf (2012a, b, c); www.ab-inbev.cn www.RedTechAdvisors.com www.chinawatch.com cnnic.net.cn

 Visit the Online Resource Centre and follow the weblinks to learn more about social networking in China.

Companies have a major presence on social networking sites as this allows them to interact with their current and potential consumers in new ways that are different from traditional advertising. Games, competitions, quizzes, and other interactive approaches enable an engagement with consumers that would not be possible in other media. Apps also offer some added function or amusement and ensure that the name of the brand is kept in front of the consumer in a much more consistent way than can be achieved through other forms of advertising.

Twitter is another important development for consumer behaviour, largely because it is an almost instant medium of communication. Twitter search, a powerful feature with searches based on real-time tweets, is perhaps one of the most important features for consumers. At the time of writing, there were over two billion searches on Twitter every day (http://www.statisticbrain.com/twitter-statistics/). Social networking sites have been important in terms of developing two-way (both consumer to consumer and consumer to supplier) rather than one-way (supplier to consumer) conversations. It is easy for consumers to share information amongst each another, and importantly people want to participate and talk about the brands and products they love and/or hate.

It is important to recognize the differences between those consumers who have grown up surrounded by computers, mobile phones, and digital technology and those who have not. An interesting, although contentious, view is offered by Prensky (2001), who compares what he calls 'digital natives' and 'digital immigrants'. In his view, the importance of the distinction is this: as digital immigrants learn to adapt to their environment, they always retain, to some degree, their 'accent', i.e. their foot in the past. The 'digital immigrant accent' can be seen in such things as turning to the internet for information second rather than first, or in reading the manual for a program rather than assuming that the program itself will teach you to use it. Marketers have to remember that they are dealing with a range of people who have learned about technology in different ways.

Mobile technology

In 2012, the World Bank estimated that three-quarters of the world's population has access to mobile technology (http://www.worldbank.org). In 2010, Morgan Stanley identified four important current trends that directly affect consumer behaviour.

1. **Location-based services**—Zipcar (Zipcar.com) is a service for people who want to be able to drive a car but not own one, and has a free app (which engages GPS and Google Maps) to allow users to locate, reserve, and unlock Zipcars.

2. **Transparent pricing**—examples of such apps, which allow consumers to scan barcodes and identify best pricing information, include Etao.com (China) and the ShopSavvy app (UK/USA).

3. **Deep discounts**—gilt.com has online 'flash' designer sales with deep discounts, offered on an invite-only basis, for a limited time.

4. **Immediate gratification**—books, music, and films are all now available instantly or within seconds.

An example of how such mobile technology can be used effectively is a promotion by Jimmy Choo from 2010. Using the location-based social networking site Four Square, Jimmy Choo sent a single pair of trainers from their trainer range to check in at fashionable

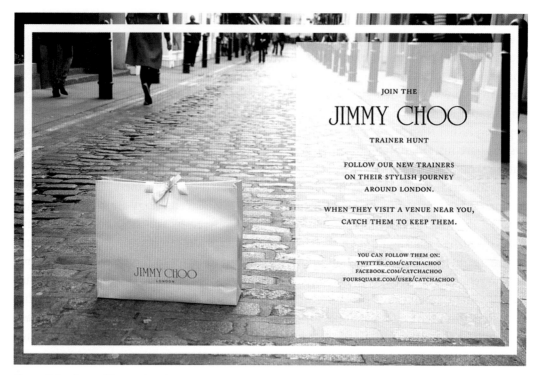

Figure 2.9 Jimmy Choo trainer hunt

Source: Image courtesy of FreshMinds (http://www.freshminds.co.uk).

hangouts around London, and sent Four Square subscribers real-time updates about their whereabouts. The trainers would only remain at each venue for a few minutes, and the person reaching a venue in time to catch the trainers would win a pair in their size (see Figure 2.9). Jimmy Choo estimated that 4,500 people took part over a three-week period, but also that their trainer sales increased by 33 per cent during the campaign (Fresh Networks, 2013).

Conclusions

In this chapter we have examined a range of very different contemporary ways of looking at how consumers behave. We identified key topics from **behavioural economics** and how they may impact consumer behaviour. In Consumer Insight 2.1 we described a number of examples from the health domain to show how behavioural economics is becoming increasingly popular as a way of influencing behaviour. We also looked at research into recycling behaviour in hotels, and demonstrated how emphasizing social norms in marketing communications leads to greater behavioural change.

We explored the theories and practices of *experiential consumption* and *consumer culture theory*, and Practitioner Insight 2, focusing on the experiences associated with buying a car in Mexico, showed how these ideas have been used in a commercial context.

Appreciating the *role of technology*, and how it impacts on consumption, is very important to help understand how consumption practices develop and change over time. In Consumer Insight 2.3 we discussed the evolution of smartphone technology, how companies are using technology to interact with consumers, and how this has empowered consumers. This illustrates some of the ways that new technologies can shape behaviour.

The *nature of innovations* was explored in depth, and we considered a range of examples, including the driverless car. We showed that the extent to which the new technology disrupts established patterns of behaviour will have most impact on how consumers react to and interact with new technological innovations.

New technological platforms have allowed the development of novel *social media* and businesses are learning how consumers are behaving with these media and what opportunities they may offer. We considered the example of the use of the Chinese social networking site Sina Weibo to promote Budweiser among youths, and take an in-depth look at Pinterest in Case Study 2. Social media will be used differently by different demographic groups and so offers many opportunities, but we must also recognize that some consumers will be more resistant or less able to use them. Above all we recognize that we cannot rely on a simple unified approach to consumer behaviour, and marketers who want to succeed in the complex marketplace need to draw on a range of theories, resources, and techniques to better understand their consumers.

Review questions

1. Explain the difference between the automatic and reflective systems.

2. What does mental accounting and priming tell us about consumer behaviour?

3. Briefly explain what is meant by loss aversion and mental accounting.

4. What do we mean by the term 'experiential consumption'?

5. Define and describe the four main research themes underpinning the consumer culture theory approach to consumer behaviour.

6. Identify three ways in which new technology has affected consumer behaviour.

7. What is the difference between a 'digital native' and a 'digital immigrant'? How might their consumer behaviour differ?

Discussion questions

1. Using behavioural economics to inform your discussions, consider campaigns that might be successfully developed for:

    a) encouraging people to take some exercise during their working day

    b) putting litter into litter bins

    c) keeping to the speed limit.

    Remember that incentives, choice, and feedback can be useful for successful choice architecture.

2. Where do you think your government might consider an 'opt out' rather than 'opt in' method for changing consumer behaviour. What might be the problems with doing this? Are there ethical issues that we should consider?

3. MyFitnessPal.com is an app designed to allow people to work out how many calories they consume in a day. Go to their website http://www.myfitnesspal.com/ and consider what benefits consumers get from using this app and website.

4. Use the four stages of consumption experience (Arnould et al., 2002) to describe a recent purchase. Try to identify what was special or ordinary about each experience stage.

5. Visit the ICM website and watch the short ethnographic film showing a consumer's daily London commute (http://www.icmresearch.com/consumer-ethnography). Analyse in terms of your understanding of consumer culture theory. As part of this analysis, think about and comment on how this material is relevant for marketing practice.

6. Consider a recent product you have adopted. How do you use this product? Has it meant that you have stopped using something else?

 Visit the Online Resource Centre to test your knowledge further and complete the Multiple Choice Questions for Chapter 2.

CASE STUDY 2

Pinterest: the new pinning craze

In this case, we examine the social media site Pinterest, providing some information about its background, history, and users and offering some insights into the consumption issues associated with this site. The Pinterest case illustrates an interesting range of behaviours that may not at first seem obvious from the nature of the site.

Pinterest (Pinterest.com) has been described as the social media's rising star as well as the darling network of brides-to-be, fashionistas, and would-be chefs and bakers. In 2012, what was perhaps most significant about this new social media business was its meteoric growth in referral traffic since its inception in 2009. A referral occurs when any hyperlink is clicked which takes a user to a new page or file in any website, the originating site being the referrer. When a user arrives at your site, referral information is captured, including the referrer URL if available and any search terms that were used. In January 2012 Pinterest beat YouTube, Reddit, Google+, and MySpace for the percentage of total referral traffic (Fox, 2012).

Ben Silbermann developed Pinterest in 2009, and the following year opened the site on an invitation-only basis. Nine months after its launch the website had 10,000 users, and by August 2011 *Time* was able to list Pinterest in its '50 Best Websites of 2011'. In December 2011 it was rated as the No. 10 social site among 6,581 properties measured by Experian Hitwise, with 11 million visits per week (Sloan, 2011). According to another analytics site, comScore, in January 2012 it had 11.7 million unique users which made it the fastest site to break through the 10 million mark (Constine, 2012), and by February 2012 this had risen by 52 per cent to 11.7 million (Kelly, 2012).

What is Pinterest?

So what is Pinterest and how is it used? Essentially it is an online pin board. Users can upload images known as pins and develop collections known as pin boards under themes such as cookery, faces, fashion, weddings, gardens, or indeed anything else. Categorization of pin boards in this way allows other users to find them easily or search for something they are interested in. Users can copy content from within or outside Pinterest.

Initially, some critics suggested that it served as little more than a scrapbook for bored housewives and was dominated by pictures of kittens and cupcakes (Everitt, 2012), but while it may serve this purpose, it is also becoming an increasingly influential medium that businesses want to be involved with. Just do a search on weddings and you will find that it is an endless source of inspiration for the bride and groom. Information comes from other brides, from commercial organizations, and from other pinners, and as all sources of pictures are identified it allows users to easily link through to the original site from which the image has been derived, many of which are commercial.

Who uses Pinterest?

To begin with Pinterest's core user base was not what might be considered a typical early US adopter profile from the west and east coasts of the USA. Instead, the Pacific and northeast regions contained many early Pinterest users; it also had a strong following in the east south central and west north central states, such as Kansas, Missouri, Minnesota, and Mississippi. Although in 2012 there were 12 million users in the USA, the number of UK users had only reached about 200,000. However, the demographics of the UK users were very different. In the USA, 83 per cent were women while in the UK the split was 44 per cent women and 56 per cent men (Chowney, 2012). UK users also seemed to be interested in a wider range of subjects including venture capital, marketing, and public relations alongside the more US favoured subjects of crafts and design. In the USA other image-based sites are being developed specifically for men—for example, Manteresting and Gentlemint. Pinterest is starting to gain popularity in other countries, and usage by country is shown in Figure 2.10.

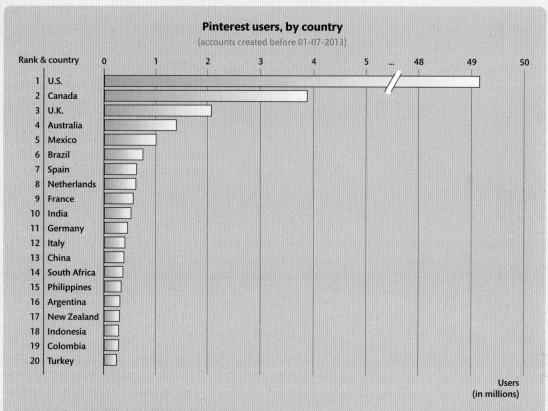

Figure 2.10   Pinterest use, by country

Source: Image reproduced with permission from Semiocast.

Marketers are already looking to identify distinct groups who use Pinterest. Research from Experian Hitwise (Ledbetter, 2012) has identified three key groups.

1. 'Boomers and Boomerangs' is a two-group segment which includes baby boomer adults and their teenage and young adult children who live at home. The boomers are often living in houses over 15 years old which suggests that they are interested in home projects.

2. 'Babies and Bliss' tend to be in large families in their thirties and forties, with the mother working full time, and are highly IT literate. They like internet shopping, and high-quality merchandise and convenience is critical.

3. Finally, the 'Families Matter Most' group includes young middle-class families with active lifestyles. Typically, they are serious parents and 'informed consumers', looking for healthy lifestyles for themselves and their families. They pride themselves on knowing better than to waste their time window-shopping.

The commercial value of Pinterest

Arts and crafts from crochet to metal work are available to view on Pinterest, but so are pin boards on finance, technology, and architecture. While many of the pictures may be folksy and of limited appeal, Pinterest is also a source of new zany artefacts and market information (see Figure 2.11). Items that are unique or different may go viral very quickly. Social media strategist Rob McNair from my-cleveragency describes it as 'a discovery tool and the products that get shared are the most unique products' (Everitt, 2012). Food and recipes are particularly popular as they are so dependent on visual stimulus; a board called Gastromomia has been re-pinned over 1.4 million times. There are many other opportunities for commercial involvement as topics such as festive occasions, holidays, and interior design are popular. A quick search on Pinterest for the top ten pinned items of the week will give you an idea of where potential customers' interests lie For marketers, the lists of most pinned items could prove a very useful tool in market research.

Figure 2.11   A Pinterest page

Source: Image kindly supplied by Karina Minteer.

Could Pinterest be a threat to businesses? The danger is that people in communities like this will be sharing ideas with one another rather than going to the specialist magazines or websites. A story in *The Washington Post* suggested that with brides and grooms finding inspiration for themselves by using Pinterest, it might threaten the wedding planning industry (Kelly, 2012). But wedding planner Febienne Laveau felt that the interest in Pinterest was likely to result in more brides thinking that they needed a wedding planner rather than risk doing it on their own. There is also extensive exposure on Pinterest not only of wedding planners but also all the other businesses linked with weddings—jewellers, bakers, venue owners, and dressmakers. One successful wedding site, 'Style Me Pretty', features vendors, inspiration, and photographic records of real-life weddings. It has seen an increase in visitors to its site referred directly from Pinterest, which now equals Google search for referral traffic. Global name brands such as Nike and Gap have lots of followers; the US retail store Nordstrom has over four million. Firms can readily show lifestyles that they want associated with their brand, such as the sporty, fit, healthy-looking images on the Wholefoods Strength page. It is also clearly a source of fashion inspiration; with thousands of fashion pins people can follow fashionistas and then pick out and re-pin the styles they like best. Pinterest offers a safe place for people to express their identity, preferences, dreams, and aspirations visually. It allows people to be witty and thoughtful. One pinner, Meghan McCabe, showed a dress in her 'Get in my closet right now' board that was re-pinned over 4,000 times. But Meghan has a range of boards with titles such as 'Crushin on Yew', 'Get Er Done', and 'You make me wanna say I do', which gives an amazing insight into the life and 'loves' of a young American woman.

Pinterest is extremely viral, more so than many other social media platforms with over 80 per cent of pins being repins. Therefore, if you are a content creator you can be fairly sure that your message will be readily spread. Adding the 'PinIt' button to a commercial site or blog can mean that people pin from your site whether or not you have a Pinterest account. For example, look on the Selfridges pin board. This is a shrine to the brand, with pictures of the store, the Selfridges logo, and images from the interior, and people shopping alongside brands sold there. This is important as one of the many common activities on Pinterest is people pinning the things that they want to buy whether they be general wish lists or specific Christmas or birthday lists. You can even add prices to pins.

Most importantly for marketers, there is also a high correlation between pinning and purchasing, with more than one in five Pinterest users having pinned an item that they later purchase. It is difficult to know the cause and effect between pinning and purchasing as Samuel (2012a) questions: 'Are people buying because they pin, or pinning what they always intended to buy? Still, the implications for marketers are clear. Pinning, especially among loyal, active Pinterest users, is intimately intertwined with buying. Pinning is a signal that says, "I'm thinking of purchasing your product too" '. Samuel (2012b) reports on the nature of the Pinterest customer and relationship. Firstly, she says that Pinterest attracts both compulsive shoppers and those who want to get in and out of stores as quickly as possible. It might be that, for some people, being involved in Pinterest actually reduces their consumption as they engage with a form of virtual acquisition which means that they don't actually have to buy the product.

Questions

1. Given Pinterest's growth, who do you think can benefit most from the social network— brands, news sources, market researchers ... who else? How might these social network members benefit?

2. Go to Pinterest.com and spend some time looking at the various boards pinned there. Can you think of any consumer groups who might be targeted (who are not already targeted)?

3. Imagine that you run a small local high street bakery. Consider the ways in which you would use Pinterest to add value to your company.

Sources: Sloan (2011); Chowney (2012); Constine (2012); Everitt (2012); Fox (2012); Hitwise.com (2012); Ledbetter (2012); Samuel (2012a,b).

 Visit the Online Resource Centre and follow the link to the authors' blog where you can keep up to date with the latest developments in consumer behaviour and further explore theories through additional articles and real-world examples.

References

Annan, G.K. (2012), 'Radio took 38 yrs to get 50 million', http://visual.ly/reaching-50-million-users (accessed 3 May 2013).

Araujo, L., Mason, K., and Spring, M. (2012), 'Self-driving cars: a case study in making new markets', *Big Innovation Centre*, 4 December, http://www.biginnovationcentre.com/Publications/25/Selfdriving-cars (accessed 6 May 2014).

Arnould, E.J. and Thompson, C. J. (2005), 'Consumer culture theory (CCT): twenty years of research', *Journal of Consumer Research*, 31, 4, 868–882.

Arnould, E., Price, L., and Zinkhan, G. (2002), *Consumers*, New York: McGraw-Hill.

BBC (2013), 'Tata Nano: world's cheapest car gets image makeover', 22 August, http://www.bbc.co.uk/news/world-asia-23792196 (accessed 13 September 2013).

Belk, R. (2010), 'Sharing', *Journal of Consumer Research*, 36, 5, 715–734.

Belk, R.W., Sherry, J.F. and Wallendorf, M. (1988), 'A naturalistic inquiry into buyer and seller behavior at a swap meet', *Journal of Consumer Research*, 14, 4, 449–470.

Belk, R.W., Wallendorf, M., and Sherry, F.J. Jr. (1989), 'The sacred and the profane in consumer behavior: theodicy on the Odyssey', *Journal of Consumer Research*, 16, June, 1–38.

Belk, R.W., Ger, G., and Askegaard, S. (2003), 'The fire of desire: a multisited inquiry into consumer passion', *Journal of Consumer Research*, 30, December, 326–351.

Bradford, T.W., Grier, S.A., and Henderson, G.R. (2012), 'Gifts and gifting in online communities', in R.W. Belk, S. Askegaard, and L. Scott (eds), *Research in Consumer Behavior*, Vol. 14, Bingley: Emerald Group, pp 29–46.

Cabinet Office (2010), 'Applying behavioural insight to health', Discussion Paper, Cabinet Office Behavioural Insights Team, London, December, https://www.gov.uk/government/publications/applying-behavioural-insight-to-health-behavioural-insights-team-paper (accessed 2 August 2014).

Carrington, D. (2012), 'Why there's only one honest objection to wind farms', *Guardian*, 21 June, http://www.guardian.co.uk/environment/damian-carrington-blog/2012/jun/21/wind-power-subsidies (accessed 4 June 2013).

Cayla, J. and Arnould, E. (2013), 'Ethnographic stories for market learning', *Journal of Marketing*, 77, July, 1–16.

Chang, R.C., Kivela, J., and Mak, A.H. (2011), 'Attributes that influence the evaluation of travel dining experience: when East meets West', *Tourism Management*, 32, 2, 307–316.

Chang, R.S. (2008), 'Tata Nano: the world's cheapest car', http://wheels.blogs.nytimes.com/2008/01/10/tata-nano-the-worlds-cheapest-car/ (accessed 20 April 2013).

Chowney, V. (2012), 'More male Pinterest users in UK than female: infographic', http://econsultancy.com/uk/blog/9021-more-male-pinterest-users-in-uk-than-female-infographic (accessed 12 December 2012).

Constine, J. (2012), Pinterest hits 10 million US monthly unique faster than any standalone site ever—comScore, http://techcrunch.com/2012/02/07/pinterest-monthly-uniques/ (accessed 6 December 2013).

Coupland, J.C. (2005), 'Invisible brands: an ethnography of households and the brands in their kitchen pantries', *Journal of Consumer Research*, 32, 1, 106–118.

Devine-Wright, P. (2005), 'Beyond NIMBYism: towards an integrated framework for understanding public perceptions of wind energy', *Wind Energy*, 8, 125–139.

Dijksterhuis, A. and Bargh, J.A. (2001), 'The perception-behavior expressway: automatic effects of social perception on social behavior', *Advances in Experimental Social Psychology*, 33, 1–40.

Dumanovsky, T., Huang, C.Y., Nonas, C.A., Matte, T.D., Bassett, M.T., and Silver, L.D. (2011), 'Changes in energy content of lunchtime purchases from fast food restaurants after introduction of calorie labelling: cross sectional customer surveys', *British Medical Journal*, 343, d4464.

Ebhohimhen, P.V. and Avenell, A. (2008), 'Systematic review of the use of financial incentives in treatments for obesity and overweight', *Obesity Review*, 9, 4, 355–367.

Elbel, B., Kersh, R., Brescoll, V.L., and Dixon, L.B. (2009), 'Calorie labeling and food choices: a first look at the effects on low-income people in New York City', *Obesity* 28, 6 w1110–w1121.

energychest.net (nd), http://www.energychest.net/energy_sources/activity_centre/windofchange.html (accessed 2 February 2013).

Everitt, L. (2012), 'Pinterest: just what exactly is on it?', http://www.bbc.co.uk/news/magazine-17204313 (accessed 7 December 2012).

Fox, Z. (2012), 'Pinterest drives more traffic than Google+, YouTube and LinkedIn combined', http://mashable.com/2012/02/01/pinterest-traffic-study/ (accessed 6 December 2012).

Fresh Networks (2013), 'Supporting global brands: Jimmy Choo', http://www.slideshare.net/freshnetworks/jimmy-choo-pep-foursquare-web-4667255 (accessed 2 August 2014).

Goldstein, N.J., Cialdini, R.B., and Griskevicius, V. (2008), 'A room with a viewpoint: using social norms to motivate environmental conservation in hotels', *Journal of Consumer Research*, 35, 3, 472–482.

Gross, D.B and Souleles, N.S. (2002), 'Do liquidity constraints and interest rates matter for consumer behaviour? Evidence from credit card data', *Quarterly Journal of Economics*, 117, 149–185.

Hastorf, A.H. and Cantril, H. (1954), 'They saw a game: a case study', *Journal of Abnormal Psychology*, 49, 129–134.

Holbrook, M. (2006), 'Consumption experience, customer value, and subjective personal introspection: an illustrative photographic essay', *Journal of Business Research*, 59, 6, 714–725.

Holbrook, M.B. and Hirschman, E.C. (1982), 'The experiential aspects of consumption: consumer fantasies, feelings and fun', *Journal of Consumer Research*, 9, 2, 132–140.

Holland, R.W., Hendriks, M., and Aarts, H. (2005), 'Smells like clean spirit, non-conscious effects on of scent on cognition and behaviour', *Psychological Science*, 16, 9, 689–693.

Hoyer, W.D. and MacInnis, D. (2008), *Consumer behavior*, Boston, MA: Cengage Learning.

Huh, Y.E. and Kim, S.-H. (2008), 'Do early adopters upgrade early? Role of post-adoption behavior in the purchase of next-generation products', *Journal of Business Research*, 61, 1, 40–46.

Johnson, E.J. and Goldstein, D. (2003), 'Medicine: do defaults save lives?', *Science*, 302, 5649, 1338–1339.

Just, D. and Wansink, B. (2009), 'Smarter lunchrooms: using behavioral economics to improve meal selection', *Choice*, 29, 3.

Kelly, C. (2012), 'Wedding planning: Pinterest or professionals', http://www.washingtonpost.com/lifestyle/weddings/wedding-planning-pinterest-or-professionals/2012/05/31/gJQAOYwD5U_story.html (accessed 8 November 2012).

Kirkup, J. (2012), 'Living next to a wind farm is good for you, says minister Ed Davey', *Daily Telegraph*, 12 March 2012, http://www.telegraph.co.uk/earth/energy/windpower/9137224/Living-next-to-a-wind-farm-is-good-for-you-says-minister-Ed-Davey.html (accessed 8 March 2013).

Lawrence, F. (2010), 'First goal of David Cameron's 'nudge unit' is to encourage healthy living', *Guardian*, 12 November, http://www.guardian.co.uk/politics/2010/nov/12/david-cameron-nudge-unit (accessed 26 January 2013).

Ledbetter, E. (2012), 'Pinterest demographic data: the marketers guide to people who pin', http://www.ignitesocialmedia.com/social-networks/pinterest-demographic-data/ (accessed 3 January 2014).

Martin, S. (2012), '98% of HBR readers love this article', *Harvard Business Review*, October, 23–25.

Mintel (2012), 'Digital cameras UK', http://store.mintel.com/digital-cameras-uk-may-2012 (accessed 2 August 2014).

Montanari, A. (2012), 'Beyond subjective to confirmatory personal introspection: interpreting events and meaning of a long-term visit in Sweden', *Journal of Business Research*, 66, 11, 2363–2368.

Morgan Stanley (2010), https://www.datam.co.nz/Files/Whitepaper-Internet-Trends-apr2010.pdf (accessed 8 July 2013).

Nagiah, N. (2013), 'Consumer empowerment is an illusion', *Huffington Post*, 23 July, http://www.huffingtonpost.com/navin-nagiah/consumer-empowerment-is-a_b_3635067.html (accessed 2 August 2014).

O'Guinn, T.C. and Faber, R.J. (1989), 'Compulsive buying: a phenomenological exploration', *Journal of Consumer Research*, 16, 2, 147–157.

Pine, B.J. and Gilmore, J.H. (1998), 'Welcome to the experience economy', *Harvard Business Review*, 76, 97–105.

Prensky, M. (2001), 'Digital natives, digital immigrants: Part 1', *On the Horizon*, 9, 5, 1–6.

Rogers, E.M. (1995), *Diffusion of innovations* (4th edn), New York: Free Press.

Rook, D.W. (1988), 'Researching consumer fantasy', *Research in Consumer Behavior*, 3, 247–270.

Samuel, A. (2012a), 'Moving customers from pinning to purchasing', http://blogs.hbr.org/2012/05/from-pinterest-to-purchase/ (accessed 2 August 2014).

Samuel, A. (2012b), 'Meet your Pinterest customer', http://blogs.hbr.org/2012/03/meet-your-pinterest-customer/ (accessed 2 August 2014).

Schembri, S., Merrilees, B., and Kristiansen, S. (2010), 'Brand consumption and narrative of the self', *Psychology and Marketing*, 27, 6, 623–637.

Schultz, S.P., Nolan, J.M., Cialdini, R.B., Goldstein, N.J., and Griskevicius, V. (2007), 'The constructive, destructive, and reconstructive power of social norms', *Psychological Science*, 18, 429–434.

Shankar, A. (2000), 'Lost in music: subjective personal introspection and popular music consumption', *Qualitative Market Research*, 3, 1, 27–37.

Sloan, P. (2011), 'Pinterest: crazy growth lands it as top 10 social site', http://news.cnet.com/8301-1023_3-57347187-93/pinterest-crazy-growth-lands-it-as-top-10-social-site/?tag=mncol;txt (accessed 9 November 2012).

Social Media Today (2013), http://socialmediatoday.com/socialbarrel/1650226/second-largest-search-engine-infographic (accessed 26 November 2013).

Stern, B., Thompson, C., and Arnould, E. (1998) 'Narrative analysis of a marketing relationship: the consumers' perspective', *Psychology and Marketing*, 15, 3, 195–214.

Surridge, K. (2001), 'More than a great poster: Lord Kitchener and the image of the military hero', *Historical Research*, 74, 185, 298–313.

Thaler, R.H. and Sunstein, C.R. (2009), *Nudge: improving decisions about health wealth and happiness*, London: Penguin Books.

Volpp, J., John, L.K., Troxel, A.B., Norton, L, Fassbender J., and Lowenstein, G. (2008). 'Financial incentive-based approaches for weight loss: a randomized trial', *JAMA*, 330, 22, 2631–2637.

Wansink, B. and Kim, J. (2006), 'Bad popcorn in big buckets: portion size can influence intake as much as taste', *Journal of Nutrition, Education and Behavior*, 37, 5, 242–245.

Warren, C.R., Lumsden, C., O'Dowd, S., and Birnie, R. V. (2005), 'Green on green: public perceptions of wind power in Scotland and Ireland', *Journal of Environmental Planning and Management*, 48, 6, 853–875.

Wolf, D. (2012a), 'China's social networks: choosing the right site', http://www.warc.com

Wolf, D. (2012b), 'Marketers and China's microblogs: Sina Weibo vs Tencent Weibo', http://www.warc.com

Wolf, D. (2012c), 'Social media in China: a marketer's guide', http://www.warc.com

World Bank (2012), http://www.worldbank.org/en/news/press-release/2012/07/17/mobile-phone-access-reaches-three-quarters-planets-population (accessed 26 November 2013).

Wryobeck, J. and Chen, Y. (2003), 'Using priming techniques to facilitate health behaviours', *Clinical Psychologist*, 7, 2, 105–108.

PART 2

MICRO-VIEW OF CONSUMPTION

Where are we going?

**Future Trends in
Consumer Behaviour**

Macro-view

**Consumers in society and
the market: groups,
social processes, culture
and repeat purchasing
behaviour**

Micro-view

**The individual consumer:
Individual decision
making, learning,
perception, attitudes,
personality and
motivation**

How we arrived here

**Historical context and
contemporary
perspectives on
consumption**

3

DECISION-MAKING AND INVOLVEMENT

Introduction

When you buy a product for the first time, how much do you think about what you are buying? Do you ever go shopping in the supermarket intending to buy one brand and come out with a completely different one? If you buy the same brand for three weeks in a row, does that mean you are brand loyal?

When and how we shop, the decisions we make about whether or not to purchase, and what we buy and how we feel after we have bought something are the concerns of this chapter. How rational are consumers in their choices? Do we use shortcuts to make decisions? And how involved are we with what we purchase? These are all questions important to marketers in understanding consumer behaviour and for finding the best marketing strategy to ensure that their products and brands are purchased and purchased again.

LEARNING OUTCOMES

Having read this chapter, you will be able to:

1. Explain **decision-making** in low and high involvement situations.

2. Understand the nature of **involvement** and how this affects people's decision-making.

3. Examine the *stages in the decision-making process*.

4. Understand *shopping behaviour* and consumer shopping motives.

5. Identify the problems that people have with choice, and the strategies used to deal with choice situations such as *satisficing and maximizing behaviour, and the use of heuristics, anchoring, and framing*.

From choice to decision-making

We make decisions every day. While some of these are important and may have a long-term impact on our lives (such as choosing which university course to take), many are trivial (such as whether to have toast or cereal for breakfast) and sometimes we may not even notice that we have made a decision. The decision-making process assumes that we seek to solve a problem or achieve a desired goal. We may want to lose weight or move to a new city. We may feel thirsty or hungry. While the solutions to some of these may be relatively simple, others are more complex and involve a number of decisions regarding choices and actions to achieve our goal. There will be significant differences in how the decision comes about depending on the problem to be solved and the nature and context of the person deciding. The level of involvement consumers have with a purchase is a key factor influencing the decision-making process. **Involvement** *is the perceived relevance of a purchase to the consumer.*

Some decision-making, such as choosing our university course, is important as it will affect aspects of our life (such as the career we can follow). We refer to these as high involvement decisions. Others decisions are of less importance. When a consumer is thirsty they are likely to choose a pleasant tasting drink that quenches their thirst. If they do not like the drink chosen, they may buy another or not buy that brand again, but the outcome is not likely to be very important. Such decisions are referred to as low involvement. Figure 3.1 provides a simplified comparison of decision-making in low and high involvement contexts.

What are the differences between these two decision-making processes? The main difference of significance to marketers is that in the high involvement decision a choice is made following a process of search and evaluation, where some kind of evaluative criteria will be applied. In the low involvement decision the choice is made without these intervening steps. Obviously there are shades of grey, and some researchers distinguish between what is referred to as extended problem-solving (high involvement) and habitual decision-making (low involvement). Limited problem-solving occurs in situations where the consumer is less motivated to search for information or evaluate alternatives in as rigorous a way as they would for an extended problem-solving choice. In such cases consumers may use simple evaluation criteria or decision rules such as 'it must be under £5' or 'it must fit into the space in the corner'. In the low involvement decision the outcomes of the purchase

Figure 3.1   High and low involvement decision-making

may also affect evaluative criteria, although the impact may be more limited (identified by the dashed line in Figure 3.1). A key difference between high and low involvement from a marketing perspective is that in high-involvement consumers are in an active manner as outlined in Table 3.1.

In the consumer behaviour context **active learning** *involves the acquisition of knowledge before purchase, and therefore extensive information search* (Erdem et al., 2005). Here we want to learn more about the brands we are considering buying because the purchase decision is important to us, i.e. it is one of high involvement. Although problem recognition occurs in a low involvement decision, just as it does in high involvement, the consumer uses beliefs formed from passive learning in order to make their choice. **Passive learning** *is the acquisition of knowledge*

Low involvement hierarchy	High involvement hierarchy
Brand beliefs are formed through **passive** learning	Brand beliefs are formed through **active** learning
A purchase decision is then made	Brands are then evaluated
The brand may or may not be evaluated	A purchase decision is made

Table 3.1   Learning in low and highinvolvement decision-making

without active learning. The idea of passive learning was developed by Krugman and Hartley (1970) who studied how people watched television and which advertisements were recalled. They found that watching TV required little effort from the audience; viewers did not need to be actively involved. Messages received by consumers were stored in a passive dormant state until stimulated by recognition of the brand, perhaps the next time that they went to the supermarket. Awareness of the brand at this point could produce behaviour resulting in a purchase. Once the consumer had tried the brand and evaluated it, their attitudes towards it would be formed. An important aspect of passive learning is an absence of resistance to what is learned. As active learning is by its nature exciting and engaging, it may bring about more resistance. If you are looking for a new refrigerator you search catalogues, internet sites, and shops, and in the process you will identify brands that you like (e.g. Smeg, Neff, Miele), but also those you dislike or you think are not right for your needs (e.g. Beko, Indesit, LEC). This represents a form of resistance developed through the active search process.

However, there are times when the decision is still important but we do not go through the extensive decision-making process outlined above. When someone buys a new car they may spend considerable time looking at different brands and types within their price bracket and evoked or consideration set. The **evoked set** refers *to all brands they are aware which might meet their needs*, while the **consideration set** refers *to those they might actually consider buying.* Alternatively, they may already have a well-formed intention of what they want to buy. Perhaps their current car is a BMW Mini and the only reason they want to change is because it has reached a high mileage. In this case they may limit themselves to looking at new models of the Mini. They have a well-formed intention to make a particular choice, and this process is shown in Figure 3.2 where intention comes directly after problem recognition. Of course, if as a result of this purchase they are not happy with their choice, they will probably reconsider and revert to a more actively oriented decision process as shown in Figure 3.1. In Figure 3.2, however, for the purchase to become a more routine decision, a positive outcome has to feed back to a future intention to buy the same brand.

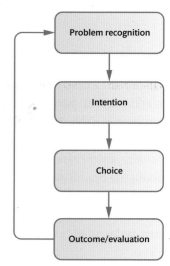

Figure 3.2 Routine decision process in a high involvement situation

Before examining the stages in the decision-making process in more detail, other types of involvement that might impact decision-making and the importance of involvement to marketing are considered in more detail (see Research Insight 3.1).

Involvement and decision-making

As discussed already, the level of involvement and relevance of purchases for consumers can bring about different decision-making processes, as shown in Table 3.2.

RESEARCH INSIGHT 3.1

Arsel, Z. and Bean, J. (2013), 'Taste regimes and market-mediated practice', *Journal of Consumer Research*, 39, 5, 899–917

This paper considers an aspect of consumers' decisions that influences how and what they consume—the concept of taste. Taking a consumer culture theory approach, the authors explore how consumers develop a sense of good taste in interior design and how they incorporate it into their homes. By analysing a popular home design blog, Apartment Therapy, the authors undertake a qualitative and quantitative investigation of participants on this blog to develop a deeper understanding of how consumers develop their sense of taste.

 Visit the Online Resource Centre to read the abstract and access the full paper.

In a low involvement process, where there are few differences among brands, a consumer may not be too concerned about their choices. This could result in inertia which may manifest itself in apparent loyalty, i.e. buying the same brand of tinned tomatoes every week. While the consumer may appear loyal, a price promotion on a similar brand may find them switching brands. Similarly, a consumer may equally follow a random choice routine where they pick up the first brand they notice within their price range or that appeals to them because of packaging or promotion. However, if the choice is a high involvement decision which may include an element of risk, the consumer is likely to engage in dissonance reduction strategies (see Chapter 6) to ensure that they make the right choice. This may mean that they engage in an extended search and look for reassurance after purchase that they have made the right choice.

In a recent advertisement for Swinburne University of Technology in Melbourne, Australia, the copy in the advertisement states 'Am I making the right choice or the safe one?', thereby asking the prospective student if they are confident to look beyond the hype and choose a university based on its merits. This approach reflects Swinburne's recognition that university choice is difficult and that older more established names may be seen as a safer bet. Swinburne tackled high involvement choice head on by trying to alleviate the dissonance a student might feel by emphasizing that Swinburne may be the right (if not the safe) choice. Of course there may be some students who wish to choose a safe option, but many young people will be influenced by an argument that attacks the 'safe' position.

When there are many differences among brands in a low involvement decision there is more incentive for the consumer to engage in variety seeking and try different brands, as noted in Table 3.2. This is often the case in products such as soft drinks, confectionery, and ready-to-eat cereals. Variety-seeking behaviour provides an important opportunity for businesses to develop new flavours, formulations, and packaging as consumers may

	Low involvement (low price, low risk)	High involvement (high price, high risk)
Few differences among brands	Inertia or spurious loyalty Random choice	Complex decision-making and dissonance reduction
Significant difference among brands	Variety seeking Random choice Experimentation	Complex decision-making or brand loyalty

Table 3.2 High and low involvement purchases

be prepared to experiment because the cost of disappointment is low. Equally, as it is a low involvement purchase, they may also follow the random choice process highlighted in Table 3.2. In the high involvement situation the consumer has more reason to engage in active decision-making to ensure that they examine all possibilities. However, they may also follow a routine process once they have found their preferred brand, as described in Figure 3.2, reducing the effort that they put into the new purchase.

Other forms of involvement

While we categorize decision-making by high or low involvement, a consumer's level of involvement will depend on how relevant the purchasing decision is to them. Different people will exhibit varying levels of involvement with regard to the same product because of differences in their personality, socio-economic and demographic factors, previous experience, and the product's relevance to them and their situation (Antil, 1984). In this section we shall consider the following types of involvement.

- **Product involvement** *is the perceived personal relevance of the product, based on needs, values or interest* (Zaichkowsky 1985, 1986).

- **Message-response involvement** *reflects the consumer's interest in marketing communications* (Batra and Ray, 1983).

- **Enduring involvement** which is 'the pre-existing relationship between an individual and the object of concern' (Houston and Rothschild, 1978: 3).

- **Ego involvement** *when consumers perceive products or brands as relevant to their personal interests* (Foxall, 1993).

While companies are often concerned with developing advertisements to convince consumers to purchase a product, advertising agencies know that it is often most important to get the consumer involved with the message as persuasion may follow (see Consumer Insight 3.1).

Foxall's (1993) research reminds us that involvement is a relationship between the product and the consumer, and that some consumers may be more involved with a typically low involvement product field. While personal factors and a long-term interest in a product may affect our level of involvement, such factors may also change depending upon the

CONSUMER INSIGHT 3.1

How to achieve enduring involvement through emotion

The advertising agency Fallon was tasked with building a feeling of love towards Cadbury's Dairy Milk, especially among younger consumers who had not grown up with Cadbury Dairy Milk being the 'default' chocolate bar as their parents' generations had. The agency felt that the brand needed what they referred to as 'fame'. The creative brief was to 'Give people the feeling they have when eating our chocolate'; they needed to imbue the advertisements with emotion. The juxtaposition of a gorilla playing drums to a track by the former Genesis drummer and vocalist Phil Collins was designed to make people smile (see Figure 3.3).

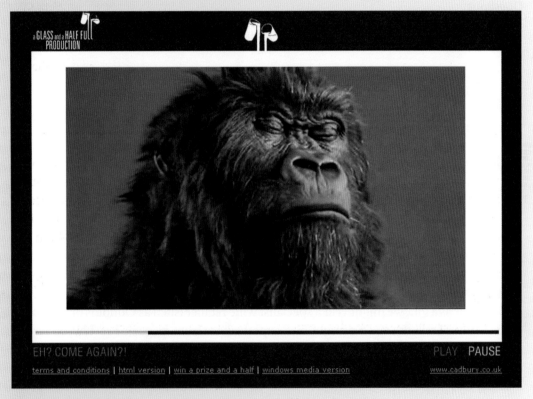

Figure 3.3   Screen shot from the Cadbury's 'Glass and a half full production'
Source: Image printed with permission from Cadbury's Ltd.

In testing the advertisements the key criterion of success was generating a smile; the agency recorded facial expressions. In further quantitative analysis the impact and involvement for the advertisement was high, with spontaneous brand recall at 80 per cent.

A very different approach was used by John Lewis in an advertisement showing a woman's life from a baby to an elderly woman, supported throughout with products from the department store and accompanied by the song *Always a Woman*. The advertisement illustrates how it is possible to resonate with the nature of both a customer's product and enduring involvement. The campaign is aimed to reinforce in consumers' minds that the company makes a lifelong commitment to quality, fair pricing, and excellent service.

It was a phenomenally successful campaign, and Robert Bain, the Head of Strategy for John Lewis, put its success down to how the advertisement reflected the 'lifelong commitment and emotional bond that people build with the brand. It's the idea that John Lewis is there throughout all key stages of your life—a birth, a wedding, moving home. They're events that stir strong emotion, and I think the advertisement was able to reflect that. Part of the foundation of what we believe John Lewis offers is trust. The ability to come back over all those stages of your life and get the same level of service, the same quality of goods is important. The emotional affinity people felt with the advertisement made it the success it was.'

Questions

1. Take a look at the two advertisements on YouTube. How do they engage with the consumer?

2. What different techniques are used in the advertisements?

3. Do you think they are successful? Why do you think this?

Sources: Barreyat-Baron and Barrie (2008); Bain (2010); www.utalkmarketing.com

 Visit the Online Resource Centre and follow the weblink to learn more about achieving enduring involvement through emotion.

purchase situation. Situational involvement tends to depend on some particular event or time in our lives. Buying a bottle of wine as a gift is different from buying a bottle of wine to drink at home at the weekend. This reflects our different levels of involvement. If we are buying wine as a gift, we might visit a specialist wine retailer (such as Oddbins or Indigo, an online wine merchant), and we might seek expert advice from magazine reviews to ensure that we buy the 'right' gift. Wine bought to drink at home might be purchased at the supermarket, perhaps influenced by price deals and expert recommendations (a trend in supermarkets is to note 'As recommended by...' alongside wines on display).

How to increase involvement

Marketers want to increase involvement with both their products and their messages so that customers have positive associations with them when making high or low purchase decisions. There are a number of ways that they can achieve this.

Link the brand to hedonic needs Häagen Dazs ran a series of advertisements that directly associated the eating of ice cream with sex, while Pot Noodles presented their brand as a dark and rather naughty pleasure (Figure 3.4). For some time Pot Noodles used the line 'the slag of all snacks' but this had to be removed after a number of complaints. Nevertheless, this

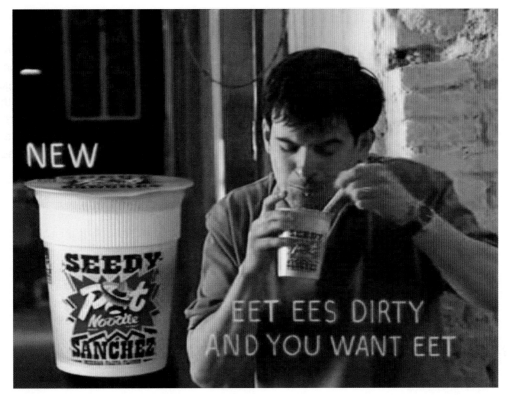

Figure 3.4   Increasing involvement through hedonism

Source: Image supplied by The Advertising Archives.

positioning as a cheap and easy form of instant food gratification has continued.

Use distinctive or novel ways of communicating your product The packaging for the Korean laundry detergent Spark (Figure 3.5) is distinctive and novel, quickly facilitating communication about the product and its use. In addition, the packaging allows the consumer to see how much is left in the box, making re-purchase easier.

Use celebrities Celebrities can be very useful for creating greater involvement with a brand (see Consumer Insight 3.2). Walkers crisps used Gary Lineker as the notorious 'crisp stealer' to communicate their brand for many years. Walkers have managed to involve many other sports personalities to appear with Gary Lineker to extend the creative use of the celebrity and to introduce new flavours

Figure 3.5   Using novel ways of communication to increase involvement

Source: Image printed with permission of Aekyung Industrial Co., Ltd.

CONSUMER INSIGHT 3.2

Finding the right celebrity endorser around the world

In Asian countries American celebrities have extensively endorsed local brands. In Japan, Arnold Schwarzenegger has advertised Nissin instant noodles, while Keanu Reeves promotes Suntory Reserve. China is particularly celebrity prone, although the use of some celebrities such as Bill Clinton, Warren Buffet, and Bill Gates has clearly been achieved without their permission. Brands like L'Oréal have used a successful mix of local and global ambassadors including actor Andy Lau and movie star Li Bingbing in China, and former Miss World and Bollywood actress Aishwarya Rai in India.

In Taiwan Magiclean used a celebrity mum to advertise their cleaning products. A successful TV star and mother of three children, Dee Hsu was seen as epitomising the modern Taiwanese working woman trying to strike a balance between family and career. According to this campaign, people like Dee Hsu don't have much time to clean their kitchens and bathrooms and are looking for a quick and easy solution, which Magiclean provides.

The internet and social media have led to celebrity endorsement being extended across channels, critical in these times when young people are using their mobile phone screens for media consumption. Fans of celebrities will purchase the brands they endorse, collecting and sharing information through social media. Fans will post reactions to new commercials on social media and blogs, and will visit the corporate sponsors to watch the advertising in which their idol is represented. One such idol in Japan is Ninomiya Kazunari, a member of the boy band Arashi. On the corporate webpage for the cooking oil he endorses, Nisshin OilliO, fans can view longer commercials and videos of the making of the commercials as well as downloadable PC wallpaper and recipes for their idol's favourite food.

Questions

1. What do you think are the advantages and disadvantages of using local celebrities to increase involvement?

2. Think of ways that you might use social media to increase involvement with celebrities for:

- a new brand of chocolate bar

- Gardening tools.

Sources: www.howstuffworks.com; www.guardian.co.uk; www.asiapacificmemo; Lee (2012).

 Visit the Online Resource Centre and follow the weblinks to learn more about campaigns that have used celebrities.

linked to other celebrities; for example, Gordon Ramsay is featured in the advertisement for the Great British Dinner flavours.

Tell a story This is particularly effective where there is a longer period of time to present a narrative such as in cinema advertising or on the internet. A famous example is the Chanel No. 5 advertisement using the actor Nicole Kidman, directed by the film director Baz Luhrmann. Throughout this film the Chanel entwined C is prominent on the rooftop and in the mythical metropolis to ensure that the story is linked to the brand. Nescafé Philippines told stories of community spirit and passion for music in their Red Mug Sessions, which show inspiring stories and experiences of Filipino musicians that were shared on Nescafé Philippines social media platforms. Nescafé was linked to supporting local talent and giving musicians an outlet for their music, but importantly these videos were not used as a vehicle for highlighting Nescafe's attributes although the beverage was always in the background. The Red Mug Sessions achieved over 500,000 views on YouTube and over 1.8 million fans on Facebook (Quek, 2013).

Build a relationship Companies that invest in a particular communications message can build a relationship between the viewer and that message. Whether or not the consumer is involved with the brand, they will, over time, build knowledge of what the brand stands for. Oxo famously used a family to advertise its stock cubes for many years. Viewers learnt about how the family developed over time, with the children growing up and eventually leaving home, and throughout the campaign the central focus was the family meal made with Oxo cubes. More recently BT have used a modern romance that both tells a story of a couple (Adam and Jane meeting, falling in love, and marrying) and builds a relationship with the viewer (by getting the viewer to choose what happens in the next advertisements). In 2011, viewers were asked to vote, through a Facebook page, for Jane's wedding dress and car. Throughout the series of advertisements BT align products with the story; for example, as the couple are about to move house, BT links this with a new easy form of telephone connection for people moving home. While the internet and social media platforms are increasingly important for building relationships, this example shows that television remains important. This theme is continued in Practitioner Insight 3 where we

PRACTITIONER INSIGHT 3

Simon Tunstill, Head of Communications, Thinkbox

Watching TV is sometimes described as a 'passive' or 'lean back' experience. The theory goes that, unlike holding and reading a book or scrolling, browsing, and clicking your way around the internet, with TV you nestle into your sofa and let it all wash over you. There's not much more to do beyond choosing your channel and adjusting the volume.

But our brains are very much in motion; they are incredibly active. The term 'passive' doesn't quite do justice to the time we spend watching TV and deciphering plots, or chewing over quiz questions, or being gripped by a match, or laughing at jokes, or following a recipe, or any of the other countless things our brains process when we watch TV.

The blend of conscious and semiconscious activity that goes together to enable us to enjoy TV is described by Dr Robert Heath in *The Hidden Power of Advertising* as 'low involvement processing'. Much of it involves 'implicit' learning which takes place without us knowing that we are learning. This sort of information is filed in our long-term memory without any of the conscious filtering which would increase the risk of rejection. As such, it is an incredibly effective way of increasing a set of associations around a brand and is well suited to thematic or brand messages that need to be remembered over the long-term.

The way our minds interact with TV and its advertising is at the heart of why TV advertising is so powerful and memorable, and central to this is the emotional connection TV creates between viewer and brand. The role of emotion in advertising has risen to greater prominence in recent years, as what is clear from the major research is that emotion is fundamental to advertising effectiveness. Just ask John Lewis.

The context in which we normally watch TV is also very important. TV is generally a shared experience; we watch it with other people (either in the room with us or connected to us via the internet and social media—more of that later). Half our TV viewing is shared with loved ones in the room with us (sometimes with unloved ones too). This rises to over 70 per cent during peak viewing in the evening.

Because we share the experience, TV creates conversations—both immediately as we watch and subsequently in our daily discourse. TV has always been one of our favourite topics of conversation, and this devotion to discussing what we've watched is another reason why TV is so memorable. And these conversations are often about brands as well as programmes; that pasta sauce, visit that website, adopt that Meerkat. They can also lead to instant personal recommendations ('I've tried that, it was great. You should try it'), which is a very powerful motivator. Thinkbox's POETIC research—'Paid, Owned, Earned: TV's Influence Calculated' (http://www.thinkbox.tv/server/show/nav.2383)—revealed that TV advertising is behind 51 per cent of new conversations about brands. Nothing else comes close.

In recent years the power of the shared TV experience has increased because now, thanks to the internet, we are sitting on a virtual sofa as well as on our actual sofa. Even if we are not watching TV with someone else in the room, we can connect with people across the globe to share our views and opinions—good or bad—about what we're watching via a companion internet-enabled screen such as a laptop, tablet, or smartphone. Twitter tells us that 40 per cent of prime-time tweets are TV-related. The phenomenon of multi-screening, as it is known, enables us to chat, play, discover, and even buy things as we watch TV. We can upload our own pastiches to YouTube, join TV-related Facebook groups, and follow and comment on TV-associated hashtags on Twitter. Multi-screening has expanded the world of TV.

In Thinkbox's 'Screen Life: the view from the sofa' research, we examined exactly what was going on in people's living rooms as they multi-screened. People have always multi-tasked when watching TV—multi-screening is the latest accompaniment, albeit an incredibly complementary one. We discovered that multi-screening is now establishing itself in the living room: 86 per cent of people in the UK (with access to TV and the internet) had multi-screened, with 34 per cent of our sample claiming to multi-screen regularly.

Because of the immediate public—potentially global—sharing of TV that can now happen, social media offer a great window into the effects that broadcast TV creates. Broadcasters and programme-makers can, and are, using these insights and interactions to shape output and market TV in an agile cost-effective way. However, it is worth being cautious about acting on what you discover that people are saying online. Keller Fay, the US word-of-mouth specialist, has estimated that 90 per cent of brand conversations happen offline anyway.

For TV advertisers, multi-screening means that many viewers have a device to hand primed for response to their advertisements. One of the key findings from the Screen Life research was that multi-screeners are even more open, welcoming, and positive about advertising than single-screeners. It also revealed that multi-screening keeps viewers present for advertisement breaks, encourages more TV viewing, does not affect advertisement recognition, brings people closer to TV and its advertisements, and even appears to encourage more shared and family TV viewing. It is good news for marketers.

So, with multiple screens come multiple opportunities. TV is now a point-of-sale medium; the living room is the high street, and viewers are able to act and transact on what they see on TV immediately via a second screen. This is why there has been a gold rush of companies wanting to develop and own the accompanying interactive platform for TV; it's so easy for consumers to take the next step into e-commerce. The advertisement break now enables viewers to go straight from engagement with a TV advertisement to interaction with it to purchase. So much for passive TV viewing.

spoke to Simon Tunstill, Head of Communications at Thinkbox, about how consumers 'use' television in the twenty-first century.

Get the consumer to participate With social media the opportunities for active involvement are huge, and companies are increasingly looking for ways to engage consumers by involving them with their marketing communications. The Singaporean communications company SingTel engaged in a real-time marketing experiment on Twitter, asking followers to describe useful situations for a high-speed 4G mobile connection. Within nine hours the company had turned the suggestions into improvised comedy sketches on YouTube and tweeted the contributors. The #Need4GSpeed hashtag was trending for more than 24 hours and increased traffic for the 4G website by 39 per cent (Quek, 2013).

Having looked at involvement and ways to increase it in detail we shall now look at the stages in the decision-making process, starting with problem recognition.

Stages in the decision-making process

Problem recognition

Problem recognition *is a realization that a problem needs to be solved through purchase.* It may be triggered by internal factors such as hunger or thirst, or external factors such as having to buy a birthday present. Problem recognition occurs in high and low involvement decision-making when we recognize (not necessarily consciously) the difference between our actual state and an ideal state. Figure 3.6 shows two ways in which problem recognition may manifest itself. In each case there

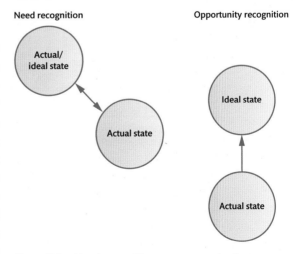

Figure 3.6   Need recognition versus opportunity recognition

is a difference between the actual and the ideal state. The need recognition example shows a situation where one moves easily between an actual and an ideal state, and that is why the top circle is labelled as both ideal and actual. A person can readily bring themselves back to the ideal state through a simple consumption decision. So when hungry (actual state) at lunchtime, we buy a sandwich and some fruit and are no longer hungry (ideal state); although our actual state was, briefly, not our ideal one we were able to rectify it easily. Opportunity recognition, however, is a situation where the consumer may recognize a lack in their actual state that they were not aware of before. Perhaps they see an advertisement for a new mobile phone, or a friend tells them about the holiday that they are about to go on. Although previously content with their actual state, seeing the advertisement or having the conversation affects them so that they wish to upgrade their phone or book a holiday to bring about the ideal state, which may take considerable effort and cost. Therefore opportunity recognition as illustrated in Figure 3.7 shows the distance between actual and ideal state as greater and the arrow is shown pointing in one direction.

Information search

Information search *is the process by which we identify appropriate information to help aid our choice in a decision-making situation.* In the case of need recognition our information search may be quite simple. We may already know from previous experience (ongoing search) the location of the nearest preferred sandwich bar. Our search is mostly at the point of sale in terms of choosing what we want, and here marketers help us choose by clearly presenting a variety of different food deals to help us decide (see Figure 3.7).

Figure 3.7   Food-to-go counter

Source: Image courtesy of Appleby Westward Group.

In an opportunity recognition situation our search may be more complex as we may not have the information necessary to make the decision. While we may use pre-purchase search to facilitate decision-making for a specific goal, many of us are searching with no particular plan to buy (Bloch, 1986). Such ongoing search occurs independently of a specific immediate purchase problem (Bloch et al., 1986). Information search is not purely functional; it is often just fun to browse the shops, trying things on and comparing different possibilities. Vogt and Fesenmaier (1998) identified five classes of information need: functional, hedonic, sign, innovation, and aesthetic.

- *Functional needs* are the acquisition of knowledge from one's own experiences and, those of others, and through stimuli such as advertising or articles to increase knowledge and reduce risk. These act as a way of educating a consumer about the product's utility, attributes, and applications.

- *Hedonic needs* relate to the elements of pleasurable experiences that may occur during decision-making.

- *Sign needs* are the social and identity aspects of information search—what the product might say about us. Information may be passed on or sought as part of signifying our social position (see Chapter 1 on sign value).

- *Innovation needs* relate to the search for something that is new or different to the consumer.

- *Aesthetic needs* are where information is viewed as a stimulus to visual thinking, to imagining the product and how it looks in your life.

We may already have resources from previous experiences to draw upon (internal search), while a novel or difficult purchase may require an external search. While much searching will be deliberate, i.e. actively looking for information, we often also receive incidental information through talking to people or noticing an advertisement or editorial when we are not actively seeking information. Marketers have to consider carefully when, where, and how often they place advertisements in the hope that they will initiate needs in their customers.

Alternative evaluation

Following an information search we face choice alternatives. These may not just be different brands or products; they might include make-or-buy decisions, such as hosting a dinner party and considering whether to make or buy a dessert. Marketers can exploit these choice situations through campaigns such as the Waitrose's '£20 Valentine's dinner for two' campaign (see Figure 3.8) which offers the option of a ready-made dinner rather than having to make the dinner from scratch.

There may be brands that you are familiar with and brands you have used before. Your information search may also have resulted in new unfamiliar brands. At this point we can

Figure 3.8 Dinner for two from Waitrose

Source: Image courtesy of Waitrose.

place the results of the information search into different categories (Narayana and Markin, 1975).

- The **evoked set** includes *the possible brands already known to the consumer from which to choose.*

- The **consideration set** includes *brands from the evoked set that you might actually consider buying.*

- The **inept set** are *those brands that the consumer may have come across during their search or from previous experience but would not consider for this decision.*

- The **inert set** includes *those brands not under consideration at all.*

An example of such a categorization might be when a consumer is purchasing a fragrance for their mother. The inert set might include brands they are aware of but which they would just never consider buying, say in this case Katie Price's Besotted. There may be certain brands that they like but do not think would be suitable for her (inept) such as Clinique's Happy. Inevitably brands that are familiar are likely to be in a consumer's evoked set; here it might be Chanel No. 5 and Elizabeth Arden, and this in turn means that businesses need to ensure that consumers are familiar with their brands and that these are readily available to them. This is important for both how much a company spends on marketing communications and its distribution strategy.

Evaluation

In an active decision-making situation we may consciously use **evaluative criteria** which are *those factors that we use to compare offerings to help make a choice.* Figure 3.1 includes beliefs, attitudes, and intentions. As we shall see in Chapter 6, the formation of beliefs and positive attitudes can lead to an intention to purchase. These will be part of one's evaluative criteria, but it does not necessarily follow that a person will purchase a product that they have positive attitudes towards or even an intention to buy (see Research Insight 3.2). For example,

RESEARCH INSIGHT 3.2

Court, D., Elzinga, D., Mulder, S., and Vetvick, O. (2009), 'The consumer decision journey', www. mckinseyquarterly.com

In 2009, *McKinsey Quarterly* published 'The consumer decision journey' which questioned the traditional 'funnel approach' to consumer decision-making. This approach suggests that consumers start with a potential number of brands which gradually reduces as they move towards their final choice. Drawing on purchase decision data from almost 20,000 consumers across five industries and three continents, Court et al. suggest that rather than a linear process, most consumers are engaged in a more circular journey with four key points where a brand may win or lose (see Figure 3.9).

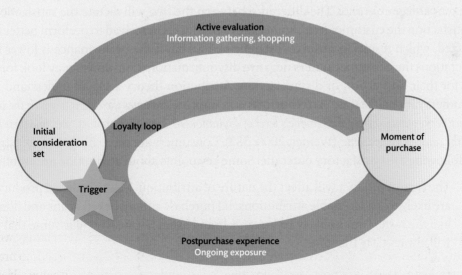

Figure 3.9   Exhibit from 'The consumer decision journey', June 2009, *McKinsey Quarterly*, www.mckinsey.com/insights/mckinsey_quarterly McKinsey & Company. Reprinted by permission

1. The consumer makes their initial choice set based on existing brand perceptions and recent touch points (i.e. advertisements, conversations with friends, product experiences).

2. Consumers bring in new brands and lose others as they evaluate what they want.

3. A brand is selected at the point of purchase.

4. The consumer assesses the purchase which will inform the next decision journey.

 Visit the Online Resource Centre to read the abstract and access the full paper.

after much consideration a consumer may have decided to buy their mother Chanel No. 5 perfume but may find that the store does not have it in stock. At this point they may go to another store or choose to purchase their second-choice brand Elizabeth Arden.

Outcomes of choice

Businesses are concerned that their customers are happy with their purchase. Generally that is the main concern of marketing, but an outcome of purchase may ultimately be disposal, whether it is throwing something away when it is no longer working or useful or selling it on when you want a replacement, such as with a car or house. There are a number of outcomes of decision-making that impact on marketers, including disposal, which we examine.

Both happy and unhappy customers may tell others about their purchase experience (word of mouth) as in the example in Consumer Insight 3.3. The **disconfirmation paradigm** is *the difference between a consumer's pre-purchase expectations of the product's performance and their post-purchase experience*. The difference between the two will dictate the satisfaction or dissatisfaction the customer feels. Sometimes a product is perceived to perform better than expected, which results in positive disconfirmation, but if the performance is lower than expectations the consumer suffers negative disconfirmation. Consumers may look for reasons for their satisfaction or dissatisfaction. Attribution theory seeks to understand how consumers rationalize this. '**Attributions** *arise when one evaluates the extent to which the initial product performance corresponds to one's level of aspiration vis-à-vis that product, and one then questions the cause of the outcome*' (Weiner, 2000: 383). Consumers are more likely to seek attribution following a dissatisfactory outcome. Some key points about attribution are as follows.

1. The type of product will affect the nature of attribution. Mass produced products are likely to lead to stable attributions. If I purchase a tin of baked beans and don't like the taste, I am unlikely to buy this brand again because I will assume that it will always taste the same.

2. Unstable attributions are more likely to occur when the nature of the product means that the quality could vary. Service businesses such as banks and airlines

CONSUMER INSIGHT 3.3

Happy with your purchase?

If you are unhappy with your purchase, what do you do? Today it is relatively easy to get a refund for something you don't like or doesn't fit you. But what if you want to complain about your purchase? A number of research studies (summarized in Figure 3.10) have examined what we might do in such situations. 'Action/no-action' discrimination (Day and Landon, 1977) is the first step of complaining behaviour. The most basic distinction in complaining is exit or voice division (Hirschman, 1970): does the consumer decide to respond to their unsatisfactory experience through exiting, i.e. not purchasing again, or with voice, i.e. communicating their dissatisfaction? If the latter, they may do it publicly, to the company or to other third parties such as regulatory authorities or the media, or privately, to family and friends. Finally, the consumer may seek redress, which might include monetary compensation, again either from the company or third parties.

Today one of the most popular and seemingly successful ways of complaining is using social media. Companies such as BT, Fitness First, and Halifax have dedicated Twitter accounts for customer feedback. Companies are concerned about the viral capacity of social media. *The Observer* (Bachelor, 2012) recently reported that a customer had spent three months trying to get a refund from a travel company using letters, email, and phone and finally threatened to send a tweet; he received a full refund the same day plus additional compensation.

Figure 3.10 The integrated model of customer complaining behaviour
Source: Istanbulluoglu (2013).

Questions

1. Do you complain? When would you complain to the company and when to friends and family? What methods do you use to complain?

2. Why is social media becoming popular for complaining?

3. Do companies make it easy for you to complain?

Sources: Hirschman (1970); Day and Landon (1977); Bachelor (2012); Istanbulluoglu (2013).

 Visit the Online Resource Centre and follow the weblinks to learn more about how consumers register their complaints.

are subject to such unstable attributions. If I travel on an airline and receive excellent service and the next time the service is not so good, I may well continue to use the airline believing that poor service is not typical.

3. Once a consumer has a well-formed expectation of a satisfactory or unsatisfactory experience they can become 'frozen' and difficult to change. Škoda was associated with unreliability and cheapness when it was produced in the former Eastern Bloc state of Czechoslovakia before 1989. In 2000, following the fall of the Berlin Wall, Volkswagen took 100 per cent share in Škoda and developed a major advertising campaign which aimed to convince people that the quality and reliability of the Škoda had changed. This was done in a tongue-in-cheek manner where potential customers would test drive the car but could not come to terms with a car that good being a Škoda and so were shown running away from the car dealership—a clear case of an attempt to shift a 'frozen' image.

4. Causal locus is where the cause of the attribution is with or outside the control of the consumer. Therefore on occasions we may blame ourselves for our decision such as, 'I'll never get the hang of this mobile phone', or we may attribute the problem to the product: 'The instructions with this mobile phone are incomprehensible'. Marketers need to be aware of the likely type of attribution their products will be subject to and ensure that they respond appropriately. Commodity products such as margarine need to be regularly taste-tested so that they meet consumers' preferences. Service businesses often use 'mystery shoppers' to ensure that they are providing the appropriate level of service. In both cases the issue is that if standards are not maintained, eventually the customer will reassess their attribution.

Disposal of goods

As mentioned already, one final outcome is disposal. At a time when environmental concerns are of greater importance than ever before, marketers need to be aware of how their customers dispose of goods. Dealing with the disposal of goods is a business in itself and companies involved in this may want to attract customers to use their service. When we purchase something we are probably not thinking about when or how we are going to dispose of it. We dispose of packaging every week when we shop and increasingly we are encouraged to recycle such packaging. For some consumers their choice of product or brand may depend on the amount of packaging—for example, choosing loose fruit and vegetables rather than pre-packaged. We dispose of things in numerous ways and some are listed here:

1. to friends and family or given away freely through specialized sites such as Freecycle (http://uk.freecycle.org/)

2. to charity

3. direct disposal either in general rubbish or recycled

4. by exchanging for another item

5. through car boot sales, private advertisements, auction sites.

One issue to consider is the impact our consumption has on the environment. This is a particular concern as the world population grows, alongside the increase in the number of products and their packaging. One message that has been used across continents is 'Reduce, Reuse, Recycle' (Figure 3.11). The idea is that before we think about recycling we also need to consider whether our consumption could be reduced and whether we have products that could be reused either by ourselves or others. For example, this might mean mending clothes rather than throwing them away if they have a tear. Of course, there are forces that work against this approach, such as the increased availability of cheap clothes, and the fact that many products are made with built-in

Figure 3.11   Reduce, reuse, recycle
Source: © Yobidaba/Shutterstock.com.

obsolescence, meaning that they either stop working after a period of time or that new more fashionable versions are introduced.

One of the biggest problems of consumption is the environmental impact of waste. Plastic in the world's seas is killing, and changing, marine life. Some countries, such as Ireland, Israel, and Uganda, are using legislation to reduce waste. In 2002 Ireland became the first country to introduce a tax on plastic bags, the Plas Tax. The Plas Tax had a dramatic impact, with reduction of around 90 per cent in plastic bag consumption and less litter (Harrison, 2013).

The purpose of such a tax is not to generate revenue but to encourage consumers to reduce and reuse. Although East African countries banned certain types of plastic bags in 2007, implementation has proved tricky where it is difficult to ensure compliance. In countries in South America and Africa waste is a much more complex problem. Many countries place their refuse in huge dumpsites where people scavenge for plastic waste which they sell on to contractors. Others benefit, meaning that waste provides jobs for some of the poorest in these societies thus making waste a productive product for some.

Shopping behaviour

To make our purchases we have to shop, whether with a major retailer, on the internet, or in a local shop or market. Researchers have considered how and why people shop and the role that shopping plays in their lives. For most people there is a difference between 'going shopping' and 'doing the shopping'. The former is often a pleasurable activity, where you may spend time and money perhaps with a friend or partner, just enjoying the experience of shopping, whereas 'doing the shopping' is often an obligation or a routine chore (Bowlby, 1997). Since the early 1950s there have been attempts to segment people by how they shop (e.g. Stone, 1954). Westbrook and Black (1985) examined eight previous studies and found many different shopper types, but only a few appeared consistently across studies. These were:

- *economic*, price-conscious people looking for a bargain

- *social*, those who enjoyed the social experience of going shopping

- *apathetic*, uninterested in shopping and not really enjoying it.

A more recent study by Ganesh et al. (2007) found five different types of shopper: apathetic shoppers (indifferent to shopping), enthusiasts (who enjoy all aspects of shopping), destination shoppers (focused on finding the right place to buy the brand or product they are after), basic shoppers (those with a clear idea of what they want, they shop quickly and easily, having no interest in the social or experience aspects of shopping), and bargain seekers (motivated to find a good deal and to achieve choice optimization).

There are also those who are very involved with the shopping experience, often known as 'market mavens' (Feick and Price, 1987). Market **mavens** are *active information-seeking consumers or smart shoppers (similar to the recreational shoppers and information seekers identified in other studies), and they like to communicate, providing information to others on a broad variety of goods, services, and marketplace characteristics* (Slama and Williams, 1990).

Shopping motivation—on- and offline

The pleasure we get from shopping and how our motivations and even personalities affect how we shop are important to marketing (see Research Insight 3.3). Knowing how and why

RESEARCH INSIGHT 3.3

Arnold, M.J. and Reynolds, K.E. (2003), 'Hedonic shopping motivations', *Journal of Retailing*, 79, 2, 1–20.

In this paper the authors differentiate between social shopping and value shopping, the former with friends or family for enjoyment and the latter when hunting for bargains. This differentiation implies that the same person can be engaged in either of these activities at different times.

 Visit the Online Resource Centre to read the abstract and access the full paper.

consumers shop the way they do enables marketers to provide the appropriate shopping experience. In 1972, Tauber published an exploratory review of 30 people aged between 20 and 47, and from this hypothesized both personal and social motives for shopping. Here we discuss how relevant these may be for the twenty-first century consumer.

Personal motives for shopping

Role playing According to Tauber, shopping is related to certain roles in society, and for some women grocery shopping offered the opportunity to express their housewife role. Today the internet provides one way for time-constrained working consumers to enact the traditional role of household shopper since they can do so at a time that is convenient for them (Parsons, 2002).

What!?

Diversion Tauber suggested that shopping can be a recreational activity, a diversion from everyday life. The development of shopping malls, where many shopping, entertainment, and catering resources are commonly in one place protected from the weather, shows how marketing has responded to this. Similarly, online window-shopping may act as a diversion for people at any time of the day within their own homes. The internet also gives consumers a chance to shop at store types that would otherwise be unreachable because of their location or opening hours.

Self-gratification Shopping may offer a compensation for other problems in consumer's lives. Escapism and reward are part of this type of shopping motivation. When only offline shopping was available, we had to make a certain amount of effort to go out and shop, but now consumers can reward themselves whenever they want by just logging on to their favourite shopping sites.

Learning about new trends Going around the shops allows people to keep up to date with new trends. If you go into most city centres in western economies at the weekend you will see young people checking out what the shops have to offer and also what their peers are wearing. Computer and electronics shops let people 'play' with their products to get an idea of what they can do. Whereas in the past we had to search out new trends, the internet

Figure 3.12 Christmas at Selfridges   *Source*: Image courtesy of Selfridges & Co.

means that they are brought to us on a daily basis. If you sign up for any shopping site you will get regular updates of 'What's New'.

Physical activity This refers to people shopping for physical exercise, and indeed there is a trend towards the shopping mall as a place for exercise, with reports from Doha, Qatar, of initiatives to encourage consumers to use the mall as a place for exercise (Nordland, 2013). Clearly internet shopping detracts from this physical activity, although using the internet to shop could free up time for physical exercise (Parsons, 2002).

Sensory stimulation Walk into a big department store in any major city and you will be bombarded with sights, sounds, and smells. Christmas shopping in Selfridges in London is enlivened by Christmas Carol singers and food tastings to add to the Christmas feeling (see Figure 3.12). Clearly it is more difficult to achieve this sensory experience online, but increasingly companies are enhancing their sites by using music, videos of their products, and even real-time fashion shows. New techniques such as Vine (the video-sharing app owned by Twitter) allow companies such as Calvin Klein to use multiple platforms to provide such experiences. Calvin Klein made use of Vine to share short videos of model Matthew Terry (who featured in their advertising campaign) exercising in his Calvin Klein boxers.

Social motives for shopping

Social experiences Some shopping situations may become social events. When pressed for time, shopping for food for dinner may not seem very social. However, a Sunday morning trip to a farmers' market can be a very different food shopping experience, with both buyers and sellers often happy to discuss the produce and interact in a relaxed fashion. On a

Sunday in Singapore you will often see families eating picnics outside shops waiting for them to open. Social media has become one of the biggest opportunities for sharing social experiences as consumers contact one another about new products, or show themselves wearing or using or even eating their purchases.

Communicating with others who have similar interests Special interest and sports shops are often the focus of conversation and comparisons among shoppers and staff. Staff with a particular expertise may be employed specifically so that they can talk knowledgeably to customers. If you go into an electronics or gaming shop, or a specialist running store, you will see much interaction alongside the act of purchasing, and often the store environment is set up to encourage this. Again, the internet has become an important vehicle for shared interest, particularly on community sites dedicated to sharing information about favourite brands. In their study of the Zara virtual brand community, Royo-Vela and Casamassima (2010) concluded that brand communities can be used by companies to increase customers' levels of satisfaction and commitment, and enhance positive word of mouth communication.

Peer group attraction In some cases people are attracted to certain shops because they associate them with an aspirational group. If you read a celebrity magazine and see a picture of a pop star shopping in Gucci or Prada you might wish to go there for some of the celebrity glamour to rub off even if you don't end up buying anything! The same peer group attraction effect can be achieved on the internet with fashion sites such as ASOS Fashion Finder, which matches looks worn by celebrities with their own products.

Status and authority Some shops still have shop assistants attending to your needs, which may give you the feeling of being special. If you have a suit made in London's Savile Row you would expect such service. While you might imagine that the internet would not be able to offer such personal service, a number of sites now offer web chat to help customers make the best choice when shopping online.

Pleasure of bargaining There are still many opportunities for people to either haggle or feel that they can get a bargain (see Figure 3.13). eBay and other auction sites allow you to bid for goods while car boot sales allow direct bargaining.

Although all these motivations can be important, shopping is a cost-incurring activity. As Consumer Insight 3.4 shows, consumers around the world are still concerned about the price they pay for goods, with many cash-strapped shoppers motivated by the desire to find a bargain.

Is shopping different on the internet?

Do we shop differently on the internet and how does it compare with shopping in person? Researchers have developed consumer categorizations specific to internet shopping habits to help understand what motivates people to use the internet for shopping and whether

Figure 3.13 Haggling at a street market in Singapore *Source*: Image courtesy of Isabelle Szmigin.

they shop differently there. In research with online grocery shoppers, Rohm and Swaminathan (2004) identified four groups.

1. The **convenience shopper** (11 per cent of sample) was motivated by the convenience of online shopping; they were less concerned by immediate possession of goods and didn't particularly seek variety across retail channels.

2. The **variety seeker** (41 per cent) was most interested by variety seeking across retail alternatives, products, and brands, while still motivated by online shopping convenience.

3. The **balanced buyer** (33 per cent) showed a lower likelihood to plan purchases and therefore might be a more impulsive online shopper

4. The **store-oriented shopper** (15 per cent) showed the lowest level of online shopping convenience, preferring the physical orientations of the store and the immediate possession of goods.

Shopping online is a different experience from shopping in store where you can touch and smell goods and ask assistants for advice. Online stores aim to replicate some of the

CONSUMER INSIGHT 3.4

The growth of the discount store

There has been a huge growth in discount stores such as Poundland in the UK, Dollar King in Australia (Figure 3.14), and 100 yen shops in Japan. Recent analysis has suggested that this trend will outlive the recession (*Economist*, 2013). What is sold in these stores varies greatly over time depending on the purchasing strategies and abilities of their owners. The names of these stores are usually based on the price points at which they sell, and in some places, such as Hong Kong, this in itself has become a point of competition with 10 dollar, 8 dollar, and even 2 dollar shops opening.

Figure 3.14 Dollar King store in Australia   *Source*: Image courtesy of Dollar King.

In 2010 the UK store Poundland announced an increase in profits of 130 per cent to £19.8m. Founded in 1990, Poundland sells thousands of items all for £1. Now there are hundreds of stores all over Britain, in affluent areas as well as those less economically well off. Countries all over the world have shops whose rationale is a price level offer. Such shops first opened in the USA in the 1950s. Poundland offers many branded goods, such as Heinz, Cadbury's, and Colgate, at prices less than supermarkets. While Poundland draws most of its customers from lower socio-economic groups, people from higher-income groups are increasingly shopping there. A recent poll by the *Guardian* newspaper found that 72.4 per cent of people would accept discount stores in more upmarket shopping malls as they reflected our changing shopping habits, and only 27.6 per cent said that shopping centres are supposed to offer a more upmarket retail experience.

Source: Kollewe (2012); Roberts (2012); Wood (2012); *Economist* (2013).

Questions

1. Refer back to the shopping types illustrated at the end of Case Study 1. How do you think the different groups will use the discount stores described in this Consumer Insight?

2. What other factors might affect consumers' decisions to shop in such stores?

 Visit the Online Resource Centre and follow the weblinks to learn more about the growth of discount stores around the world.

advantages of bricks and mortar stores by having online assistants to answer questions, and reduce the risk of making the wrong decision through ease of returning goods. An important aspect for many shoppers is the ability to comparison shop online without having to physically go from store to store. Comparison shoppers typically compare product features, prices, and brands before making their purchases and actively look for promotional offers. Another feature of online shopping is customer reviews. Most companies encourage customers to give feedback on their purchases, which can provide information to other customers. We should also be aware that 'blended shopping' is increasing, where consumers mix and match between the internet and the online store, sometimes ordering online and collecting in store, or doing their information search in store and then making their final choice online.

Shopping on impulse

Most of us will have had the experience of **impulse purchasing** described by Rook (1987) *as a sudden, powerful urge to buy a product with little regard to the consequences of what we are buying.* There is normally little outcome if we buy a low value item, such as a bar of chocolate or some make-up, but we can also impulse purchase much higher value goods such as clothes or even a car. The environment we shop in may increase our likelihood to impulse purchase—for example, buying clothes on the internet or a book using an electronic device such as a Kindle. It is also likely that *how* we buy may affect our likelihood to impulse purchase. Thompson et al. (1990) describe impulse purchasing as an emotional rather than intellectual experience. However, as we discuss below, an impulse purchase is not necessarily an irrational purchase. Thompson et al. (1990: 354) discuss one unsatisfactory impulse purchase that was described as actually too practical. A respondent described buying a skirt on impulse in a sale just because it fitted her. She needed another skirt and it was on sale, but it did not excite her, leading her to conclude 'I was being too practical'.

Other researchers have tried to identify types of impulse purchasing. Bayley and Nancarrow (1998) identified four styles of impulse shopping:

1. **Accelerator impulse**—consumers are motivated to stockpile, purchasing in advance of some future need. Sales promotions such as BOGOF (buy one get one free) appeal to this type of impulse, as consumers can rationalize the purchase as likely to be used in the future.

2. **Compensatory impulse**—consumers make impulse purchases as a reward for success or as compensation for failure. Advertisements for confectionery or snacks often suggest that we deserve compensation or reward through food. An example of this is the 'Have a break, have a Kit Kat' slogan where the marketer makes the association of a rest from work with a chocolate snack.

3. **Breakthrough impulse**—this type of impulse relates to the sudden need to make a purchase, often triggered by some kind of unconscious problem or issue. The researchers suggest that it can be life changing as well as dealing with particular issues suffered by the person. For example, on impulse a man may see a ring in a jewellery shop, buy it, and propose to his girlfriend. Advertisements shown around Valentine's Day often try to encourage such impulsive behaviour.

4. **Blind impulse**—this refers to impulse buys that are not easily explained or rationalized by the consumer. Often this occurs when a consumer is overwhelmed by the product and feels that they just have to have it immediately, without any thought for the cost implications.

Is choosing a problem?

In the twenty-first century those of us living in the developed world face more choice in terms of products and brands we can buy than ever before. But is having such choice always a good thing? Choice means that we can have more variety in style, price, and content, but some think that it leads to confusion and even discomfort. In the opening chapter of *The Paradox of Choice* Schwartz (2009: 1), the author describes buying a pair of jeans. This is his interaction with the sales clerk:

> 'Do you want them slim fit, easy fit, relaxed fit, baggy, or extra baggy?' she replied. 'Do you want them stonewashed, acid-washed, or distressed? Do you want them button-fly or zipper-fly? Do you want them faded or regular?'

He goes on to list the 61 varieties of suntan lotion and 80 different pain relievers in the pharmaceutical aisle of his supermarket to add to his argument that more choice can lead to confusion as we cannot check out all the alternatives. Marketers need to understand when choice is good for the consumer and when it may lead to problems such as confusion or information overload. The lessons for marketers will be discussed further in the following sections.

Satisficing and maximizing

Have you ever stood in front of a display of shampoos unsure which to buy? You may be wondering whether your hair is fine, coloured, heat damaged, or all three. You may consider whether you need a separate conditioner and shampoo, or even just what size to buy.

Some people will take the time to look at the ingredients on the bottles and others will use heuristics (discussed in the following sections) to help them make a decision, but for many of us a good enough decision will suffice. So rather than assume, as traditional economics might, that consumers have complete information about the costs and benefits of all possible choices, information itself may be considered a commodity with its own price, whether in money or time or effort (Schwartz et al., 2002).

When we make such 'good enough' decisions we are doing what Herbert Simon (1956) referred to as 'satisficing'. We are almost always limited by the complexity of the environment and our own cognitive limitations, i.e. how we manage to keep and recall information and do the mental calculations to arrive at the 'best' choice. A satisficer will choose a brand based on some kind of threshold, such as price. In future they may find another brand that surpasses their original choice and so reject their previously chosen item. We might buy a spray window-cleaning product on one occasion and then on the next we may buy cleaning wipes and find that we prefer them because they are easier to use. Marketers use the information from purchasing statistics to identify where to invest and what products to keep in production and what to phase out, or indeed whether it is better to offer consumers a range of choice.

Maximizers tend to be people who consider all alternatives and seek the best option. Research shows that in some situations consumers are more likely to make a purchase if fewer choices are made available to them. Iyengar and Lepper (1999, 2000) found that too many choices could be demotivating, and consumers were more likely to choose and buy goods (in their studies, jams and chocolate bars) when fewer options were available. There may be some problems for those consumers who maximize their options. Firstly, it is often difficult to assess whether all alternatives have been considered, and if it is not practical to examine all options they may have doubts as to whether they have made the best choice. This may mean that they are less happy with their choice (Schwartz et al., 2002). Finding the 'best' may just be very difficult, especially in environments where there is a lot to choose from. Although maximizers may achieve better objective outcomes, they may not feel that they have made a better choice because of the high bar they set themselves, and where an exhaustive search is just not possible they may suffer regret at the 'better' options they may have chosen. There are some situations where being a maximizer is probably the best approach—for example, when one is looking for medical treatment. If it is a matter of life or death, most people will be looking for something better than 'good enough'. So companies need to identify when they should be providing the best and when 'good enough' will do.

Heuristics to aid choice

Heuristics are *methods to aid decision-making to arrive at satisfactory solutions by simplifying the complexity of assessing the probability and prediction of value in a choice situation.* They are often referred to as mental short cuts or rules of thumb to help aid decision-making. Heuristics are particularly useful for consumers in situations where there is a lot of choice but little difference between brands and the outcome of the choice will not matter greatly, perhaps because the item is relatively cheap. Consumers use heuristics for effort reduction (Shah and Oppenheimer, 2008). There are many different categories of heuristics, but we shall consider a few of particular interest to how consumers behave. Jansson-Boyd (2010) categorizes heuristics into four types: prediction, persuasion, choice, and compliance.

- **Prediction heuristics** are *where the consumer is trying to predict an outcome such as 'If I buy a new mobile phone now, when will I need to update it'.* Important examples of prediction heuristics are the availability and representativeness heuristics.

  - The **availability heuristic** *refers to a situation where people judge the likelihood or frequency of something happening in the future by how easy it is to remember similar events.* Consumers use the mental images they have available to act as a cue for the likelihood of an event. An important aspect of the availability heuristic is its salience or vividness, with more salient and vivid images coming more easily to mind in consumption contexts. Therefore if you have a strong memory of news reports of accidents at funfairs this may make you fearful of attending such fairs.

  - The **representativeness heuristic** is when we *judge something on the basis of how similar it is to something else.* We often make decisions about the probability of an event by assessing it against some stereotypical case. A problem with this is that it ignores other information to help make a better decision. Tversky and Kahneman (1974) found that people typecast features and make assumptions on the basis of stereotyping. We make assessments using the representativeness heuristic all the time in our purchase decisions, choosing products or brands because they look similar to others and therefore we have an expectation of their performance or taste.

- **Persuasion heuristics** refer to how *consumers take short cuts when processing advertisers' messages.* Rather than processing all the information available, people may refer to previous experiences or other cues to reduce demands on their thinking. Consumers may follow the consensus rule (Chaiken et al., 1989) where a majority opinion is used for guidance, such as when an advertisement suggests that in trials the majority of people will use a particular brand (see Figure 3.15). Similarly, expertise (e.g. using a dentist in an advertisement to endorse a brand of toothpaste) may act as a short cut to assuming that the brand must be better than if advertised by an actor (Ratneshwar and Chaiken, 1991).

- **Choice heuristics** *allows us to reduce the number of attributes to be considered for the possible alternative choices.* Choice heuristics are orientated towards reducing cognitive effort, particularly in situations where the product class is not very important or where there are a lot of brands to choose from. People often use what is known as the lexicographic heuristic (Fishburn, 1974). Here consumers decide which attribute is the most important (e.g. price) and then select which brand offers the best value for this attribute. If a number of brands tie, then

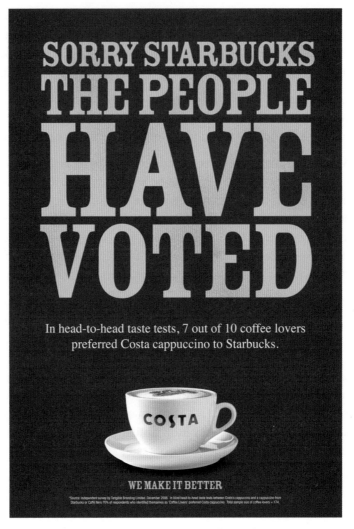

Figure 3.15 Costa's use of persuasion heuristics   *Source*: Image courtesy of Whitbread PLC.

consumers will look to the second most important attribute and so on until a choice is made.

- **Compliance heuristics** *are those built around the likelihood of choosing something based on complying with a request.* The knowledge that people will do this is used extensively in marketing. One compliance heuristic, scarcity (Brannon and Brock, 2001), means that we place higher value on something judged to be rare or scarce; websites often have messages saying 'Hurry low stock!' to encourage us to purchase. Another compliance heuristic, reciprocity (Langer, 1989), involves the apparent return of a favour, so if a sales person does the make-up for a customer in store, the customer may reciprocate by purchasing products.

While these heuristics may appear quite different, with some based on functional aspects such as specific attributes and some on attitudinal or even emotional responses, the key to their commonality is that they all act to reduce the effort associated with decision-making. By understanding how people make such short cuts, marketers can design communications to take such behaviour into account. Of course, it could also be said that marketing exploits this knowledge, and as consumers we should also be aware that using such heuristics may not always give us the 'best' solution.

Other methods we use to help us choose—anchoring and framing

Some methods to help us choose, such as satisficing and heuristics, aid decision-making in complex situations whilst others may determine, apparently arbitrarily, what we are prepared to pay for a product. This is known as anchoring. We often compare the prices of goods on the basis of other items in the same store. A person may see one pair of shoes in a shop for £200 when all the others are priced at over £300 and think that the £200 pair is a bargain. But if this same person were to look at other stores and see that similar shoes were priced under £100, they might not feel that the £200 pair was such a good deal. Such **anchoring** *is over-reliance on one piece of often irrelevant information to make a decision.* Anchoring is also referred to as arbitrary coherence. The initial price of the pair of shoes was arbitrary; the person could have started their shoe search in a cheaper or more expensive shop. However, once the price is established in our minds, this shapes what we are willing to pay for this and similar items and hence becomes coherent (Arierly, 2008). So within one shop we expect to see similar prices, and such anchoring may lower our resistance to purchasing.

Framing refers to how we make a decision *through the context in which a choice is presented to us*. Perception, language, and the way items are ordered may all make us see things differently. Tversky and Kahneman (1981), in their study on framing decisions, compared this to travelling in a mountain range. As you move through the range you notice that the apparent relative height of the mountain peaks appears to vary depending on where you are; at one point a mountain peak may look higher than others, but as you move forward this will change as the relative positions of the mountains change. Framing produces the same effect, such that the relative attractiveness of options changes when presented or framed differently. If you imagine that you want to book a cheap flight on the internet, you might come across a message such as this on a website:

'Pay by debit card for a £20 discount'.

Another website might have the following announcement:

'All credit card transactions are subject to a £20 surcharge'.

Effectively both sites are presenting the same offer but they are framed differently. In the first you are drawn to the idea of a discount if you use a debit card, but effectively it is the same as the second offer because if you pay with a credit card (the only other payment option) in the first example you will be paying £20 more than if you paid with your debit card. Framing effects may be used to manipulate decision-making. This is most obvious in how the content of food products is described. Advertisers have learned that labelling a food product 75 per cent fat free is likely to have a more favourable impact on sales than labelling it as having a 25 per cent fat content.

Conclusions

Understanding **decision-making**, and how the nature of **involvement** in the purchase may impact it, is important in terms of how and when marketers communicate with consumers along the decision-making journey. We examined a range of examples to show the complexity of consumer involvement. Companies generally aim to increase involvement with their brand in an attempt to make it more likely to be purchased, and Consumer Insight 3.1 explained how the Cadbury's Gorilla advertising campaign was used to increase enduring involvement with the brand.

We examined the **stages in the decision-making process**, drawing on a range of examples to illustrate the stages. In Research Insight 3.2 we introduced the concept of the consumer decision journey to show how companies might benefit from thinking in terms of consumers engaged in a more circular journey. Case Study 3 examined the decision-making processes associated with buying a sofa, to show how a decision can depend on many factors.

Consumer behaviour involves understanding both purchasing and consuming behaviour, and therefore we have looked at aspects of **shopping behaviour** alongside consuming behaviour. Shopping motivations were examined in more detail, and we compared the different motives for online and offline shopping. The growth of the discount store was the focus of Consumer Insight 3.4, where we looked at this phenomenon across the globe.

Whether we have too much choice in the market place today is open to question: while some think that it would be easier for many to have less choice, many other consumers feel that they benefit from the range and variety available. In some situations, consumers are prepared to accept a good-enough solution, known as **satisficing**, while in others we need to be more sure that we are really getting the best solution to a problem. In such cases we are **maximizing** our choices.

Decision-making may be thoughtful or impulsive, and may be affected by many factors including **heuristics**, **anchoring**, and **framing**. At times people's behaviour when they are using heuristics may appear irrational, but often there are reasons, some conscious and others unconscious, for the decisions made.

Review questions

1. Compare and differentiate low and high involvement decision-making.

2. Explain the difference between need and opportunity recognition.

3. Explain the difference between enduring involvement and situational involvement

4. Which methods would you consider for increasing involvement with a chocolate bar and why?

5. Identify three motivations for shopping.

6. Distinguish between different types of impulse purchasing.

7. What are the key differences between a maximizer and a satisficer? Identify a situation where it would be better to be a maximizer and one where it would be better to be a satisficer.

8. Explain the difference between heuristics, framing, and anchoring.

Discussion questions

1. Take a look at http://hardshipandhope.blogspot.co.uk/ What tactics do you use when shopping to keep the cost of your shopping down? Can you recognize situations where you are a different kind of shopper to others? Use any of the categories of shopper identified in this chapter and consider an incident when you have shopped in that way. Are there different ways that you shop which are not mentioned in any of the typologies?

2. Consider an impulse purchase that you have made. Does it fall into any of the categories discussed in this chapter? Was it a low or high value item? Try to recall how you felt when you bought it and how you felt afterwards. Did you keep it or return it? Were you pleased that you made the purchase?

3. Think of a situation where a consumer might use an availability heuristic, a compliance heuristic, and a lexicographic heuristic. Examine how using such heuristics in the situations you have chosen can be explained by the effort reduction they offer.

4. Consider the decision process that you go through for:

    a) purchasing tea or coffee

    b) purchasing a new winter coat.

    How do they differ? Do they correspond to the high and low involvement decision-making models? If not, how and why do you think that they differ?

5. Think of two or three brands that you regularly buy. Consider the type of involvement you have with them. Do you remember the advertisements (message-response)? Are they high or low involvement products for you? Do you have enduring involvement with these brands? Also think about situations where you might buy different brands of the same product category. What influences your different choice of brand?

 Visit the Online Resource Centre to test your knowledge further and complete the Multiple Choice Questions for Chapter 3.

CASE STUDY 3

George buys a sofa

While we have considered decision-making from a theoretical perspective of high and low involvement, it is important to recognize that individuals vary in how they make decisions based on many factors. In this case we see one example of a fairly ordinary decision, but one which appears to be dependent on many different factors. One issue to consider in this case is how closely George's decision process matches those we have studied in this chapter.

George had just moved into his new flat and wanted to buy a sofa for his living room. He had an old sofa that his brother had loaned him, but it was uncomfortable and the material was fraying. George had only just started working so didn't have a lot of money to spend. His living room was quite small so his first limitation was the size of the sofa. He began with a Google search in which he had included the size he thought would be best for the space. There was very little available in the preferred size. That evening his friend came round and George told him his problem. His friend suggested that George could have a larger sofa if he moved some of his other furniture around. Back on the internet, George found much more choice in this larger size and also found sites where he could input his preferred price ranges. Next George wondered what colour the sofa should be. He had only just painted the living room and decided that he couldn't change it again just for the sofa. George remembered from his previous search a sofa in the right colour, but at the time he thought it would be too big. He decided to go back online and buy it. Unfortunately, he found it was now out of stock and not available for another two months.

That evening, George's girlfriend came round and they decided to visit some shops together at the weekend. George wanted to go to the city centre to a department store from which he had bought other items for his house. George's girlfriend wanted to go to a new shopping mall which had a number of bargain furniture stores. George was not familiar with these stores and was not very happy to go as in general he felt that such stores did not sell good quality furniture, but he agreed to take a look as long as they visited the department store afterwards. Although the bargain stores had a number of sofas of the right size they were all in very bright colours and George did not think they would suit the colour scheme.

In the department store, they were immediately helped by a sales assistant who carefully noted George's requirements. He spent over an hour helping them find a suitable sofa. However, nothing that they liked was in their price range. Because the salesperson had been so helpful, George decided to buy a pair of table lamps to compensate for not buying a sofa. The salesperson also suggested that they look on the department store's website as he thought there might be some styles not held in store.

That night George called his parents to talk through how far he had got with the purchase. He felt that it had taken a long time and he still had not found the right sofa. His parents suggested that two armchairs might be just as good. They also said that they might want to get rid of one of their sofas, and if he was interested they could arrange for a van to bring it over to his house. George had a lot to think about at work next week and found little time to put more effort into his search. However, he decided that he definitely needed a sofa rather than armchairs and thought that his parents' sofa would be too old-fashioned.

On Friday night he decided that he was not going to spend any more time on the decision; if he couldn't find anything in one last internet search, he would go back to the bargain store and buy one of the sofas in a bright colour and repaint his room when he had time. He went back to the website of the department store he had visited at the weekend where he saw that one of the sofas he had previously seen in store was available in a smaller size online, but the site told him that there was now only one left in store. He had liked the colour when he saw it in store and he knew his girlfriend had too. He immediately decided to buy the sofa and started to put in his details. He had just put in his credit card number when he noted that deliveries were usually only between 9.00 and 17.00, with no specified time. This was difficult for George as he was expected to be at work by 9.00 and he was reluctant to take a whole day off just to wait for his sofa. Just as he was about to put off the decision and close his computer he noticed a special delivery section; for an extra £20 he could have the sofa delivered on a weekday between 7.00 and 8.00. George thought that this was a price worth paying and clicked 'pay'. George waited for the sofa the following week but it did not arrive. He had to leave for work and rang the store to convey his disappointment. They apologized and promised the sofa would be delivered the following day at the specified time; the company also compensated George for the £20 he had paid and an added in a £20 gift voucher for his trouble. The sofa was delivered and George was happy with his purchase, although he had a lot of packaging to get rid of.

Questions

1. Outline George's decision-making process. How does his decision-making process compare with those outlined in the chapter?

2. How many decisions did George make?

3. Identify any heuristics used in his decision-making.

4. What were his key evaluative criteria?

5. Do you think he will purchase from the store again?

6. Are there any lessons to be drawn for companies marketing their products on the internet?

 Visit the Online Resource Centre and follow the link to the authors' blog where you can keep up to date with the latest developments in consumer behaviour and further explore theories through additional articles and real-world examples.

References

Antil, J.H. (1984), 'Conceptualization and operationalization of involvement', in T.C. Kinnear (ed.), *Advances in consumer research*, Vol. 11, Provo, UT: Association for Consumer Research, pp 203–209.

Arierly, D. (2008), *Predictably irrational: the hidden forces that shape our decisions*, London: Harper Collins.

Arnold, M.J. and Reynolds, K.E. (2003), 'Hedonic shopping motivations', *Journal of Retailing*, 79, 2, 1–20.

Arsel, Z. and Bean, J. (2013), 'Taste regimes and market-mediated practice', *Journal of Consumer Research*, 39, 5, 899–917.

Bachelor, L. (2012), 'Complain on Twitter for an instant response', *The Observer*, 12 May, http://www.theguardian.com/money/2012/may/12/complaint-air-on-twitter (accessed 30 July 2014).

Bain, R. (2010), 'In partnership', *Research*, http://www.research-live.com/magazine/in-partnership/4004253.article (accessed 15 May 2014).

Barreyat-Baron, M. and Barrie, R. (2008), 'Cadbury—how a drumming gorilla beat a path back to profitable growth: a real-time effectiveness case study, IPA Effectiveness Awards', WARC https://www.warc.com/Content/ContentViewer.aspx?MasterContentRef=ded7d8eb-9cfd-460b-9d17-b2f91fb9238a&q=AID%3a88470&CID=A88470&PUB=IPA (accessed 15 February 2012).

Batra, R. and Ray, M.L. (1983), 'Operationalizing involvement as depth and quality of cognitive responses', in A. Tybout and R. Bagozzi (eds), *Advances in Consumer Research*, Vol. 10, Ann Arbor, MI: Association for consumer Research, pp 309–313.

Bloch, P.H. (1986), 'The product enthusiast: implications for marketing strategy', *Journal of Consumer Marketing*, 3, 3, 51–62.

Bloch, P.H., Sherrell, D.L., and Ridgway, N. (1986), 'Consumer search: an extended framework', *Journal of Consumer Research*, 13, 1, 119–126.

Bayley, G. and Nancarrow, C. (1998), 'Impulse purchasing: a qualitative exploration of the phenomenon', *Qualitative Market Research*, 1, 2, 99–114.

Bowlby, R. (1997), 'Supermarket futures', in P. Falk and C. Campbell (eds), *The Shopping Experience*, London: SAGE.

Brannon, L.A. and Brock, T.C. (2001), 'Norms against voting for coerced reform', *Journal of Personality and Social Psychology*, 64, 347–355.

Chaiken, S., Liberman, A., and Eagly, A.H. (1989), 'Heuristic and systematic processing within and beyond the persuasion context', in J.S. Uleman and J.A. Barg (eds), *Unintended thought*, New York: Guilford Press, pp 215–252.

Court, D., Elzinga, D., Mulder, S., and Vetvick, O. (2009), 'The consumer decision journey', www.mckinseyquarterly.com (accessed 9 January 2013).

Day, R. and Landon, L. (1977), 'Towards a theory of consumer complaining behavior', in A. Woodside, J.N. Sheth, and P. Bennett (eds), *Consumer and industrial buying behavior*, Amsterdam: North-Holland.

Day, R., Grabicke, K., Schaetzle, T., and Staubach, F. (1981), 'The hidden agenda of consumer complaining', *Journal of Retailing*, 57, 3, 86–106.

Erdem, T., Keane, M.P., SabriÖncü, T., and Strebel, J. (2005), 'Learning about computers: an analysis of information search and technology choice', *Quantitative Marketing and Economics*, 3, 3, 207–247.

Economist (2013), 'Shopping habits: in for a pound', *Economist*, http://www.economist.com/news/britain/21578107-middle-classes-are-turning-keen-bargain-hunters-pound (accessed 9 July 2013).

Feick, L. and Price, L. (1987), 'The market maven: a diffuser of marketplace information', *Journal of Marketing*, 51, 1, 83–97.

Fishburn, P.C. (1974), 'Lexicographic orders, utilities and decision rules: a survey', *Management Science*, 20, 142–147.

Foxall, G.R. (1993), 'The influence of cognitive style on consumers' variety seeking among food innovations', *British Food Journal*, 95, 9, 32–36.

Harrison, S. (2013), 'Northern Ireland bag levy could reduce litter', BBC News, 8 April, http://www.bbc.co.uk/news/uk-northern-ireland-22037034 (accessed 25 November 2012).

Hirschman, A. (1970), *Exit, voice, and loyalty: responses to decline in firms, organizations, and states*, Boston, MA: Harvard University Press.

Houston, M.J. and Rothschild, M.L. (1978), 'Conceptual and methodological perspectives on involvement', in S. Jain (ed.), *Research frontiers in marketing: dialogues and directions, 1978 educators' proceedings*, Chicago, IL: American Marketing Association, pp 184–187.

Istanbulluoglu, D. (2013), 'An exploration of consumers' online complaining behaviours on Facebook', unpublished PhD thesis.

Iyengar, S.S. and Lepper, M. R. (1999), 'Rethinking the value of choice: a cultural perspective on intrinsic motivation', *Journal of Personality and Social Psychology*, 76, 349–366.

Iyengar, S.S. and Lepper, M.R. (2000), 'When choice is demotivating', *Journal of Personality and Social Psychology*, 79, 995–1006.

Ganesh, J., Reynolds, K., and Luckett, M. (2007), 'Retail patronage behaviour and shopper typologies: a replication and extension using a multi-format, multi-method approach', *Journal of the Academy of Marketing Science*, 35, 3, 369–381.

Jansson-Boyd, C.V. (2010), *Consumer Psychology*, Maidenhead: Open University Press.

Kollewe, J. (2012), 'Discounters take over UK malls', *Guardian*, 18 April, http://www.theguardian.com/business/2011/apr/18/discounters-take-over-uk-malls (accessed 9 April 2014).

Krugman, H.E. and Hartley, E.L. (1970), 'Passive learning from television', *Public Opinion Quarterly*, 342, 184–119.

Langer, E.J. (1989), *Mindfulness*, Reading, MA: Addison-Wesley.

Lee, W. (2012), 'Magiclean: Celebrity mom kidnapping', http://www.warc.com/Content/ContentViewer.aspx?ID=e68b68f3-b312-4701-949a-8196417ddf17&MasterContentRef=e68b68f3-b312-4701-949a-8196417ddf17 (accessed 17 August 2013).

Narayana, C.L. and Markin, R.J. (1975), 'Consumer behavior and product performance: an alternative conceptualization', *Journal of Marketing*, 39, 4, 1–6.

Nordland, R. (2013), 'Too hot to exercise (and who really wants to?)', *New York Times*, 7 July, http://www.nytimes.com/2013/07/08/world/middleeast/in-qatar-too-hot-to-exercise-and-who-really-wants-to.html?_r=0 (accessed 9 April 2014).

Parsons, A.G. (2002), 'Non-functional motives for online shoppers: why we click', *Journal of Consumer Marketing*, 19, 5, 380–392.

Quek, C. (2013), 'Make your brand story meaningful', *Harvard Business Review*, http://blogs.hbr.org/2013/06/make-your-brand-story-meaningf/ (accessed 30 July 2014).

Ratneshwar, S. and Chaiken, S. (1991), 'Recognition is used as one cue among others in judgement and decision making', *Journal of Experimental Psychology: Learning, Memory and Cognition*, 32, 150–162.

Roberts, H. (2012), 'Top of the shops: discount stores are booming in recession as thrifty customers seek out bargains', *Daily Mail*, 3 April, http://www.dailymail.co.uk/news/article-2124263/Discount-stores-thrive-recession-thrifty-seek-bargains.html (accessed 9 April 2014).

Rohm, A.J. and Swaminathan, V. (2004), 'A typology of online shoppers based on shopping motivations', *Journal of Business Research*, 57, 748–757.

Rook, D. (1987), 'The buying impulse', *Journal of Consumer Research*, 14, 2, 189–199.

Royo-Vela, M., and Casamassima, P. (2010), 'The influence of belonging to virtual brand communities on consumers' affective commitment, satisfaction and word-of-mouth advertising: the Zara case', *Online Information Review*, 35, 4, 517–542.

Schwartz, B. (2004), *The paradox of choice: why more is less*, New York: HarperCollins.

Schwartz, B., Ward, A., Monterosso, J., Lyubomirsky, S., White, K., and Lehman, D. R. (2002), 'Maximizing versus satisficing: happiness is a matter of choice', *Journal of Personality and Social Psychology*, 83, 5, 1178–1197.

Shah, A.K. and Oppenheimer, D.M. (2008), 'Heuristics made easy: an effort-reduction framework', *Psychological Bulletin*, 134, 2, 207–222.

Simon, H.A. (1956), 'Rational choice and the structure of the environment', *Psychological Review*, 63, 129–138.

Slama, M. and Williams, T. (1990), 'Generalization of the market maven's information provision tendency across product categories', *Advances in Consumer Research*, 17, 48–52.

Stone, G. (1954), 'City shoppers and urban identification', *American Journal of Sociology*, 60, 1, 36–45.

Tauber, E.M. (1972), 'Why do people shop? ', *Journal of Marketing*, 36, 4, 46–49.

Thompson, C.J., Locander, W.B., and Pollio, H.R (1990), 'The lived meaning of free choice: an existential-phenomenological description of everyday consumer experiences of contemporary married women', *Journal of Consumer Research*, 17, 3, 346–361.

Tversky, A. and Kahneman, D. (1974), 'Judgement under uncertainty: heuristics and biases', *Science*, 185, 4157, 1124–1131

Tversky, A. and Kahneman, D. (1981), 'The framing of decisions and the psychology of choice', *Science*, 211, 4481, 453–458.

utalkmarketing.com (2008), Editor's pick: John Lewis 'Always a Woman' advert, http://www.utalkmarketing.com/Pages/CreativeShowcase.aspx?ArticleID=17464&Filter=0&Keywords=&Order=&Page=8&Title=Editor%E2%80%99s_Pick._John_Lewis_%E2%80%98Always_a_Woman%E2%80%99_advert (accessed 30 July 2014).

Vogt, C.A. and Fesenmaier, D.R. (1998), 'Expanding the functional informational search model', *Annals of Tourism Research*, 25, 3, 551–578.

Westbrook, R. and Black, W. (1985), 'A motivation-based shopper typology', *Journal of Retailing*, 61, 1, 78–103.

B. (2000), 'Attributional thoughts about consumer behaviour', *Journal of Consumer Research*, 27, 3, 382–387.

Wood, Z. (2012), 'Discount stores boom as upmarket shoppers boast of saving money', *Observer*, 26 August, p 43, http://www.theguardian.com/business/2012/aug/26/discount-stores-boom-upmarket-shoppers (accessed 9 April 2014).

Zaichkowsky, J.L. (1985), 'Measuring the involvement construct', *Journal of Consumer Research*, 12, 341–352.

Zaichkowsky, J.L. (1986), 'Conceptualizing involvement', *Journal of Advertising*, 15, 2, 4–14.

4

LEARNING AND MEMORY

Introduction

When Apple introduced the iPhone in 2007, the company spent time and effort teaching consumers how to use it, with every advertisement showcasing one iPhone feature. This process of teaching consumers how to use a relatively new product category was important for bringing smartphones to the mass market, and for helping consumers engage with other devices such as tablets. How consumers learn is the focus of this chapter. We are all familiar with the rigours of learning, whether it is cramming for an exam or trying to master a new language. Learning extends into many areas, and is linked with other human characteristics, including personalities, motivations, perception, and attitudes.

Consumption inevitably has a learning aspect which is manifested in various ways. Businesses rely on consumers remembering brand names, their attributes, how they can be used, what price they are compared with their competitors, and of course how they feel about the brand. For consumers to retain this information they need to store it in their memory, and to do this they must have gone through the process of learning about the brand. Marketers need to know how consumers learn to enable them to communicate appropriately with buyers. In particular, they need to identify the best ways to reinforce learning about their brands, while being aware of the limitations of consumers' cognitive capacity to take many new ideas on board.

LEARNING OBJECTIVES

Having read this chapter you will be able to:

1. Understand the *main approaches to learning*.

2. Examine *behavioural learning*, and specifically the difference between classical and operant conditioning.

3. Describe the different *modes of cognitive learning*.

4. Explain the different functions of *sensory, short-, and long-term memory*.

5. Understand the role of memory in *retaining and retrieving information*.

6. Explore the issues around *social learning*, including observational and vicarious learning.

Main approaches to learning: behavioural and cognitive learning

Learning *is the activity or process of acquiring knowledge or skill by studying, practicing, or experiencing something.* Learning is important in the field of consumer behaviour as it often leads to changes in attitudes, beliefs, or behaviour. We consider two major categories: behavioural and cognitive. Figure 4.1 identifies the different branches of learning theory that will be discussed.

Behavioural learning *is concerned with learning as a response to changes in our environment.* Here, environment is the key to shaping learning and behaviour; it rejects the need to consider internal mental processes of thoughts and feelings. A behavioural view of learning

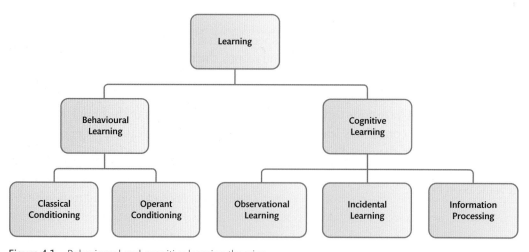

Figure 4.1   Behavioural and cognitive learning theories

expects a consumer to respond to an external stimulus, such as seeing a brand of soft drink for sale and, having had a previous positive experience with the brand, making a decision to buy it again. This model of learning has known limitations, but there is a long tradition of its use in marketing since the 1950s and it has been widely used as a model for the interpretation and understanding of advertising.

Cognitive learning *theories focus on learning through internal mental processes and conscious thought.* Such theories regard learning primarily as a process of mental activity where we are thinking through our actions to some degree. This is particularly true for information processing, which will be discussed later in this chapter. A consumer deciding whether to buy a major household appliance, such as a new washing machine, might carefully read advertisements and customer reviews, talk to people, consider all the attributes and prices, and evaluate what is best for them, as in the high involvement decision process discussed in Chapter 3. During this decision process the consumer is taking in and learning new information, some of which will be committed to memory. With cognitive learning, we might expect consumers to have gone through a process of search and evaluation from their memory of previous experiences (internal) and from new information available to them (external).

Behavioural learning

Classical conditioning

In this section we shall consider classical conditioning as a form of behavioural learning and consider what are known as first-order conditioning and higher-order conditioning. We shall look at stimulus generalization and discrimination as part of classical conditioning. These theories stem originally from Ivan Pavlov, a Russian physiologist who was researching digestive processes in dogs when he identified what is now referred to as classical conditioning. Pavlov noted that when an assistant entered the dogs' room they began to salivate because they associated the assistant with feeding time. Salivation is a reflexive process, not within the control of the dog or, more usefully, humans. Imagine coming home hungry after a long walk, entering your house, and smelling enticing cooking smells; your saliva glands are probably activated in a similar fashion to those of Pavlov's dogs. What was unusual was that the dogs began to salivate when the assistant entered the room, even when there was no food present, and this could not be explained physiologically. Pavlov then experimented with a bell which was rung each time food was presented and again the dogs salivated as they were about to be fed. After a period of time of repeatedly ringing the bell in the presence of food, the bell was rung but no food was given to the dogs. The dogs still salivated, suggesting that the salivation process had been conditioned by the presence of the bell. This led Pavlov to explain the link between the unconditioned stimulus (US)—the food—and the conditioned stimulus (CS)—the bell. The dogs' physiological response to food is unconditioned and is referred to as the unconditioned response (UR).

When the dogs salivated and there was no food present, clearly they had been conditioned by the previous contiguity of the bell and the food, thus producing a conditioned response (CR).

Figure 4.2 provides an explanation of these links between the unconditioned, neutral and conditioned stimuli and responses. The unconditioned stimulus produces an unconditioned response, and the unconditioned stimulus (food) linked with a neutral stimulus (bell) produces an unconditioned response. Over time, this repeated pairing results in the bell acting as a conditioned stimulus that produces a conditioned response (salivation).

First-order conditioning

The example of Pavlov's dogs is known as **first-order conditioning**, and occurs when *a conditioned stimulus acquires motivational importance by being paired with an unconditioned stimulus which is intrinsically aversive or rewarding,*

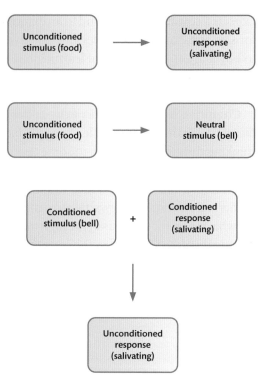

Figure 4.2   Producing a conditioned response

such as a painful shock or food (Gewirtz and Davis, 2000). In first-order conditioning the US needs to come almost immediately before exposure to the CS, which is typically a biological stimulus, such as food, sex, or pain, that elicits a natural physiological response. This may explain why sexual images are so often used in advertising for products such as expensive fast cars. In such advertisements, a woman (US) is directly associated with the sports car (CS), suggesting to the viewer that the two are connected. Sex is a basic biological instinct (see Chapter 7) and the association here is between driving an expensive car and the appeal that this will have to the opposite sex. Women are not excluded from such sexual connections; for a number of years, Diet Coke has used the image of an attractive and fit young man drinking coke while being watched by women. In their recent advertising a group of girls send a can of Diet Coke down to a gardener mowing a lawn. He opens the can and the Coke splashes over him, making him take his top off, with Etta James singing 'I just wanna make love to you' in the background. The link between Diet Coke and sex may be more difficult to discern, but there is a direct biological connection between a diet product and a fit body!

Classical conditioning depends on the continued pairing of the CS and the US. If the unconditioned stimulus is removed from the conditioned stimulus, over time the response will be removed. This is known as **extinction**. If Pavlov had continued to ring the bell but not produce food, eventually the dogs would have ceased salivating as they would no longer connect the bell with food. Classical conditioning is contingent on many factors, and experiments over the years have not always provided such conclusive results as those of Pavlov (Bitterman, 2006). A recent investigation into the application of classical conditioning in consumer behaviour and advertising contexts suggests that its effectiveness may be exaggerated (Pornpitakpan, 2012). For examples of the appication of classical conditioning to advertising see Consumer Insight 4.1.

CONSUMER INSIGHT 4.1

Celebrity endorsers and classical conditioning

Celebrity endorsement is widely used in advertising (see Figure 4.3). The 'match-up' hypothesis (Till and Busler, 2000) suggests that celebrities are most useful when there is commonality between them and the product they are endorsing. So, while Rihanna would be an unlikely endorser of Halford's bikes, the Olympic gold medal winner Victoria Pendleton matches up with the product and brings credibility to the endorsement. Nike makes extensive use of celebrity endorsement across the world, for example the use of Liu Xiang, the Chinese Olympic hurdler, as an endorser of Nike to promote the spirit of Nike—'Nike: Find Your Greatness'.

In experimental studies Till et al. (2008) found support for the use of celebrities as unconditioned stimuli. They also found that highly congruent celebrities will result in greater conditioning. Associating the basketball player Michael Jordan with a sports drink resulted in stronger conditioning than when the sports drink was paired with actor Pierce Brosnan.

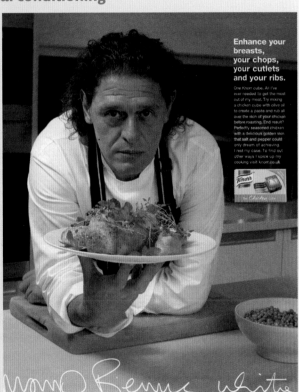

Figure 4.3   The chef Marco Pierre White advertising Knorr stock cubes

Source: Image supplied by The Advertising Archives.

There are drawbacks to using celebrities for classical conditioning; if a celebrity has built up a strong connection with one brand, it may be difficult to use the same celebrity for another product as the previous connection could suppress the formation of a new association (Pornpitakpan, 2012). However, there are some celebrities for whom the unconditioned response is carried across readily from one brand to another. Kate Moss endorsed the luxury brand Chanel, but also has endorsed

TopShop, and both brands were enhanced by their links with the model. The unconditioned stimulus Kate Moss is readily linked with a variety of conditioned stimuli from fashion to make-up.

Questions

1. Pick three or four different brands that use celebrity endorsers and assess their 'match-up'. Try to pick different product types and also consider different celebrities who are used by different brands in the same product class.

2. Assess to what extent you think congruency matters in the use of celebrity endorsement. Are there any apparently mismatched celebrities whom you still think work as unconditioned stimuli?

Sources: Till and Busler (2000); Till et al. (2008); Pornpitakpan (2012).

 Visit the Online Resource Centre and follow the weblinks to learn more about the use of celebrity endorsements.

Higher-order conditioning

Whereas first-order conditioning relies on the connection between the unconditioned and conditioned stimulus, **higher-order conditioning** is *the pairing of two conditioned stimuli.* Higher-order conditioning can occur when a conditioned stimulus (CS1) acquires associative strength through being connected to a second conditioned stimulus (CS2) (rather than an unconditioned stimulus). The pairing of CS1 and CS2 may occur before or after the first conditioned stimulus (CS1) is paired with an unconditioned stimulus (US).

Music acts as a particularly powerful form of higher-order conditioning. The use of well-known songs in advertising has become increasingly popular and successful. In the media this trend is known as 'synchronization' which reflects the appropriate pairing of song and brand (*Economist*, 2003). In the 1960s, Bob Dylan released the song 'Blowin' in the Wind', which was an anti-establishment anthem for young people of that era, asking when change would come about. This song was already conditioned in (older) people's minds associated with the need for change for the better. In 2009, Dylan granted permission for the UK-based group The Co-operative to use it in an advertisement. The advertisement carefully linked visually with the song from the opening shot of a dandelion blowing its seeds in the wind which blew across many lands showing people working to produce goods sold by the Co-Op (see Figure 4.4). The closing lines of the advertisement were: 'From community projects to a share of the profits. From renewable energy to Fair Trade products, The Co-operative believes that when benefits are passed on it's good for everyone', thus successfully pairing the associations of The Co-operative with the already conditioned song as a movement for change. Hence, two conditioned responses (anti-establishment conditioning associated with the song and community orientation associated with The Co-operative) produce a powerful associative response.

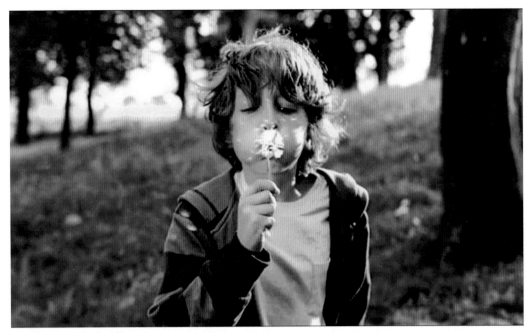

Figure 4.4   Still from The Co-operative's 'Blowin' in the Wind' advertisement

Source: Image supplied by The Advertising Archives.

Stimulus generalization

Stimulus generalization *occurs when a stimulus similar to a conditioned stimulus elicits a similar conditioned response.* Stimulus generalization stems from the fact that people often respond in the same way to stimuli that are similar. The importance of stimulus generalization to marketing is how consumers respond to brand extensions and private-label marketing. Consumers form impressions and judgements about new product lines and extensions based on their general feeling towards the brand derived from previous experiences with it. Brand extensions are important for companies as they allow them to innovate, increase market share, and move into other markets, but they are also risky for companies in terms of consumer acceptance. Where there is transfer of positive feelings from the parent brand to the extension, the risk will be reduced. Stimulus generalization is a mechanism for such positive transfer (Till and Priluck, 2000), with the assumption that it is most likely when there is similarity between the two products (Broniarczyk and Alba, 1994).

Heinz is a brand that has successfully managed product innovation while benefiting from stimulus generalization. From ketchup to beans to baby food, the Heinz brand is well known. If Heinz brings out new products such as hot sauces, the process of stimulus generalization acts as insurance to the consumer and may encourage them to try something new. In Figure 4.5 we see three products from Heinz. Most people will be familiar with the shape of the bottle and label on Heinz ketchup, and this has been transferred to two other products—relish and mustard. Therefore the familiarity of the ketchup bottle and labelling is transferred to the other products in this stimulus generalization example. Heinz often uses tag lines such as 'It has to be Heinz' to enforce the reassurance of choosing the brand even if the product is unfamiliar.

Another area where stimulus generalization has an impact is private-label marketing. Many retailers offer private labels in their stores to compete with national brands. These private-label products often use similar colours, fonts, package shapes, etc. to those of the major brands with which they are competing. Consumers may be confused or pick up own-label brands quickly, or through stimulus generalization the private-label brands may simply benefit from a transfer of positive attitude from the main-line brands. Major companies, such as Proctor & Gamble and United Biscuits (see Consumer Insight 4.2), have successfully sued private-label brands that they see as feeding off the goodwill of their name (Narisetti, 1994).

Figure 4.5   Heinz product extensions
Source: © iStock.com/cnicbc.

CONSUMER INSIGHT 4.2

Passing off: Penguin versus Puffin

Passing off is *the marketing of a good in a way that enables it to be mistaken for another brand, and it relies on the phenomenon of stimulus generalization.* From a legal perspective, the essence of passing off is that the goodwill of one brand is taken advantage of by another to the detriment

Figure 4.6   Penguin packaging
Source: Image courtesy of United Biscuits.

of the first. Passing off relies on consumers associating the benefits of a well-known brand with another brand that looks similar through stimulus generalization (Warlop and Alba, 2004). Typically such 'copycat' brands use perceptual elements, such as colour, shape, and imagery, from the brand they are imitating (Miceli and Pieters, 2010). An important case of passing off was between United Biscuits, the makers of the Penguin chocolate biscuit, and UK supermarket Asda, who sold an own-label biscuit called Puffin in their stores in their stores from 1997. This was the first time that a copycat case went to trial. It was also interesting because United Biscuits' products were sold in Asda stores. Penguins were chocolate-coated biscuits sold in red packaging with a yellow band across and the brand name horizontally placed in black lettering, and the packs also displayed images of penguins (see Figure 4.6). United Biscuits used the slogan 'Pick up a Penguin' in its advertising. The Asda lookalike brand was also in red packaging with black lettering and had a cartoon Puffin on the front. In promotional material Asda used the phrase 'Pick up a Puffin'. Puffin was sold in Asda stores alongside Penguin, but at a lower price. In a BBC Money Programme, Justin King, then the product development manager of Asda, said, 'We feel it is very important that we are able to continue to offer the value that own-label products deliver to our customers'. Two witnesses said that they had thought they were buying Penguins when they were actually buying Puffins, and another two witnesses said that they thought Puffin must be made by the same company that made Penguin.

In this case the judge upheld the complaint by United Biscuits of misrepresentation, recognizing the similarity between the packaging and the use of a bird similar to a penguin (marketingweek.com). 'The judge said that had the Asda product been called "Bison" with an appropriate cartoon, the case would never have been brought and concluded, "The Puffin packaging and get up was, in the material sense, deceptively similar to those of the Penguin"' (Burrell, 1997).

Questions

1. Despite the ruling in 1997 there are still many lookalike brands. Choose a couple of own-label brands from a supermarket that you think look particularly similar to leading brands. Identify what elements are similar, e.g. size and shape of packaging, the name, the colours used. What is the price difference?

2. For your chosen brands, assess whether you think your chosen brands are passing off or that customers would recognize the differences. Why?

Sources: Burrell (1997); Warlop and Alba (2004); Miceli and Pieters (2010); marketingweek.com

 Visit the Online Resource Centre and follow the weblinks to learn more about brand misrepresentation.

Stimulus discrimination

Just as we can generalize from one stimulus to another, we can also learn to discriminate between similar stimuli. For example, dogs can be trained to discriminate so that they only respond to the particular sound of their master's whistle. If a conditioned stimulus is not followed by an unconditioned stimulus, the response will decline and hence we discriminate against that conditioned stimulus. If we buy an own-label product and find that it does not perform to the same standards as the branded product, we are likely to discriminate against this product by switching back to the manufacturer's brand. Manufacturers have a vested interest in consumers recognizing their brand in a sea of own-labels and competitor brands, and will often indicate their uniqueness and quality with lines such as Tetley's 'Original and the best' slogan. Manufacturers can also use stimulus discrimination more positively to enable consumers to distinguish between products in their brand range. Typically, cosmetics manufacturers choose one or two colours with which to associate their brand, but introduce more variety in packaging, such as tubs, jars, and tubes, to enable consumers to recognize additions to their product range easily.

Operant conditioning

Operant conditioning, also known as instrumental learning, was identified by B.F. Skinner (1953). **Operant conditioning** is *the changing of behaviour through reinforcement* *following a desired response.* Skinner showed that learning can occur when behaviour is changed or modified as a result of the outcome of previous behaviour. Skinner kept a number of pigeons in a box, always at three-quarters of their ideal weight to ensure that they were hungry. In the box was a lever that dropped food when pushed. The pigeons learnt to press this lever to receive food. The behaviour of pressing the lever was reinforced by the appearance of the food. Table 4.1 describes the different responses and outcomes that are found in operant conditioning.

Imagine that a new coffee shop opens on your way to work. You decide to try it one day instead of your usual shop. You find that the coffee is very good and cheaper than that you usually buy, so you decide to go there again. Here you have acquired learning through behaviour which has produced a positive outcome, or what is known as positive reinforcement. Your behaviour may also be affected by negative reinforcement. This is where something unpleasant is removed following a particular behaviour or where you behave in a certain way to avoid something unpleasant. You might have a stain on your favourite shirt and find a product that removes it—this is an example of negative reinforcement. In addition, some behaviours may neither increase nor decrease the likelihood of repetition; perhaps the behaviour was not important enough or the response was neutral. You might buy some stock items such as biscuits or tea; if there was nothing particularly good or bad about them you might not notice the brand, and next time you might or might not buy them again. These are referred to as *neutral operants*. Some responses decrease the likelihood of repeating the behaviour; i.e. they lead to a weakening response. If you buy a new flavour of ice cream and neither you nor your family like it, you are effectively being *punished* for your choice and are unlikely to purchase it again. Finally, if a behaviour is repeated but no longer leads to a positive outcome, extinction will occur and the behaviour will be less likely to continue.

	Condition	Response	Outcome
Strengthens response	Positive reinforcement	Shopping at a retail outlet you find many shops and bargains on designer brands	This increases the likelihood that you will return to shop at the outlet
	Negative reinforcement	You suffer from hay fever but when you take antihistamine tablets your symptoms decrease	You ensure that you have antihistamine tablets with you during the hay fever season
Weakens response	Punishment	The boots you bought for winter let in water and don't keep you warm	You will not return to the shop from which you bought the boots
	Extinction	The internet site that offered free shipping and returns removes this service feature	Decreases the likelihood of your using this site

Table 4.1   How operant conditioning works

Marketers want to create positive reinforcement for their brands. Free samples are a useful way of encouraging consumers to try products and, if the brand meets consumers' expectations, are a form of positive reinforcement for them. Lillet, the long-established French aperitif brand, made extensive use of free samples of its drink to broaden awareness of the brand among a young adult audience.

At the most basic level companies want to be sure that their brand is good enough for the item to be purchased again, but they may also provide other positive attributes which may help in a customer's choice and repeat purchasing. Internet retailers are increasingly offering free delivery and returns to customers, effectively giving them a reduction in price and an incentive to shop. This may act as a positive reinforcement, especially if it is offered all the time or regularly as in the case of the internet fashion company Boden (Figure 4.7).

Reinforcement schedules

An important aspect of operant conditioning relates to how and when reinforcement is applied to behaviour. Reinforcement schedules can be continuous or variable.

- A **fixed ratio schedule** *applies reinforcement after a specific number of responses.* Many loyalty schemes will make it clear how much you have to spend before you get a financial reward. Caffe Nero stamp your card every time you buy a drink

Figure 4.7   Using free delivery to reinforce purchasing   *Source*: Image courtesy of Boden.

Figure 4.8   Fixed ration cards from Caffe Nero and other food and drink outlets
Source: Image courtesy of Eatbigfish (www.eatbigfish.com).

(see Figure 4.8), and once it is stamped for nine drinks you are rewarded with a free one. See Research Insight 4.1.

- A **fixed interval schedule** *is when reinforcement is provided after a specific known period of time.* A store may advertise that it has a sale three times a year, and customers may decide only to shop there at those times.

RESEARCH INSIGHT 4.1

Nunes, J.C. and Drèze, X. (2006), 'The endowed progress effect: how artificial advancement increases effort', *Journal of Consumer Research*, 32, 4, 504–512.

In this paper, Nunez and Drèze examine and compare the level of effort and commitment involved in filling a loyalty card for a carwash. They conducted an experiment to look at the factors influencing whether or not consumers stick with reward cards to get them completely filled up (and receive the reward). They found that those who received two free stamps on a loyalty card exert more effort and are more committed to using the same carwash than those receiving no free stamps. They documented this effect as the 'endowed progress effect' whereby people provided with artificial advancement towards a goal (e.g. the two free stamps) exhibit greater persistence towards reaching the goal.

 Visit the Online Resource Centre to read the abstract and access the full paper.

- **Variable schedules** *are where reinforcement is provided on an irregular basis.* Skinner suggested that gamblers are particularly susceptible to variable schedules. This is when reinforcement is present after a variable (unknown to the person behaving) number of responses. If you play a slot machine you may win a little at one time and a lot at another, but you have no control over the response. It is the unknown but potentially positive outcome that keeps gamblers playing.

- Finally, a **variable interval** *is when the reinforcement occurs at some unknown but consistent rate.* In the lead-up to festivals, such as Diwali in India, companies typically have a range of deals and special offers to coincide with the festival. Customers expect them but they do not know exactly when, and so they may be encouraged to regularly shop and visit websites to ensure that they don't miss an offer. The Samsung campaign for Diwali 2013 is typical of this kind of promotion. With the slogan 'Samsung Home Happy Home', the company invited consumers to choose Samsung household goods (such as flat panel TVs, air conditioners and refrigerators) to make their home a happy place for the festive season.

Learning history

An important element of behavioural learning is our learning history. This is developed from similar or related experiences that the consumer has had before, and when they encounter new settings they call upon these experiences to guide behaviour. The first time you visit a gym, you may feel uncertain about what to do, how the machines work, or the gym etiquette. But you may have some experience of using sports facilities in another context, say from school, that you can draw on to help you. After you have been a few times you become familiar with the environment and feel much more comfortable. It is our past experience of these situations and their consequences that help us understand new environments. We use this experience, which comprises our learning history, to adopt appropriate behaviour (Foxall et al., 1998). Therefore it is advantageous to marketers to try to ensure that it is easy to learn how a product or service environment works.

Cognitive learning

Whereas behavioural learning focuses on how we learn through our external responses to the environment, and how this is manifested in behaviour, cognitive learning is concerned with internal mental processes. This gives it the potential to explain much more complex behaviour and decision-making processes than is possible with the behaviourist approach.

For our purposes, the key feature of cognitive learning is that it is based on the view that humans are broadly rational and use the information available in their environment to make decisions. Our responses to our environment can include a complex set of processes including gathering, processing, interpreting information, assigning it meaning, and storing it in our memory. Cognitive learning manifests itself in many aspects of our lives. It can operate in high or low involvement situations (see Chapter 3) and can be conscious or unconscious. While in some situations we may be aware of collecting information in a conscious manner, on other occasions we learn through what Krugman (1965) termed passive learning, i.e. we are not conscious that we are learning.

There are various conceptions of cognitive learning theory, but some key elements can be identified, such as an insistence that although we cannot directly observe the workings of the mind we can make inferences from behaviour, and that we create knowledge based on our experience rather than passively receive it. At the heart of most cognitive learning theory is the information processing model.

Information processing

The information processing model explains how communications are received by the consumer and then interpreted, stored in the memory, and later retrieved in a logical and sequential fashion. Information processing in high involvement situations (see Chapter 3) became of increasing interest to researchers in the late twentieth century, particularly as computers became widespread. Researchers such as Newell and Simon (1972) and Bettman (1970) often referenced explanations of how computers worked to illustrate human information processing.

When information processing takes place the consumer uses information received from the environment which passes through a cognitive process. In the case of deciding whether or not to purchase a particular brand, this involves not only new or repeat information from their environment, but also a mental assessment as to the brand's suitability, given the consumer's evaluative criteria and its integration with information stored in the memory. The process can be summarized as follows, using the example of a consumer, Jim, buying a gift, and is illustrated in Figure 4.9.

- **Exposure** *involves sensory detection and registration through receptor organs.* Jim wants to buy a birthday present for a friend. As he looks around he is exposed to many advertisements in magazines and the internet.

- **Attention** *requires the focusing of attention, leading to perception and categorization of stimuli.* Jim doesn't notice most of the information to which he is exposed, but he regularly receives an email alert from an internet bookshop and as he knows his friend is interested in history he pays more attention to this site.

- **Comprehension** *is where the consumer searches (and identifies) meaning.* Jim looks at the site in more detail and compares the information with what he has in his memory regarding his friend's taste in books and what he knows he has read. He also reads some of the reviews in more detail so that he starts to distinguish what might be the best choice.

- **Acceptance/rejection**: *the consumer considers existing choice criteria and elaborates the message received to reach a point of acceptance or rejection of the information.* Jim shortlists

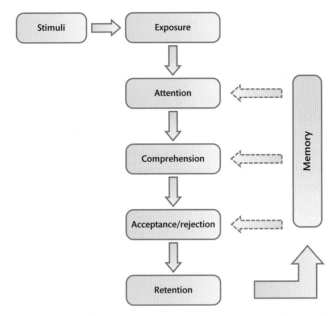

Figure 4.9   A five-stage process of information processing   *Source*: Adapted from Blackwell et al. (2006).

two books and is convinced that one of them is likely to be particularly appealing to his friend.

- **Retention**: *learning has to be retained in the memory for future use*. Jim has learnt a number of things—how to navigate the website, where to find reviews on books, and that the bookstore was offering free shipping on orders over 30 euros. He will retain some or all of this in his long-term memory.

It is believed that to reach the consumer's long-term memory, information has to go through the stages outlined in Figure 4.9. Typically, successful exposure to a stimulus depends on how closely it conforms to a consumer's past experiences and current beliefs, that the stimulus is not too complex, that it is believable, and that it relates to their current needs. However, it is worth noting that we may perceive and take note of information that is not immediately believable or relate to our current needs, but is novel or just interesting. Advertising often captures our attention with novel stimuli (see Chapter 5). We may not be immediately interested in the service or product but are attracted by the advertisement and its content. The problem that marketers face is whether such information will be rejected at a later stage of the process, or will be understood and accepted, so that it becomes a long-term memory? Novel stimuli can often gain the consumer's attention, but may not survive their information processing. In Practitioner Insight 4, Rachel Hartley tells us how the Nutracheck tool helps people to learn about their calorie intake through a process that aids comprehension and retention in their memory to enable them to manage their food intake.

PRACTITIONER INSIGHT 4

Rachel Hartley, Business Development & Marketing Director, Nutracheck

In 2005, Nutracheck developed the UK's first mobile phone program to track what you ate. Its latest barcode scanning app, together with the interactive food diary website, is designed to track your food intake and empower you with knowledge to make better choices to manage your diet for weight loss or maintenance.

Managing your diet is all about learning. Many people genuinely have no idea about the calorie content of foods and how many calories their body actually needs. Nutracheck has a food database (UK foods) of over 100,000 products. We also have the calorie content of foods that don't have nutritional labelling, such as coffee shops, alcoholic drinks, take-aways, and eating out places.

Nutracheck is an app with a dedicated website designed to help people track their calorie intake by keeping a food diary—either via the barcode scanning app or online. It is an educational tool to make people more aware of how their food choices contribute to their daily calorie allowance—and in turn affect their weight. Keeping a food diary is a very important aspect to learning and building up knowledge through repetition. All you do is search for the food you ate in the Nutracheck food database which has over 100,000 UK products—using either the app or online—and add it to the food diary which keeps track of how many calories you've consumed. Once a member has learned the basics of simply recording what they eat and staying within their calorie allowance, there are many quick short-cuts they can use to speed up keeping the food diary and this helps to make learning easier. For example, people can add favourites, they can multiple copy whole days of their diary or select foods they eat every day, and use food wizards to create popular combinations of food and add them in one go.

Another important aspect for people concerned about their weight and nutrition is how to reinforce their behaviour. We use awards of silver and gold rosettes when the 7lb and 1 stone goals have been reached. These can be displayed on their forum profile so that other members can congratulate them. A special weigh-in and progress board in the forum allows members to share their successes. We also run a team challenge where members pledge how much they wish to lose during the four- to six-week challenge and are allocated into teams. We show the teams' progress against their collective goal and members support one another. Such support is also provided by Diet Buddies who can communicate with one another through a private messaging service to help someone through a similar experience to them, such as losing baby-weight or getting ready for a special event.

Above all, learning about nutrition is the aim of Nutracheck, and once members have become familiar with the nutritional content of food and the calories they consume, this is knowledge they are unlikely to forget (especially the high calorie counts that have shocked them!), and the more they fill in their food diaries and check the calorie content the better the information will stay in their memories.

Memory

Once a consumer has been through a learning process it is important that the information is retained in their memory to enable them to use it later. This is particularly important for marketing, where companies are spending huge amounts of money to get people to remember their brand. In this section we shall go through the various stages involved in how information is contained and retrieved from memory via a process of encoding, storage, and retrieval. A simplified summary of how memory works is presented in Figure 4.10.

Figure 4.10   How the memory works

Memory *is a system and a process whereby information is received, sorted, organized, stored, and retrieved over time.* Memory is central to understanding how consumers make decisions; marketers are eager to get their brands remembered and enable retrieval from consumers' memories during the purchase decision process. However, they have to recognize the many limitations on getting their message remembered. Alongside the issues associated with perceiving a stimulus (see Chapter 5), people are often exposed to advertisements weeks or months before they intend to buy. Therefore the chance of their remembering much of the original message is low. There are three critical steps to information being remembered, encoding, storage, and retrieval.

Encoding *refers to how information enters the memory.* It is important that consumers have fully comprehended the information. While advertisers want their brands and communications to be distinctive and different, their messages must be comprehended unambiguously in order to be made sense of and stored. This can be facilitated by brand names which incorporate the main benefit of the product and can be easily encoded, such as Mr Sheen household polish or Head and Shoulders shampoo, where key characteristics of the brands are encapsulated in the brand name. Remember, in different countries very different sounding brand names may appear memorable. In France the brand Pschitt is onomatopoeic, recognized by consumers as sounding like the opening of a bottle—in English-speaking countries it has quite different connotations and associations. Brands can also present themselves in a simple form to avoid any ambiguity. If you look at the campaign for the Ronseal brand, each advertisement is very pared down and direct in its message, with the tag line, 'Does exactly what it says on the tin' as the actor presents the tin with the product description to the camera.

Storage *is how the encoded information is retained in the memory.* Once in the memory the new information is connected with other information which may impact on how and when it is retrieved. Our memories include memorable nostalgic experiences such as an important birthday or graduation (Wildschut, 2006). Zauberman et al. (2008) identified that people will use strategic memory protection in order to protect their ability to remember such important experiences. Memory pointers such as photographs or mementos may be used to help them recall these events. We may also practise memory protection through avoidance, so that our special memories are protected. For example, you might not want to go back to the restaurant where your partner proposed to you with business colleagues because the new situation may sully the memories of the more important experience. We shall see later in this chapter, in the section 'Retrieval of memory', how marketers aim to get consumers to retrieve these memories.

CONSUMER INSIGHT 4.3

Repetition and learning in advertising

Krugman (1965) identified that most people are unlikely to be involved with much of the commercial information they receive through television, but some of that information may move into their long-term memory just from repeated exposures (see Simon Tunstill's Practitioner Insight in Chapter 3 for a twenty-first century view of television viewing). This does not mean that we have been persuaded about the product or that our attitudes have changed. Krugman advised marketers to repeat brand names and slogans as often as possible, given their finite promotional budgets, because beliefs and associations stored in the memory over time may form the basis for brand choice. It is at the moment when we are at the point of purchase and see the brand that our memories are jogged, even though we may not have considered the brand consciously until then. Krugman described this as the catalyst that brings to the fore the passive learning that has occurred just from repeated contact with mass media. In such low involvement situations marketers are looking for methods to help their messages penetrate the memories of their audience.

Jingles and distinctive visual imagery may help in this process. Learning through repetition is referred to as rote learning and is one of the easiest ways that we learn. Often we find jingles or words from songs in our memories even though we have not consciously memorized them. Most people are able to memorize information that is heard or seen repeatedly. Such information can be visual (iconic rote memory) or aural (echoic rote memory). Businesses may use words or phrases that are simple but memorable.

An example of a business that successfully combines echoic and iconic rote memory is comparethemarket.com. It uses the powerful imagery of talking meerkats to increase iconic rote memory while continually raising the apparent confusion between the fictitious 'compare the meerkat.com' and its own name, thus pursuing an echoic rote memory route as well. The company has repeatedly used this combination in its advertising such that for many it is difficult not think of meerkats without thinking of comparethemarket.com.

Questions

1. Do you think that there are there any disadvantages of repetition for consumers? If so, what are they?

2. Think of some other examples where iconic and/or echoic rote memory are utilized. Are there particular types of imagery that are powerful and why?

Sources: Krugman (1965); www.comparethemarket.com

 Visit the Online Resource Centre and follow the weblinks to learn more about repetition and learning in advertising.

Memory systems

Memories are not stored in discrete areas of the brain. Although we talk about sensory, short-term, and long-term memory, these are ways of describing how we remember rather than the physical storage of memories. While not universally accepted, this model of three levels of memory—sensory, short-term, and long-term—helps us to understand how and why some things are remembered and some are not. This system is referred to as the multiple store of memory.

Sensory memory

Here information is received in its sensory form—sight, smell, touch, taste, or hearing—and retained for a very brief period, no longer than the amount of time that the sensation is experienced. Imagine that you are walking through a fairground. You will pass many colourful sights, fascinating smells, and noisy sounds, you may taste a bit of your friend's candyfloss and touch a teddy bear that someone has won, but all these moments are fragmentary. When you get home you may have a general sense of what you experienced and one or two things may have stayed with you (transferred to short-term memory), but much will have been forgotten as visual information only stays in the sensory memory for about half a second and auditory information for about two seconds (Jansson-Boyd, 2010). The reason for this is that sensory memory is essentially automatic and does not involve any particular attention or interpretation.

Short-term memory

This is where current information is processed. An important aspect of short-term memory is that it is limited to only holding small amounts of information in mind for short periods of time. In a classic study from the 1950s, Miller (1956) conducted a number of experiments where he found that in a uni-dimensional task (i.e. where a person is being asked to remember one type of thing at a time, such as numbers, loudness, etc.) most people can remember a series of up to seven items plus or minus one or two. Around seven items in some kind of sequence appears to be the maximum capacity of the short-term memory. One way that marketers can help their messages to be retained is through **chunking** *which is the grouping together of similar or meaningful pieces of information* (MacGregor, 1987). A chunk may be small or large, but as long as it is meaningful then it can be remembered as a whole; people can remember around seven chunks of such information (see Research Insight 4.2). Imagine that someone writes down their phone number for you. It might look like 0204156543, but to remember it you might recall it in three chunks of three or four numbers 020 425 6543; the latter is much easier for the brain to process and remember. Take a look at the debit or credit card in your wallet; the long number will be presented as four chunks of grouped numbers which are easier both to say and to remember.

Long-term memory

Our long-term memory has the potential to remember for ever. But first, memories have to get to the long-term memory and few do, otherwise we would be overloaded with mostly useless memories. Getting memories into the long-term memory is achieved by encoding

RESEARCH INSIGHT 4.2

Vanhuele, M., Laurent, G., and Drèze, X. (2006), 'Consumers' immediate memory for prices', *Journal of Consumer Research*, 33, 2, 163–172.

Vanhuele et al. (2006) found two important properties in remembering prices. One was the verbal length of the price stimulus and the other was the nature of its pattern. Consumers may aid retention of prices in their memory by using different recall strategies that decrease the number of syllables they have to remember. A price of $173 may be remembered as 'one hundred and seventy-three', 'one hundred seventy-three' 'one seventy-three, or 'one seven three'—anything from four to eight syllables.

 Visit the Online Resource Centre to read the abstract and access the full paper.

them through **engrams** *which are neural networks connecting new memories with old* (Schacter, 1996). This involves the rehearsal of information in the short-term memory and linkage of this information with that stored in the long-term memory. Heath (2012) suggests that an engram for a brand would connect with its advertising and with that of other brands and their advertisements to produce an extensive network of interlinked memories or associative networks as shown in Figure 4.11.

Memory can be affected by the processing effort required, with more effort (deep processing) more likely to result in long-term memory. It is probably best not to think of long-term memory as being completely discrete from short-term memory as there is much movement between the two. Information can be envisaged as being stored in the memory

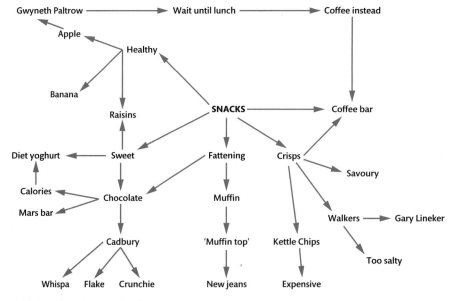

Figure 4.11   Associative network

in a complex set of linked packets of information forming what is referred to as an associative network (Anderson, 1993). The networks are made up of nodes, which are concepts such as a place, time, person or brand, taste, smell, etc., and they are linked through different associations and pathways to form a network. Some associations may be stronger than others and some elements may have more links to items than others. One of the typical packets of information, and a key element in how memory works, is the schema, which is an abstraction about an entity based on a range of experiences with that entity. So we may have a café and restaurant schema which contains such information as the various features of tables, chairs, menus, counter, coffee machine, till, and toilets, and also information about the typical spatial arrangement of these features, such as the counter being near the entrance and the toilets at the back. Associated with this may well be a script. This is a special type of schema where we have a well-developed concept of what to do in a certain situation. This may be built up from our learning history (see the section on 'Operant conditioning') where, from experience, we know what we will do in certain situations. Therefore in this example we may have a script for going to a café which involves elements such as reading the menu, attracting the waiter's attention, ordering, waiting, eating, and paying the bill. Figure 4.11 shows a possible associative network for someone thinking about a snack. The first words that occur in the memory might include crisps, healthy, and sweet—the person might like a bag of crisps but is also thinking of something healthier to have and that an alternative might be something sweet. Each of these words is linked to other items, perhaps specific products such as an apple (healthy) and chocolate (sweet), and in turn these can be linked to specific types (e.g. New Zealand Braeburn apples or Japanese Crispin apples) or brands (e.g. Cadbury's Dairy Milk or Hershey's Milk Chocolate), but may also be linked to consequences (e.g. satisfying; fattening). Some of the links may even lead to people, such as the healthy apple and Gwyneth Paltrow (her daughter's name is Apple), and for the crisps there may be similar associations such as footballer Gary Lineker, who has been a celebrity endorser for the Walkers brand of crisps in the UK or Mahendra Singh Dhoni who is endorsing Lay's crisps in India.

A company interested in identifying what an associative network might look like can use a number of research techniques. One is the response-time method where statements regarding a brand can be presented and respondents agree or disagree. Not only can the links with statements be mapped out visually but the response times can be measured, with longer times suggesting that the association is further away and vice versa. Another approach is the Kelly Repertory Grid (Kelly, 1955). This method is used to map associations with brands and allows respondents to identify the stimulus brands, and then assess the dimensions on which to compare and differentiate the brands. Respondents can then compare groups of three brands at a time. Here they are asked in what way two brands are alike and the third is different. So if the research was looking at snacks, one triad of brands might be Twiglets, Frito-Lay's potato chips, and Cadbury's Dairy Milk chocolate. An obvious similarity would be between the first two as savoury snacks, while the final one is sweet. Another might be Cadbury's Dairy Milk with Picnic and Mars Bar; here a respondent might group the last two together as chocolate bars for eating on your own and the Cadbury's Dairy Milk for sharing. Over multiple combinations dimensions can be identified along which the brands can be evaluated and positioned on associative maps. Then the associative maps can be used by marketing managers to better understand the links that consumers make between different brands, different products, when they are used, and who or what they are associated with. This kind of map helps marketers understand how consumers actually see connections between different products, brands, and other associations and can be used for new product development and marketing communications.

Types of long-term memory

The long-term memory can be subdivided into two types of memory: knowing how to do things (*procedural memory*) and memory of events that have taken place (*declarative memory*), as shown in Figure 4.12.

- **Procedural memory** *allows us to remember how to perform tasks and actions—riding a bike, typing on a computer, making a cup of tea.* We learn how to tie our shoelaces as children, and it is often difficult to remember when we learnt this as it has become an automatic action.

- **Declarative memory** *is specifically about knowing things.* It is made up of two different types of memory systems, episodic memory and semantic memory, which remember different types of event.

Episodic memory *refers to our memories of specific events and experiences which have formed our auto-biographical time line.* We remember significant events in our lives, perhaps getting examination results, an important boyfriend or girlfriend, and our graduation or wedding (see Figure 4.13). Places, times, the season when a significant event happened are all associated with other contextual elements to form these memories, which are often emotionally charged.

Semantic memory *involves the structuring of specific records, facts, concepts, and knowledge about the world we live in.* It can include factual data, such as who was the first man on the Moon or the names of capital cities, and can also include generally held customs or how to play games or more abstract ideas, such as the meanings associated with certain people or well-known characters such as Harry Potter or Bart Simpson. Heath (2012) suggests that the reason specific advertisements are difficult to remember is that they involve episodic memory, which requires more thorough encoding than semantic memory. He says that in order to recall an advertisement we have to have encoded it sufficiently to have a picture in our mind and possibly an idea of when we saw it. This may explain why

Figure 4.12 The organization of long-term memory

Figure 4.13   Episodic memory includes important life events   *Source*: © iStock.com/monkeybusinessimages.

advertisers have increasingly used nostalgia in their advertisements, possibly to try to link their brands with happy memories from our past. In the UK, Robinsons Barley Water tried to create the feeling of being young again with this copy: 'Think about it, a hot day in an endless summer and you're waiting expectantly for a large frothing glass, you drain it to the last drop and wipe the barley moustache from your lips. A butterfly circles and lands on your arm'. Here there is a clear attempt to encode Robinsons through the memory of a hot summer day as a child, probably for most people a pleasant memory that they would be happy to recreate.

CONSUMER INSIGHT 4.4

'Dumb Ways to Die'—learning through songs

Metro Trains, Melbourne, Australia, released a three-minute cartoon message designed to encourage young people to behave safely around trains. Generally this might be considered a rather boring message and not one to which young people are going to pay attention. But this cartoon showed a number of 'jelly bean' men meeting a range of sticky ends, including being hit by a train, all to the catchy tune 'Dumb Ways to Die'. Animated gifs were released on Tumblr, on radio, in posters, and throughout the Metro Trains network. Within days the YouTube video amassed millions of views and was on the front page of Reddit for hours, and had 'gone nuts on Tumblr' (John Mescall, McCann ECD, who wrote the advert).

   Why did it work so well? It has a catchy song which leaves the safety message right until the end. It is likeable—you want to share it because of the lovely jelly bean characters who all find dumb ways to die, for example offering their private parts as piranha bait or poking a stick at a grizzly bear, and yet all continue to sing and dance even with no heads or bodies, or burnt to a crisp (see Figure 4.14).

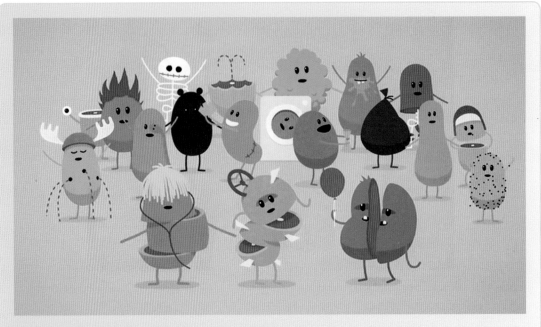

Figure 4.14   'Dumb Ways to Die'

Source: Image printed with permission of McCann and Metro Trains Melbourne and screenshot taken from http://www. dumbwaystodie.com

Above all it is not didactic; it is not telling young people what to do but having a laugh with them about dumb things they might just consider doing.

The use of strong visual imagery and catchy song (iconic and echoic rote memory) help to make a difficult message memorable. Now 'Dumb Ways to Die' has been released as a ringtone and a smartphone app where you have to save as many of the characters as you can. You have to flick the piranhas away from the private parts and swat the wasps as quickly as you can, remove forks from toasters carefully and above all keep idiots away from the platform edge.

Questions

1. Identify any theories used in this chapter so far which indicate why this should be such a successful campaign.

2. What other marketing techniques might be used to extend the value of this marketing communication?

3. This ad uses humour to aid learning, but many other campaigns use different approaches. Consider some other approaches that you are familiar with to communicate safety messages and comment on what you consider their pros and cons are in compared with 'Dumb Ways to Die'.

Sources: theinspirationroom.com econsultancy.com

 Visit the Online Resource Centre and follow the weblink to learn more about this campaign.

Retrieval of memory

Retrieval *is the process whereby we remember and access our stored memories.* There are different ways that we retrieve information from our memories including recollection, recognition, and relearning.

- **Recollection** *is when we reconstruct memory through a range of different narratives and bits of memory.* If we are in a store we may see a product, remember someone telling us about it, and then recall having seen an advertisement in a magazine; the partial memories come together to form a greater whole.

- **Recognition** *requires the memory to retrieve information by experiencing it again.* So you may be looking in the supermarket for snacks and recognize a new product that you had seen advertised on TV. You had to visually recognize the product to recall it.

- **Relearning** *is when you relearn something that you had previously learned, and the process of relearning helps you to remember and retrieve.* You may have used the automatic check-in at an airport but often you have to relearn how to use it if some time has elapsed between uses. The more you use the check-in, the easier it is to retrieve the information you need to help you manage it easily.

In some cases it may be beneficial for a company if their customers forget things. Consider all the different attributes that you had to learn when choosing a new mobile phone. A year or two after going through this learning process a new product type is launched on the market, and that means learning new product features in order to decide which brand to buy. When trying to remember the new and important attributes of a product, some of the older features may interfere with the most recent ones. This is a process known as *proactive interference.* On the other hand, *retroactive interference* is when new information you have had to learn excludes previously learnt old information which may still be important to product choice. If you only remember the new attributes plus any of the old ones that are still pertinent, you are experiencing what has been termed the *benefit of forgetting,* i.e. the right balance of remembering the old and the new. Such intentional forgetting can be useful to marketers as it means that customers are making room in their memories for new information about brands (Shapiro et al., 2006).

Explicit and implicit memory

Researchers distinguish between explicit and implicit memory. **Explicit memory** *is the conscious recollection of an experience* while **implicit memory** *is remembering without conscious awareness.* Explicit memory requires a conscious recollection of something. Market research agencies will often measure explicit memory in day-after recall tests where they may ask you how much you can remember of an advertisement you watched on the television the previous night. You will use explicit memory through recognition or recall. Marketers will use devices such as colours, packaging, and logos to aid your recognition. Sometimes it

Figure 4.15   Recognition of a cereal

Source: © iStock.com/monkeybusinessimages.

may be confusing when in a supermarket to immediately identify the brand you want to buy, and so you may rely on the marketers' devices to aid rapid recognition by looking for the familiar colour or logo. Children can often readily pick out logos that they are familiar with (Figure 4.15).

Implicit memory occurs when previous experiences help performance of a task despite the person involved having no memory of a prior event. People may be unaware of using information they have been recently exposed to when performing a subsequent task. Imagine you were walking through a department store (e.g. Debenhams or El Corte Ingles in Spain) and to get to the department you wished to visit you passed through the sports section. You did not consciously look at anything, but later when a friend asks you for ideas of where you might buy tennis shorts you bring to mind the section in the department store you passed through. The impact of implicit memory often depends on whether or not the consumer has existing strong brand preferences, as a dominant brand is more likely to be chosen because it is both more preferred and more easily accessed in the memory (Lee, 2002). So while you might have passed a number of different brands, it may only be well-known brands like Adidas and Nike you remember. From a marketing perspective it is important to remember that exposure to stimuli is often momentary and failure to remember does not mean that the consumer has not been affected by this exposure (Holden and Vanhuele, 1999). This explains why companies continue to spend money on billboards that may only be glanced at.

Aiding memory

Marketers ultimately want their products and brands remembered and for consumers to recall them at the time of purchase or at other important points during the decision-making process. Research suggests that a number of techniques can help the retrieval of memory and therefore are useful for marketers to understand in order to capitalize on them in their marketing.

Repetition and spacing

If a consumer is repeatedly exposed to marketing stimuli for a particular brand, their likelihood of recalling it increases. Unnava and Burnkrant (1991) found that this does not have to be exactly the same message, and indeed variation can improve the chance of recall. Variation in spacing can also help recall. So rather than repeating an advertisement regularly over a short period of time, it may be better to space the communication over a longer period. The evidence seems to show that various combinations of the space and content of advertisements may work together to provide different results with memory.

Position and duration

The position and duration of the advertisement may also help recall (however, see Research Insight 4.3). The time elapsed from the start of a commercial break until the beginning of a commercial may significantly negatively impact unaided brand recall, with the first and last commercial in a break having an advantage over those in the middle (Pieters and Bijmolt, 1997). In many countries a premium is charged for advertisements at the start of the commercial break, and in real life advertisers may lose viewers who do something else during a break but catch the first advertisement. It is also important to remember that increasing numbers of consumers will have pre-recorded programmes and may notice the first ad but then zap to the end of the commercial break, making it more difficult for advertisers to capitalize on order effect.

RESEARCH INSIGHT 4.3

Mulhern, F. (2009), 'Integrated marketing communications: from media channels to digital connectivity', *Journal of Marketing Communications*, 15, 2/3, 85–101.

In a digital age position and duration may no longer be of so much importance to advertisers or consumers. In this paper Mulhern describes how the digitization of media represents a major step change with data-driven ad placement being principally about logistics. Advertising algorithms will place advertisements in contextually appropriate locations. They are placed in real time and the algorithm becomess smarter every time someone clicks on the ad. The advertisements are interacting with and learning the consumer's online behaviour and in so doing can generate higher levels of precision in targeting.

 Visit the Online Resource Centre to read the abstract and access the full paper.

Pictorial and verbal cues

When we look at a visual stimulus, like an advertisement, we tend to take in the images before we consider the text (Kroeber-Riel, 1986). However, while we may notice a picture we may not comprehend it fully just through the pictorial cue and use the text to support our understanding. Research shows that pictures have an advantage over words for memory retrieval. However, some words will evoke images better than others and have higher levels of 'imagery value'. If you think of the word 'bed' or 'chair', an image is likely to be called to mind more easily than words such as justice or fairness. Such high imagery words are better remembered than low imagery ones (Richardson, 1980) because they are able to form both verbal and visual codes in the memory. Unnava and Burnkrant (1991) give the example of advertising the features of a camera. If you used the line 'brand X camera captures fast movement' the reader might form a verbal code, but the words are unlikely to produce an image. However, if a picture, such as people in a roller coaster, is used together with the claim, the addition of the picture would help the attribute 'captures fast movement' to be remembered as both a verbal code and an image. The dual codes should make the brand more likely to be retrieved. Microsoft launched its Surface Tablet with a strong visual commercial, but added a rhythmic background sound illustrating the magnetic click of the keyboard with the screen, underlining one of the key functionalities of the product that it could be used just as a tablet or with the keyboard. This can be extended to the actual brand name, which can use high imagery words and appropriate visual imagery together—for example, the Apple brand with its distinctive logo (see Figure 4.16).

Figure 4.16   Apple—a brand with high imagery value
Source: Image courtesy of Barry Doyon.

Social learning: observational or vicarious learning

Much of our learning occurs in a social setting where we observe the behaviour of others and learn from it. This is built upon the theory of social learning and in particular the work of the psychologist Albert Bandura (1965, 1969). Social learning theory is concerned with the role played by vicarious, symbolic, and self-regulatory processes in people's behaviour. It sees human behaviour as influenced by observation, that humans use symbols to help analyse their experiences, and that people select and organize the stimuli around them in a self-regulatory manner. Observational learning is often used in marketing, as we regularly learn the specifics of how to do something by observing others.

If you are in a new country and want to use the buses you may first observe what others are doing. Similarly, if you are using an automatic ticketing machine at an airport, you learn by observing others around you (see Figure 4.17). That we are prepared to learn like this is important, as it means that consumers will do some of the work for marketers and it may even mean that businesses can reduce staff costs where consumers help themselves.

Figure 4.17 Observational learning may occur by watching others

Source: © iStock.com/Mlenny.

Observing the behaviour of others may also lead to us replicating such behaviour. As an example, we might watch the James Bond film *Skyfall* and see James Bond sipping from a bottle of Heineken or Q solving complex problems on his Sony Vaio. If we retain these images and are motivated to replicate them, millions of pounds worth of product placement investment will have been worthwhile. Utilizing observational learning is beneficial to marketers to explain how to use their products. Didactic or educational advertisements may engage the viewer with how to use a complex new product. When microwaves were introduced, many such advertisements appeared giving instructions on how to use the machine, often supplemented by in-store demonstrations. Today advertisements for smartphones often do the same to show the various applications available.

Sometimes we learn by accident, particularly if we are very interested in something. A child might be engaged in a specific activity because it is fun (such as a sport), but may be learning speech or coordination without knowing it. The use of tablet devices is said to be helping students learn because the range of apps available gives them access to more varied and enjoyable ways to learn. So again, children may feel that what they are doing is a game, but they may incidentally be learning vocabulary or maths or some other skills (see Research Insight 4.4).

RESEARCH INSIGHT 4.4

Kerrane, B. and Hogg, M.K. (2013), 'Shared or non-shared? Children's different consumer socialization experiences within the family environment', *European Journal of Marketing*, 47, 3/4, 506–524

Children learn in many different ways, including formal learning at school, but one of the most important contexts for learning is the family. This study brings a consumer culture theory perspective to understanding the processes of children's consumer socialization practices within the family. The paper highlights the great variety, within families, in terms of parenting styles and interactions, sibling relations, and communication styles.

  Visit the Online Resource Centre to read the abstract and access the full paper.

Conclusions

Understanding how consumers learn and remember is central to understanding consumer behaviour. It is particularly important to companies in their efforts to market their brands. They want to know how to spend their budgets most cost effectively to ensure the best result. The *main approaches to learning* are behavioural and cognitive learning. We may note that at times our learning may be behavioural in nature, a matter of stimulus and response or reacting to a conditioned or unconditioned stimulus. In considering *behavioural learning* we looked at the issues around both classical and operant conditioning, using a range of examples to show where each was relevant in marketing. Celebrity endorsement as an example of classical conditioning was considered in Consumer Insight 4.1, where we looked at the way that celebrities from around the world are associated with brands in order to elicit positive feelings towards those brands. We also looked at the application of operant conditioning in marketing through sales promotions and loyalty card schemes.

Alongside this approach, we know that consumers also learn about brands and are able to recall attributes and experiences of brands when they are in buying situations, and this is in line with the *cognitive learning approach*. Practitioner Insight 4, focusing on the Nutra-check app, looked at how consumers learn to manage their diet and calorie intake through a process that aids comprehension and retention in memory.

The importance of understanding *memory*, and how consumers store information in their long- and short-term memories, is critical for marketers, and was examined in Consumer Insight 4.3. Marketers need to find ways to help get their message into the long-term memory and perhaps more importantly to help the consumer *retain and retrieve information* from memory at the point of purchase. By understanding better how memory works and how we may forget and remember things, marketers should be able to devise appropriate marketing communications strategies. Finally, we examined *social learning* and in Research Insight 4.4 we explored learning within the family context.

This knowledge of learning enables organizations to make positive links to their brand. Case Study 4 focused on Havaianas flipflops to demonstrate how an understanding of learning can assist brand development.

Review questions

1. What are the key differences between operant conditioning and classical conditioning?

2. Explain the difference between observational learning and passive learning.

3. What are the stages that a consumer may go through when they are information processing?

4. Explain the key differences between sensory, short-term, and long-term memory.

Discussion questions

1. Encoding can be helped by brands which incorporate a key benefit of the product and are easily remembered. Identify three brands that do this and explain how it is achieved.

2. Name two advertisements that use classical conditioning. Identify the unconditioned and conditioned stimulus. Why do you think they work?

3. Find specific examples of different reinforcement schedules. Identify whether they are fixed or variable and make an assessment of why each type is used in this circumstance and their likely success.

4. Develop an associative network of your own. Try starting with the following, 'breakfast', 'Friday night', or 'Starbucks', or choose your own. How many different types of nodes do you get, including products, brands, actions, thoughts, and people?

 Visit the Online Resource Centre to test your knowledge further and complete the Multiple Choice Questions for Chapter 4.

CASE STUDY 4

Learning Brazilian

Most young people have heard of the Havaianas brand of flipflops. In this case study we consider the history of the brand and how we have learned what the brand stands for. While all consumers learn, this case illustrates that the brand has to ensure how they learn and that they learn the right things to ensure success.

What are the first things you think of when someone says Brazil to you?

Maybe you think of football, but then perhaps sunshine, beautiful bodies, having fun, bright colours and sunlight, beach life. And if you are on the beach you usually need a pair of flipflops. Flipflops are basically a piece of rubber with two straps. They are simple and practical, but one thing we can learn from Brazil is that even the simplest functional item can become a coveted brand. Over the last twenty years the Havaianas brand has been transformed from cheap footwear worn by maids, fishermen, and agricultural and construction workers to the chosen footwear of catwalk models and film actors, as well as consumers all over the world.

The brand was developed in the late 1950s based on the Zori sandals worn by Japanese immigrants in Brazil. These were made from fabric straps and rice straw soles, and Havaianas have maintained the textured rice pattern on the footbed of the sandals. At the beginning of their life cycle, their outstanding features were their cheapness and functionality; they were durable and sold largely in street markets—anyone could afford them. They were limited to five basic colours—black, blue, green, red, and yellow, all with a white sole. But as they were cheap and Brazilian they were often packed by tourists and taken home as souvenirs, and inevitably their fame spread. However, one of Havaianas's problems was their functionality and cheapness. They became primarily perceived merely for their practicality, and so in the 1990s sales declined and the company began to reposition the brand.

In revamping the brand what did Havaianas hope to achieve? They wanted to maintain their identity as a democratic brand, one that could be worn by everyone, but they needed to instil more of the qualities associated with being Brazilian—fun and colourfulness, and an even a bit of an irreverent attitude (see Figure 4.18). So

Figure 4.18 Havaianas as a symbol of Brazilian lifestyle
Source: Image courtesy of Havaianas.

new colours and improved styling were backed up by an extensive advertising campaign. The line of the campaign was 'Havaianas—everyone wears them' and featured famous Brazilians such as actress Malu Mader, the world champion football player Bebeto, basketball player Hortencia, and model and actress Luana Piovani. Today 30 million pairs are exported annually to 80 markets and they are worn everywhere, not just on the beach. They are still cheap, but not as cheap as they used to be—at least three to four times their original price. As the shoes were taken up by opinion leaders and stars such as Jennifer Aniston and surf champion Kelly Slater, it became socially acceptable to wear them in an ever wider variety of circumstances. In other words, they were no longer just beachwear. They even appeared on the runway during a John Paul Gaultier show and in the gift bags received by actors at the 2003 Oscars Ceremony.

The brand hasn't stood still either; it has developed a range of flipflops, including exclusive ones studded with Swarovski crystals, and it caters for all age ranges including babies. Havaianas slim were introduced with thinner straps to please the more feminine of their customers. Now Havaianas are extending their brand and their strategy. If you go on the Havaianas website you will see what other products you can buy, such as bags and boots. They opened a concept store designed by one of Brazil's best known architects, Isay Weinfeld, in São Paulo's Rua Osca to extend the Havaianas experience (see Figure 4.19). Here, Havaianas are displayed in market-like stalls, with the lighting carefully managed to give the feel of being outdoors, and you can customize your sandals in all kinds of ways.

The store, a profusion of colour and fun, has become a tourist attraction in its own right. Table 4.2 presents some of the associations identified for the brand from market research commissioned by Havaianas.

Questions

1. Use any learning theories discussed in the chapter to explain the development of the Havaianas brand.

2. Either from your own personal experience with the brand, or from what you have read here and on the Havaianas website, develop an associative network for the brand.

Figure 4.19 Havaianas concept store in Sao Paulo

Source: Image courtesy of Havaianas.

Cognitive response		Emotional response	
Before 1994	**Today**	**Before 1994**	**Today**
Original associations • Durable • Don't smell (hygiene) • Useful: 'comfort' • Worn by the poor • Good cost–benefit relation • Traditional: just one model • Only five colours	**New associations** • 'Sandal style' • Fashion sandals (more styles and colours) • 100% natural • 100% Brazilian **Maintained associations** • Excellent cost–benefit relation • Accessibility • Comfort • Durability • Hygiene	• Practical • Functional • Protects the feet of the poor at low cost, i.e. poor person's slipper	• Brazilian national identity • Tropical • Beach • Heat • Holidays • Joy and relaxation • Physical and emotional well-being • Comfort • Fashion • Customization • Sexy

Table 4.2 Havaianas brand associations—cognitive and emotional

Source: adapted from Silva et al. (2010).

3. Take another popular brand of your choice and list the emotional and cognitive responses you think that the brand produces among consumers who buy it (and if you can, those who don't).

Sources: Silva et al. (2010); WARC (2011); Khalpada et al. (nd); havaianas-store.com interbrand.com melissa.com.br/en.

 Visit the Online Resource Centre and follow the link to the authors' blog where you can keep up to date with the latest developments in consumer behaviour and further explore theories through additional articles and real-world examples.

References

Anderson, J.R. (1993), *Rules of the mind*, Hillsdale, NJ: Lawrence Erlbaum.

Bandura, A. (1965), "'Influence of models'" reinforcement contingencies on the acquisition of imitative responses', *Journal of Personality and Social Psychology*, 1, 589–595.

Bandura, A. (1969), *Principles of behaviour modification*, New York: Holt, Rinehart and Winston.

Bettman, J.R. (1970), 'Information processing models of consumer behaviour', *Journal of Market Research*, 7, 3, 370–376.

Bitterman, M.E. (2006), 'Classical conditioning since Pavlov', *Review of General Psychology*, 10, 4, 365–376.

Blackwell, R.D., Miniard, P.W., and Engel, J.F. (2006), *Consumer behaviour* (10th edn), Mason, OH: Thomson Higher Education.

Broniarczyk, S.J. and Alba, J.W. (1994), 'The importance of the brand in brand extension', *Journal of Market Research*, 31, 214–228.

Burrell, I. (1997), 'Penguin wins its suit as Puffin gets the crumbs in battle of the biscuits', *The Independent*, 19 March, http://www.independent.co.uk/news/penguin-wins-its-suit-as-puffin-gets-the-crumbs-in-battle-of-the-biscuits-1273690.html (accessed 31 July 2014).

Economist (2003), 'The death of the jingle', http://www.economist.com/node/1570553 (accessed 8 June 2012).

econsultancy.com (2012), http://econsultancy.com/uk/blog/11204-dumb-ways-to-die-smart-ways-to-do-viral (accessed 8 July 2013).

Foxall, G.R., Goldsmith, R.E., and Brown, S. (1998), *Consumer psychology for marketing* (2nd edn), London: International Thomson Business Press.

Gewirtz, J.C. and Davis, M. (2000), 'Using Pavlovian higher-order conditioning paradigms to investigate the neural substrates of emotional learning and memory', *Learning and Memory*, 7, 257–266.

Heath, R. (2012), *Seducing the subconscious*, Chichester: Wiley-Blackwell.

Holden, S.J.S. and Vanhuele, M. (1999), 'Know the name, forget the exposure: brand familiarity versus memory of exposure context', *Psychology and Marketing*, 16, 479–496.

interbrand.com, 'What about Brazilian brands', http://www.interbrand.com/Libraries/Articles/10What_about_Brazilian_Brands_english_final2_pdf.sflb.ashx (accessed 31 July 2014).

Jansson-Boyd, C.V. (2010), *Consumer psychology*, Maidenhead: Open University Press.

Kelly, G.A. (1955), *The psychology of personal constructs*, New York: Norton.

Kerrane, B. and Hogg, M.K. (2013), 'Shared or non-shared? Children's different consumer socialization experiences within the family environment', *European Journal of Marketing*, 47, 3/4, 506–524.

Khalpada, N., Lakhanpal, R., Moreira, L., Singh, J., and Sontakke, Y. (nd), 'Havaianas—international expansion', http://media2.intoday.in/businesstoday/images/Havaianas-International-Expansion-BT-version.pdf (accessed 15 May 2014).

Kroeber-Riel, W. (1986), Die inneren Bilder der Konsumenten: Messung, Verhaltenswirkung, Konsequenzen für das Marketing, *Marketing ZFP*, 8, 81–96.

Krugman, H.E. (1965), 'The impact of television advertising: learning without involvement', *Public Opinion Quarterly*, 29, 349–356.

Lee, A.Y. (2002), Effects of implicit memory on memory-based versus stimulus-based brand choice, *Journal of Marketing Research*, 39, 440–454.

MacGregor, J.N. (1987), Short-term memory capacity: limitation or optimization?', *Psychological Review*, 94, 107–108.

marketingweek.com (1997), 'Penguin forces Asda redesign', http://www.marketingmagazine.co.uk/article/60455/penguin-forces-asda-redesign (accessed 31 July 2014).

Miceli, G. and Pieters, R. (2010), 'Looking more or less alike: determinants of perceived visual similarity between copycat and leading brands,' *Journal of Business Research*, 63, 1121–1128.

Miller, G. (1956), 'The magical number seven, plus or minus two: some limits on our capacity for processing information', *Psychological Review*, 63, 81–87.

Mulhern, F. (2009), 'Integrated marketing communications: from media channels to digital connectivity', *Journal of Marketing Communications*, 15, 2/3, 85–101.

Narisetti, R. (1994), 'P&G files suit against its customer about sale of private-label products', *Wall Street Journal*, 8 September, p A2.

Newell, A. and Simon, H.A. (1972), *Human problem solving*, Englewood Cliffs, NJ: Prentice Hall.

Nunes, J.C. and Drèze, X. (2006), 'The endowed progress effect: how artificial advancement increases effort', *Journal of Consumer Research* 32, 4, 504–512.

Pieters, R.G.M. and Bijmolt, T.H.A. (1997), 'Consumer memory for television advertising: a field study of duration, serial position, and competition effects', *Journal of Consumer Research*, 23, 362–372.

Pornpitakpan, C. (2012), 'A critical review of classical conditioning effects on consumer behavior', *Australasian Marketing Journal*, 20, 282–296.

Richardson, J.T.E. (1980), *Mental imagery and human memory*, London: Macmillan.

Schacter, D.L. (1996), *Searching for memory*, New York: Perseus Books.

Shapiro, S., Lindsey, C., and Krishnan, H.S. (2006), 'Intentional forgetting as a facilitator for recalling new product attributes', *Journal of Experimental Psychology: Applied*, 12, 251–263.

Silva, S.C., Souza, M.J., and Freyre Filho, F. (2010), 'Understanding the internationalisation process of Havaianas: the important role of brand', *Encontros Científicos: Tourism and Management Studies*, 6, 9.

Skinner, B.F. (1953), *Science and human behavior*, New York: Free Press.

theinspirationroom.com (2012), http://theinspirationroom.com/daily/2012/metro-dumb-ways-to-die/ (accessed 8 July 2013).

Till, B.D. and Busler, M. (2000), 'The match-up hypothesis: physical attractiveness, expertise, and the role of fit on brand attitude, purchase intent and brand beliefs, *Journal of Advertising*, 29, 1–13.

Till, B.D. and Priluck, R.L (2000), 'Stimulus generalization in classical conditioning: an initial investigation and extension', *Psychology and Marketing*, 17, 1, 55–72.

Till, B.D., Stanley, S.M., and Priluck, R. (2008), 'Classical conditioning and celebrity endorsers: an examination of belongingness and resistance to extinction', *Psychology and Marketing*, 25, 2, 179–196.

Unnava, H.R. and Burnkrant, R.E. (1991), 'An imagery-processing view of the role of pictures in print advertisement, *Journal of Marketing Research*, 28, May, 226–231.

Vanhuele, M., Laurent, G., and Drèze, X. (2006), 'Consumers' immediate memory for prices', *Journal of Consumer Research*, 33, 2, 163–172.

WARC (2011), 'Sao Paulo Alpargatas: Havaianas—identity, Cannes Creative Lions', Sao Paulo: Creative Effectiveness Awards.

Warlop, L. and Alba, J.W. (2004), 'Sincere flattery: trade-dress imitation and consumer choice', *Journal of Consumer Psychology*, 14, 1/2, 21–27.

Wildschut, T., Sedikides, C., Arndt, J., and Rotledge, C. (2006), 'Nostalgia: content, triggers, functions', *Journal of Personality and Social Psychology*, 91, 975–993.

Zauberman, G., Ratner, R.K., and Kim, B.K. (2008), 'Memories as asset: strategic memory protection in choice over time', *Journal of Consumer Research*, 35, February, 715–728.

5

PERCEPTUAL PROCESSES

Introduction

Imagine that you are in a car, driving down a busy road into the city. On either side of the road are billboards and shops with signs above them and posters in their windows. There are bus shelters with more advertising displayed on their sides; you pass taxis and buses all with stickers advertising local businesses. You may be listening to a commercial radio station while you drive. It is not possible for you to pay attention to this vast array of stimuli; you would not want to and indeed it would not be safe to do so. The way in which stimuli are perceived, attended to, and interpreted is vital for our understanding of consumer behaviour. How and whether we notice a stimulus is dependent on our perception. Perception is closely bound up with the nature of the stimulus itself, the environment in which it is placed, and our ability and willingness to perceive the stimuli. We have to make choices about which perceptual stimuli we will attend to. Not only can perception be limited, but it is also highly subjective; our own situation, past experiences, and preferences all affect how we perceive things. Marketers need to ensure that their messages are not only perceived, but attended to and interpreted in the way that they wish them to be. An understanding of the perceptual process is integral to success in this, and ultimately an effective marketing campaign.

LEARNING OBJECTIVES

Having read this chapter, you will be able to:

1. Explain the *perceptual process*.

2. Understand the mechanisms underlying *exposure* and how this is used in marketing

3. Recognize the *nature and role that sensory receptors* play in the perceptual process.

4. Understand how consumers pay *attention* to sensory stimuli.

5. Recognize how *interpretation* of stimuli occurs, and appreciate how *gestalt psychology* is used in marketing.

6. Describe some of the ways that marketing uses this understanding of perception, such as *perceptual mapping, perceived risk, repositioning, price perception*, and semiotics.

The perceptual process

Perception *is the process through which information in the form of stimuli in the environment is selected, organized, and interpreted through the sense organs.* The process by which we perceive is illustrated in Figure 5.1, and forms the basis for the structure of this chapter.

Exposure

This sequence of steps begins with exposure to stimuli—the visual effect or the sounds we hear in market encounters.

Exposure *ensures that the stimulus is in the appropriate place for consumers to have access to it.* At this stage stimuli are only analysed for their simple physical properties with little information conveyed. Successful exposure can depend on many things. Siemon Scamell-Katz of

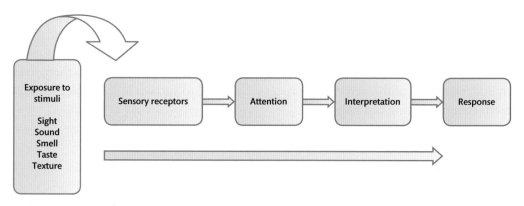

Figure 5.1 The perceptual process

TNS Magasin (an international shopper strategy consultancy) comments on the difficulties companies face when trying to ensure that their brand receives successful exposure when placed in visually noisy places such as supermarkets. He says that we can only process about five pieces of information at once, and this becomes particularly difficult when we are in an environment with over 20,000 products, each containing a number of different visual elements. One experiment, conducted by TNS Magasin to examine exposure, placed various products in unfamiliar shelves around the supermarket; for example, lager was located in the cereal aisle and chocolate bars were shelved among the cat foods. When asked, customers had not noticed the out-of-context products because they were effectively blind to what they did not expect to see.

Exposure is linked to physical positioning, and this can be managed by marketing and advertising. The Spanish organization ANAR (which deals with child abuse) developed an outdoor advertisement using lenticular print technology, a technique which gives the illusion of depth and can change or move as it is viewed from different angles. ANAR used this technology to embed a message that could only be read by people under a height of 1.35 metres (i.e. mainly children). They wanted to communicate a message to children who were potential victims of abuse, but without their adult aggressors viewing the message. Adults saw an image of an unbruised child with the message 'Sometimes child abuse is only visible to the child suffering it'. However, those under the height of 1.35 metres saw the same child with cuts and bruises with the caption, 'If somebody hurts you, phone us and we'll help'.

Consumers can also limit their own exposure to stimuli, a form of **selective exposure** which is *the active seeking and avoidance of stimuli*. During a commercial break, viewers may switch to another channel, leave the room before their TV programme resumes, or, with time delay recording, fast forward through the advertisements. Similarly, consumers can subscribe to agencies which ensure that they do not receive unsolicited mail, advertising, or telemarketing. Children are particularly susceptible to exposure to products and messages that parents may not want them to see. Increasingly, governments are looking to limit the times when advertising for products high in sugar, salt, and fat may be advertised to children, and bodies such as Ofcom in the UK, the Australian Broadcasting Authority, and the Federal Communications Commission in the USA are looking to regulate internet content deemed inappropriate for children to see.

Selective exposure may also involve perceptual vigilance and perceptual defence. **Perceptual vigilance** *is when a consumer consciously or unconsciously filters stimuli for relevance*. Perceptual vigilance will depend on the person, their situation, and the nature of the stimulus. People who do not drive are unlikely to be interested in car advertisements; someone about to get married may be very interested in advertisements for dresses and venues, but once married the relevance of these products immediately diminishes.

Perceptual defence *is when a consumer inhibits perception of potentially threatening or unpleasant stimuli*. People who are overweight may avoid advertisements for clothes they cannot wear, or smokers may avoid the government health warnings on packs of cigarettes. One

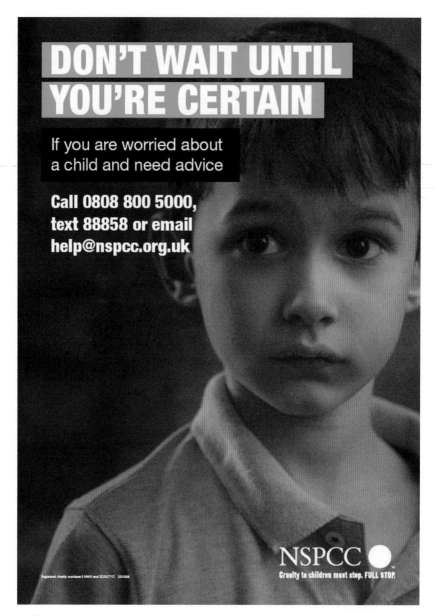

DON'T WAIT UNTIL YOU'RE CERTAIN

If you are worried about a child and need advice

Call 0808 800 5000, text 88858 or email help@nspcc.org.uk

NSPCC

Cruelty to children must stop. FULL STOP.

Figure 5.2   Different approaches to cut through perceptual defence

Source: Image courtesy of NSPCC (www.nspcc.org).

of the most common areas where people activate perceptual defence is charity advertising, largely because they feel fatigued at seeing unpleasant images or try to avoid them because they cannot or are unwilling to contribute to the charity. In response, charities have looked to break through this defence with even more shocking images or use a juxtaposition of words and pictures to create impact, such as in the advertisement for the NSPCC (Figure 5.2).

Sensation and the perceptual process

We receive sensations through our sensory receptors—eyes, ears, nose, mouth, and skin—but it is the process by which we select, attend to, organize and interpret these sensations that is most important to the marketer (see Research Insight 5.1). We may have preferences for certain colours or tastes, or we may associate particular smells with happy or sad moments in our past. Lindstrom (2008) suggests that the smell of Johnson & Johnson's baby powder has a similar impact on people the world over. As well as smell, there are numerous studies on the effects of colour, particularly in store settings. Retailers want to know if the colours they use in their stores influence consumer purchases. Babin et al. (2003) found that consumers reacted most favourably to shop interiors painted in cool colours; consumers rated and expressed relatively greater shopping intentions in a blue interior than in an orange one. However, it is clear that such preferences are very subtle, as Babin et al.'s research also showed that when colour is combined with different lighting intensities preferences can change; for example, the reaction to an orange store interior is improved when it is combined with soft lighting. Bellizzi et al. (1983) have suggested that the colour red can speed up behaviour and so may be useful in a fast food restaurant environment. Even online shopping can be influenced by differences in sensory stimuli, such as colour, borders, type style, and sound, and it has been found that the atmospherics of an online environment can influence the pleasure experienced by shoppers (Eroglu et al., 2003).

Sight

Levine (2000) suggests that sight, or visual attention, accounts for about 80 per cent of human perception. Given this central role in our perception it is not surprising that colours have deep-rooted cultural meanings. In many western countries, it is assumed that a baby dressed in blue is a boy, while girls are associated with pink clothing, an

RESEARCH INSIGHT 5.1

Simons, D.J. and Chabris, C.F. (1999), 'Gorillas in our midst: sustained inattentional blindness for dynamic events', *Perception*, 28, 1059–1074

Simons and Chabris (1999) conducted an experiment which appears to show that in many situations we do not even perceive objects that are directly in front of us—this is known as inattentional blindness. In their experiment a woman dressed as a gorilla passed in front of a group playing basketball. Observers had been asked to note the number of passes of the ball and many failed to see the gorilla. Previous research has shown that conscious perception requires attention and that when attention is fixed on another object or, as in this case, a task intentional blindness may occur.

 Visit the Online Resource Centre to read the abstract and access the full paper.

interpretation of colour that emerged around the 1940s (Paoletti, 2012). Colours can also provoke or enhance various emotions, and psychologists have attempted to map out the effect of colours on our feelings. Red is generally understood to be the colour of passion, excitement, and energy, and is often used by companies wishing to express these qualities through their brand. The Virgin group logo conveys energy and confidence, while the trade-marked red sole of Christian Louboutin shoes is a distinctive aspect of that brand, capturing its energy and glamour. In China, the colour red has traditionally symbolized health and wealth, and is associated with weddings and special occasions—bridal gowns are traditionally red, and newly-wed couples receive gifts of money in red packages. There is a strong cultural aspect to how colours are perceived, and it is important for companies operating in international contexts to be aware of this.

In addition, we often relate certain colours to certain roles in society, mainly because of the associations we make between colours and attributes. Black or dark blue is worn by the police, and white by health practitioners. Dark colours may establish authority, while the white coats worn by pharmacists, doctors, or nurses often represent hygiene and cleanliness. The association of white with purity has been used by Clinique, the skincare brand. Clinique's branding of their 'medical' skincare range uses simple crisp white packaging with pale green text—the aim of which is to emulate the cleanliness and simplicity of the product inside (see Figure 5.3). Green and white is also the colour palate used by the Simple skincare brand whose unique selling point is the lack of perfume and colour for those with sensitive skin.

But white, like most other colours, has a cultural significance and mistakes are easily made. United Airlines had to remove the white carnations their assistants had been given to wear on Pacific routes as white is strongly associated with death and mourning in that region (Aslam, 2006). Colours become associated with brands and even movements. Since the early 1990s, pink has become associated with breast cancer awareness campaigns worldwide. Brands often have to distinguish themselves by differences in colour—Pepsi uses the colour blue which distinguishes it from Coca-Cola's red (Labrecque and Milne, 2012).

Figure 5.3 Clinique skincare product

Source: © iStock.com/ AnthonyRosenberg.

Another aspect of sight relates to our expectations in relation to the shape of the products being consumed. Recent experimental research by Nestlé (Lenfant et al., 2013) has shown how the shape of dark chocolate pieces impacts on how the chocolate is regarded in terms of both texture and flavour perceptions. Round and rectangular chocolate shapes

RESEARCH INSIGHT 5.2

Soars, B. (2003), 'What every retailer should know about the way into the shopper's head', *International Journal of Retail Distribution and Management*, 31, 12, 628–637.

From a range of research studies Soars (2003) identifies the likely effects of different colours. These include yellow being the colour that the human eye normally notices, while red is often used to emphasize masculinity and play down femininity.

 Visit the Online Resource Centre to read the abstract and access the full paper.

were rated highest in terms of texture, whereas wing-shaped chocolates were perceived as most flavourful.

Visually, the size and shape of the object and the environment in which it is placed are also important. While we may be attracted by something that is large or out of the ordinary, small things can also focus our attention. The Volkswagen Beetle, known for being a small car, used this to its advantage in its advertising (Figure 5.4), by making smallness a virtue and using a tiny picture of the VW against a stark background, accompanied by lines such as '*Think small*' and '*It makes your house look bigger*'. Here, it is not only the smallness that attracts our attention but also the environment in which the object is placed.

Companies also have to ensure that their product or advertisement is seen in the 'right' environment (see Consumer Insight 5.1). Luxury brand owners will prefer their brands to be stocked in Harrods in London or Takashimaya in Singapore because the environment of the store rubs off on the brand. Similarly, advertisers take care where to place their advertisements in TV schedules, aiming to ensure a fit between the brand and the interests of the target audience's viewing interests. In-game advertising features in many popular video and PC games, and the perceptual fit between the brand being advertised and the target audience is important for the success of the campaign. An example is the case of Burger King featuring in the game Pro Evolution Soccer 2013 (Nairn and Hang, 2012).

Sound

A feature of modern life is that we are bombarded with sound as we go about our daily lives, a key source being the music we hear in shops and restaurants. Just as with colour, the music played is designed to enhance or change people's mood to encourage purchase. One early study (Millman, 1982) found that shoppers spent 38 per cent more time in a grocery store when slow music was played as compared with fast music. Lantos and Craton (2012) identify a range of factors which impact a consumer's response to music used in advertising, including their personality, social class, culture, and mood state when listening to the music. Music creates emotion, and some people may respond more to music that creates a sad response (Schellenberg et al., 2008).

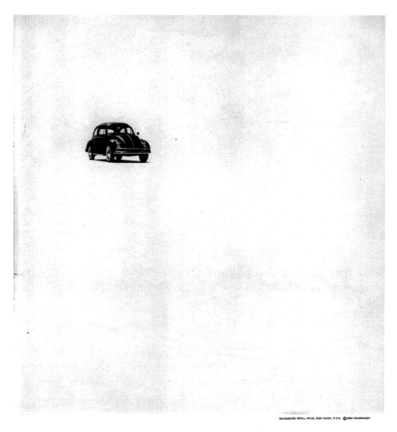

Figure 5.4   Using size to get attention

Source: Image supplied by The Advertising Archives.

Lantos and Cranton (2012) discuss how reactions to music are complex, such that a disliked genre of music may be appreciated if it is particularly upbeat and catchy. In 2012, South Korean musician PSY released 'Gangnam Style', an upbeat and remarkably catchy song, with a distinctive dance featured in the accompanying video. The song and video enjoyed worldwide popularity, and by early 2013 had over 1.42 billion views on YouTube. Now both the music and the dance moves have been taken up in a range of commercial contexts. For example, PSY appears, dancing to 'Gangnam Style', in the advertisement for Wonderful Pistachios. In the advertisement for E-Lites, a company producing electronic cigarettes, a baby's first steps are the 'Gangham Style' dance, with

CONSUMER INSIGHT 5.1

Spotting your favourite coffee shop

How we consume our coffee around the world varies hugely, but in major cities around the globe coffee shops are a common sight, and with them certain brands. How do they compete on the high street? One way is to make sure that we perceive, and pay attention to, the brand with which we are familiar (see Figure 5.5). When we spot the colour and logo of a familiar brand, be it in Melbourne or Stockholm, we know what to expect and may feel safe and comfortable. Therefore consistency and distinctiveness in the visual presentation, colour, and style are critical.

Figure 5.5   A famous coffee shop   *Source*: © iStock.com/ilbusca.

An interesting recent trend is towards ensuring that the store design retains the brand distinctiveness, but also speaks to the local market. So, for example, Starbucks has embarked on updating and revamping its London stores to reflect the variations in its markets, with the St John's Wood store having low-key branding in dark colours, while the Westfield Stratford shop uses more prominent imagery of the Starbucks branding (Handley, 2013). Similarly, Costa Coffee has reported how it adjusted its in-store design in Shanghai to relate to the younger consumers using it compared with the UK market (Mortimer, 2011)

Questions

1.   Consider two famous coffee shop logs. What is distinctive about their visual presentation?

2.   Read the paper summarized in Research Insight 5.2. Choose another high street brand and, using the colour analysis developed in this paper, try to assess what feeling they are trying to communicate to their customers.

Sources: Mortimer (2011); Handley (2013).

   Visit the Online Resource Centre and follow the weblinks to learn more about this topic.

Figure 5.6 Screenshot from the E-Lites commercial showing a baby dancing to 'Gangnam Style'
Source: Image courtesy of Zandera Ltd.

the advertisement emphasizing the importance of not missing out on your family's life because of smoking (see Figure 5.6).

Smell

Consumers generally expect certain products to have particular fragrances. Household cleaning products often have a lemony odour, while wood polish may smell of lavender. Milotic (2006) identifies the most commonly used terms to describe odours were floral, herbal, fruity, sweet, green, woody, spicy, animal, and citrus. Smells can elicit emotions in people, particularly in relation to memory, and so certain smells can evoke nostalgic thoughts and memories. Of all the senses, smell is considered to be most closely linked to emotion because the olfactory bulb in the brain detects smells and links them to the limbic system which links emotion and memory (Milotic, 2006). Fragrances are also thought to be stimulating or relaxing. We spoke to Category Director of Dettol, Frederique Hull, to understand how the senses, and especially smell, play an important part in understanding how consumers perceive different products (see Practitioner Insight 5).

Consumers also categorize pleasant and unpleasant smells. Culturally we have come to regard some smells as acceptable and others as not; we mask body odour by using deodorants and even the smell of our homes by using air fresheners. Supermarkets may ensure that the smell of freshly baked bread is pumped through the store, but are equally concerned to minimize and remove the smells from the fish counter. The advertisements for Febreze build directly on this point, showing how use of this product masks the other smells assumed to 'stick' to our clothes.

Some Asian bank brands are embracing the ideas around engaging customers' senses as a way of enhancing their service interaction. Standard Chartered in Hong Kong has created

PRACTITIONER INSIGHT **5**

Frederique Hull, Category Director of Dettol, Reckitt Benkiser, on the perception of smell

Consumers relate to hygiene and germ awareness in different ways, and this is very noticeable when you look across countries. In the USA consumers are typically very concerned and use a lot of anti-bacterial products. In Russia there is generally a lower awareness of germs, whereas in Germany while people are aware, they have a lower concern and a feeling that the immune system needs to develop to cope with germs. In some developing countries there may even be confusion as to what germs are and where they are to be found. For example, in some countries people think that insects and dust contain germs or that they grow on your skin, so understanding how consumers perceive germs and hygiene is very important to how products are developed and marketed.

One also has to consider the role that disinfectant products play in people's lives. Most of the time people are not too worried about germs; they are busy looking after their family and home and what they would prefer is a product that cleans and kills germs so they don't have to bother with an extra step in the whole cleaning process. But when there is a health scare such as A/H1N1 (swine flu), sales increase rapidly. There are also certain times when people want to use a disinfectant such as Dettol. Parents are extra vigilant when their children are sick, and people often do an extra clean and disinfect when they move into a new house.

Fragrance and texture are very important sensory stimuli in the choice of hygiene products. For Dettol antiseptic liquid, the initial perception needs to be one of a strong hospital-like smell. This gives consumers confidence and is the anchor of efficacy for the brand. The packaging also supports this; it is understated and the clear brown liquid says 'I am effective'. On the other hand, our soap products should not have a texture and fragrance that reminds someone of a hospital theatre but they still need to signal the efficacy of the brand, so we have different fragrances, but ones in keeping with the brand's attributes. Therefore it is important to get the right balance in terms of the texture and fragrance which is congruent with the product. A really unusual fragrance, such as pineapple, would create a completely different association. In the kitchen we know that lemon is a popular fragrance as people associate lemon with being able to cut through grease, but another fragrance such as vanilla might be perceived as interfering with the smell of the food and has connotations of stickiness as it is often associated with sweet things. Packaging is also very important when consumers choose products. We know from focus group research that an opaque pack or one with a sleeve is always considered to be a more effective cleaning product than one that is presented in a clear container. Therefore a product such as our Power and Pure multipurpose kitchen spray, which is designed to tackle tough kitchen cleaning tasks, is presented in an opaque package.

a special fragrance for its showcase Lan Kwai Fong branch. The fragrance is used to convey an upmarket, high quality, and warm feel for its customers, thus enhancing their experience in the branch and ultimately developing greater brand loyalty (Faure-Field, 2013).

Touch and texture

Touch is an important, but underrated, sense. Underhill (2009) says that more than ever people want to touch the things that they are going to buy, and yet this raises questions about the role of touch in online environments (see Consumer Insight 5.2). Many products are marketed on the basis of texture. In 2012, Mars revived the strapline for its Galaxy chocolate 'Why have cotton when you can have silk', emphasizing the positioning of Galaxy as a distinctively smooth-textured chocolate. Fabric conditioner is a product that was developed purely to improve the texture and feel of clothes after they have been washed; a similar job is achieved with hair conditioner. Both are products that were not readily available 50 years ago but are innovations designed to match consumers' preferences for smooth or soft textures. Preferences for texture vary greatly, giving companies a good opportunity to market food items such as juice or yoghurt as either 'smooth' or 'with bits', thus matching differences in consumer tastes. Consumer Insight 5.2 further explores issues of consumer preferences in texture.

CONSUMER INSIGHT 5.2

Are you an NFT (need for touch) consumer?

The word 'haptic' derives from the Greek and refers to the sense of touch. In the marketing context we see it used to mean 'the active seeking and pickup of information by the hands' (Peck and Childers, 2003: 36). Peck and Childers performed a number of experiments to see how people responded to different touch situations. They found that product characteristics, individual differences in people, and the nature of the situation all affected the motivation to obtain haptic product information. They were also interested in the growth of non-touch media and how it might impact on people's shopping motivations. They suggested that eventually there might be a substitute for the sense of touch, although they stated that this was probably the most difficult sense to replicate. They suggested that the internet was going to be particularly successful for marketing products that consumers do not perceive to have material properties, such as books, music, and DVDs, and therefore are not dependent on their haptic properties for sales.

Retail anthropologist Paco Underhill (2009) recognized the importance of the tactile in shopping, which is one of the few opportunities that we have to touch things without inhibition. When goods are sealed or packed away in cabinets we are deprived of this important sensory experience. Others have recognized that senses are interrelated, especially touch and smell (Krishna et al., 2010). Although some would argue that internet and catalogue shopping is restricted by consumers' inability to touch the goods before buying (Peck and Childers, 2003), there are many successful online-only clothing stores such as ASOS, MyWardrobe.com, and Figleaves. Stores such as these exist throughout the world, for example Coco Fashion, selling Asian and Korean street fashion, and Kira Plastinina in Russia. In addition, there are internet versions of well-known stores such as Gap, TopShop, and Banana Republic. Presenters on TV shopping channels often talk about the feel and touch of the product to convey its texture and weight to prospective customers.

Questions

1. How have online clothing stores managed to overcome the problem of lack of touch on the internet?

2. Imagine you are opening a new clothes shop. How would your knowledge of sensory perception influence how you would design the store?

Sources: Peck and Childers (2003); Underhill (2009); Krishna et al. (2010).

 Visit the Online Resource Centre and follow the weblinks to learn more.

We learn to expect products to have a certain type of feel or even weight about them. Lindstrom (2008) reported an experiment conducted with Bang & Olufsen remote controls. One hundred participants were given two remote controls, one with aluminium inside and the other without. The participants felt that the lighter control was broken just because it felt lighter than they expected. Even after it was explained to them that the lightweight one was completely functional, they still preferred the heavier one. Evaluations of how some product or brand feels are based on objective evaluations (e.g. how heavy it feels), but in the context of previous experiences and associations with that evaluation (e.g. heavy feels good, light feels broken). This example emphasizes the importance of appreciating the social nature of our interpretation of sensory inputs.

Taste

Taste preferences are highly specific to individuals and cultures (see Research Insight 5.3). KitKat sells a green tea flavour variant in Japan which would probably not be popular in European countries. Our taste preferences may also change as we grow older. Importantly, what tastes good to one person may not to others, which is why food product manufacturers ensure that their brands are thoroughly taste-tested before being brought to market. Marmite, the savoury spread brand, made a virtue out of the fact that people appear to be divided on whether they like the taste of the product or not, i.e. they either love or hate it. In previous advertisements, Marmite actually showed scenes of sales people chasing possible customers to get them to try the spread even though they clearly did not want to.

For those popular brands which are familiar to us and which we like, it may be difficult for our brains to distinguish the taste from our image of the brand (see Chapter 11 on neuromarketing). As Montague (2006) notes, experts in the field know that flavour is actually

RESEARCH INSIGHT 5.3

Laemmerhirt, I.-A. (2010), 'Imagining the taste: transnational food exchanges between Japan and the United States, *Japanese Journal of American Studies*, 21, 231–250.

Laemmerhirt (2010) describes how differences in food tastes and culture occurred in the initial contact between people from Japan and the USA. In this study, the Americans were suspicious of Japanese fish and seaweed, and the Japanese found the wheat, meat, and dairy products of the American diet difficult. Today the Japanese have embraced fast food such as McDonalds just as westerners enjoy Japanese food such as sushi.

 Visit the Online Resource Centre to read the abstract and access the full paper.

a composite perception only partly built from the taste (whether it is sweet, sour, or bitter, etc.). Other factors involved in our taste perception include texture, temperature, the way the product is presented, and expectations from our knowledge of the brand and our previous history with it.

There are also ethical issues about the taste of food that we should consider. In contemporary western cultures, where obesity is a major health issue, food companies are accused by some of creating food products with tastes and textures that make them more appealing, which we become addicted to, and ultimately crave. Kessler (2010) calls this 'hyperpalatability', which is defined as flavour that further stimulates the appetite. Foods rich in fat, sugar, and salt are often also combined with textures that are easy to chew to create 'feel good' tastes. Many scientists and commentators are critical of these heavily processed foods, arguing that they are damaging to health and bear more similarity 'to drugs of abuse than to the natural energy resources people consumed historically' (Gearhardt et al., 2011: 140).

Sensory thresholds

We all have limits to how well our senses are able to respond to stimuli. The **absolute threshold** *is the minimum amount of stimulation that can be picked up by any of our senses.* Advertisers have to ensure that their communications can be seen or heard; therefore getting the right level of background music on TV advertisements and the right size of print on posters can be very important for the success of their communication. The **differential threshold** *is the point at which we notice a difference between two stimuli.* If you buy a product that claims that it contains a new and improved formula, can you tell or taste the difference between this and the old version of the brand? Whether or not product changes are communicated to consumers is a concern of marketers. A company may have had to change the ingredients of a product but may prefer not to communicate the changes to customers as this might involve costs and possibly brand-switching. They may decide to conduct blind taste tests to see if consumers notice the difference in ingredients. Obviously in some cases marketers may want to inform their customers of the difference, especially if the product has been improved as part of a relaunch.

Often small differences in the size or price of a product are not noticed by customers. Referred to as 'Grocery Shrink Ray', this approach is sometimes used by marketers to reduce the size of products but charge the same amount. It may be such a small difference that most people do not notice that they are getting less product for their money. However, it is becoming a major consumerist cause; the British consumer organization Which investigated the issue of consumer goods being produced in reduced size packs but with prices remaining the same (Allen, 2012) and concluded that this was an 'underhand way to raise prices'. They called for clearer labelling to indicate packaging changes. In the USA, The Consumerist (comsumerist.com) champions the cause of the consumer and highlights what it considers to be inappropriate market behaviour. It regularly highlights brands that have suffered Grocery Shrink Ray, such as Aussi, a brand of hair care products made by Procter & Gamble, whose bottle redesign included a reduction from 33.8 to 29.2 fluid ounces.

In perceptual terms, the **just noticeable difference (JND)** *is the minimum change in a stimulus to be noticed by the majority of people.* The nineteenth-century experimental psychologist Ernst Weber identified that the size of the just noticeable difference threshold appeared to be related in a law-like way to the magnitude of the initial stimulus. **Weber's law** tells us that *the stronger the initial stimulus, the more difference would be required for the change to be noticed.* In marketing, Weber's law has mostly been applied to the small changes in the design of packaging one sees over time, which are difficult for most consumers to notice individually. Take a look at the brands of sweets and chocolates shown in Figure 5.7 from the Museum of Brands and Packaging and see which wrappers look familiar. You will notice that some no longer exist, but there will be others that you recognize for their distinctiveness and similarity to the brands you see on the shelves today, such as Rolo, Bounty, Bournville, and Fry's Turkish Delight.

Crucially, Weber's law is also very important for pricing as it determines the levels of price differences that consumers will notice and respond to. When shopping for groceries we are typically happy if we find a promotion or item on sale that has 50p or 50 cents off. However, if we visited a major designer shop during sales time, a reduction of 50p would seem ludicrous and inappropriate in that context. This is because the initial stimulus of the much higher price has to be recognized by a similarly large change in the sale price. This is why promotions are often represented in terms of percentages.

Adaptation

Adaptation *is the extent to which people's awareness of a stimulus diminishes over a period of time.* Schwarz (2004) reported that in 1973 only 13 per cent of Americans thought that air-conditioning in cars was necessary, whereas in 2004 this figure was 41 per cent and today it is probably even higher. When we become accustomed to something, it becomes the norm. Sensory adaptation is when our sensory receptors diminish in sensitivity, enabling the body to function in unfamiliar situations by filtering out the initial strength of the stimulus. Four areas where sensory adaptation is important are sight, touch, smell, and sound. In consumer behaviour, marketers need to be aware that what was once unusual will gradually become unremarkable. This is important for developing the creative content

Figure 5.7 How chocolate wrappers have changed

Source: Image courtesy of Robert Opie and The Museum of Brands.

of advertisements and for businesses to consider when they need to try something different to overcome adaptation.

Attention

Attention *is the mental activity given to a stimulus.* One of the most important aspects of attention is that it is selective. We are exposed to such a large amount and variety of marketing stimuli that we have to select what we pay attention to. Pieters and Wedel (2007) found that attention varied depending on the different processing goals that consumers had. For example, in situations where the consumer is trying to learn about the brand (brand evaluation) there is greater attention placed on the textual information associated with the brand, and less on the visuals. This is relevant to those contexts where a consumer is buying a product for the first time. They are likely to undertake a brand-evaluation process, whereby attention is paid to the detail of what is said about the brand on the packet, but with brand familiarity this becomes less important for future purchases.

We can also divide our attention between different activities, which means that we may be looking at content and advertisements on multiple screens (e.g. PCs, tablets, TV, smartphones) almost simultaneously. Polychronic or multitasking behaviour is increasing, with media multitasking in the home reportedly having risen by 35 per cent in 2009 alone (Brasel and Gips, 2011). It is important for marketers to try to understand how consumers allocate their attention over multiple screens. Although studies have established that younger people are most likely to use multiple media simultaneously (Jeong and Fishbein, 2007), there is evidence that the gap across generations is closing, with one European study showing a 75 per cent growth in media multitasking in those aged over 55 (European Interactive Advertising Association, 2009). Given that there are more TV channels than ever before and more types of media, marketers increasingly have to deal with advertising clutter. There are various estimates of the thousands of promotional messages that targeted us each day, but what is evident is that companies are finding increasingly innovative ways of cutting through this clutter (see Consumer Insight 5.3).

CONSUMER INSIGHT 5.3

Gaining and retaining attention through social media

In 2003, Old Spice introduced body wash for men and amassed millions of fans with a campaign that targeted men and women, promoting what might happen if Old Spice body wash was used. The success was largely due to the presence, style, and charisma of American actor Isaiah Mustafa, also known as 'The Man Your Man Could Smell Like'.

In 2011 the company wanted to increase the fan base on YouTube, Facebook, and Twitter. It created an interactive experience where 'The Man Your Man Could Smell Like' responded directly to his fans on the internet, answering questions, or making suggestions related to questions that they had about Old Spice, i.e. highly personalised messages to fans.

How did Old Spice do this? The company began by using YouTube as it allowed comments and had a wide existing fan base for Old Spice. Using a programme that identified mentions of Old Spice from a range of social networking sites, the company wrote and produced nearly 200 personalized videos. They began by hitting mainstream celebrities, influencers, and fans of Old Spice, but about 70 per cent were created in response to the man or woman in the street. On Twitter, Old Spice gave consumers a timeline to watch the campaign unfold and allowed additional questions to 'The Man Your Man Could Smell Like'. The company also posted responses on Old Spice's Facebook page for increased word of mouth. Thus the concept of a brand message swiftly became a brand conversation across platforms and media.

On the first day of the campaign there were 5.9 million YouTube views and by the end of the week this had increased to 40 million. Twitter followers increased by 2700 per cent. Over three days 'The Man Your Man Could Smell Like' offered President Obama tips on how to court a lady, gave his support to libraries, and introduced a new catchphrase to the world. Nobel (2013) reports on research from Harvard Business School which identifies successful viral advertising as having four steps:

- attracting viewers' attention

- retaining their attention

- getting viewers to share what they have seen with others

- persuading viewers.

In the case of Old Spice the key aspect is that the viewer's attention is grabbed and retained by the fact that the attention is actually focused on them—the Old Spice man is speaking directly to you!

Questions

1. Think of some examples of social media advertising that have gained and retained your attention. How have they done it?

2. Many believe that the success of social media advertising is sharing with others. What makes you want to share an advertisement with your friends? Think about how you would use this to market a product of your own.

Sources: Fernandez (2011); WARC (2011); Nobel (2013).

 Visit the Online Resource Centre and follow the weblinks to learn more.

Getting the consumer's attention

To gain consumers' attention in a cluttered environment companies have to think of novel, different, and relevant ways to get noticed. Movement can grab people's attention, particularly when they are not expecting it. Therefore while we expect movement in a TV or cinema advertisement, we are not expecting it in a magazine or on a billboard poster. Such approaches disrupt our expectations of the world around us, expectations which are based on schemas, beliefs, and feelings that we build up over time and through learning about our environment. To gain consumers' attention in a cluttered environment companies have to think of novel, different, and relevant ways to get noticed. Movement can grab people's attention, particularly when they are not expecting it. Therefore while we expect movement in a TV or cinema advertisement, we are not expecting it in a magazine, billboard poster, or sign. The neon cowboy sign in Las Vegas uses movement to capture attention (see Figure 5.8). Digital displays that change every so often use movement to grab our attention; other billboards may create a feeling of movement—for example, showing a bottle being poured. Movement breaks through to grab our attention even when we were not previously looking at the advertisement.

Schemas *are cognitive frameworks which are used to organize and interpret information*. Schemas help us to organize our world and interpret stimuli easily. We take shortcuts to interpret similar things because we have had experience of them before. So if we travel to Asia and are offered tea in a cup without handles we can still interpret it as an object for containing liquid as it is similar enough to the schema of a teacup that we are used to.

Another technique to cut through clutter is to place something in an unusual or unlikely setting. Berns et al. (1997: 1272) express **novelty** as a '*deviation from the expected likelihood of*

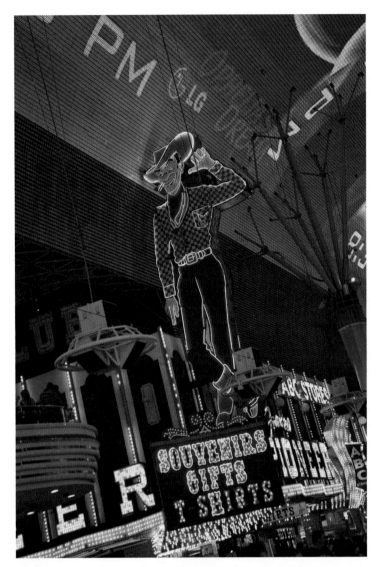

Figure 5.8   Neon cowboy sign in Fremont Street, Las Vegas   *Source:* © iStock.com/slearmonth2.

an event on the basis of both previous information and internal estimates of conditional probabilities'. Something can be novel because the stimulus has not been seen before or because it is in an unusual context. They found that certain parts of the brain respond to novel stimuli often without any conscious awareness. Contrast may also be used to gain people's attention, such as the use of black and white advertisements in a magazine or on television where we are expecting to see colour.

Sound may also be used as a contrast, and advertisers often use a combination of sound and visually arresting images to aid recall. The British financial services comparison website Gocompare.com used the strong visual image of a caricatured opera singer (with comic-like hair and corkscrew moustache in full evening dress) singing the benefits of the company, in opera style, to prospective customers. Sex can also attract attention, although advertisers need to be cautious that viewers' attention is not focused on the sexual content over the brand. Sex can appear in many guises, and a recent TV campaign by Marks & Spencer was described as 'food porn' (Brownsell, 2010) because of the way the food was temptingly shown, and the use of a soft and sultry female voice-over and music, all designed to seduce the viewer. Emotion can also attract the consumer's attention. Particular images or sounds resonate with our emotions. The John Lewis Christmas advertisements are particularly successful in depicting scenarios that form deep emotional resonance with customers through the use of character, story, and music. The 2013 campaign (Figure 5.9), which told the story of a bear who has never experienced Christmas because he always hibernates through winter, attracted a great deal of media attention and analysis in the run-up to Christmas 2013.

The use of shock to gain attention

The use of shock to gain attention is perhaps the most interesting and controversial way in which advertisers gain awareness, but it can be fraught with danger as businesses have to ensure that they do not alienate existing and potential customers. Experiments have shown that shock advertising can increase attention and memory and influence behaviour in appropriate contexts (Dahl et al., 2003). One of the most famous businesses to use shocking images regularly in its advertising campaigns is Benetton. In the 1980s and 1990s, Benetton provoked controversy with advertisements showing a nun kissing a priest, a dying AIDS victim, and a child soldier holding a human bone. One of the most disliked images was of a newborn baby still covered in blood.

The images provoked varying responses, particularly in different cultures. The nun kissing the priest was condemned in many Catholic countries, while the UK seemed to take a particular dislike to the newborn baby. Despite this, many of the advertisements received awards. Today Benetton advertisements still court controversy. They recently produced an advertisement in their so-called 'Unhate' campaign showing Pope Benedict XVI kissing

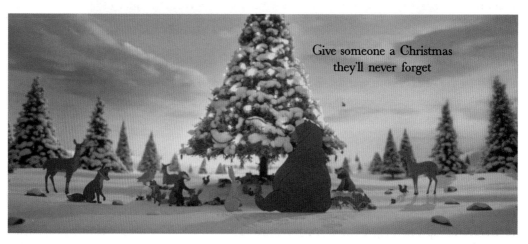

Figure 5.9   A still from the John Lewis Christmas 2013 advertisement   *Source*: Image courtesy of John Lewis.

Ahmed el-Tayeb, a senior Egyptian imam. The Vatican threatened to take legal action unless the advertisement was removed. Benetton's advertisements gain attention largely because they are challenging our expectations.

There are numerous images and messages that shock. These can be sexual, involve age or religion, or just be unusual behaviour. What people find shocking in advertisements is often culturally defined. In 2005 one of the TV advertisements that provoked the most complaints in the UK was for KFC, showing women in a call centre speaking with their mouths full. Of the 1,671 complainants to the Advertising Standards Authority (www.asa. org), many were particularly concerned about the example it might be setting children in terms of bad table manners.

Shocking advertisements can backfire on the company. A Brazilian advertisement for the World Wildlife Fund brought strong condemnation for the line 'the tsunami killed 100 times more people than 9/11' and showing a host of airplanes flying into New York. In a somewhat different example, the Italian firm Dolce & Gabbana had to remove an advertisement that showed a man towering over a woman, with other men in the background, because of its aggressive sexual implications.

Interpretation

Once people have attended to a stimulus, whether it is an advertisement or a new brand on the supermarket shelf, they may allocate a meaning to it. Perception is highly subjective, and two people seeing the same advertisement or event may visualize and interpret it quite differently. Our interpretation may depend on our existing schemas, and in some cases interpretation may be primed by the use of certain images or colours already associated with the brand. This might be the case when we see the colour purple and think of Cadbury's Dairy Milk chocolate, or the dark green of a Gordon's Gin bottle. Interpretation will also depend on the personal relevance of the stimulus and our particular preferences. In three experimental studies, Chernev (2001) found that participants regularly interpreted information that supported their existing established preferences more than information that countered their beliefs. Finally, companies have to bear in mind that even if an advertisement or the packaging on a brand is powerful in accosting the senses and grabbing attention, if it is for a product category that the customer is not interested in, the likelihood of personal relevance is limited and therefore there is no motivation to interpret the message.

Interpretation and organization: Gestalt psychology

The stimuli in our environment are not perceived discretely. Perception in practice is largely about putting meanings to the things we see around us, and therefore we use our memory and experience to interpret the images we see. This often means that we add something to ensure completeness, as naturally we want to make sense of our environment. Gestalt psychology explains much of how the human brain looks for completeness. The meaning of **Gestalt** is roughly 'whole' but above all it refers to *how people look for meaning and patterns in the stimuli in the environment.* The implications of Gestalt for consumer behaviour were developed by a group of German psychologists in the late 1800s and early 1900s who examined how people interpreted the whole above individual features. Above all they were interested in how people organized stimuli into shapes and patterns for completeness and order. A number of principles which reflect how people organize their environment have been derived from Gestalt psychology.

Principle of closure

Closure *is the tendency for people to fill in the 'missing' elements of an incomplete picture.* When we see an incomplete stimulus there is a tension which is released when we complete it. Figure 5.10 shows two triangles which are incomplete, but we can readily make them out.

The principle of closure is used by advertisers to involve the consumer and potentially promote retention. Well-known lyrics may be used with some words missing or slogans will be incomplete, encouraging the consumer to complete them mentally. Visual closure may be successful with either words or images. A classic example using words was a Christmas campaign for J&B whiskey where the letters J and B were left out of the words Jingle Bells. A more recent example can be seen in the Audi campaign shown in Figure 5.11.

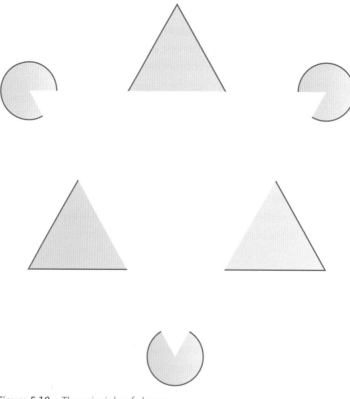

Figure 5.10   The principle of closure

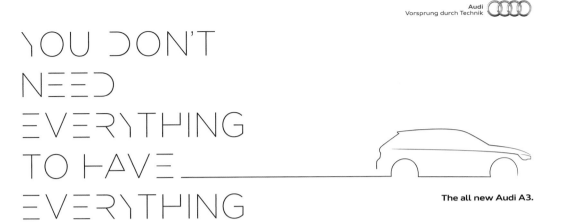

Audi
Vorsprung durch Technik

YOU DON'T NEED EVERYTHING TO HAVE EVERYTHING

The all new Audi A3.

Official fuel consumption figures for the all new Audi A3 range in mpg (l/100km) from: Urban 40.4 (7.0) – 61.4 (4.6), Extra Urban 58.9 (4.8) – 85.6 (3.3), Combined 50.4 (5.6) – 74.3 (3.8) CO_2 emissions 130 – 99 g/km.

Figure 5.11   This Audi advertisement provides a good example of the principle of closure

Source: Image printed with permission of Audi and courtesy of Bartle Bogle Hegarty (www.bartleboglehegarty.com).

Principle of similarity

Humans naturally group objects of similar physical similarity together. **Similarity** *refers to how things that are similar to one another are perceived to be more related that those that are dissimilar.* In Figure 5.12 it is easy to pick out the cross in the centre of the image because it is made up of similar square shapes, and is distinct from the other shapes in the picture. When manufacturers extend product lines they usually maintain the design of the packaging so that consumers can easily categorize the new product as part of the existing brand. By the same principle own-label products often use similar colours and shapes to those of well-known brand names.

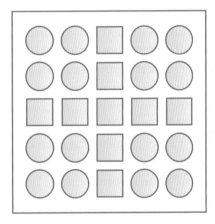

Figure 5.12   The principle of similarity

The principle of proximity

When we see visual stimuli close together we are more likely to assign them to a group. The **principle of proximity** states *that the things we see close together are perceived to be more related than things that are seen as farther apart.* In Figure 5.13, the viewer is more likely to see three groups of black and red circles, rather than a set of black dotted lines and a set of red dotted lines. The nearness (or proximity) of the lines is stronger than the similarity of the colours.

In marketing practice, retailers tend to group together products that complement one another, such as tights near to shoes and handbags in a department store or hamburgers and buns alongside barbeque equipment.

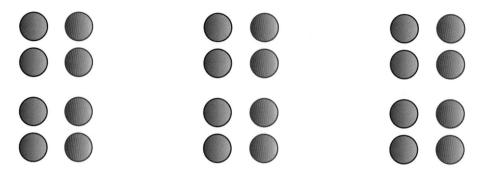

Figure 5.13   The principle of proximity

The principle of figure and ground

In organizing stimuli, individuals tend to distinguish those that are prominent in the environment. The prominent element is the figure and the context in which it is seen is the ground. The more familiar the figure is the more likely it is to be noted, but sometimes it is unclear which part is the figure and which is the ground. Figure 5.14 shows a classic example of figure and ground; some people may see a vase as the dominant image, whereas others may be more likely to pick out the two men's profiles as the dominant figure.

Advertisers aim to ensure that the dominant message in their communications is not drowned out by the context (the story, the setting, or even the personalities used). However, on occasion they may wish to get the viewer to work harder to view the message of their advertisement and even blend the 'figure' into the 'ground'. Figure 5.15 shows a German advertisement for the World Wildlife Trust with the line 'The rainforest does not die alone', showing parched earth but also the clear outline of a parrot against it. This appears to symbolize the connection between the rainforest and the creatures within it, and is a powerful image created from the use of the Gestalt principle of figure and ground.

Figure 5.14   The principle of figure and ground

Source: Image supplied by Shutterstock.

Marketing and perception

There are a number of areas in marketing where the nature of perception and how companies are able to manage their consumers' perceptions are particularly important. We shall examine perceptual mapping, perceived risk, repositioning, and semiotics.

Figure 5.15   *Tropical trees never die alone*
Source: Image courtesy of Ogilvy & Mather.

Perceptual mapping

Perceptual maps are visual representations of the marketplace from the customers' perspective. They effectively provide managers with a map of how consumers view the products and brands in the market in comparison with other brands, and also in relation to how the company sees the brands. By giving a visual representation of the market, companies may be able to ascertain clearly where their brand lies against its competition (Kim et al., 2007; Nestrud and Lawless, 2008). Perceptual maps are developed from attribute ratings, whereby a selection of product attributes are scored by consumers along semantic scales (e.g. very good through to very bad) or bipolar scales (e.g. firm versus soft). Such judgements

Figure 5.16 Perceptual map for laptops
Source: Image courtesy of Brandon Ford.

are then analysed to identify key variables influencing consumers' choices and preferences. Customer familiarity with products is important for companies, but the visual representations used to remind consumers of different brands are also important. The products are evaluated by participants who may rate a product by attribute or consider similarities and differences between groups of alternatives. Brands are then represented on a visual map of perceived space as shown in Figure 5.16. Judgement from managers and researchers is required when labelling and interpreting such diagrams, because the computer generating the analysis is unable to label or interpret the axes.

Perceptual maps are useful for a number of reasons. First, they are a visual representation from the consumers' rather than the company's perspective of brands and their relations with other brands. Secondly, they can show where there may be potential gaps in the market for new product development, and finally, by showing the company where their brand lies compared with their competitors, they can consider changes to their brand that might improve its position. These may be real in the sense of product improvements or changes in message to communicate to the consumers attributes of the brand that they currently do not perceive as being associated with it.

The perceptual map shown in Figure 5.16 is specific to brands of laptops and the axes show important discriminatory perceptions by consumers, namely performance and aesthetic appearance. Perceptual maps can also be used for identifying usage differences among products. If you think about eating cereal and toast, are these only perceived as breakfast foods or are they also used as an afternoon or evening snack by some people?

Perceived risk

While there may be a degree of objective risk in choosing to drive a fast car or going for a bungee jump, many of a consumer's decisions are also informed by perceived risk. The degree of perceived risk may depend on the nature of the consumer, and how they perceive the information provided to them. Bauer (1960) first introduced the idea of perceived risk which he envisaged as having two dimensions, uncertainty and adverse consequences. In three experimental studies Fedorikhin and Cole (2004) found that mood was important, and specifically that people in a positive mood buying a new product were less risk averse than consumers who were in a negative mood. Like other aspects of perception, perceived risk is relative, and people's behaviour is mediated by their subjective perceptions of risk. There are a number of situations where perceived risk is likely to increase. These include the following:

- **A completely new offering to the market**, although probably less risk is involved in a new fast food product than in a new type of digital device which may also incur risk through its technological complexity.

- **Where there is little information about the product or service**, so travelling to a relatively unknown holiday destination may produce more perceived risk.

- **Where there are major differences among brands**, so there is a risk of inferior choice.

- **Where the consumer has limited experience of the product class**.

- **Where the purchaser may be likely to be judged by others for the purchase decision**.

In some cases marketers will want to reduce consumer's perception of risk, such as when marketing financial loans or more risky financial products such as stocks and shares. In other cases marketers may actually want to heighten consumer's perception of risk. Advertising for toothpaste regularly shows the consequences that plaque may bring about, amplifying consumer's fears and worries about the risks of tooth decay, and thus encouraging them to buy certain brands of toothpaste. A recent advertisement for Cancer Research UK cleverly juxtaposes a young girl eating a cake, an image that most would find inoffensive, with information regarding the potential consequences of overeating, thus trying to get across the idea that even apparently harmless food consumption has potential consequences as overweight and obese people have a greater propensity to certain cancers. Another example of perception of risk is shown in Research Insight 5.4.

RESEARCH INSIGHT 5.4

Bjerklie, D. (2006), 'The hidden danger of seat belts', *Time*, 30 November.

This article outlined how Emeritus Professor John Adams of University College London revealed the problems of risk compensation in relations to seat-belt wearing. He found that the compulsory wearing of seat belts in 18 countries resulted in some cases in an increase in road accident deaths. His conclusion is that a process known as risk compensation occurs, where consumers adjust their behaviour in response to levels of perceived risk.

 Visit the Online Resource Centre to follow the link and read the full article.

Six types of perceived risk are most commonly recognized as affecting consumer behaviour.

Financial risk *is the perception of a likely financial loss.* Financial risk is relative. Those with little money may perceive greater financial risk in buying situations where those with more money would not (Bertrand et al., 2006). Updating a mobile phone may seem like a small outgoing for some, while for others it will represent a major purchase and therefore being sure to buy the most appropriate one for their needs is important.

Performance or functional risk *is the perception of how well the product will perform its expected task.* This may involve the technical aspects of a product, such as face creams which advertise that they will reduce the appearance of wrinkles or sanitizers that say they kill 99.9 per cent of germs. It may also be more intangible, as when someone buys a new suit for work with the hope that it may make them appear more business-like. Companies may issue money-back guarantees to help reduce perceived performance risk before purchase.

Physical risk *is the perception of harm that a product or service might have.* Most prescription drugs now have lengthy descriptions of their potential side effects. Consumers often find it difficult to know when food is past its best and may cause a risk to their health. In 2011, the UK government decided that food should only carry 'use by' or 'best before' dates (indicating the point after which the food was unsafe), while 'sell by' and 'display until' labels (which emphasize the optimum time for eating) were removed to deter consumers from throwing out food that could still be consumed safely. This change was meant to give the labels greater clarity and to reduce consumer confusion, although recent reports suggest that these terms are still not clear in consumer's minds (WRAP, 2013). Other countries follow similar practices; for example the Foods Standards Code of Australia and New Zealand has guidelines for 'best before' and 'use by' dates.

Social risk *is the personal and social risk that may arise from a purchase.* Social risk is associated with having the 'wrong' product or brand. For example, teenagers may feel that it is very important to have the 'right' brand of mobile phone or to wear the coolest clothing

Figure 5.17 The nutcase logo and model wearing nutcase helmet

Source: Images courtesy of Nutcase Helmets.

brand (Piacentini and Mailer, 2004). In Copenhagen, many young people cycle, but wearing a helmet is regarded by some as unstylish and thereby carries a social risk. The company Nutcase developed its marketing and promotions strategy for cycling helmets ('I love my brain') to counteract this social risk and in so doing reduce the physical risk to cyclists. The company launched the 'Outdoor Fitting Room', a series of poles around Copenhagen, each indented with a helmet. People are invited to lean over and try out the helmet, and are encouraged to have their photo taken and placed on the Nutcase Denmark Facebook page through the incentive of the chance of winning a free helmet (see Figure 5.17).

Psychological risk *is the risk which reflects the individual's perception of themselves.* It reflects how well purchases fit with a consumer's self-perception (discussed in more depth in Chapter 7). For example, many consumers believe themselves to be highly ethical but still make purchases from companies that they do not consider to be so. The psychological risk is embodied in how they feel about such purchases (Szmigin et al., 2009) and how it reflects on their self-identity.

Time risk *is the risk embodied in the uncertainty regarding the time required to buy or learn to use the product.* Time is critical to marketing as many products and services are time-bound and require consumer time as an input, for example choosing convenience food or traditional cooking (Usunier and Valette-Florence, 2007). People may choose to put their savings into a building society or bank rather than in shares as the time involved in learning how to use the financial markets may seem like too great a commitment. Similarly we might decide not to try to learn a new language because of the potential time commitment to become proficient in the language.

Repositioning

As perception is a subjective phenomenon it can be difficult for companies to manage how people perceive their brands. A key aspect of repositioning is to find ways of changing people's existing perceptions of a brand (see Consumer Insight 5.4). Of course, this may be difficult if a company has invested money over a period of time.

CONSUMER INSIGHT 5.4

Repositioning Lucozade

Lucozade was invented by a British chemist in the 1920s, and was found to be particularly effective for people who had been ill and lost their appetite since the glucose was in a form (a drink) that was easily assimilated by the body. The brand was bought by Beecham in 1938, and throughout the 1950s and 1960s it was very successful, positioned as a drink for times of illness. However, between 1974 and 1978 the brand's sales declined by 30 per cent, largely as a result of lower levels of sickness, fewer flu epidemics, and increased vaccination. In the 1980s Beecham completely repositioned the brand as a carbonated energy drink aimed at a broader market. To accomplish this, a new marketing campaign was developed involving a focus on sport and exercise, promoting the drink as a delicious, refreshing energy drink. Daley Thompson, a British Olympic gold medal winning athlete, was chosen to advertise Lucozade as a refreshing drink that restores energy. From a perceptual perspective, Beecham successfully moved people's subjective perception of Lucozade as a drink for convalescents to a drink that supports sporting activity and revives energy (see Figure 5.18).

Since then the brand has developed its position in what is known as the energy drink sector, a growth sector of the soft drinks market, against competitors such as Red Bull and Powerade. It provides a number of different products

Figure 5.18   Lucozade before and after repositioning

Source: Image of the classic Lucozade advert before repositioning is courtesy of Paul Carrington. The image of Lucozade after repositioning is supplied by The Advertising Archives.

aimed at satisfying hydration and energy needs. Over the years the brand has used many sporting superstars to advertise the brand including footballer Michael Owen and rugby union player Jonny Wilkinson. With a target age range of 16–24, Lucozade has also used musicians such as British rapper Tinie Tempah and former Blink 182 drummer Travis Barker in its 'celebration of energy' campaign. The latest addition to Lucozade products is Revive, an enhanced and flavoured water marketed alongside its energy drinks.

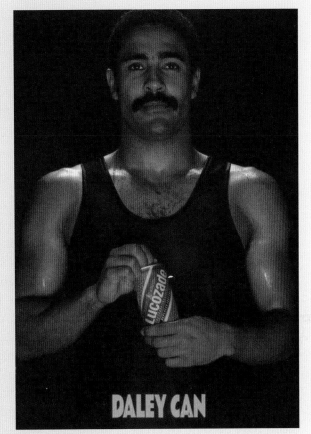

DALEY CAN

Questions

1. Can you think of other brands that have repositioned themselves? Why did they? What was the nature of their repositioning and how successful do you think they have been?

2. If you were developing a new soft drink today for this age group, how might you position it against existing brands in the market?

Sources: Smith (1992); O'Reilly (2011); www.brandrepublic.com

 Visit the Online Resource Centre and follow the weblinks to learn more about brand repositioning.

Price perception

Price perception is another important issue for marketing. Consumers often make assumptions about the quality of products based on price. Similarly, they will make assessments of what the price of goods is likely to be based on the environment in which they are placed. Therefore it is very important for brand owners to ensure that their products are stocked in the stores that best reflect the price being charged. Customers become familiar with stores such as H&M and TopShop having clothes that are reasonably priced. Recently, these stores have introduced guest designers such as Stella McCartney and Jimmy Choo for H&M, and Top Shop has also introduced a set of limited edition designs collections. Both Stella McCartney clothes and Jimmy Choo shoes are associated with high-end prices, and the collaboration with high street stores may suggest that the shops are trying to associate their brands with higher prices. Once connected with high-end brand names, customers may be more willing to pay the higher price charged for these products, or for products in those stores more generally. However, price perceptions work both ways, and in the past high-end brands have introduced diffusion ranges at lower prices. In 2013 the exclusive designer Oscar de la Renta announced that it would be producing an exclusive diffusion line for the online retailer The Outnet. While such moves may result in capture of a larger share of the market, it can also change their consumers' perception of the brand and reduce its perceived status.

Semiotics

It is clear that perception is subjective and open to interpretation, and therefore much of our reading of marketing communications is through the signs we take in and interpret from advertising, packaging, and even the layout of shops. We use mental shortcuts based on our existing knowledge, experience, culture, and social preferences to simplify and manage the world. Shortcuts are often triggered by signs that bring about our interpretation. From our experience, certain colours, shapes, clothing, and even jobs are associated with certain other things; many of these associations are deeply embedded and difficult to change. If we think about Christmas and the image associated with it, certain colours may spring to mind (red, green, gold), but importantly we often focus on the social aspects of the festival, perhaps the family meal and being with friends. Over time, Coca-Cola has associated itself successfully with Christmas, and indeed Coca-Cola's Christmas advertisements have become an event in themselves. One of the associations that Coca-Cola has with Christmas relates to 'the family Christmas' because of the advertising imagery that has been built by the brand. In 1931, Coca-Cola commissioned Swedish-American artist Haddon Sundblom to paint Santa Claus for the company's Christmas adverts. Sundblom created a portly warm character with a beard, purposefully crafted to look like a grandfather (see Figure 5.19). The colour red, synonymous with Coca-Cola, is also the traditional colour used for Santa Claus's outfit. The company benefited from the associations it was able to build between Coca-Cola and the family values associated with Christmas through a series of advertisements, to the extent that, for many people, Coca-Cola represents American traditions and values (Oswald, 2012). This is a case of marketing semiotics, where the brand is linked through 'semiotic networks' with the consumer's view of the world.

Semiotics 'interprets reality in terms of cultural codes that structure phenomena into signs and meanings' (Oswald, 2012: 9). **Semiotics** *is concerned with exploring the links between signs and symbols and the meanings they signify and convey.* The use of signs to interpret our world goes back as far as Hippocrates, who looked at medical symptoms as signs on the body. But the origins of semiotics were developed by the Swiss linguist Ferdinand de Saussure and the American philosopher Charles Sanders Pierce. Pierce represented semiotics as comprising three elements: an object, a sign, and an interpretant in a triadic relationship (see Figure 5.20).

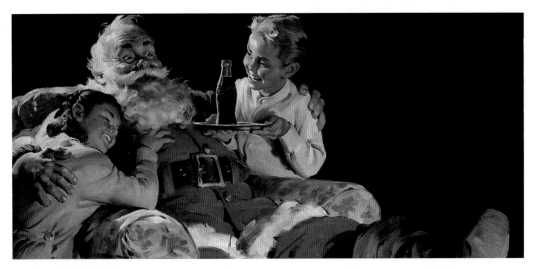

Figure 5.19   Coca-Cola Christmas advertising   *Source*: Image supplied by The Advertising Archives.

A sign is just that—a sign. On its own, this element may be just a word, a colour, a smell, or a flavour, and has no intrinsic meaning until linked with something else. A sign always stands for something else in the mind of others in a particular context or culture, and this is where the link to the interpretant is made. Red is just a colour, but it may stand for different things for different people, such as danger or stop or hot water or Santa Claus. 'Red' creates a sign in the mind of someone, and this effect of the initial sign (red) on the person taking it in is known as the interpretant of the initial sign. The interpretant is the effect or the mental concept developed in someone's mind, and therefore represents a process of the sign's meaning forming into a further sign by interpretation. In the case of the Christmas advertisement for Coca-Cola, which on its own is just an image (the sign), the interpretant is what it represents in terms of being part of a family, celebrating, giving presents. For another person, the word Christmas might have a very different interpretant, perhaps a more religious effect or, if Christmas is not a feature of their cultural context, very little effect at all. As Mick (1986: 199) notes, 'Ultimately, the interpretant is transformed into a language or other symbolic code by which it is shared with and transmitted through the social environment'. The object is the thing that the sign is referring to, and thus the sign represents the object. In this example, the object is the drink Coca-Cola.

The symbolic function of a good depends on context and culture. As

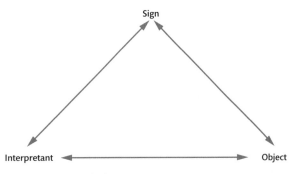

Figure 5.20   Triad of semiotics

Source: John Fiske, *Introduction to communication studies* (2nd edn), London and New York: Routledge, 1990, p 42.

RESEARCH INSIGHT 5.5

Levy, S. (1981), 'Interpreting consumer mythology: a structural approach to consumer behaviour', *Journal of Marketing*, 45, 3, 49–61.

In this classic paper from the 1980s, Sidney Levy analyses the myths and interpretations associated with food preparation and consumption by American housewives. While he talks here about associations such as raw food and representing avant-garde dining, similar interpretations might be made with today's food choices.

 Visit the Online Resource Centre to read the abstract and access the full paper.

Oswald (2012) notes, when DeBeers entered the Chinese market in 1994, diamond rings were not symbolic of weddings in China. While in the west the diamond ring had been associated with long-lasting love and romance, the Chinese recognized the need for persistence in the marriage commitment, somewhat different to the romantic western ideals. Therefore the diamond ring was positioned by DeBeers for the Chinese man to affirm his reliability rather than a sign of romantic love. DeBeers successfully entered this market by understanding that marriage in China is about persistence and commitment, and that associating the diamond ring with these values would be important for growing this market.

When a symbolic association becomes embedded in society or convention, the association acts as a code shaping how people behave—so in many countries a diamond engagement ring is part of the code for marriage. Similarly, a mother seeing an advertisement showing a family picnic on a sunny day, featuring a particular brand of suntan lotion, may think of family values and enjoying time safely with her children where they are not at risk of getting sunburn. But as Levy (1959) notes, teenagers may interpret the family picnic as 'kid stuff' from which they want to break away (see also Research Insight 5.5).

Conclusions

The **perceptual process** was explored, and we examined the stages and explained each through a number of advertising and communications examples. We looked at the mechanisms underlying **exposure** and how this is used in marketing. The example of the Spanish organization ANAR provided insights into how technology can be used to manage consumer's exposure to stimuli.

We considered the **nature and role of sensory receptors**, and the effect of sight, sound, smell, taste, and texture on how consumers behave. In Consumer Insight 5.1 we examined the role of the senses in helping consumers to pick out their preferred brand from an abundant set of choices—in this case, spotting their favourite coffee shop. Practitioner

Insight 5 further examined how marketers use this understanding of the sensory aspects of consumption when devising product formulations, packaging, and promotions for disinfectants.

When exploring how consumers pay **attention** to stimuli, we looked at how social media was used in the case of Old Spice (Consumer Insight 5.3) to ensure that attention was on the brand and that the brand message was retained by consumers.

Interpretation was considered, and the principles of **Gestalt psychology** were described and illustrated through examples from marketing.

We described the techniques derived from an understanding of perception. **Perceptual mapping** was introduced, with the illustration of laptop brands, and we also looked at **perceived risk**, with Research Insight 5.4 focusing on seat-belt usage to explore some of the issues around how consumers make adjustments to their behaviour based on risk assessments. **Repositioning** was explored in Consumer Insight 5.4, where we examined how Lucozade had been repositioned over the years. Finally, we examined how **semiotics** is used in interpreting consumer behaviour, and also how **price perceptions** are formed.

Review questions

1. Highlight the key importance of each of the senses for marketing. Where do you consider each sense to be of most importance?

2. Explain what is required for successful exposure and attention. How are these related to successful interpretation?

3. What is meant by Gestalt? Explain the importance of figure and ground for successful interpretation of an advertisement.

4. For each type of perceptual risk consider an example which might help or hinder marketers.

Discussion questions

1. Look at the colours and lettering used by any two fast food restaurants that you are familiar with. How do you think the colours work for the brand? What alternative colours might they have used and why?

2. Consider tastes you do and don't like and analyse why. Are there cultural differences which affect the foods you prefer?

3. Soars (2003) suggests the following scents and their effects:

   - sweet basil lifts mood, improves mental clarity and memory

   - bay relieves nervous exhaustion and melancholy

   - ginger relieves confusion, loneliness, and anxiety

   - Lime cheers, uplifts, and purifies.

   Suggest where each scent might be successfully used for marketing purposes.

4. Choose a Benetton advert from their 'Unhate' campaign. What do you think they were trying to achieve with this campaign? Why is this campaign in particular shocking?

5. Draw a conceptualized perceptual map for brands of toothpaste and breakfast cereal and assign appropriate axes. Are there key differences between brands and are they similar across product categories?

6. Consider what elements there might be in a semiotic triad for the following signs: 'blue', 'Italian', and 'silk'. In each case try to link them with a brand or product category if possible.

 Visit the Online Resource Centre to test your knowledge further and complete the Multiple Choice Questions for Chapter 5.

CASE STUDY 5

Real or fake: how consumers perceive brand symbolism in the luxury handbag market

In this case we look at the luxury handbag market, and focus on consumer perceptions towards brand symbols and their prominence for both authentic and counterfeit brands. We introduce a consumer taxonomy based on wealth and need for status, and consider how this translates into how brands are perceived and used for status signalling. We then consider some of the issues around counterfeit brands and how they are perceived by consumers.

Luxury handbags

Luxury goods and brands are a massive market, and seem to be impervious to the global recession. In the UK, the luxury sector is expected to grow to £12.2 billion by 2017, representing a doubling in size over five years (Taylor, 2013). Luxury handbags are a particularly buoyant market, representing one of the fastest growing segments in the overall luxury market. The consumer base for luxury brands has grown in recent years because of the rising number of wealthy consumers worldwide (especially in developing markets such as India and China), the growing global middle class globally, and the increasing consumer demand for branded products (Research and Markets, 2013). Much of the appeal of these highly priced bags lies in their ability to signal status and exclusivity to other consumers, using a code that is recognizable only in certain groups. This form of brand communication requires an understanding of the brand language and codes, which in turn relies on consumers being able to perceive and interpret the language of the luxury brand. But this is a complex language of symbols and styling, and brands mark their products differently in order to be more or less visible.

Consumers and brand prominence

Recent research by Han et al. (2010) has introduced the idea of brand prominence, which refers to the extent to which the branded product is visibly marked. They describe 'loud' and conspicuous branding, readily perceived and recognized by consumers, which contrasts with 'quiet' or discrete branding that is recognizable only to a select few. Both Louis Vuitton and Chanel bags might be described as loud brands, since they have visual cues that are instantly recognizable, in contrast with the more discrete cues represented by brands such as Hermès and Bottega Veneta, which are considered to be quieter.

Han et al. (2010) propose that luxury handbag consumers can be placed into a taxonomy which categorizes consumers into four main classes based on wealth and their need for status. This taxonomy enables a better understanding of how consumers perceive and relate to different brands to be achieved. The categories are as follows.

Patrician This group possesses significant wealth, and have a low need to consume for the sake of prestige. They will pay a premium for understated brands—those considered quiet or discreet. They are principally concerned with associating with other patricians (rather than dissociating from other groups) and use brand cues as a way of doing so. A typical brand that might appeal would be Hermès, with its very quiet and subtle brand markings.

Parvenus This group has considerable wealth but not the connoisseurship necessary to interpret subtle signals, and they use more obvious brand cues to signal their status. They are concerned with dissociating themselves from the 'have-nots', while clearly associating with the 'haves'. This group would be drawn to the distinctive LV of the Louis Vuitton bag.

Poseurs These consumers are highly motivated to consume for the sake of it, but tend to be less wealthy. They are motivated to associate with those they perceive as having wealth (the parvenus) and thus are more likely to turn to counterfeit products in place of authentic or original brands. This group seek out fake versions of loud or conspicuous brands, such as those favoured by parvenus.

Proletarians In this context, this term refers to people who are not driven to consume for the sake of status or interested in signalling prestige through consumption. They are not particularly interested in luxury brands.

How brands are perceived will vary for each consumer class, but it is important to recognize the role of fake brands, and how they are perceived, in relation to the luxury handbag market.

Counterfeit brands

Authentic luxury brands communicate exclusivity and status through high price, but for many consumers, these high prices mean that these brands are not available to them, which in turn feeds the market for counterfeit goods (Geiger-Oneto et al., 2013). Counterfeit goods are identical in appearance to authentic brands, displaying the brand name, but selling at a vastly reduced price (see Figure 5.21).

Figure 5.21 Market stall selling counterfeit handbags   *Source*: © iStock.com/contrastaddict

A fake Louis Vuitton wallet can sell for $40, while an authentic one costs $765 in the Louis Vuitton store (Ortiz, 2013). A consumer considering buying both may use a range of visual cues to assist the purchase. On visual cues alone, the two look very similar, although close scrutiny will reveal a number of differences, mainly in terms of quality of material used and attention to detail in production. However, at a superficial level, the fake could pass as an authentic wallet.

Why do consumers buy fake brands? For those who are seeking to associate with prestige in some way (the poseurs) counterfeit luxury brands provide one way of signalling their status to other people at a fraction of the price (Wiedmann et al., 2012). This is the main reason for their purchase, but in a very disposable culture they allow consumers to keep up with handbag trends without a massive financial outlay (Gentry et al., 2006). However, in other respects counterfeits are limited in the value offered to consumers. Frequently, these products are not up to standard, may break down or fade, or even be damaging to consumers (Wiedmann et al., 2012). Also, these products may have limited social value, since those in the know (parvenus and patricians) are likely to perceive these goods to be of inferior quality and judge the counterfeit consumers accordingly (Oneto and Sundie, 2006).

Questions

1. From your understanding of consumers' perceptions of luxury handbags, what advice would you offer Louis Vuitton to minimize brand damage caused by fake versions of its products?

2. This YouTube video (http://www.youtube.com/watch?v=9Vp8LXXMZwQ#at=67) shows a range of differences between authentic and fake versions of the Chanel 2.55 handbags. Watch it and list as many differences as you can between the two. What steps does Chanel take to minimize and protect its brand?

3. From your understanding of perceived risk (outlined in this chapter) provide a detailed analysis of the types of risk associated with (a) luxury handbags and (b) fake handbags.

4. Taking another luxury product category (e.g. watches or shoes) find examples of quiet and loud brands, and analyse these in terms of types of consumers of the brands. Can you find any

limitations of the four-class approach (Han et al., 2010)? Can you find luxury contexts where it does not apply neatly? Have you any suggestions for how this model might be improved upon?

Sources: Oneto and Sundie (1999); Gentry et al. (2006); Han et al. (2010); Wiedmann et al. (2012); Geiger-Oneto et al. (2013); Ortiz (2013); Research and Markets (2013); Taylor (2013).

 Visit the Online Resource Centre and follow the link to the authors' blog where you can keep up to date with the latest developments in consumer behaviour and further explore theories through additional articles and real-world examples.

References

Allen, E. (2012), 'Supermarket "Shrink Ray": how shoppers are paying the same for ever smaller products', *Daily Mail*, 19 April, http://www.dailymail.co.uk/news/article-2131927/Our-shrinking-foods-How-manufacturers-making-everyday-products-smaller-keeping-prices-same.html (accessed 8 April 2014).

Aslam, M.M. (2006), 'Are you selling the right colour? A cross-cultural review of colour as a marketing cue', *Journal of Marketing Communications*, 12, 1, 15–30.

Advertising Standards Association (nd), www.asa.org.uk/About-ASA/Our-history.aspx (accessed 19 June 2013).

Babin, B.J., Hardesty, D.M., and Suter, T.A. (2003), 'Color and shopping intentions: the intervening effect of price fairness and perceived effect', *Journal of Business Research*, 56, 7, 541–551.

Bauer, R.A. (1960), '*Consumer behaviour as risk taking*', in R.S. Hancock, (ed.), *Dynamic marketing for a changing world*, Chicago, IL: American Marketing Association, pp 389–398.

Bellizzi, J.A., Crowley, A.E., and Hasty, R.E. (1983). 'The effects of color in store design', *Journal of Retailing*, 59, 1, 21–44.

Berns, G.S., Cohen, J.D., and Mintun, M.A. (1997), 'Brain regions responsive to novelty in the absence of awareness', *Science*, 276, 1272–1275.

Bertrand, M., Mullainathan, S., and Shafir, E. (2006), 'Behavioral economics and marketing in aid of decision making among the poor', *Journal of Public Policy & Marketing*, 25, 1, 8–23.

Bjerklie, D. (2006), 'The hidden danger of seat belts', *Time*, 30 November, www.time.com/time/nation/article/0,8599,1564465,00.html (accessed 8 March 2012).

Brasel, S.A. and Gips, J. (2011), 'Media multitasking behavior: concurrent television and computer usage', *Cyberpsychology, Behaviour and Social Networking*, 14, 9, 527–534.

Brownsell, A. (2010), 'M&S axes long-running "food porn" ad strategy', *Marketing Magazine*, 22 March, http://www.marketingmagazine.co.uk/article/991680/m-s-axes-long-running-food-porn-ad-strategy (accessed 17 October 2013).

Chernev, A. (2001), 'The impact of common features on consumer preferences: a case of confirmatory reasoning', *Journal of Consumer Research*, 27, 475–488.

Dahl, D.W., Frankenberger, K.D., and Manchanda, R.V. (2003), 'Does it pay to shock? Reactions to shocking and nonshocking advertising content among university students', *Journal of Advertising Research*, 43, 3, 268–280.

Eroglu, S.A., Machleit, K.A., and Davis, L.M. (2003), 'Empirical testing of a model of online store atmospherics and shopper responses', *Psychology & Marketing*, 20, 2, 139–150.

European Interactive Advertising Association (2009), 'EIAA media multi-tasking report', www.eiaa.co.uk (accessed 20 May 2014).

Faure-Field, S. (2013), 'Why customer "sensation" is important in Asian retail and premium banking (Part 2)', *Asian Banking and Finance*, 11 September, http://asianbankingandfinance.net/retail-banking/commentary/why-customer-sensation-important-in-asian-retail-and-premium-banking-part-0 (accessed 18 October 2013).

Fedorikhin, A. and Cole, C.A. (2004), 'Mood effects on attitudes, perceived risk and choice: moderators and mediators', *Journal of Consumer Psychology*, 14, 1/2, 2–12.

Fernandez, J. (2011), 'How the Old Spice hunk took over the world', *Marketing Week*, http://www.marketing-week.co.uk/how-the-old-spice-hunk-took-over-the-world/3030137.article (accessed 8 June 2013).

Gearhardt, A.N., Davis, C., Kuschner, R., and Brownell, K.D. (2011), 'The addiction potential of hyperpalatable foods', *Current Drug Abuse Reviews*, 4, 140–145.

Geiger-Oneto, S., Gelb, B.D., Walker, D., and Hess, J.D. (2013), ' "Buying status" by choosing or rejecting luxury brands and their counterfeits', *Journal of the Academy of Marketing Science*, 41, 3, 357–372.

Gentry, J.W., Putrevu, S., and Shultz, C.J. (2006), 'The effects of counterfeiting on consumer search', *Journal of Consumer Behaviour*, 5, 3, 1–12.

Han, Y.J., Nunes, J.C., and Drèze, X. (2010), 'Signaling status with luxury goods: the role of brand prominence', *Journal of Marketing*, 74, 4, 15–30.

Handley, L. (2013), 'Starbucks wants bespoke design for every store', *Marketing Week*, 26 June, http://www.marketingweek.co.uk/news/starbucks-wants-bespoke-design-for-every-store/4007167.article (accessed 8 June 2013).

Jeong, S. and Fishbein, M. (2007), 'Predictors of multitasking with media: media factors and audience factors', *Media Psychology*, 10, 364–384.

Kessler, D. (2010), *The end of overeating: taking control of our insatiable appetite*, London: Penguin.

Kim, D.J., Kim, W.G., and Han, J.S. (2007), 'A perceptual mapping of online travel agencies and preference attributes', *Tourism Management*, 28, 591–603.

Krishna, A., Elder, R.S., and Caldara, C. (2010), 'Feminine to smell but masculine to touch? Multisensory congruence and its effect on the aesthetic experience', *Journal of Consumer Psychology*, 20, 410–418.

Labrecque, L.I. and Milne, G.R. (2012), 'Exciting red and competent blue: the importance of color in marketing', *Journal of the Academy of Marketing Science*, 40, 5, 711–727.

Laemmerhirt, I.-A. (2010), 'Imagining the taste: transnational food exchanges between Japan and the United States', *Japanese Journal of American Studies*, 21, 231–250.

Lantos, G.P. and Craton, L.G. (2012), 'A model of consumer response to advertising music', *Journal of Consumer Marketing*, 29, 1, 22–42.

Lenfant, F., Hartmann, C., Watzke, B., Breton, O., Loret, C., and Martin, N. (2013), 'Impact of the shape on sensory properties of individual dark chocolate pieces', *LWT-Food Science and Technology*, 51, 2, 545–552.

Levine, M.W. (2000), *Levine and Shefner's fundamentals of sensation and perception* (3rd edn), Oxford: Oxford University Press.

Levy, S. (1959), 'Symbols for sale', *Harvard Business Review*, July/August, 117–124, reprinted in Rook D. (ed.), *Brands, consumers, symbols, and research*, Thousand Oaks, CA: SAGE, 1999, pp 203–212.

Levy, S. (1981), 'Interpreting consumer mythology: a structural approach to consumer behaviour', *Journal of Marketing*, 45, 3, 49–61, reprinted in D. Rook (ed.), *Brands, consumers, symbols, and research*, Thousand Oaks, CA: SAGE, 1999, pp 514–529.

Lindstrom, M. (2008), *Buyology: how everything we believe about why we buy is wrong*, London: Random House.

Mick, D.G. (1986), 'Consumer research and semiotics: exploring the morphology of signs, symbols, and significance'. *Journal of Consumer Research*, 13, 196–213.

Millman, R.E. (1982), 'Using background music to affect the behavior of supermarket shoppers', *Journal of Marketing*, 46, 86–91.

Milotic, D. (2006), 'The impact of fragrance on consumer choice', *Journal of Consumer Behaviour*, 3, 2, 179–191.

Montague, R. (2006), *Why choose this book? How we make decisions*, New York: Dutton.

Mortimer, R. (2011), 'Costa's £10m tongue', *Marketing Week*, 6 October, http://www.marketingweek.co.uk/analysis/essential-reads/costas-10m-tongue/3030691.article (accessed 8 April 2014)

Nairn, A. and Hang, H. (2012), 'Advergames: it's not child's play. A review of research', http://www.bath.ac.uk/management/news_events/pdf/advergames-report-december2012.pdf (accessed 8 April 2014).

Nestrud, M.A. and Lawless, H.T. (2008), 'Perceptual mapping of citrus juices using projective mapping and profiling data from culinary professionals and consumers', *Food and Quality Preference*, 19, 431–438.

Nobel, C. (2013), 'Advertising symbiosis: the key to viral videos', *Harvard Business School Working Knowledge*, http://hbswk.hbs.edu/item/7267.html (accessed 19 June 2013).

Oneto, S. and Sundie, J.M. (1999), 'Perceptions of counterfeit consumers', *Economic Psychology*, 20, 2, 147–182.

O'Reilly, L (2011), 'Lucozade features musicians for first time in brand repositioning', *Marketing Week*, http://www.marketingweek.co.uk/lucozade-features-musicians-for-first-time-in-brand-repositioning/3024936.article (accessed 9 January 2013).

Ortiz, P. (2013), 'Fake designer handbags: hard to find and easy on the eye but feeling is believing'. *Daily News*, 14 June, http://www.nydailynews.com/new-york/feeling-believing-fake-handbags-article-1.1373364#ixzz2a3NDezVO (accessed 12 June 2013).

Oswald, L.R. (2012), '*Marketing semiotics: signs, strategies, and brand value*, Oxford: Oxford University Press.

Paoletti, J.B. (2012), *Pink and blue: telling the boys from the girls in America*, Bloomington, IN: Indiana University Press.

Peck, J. and Childers, T. (2003), 'To have and to hold: the influence of haptic information on product judgements', *Journal of Marketing*, 67, 35–48.

Piacentini, M. and Mailer, G. (2004), 'Symbolic consumption in teenagers' clothing choices', *Journal of Consumer Behaviour*, 3, 3, 251–262.

Pieters, R. and Wedel, M. (2007), 'Goal control of attention to advertising: the Yarbus implication', *Journal of Consumer Research*, 34, 2, 224–233.

Research and Markets (2013), 'Global handbags market report—2013 edition', http://www.researchandmarkets.com/research/hpzxpm/global_handbags (accessed 19 July 2013).

Schellenberg, E.G., Peretz, I., and Vieillard, S. (2008), 'Liking for happy- and sad-sounding music: effects of exposure', *Cognition and Emotion*, 22, 218–237.

Schwarz, B. (2004), *The paradox of choice: why more is less*, New York: HarperCollins.

Simons, D.J. and Chabris, C.F. (1999), 'Gorillas in our midst: sustained inattentional blindness for dynamic events', *Perception*, 28, 1059–1074.

Smith, G. (1992), 'Lucozade: a case history', *IPA Effectiveness Awards*, www.warc.com

Soars, B. (2003), 'What every retailer should know about the way into the shopper's head', *International Journal of Retail Distribution and Management*, 31, 12, 628–637.

Szmigin, I., Carrigan, M., and McEachern, M. (2009), 'The conscious consumer: taking a flexible approach to ethical behaviour', *International Journal of Consumer Studies*, 33, 224–231.

Taylor, G. (2013), 'UK luxury sector "to double in size" by 2017', *Retail Gazette*, http://www.retailgazette.co.uk/articles/21403-uk-luxury-sector-to-double-in-size-by-2017 (accessed 9 July 2013).

Underhill, P. (2009), *Why we buy*, New York: Simon & Schuster.

Usunier, J.-C. and Valette-Florence, P. (2007), 'The time styles scale: a review of developments and replications over 15 years', *Time and Society*, 16, 2/3, 333–366.

WARC (2011), 'Old Spice: the man your man could smell like', http://www.warc.com.ezproxye.bham.ac.uk/Content/ContentViewer.aspx?MasterContentRef=bbdb1157-4f4e-4bac-a2f6-c587ab561816&q=old+spice (accessed 18 May 2013).

Wiedmann, K. P., Hennigs, N., and Klarmann, C. (2012), 'Luxury consumption in the trade-off between genuine and counterfeit goods: what are the consumers' underlying motives and value-based drivers?', *Journal of Brand Management*, 19, 544–566.

WRAP (2013), 'Consumer attitudes to food waste and food packaging: summary of research findings', http://www.wrap.org.uk/sites/files/wrap/Slides%20-%20Consumer%20attitudes%20to%20food%20waste%20and%20food%20packaging.pdf (accessed 8 July 2013).

6

ATTITUDE THEORY AND BEHAVIOUR CHANGE

Introduction

Encouraging consumers to feel positively towards products and brands is an important goal for marketing. Companies recognize that consumers are more likely to buy products that they feel good about. Take, for example, Triodos Bank (Figure 6.1) which started operations in the Netherlands in the late 1960s and has since opened further branches in European countries. It has a mission to make its customers' money work for positive social, environmental, and cultural change and to promote sustainable development. Triodos Bank's objectives are promoted in communications to consumers, enhancing their feelings about the bank and encouraging development of positive attitudes towards banking with them. Consumer attitudes are important in marketing terms, since they represent the deeply held set of beliefs and evaluations that consumers hold towards marketing offerings. A key aspect of attitudes is their role in influencing behaviour. Some consumers may form favourable attitudes towards a brand and then purchase it, while others may have negative attitudes and thus avoid buying or consuming it. Aside from influencing how we consume products and brands, consumer attitudes can also influence other aspects of consumption, such as how we talk about our experiences with brands to other consumers, thus spreading word-of-mouth communications (see Chapter 8). Attitudes and their links to consumer behaviour are the focus of this chapter.

Make your money make a difference

Figure 6.1 Banking with Triodos

Source: Image printed with permission from Triodos Bank.

LEARNING OBJECTIVES

Having read this chapter, you will be able to:

1. *Define the concept of attitudes* as used in consumer marketing.

2. Describe the *main components of attitudes*—the tri-component model, the uni-dimensionalist model, and the hierarchy of effects model.

3. Discuss the *main approaches* to attitude theory.

4. Recognize the differences between *compensatory and non-compensatory* models and understand how they may be used in consumer decision-making.

5. Explain the various approaches *to attitude change*, including persuasion models such as the elaboration likelihood model.

6. Demonstrate the value of attitude theory for marketing practice.

Defining attitudes

At the simplest level, an attitude is made up of what you think, what you feel, and what you do. The definition proposed by Fishbein and Ajzen (1975: 6) suggests that **attitude** is *'a learned predisposition to respond in a consistently favourable or unfavourable manner in relation to some object'*. From this definition it is clear that attitudes are *learned* (through experiences in the world), have an *evaluative dimension* (favourable/unfavourable), have *intensity* (strong attitudes versus weak attitudes) and have *consistency* and *stability* (do not tend to change much and align with our other attitudes) (Oskamp and Schulz, 2005). Importantly, this definition suggests that attitudes have a link to behaviour, giving a predisposition to act in a certain way. It is this link with behaviour that makes the study of attitudes so interesting to marketers. When discussing attitudes it is important to specify the target object about which attitudes are being gathered and explored. This is known as the **attitude object/act** which can be defined as the *thing about which the attitude is held, and can include brands, services, ideas, people, and behaviours* (Herr and Fazio, 1993). This may be behaviour (e.g. smoking), an object (e.g. Marlboro cigarettes), or a person (e.g. Brad Pitt).

If we think about consumer attitudes towards debt, the various aspects of this definition will become clearer. Consumers learn about and form views on debt through interactions with family, friends, other consumers, and various media, as well as the marketplace offerings they are exposed to. From these interactions and experiences, consumers are likely to hold a relatively stable position (positive or negative) towards debt, which in turn informs and influences their behaviour towards debt. If you come from a family setting where saving is valued and borrowing discouraged, you are likely to avoid building up large debts. However, there are situations where it is difficult to avoid accumulating debt (if you are getting a mortgage, or taking out a student loan to pay for fees), and in those contexts you are likely to adjust your attitude and behaviour. Therefore contexts of consumption are mportant as a key influence on consumer attitudes and subsequent behaviour, as is evident in Consumer Insight 6.1 where the changing environment around credit and debt is discussed.

CONSUMER INSIGHT 6.1

Attitudes to credit and debt

Credit has become a common feature of consumer lives in the late twentieth and early twenty-first centuries. This has been an almost worldwide phenomenon, with credit card usage in some Asian countries increased by up to 500 per cent (Kang and Ma, 2007). Peñaloza and Barnhart (2011) studied the cultural meanings that white middle-class Americans associated with credit and debt, and considered how attitudes compared with the previous generation's views. A dominant theme emerged that debt was necessary in order to fund the 'must haves' associated with a middle-class American lifestyle—buying a house, a car, a college (university) education. Taking on debt was a *normal* way of funding this lifestyle.

O'Loughlin and Szmigin (2006) found that students in the UK and Ireland also accepted debt as part of normal life. This increased debt resulted in students being more confident in their consumer roles; they were also less thrifty in an environment where credit was the norm.

Recent data from the UK suggests that attitudes towards debt have changed. While UK consumers became more debt-tolerant from the 1990s up to around 2005, there has since been a shift to a more cautious approach, prompted by the economic climate. Consumers realize that they cannot refinance their mortgages in the ways they might have done previously. Research by Mintel (2011) suggests that the recession has prompted half of all adults to reassess their attitudes towards debt. Such behaviour is matched in EU countries, including Greece, Portugal, Ireland, Spain, and Italy, as the economic crisis has led to cuts to public jobs, healthcare, education, and many other entitlements which have increased the hardship felt by a diverse array of stakeholders across society (Lane, 2012).

Questions

1. Ask three people you know, ideally of different ages, about their thoughts and attitudes towards debt. Ask them if they have tried to reduce their debt in the last few years and why?

2. From these discussions outline how you think their current attitudes to debt might be described.

Sources: Kang and Ma (2007); Szmigin and O'Loughlin (2010); Mintel (2011); Peñaloza and Barnhart (2011); Lane (2012).

 Visit the Online Resource Centre and follow the weblinks to learn more about consumer debt.

Main components of attitudes

The tricomponent model

Generally, attitudes are thought to comprise three main components: *affect* or feelings, *behaviour* or conations, and *cognitions* or beliefs (Henderson and Hoque, 2010).

The **affective component** relates to *the emotional connection the consumer has with the target object about which the attitude is formed*. If we think about the emotional aspect of our attitude towards buying books on Amazon, we may feel enthusiastic about the prospect of a bargain, but we may also feel angry as we recall stories about Amazon avoiding paying tax in the UK. The affect refers to the fundamental feelings related to the attitude, which are often represented as liking or disliking.

The **behavioural component** refers to *the action or behaviours associated with the attitude object*. This may be an intention to stop smoking, or an intention to start composting household waste. This component covers the 'doing' aspect of the attitude, the action about which the attitude is formed. Note, however, that intended actions are not necessarily carried out.

The **cognitive component** refers to the beliefs and thoughts the individual has in relation to the target attitude object, its character, and its relations to other things. We may hold a belief that running every day is good for our fitness. We may also believe that being fit is preferable to being unfit and perhaps overweight. These are cognitions that can be related to the behaviour of buying new running shoes.

Together, these elements combine to give the tri-component model, also called the ABC model: affect (feeling), behaviour (doing), and cognition (knowing). The ABC model is useful in terms of thinking about the components of attitudes, but does not provide marketers with a sense of how these elements are related, or how they combine to produce attitudes (Grimm, 2005).

The following example makes this clear. The Livescribe Smartpen is a ballpoint pen with an embedded computer and digital audio-recorder, and its main function is to save written words (through transferring them onto a computer) and to synchronize these notes with any audio-recording that is made (see Figure 6.2). The Livescribe Smartpen is aimed at situations where notes are taken (e.g. in meetings or classrooms) and its main benefit is

Figure 6.2 Livescribe Smartpen   *Source*: Image courtesy of Honcho PR.

captured in the strapline 'Never miss a word' (see the company website http://www.live-scribe.com/uk/).

If we analyse this product in terms of the tri-component model, it can be seen how each of the ABC elements are related.

A. Affect—in terms of affect (feelings), the consumer may be positive, excited, and enthusiastic about trying the Livescribe Smartpen.

B. Behavioural (conations)—the consumer decides to buy and use the Livescribe Smartpen, based on their feelings and beliefs about it.

C. Cognitions (beliefs)—the consumer may form cognitions (beliefs) about the Livescribe Smartpen along the lines that it has great functionality and will improve their note-taking skills. While consumers may be able to generate many beliefs associated with the target attitude object (in this case the Livescribe Smartpen), only those that are *important* to consumers, known as salient beliefs, will inform the attitude they form in relation to it. **Salient beliefs** *are the most relevant beliefs for any given person at the time the attitude is considered.*

Together these three components may translate into the attitude, but this model does not tell us how these elements come together. We have no idea how important one is in relation to the others, and therefore it is difficult for marketers to influence attitudes using this approach. However, the three main components of attitudes found in this model (affect/feelings, behaviour, and cognitions/beliefs) do form the basis of many of the more structured models of attitudes, as we shall see in our treatment of the multi-attribute models of attitudes.

RESEARCH INSIGHT 6.1

Sela, A.S., Wheeler, C., and Sarial-Abi, G. (2012), 'We are not the same as you and I: causal effects of minor language variations on consumers' attitudes toward brands', *Journal of Consumer Research*, 39, 3, 644–661

In this paper the authors seek to identify whether subtle wording changes in marketing communications can affect the emotional connections consumers develop with the brand and thus the attitude formed. The researchers discover that language can have important effects on consumers' attitudes. They found that when consumers expect to have a close relationship with brands (both real and hypothetical brands), they held more positive attitudes towards the brand after reading a message that referred to the brand and the consumer in terms of the collective pronoun 'we' rather than the phrase 'you and the brand' that emphasizes a separation.

 Visit the Online Resource Centre to read the abstract and access the full paper.

Hierarchy of effects

Although the ABC model does not indicate the level of contribution and interrelationship of the three attitude components, it represents a sequence of steps that arise when consumers form attitudes (Alexandris et al., 2012). Using this approach, the starting point for attitude formation can be any of the components (affect, behaviour, or cognition), and different implications for marketers emerge depending on the starting point (Beatty and Kahle, 1988). This is known as the hierarchy of effects, and there are four main types of hierarchy that are useful for marketers which are summarized in Table 6.1.

The *high involvement or standard learning hierarchy*, represented by the sequence 'cognitions → affect → behaviour', assumes that the consumer is actively engaged in a rational decision-making process. This hierarchy is relevant for attitude formation in high

Hierarchy and sequence	Main emphasis
High involvement (standard learning) hierarchy: cognitions → affect → behaviour	High involvement, consumer engaged in extensive research to develop beliefs, emphasis on cognitive information processing
Low involvement hierarchy: cognitions → behaviour → affect	Consumer drawing on limited knowledge, behavioural learning important here
Behavioural hierarchy: behaviour → cognitions → affect	Emphasis on consumers responding to consumer context, impulse type buys, behavioural approach important.
Emotional hierarchy: affect → behaviour → cognitions	Experiential aspects of the consumption setting, importance of hedonic consumption

Table 6.1   Hierarchy of effects

involvement consumption contexts, such as when a consumer is considering purchasing a tablet. The consumer undertakes an extensive search, but also develops an affective or emotional connection with the brands available. This is demonstrated in the 2013 advertising campaign 'Made for what matters' for Google Nexus, which tells the story of a teenage boy struggling with public speaking and using the tablet as a source of inspiration and communication to overcome his fear. Finally, the consumer acts (makes a purchase) based on the evaluation of their beliefs and feelings. In this example beliefs dominate the attitude formation process.

The *low involvement hierarchy* has the sequence 'cognitions → behaviour → affect'. The difference in this context is that the consumer starts with a set of beliefs about the consumption object, but the knowledge they are drawing on may be limited, and it is not as essential for the consumer to undertake extensive research. Often, the thinking and action stages are quite close, with the consumer forming an emotional response (how they feel about the brand or service) after the purchase. Consider going to buy a new pair of trainers. You will have some knowledge to draw on—for example, about the type of trainer required, the shops where they can be bought, and an acceptable price range. However, going to a store such as Decathalon, and seeing what products are available in your size and price range, will greatly impact on the purchase made. Following purchase, the consumer may establish an emotional connection to the product/brand purchased. This hierarchy is distinctive in that it is relevant for relatively low involvement contexts and familiar consumption situations. In such contexts, the consumer relies greatly on their own knowledge and beliefs to inform their attitudes towards the consumption object.

The *behavioural hierarchy*, represented by 'behaviour → cognitions → affect', emphasizes behaviour first, and from this the consumer forms beliefs and then feelings in relation to the consumption object. A consumer may impulsively purchase a new Essie nail polish shade, but it is only through the act of wearing the nail polish that she feels that this colour suits her (or not) and thus forms an attitude towards the nail polish, and perhaps towards the Essie brand in particular.

The *emotional hierarchy*, represented by 'affect → behaviour → cognitions', is more experiential in nature, assuming that a consumer acts based on emotional triggers. The feeling comes first, followed by consumption. After consumption the consumer will think through and form an attitude towards the target attitude object. A consumer may be looking for a new dress for a special occasion, such as her twenty-first birthday party. In this context, she may make her decision based on how a dress makes her feel—glamorous, 'just right'—then she makes the purchase, and, following that, evaluates and forms beliefs about the item. Was the price right? Can she wear it for other occasions, etc.? In this hierarchy, emotions and feelings dominate the attitude formation process.

Examining the various hierarchies of effects underpinning attitude formation in different types of consumer contexts is useful for marketers, since it has implications for the ways that marketing efforts may be emphasized. An example of the emotional hierarchy can be seen with the American lifestyle clothing brand Hollister Co. Hollister places great emphasis on the experiential aspects of the in-store retail environment, trying to emulate a multisensory experience (using smells, textures, music, visuals, and lighting) to encourage an emotional connection with, and affective response to, the brand. This emotional connection is the main underpinning component of attitudes towards the brand, from which beliefs and action towards the brand emerge, and is a vital part of Hollister's retailing strategy.

Contrast this with the marketing of personal computers, where beliefs are likely to dominate attitude formation and hence it is important for marketers to ensure that their brands are promoted in such a way as to emphasize the brand attributes most important to consumers. Chillblast is a UK-based computer manufacturer, launched in 2001 (http://www.chillblast.com/). It very quickly developed a reputation for offering high specification, high quality PCs at a reasonable price, supported by outstanding customer service. Chillblast has won a series of major awards in the UK computer press (the PC Pro awards 2010 and 2011; PC Advisor Winner 2012), and the company highlights these successes in all their communications as an assurance to consumers of the quality of the product and service offering (see Figure 6.3). This kind of communication influences the development of consumer beliefs in a highly complex and involved consumer context.

Figure 6.3   Screenshot of the Chillblast website

Source: Printed with permission from Chillblast at www.chillblast.com

The uni-dimensionalist model

An alternative way of considering attitudes is the uni-dimensionalist model (Lutz, 1990). This can be viewed as an evolution of the tripartite approach because, while the same three components are present, their conceptual status is different. The cognitive and behavioural components are separated from attitude such that attitude is considered to be uni-dimensional, i.e. consisting of only the component affect which can be described as the degree of liking/disliking, favourability/unfavourability towards the attitude object. Therefore the belief and behavioural elements present in the tripartite model are now considered to be antecedents (beliefs) or consequences (intention to behave) of attitude. Thus the uni-dimensionalist view proposes that we can see a causal flow through the

Figure 6.4 The uni-dimensionalist model   *Source*: Lutz (1991).

components from beliefs to behaviour which reflects the consistency of the tripartite model (see Figure 6.4).

Main theoretical perspectives on attitudes

There are three main categories of attitude theories: balance theories, motivational theories, and multi-attribute expectancy-value theories.

Balance theory of attitudes

Heider's balance theory of attitudes considers the relationship between a person (a consumer), that person's perception of an attitude object (often a brand), and the consumer's perception of some other person or object that has a connection with this brand (e.g. a celebrity) (Lee et al., 2011). The person seeks a balance or alignment between these three elements, and when they are unbalanced adjusts their perception to bring them into balance (Dalakas and Levin, 2005). A consumer may have a positive impression of cyclist Lance Armstrong, who was associated with the brand Nike, and so feel similarly positively towards Nike because of its connection with Armstrong. However, in 2012 it emerged that Armstrong took performance-enhancing drugs, which seriously damaged his reputation. Nike dropped their sponsorship of Armstrong in order to minimize the damage and to reduce any imbalance consumers may feel in relation to the Nike–Armstrong association.

Balance theory can also be considered when looking at the tri-component model of attitudes (affect, behaviour, and cognitions). There is a psychological drive to ensure that all three elements are balanced; if they are not, feelings of discomfort may arise and the consumer may adjust one of the components to bring them into line (Woodside and Chebat, 2001). Many people eat fast food (behaviour) and enjoy its taste and convenience (affect), but recognize that too much fast food is bad for their health and may lead to obesity (cognitions). From a balance theory perspective, these are not in line with each other, and therefore the consumer changes one element to bring them to a more consistent direction. They could stop eating fast food (i.e. bring their behaviour in line with their thoughts about fast food and health), but they may also adjust their thoughts to support their fast food consumption. A common view expressed by people is that 'I do not eat enough of it to impact my weight or health'. This shift in cognition allows the three elements to be balanced and for the consumer to develop an attitude that is in line with their behaviour—consuming fast food.

RESEARCH INSIGHT 6.2

George, B.P. and Yaoyuneyong, G. (2010), 'Impulse buying and cognitive dissonance: a study conducted among the Spring Break student shoppers', *Young Consumers*, 11, 4, 291–306.

In this study, the authors explore the extent to which students experience cognitive dissonance linked to impulse purchases that they make during their Spring Break shopping trips. Contrary to expectations, they found that impulse buyers appear to experience less post-purchase regret than shoppers who have done more planning. Insights into why this was the case include the idea that impulse buying is a coping strategy and a form of emotional release for some students.

 Visit the Online Resource Centre to read the abstract and access the full paper.

Linked to balance theory is the **theory of cognitive dissonance** (Festinger, 1957). **Cognitive dissonance** *is the state of having inconsistent beliefs and attitudes.* In consumer behaviour, cognitive dissonance is important as it is based on the belief that people need consistency or consonance between their behaviour and their attitudes. People will change their behaviour or their attitudes to maintain consistency and reduce feelings of unease (dissonance) that are present where an attitude or behaviour is inconsistent with some other information. This is seen in the case of eating fast food, where the consumer may try to downplay the health problems associated with it, and perhaps increase its convenience benefits.

Motivational theories: the functional theory of attitudes

The functional theory of attitudes was proposed by Katz (1960). This approach is called a motivational theory of attitudes, since an understanding of motives (or functions) underpinning the attitudes is required before attitude change can occur (Kardes, 1993). According to this theory, advertising and marketing campaigns are most persuasive when they address the motives underlying the attitude targeted for change. This is an important theory for understanding consumer behaviour.

There are four main functions that attitudes can serve for people: *utilitarian, value-expressive, ego-defensive,* and *knowledge based* (Russell-Bennett et al., 2013). The first is the **utilitarian function**, which stems from the idea that *consumers seek maximum utility and value from their consumption* (Grewal et al., 2004). The utilitarian function of attitudes is characterized by consumers seeking (and maximizing) rewards and avoiding punishment. If you think about bottled water, you might think that the product fulfils your need for thirst, but is also portable and handy when you are out and about. You place value on these useful aspects of the bottled water, and therefore you are seeking to fulfil a utilitarian motivation through your consumption, which informs your positive attitudes towards it.

Marketers of products and brands serving utilitarian functions benefit from recognizing that there is a greater likelihood that consumers will form positive attitudes if there is a

Figure 6.5 Nurofen as an example of utilitarian function

Source: Image courtesy of Reckitt Benckiser.

good match between the consumer need and the brand which satisfies that need. Looking to other product categories, a consumer suffering from a headache may take ibuprofen for pain relief, which removes the pain they are suffering; this is a form of reward in theoretical terms. The packaging for Nurofen (Figure 6.5) illustrates the utilitarian function of attitudes, emphasizing the benefits following use of this brand—easy to swallow, fast and effective pain relief.

The second motivational function is the **ego-defensive** function. Here attitudes have the function of defending our self-image, making us feel better about ourselves (Kardes, 2001). Think about the grooming routines and rituals we undertake in the morning. We gargle with mouthwash to ensure that we don't have smelly breath and we put on deodorant to mask our natural body odours. We are hiding aspects of ourselves that we do not want others to experience. Fundamentally, this is what the ego-defensive function of attitudes is concerned with—protection of our sense of self, and ensuring that we control aspects of our selves that are deemed unacceptable in some way. Threats to our ego usually arouse the ego-defensive attitude, which can be influenced by a suggestion which removes that threat. Personal hygiene products such as Nivea's deodorant Invisible for Black and White (see Figure 6.6) are often discussed in terms of ego-defensive attitudes. This product incorporates a formula which does not stain black (or dark clothes) and also prevents white clothes from yellowing,

Figure 6.6 Nivea Invisible for Black & White deodorant

Source: © iStock.com/mrtom-uk.

thus protecting the consumer from having unsightly stains on their clothes which may make them feel self-conscious. In addition, the deodorant offers 48 hour dryness, giving the consumer confidence and security.

The third motivational function is the **value-expressive function**, or the social identity function (Schossler, 1998; Shavitt, 1990). This is concerned with *the drive to express important aspects of the self* (Grewal et al., 2004) and, linked to this, of the self that one aspires to be. This function is characterized by consumers using products and brands to project, rather than hide, some aspect of themselves or of how they would like to be perceived. A teenager may choose to get her tongue pierced to establish her identity or fit in with her peer group, and express independence from parental control. An example of value-expressive function of brands is found in the luxury brand Louis Vuitton which expresses the values of

Figure 6.7   The Louis Vuitton/Kusama Collaboration
Source: iStock by Getty Images.

luxury, quality, and authenticity to the consumer, and thus communicates the status of the wearer. Louis Vuitton has collaborated with artists, notably the Japanese artists Takashi Murakama and Yayoi Kusama (see Figure 6.7) to emphasize further symbolic meanings for the brand around cultural values and cultural authenticity. Wearing a bag designed by a great artist brings the consumer closer to the artist, expressing the consumer's cultural capital.

Finally, the **knowledge function** *relates to the human need to have a meaningful, stable, and organized view of the world*, 'involving forming accurate judgements about an object or issue' (Kardes, 1993: 169). Often consumers find that they are looking to change their mobile phone, perhaps because they have finished their contract and are eligible for a new one. If your current handset is a Nokia and you have been happy with this brand, you are likely to draw on your positive experience and knowledge about Nokia as you look to get a new handset. In this context, knowledge-based attitudes, built around brand and product information, act as a frame of reference to help the consumer understand and make sense of the consumption context of upgrading their phone.

These knowledge-based attitudes provide structure for consumers to evaluate new information (Grewal et al., 2004). Another example may be a mother who has a positive

Figure 6.8 Johnson & Johnson baby skincare products

Source: © iStock.com/evemilla.

attitude towards Johnson & Johnson baby skincare products (see Figure 6.8), based on her experience with the brand. If Johnson & Johnson were to launch a new range of baby toy products, parents with a positive attitude towards Johnson & Johnson, based on their knowledge function, may be willing to try it. The knowledge-based function is important for marketing in helping to understand and predict consumer attitudes towards brand extensions and diversifications, since it helps consumers to organize and simplify new experiences.

Products, services, and brands can activate the motivational concerns of consumers. The examples outlined in this section provide instances where a product can be categorized as satisfying a predominantly singular function, but products and brands can often serve multiple functions (Shavitt, 1989, 1990). A car is a good illustration of a multi-functioned product, since it can relate to both utilitarian concerns (e.g. around safety and performance) and value-expressive concerns (such as implied social status). Another example of a multi-functioned product is described in Consumer Insight 6.2.

CONSUMER INSIGHT 6.2

Attitudes towards tents from a functional theory perspective

Oase Outdoors is a Danish company that specializes in camping equipment, and is the parent company of the popular tent brands Outwell and EasyCamp (see Figure 6.9). These brands serve different markets. Outwell is an innovative camping brand, aimed at the family market, where quality and reliability

Figure 6.9 Outwell tent and EasyCamp Carnival tent

Source: Images courtesy of Oase Outdoors.

are important. In contrast, EasyCamp is a budget range, producing easy-to-pitch tents at a reasonable price. They have a range called Carnival, aimed at the festival market, which is 'light and bright, easy to use and exudes an element of fun'.

From a functional theory of attitudes perspective, these tents are satisfying different motivational functions. For the young person buying a tent for a festival, the EasyCamp brand meets their utilitarian needs of being cheap and easy to pitch. Longevity of use (and re-use) is not a primary concern. For festival-goers, the tent may serve a secondary value–expressive function around having a bright, colourful, and trendy tent

Figure 6.10   Outwell brand extensions

Source: Image courtesy of Oase Outdoors.

that matches the mood of the festival event, allowing them to express their social identity through use.

For the middle-class family buying a tent, there may be similar motivational functions in place, but they operate differently. The utilitarian function may be very important, not just in terms of how easy the tent is to pitch, but also in terms of its innovative materials and design features, such as ventilation, window design, and living space. Additionally, there is a strong value-expressive aspect to the Outwell brand, as it is viewed as a lifestyle tent brand. Ego-defensive motivations may also be at play, in terms of the middle-class family being assured that they have the 'right' brand of tent that enables them to project their aspirational self-image relating to their family role. Knowledge functions operate in terms of helping buyers make sense of product information and lines available, as well as buying affiliated products (brand extensions), such as an Outwell carpet for inside the tent (see Figure 6.10).

Questions

1. How might a camping equipment company use the ideas of differing motivational functions to market its products to different consumer segments?

2. Think of another brand that markets products to different target groups and identify the motivational functions served by their different products.

Sources: Kardes (1993); Young (2010); Shooter (2010); Weaver (2013).

  Visit the Online Resource Centre and follow the weblinks to learn more.

Multi-attribute models of attitudes

Multi-attribute models are used to understand and measure attitudes, and they work by unpacking the many aspects or attributes of the attitude object (remember, this is what we are forming our attitude about) and attempting to work out how important each of these is to consumers.

The expectancy-value model

The basic multi-attribute model has three elements:

- attributes are the characteristics or features of the attitude object

- beliefs about the extent to which the object has the attributes

- evaluations are the levels of importance attached to the attributes.

Very
nice
Example

If we take the example of attitudes towards Nespresso coffee (attitude object), attributes might include flavour strength, caffeine level, aroma, colour, and coffee density. Beliefs would be the extent to which the consumer believes that Nespresso has these attributes. For example, a consumer may believe that the flavour is not strong enough, and so rate the coffee low on that belief. Finally, the evaluation measure is trying to gain a sense of how important that attribute is to the consumer. The same consumer may feel that the flavour strength is extremely important, and if he believes that Nespresso is lacking in that attribute then this is likely to reduce how he rates Nespresso overall. This model offers a way for marketers to unpack the range of factors that influence our overall attitude and evaluation of a brand, and to gain a sense of how important these factors are to consumers. Such an understanding can inform many aspects of product and brand development from the actual product design itself through to devising advertising campaigns to emphasize attributes viewed as important by consumers.

The most influential multi-attribute model—the Fishbein model—also uses three components of attitude and, in a similar fashion, aims to establish the relative importance of each and how they inform consumer attitudes. This model aims to represent the mental calculations that consumers perform when developing attitudes and represents this by a numerical score. This model is also known as the **expectancy-value model** which suggests that *people form attitudes towards objects (e.g. brands) based on their expectations and evaluations of the attributes that make up the brand.* Such models describe how these components relate to each other in order to produce attitudes. They have had a wide range of applications, including attitudes towards condom use in social marketing (Gabler et al., 2004), attitudes and intentions towards music piracy (Chiou et al., 2005), and attitudes towards counterfeit luxury goods (Phau and Teah, 2009). In order to explain this model more fully, it is useful to unpack and revisit some key terms.

The first is **attitude object** which is *anything towards which we hold an attitude* (as discussed already in this chapter). As stated earlier, this can be a product, brand, service, or even idea, but the attitude object must be clearly defined. Microsoft may be interested in consumer attitudes towards Microsoft generally, but perhaps more useful for the company is to establish attitudes towards Microsoft Xbox specifically as the attitude object (or indeed any of its specific brands). In fact, Fishbein was concerned that the attitude measured was as specific as possible, and therefore he suggested that we measure the attitude towards a behaviour, rather than an object (e.g. the attitude to buying the Microsoft Xbox for a Christmas present).

Next it is important to revisit beliefs. **Beliefs** are the *thoughts the consumer holds which describe the object of the attitude, its characteristics, and its relations to other objects.* While a consumer may hold many beliefs in relation to the attitude object, some, known as the salient beliefs (already described in this chapter), will have greater importance for the consumer in that context. This is important for attitude studies, since the attitude is formed based on the beliefs that are important to the consumer. Remember, beliefs in themselves do not indicate a particular attitude, i.e. beliefs do not have an affective (good or bad) component. For example, you may hold beliefs about different brands of mobile phone, but that in itself does not indicate whether you feel positively or negatively towards them.

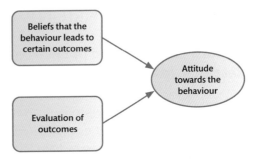

Figure 6.11   Relationship between beliefs, evaluations, and attitudes

Evaluation refers *to the process of determining how valuable, or important, something is to us.* In the context of attitudes, evaluation refers to the process of judging the consequences of the beliefs associated with the attitude object. The evaluation of beliefs provides a way of unpacking the importance attached to each salient belief influencing attitude formation, since it provides a sense of how important each belief is to the consumer's attitude towards the object. Figure 6.11 shows graphically how these elements are related.

These elements form the building blocks of multi-attribute attitude models. The purpose of this approach is to express the relationships between these three elements as a way of representing how consumers form attitudes from a number of key criteria. In the consumer's mind, each belief is assigned a value and this is multiplied by their evaluation scores. These values are combined across all the beliefs, and finally added to provide an overall attitude score.

Taking this approach to understanding attitudes requires that the person commissioning the research accepts that consumers can and do mentally assign values to each of the belief and evaluation components and the multiplication of these can produce a score which represents their attitude towards an object. The beliefs must be salient, and these tend to be the first few that a respondent gives to an open-ended question such as 'Tell me what you think about …'. They may be different in different situations; for example, your beliefs regarding buying a turkey for dinner will be different in the middle of summer than a couple of days before Christmas. We spoke to Edward Langley, Head of Environment Research at Ipsos MORI (the leading provider of social research to the public services in the UK), to discover just how important research into consumer attitudes and beliefs is when planning environmental initiatives. He also provides some insights into how attitudes are measured and tracked.

Theory of planned behaviour

Attitude theory has evolved to represent more fully the range of influences on attitude formation and intentions to behave in a certain way, and a revised and expanded version is the theory of planned behaviour (Figure 6.12).

The revised model includes **behavioural intention**, which is the *intention to act in some way.* The idea behind this is that behaviour is determined by intentions, which are influenced by our attitudes. To illustrate, instead of investigating consumers' attitudes towards Saucony

PRACTITIONER INSIGHT 6

Edward Langley, Head of Environment Research, Ipsos MORI

For some areas of consumer behaviour, it is very important to get a picture of the differences in people's beliefs and attitudes. Where there are issues that can divide communities, such as forms of energy, housing, or new transport links, it is very important for those involved to really understand how people differ in their positions.

In 2009, the Welsh Government launched the new Sustainable Development Scheme *One Wales: One Planet*. This scheme defined sustainable development as enhancing the economic, social, and environmental well-being of people and communities, achieving a better quality of life for our own and future generations in ways which promote social justice and equality of opportunity; and enhance the natural and cultural environment and respect its limits. In order to further the Sustainable Development Scheme the Welsh Government wanted to understand differences in people's beliefs and attitudes around sustainability. In 2012, we produced a survey for them which identified the Welsh population segmented on the basis of their values, beliefs, attitudes, and behaviours, with a view to help target and support interventions designed to deliver sustainable behaviours. To do this we had to identify the nature of relevant values (e.g. self-enhancement, openness to change, beliefs related to environmental and economic sustainability, and attitudes to such things as living in Wales, climate change, and sustainable lifestyles). Appropriate questions were developed and administered to a sample of over 1,500 people from across Wales, the responses from which enabled the project partnership to build a segmentation model. Six segments were identified: enthusiasts (17 per cent), pragmatists (21 per cent), aspirers (15 per cent), community-focused (20 per cent), commentators (12 per cent), and self-reliant (16 per cent). We also looked at the nature of each group in terms of demographic dimensions. From this we were able to build up a picture of the type of sustainable behaviours and attitudes prevalent in Wales; we could also see where consistencies and inconsistencies between attitudes and behaviour may lie. The community-focused segment favoured the economy over the environment, which they viewed as the concern of an 'alternative lifestyle'. Despite this they are concerned about waste, are committed recyclers, and are the second most likely group to say that they don't throw away much food. The youngest segment, with nearly half under 35, is aspirers. While they are concerned about the environment and climate change, they also consider success and wealth to be important values and are below average for 'recycling everything'. Such detailed analyses of attitudes will give policy-makers a much more nuanced understanding of how consumers may respond to initiatives and how they see such measures fitting in with their own beliefs and lifestyles. It can help to develop appropriate and targeted actions and communications.

This study was delivered in partnership with AD Research & Analysis Ltd and Cardiff University.

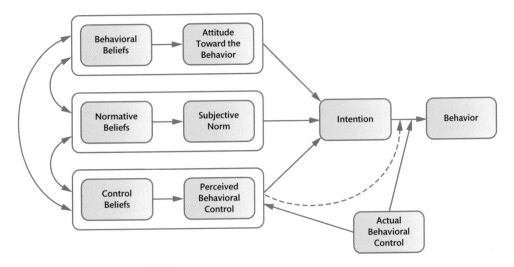

Figure 6.12   Theory of planned behaviour

Source: Ajzen (2005). Image reproduced with permission from Icek Ajzen.

training shoes, the theory of reasoned action would investigate consumers' attitudes towards running in Saucony training shoes. The subtle shift in emphasis focuses attention on the consumer's attitude towards the behaviour attached to using the product, brand, or service, and provides a more accurate predictor of whether or not the behaviour will take place.

Here, behavioural intention is also influenced by the way in which the consumer pays attention to, and takes on board, the beliefs of key social influencers. Social influences are represented by the **subjective norm** concept, which *represents perceptions of specific significant others' preferences as to whether one should or should not engage in the behaviour* (Han et al., 2010). The subjective norm captures the people who may influence the consumer in their consumption lives (e.g. parents, siblings, partner/spouse, friends, boss) and will vary from context to context. Staying with the running shoes example, relevant significant social influences may include friends or people from your running club. Your boss may be an important social influencer in terms of the clothes you wear to work, but your friends are likely to be more influential regarding the clothes you wear on a Friday night.

Just as the expectancy-value model focuses on calculating the scores for attitudes based on beliefs and evaluations, a similar approach is adopted in the theory of planned behaviour. However, additionally scores are calculated for the subjective norm and perceived behaviour control concepts. There are two aspects to the subjective norm. First, we have **normative beliefs** which are the *individual's perception about relevant or significant others' beliefs that the individual should engage in the behaviour or not* (Ajzen, 2012). In the running example, a normative belief might be 'My friends think that it is a good thing for me to wear Saucony running shoes when I go out running'. It is worth pointing out that the response to a statement such as this represents the subjective perception of the participant, rather than an objective account of whether the friends really would think it a good thing to wear Saucony shoes. The second aspect of the subjective norm is the **motivation to comply** which is *the extent to which the* *consumer wishes to comply with or conform to the perceived preferences of these important people* (Ajzen, 2012). A motivation to comply item might be 'It is important to me that my friends think I am wearing good running shoes'. The subjective norm score is calculated by multiplying the various normative belief and motivation to comply scores and then adding them together.

The theory of planned behaviour includes the concept of **perceived behavioural control**, which is *the person's perception of how easy or difficult it is for them to perform the behaviour*. Perceived behavioural control gives an indication of an individual's own confidence in successfully performing the behaviour. For example, a consumer may have the intention of travelling to an IKEA store to buy a flatpack shelf unit. Perceived behavioural control may relate to how confident the consumer feels that the store stocks the item he wants; it may also include his confidence in his DIY skills and ability to follow the instructions. Other factors can also interfere with the consumer's control over their intended behaviour, including skills, abilities, and knowledge (internal), and time, opportunity, and dependence on others (external). The point is that perceived behavioural control accesses the range of factors that may intervene between deciding to do something and actually managing to do so.

Finally, the attitude, subjective norm, and perceived behavioural control scores are weighted (with respect to the relative importance of each of these components) and are then added together to provide a measure of the behavioural intention to perform the behaviour. Applications of the theory of planned behaviour include a wide range of subject areas from physical exercise (Ajzen and Driver, 1992) through to problem or addictive behaviours (Morojele and Stephenson, 1992; Schlegl et al., 1992; Devries and Backbier, 1994) to more consumption-related behaviours such as recycling (Boldero, 1995) and gift buying (Netemeyer et al., 1993).

See Research Insight 6.3 and Consumer Insight 6.3 for more examples of attitude and behavioural change.

RESEARCH INSIGHT 6.3

Jiang, L., Hoegg, J., Dahl, D.W., and Chattopadhyay. A. (2010), 'The persuasive role of incidental similarity on attitudes and purchase intentions in a sales context', *Journal of Consumer Research*, 36, 5, 778–791.

According to research by Jiang et al. (2010), if a salesperson shares a birthday or a birthplace with you, you are more likely to form a favourable attitude towards the brand or product, as well as make a more expensive purchase. Under experimental conditions, the researchers examined *incidental similarities* between salespeople and consumers across a range of contexts (signing up to a fitness programme and evaluation of dental providers). They found that when consumers shared a birthday or a birthplace with the provider this led to a more favourable attitude towards the provider, and a higher behavioural intention.

    Visit the Online Resource Centre to read the abstract and access the full paper.

CONSUMER INSIGHT 6.3

Attitudes towards road safety

Within social marketing, attitude theories are fairly widely used to inform interventions aimed at attitude and behavioural change. Such strategies often aim to influence and change behaviour by modifying the beliefs that individuals hold which underlie their attitudes, their perceptions of social norms and their motivations to comply, and their sense of personal control over the situations in which the behaviour takes place.

Examples of attitude change applied to road safety are as follows.

- 'Arrive alive DRIVE SOBER®' is a Canadian campaign, which has been running for 25 years, which aims to change attitudes towards drink driving and encourage sober driving. This campaign uses a wide range of marketing communications techniques, including social media such as Facebook and a mobile phone app, the 'Arrive Alive App' (Leonard, 2013), to raise awareness of the risks associated with drink driving.

- Think! Campaign (2012)—this UK-wide social marketing campaign covers many aspects of road safety, including driving under the influence of drugs or alcohol, use of mobile phones while driving; wearing seat belts, and speeding. The main aim is to influence the British public's attitudes and behaviour towards road safety and an annual survey is performed to monitor change (Think!, 2013).

- Between 2007 and 2009 the New South Wales Roads and Traffic Authority in Australia launched the Pinkie campaign that focused on subjective norms around young men speeding. The aim was to undermine the social acceptability of speeding by using the well-known 'pinkie' gesture to emasculate the driver's behaviour.

Sources: Think! (2012); Leonard (2013); www.advertising.nsw.gov.au

Questions

1. From your understanding of attitude theory, devise a set of questions you might use to inform a study tracking attitudes towards road safety? Look back over the various theories covered in this chapter, and try and map your questions onto the theoretical concepts (such as listing beliefs, evaluations of beliefs).

2. What do you think are the benefits and disadvantages associated with measuring and tracking attitude change?

3. Consider the kind of communications campaign you might put together using attitude theory to lessen the impact of binge drinking in the urban night-time economy. Consider who your targets would be and what the different elements of your campaign would include.

 Visit the Online Resource Centre and follow the weblinks to learn more about campaigns against speeding.

Critique of multi-attribute models of attitudes

While these theories have been widely used in academic research in social marketing and health sciences, their use in commercial marketing has not been widespread. There are a number of reasons for this. As the expectancy-value model takes account of the impact of social influences through the subjective norm construct, it works best for behaviours under the individual's volitional control, i.e. behaviours for which they are solely responsible. The emotional aspects of consumption are also not clearly dealt with in this model, although some studies have overcome this limitation by including emotions (such as regret or guilt) as moderating variables in the model (Ajzen, 2011). In such cases, the predictive power of the model has increased, suggesting that emotions are important for predicting intentions and behaviours. Finally, these models can be difficult to administer in practice, since there are a number of elements to be measured, leading to fairly lengthy questionnaires. Generally these models have proved most useful where people have quite strong opinions and are aware of the opinions of others, including social and personal issues such as contraception, smoking, and health-related topics. However, it is important to recognize the contribution that such models have made to understanding consumer behaviour. First, they have reduced to clear and simple terms the key elements that contribute to behavioural intentions. Secondly, their diagnostic properties have been found useful for identifying how people perceive and evaluate the attributes of a brand. In terms of understanding an attitude to a particular brand, if it is possible to determine a person's beliefs and evaluations of those beliefs, the company can identify what it might do in terms of changing any of those elements or introducing new beliefs that might be relevant to their brand.

Compensatory and non-compensatory models

An important feature of the multi-attribute models discussed so far is that they are compensatory in nature. **Compensatory models** *are made up of a number of beliefs and use a scoring system to derive a final score—a low score in one belief/evaluation can be compensated by a higher score in another.* In attitude research, the beliefs are often weighted equally, implying that they have the same importance. However, we know that for some purchase decisions just one belief or evaluation of belief may be the overriding factor in behavioural intent. Consumers may use different types of **decision rules** to identify what is the best choice for them. For example, if you are choosing a new TV but you live in a small flat, while you might have many positive beliefs regarding the quality and style of alternative brands, your decision might be totally dependent on the size of the TV—this is what we call a **non-compensatory model**, i.e. *one overriding factor or attitude is dominant in the choice process.* A number of different decision rules may be used in non-compensatory models. If a customer uses the **conjunctive rule** it implies that *they will choose a brand based on minimum levels for each of any key evaluative attributes.* Any brand that meets all the cut-off points will be considered for purchase. Using the **lexicographic rule** the customer would *rank the evaluative attributes by their importance.* They would then begin by considering the attribute most important to them and pick the brand that performs best. If brands tie, the consumer looks to the next most important attribute and so on. The **elimination-by-aspects rule** *ranks evaluative aspects by importance again and establishes a minimum cut-off point for each attribute.* Ranking begins with the most important attribute; a brand that does not meet the satisfactory cut-off point is eliminated and the remaining brands are evaluated on the next most important and so on until one brand remains. Full examples of all these rules are provided in Case Study 6.

Attitudes and behaviour change

As we discussed earlier in this chapter, attitudes are learned, and are amenable to change and influence using the processes associated with consumer learning (Chapter 4). The influences on attitude formation are wide-ranging, but can relate to personal experiences, social influences, and marketing. The main opportunities for marketing to influence attitudes relate to the theoretical explanations offered for attitude formation, and building on the main approaches covered in this chapter we will now consider how attitudes may be changed.

Changing the basic motivational function

This strategy builds on Katz's motivational theory of attitudes, which comprises four functions: utilitarian, value-expressive, ego-defensive, and knowledge. This approach to attitude change involves understanding the motivational needs driving attitude formation, and ensuring that there is a match between the consumer need and the ability of the product or brand to meet this need. The launch of 'Simply M&S' food by the British retailer Marks & Spencer might be considered as satisfying utilitarian needs—offering good value for money, a simple product, at a particular quality level. The 'Simply M&S' label contrasts with the 'Your M&S' slogan, which ran across all product lines, including food, and served a more value-expressive social identity function, where cost and value were emphasized less, and the link to identity was provided through the use of the word 'your'. Both campaigns are shown in Figure 6.13.

Altering components of the multi-attribute model

Marketers need to understand attitudes not only towards their products and brands, but also towards those of their competitors. Companies engage in brand-tracking exercises examining consumer attitudes towards their brands, and from this try to establish key aspects of the brand attributes that appeal to consumers. If companies understand how consumers feel about their offerings and those of their competitors, they are in a better position to understand what it is about the product category that is important to consumers, and thus to adjust or add new attributes based on this research. Linked to

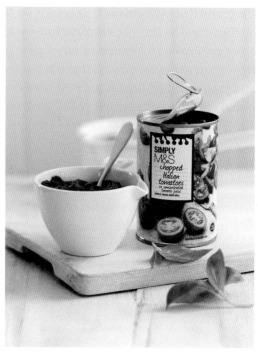

Figure 6.13 Comparing 'Simply M&S' with 'Your M&S' labels

Source: Images courtesy of Marks & Spencer.

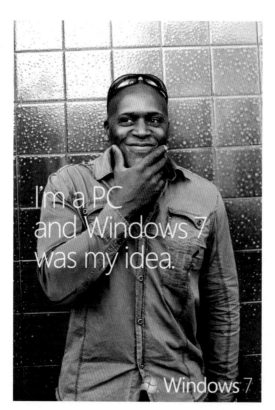

this approach, companies may attempt to change consumer beliefs about their offering. The Windows 'Life Without Walls: I'm a PC' campaign (Figure 6.14) aimed to change public perceptions of its operating system through a campaign which emphasized that Windows consumers were using the system in innovative ways that enabled them to lead unconventional lives. In so doing, the campaign helped to address the stereotypical image of a Microsoft PC user that featured in the Apple 'Get a Mac' campaign (described in Chapter 7, 'Personality, self, and motivation').

It is clear from the expectancy-value model and the theory of reasoned action/theory of planned behaviour models, that

Figure 6.14 Microsoft 'Life Without Walls: I'm a PC'

Source: Image courtesy of Microsoft.

evaluations of beliefs are also important, and this may be a useful route for influencing or adjusting consumer attitudes. Governments aiming to discourage young people from excessive alcohol consumption may seek to use social marketing efforts to influence them to change their evaluation of the consequences of drinking heavily. This approach was used in the Alcohol Advisory Council of New Zealand's 'Big Glasses' campaign which sent out powerful messages about the consequences of excessive drinking, with the strapline 'Was last night really worth it?'. By showing a range of consequences across different contexts (such as a girl on a hospital bed looking bruised and dishevelled; and a family scene where a father figure is sitting alone looking ashamed of himself), the campaign encouraged consumers to pause and think about the potential consequences of heavy drinking, and ultimately, through changing beliefs, to influence attitudes and behaviour with respect to heavy drinking.

Companies can also seek to influence competitors' ratings through an understanding of what is important to consumers, as evidenced by an advertisement for the UK airline easyJet in 2010. The company made a direct comparison with its Irish competitor Ryanair, suggesting that the actual airport that Ryanair flew to was some distance from the destination city. Clearly, easyJet was aiming to influence the way the competitor was viewed in consumer's minds, i.e. beliefs about the brand. In this case, the Advertising Standards Authority upheld a complaint by Ryanair as they did not feel that the company had misled customers as to their destination airport. This argument might suggest that such comparative advertising is a dangerous tactic to pursue, but it also produced a huge amount of newspaper coverage for both companies.

Consumer Insight 6.4 provides another example of influencing consumer attitudes.

CONSUMER INSIGHT 6.4

Attitudes to digital marketing

Companies use new technology to interact with consumers and to get their products to them in innovative ways. But how are these innovations received by consumers, and what are the issues for them? Recent research has shown that consumers are receptive to digital marketing applications when they perceive that the technology is easy to use and is useful to them, and when they trust the technology and the mobile marketing company (Zhang and Mao, 2008; Gao et al., 2013). It is also important that the marketing messages are relevant to consumers, especially when they are interacting with push-type technologies, such as SMS advertising. Varnali et al. (2012) found that SMS messages were not considered to be intrusive as long as the messages were viewed as relevant.

Recent commercial research shows that, overall, younger consumers tend to have more positive attitudes towards digital marketing, recognizing its importance to the future of media (Sharp, 2012). For companies targeting a youth audience, there is an interest in ever more sophisticated and creative uses of digital marketing in their campaigns. Another recent trend is the increased uses of QR codes to bridge the gap between offline and mobile media. For consumers, this requires a bit more effort to take a picture of the QR code, but they are likely to have increased engagement with the marketing content (Fernando, 2010).

An interesting example of the use of a range of digital marketing tools is the recent case of the German shoe brand Goertz, which has devised an interactive retail installation where people can try on shoes virtually and then make purchases. A digital billboard and Microsoft Kinect Sensors, are used to scan people's feet and reproduce them on the screen—they can then choose any model and size from Goertz's online store and see how the shoes fit in real time. The experience is integrated with social media, allowing people to share snapshots with their friends on Facebook. QR codes are also used to direct consumers to the online shop where they can buy the shoe they like and have it delivered the next day.

Questions

1. Why do you think consumers would use this interactive retail store for buying shoes?

2. Using your knowledge of consumer attitude theory, analyse and deconstruct consumer attitudes towards buying shoes online and specifically using this interactive format. Analyse consumer attitudes from two different perspectives. Which theory of attitudes is most useful?

Sources: Fernando (2010); Sharp (2012); Varnali (2012); Gao et al. (2013)

 Visit the Online Resource Centre and follow the weblink to learn more.

Elaboration likelihood model

One model that is useful for considering the mechanisms of attitude change is the elaboration likelihood model (ELM) (Petty and Cacioppo, 1986), which focuses on the ways that consumers respond to communication messages. The model is shown in Figure 6.15.

The ELM details the psychological processes by which attitudes are created and changed, providing insights into how attitudes can be formed or modified. Central to this model is the **elaboration continuum**, *which describes the amount of thought (elaboration) given to an advertising message or persuasive communication* (Petty and Briñol, 2012). Elaboration likelihood ranges from high (deep, critical engagement) to low (less engagement), and the ways in which information is processed will depend on the level of engagement. As shown in Figure 6.15, high elaboration (greater thinking and engagement) leads to central route processing, and low elaboration (less thinking) leads to peripheral route processing.

High elaboration tends to accompany highly involved consumer situations, and typically involves the consumer systematically and critically engaging with the information in the

Figure 6.15   The elaboration likelihood model

Source: Petty, R.E. and Cacioppo, J.T. (1986), *Communication and persuasion: central and peripheral routes to attitude change*, New York: Springer-Verlag; reproduced from the original source with kind permission of Springer Science+Business Media.

advertising message (O'Keefe, 2008). The highly involved consumer is likely to pay attention to the information, and then carefully evaluate new information in relation to their existing knowledge and develop an attitude based on logical reasoning. When consumers are motivated to pay attention to an advertising message, they consciously think about the ad and tend to take a logical central route to decision-making. This is known as *central route processing*, where they make greater use of information which relates to the product features in evaluating the product (Rucker and Petty, 2006). The advertisement for the Olympus PEN camera (Figure 6.16) provides a good illustration of a persuasive communication that mainly aims to encourage central route processing to elicit deep thinking and engagement about the brand. This advertisement is not only engaging and information oriented (good use of text and engaging images), but it also has a QR code which takes consumers to the online TV advertisement ('Watch the TV ad'), encouraging deeper engagement with the brand.

When elaboration likelihood is low, i.e. when people are less likely to pay attention to persuasive messages, they make less effort to evaluate new information and bring less of their own information to bear in forming their attitude to the product or service (Petty and Briñol, 2012). Here, *peripheral route processing* occurs, whereby consumers pay less attention

Figure 6.16 Olympus PEN camera advertising campaign
Source: Image courtesy of Wallop Design.

to the persuasive arguments in advertising messages but instead are influenced by the surface characteristics of the advertisement or product. The emphasis here is on the images used, the speakers (often celebrities), and the use of emotional connections between the product/brand and the consumer. The print advertisement for Swiss Pastorini Spielzeug Toystore provides a good illustration of peripheral route processing for a fairly low involvement product choice. The intriguing image shows a boy towering over a bridge and fields where toy bricks are strewn, suggesting the connection between the real world (the bridge and fields) and the child's imagination (the toy bricks). This is a simple and effective message operating at the emotional level of feeding a child's imagination and creativity.

Communications messages can draw on both central and peripheral routes to encourage deeper elaboration and engagement, as demonstrated in the award-winning print advert for Prostate Cancer Foundation (Figure 6.17). This image is definitely eye-catching and captures the viewer's attention (peripheral processing route), but then draws you in to read the small print which informs you about detection methods for prostate cancer, which are connected to the image in the advertisement ('The early detection examination for prostate cancer no longer takes place where it would be expected. A simple blood test in the crook of the arm suffices. Preferably early on. Ask your doctor and gain information on www.prostatekrebs.ch'). The textual part of the advertisement encourages deeper engagement, and hence a central processing route.

Understanding the routes to persuasion is important for marketers, since it encourages a deeper appreciation of the circumstances under which the different routes to attitude formation and change are likely to occur. Knowing the impact that levels of involvement and motivation have on the ways that consumers engage with and

Figure 6.17 Prostate Cancer Foundation

Source: Image courtesy of Jung von Matt (www.jvm.com).

process marketing cues is a useful starting point when devising content and messages for marketing strategies.

Conclusions

Attitudes are important for marketers and can act as both an obstacle to their strategies and as a way of helping to ensure that they fully understand their consumers. In this chapter, we **defined the concept of attitudes** as used in consumer marketing, emphasizing the importance of the link between attitudes and behaviour, as explored in Consumer Insight 6.1 which examined attitudes towards credit and debt. We then discussed the **various components** of attitudes, drawing on theory from a range of socio-psychological studies, in order to show the range of issues that are important to consider when trying to examine consumer attitudes. Research Insight 6.1 focused on the language used in marketing communications and how this influenced the emotional aspects of brand attitudes formed by consumers.

The **main theoretical approaches to attitudes** were presented, including the balance theory of attitudes, the functional theory of attitudes, and the multi-attribute models of attitudes. The approaches taken by academics when studying attitudes do not always neatly align with the methods used by marketing practice (as demonstrated in Consumer Insight 6.3, which described various approaches used to look at attitudes towards road safety), and yet 'consumer attitudes' are frequently examined and called upon in commercial marketing contexts. The mismatch in approach may be due to some of the issues with and limitations of the theories discussed in this chapter.

The importance of **compensatory and non-compensatory models** and how they can be used in consumer decision making was then covered, with Case Study 6 examining these decision rules in the context of buying a house.

A number of approaches to **attitude change** were also presented, and Consumer Insight 6.4 focused on Goertz shoes, exploring some of the issues in relation to shifting attitudes to become more favourable to digital interactive modes of purchasing.

In this chapter, we have drawn on a wide range of illustrative examples from both commercial and social or not-for-profit marketing to show how relevant and important attitudes are to understanding consumer behaviour, and **how marketing practice might work with and build on this theory**. Above all, understanding the components of attitudes can help marketing professionals better position and reposition their brands in the market.

Review questions

1. Define attitudes, and comment on the various components of attitudes.

2. What do you understand by the term 'hierarchy of effects'? Provide illustrations of your own from four different contexts.

3. What is balance theory, and how is it useful for marketing?

4. Explain cognitive dissonance theory, and show how marketers can use this theory to inform their activities.

5. Explain the functional theory of attitudes and illustrate with examples.

6. Describe the evolution of, and the components within, the theory of reasoned action.

7. What is meant by compensatory and non-compensatory models?

8. What are the main approaches to attitudinal change? Give illustrations drawing on each of the main theoretical approaches to attitudes.

Discussion questions

1. Choose any consumer context, and analyse a range of brand offerings within that category in terms of the functional theory of attitudes (you may wish to revisit the analysis of the tents provided in Consumer Insight 6.2).

2. Attitudes are commonly referred to and used in marketing practice, but marketing managers rarely draw on the theory of reasoned action or planned behaviour to inform their studies of consumer attitudes. Why do you think this might be the case? What evidence can you find to back this up?

3. You have been invited by your local council to develop a strategy to encourage greater use of public transport. Based on your understanding of attitude theory, what would you advise them?

4. Visit the Online Resource Centre and follow the weblink to watch a clip about outdoor patio heaters. Use your knowledge of attitude theory and measurement to work out how you would examine attitudes towards patio heaters. Approach this issue using two completely different theories. Which one is most useful/appropriate? What recommendations would you make for marketing managers trying to measure attitudes?

 Visit the Online Resource Centre to test your knowledge further and complete the Multiple Choice Questions for Chapter 6.

CASE STUDY 6

Decision rules when buying a house

In this exercise, we consider the case of a consumer buying a house, and specifically how a consumer might come to a purchase decision based on the type of decision rule they use. You must be familiar with the material in this chapter on both the compensatory and non-compensatory decision rules (conjunctive, lexicographic, elimination by aspect) in order to analyse this material.

Imagine you are buying a new family house. While there are likely to be a number of key features or attributes of the house that would be important to you, you are probably aware that your perfect house may not exist or will be too expensive or at the very least will have some drawbacks. Often in decisions like this we have to consider what is most important to us, and even make compromises in areas that are less important. We are going to look at a range of attributes and their evaluations, and consider how the different models (and rules) might lead to the development of different attitude scores and ultimately decisions.

Attributes and evaluation scores

Table 6.2 contains information comparing four potential houses in terms of attributes that you might consider to be important when making a house purchase. Taking each attribute in turn, we have come up with a hypothetical rating for each house according to the importance of that attribute. Looking at 'price', house 4 ranks best on this feature, since it is the highest score of 6. For 'location', houses 1 and 2 rate the highest (scored 6 and 5, respectively).

Attributes (B_i)	House 1	House 2	House 3	House 4
Price	4	5	3	6
Proximity to school	2	4	6	4
Size of garden	2	3	4	4
Location	6	5	2	3
Renovation required	4	3	4	1
Size of kitchen	6	5	5	4

Table 6.2   Key attributes rated for each house

In Table 6.3, we provide an evaluation of these attributes, which is the weighting for the importance of each of these attributes to the consumer. For this house buyer, 'location' and 'size of kitchen' are the most important attributes, and hence are given the highest evaluation scores (4 each), while the size of the garden is the least important feature (with a score of 1).

Attributes (B_i)	Evaluation score (E_i)
Price	3
Proximity to school	2
Size of garden	1
Location	4
Renovation required	1.5
Size of kitchen	4

Table 6.3   Evaluation scores for each attribute

Application of compensatory model

You will recall that the compensatory model is one where all the key attributes and evaluations are included. Compensation occurs because a low evaluation on one particular attribute can be compensated for by a high evaluation on another attribute.

Using this approach to determine the attitude towards each house, you need to use the following calculation:

$$\text{Attitude} = \Sigma B_i \times E_i \qquad i = 1, \ldots, n$$

where

Σ = sum total

B_i = attribute ranking for each house

E_i = numerical evaluation rating for each attribute

n = total number of attributes.

All the numerical scores required to find the attitude values are provided in Tables 6.2 and 6.3. From this information and the equation, you can calculate the attitude score for each house. Table 6.4 provides the calculations for house 1, to show this process.

Calculate the attitude scores for the other houses, and from this information work out which house would be chosen.

Attributes (B_i)	Evaluation score (E_i)	House 1	House 2	House 3	House 4
Price	3	4 × 3 = 12			
Proximity to school	2	2 × 2 = 4			
Size of garden	1	2 × 1 = 2			
Location	4	6 × 4 = 24			
Renovation required	1.5	4 × 1.5 = 6			
Size of kitchen	4	6 × 4 = 24			
Total attitude score $\Sigma B_i \times E_i$		72			

Table 6.4   Attitude calculations based on compensatory model

Application of non-compensatory models

Conjunctive decision rule

Now consider that, rather than using a compensatory rule, you use the *conjunctive decision rule*, where you choose a product or brand based on the minimum attribute score for each of any key attributes. Any brand that meets *all* the cut-off points will be considered for purchase. In our example, the cut-off point for attributes is 3 for every attribute *except* 'price', where the cut off is 4, and 'location', with a cut-off of 5 (see Table 6.6). Table 6.5 gives the calculations for house 1, to show this process.

Now, calculate the cut-offs for the other houses, and from this information work out which house would be chosen. Remember, use the key attributes provided in Table 6.2 (you do not need to use the evaluation scores this time). Is the same house chosen as when applying the compensatory model?

Lexicographic decision rule

Looking at the other non-compensatory rules, now try and apply the *lexicographic decision rule* to calculate attitudes towards the houses. Using the lexicographic rule the customer would rank the evaluative attributes by their importance, and would then choose the house (or brand or product) which performs best on the attribute most important to them. In the event of a tie between two options, the consumer looks to the next most important attribute and so on. Using Table 6.6 where attributes are ranked in importance with price most and size of kitchen least important, you can work out which house would be chosen based on the lexicographic rule.

Attributes (B_i)	Cut-off	House 1	House 2	House 3	House 4
Price	4	4 (yes)			
Proximity to school	3	2 (No)			
Size of garden	3	2 (No)			
Location	5	6 (Yes)			
Renovation required	3	4 (yes)			
Size of kitchen	3	6 (yes)			
Meets all attribute cut-offs		NO			

Table 6.5 Calculations based on non-compensatory model: conjunctive rule

Elimination-by-aspects decision rule

Finally, you can work out which house would be chosen based on the *elimination-by-aspects decision rule*, where evaluative aspects are ranked by importance and a minimum cut-off point is established for each attribute. Ranking begins with the most important and a brand that does not meet the satisfactory cut-off is eliminated; the remaining brands are evaluated on the next most important and so on until one brand remains. Using the information provided in Table 6.6 about ranking and cut-off points, calculate which house would be chosen using this approach.

Attributes (B_i)	Ranking	Cut-off points
Price	1	4
Proximity to school	2	3
Size of garden	3	3
Location	4	5
Renovation required	5	3
Size of kitchen	6	3

Table 6.6 Ranking and cut-off points

General questions

Once you have completed the exercise discuss with your classmates what differences you note. What did you notice about how different the results were and why they were different? Were there any surprising results? What recommendations for marketing do you have following this exercise?

 Visit the Online Resource Centre and follow the link to the authors' blog where you can keep up to date with the latest developments in consumer behaviour and further explore theories through additional articles and real-world examples.

References

Ajzen, I. (2005), *Attitudes, personality and behaviour*, Maidenhead: Open University Press.

Ajzen, I. (2011), 'The theory of planned behaviour: reactions and reflections', *Psychology & Health*, 26, 9, 1113–1127.

Ajzen, I. (2012), 'Theory of planned behavior', in P.A.M. Van Lange, A.W. Kruglanski, and E.T. Higgins (eds), *Handbook of Theories of Social Psychology*, Vol. 1, London: SAGE, pp 438–459.

Ajzen, I. and Driver, B.L. (1992), 'Application of the theory of planned behaviour to leisure choice', *Journal of Leisure Research*, 24, 3, 207–224.

Alexandris, K., Tsiotsou, R., and James, J. (2012), 'Testing a hierarchy of effects model of sponsorship effectiveness', *Journal of Sport Management*, 26, 5, 363–378.

Beatty, S. E. and Kahle, L. R. (1988), 'Alternative hierarchies of the attitude-behavior relationship: the impact of brand commitment and habit', *Journal of the Academy of Marketing Science*, 16, 2, 1–10.

Boldero, J. (1995), 'The prediction of household recycling of newspapers—the role of attitudes, intentions and situational factors', *Journal of Applied Psychology*, 25, 5, 440–462.

Chiou, J.S., Huang, C.Y., and Lee, H.H. (2005), 'The antecedents of music piracy attitudes and intentions', *Journal of Business Ethics*, 57, 2, 161–174.

Dalakas, V. and Levin, A.M. (2005), 'The balance theory domino: how sponsorships may elicit negative consumer attitudes', *Advances in Consumer Research*, 32, 91–97.

Devries, H. and Backbier, E. (1994), 'Self-efficacy as an important determinant of quitting among pregnant women who smoke: the phi pattern', *Preventive Medicine*, 23, 2, 27–37.

Fernando, A. (2010), 'Start talking in code', *Communication World*, 27, 1, 8–9.

Festinger, L. (1957), *A theory of cognitive dissonance*, Stanford, CA: Stanford University Press.

Fishbein, M. and Ajzen, I (1975), *Belief, attitude, intention and behavior*, Reading, MA: Addison-Wesley.

Gabler, J., Kropp, F., Silvera, D.H., and Lavack, A.M. (2004), 'The role of attitudes and self-efficacy in predicting condom use and purchase intentions', *Health Marketing Quarterly*, 21, 3, 63–78.

Gao, T.T., Rohm, A.J., Sultan, F., and Pagani, M. (2013), 'Consumers untethered: a three-market empirical study of consumers' mobile marketing acceptance', *Journal of Business Research*, 66, 12, 2536–2544.

George, B. P. and Yaoyuneyong, G. (2010), 'Impulse buying and cognitive dissonance: a study conducted among the Spring Break student shoppers', *Young Consumers*, 11, 4, 291–306.

Grewal, R., Mehta, R., and Kardes, F.R. (2004), 'The timing of repeat purchases of consumer durable goods: the role of functional bases of consumer attitudes', *Journal of Marketing Research*, 41, 1, 101–115.

Grimm, P.E. (2005), 'Ab components' impact on brand preference', *Journal of Business Research*, 58, 4, 508–517.

Han, H., Hsu, L.T.J., and Sheu, C. (2010), 'Application of the theory of planned behavior to green hotel choice: testing the effect of environmental friendly activities', *Tourism Management*, 31, 3, 325–334.

Henderson, S. and Hoque, S.F. (2010), 'The ethnicity impact on attitudes toward country of origin for products with different involvement levels', *Journal of International Consumer Marketing*, 22, 3, 271–291.

Herr, P.M. and Fazio, R.H. (1993), 'The attitude-to-behavior process: implications', in A. Mitchell (ed.), *Advertising exposure, memory and choice*, Hillsdale, NJ: Lawrence Erlbaum, pp 119–140.

Jiang, L., Hoegg, J., Dahl, D.W., and Chattopadhyay. A. (2010) 'The persuasive role of incidental similarity on attitudes and purchase intentions in a sales context', *Journal of Consumer Research*, 36, 5, 778–791.

Kang, T.S. and Ma, G. (2007) 'Recent episodes of credit card distress in Asia', *BIS Quarterly*, June, 55–68.

Kardes, F.R. (1993) 'Consumer inference: determinants, consequences and implications for advertising' in A. Mitchell (ed.), *Advertising exposure, memory and choice*, Hillsdale, NJ: Lawrence Erlbaum, pp 163–193.

Kardes. F.R. (2001) *Consumer behaviour and managerial decision making* (2nd edn), Upper Saddle River, NJ: Prentice Hall.

Katz, D. (1960), 'The functional approach to the study of attitudes,' *Public Opinion Quarterly*, 24, 163–204.

Lane, P. (2012), 'Austerity's children', *Harvard International Review, From the Blogs*, Summer, 4–5, http://hir.harvard.edu/archives/2915 (accessed 1 August 2014).

Lee, H.M., Lee, C.C., and Wu, C.C. (2011), 'Brand image strategy affects brand equity after M&A', *European Journal of Marketing*, 45, 7/8, 1091–1111.

Leonard, A. (2013), 'Arrive Alive app—a road map', presented at World Social Marketing Conference, Toronto, 21–23 April.

Lutz, R.J. (1991), *'The role of attitude theory in marketing'*, in H.H. Kassarijian and T.S. Robertson(eds), *Perspectives in Consumer Behavior* (4th edn), Glenview: IL: Scott, Foresman, pp 317–339.

Mintel (2011), *Consumer attitudes towards debt—UK*, http://oxygen.mintel.com/display/638223/# (accessed 22 May 2014).

Morojele, N.K. and Stephenson, G.M. (1992), 'The Minnesota model in the treatment of addictions: a social psychological assessment of changes in beliefs and attributions', *Journal of Community and Applied Social Psychology*, 2, 1, 25–41.

Netemeyer, R.G., Andrews, J.C., and Durvasula, S. (1993), 'A comparison of three behavioural intentions models: the case of Valentine's Day gift giving', *Advances in Consumer Research*, 20, 1, 135–141.

O'Keefe, D.J. (2008) 'The elaboration likelihood model', in W. Donsbach (ed.), *International encyclopaedia of communication*, Vol. 4, Boston, MA: Blackwell, pp 1475–1480.

O'Loughlin, D. and Szmigin, I. (2006) ' "I'll always be in debt": Irish and UK student behaviour in a credit led environment', *Journal of Consumer Marketing*, 23, 6, 335–343.

Oskamp, S. and Schultz, W. (2005), *Attitudes and opinions*, Hillsdale, NJ: Lawrence Erlbaum.

Peñaloza, L. and Barnhart, M. (2011), 'Living U.S. capitalism: the normalization of credit/debt', *Journal of Consumer Research*, 38, 4, 743–762.

Petty, R.E. and Briñol, P. (2012), 'The elaboration likelihood model', in P.A.M. Van Lange, A.W. Kruglanski, and E.T. Higgins (eds), *Handbook of Theories of Social Psychology*, Vol. 1, London: SAGE, pp 224–245.

Petty, R.E. and Cacioppo, J.T. (1986), *Communication and persuasion: central and peripheral routes to attitude change*, New York: Springer-Verlag.

Phau, I. and Teah, M. (2009), 'Devil wears (counterfeit) Prada: a study of antecedents and outcomes of attitudes towards counterfeits of luxury brands', *Journal of Consumer Marketing*, 26, 1, 15–27.

Rucker, D.D. and Petty, R.E. (2006), 'Increasing the effectiveness of communications to consumers: recommendations based on elaboration likelihood and attitude certainty perspectives', *Journal of Public Policy and Marketing*, 25, 1, 39–52.

Russell-Bennett, R., Härtel, C.E., and Worthington, S. (2013), 'Exploring a functional approach to attitudinal brand loyalty', *Australasian Marketing Journal*, 21, 1, 43–51.

Schlegl, R.P., Davernas, J.R., and Zanna, M.P. (1992), 'Problem drinking: a problem for the theory of reasoned action', *Journal of Applied Social Psychology*, 22, 5, 358–385.

Schossler, A. (1998), 'Applying the functional theory of attitudes to understanding the influence of store atmosphere on store inferences', *Journal of Consumer Psychology*, 7, 4, 345–369.

Sela, A.S., Wheeler, C., and Sarial-Abi, G. (2012), 'We are not the same as *You and I*: causal effects of minor language variations on consumers' attitudes toward brands', *Journal of Consumer Research*, 39, 3, 644–661.

Sharp, R. (2012), 'How the natives will shape the future of digital marketing', http://www.brandrepublic.com/research/1147939/how-natives-will-shape-future-digital-marketing/ (accessed 18 May 2013).

Shavitt, S. (1989), 'Operationalizing functional theories of attitude', in A.R. Pratkanis, S.J. Breckler, and A.G. Greenwald (eds), *Attitude structure and function*, Hillsdale, NJ: Lawrence Erlbaum.

Shavitt, S. (1990), 'The role of attitude objects in attitude functions', *Journal of Experimental Social Psychology*, 26, 124–148.

Shooter, A. (2010), 'Carry on glamping! That's GLAMOROUS camping…and here's how you do it with your family this summer', *Daily Mail*, 8 July, www.dailymail.co.uk/femail/article-1292925/Carry-glamping-Thats-GLAMOROUS-camping-heres-family-summer.html (accessed 19 May 2012).

Szmigin, I. and O'Loughlin, D. (2010), 'Students and the consumer credit market: towards a social policy agenda', *Social Policy and Administration*, 44, 5, 598–619.

Think! (2013), 'Think! Annual Survey TNS-BMRB Report', https://www.gov.uk/government/publications/think-research (accessed 12 March 2013).

Varnali, K. (2012), 'SMS advertising: how message relevance linked to the attitude toward the brand?', *Journal of Marketing Communications*, 19 July, 1–13.

Weaver, C. (2013), 'Reuse, recycle, retent: the aftermath of festivals…what really happens?', http://eventsmanagementnews.com/reuse-recycle-retent-the-aftermath-of-festivals-what-really-happens/ (accessed 8 July 2013).

Woodside, A.G. and Chebat, J.C. (2001), 'Updating Heider's balance theory in consumer behavior: a Jewish couple buys a German car and additional buying-consuming transformation stories', *Psychology & Marketing*, 18, 5, 475–495.

Young, T. (2010) 'How on earth did sleeping in a tent become a high-status indicator?', *Daily Telegraph*, 27 July, http://blogs.telegraph.co.uk/news/tobyyoung/100048656/how-on-earth-did-sleeping-in-a-tent-become-a-high-status-indicator/ (accessed 18 October 2012).

Zhang, J. and Mao, E. (2008), 'Understanding the acceptance of mobile SMS advertising among young Chinese consumers', *Psychology & Marketing*, 25, 8, 787–805.

7

PERSONALITY, SELF, AND MOTIVATION

Introduction

Consumption is central to how we define and think about ourselves. The brands we use, and how we use them, can act as signifiers to others about who we are and how we see ourselves. While just a few generations ago people were mainly defined in terms of their occupation, now consumption is central to many people's sense of identity. How we see ourselves influences how we perceive products, brands, and marketing stimuli. When thinking about personality and self, it is important to recognize how personality impacts on our motivations in life. The first part of this chapter examines a range of perspectives on personality, self, and identity, and then considers different ways to conceptualize notions of self to aid understanding of consumer behaviour. We consider how these concepts apply in marketing, and finally examine the key concepts of motivation theory and the methods used for researching motivation.

LEARNING OBJECTIVES

Having read this chapter, you will be able to:

1. Explain the **main perspectives on personality and self**, focusing on psychological and socially oriented perspectives.

2. Understand the *multiplicity of self*, and define the different aspects of self.

3. Recognize the links between *personality and self in marketing practice*, including the mechanisms of symbolic consumption, the association between personality, values and lifestyles, and the main approaches to psychographics.

4. Define the key concepts of *motivation*, including a consideration of needs and wants, motivational conflict, and Maslow's Hierarchy of Needs.

5. Provide an overview of the main approaches to *researching motivation*.

Different perspectives on personality and self

In pre-modern society, an individual's identity was determined by just a few factors, such as power and status in society, as well as occupation. For those born into nobility there was a code for behaving, speaking, and dressing; the same could be said for someone born a servant (Kellner, 1992). Roles and expectations were established and static. Things are very different in today's world. There is more freedom, and identity is no longer entirely dependent on a person's place of birth or social status. A number of variables now come into play, with brands and consumption playing a key role as distinguishers of identity.

Many marketing practitioners recognize that how people make decisions around consumption are influenced by their perceptions of themselves and how they would like to be seen. Underpinning the Apple Mac campaign of 2007 (I'm a Mac, I'm a PC) was the strong identification consumers had with the Apple brand, and the distance they felt between themselves and Microsoft products. If you haven't seen the advertisement, you can watch it on YouTube. This campaign is an example of self-image and brand image alignment (or congruence). The idea was for the viewer to associate with the qualities of the more desirable person (the Mac). The campaign also emphasized the *avoidance* of brands (the PC) for which there was an incongruence between self-image and brand image. Both brands were effectively anthropomorphized—they became people.

Marketers aim to ensure that brand image is consistent with the consumer's self-image. However, this is a complex arena, where identifications with brands are often based on how consumers see themselves now and in their past, and how they imagine and aspire to be in the future. When thinking about personality and identity, there are a number of key perspectives that are relevant to consumer research, falling into more individualist psychological perspectives in comparison with socially oriented perspectives. Both approaches are relevant to understanding the role of personality and identity in relation to consumer behaviour, and each can provide useful insights into identity and consumption. How personality and identity are defined will vary depending on the theoretical approach taken, and in the course of this chapter that will become clearer.

Psychological perspectives on personality

The psychological perspective defines **personality** *as the combination of the characteristic patterns of thoughts, feelings, and behaviours that make up an individual's distinctive character* (Kassarjian, 1971). Personality stems from within the individual and remains fairly stable throughout life. This perspective includes psychoanalytic theories and trait theories.

Psychoanalytic theories

Psychoanalytic theory holds that there are inner forces outside our awareness or consciousness that are directing our behaviour. The founder of psychoanalytic theory was Austrian neurologist Sigmund Freud (1923). While his theories have been the source of much debate, his work has had a major effect on motivation and personality research in marketing and consumer behaviour.

According to Freud, the mind is divided into the conscious and the unconscious. The conscious includes everything we are aware of (including memory since it can be retrieved easily and brought into our awareness), while the unconscious refers to the feelings, thoughts, urges, and memories that lie outside our conscious awareness. It is the unconscious that drives all human motivation and, according to Freud, personality is made up of the interplay between three elements—the id, the superego, and the ego.

- The **id** *corresponds to primary needs, focused on immediate gratification, directing a person's psychic energy towards pleasurable acts without regard to the consequences.* This represents the biological forces driving humans.

- The **superego** *reflects the rules, values, and norms imposed by society, and serves as the person's conscience working to prevent the id from seeking selfish gratification.* This represents a form of societal force.

- The **ego** *represents the interests of the individual, ensuring the necessary arbitration between the demands of id and constraints of superego.* This is a form of human consciousness.

While Freudian analysis may provide some interesting insights into the underlying forces at play, such analyses are rarely applied in marketing and consumer behaviour research. However, Freudian psychology informed the methods and tools of in-depth interviewing to delve into consumer motives, often located below the level of conscious awareness, which have had a lasting impact. A psychoanalytical approach to understanding why someone engages in a high risk sport (e.g. paragliding), would ask questions that aim to dig deep into the underlying motives of behaviour, and how the individual balances the pleasures of participating in consumption activities against societal norms and expectations around risky behaviours.

Some theorists developed their own version of psychoanalytic theory, such as Swiss psychiatrist Carl Jung in his work on archetypes. Jung's concept of the **archetype** relates to *the stable characters that capture basic ideas, feelings, fantasies, and visions that seem constant and frequently* *re-emerge across different times and places.* These characters, such as the hero, the outlaw, and the sage, are recognizable across cultures, and appear over and over again in films, songs, novels, and popular culture (Woodside, 2010). According to Jung, these archetypes prompt humans to react to the world in a selective fashion, and help explain why people can hold certain myths and images across cultures. The success of the Oprah Winfrey brand draws on the 'sage' archetype, with Oprah viewed as an individual with wisdom and experience of life who is looked to for guidance. The Oprah brand is hugely successful not only in the USA, but also in other countries, such as Saudi Arabia, where she is viewed as an inspiration for many women who feel trapped (Zoepf, 2008). Angela Merkel in Germany and Aung San Suu Kyi in Burma occupy similar roles of the sage archetype in their own countries and across the world. In marketing and advertising, archetypes are used as a way of making connections with consumers, to develop more compelling brand stories for communicating with consumers. An example of the use of archetypes in practice is found in the work of the market research company Millward Brown (see Practitioner Insight 7). We spoke to the group account director Graham Staplehurst to get an understanding of how they put Jung's theory of archetypes into practice.

PRACTITIONER INSIGHT **7**

Graham Staplehurst, Group Account Director, Brand & Communications, Millward Brown, on using measures of brand personality in marketing

Since brands communicate with consumers, and consumers listen, they develop a relationship with those brands based both on *what* the brand says and *how* it says it. The tone of voice adopted by a brand is part of the set of mental associations—the knowledge, memories, and feelings that create the brand's representation in the consumer's mind. Market researchers have found that consumers can describe the impact of this tone of voice—an otherwise intangible quality—through measures of brand personality.

Brand personality is particularly suited to investigation using sensitive and careful techniques. Its earliest use was in qualitative research, when moderators started using projective techniques to help consumers articulate their feelings about brands and provide depth to their descriptions of brands. A typical projective technique would be to ask the respondent to imagine that the brand 'comes to life' and you meet them at a party. Answers to probing questions about how the brand looks, how it is dressed, who it is with, what it drinks, what car it drives, and so on can help identify the nature of the brand as it exists in the consumer's mind, and help marketers understand what and how they should communicate in future. Most brands play only very superficial roles in consumers' lives, and it is only through constant repetition that advertising imprints upon the brain.

Therefore a measure used to determine the existence and nature of any brand personality must act upon simple and slender perceptions, particularly when qualitative research is not available. The CharacterZ approach developed by Millward Brown is based on archetypes. Archetypes are easily recognized personality types or characters commonly found in story-telling across all cultures. The archetypes are based on universal metaphors rooted in psychological and sociological analysis of stories and dreams, for example by Jung and Campbell. An archetype can be quickly sketched and recognized. It is this instant recognition that makes it such an appropriate model to apply to the measurement and description of brands. CharacterZ uses a system of ten archetypes: Joker, Seductress, Rebel, Hero, Wise, King, Mother, Friend, Maiden, and Dreamer (see Figure 7.1). For example, the King archetype expresses a personality with power, leadership, strength, importance, and charisma.

Figure 7.1 Millward Brown brand personality archetypes
Source: Image courtesy of Millward Brown.

Respondents are asked to choose at least four words to describe a brand from a list of 24, which were selected through extensive qualitative and quantitative piloting. The relative levels of association of each word with a brand determine its strongest traits and these in turn determine its archetype. Many of the strongest brands historically are Wise—they are trustworthy expert partners for the consumer, skilled at the product or service they provide. IKEA is a Dreamer, providing creative ideas and preaching its unique ideals. Red Bull is a true Hero, brave and adventurous, while Irn Bru is a Rebel, defiantly different. Brands can change. IBM, which had been seen as a Wise brand, has recently evolved into a King, its growing business success reflected in more confident assertive messages.

CharacterZ was used to help Burger King understand its brand better in the UK. Analysis showed that Burger King and its key competitors McDonald's and KFC were all seen at the simplest level as Joker archetypes. None are 'serious' food, their communications often feature toys, children, and families, and their consumer experience is one of fun. CharacterZ was able to probe below this level and identify some revealing differences about the brands. McDonald's was more of a 'straight' Joker—playful, fun, and friendly. Its personality related to humorous communications, including the clown Ronald McDonald. KFC in contrast had aspects of the Mother about it—generous sharing qualities typified by the 'bucket' sharing offers for families. Burger King had two distinct aspects not present in either of these competitors—the Rebel and the Seductress. Burger King communications had used a stronger American tone and its King advertising character was designed to have a more edgy appeal to younger adults. The Seductress was the more desirable nature of the food itself—perceived to be more authentically sourced and cooked. These insights helped the advertising agency create a new campaign with a tone of voice absolutely suited to the brand, ensuring that the message resonated with the target group and built on existing brand memories.

While psychoanalytic theories laid the groundwork for much research in the area of personality, trait-based theories have been used extensively in studies into the effect of personality on consumption.

The trait-based view of personality

According to the **trait-based approach**, *personality is regarded the sum of a set of traits or qualities about a person, and these can be used to predict or explain consumption behaviour.* This view works on the basis that traits can be assessed and evaluated. The trait-based approach assumes a *quantitative approach* to personality, which is viewed as comprising of a set of traits. According to the trait-based view of the self, an individual's personality is composed of definite predispositional attributes (traits) and they can be described in terms of a particular combination of these traits. It is assumed that traits are common to many individuals, but the exact combination reflects the personality of the individual. Traits are relatively stable and exert fairly universal effects on behaviour regardless of environment.

Some consumer researchers distinguish between single-trait and multi-trait approaches to personality. In the **single-trait approach** the *focus is on one trait that is particularly relevant to a situation.* This approach does not suggest that other traits are irrelevant, but rather focuses on how one trait alone can impact on consumption. For example, a social marketing researcher may be trying to establish the links between smoking and personality. Here they may look at the effect of the personality trait 'anxiety' on smoking. Table 7.1 provides details of some of the key traits that have been used in consumer behaviour and marketing.

Trait	Definition and key study
Materialism	The degree to which a consumer is overly concerned with physical objects and material goods (Richins and Dawson, 1992)
Consumer innovativeness	Generalized tendency toward innovations applicable across product classes (Goldsmith and Hofacker, 1991)
Consumer ethnocentrism	The idea that ethnocentric individuals view their group (or culture) as superior to others, and therefore that in consumer terms there is a strong preference towards buying domestic rather than foreign-produced goods (Shimp and Sharma, 1987).
Frugality	'The degree to which consumers are both restrained in acquiring and in resourcefully using economic goods and services to achieve longer-term goals' (Lastovicka et al., 1999: 88).
Consumers' spending self-control	'The ability to monitor and regulate one's spending-related thoughts and decisions in accordance with self-imposed standards' (Haws et al., 2012: 697).

Table 7.1   Examples of single-trait theories

The **multi-trait approach** is *concerned with a number of personality traits taken together and how they combine to effect consumption.* So, returning to the smoking example, the researcher would be interested in the effect of anxiety in combination with other personality variables (such as shyness, conscientiousness, openness) on smoking. For both these approaches, prediction of behaviour is important to researchers, and multi-trait approaches have generally been used to enable prediction of behaviour since they offer a more detailed and complex picture of the relationships between personality and behaviour.

Many psychologists agree that there are five main personality types which constitute a stable and robust structure of personality. The 'Big-Five' factor structure, developed by McCrae and Costa (1990), proposes the main traits of extroversion, agreeableness, conscientiousness, neuroticism (or emotional stability), and openness (sometimes referred to as intellect). This model has been widely applied in social psychology and consumer research, such as studies of customer service performance and personality (Harris and Fleming, 2005) and smoking and personality (Adams and Nettle, 2009). A recent Swedish study (Axelsson et al., 2011) showed how personality impacted on how likely people are to take medicine. People who score highly on the neuroticism scale (likely to be fairly anxious) were found to be less likely to stick to their doctor's prescribed medication. On the other hand, people who are influenced by conscientiousness tend to be very careful and methodical in following the doctor's prescription. A study such as this can inform social marketing campaigns, recognizing that different consumer communication and education may be needed depending on personality type.

According to recent research from the psychographic agency Mindset Media, there is a link between common personality traits and consumers' TV viewing choices (Bulik, 2010). For instance, viewers of *Dancing with the Stars*, the American reality dance show, tend to be traditional in their personalities, unlike viewers of the cartoon comedy *Family Guy*, who are more likely to be 'rule-breakers' or rebels. Knowing this link between personality traits and viewing preferences might help marketers to match brands to audiences in the commercial breaks for these shows. Brands associated with risk-taking (e.g. Harley-Davidson) are more likely to connect with viewers of *Family Guy* than safe brands (e.g. Volvo), which may appeal to the traditionalists watching *Dancing with the Stars*. This approach has some appeal for marketing on the basis that consumers may choose products that fit their personality or that boost their personality in areas where they feel weak.

Brand personality and traits

Once we understand the nature of people's personality we can apply such theories to brands. Some brands even use characters to represent the brand. The Energizer Bunny appears to signify an upbeat, happy, and indefatigable personality, in line with the idea of the long-lasting batteries. The French Michelin Man has existed since 1898, and not only does he visually capture the tyre brand but he represents friendliness, gentleness, and above all safety. Aaker (1997) devised a **brand personality scale** which *describes the underlying brand dimensions of sincerity, excitement, competence, sophistication, and ruggedness.* These dimensions can apply to both retail and product brands (Möller and Herm, 2013). There is some overlap with human personality traits (e.g. sincerity–agreeableness, excitement–extroversion, competence–conscientiousness), although the brand personality dimensions of sophistication and ruggedness do not obviously map onto the human personality dimensions. Aaker explains that these dimensions tap into those things that consumers desire but do not necessarily have. High-end brands (such as Cartier and Chanel) encourage consumer aspirations around class and glamour (see Research Insight 7.1), while more rugged brands (such as G-SHOCK or Marlboro) emphasize ideals of strength and masculinity (Figure 7.2).

RESEARCH INSIGHT 7.1

Park, J.K. and John, D.R. (2010), 'Got to get you into my life: do brand personalities rub off on consumers?', *Journal of Consumer Research*, 37, 4, 655–669.

In this study, Park and John show how we might actually change our personality to match the 'personality' of a brand. Looking at the brands Victoria's Secret (lingerie) and MIT (Massachusetts Institute of Technology), the authors found that some consumers take on the brand personality when using the brand. Consumers who carried a Victoria's Secret shopping bag felt more glamorous, good-looking, and feminine when doing so than those who carried a plain shopping bag. Similarly, those using the MIT-embossed pen felt more intelligent, hardworking, and leader-like than those using a plain pen.

 Visit the Online Resource Centre to read the abstract and access the full paper.

Figure 7.2 Advertisements for Cartier and G-SHOCK watches illustrating the sophistication of the former contrasted with the ruggedness of the latter. The idea is that consumers choose brands with distinctive personalities that represent aspects of the self which they wish to express or enhance.

Source: Images courtesy of Cartier and Casio.

A social perspective on identity and self

Sociology has made distinctive contributions to the study of personality, mainly in terms of broadening understanding of personality and identity to encompass the influence of social forms and social arrangements, and their impact on how people view themselves (Heine, 1971). One major theoretical perspective on this is symbolic interactionism.

Symbolic interactionism

A more socially oriented view of identity follows the **symbolic interactionist perspective** which *sees the self as emerging out of the mind, which develops out of social interaction, and patterned social interaction as forming the basis of social structure* (Mead, 1913).The mind is the thinking part of the self (Stets and Burke, 2003: 130), but this perspective stresses the *importance of other people* in forming how we think about ourself, particularly in relation to the ways that meanings are defined by social consensus (Ligas and Cotte, 1999). We tend to behave in ways that match how we imagine other people will react towards us. Consumers want to fit in with other people's expectations, but how does our understanding of ourselves fit with others' understanding of who we are? The **self-concept** refers to *the sum total of our thoughts, feelings, and imaginations as to who we are* (Rosenberg, 1979). This approach is based on the idea that people define themselves by how others judge them and how they believe that others judge them. While the self-concept represents the content and structure of the beliefs that a person holds about him/herself, and how these are evaluated, these self-assessments can be distorted. People are particularly conscious of their physical appearance. The leisure, beauty, dieting, fashion, and clothing markets thrive on people wanting to send out the 'correct' messages to others as to the way they look in order to stimulate preferable judgements about themselves.

The Adidas 2011/2012 'All Originals' advertisement builds on this idea by showing how you can show your individuality by wearing Adidas, but still connect with other people more widely. The 2012 TV advertising showed people from around the world, representing their home, their passions, and their joy of life, connected by tagline 'Adidas is All In'—the word 'All' connecting them to a bigger whole. The 2011 print campaign featured shots from gigs of four of the UK's top music artists (Plan B, Example, DJ Caspa, and The Enemy), all wearing Adidas clothing, with the tagline 'All Originals', emphasizing the message that everyone can be individual when wearing this brand.

Multiplicity of self

Recent consumer research has moved away from the idea that identity is unitary, fixed, and stable and instead views it as dynamic (Shankar et al., 2009), comprising different aspects of the self associated with the different roles and situations we occupy in our lives. Some roles are more active than others, depending on the situations we are in and how central to our sense of self they are. Your role as a student or employee may be more active and central than your role as a cyclist, which may only emerge at weekends or on vacation. Table 7.2 gives a set of the key definitions used in the literature to refer to the multiplicity of self:

Research Insight 7.2 provides an example of how the negative self has been used in the domain of brand avoidance and anti-consumption.

The importance of situation and context is captured in the idea of the **malleable self** (Aaker, 1999), which acknowledges *that people will act differently according to the situation, influenced by social roles, cues, and the need for self-presentation.* Take, for example, the act of 'going out for lunch' (Figure 7.3). This can be analysed in terms of the selves that are activated in different consumption contexts—each of these selves may reflect a form of social self, but they differ in relation to situational contexts. For a young mother, a visit to Pizza Hut for a child's birthday party reflects her actual self, enacting her 'mother identity', whereas a trip to Zizzi, a more upmarket chain of restaurants, may be reflective of a social self, the type of place she would perhaps go with a group of girlfriends, where good food is the priority but is still within a fairly reasonable price range. Finally River Café, an upmarket restaurant

Aspect of self	Definition	Summary statement
Actual self	The core sense of self which is enduring and stable across situations	'The person that I believe I actually am'
Ideal self	The self we aspire to be like, often as important to what we do in the consumption arena as our sense of our actual self	'The person that I would ideally like to be'
Social self	Sometimes referred to as the 'looking glass self', this is how consumers believe that they are seen by significant others	'The person that I believe others see me as being'
Ideal social self	How consumers would like to be seen by significant others	'The person that I would ideally like others to see me as being'
Situational self	Recognizes the self-concept as a dynamic entity, where different aspects of self are activated depending on different situations the consumer is in, and who they are interacting with in that situation.	'The person I believe I am in particular situations'
Extended self	The idea that our possessions and belongings form such a close connection to us and our past that they come to represent us in some way; the extended self can explain a variety of consumer and human behaviour, and helps us to understand the connections that we feel towards items and brands that are special to us in some way (Belk, 1988)	'The way that my personal possessions are linked to me'
Possible selves	'Personalized representations of one's self in future states' (Cross and Markus, 1991: 230): these can be both positive selves (how they might aspire to be) and negative selves (the imagined futures they wish to avoid), and this motivates behaviour both towards and away from certain consumption practices	'The person I would like to become, could become, may be afraid of becoming'
Negative selves	Refers to the person you are not, and do not want to become. Banister and Hogg (2001) have examined the negative self in depth, arguing that the 'push' of the negative self (away from what you do not want to be) is more powerful than the 'pull' of the ideal self (towards what you want to be); they also distinguish between the undesired self ('so not me') and the avoidance self ('just not me')	'The person I am not, or do not want to be'

Table 7.2   Aspects of self

RESEARCH INSIGHT 7.2

Lee, M., Motion, J., and Conroy, D. (2009), 'Anti-consumption and brand avoidance', *Journal of Business Research*, 62, 2, 169–180.

This study asks why some consumers avoid certain brands and products. Is it because they see a different 'self' in themselves to the 'self' of the brand or product? Or are they driven to avoid certain brands for other reasons? What are the reasons behind consumers avoiding certain brands?

 Visit the Online Resource Centre to read the abstract and access the full paper.

Figure 7.3 'Going out for lunch'—different selves in different consumption contexts

Source: Zizzi images courtesy of Zizzi, Pizza Hut image: © Radu Bercan/Shutterstock.com.

in Hammersmith, London where Jamie Oliver worked before becoming a TV chef, may be reflective of a more ideal social self, a possible self, and one perhaps not easily available to her, but nonetheless desirable in terms of status attached to the venue.

The idea of multiple selves is important for marketers, especially in terms of understanding consumers' aspirations and ideals of who they *want* to be, as much as their ideas of who they *do not want* to be. The ideal self is relevant to consumption in terms of people buying brands they believe will help them achieve their ideal self. The perfume industry benefits from consumer's aspirations to access designer lifestyles. While designer clothes are beyond the financial means of many consumers, perfumes represent a more affordable way of experiencing the designer brand. Similarly, negative possible selves can act as incentives for future behaviour, representing the idea of ourselves that we reject or wish to avoid. Consumer Insight 7.1 provides an example of the negative self in action, and how the company Abercrombie & Fitch responded to the wearing of their brand by celebrities they did not want associated with the brand.

The symbolic interactionist perspective implies that each of us has many selves, and different products are required to support these selves. Valued objects such as cars, homes, and even attachments to sports teams or national monuments are used to define the self

CONSUMER INSIGHT 7.1

Abercrombie & Fitch and Mike 'The Situation' Sorrentino

While many companies enjoy celebrity endorsement of their brands, in some instances this backfires, as was the case when Abercrombie & Fitch's clothes were worn by the cast members of the US MTV show *Jersey Shore*. The company put out a press release announcing that it had offered compensation to Mike 'The Situation' Sorrentino, one of the show's stars, to get him to stop wearing the company's products on the show. The retailer was concerned that associating the brand with the raucous behaviour of Sorrentino would damage its image. In this context, Mike Sorrentino did not fit the company's customer aspirations, and was indeed a version of a negative or avoidance self for those consumers. However, the *Jersey Shore* star alleged that the offer never happened, and that the company concocted the press release as a publicity stunt to create brand awareness.

Questions

1. Can you find any examples of consumers using brands in ways deemed unacceptable to the brand owner?

2. What would you recommend the company to do in this situation?

Sources: Hughes (2011); http://www.abercrombie.co.uk/anf/investors/investorrelations.html

 Visit the Online Resource Centre to learn more.

when these are incorporated into the extended self. Consumer identity can be developed through the products and brands consumed to help us construct the 'story of ourself' (Shankar et al., 2009). If you imagine getting ready for a night out, you might use special shower gel (e.g. Gucci Envy rather than Nivea shower gel), you might mix high street fashion with some designer items (e.g. wearing TopShop skinny jeans with a D&G top), you might wear your 'going out' Diesel shoes, and straighten your hair with GHD straighteners. Together, these items help you to get ready but also enable you to become the 'you' you want to display to the world. These examples show how brands can become a central part of how we see ourselves, and are so wrapped up in our identity that they are almost part of us.

This fits with Belk's extended self (see Table 7.2), where people consume goods and brands as part of an overall 'identity project'. They are engaged in constructing an identity and using consumption as a means to do so (Ahuvia, 2005). This is what is meant when we talk about the narrative approach to identity, and this fits with the consumer culture theory (CCT) perspective of the consumer (Arnould and Thompson, 2005: 871). According to this perspective, identity is a major and continuous preoccupation of individuals, residing in a personal narrative—the story that consumers construct and play out as they make life choices and decisions (see also Consumer Insight 7.2).

CONSUMER INSIGHT 7.2

Virtual displays of self

With the rise of social media, and in particular apps such as Pinterest and Instagram, a key trend has been towards consumers showing off their consumption activities through the pictures they post (Chahal, 2013). Whether it be pinning on Pinterest of products you own or aspire to own, or postings on Instagram and Facebook of cakes baked and craft items produced, consumers are increasingly using photography to communicate quickly with others. In doing this, they are also producing and reproducing something of themselves in these formats, and thus these postings are a form of identity display and expression. The idea of consumers using brands to communicate various aspects of themselves has emerged in recent research (Hollenbeck and Kaikati, 2013). However, a form of impression management is taking place (Goffman, 1959), with consumers navigating clashes between their actual and ideal selves through their posts (including hiding consumption of certain brands).

Another interesting aspect of this is how viewers use social media during commercial breaks. For years, marketers have known that consumers do many things during the commercial break (making a cup of tea, flicking through channels, etc.), but recently viewers have turned to 'second screen conversations' on Twitter and other social media during ad breaks, checking out what other viewers are saying about the show. Brands are trying to find ways to connect to viewers during commercial breaks, and inserting messages through Twitter appears to be one way of doing so. A viewer watching the US TV show *Glee* may turn to her smartphone during the break to see what other Gleeks (Glee fans) are tweeting about the show. While she may not be watching the TV when a Pepsi ad appears on the screen, she might see when Pepsi's Twitter account sends a related message with the hashtag #Glee. In this way the brand is connecting with the viewer at the heart of the conversation taking place on Twitter. The success or failure of this approach will relate to how convincing the presence of the brand is and the fit between the brand and viewer personality.

Questions

1. Spend some time on the various social media you use (e.g. Facebook, Pinterest) and consider the extent to which you and your friends construct your identities through your consumption activities. Do you do this? Do you see any patterns in who does/does not use consumption in this way?

2. How might this awareness of consumers' use of social media as a way of expressing their brand use and identity be useful for marketers?

Sources: Goffman (1959); Lawler (2011); Hollenbeck and Kaikati (2012); Chahal (2013).

 Visit the Online Resource Centre and follow the weblinks to learn more about the importance of social media to marketers.

People are able to find identities to associate with through many websites and blogs, often linked to fashion. The blog of Italian fashionista Nicoletta Reggio shows her daily life with links to specific brands she buys (Figure 7.4) but all set within an enviable Italian identity (www.scentofobsession.com). Other sites, such as Donnamoderna.com, show a wider range of identity roles including health and food, but also look for real-life models to be represented on their pages, thus making a link to people's real lives.

Reebok used a narrative approach to self as the basis for its 2005 campaign, which took

Figure 7.4 An image of Nicoletta Reggio from the 'My Closet' section on her blog

Source: Image printed with kind permission from Nicoletta Reggio from www.scentofobsession.com.

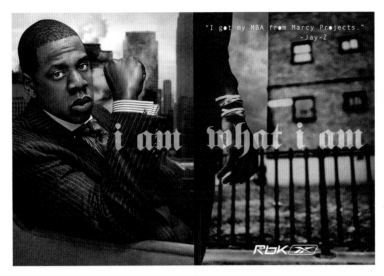

Figure 7.5 Reebok 'I am what I am' campaign *Source*: Image supplied by The Advertising Archives.

the form of various celebrities from the worlds of sport and music talking about their 'journey' through life (Figure 7.5). This campaign was based on the idea of narratives of self, that we can be who we want to be, and the stories we tell about ourselves emphasize and draw on aspects of what makes us who we are: for Manchester United's Ryan Giggs, the narrative was around national identity; for Jay Z, it was about coming from an impoverished and tough housing estate (Marcy Estate) and the lessons learned on the streets ('I got my MBA from Marcy Projects'). The campaign tagline was 'I am what I am', with the brand proposition being that Reebok plays a role in supporting you to be who you are.

Personality and self in marketing practice

Symbolic consumption

Symbolic consumption is the *tendency of consumers to rely and focus on the meanings attached to goods, beyond their physical properties,* and provides an important means by which consumers define themselves. Consumer goods are capable of serving consumers in this way because of the symbolic meaning that is embedded in the offering. Contained within the symbolism are the messages that an individual may wish to transmit to socially significant referents. However, these messages will only be successfully communicated if the symbolism in the offering is socially recognized. Therefore a shared understanding of symbolic meaning facilitates the capabilities of products as communicators of self-identity, and depends upon the individual's knowledge of the codes involved.

Thus consumption symbols provide an important way of communicating with others in the world. Yet not all product categories serve as identical means of communication.

Products such as cars, clothes, homes, and leisure activities are very visible and are used by many to make a statement. A consumer wearing a Rolex watch may be communicating success, wealth, and status to others. We attach meanings to symbols in our constructed realities (Elliott and Wattanasuwan, 1998), and the ability to recognize such meanings is at the heart of marketing culture. These symbols are associated with self-definition, which leads to symbolic consumption. Grubb and Grathwohl (1967) proposed a framework mapping out the relationships between symbolic meaning of products/brands, consumers' self-concepts, and related audiences (see Figure 7.6).

Figure 7.6 Symbolic meaning of goods, consumer self-concepts, and related audience

Source: Grubb and Grathwohl (1967: 25). Printed with permission from The American Marketing Association.

A person (individual A) uses a product or brand (Symbol X) to achieve self-enhancement. This process relies on the socially agreed meanings attached to the product/brand (Symbol X) being transferred to and associated with the consumer. Critical to this process is the role of other significant people or audiences, and their attributions of meanings and associations with the brand. The person uses the brand in the hope that significant others notice and that the positive associations the person has with the brand are also held by significant others (friends, peers, family), and that, by extension, significant others transfer that meaning to the person. To illustrate, consider a nine-year-old boy who is a keen footballer and rates Cristiano Ronaldo as a player (Figure 7.7).

Figure 7.7 Application of the process of the symbolic meaning of goods attached to brands

Source: Image of Ronaldo's football boots is taken from the Summer 2013 CR7 collection, courtesy of Nike Inc.

Ronaldo wears Nike football boots, and so the child wears the boots in order to enhance his sense of footballing self ('I can play football like Ronaldo'), but also to enhance his status and standing in the eyes of other children who interpret the wearing of these boots as a signal of high football performance. By wearing the football boots he transfers and communicates the socially agreed meaning of the boots to himself and in the process achieves self-enhancement in both a private and public sense—the child is transferring the socially attributed meanings of the product or brand to himself.

It is obviously important that the brand and its associations are congruent with the image consumers have or want to have of themselves. According to Ericksen and Sirgy (1992: 409), '**self-congruity** *refers to the extent to which a product image matches a consumer's self-image, and ideal congruity refers to the extent to which the product image matches the ideal self-image*'. The theory of 'image congruency' recognizes that consumers select products, brands, and retailers that correspond to their self-concept (Sirgy, 1982).

Linking identity and values

Increasingly, companies are recognizing the importance of understanding consumer values and making clear links to the identity of the organization. Asda in the UK has talked recently about its efforts to ensure that the brand personality ('cheeky and honest', emphasizing everyday low prices) resonates with consumer values across all its marketing communications (Baker, 2013).

Values are *our desired end-states in life and preferred paths to achieving them, constituting the purposes and goals for which we believe human life should be lived*. Rokeach's list of values (Table 7.3) proposes that there are two main sets of values guiding our behaviour: terminal values, linked to the goals we seek in life, and instrumental values, representing the means, paths, and behavioural standards by which we pursue these goals (Rokeach, 1974).

An example of the use of values in consumer marketing can be found on Martin Lewis's money saving website moneysavingexpert.com. This site is a forum for consumer tips across many consumer domains and sectors, encouraging consumer-to-consumer interactions and communications. A key theme underpinning the resource is one of consumer empowerment, celebrating frugal and shrewd consumer behaviour. In terms of values, this taps into primary terminal values around security and a sense of accomplishment, but also speaks to secondary instrumental values, especially demonstrating self-control and imagination to make savings based on information gleaned from the website. Examples of companies that adapt and respond to consumer trends and values include John Lewis and Innocent, both companies that build their core brand values in line with consumer needs and values (Cuddeford-Jones, 2013).

Psychographics

It is intuitively plausible that personality differences are related to the types of product/brand purchased, and the assumption of links between character and consumption is evident in many perfume and car advertisements. However, reviews of research (Kassarjian and Sheffet,

Terminal values	Instrumental values
A comfortable life	Imaginative
A sense of accomplishment	Ambition
A world at peace	Broad-mindedness
A world of beauty	Capable
An exciting life	Cheerful
Equality	Clean
Family security	Courageous
Freedom	Forgiving
Happiness	Independent
Inner harmony	Intellect
Mature love	Obedience
National security	Helpful
Pleasure	Polite
Salvation	Logic
Self-respect	Love
Social recognition	Honest
True friendship	Responsibility
Wisdom	Self-control

Table 7.3 Rokeach's list of values

1981; Foxall and Goldsmith, 1988) show that findings linking personality to brand and product are equivocal, with empirical results generally not repeated. At best, personality measures explained about 10 per cent of variation in consumer behaviour. Lifestyle segmentation, referred to as **psychographics** is based on *building a picture (sometimes literally) based on demographics, alongside activities, interests, and opinion variables.* Lifestyle and personality are different but closely related; personality refers to internal characteristics, and lifestyle refers to external manifestations of how a person lives. The advantage of lifestyle segmentation such as psychographics is that it can be done at a very general level (i.e. a population), at a product level (i.e. by typifying people by their attitude to healthy food or fashion), or by brand (i.e. the different types of purchasers of a particular car brand).

VALS™ framework: a lifestyle segmentation tool

VALS™ (acronym for Values and Lifestyle) is *a trade-marked segmentation system, based on US adult consumers, where subjects are grouped into eight segments using the VALS™ questionnaire,* *which consists of questions around primary motivations and resources* (Strategic Business Insights, 2013). Originally created in the 1970s, this revised framework has been developed to improve its ability to explain and predict consumer behaviour. The VALS™ framework arranges people into groups based on the two main dimensions of primary motivation (ideals, achievement, and self-expression) and resources (income, education, self-confidence, intelligence, leadership skills, and energy).

The central idea is that these traits, in combination with consumer demographics, can explain and predict behaviour. The VALS™ system has eight main segments, based on the subject's resource base (generally categorized as high or low) and the extent to which they are motivated in life by their ideals, by achievement, or towards self-expression. Figure 7.8 provides an overview of the segments, linking each to some key forms of consumer behaviour such as internet usage, purchase of organic foods, and exercise habits.

The value of a system such as this lies with its ability to explore in depth consumers who are similar demographically, but display different consumption habits and behaviour. Innovators and Achievers may be similar in terms of age and work patterns, but Achievers are much less likely to buy organic foods than Innovators, which may be explained in terms of their goals and drives.

Demographic and Behavior Snapshots Highlight the Vibrancy of Using VALS™

Primary Motivation		Ideals		Achievement		Self-Expression		
	Innovators	Thinkers	Believers	Achievers	Strivers	Experiencers	Makers	Survivors
Psychological Descriptors	Sophisticated In Charge Curious	Informed Reflective Content	Literal Loyal Moralistic	Goal Oriented Brand Conscious Conventional	Contemporary Imitative Style Conscious	Trend Seeking Impulsive Variety Seeking	Responsible Practical Self-Sufficient	Nostalgic Constrained Cautious
	Percent of Innovators	Percent of Thinkers	Percent of Believers	Percent of Achievers	Percent of Strivers	Percent of Experiencers	Percent of Makers	Percent of Survivors
Total US	10	11.3	16.5	14	11.5	12.7	11.8	12
Median age	47	58	53	41	30	24	48	69
Married	62	73	62	70	32	20	64	45
Work full time	67	52	40	65	45	42	56	13
Own a tablet or e-reader	36	25	9	19	6	14	7	4
Contributed to environmental organization in past year	20	11	2	4	2	3	4	1
Own a dog	39	40	43	52	44	41	57	38
Bought new or different auto-insurance policy in past year	17	16	16	18	15	16	22	14
Buy food labeled natural or organic	24	15	8	10	4	9	8	4
Used hair color at home to cover gray	7	11	15	9	2	1	9	11
Media trusted the most:								
TV	11	25	43	26	38	24	33	54
Radio	15	11	7	7	7	6	12	11
Internet	42	30	21	35	32	48	26	4
Magazines	10	9	7	7	4	3	7	5
Newspapers	23	25	23	24	18	19	22	24

Source: VALS™/GfK MRI Spring 2012

Figure 7.8   Overview of VALS™ segments

Source: Strategic Business Insights (SBI); www.strategicbusinessinsights.com/VALS

Not all companies use the VALS™ system, but many take a similar approach for segmenting consumers based on lifestyle characteristics. Recent research sponsored by Coca-Cola Retailing Research Council (2012) considers different *social media personas* (or identities) and how these might impact on different types of shopping behaviours — Creators, Professionals, Bonders, and Sharers (see Figure 7.9). By categorizing consumers into a typology based on their personality and other variables, marketers can anticipate the brand categories that these consumers are most engaged with. For example, members of the category Shar-

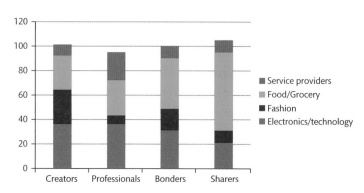

Figure 7.9   Personality segments and brand categories

Source: Data taken from Coca-Cola Retailing Research Council (2012).

ers are primarily concerned with building strong relationships, and their main use of social media is to spread the word about what is going on in their lives, to keep up to date with others, and to post information that they hope will be of value. In terms of brand engagement, they are mainly interested in food and grocery brands, possibly reflecting their primary concerns with sharing information of everyday benefit to other people.

Psychographics provide very useful information about consumers, drawing on multiple data sources which results in a detailed categorization of the drivers of consumers' behaviour (Beckland, 2011). This focused categorization allows for more targeted marketing.

Motivation

Motivation *describes the processes that cause people to behave in a particular way.* Why does one person choose chocolate for a snack while another chooses an apple? Why do some people spend time following the latest celebrities while others investigate their family genealogy? What needs and wants are being fulfilled for people by different products and activities? Marketers want to know the answers to such questions in order to communicate appropriately in terms of what needs and wants their products will fulfil. In addition, marketers need to understand their consumers' motivations to develop new products and services that people do not even know that they need or want yet. Imagine a life without your mobile phone, laptop, or tablet. These are all relatively new inventions, the benefits of which were unknown to people fifty years ago, yet are now considered to be necessities by many. People's motivations for purchase may be purely functional in some cases, such as buying a sandwich when we are hungry; the motivations for purchase of many other products can be more complex. Many people consider more than just their need for telling the time when buying a watch. Wearing an Omega watch says something about the wearer, their social status, and the distinction that the watch conveys.

Needs and wants

A person is motivated when a need is aroused that they wish to satisfy. This motivation relates to a state of tension that exists when there is a difference between our actual and our desired state. The motivation is the drive to remove this tension. You may be thirsty, which leads to a tension in how you actually feel (thirsty) compared with how you would like to feel (satiated). You will be motivated to drink a glass of water, or a cup of tea, or a bottle of beer to satisfy your thirst. **Needs** are *the result of the difference between the actual and desired states*, such as not having any music to play at the gym, while **wants** are *specific manifestations of the motives and are linked to a specific goal object* such as having an iPod so you can listen to music at the gym.

How consumers choose to reduce the tension arising from the difference between their actual and ideal state is an important question for marketers, since companies want consumers to use their products and brands to close this gap. Companies engage with consumers in order to show them how their brand offers benefits that can satisfy some need, whether functional or symbolic. Consumer choices are driven by a range of factors. If we consider the example of buying a car, it is clear that cars can serve different needs. For a recent graduate starting their first job some distance away from her home, with no public transport connections, a car serves primarily a utilitarian need, as she needs to travel to and from work. In contrast, cars can also satisfy more hedonic needs, as demonstrated by the tag line 'the ultimate driving machine' used by BMW to indicate the pleasure to be gained from driving a high performance car.

When consumers are compelled to act in a way that removes or reduces the tension between their actual and desired state, there has to be a goal which the person is trying to achieve or accomplish. Such goals may be generic, product-specific, or brand-specific (Jansson-Boyd, 2010).

At work in the morning you may feel like a cup of coffee and do not mind making yourself a cup of instant coffee. This would be a generic goal. Alternatively, you might want to have a latte or cappuccino and decide to go to a café; this would be product-specific. However, you might also have a preference for a specific brand, such as Starbucks or Caffe Nero, and with such a brand-specific goal you might be motivated to walk for five minutes to your favourite supplier. This process may be influenced by a range of factors, including personality, perception, learning, and attitudes. In Consumer Insight 7.3, we describe the motivations around the development and adoption of innovative products, using the Sony Walkman as an example.

Cultural differences determine how needs are translated into consumption. While we all need food and shelter, the houses we live in and the food we eat differ hugely across

CONSUMER INSIGHT 7.3

Adopting innovations and motivations

In 1979, the Sony Walkman, a portable cassette player with headphones, was introduced to the market. Sony's co-founder, Masaru Ibuka, did a lot of business travelling and enjoyed listening to music but did not want to lug a portable player around with him. He commissioned one of his colleagues to produce a compact portable music player. Reportedly, he then took the resulting product to Akio Morita, the Chairman of Sony, suggesting the marketing possibilities of a stereo player that you could listen to while doing other things (Haire, 2009).

What Sony did not envisage was how popular the Walkman would be. Predicted to sell about 5,000 units a month, in fact it sold 50,000 in its first two months (Haire, 2009). The Walkman was providing a solution to an unmet need. It could be taken anywhere and it did not annoy others as it had headphones but no external speaker (see Figure 7.10). People were also becoming more aware of their health, with gym membership and activities such as aerobics becoming more popular in the 1980s. The Walkman made working out entertaining and more enjoyable. Others have

Figure 7.10   Sony Walkman in use
Source: © iStock.com/ArtMarie.

suggested a wider cultural significance to the Sony Walkman which we may recognize as continuing today with products such as smartphones and tablets. In particular, du Gay et al. (1997) highlighted the ways that people did things with the Walkman that provided meaning to their cultural life and made it distinctive—for example, the practice of being able to do two things at once.

Questions

1. Think of two innovations that have been introduced in your lifetime and which you use. List the needs that these innovations satisfy.

2. Have they allowed you to do things in a different way and if so how? How have they become part of your cultural life? How would your life be different without them?

Sources: du Gay et al. (1997); Haire (2009)

  Visit the Online Resource Centre and follow the weblinks to learn more.

continents. Sometimes this is determined by the geography and climate, but it is also influenced by our cultural preferences. So, while a British student might choose a sandwich for lunch, a Singaporean might have have dumplings or satay. Needs can also be classified as biogenic or psychogenic. **Biogenic needs** *or innate needs enable us to survive* and include the need for food, water, and shelter, while **psychogenic needs** *are socially acquired needs and include the need for status, affiliation, self-esteem, and prestige.* While we all need food to survive, it may also answer psychogenic needs. What you choose to eat may be affected by cultural differences, making you averse to eating certain foods (e.g. in Thailand crickets are commonly eaten, but this is unpalatable to US and UK consumers), while eating in particular restaurants may be answering your need for status or prestige. Restaurants in major cities are often booked up months in advance, but this seems to make such places even more desirable to consumers who want to eat and be seen in such places. Research Insight 7.3 expands some of the issues around functional and hedonic needs.

RESEARCH INSIGHT 7.3

Lowe, M.R. and Butryn, M.L. (2007), 'Hedonic hunger: a new dimension of appetite?', *Psychology & Behavior*, 91, 432–439.

In this paper the authors argue that, for many people, food consumption is increasingly driven by pleasure rather than the functional need for calories. The environment is such that for most people there is a constant availability of highly palatable food '… some individuals experience frequent thoughts, feelings and urges about food in the absence of any short- or long-term energy deficit'. The authors refer to this as 'hedonic hunger', reflecting the psychogenic qualities that food has today.

 Visit the Online Resource Centre to read the abstract and access the full paper.

Motivational conflict

People are driven to avoid negative results as well as to achieve positive goals. In some cases this may result in a conflict—for example, you want to lose weight but you are tempted to indulge in choosing a dessert. Research also shows that people differ in their motivational profiles (Kramer and Yoon, 2007). Some people have a greater inclination to approach specific goals and therefore will have a greater sensitivity to positive outcomes, while others may be more sensitive to avoiding negative outcomes. There are three main motivational conflicts that marketers need to be aware of and which they can use to their advantage.

    Approach–avoidance conflict *is when a desired goal also has negative consequences.* If you buy (approach) designer label clothes you may not want (avoid) people knowing how much you paid for them. Perhaps the most obvious approach–avoidance conflict concerns food,

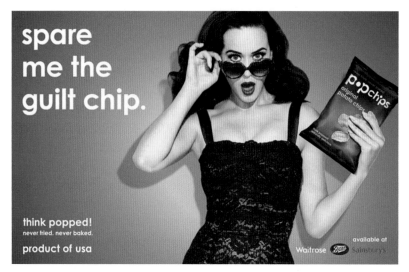

Figure 7.11 Pop chips advertisement with US star Katy Perry

Source: Image courtesy of Pop Chips (www.popchips.com).

and particularly food high in calories such as chocolate or cakes. Often marketers will position their products in a way that recognizes their indulgence but also suggests that the consumer deserves it. A classic line which was used to advertise dairy cream cakes was 'Naughty … but Nice', thus recognizing a consumer's potential approach–avoidance conflict with a highly calorific but enjoyable food. However, today, manufacturers are looking to make traditionally indulgent products such as potato crisps with fewer calories, often aiming them directly at those concerned about their weight and ostentatiously promoting their guilt-free status as in the example of Pop Chips (Figure 7.11) which have less than 100 calories per serving.

As almost all consumer behaviour is about choosing among alternatives, most of us experience what is termed approach–approach conflict on a regular basis. **Approach–approach conflict** *is when you have to choose between two or more equally attractive alternatives.* If you imagine being in a restaurant choosing a main course, there may be two or three dishes that you would like. In making the final choice you probably experience some approach–approach conflict as you would really like to taste them all, but you try to ensure that you make a choice you will be happy with, and not feel any dissatisfaction about—a form of cognitive dissonance (see Chapter 6). Some restaurants deal with this approach–approach conflict by providing tasting menus where you can have a selection of small dishes.

The final motivational conflict is known as avoidance–avoidance conflict. In **avoidance–avoidance conflict** *the choices available all have some apparent negative consequence.* Finance is an area of potential avoidance–avoidance conflict as consumers often do not see the benefit of an insurance plan or savings scheme, may be concerned about the risk associated with stocks and shares, and so have to be persuaded of the benefits of financial products. An advertisement for the US Bank of Mauston Christmas Saving Club has the tagline 'The Bank of Mauston makes saving for Christmas worth the wait with its Christmas Club account'. The campaign attempts to resolve two potential avoidance goals—saving (for Christmas) throughout the year set against the other possibility which is dealing with all Christmas costs in one go or, worse, getting into debt for Christmas.

Maslow's Hierarchy of Needs

Maslow's hierarchy of needs (Figure 7.12) is one of the most frequently quoted theories of motivation (Maslow, 1954). It is important for many reasons, not least because it differentiated between intrinsic and extrinsic needs and emphasized the importance of intrinsic needs for human development. An **intrinsic need** is *an internal motivation* that comes from within the person, such as the need for food, water, and sex, but it can also be emotional such as the need for love and friendship. On the other hand, an **extrinsic need** will *require some return or goal from the external environment*, such as a reward in the form of money or prestige. Con-

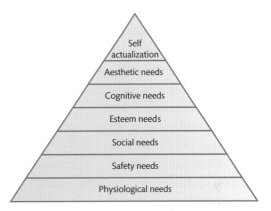

Figure 7.12   Diagrammatic representation of Maslow's hierarchy of needs

sider how people are motivated to play computer games; some may enjoy just playing on their own or with friends (intrinsic motivation), while others may prefer to go on gaming sites that offer financial rewards (extrinsic motivation). Prior to Maslow, researchers had emphasized biological needs in relation to human motivation, but Maslow introduced the idea of people having deficiency needs and growth needs. In Maslow's theory one has to achieve each level of deficiency need (physiological, safety, social, and esteem needs) before moving to the next level. According to Maslow's hierarchy, if you did not feel safe it would be difficult to move to the level of looking for social relations and affiliation with others, and similarly if these social needs had not been met, looking for recognition and esteem would be difficult. Once these deficiency needs were met the individual could move to growth needs. Originally Maslow only included self-actualization as a growth need, but later this was reclassified to include cognitive (the need to understand and explore) and aesthetic (the need for beauty and order) below self-actualization (the realization of one's potential), which in turn is below self-transcendence where the fulfilment goes beyond the self to help others realize their potential (Maslow, 1971).

There are many criticisms of Maslow's theory. First, this is theory that is abstract, not based on any empirical, experimental, or clinical data. Secondly, Maslow believed that a person has to satisfy each level before moving to the next; it would not be possible to move to the social needs before the physiological needs were satisfied, which would suggest that

poor people could not have meaningful relationships. Culturally, there are many differences in what motivates people—people can starve or give up their lives for a cause, which
would suggest that they can reach a level of self-actualization or transcendence by negating
some of the lower levels of the hierarchy. Finally, times change, and different needs may
take on differential importance. In many countries people are aware of the dangers of ter-
rorism, and that bombs may be planted on public transport or in other places. We have to
take these factors into account as we function in our lives, but it does not mean that we feel
completely safe while we carry out our daily activities. Indeed, safety is a need that seems
to pervade much of what we do. We want to be safe on the roads; we want to be sure that
the food we eat and the medicines we take are safe. Volvo have used the need for safety to
market their cars for years, recognizing that people will feel more secure in a brand of car
which advertises its safety record. Their recent campaign, shown in Figure 7.13, emphasizes their Whiplash Protection System (WHPS) which reduces the likelihood of whiplash
damage in an accident.

It is clear to see how marketing recognizes the deficiency needs; even if most people in
the western world have food and shelter, they may still be enticed by advertisements that
offer additional qualities (e.g. nutritional value) or amounts (two for the price of one) and
security such as in gated communities. In Research Insight 7.4, we describe work looking
at the how the hierarchy of needs applies in consumer lives.

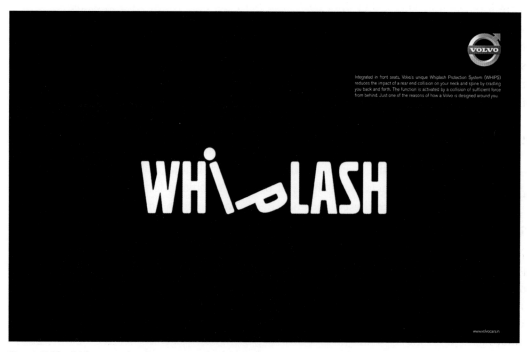

Figure 7.13   Volvo car advertisement emphasizing safety

Source: Image courtesy of Volvo Cars (www.volvocars.com).

RESEARCH INSIGHT 7.4

Csikszentmihalyi, M. (2000), 'The cost and benefits of consuming', *Journal of Consumer Research*, 27, 267–272

In this paper Csikszentmihalyi analyses how the levels of Maslow's hierarchy of needs may be played out in people's lives, detailing how products may fulfil various needs.

Goods that fulfil esteem needs are symbolic in nature, even though they often serve other motives as well. For instance, one's car could be used to drive to work, and thus satisfy survival needs; it could also have been purchased because it is safe and reliable. But if we pay extra for status attributes, the car will then become a symbol indicating our superiority and social worth.

 Visit the Online Resource Centre to read the abstract and access the full paper.

Motivation research

Motivation research became popular in the 1950s. It developed from Ernest Dichter's work with companies, which stressed the psychological and emotional content of consumption choices (see Chapter 1), and from Freudian theories that emphasized unconscious motives. An important aspect of the Freudian approach is to identify hidden and often suppressed motives which people are unable to express in a straightforward survey or interview. Marketers were interested in identifying the symbolic role that products played in people's lives but were difficult to express. As discussed already, motivation research tried to understand the true motives for consumers' choice or rejection of a brand or product, i.e. what that product symbolized for them. Motivation research comes in many forms, such as projective techniques, role play, word associations, and even clay modelling. Consumer Insight 7.4 provides information about one such technique, the thematic apperception test (TAT).

Commentators such as Vance Packard (1957) criticized motivation research because they thought it had the potential to manipulate consumers (see Chapter 1). Some

CONSUMER INSIGHT 7.4

The thematic apperception test

The thematic apperception test was developed by the clinical psychologists Christiana Morgan and Henry Murray in the 1930s (Morgan and Murray, 1935). It consisted of a series of often ambiguous pictures which participants were asked to talk about. It has been used primarily for clinical research, in particular personality disorders, but it has also been widely used in personality research and marketing contexts (Rook and Levy, 1983). In Rook and Levy's study, which showed men and women in various grooming rituals including applying makeup and blow-drying hair, participants were asked to write stories about and around these pictures. The stories revealed issues that participants had with social norms around grooming rituals, and some complex motives and fantasies. The authors concluded:

> So far these various grooming tales show that the consumption of bathroom furnishings, hair dryers, soaps, makeup, shampoos, colognes, shavers, underwear, and so on, affords complex ways of expressing one's sexual and social striving. The products are not merely aids to cleanliness and sensory pleasure; they are means to coping systematically with the demands for growing up in particular ways in American society.
>
> (Rook and Levy, 1983: 333)

Studies such as these help marketers and especially creatives in advertising agencies understand and identify appropriate ways to communicate their brands in line with how they are perceived by their customers.

Figure 7.14   An example of a thematic apperception test

Source: Ueda, T. (2012), 'Creating value with sales promotion strategies that avoid price discounting', in G.E. Smith (ed.), *Visionary pricing: reflections and advances in honor of Dan Nimer (Advances in Business Marketing and Purchasing,* Vol.19), Emerald Group Publishing, Bingley, pp 213–256.

Questions

1. Look at the picture in Figure 7.14. Discuss with a colleague what you think might have just happened and what might happen next.

2. What products and brands might these people be using? What products and brands might they not use?

Sources: Morgan and Murray (1935); Rook and Levy (1983).

 Visit the Online Resource Centre and follow the weblinks to learn more about the use of thematic apperception tests and see more examples of them.

psychoanalysts criticized motivation research for misapplying their techniques in a business situation. Another problem with motivation research is that the results depend on the researcher's interpretation, and different researchers may produce different results. It also requires an understanding of often very complex data in which the researcher needs to be carefully trained (Donoghue, 2000). Participants themselves may also feel uncomfortable about being asked to engage in role-playing exercises (Steinman, 2008).

However, it is important to recognize that, despite these arguments, motivation research still has value since it has the potential to be a rich source of data regarding consumers' beliefs and motivations which might not be reached using traditional survey methods. In particular, participants are unlikely to be aware of the purpose of the exercise, and so are unaware of what their responses might mean and therefore are less likely to give the answer that they think the interviewer is looking for. Motivation research also offers a further dimension to other research methods. It provides additional information about consumers' behaviour and decision-making, and often hypotheses developed from such research are further verified using other techniques (Steinman, 2008). These insights into motivations are useful for marketers as they reveal the deep-rooted reasons driving behaviour and thus enable companies to form deeper connections with consumers through their brand communications.

Conclusions

This chapter focused on the central role that personality and identity play in consumer behaviour, and also made connections to motivation theory. While there are many different *perspectives on personality and self*, in this chapter we discussed the main approaches in terms of definitions of self, the extent to which the internal or external aspects of self are emphasized, and the primary functions of the self-concept in each approach. Practitioner Insight 7 described how psychoanalytic theory has been used by Millward Brown in the development of CharacterZ, a system of ten archetypes which they have used in their commercial work for global brands including Burger King.

When explaining the *multiplicity of self*, we defined the many aspects of self, including actual, ideal, and social selves, as well as extended, situational, possible, and negative selves. The concept of negative self featured in Research Insight 7.2, which raised questions about consumer reasons for brand avoidance, and how this linked to aspects of self. Consumer Insight 7.2 focused on multiple self in virtual spaces, and how consumers use social media as a way of expressing self-identity.

Relating *personality to marketing practice*, it is important to appreciate that an individual's personality represents a set of characteristics that can be used to describe consumer segments. This has been the backdrop to the sections about the way that the concepts of personality and identity apply in marketing contexts. We explained in detail one approach to segmentation using personality and identity variables, namely the VALS™ psychographics and lifestyle scheme.

The final part of this chapter considered *motivation* and the role it plays in our choices of products and brands. Consumer Insight 7.3 explored some of the issues around motivations for adoption of innovative products, looking at the history of the Sony Walkman. Finally, we explored some of the techniques involved in *motivation research* and how they might be used in marketing.

Review questions

1. Explain how the id, ego, and superego contribute to personality.

2. Define the different aspects of self, and provide an example of each from your own experience.

3. What is symbolic consumption? Why is this useful for marketers?

4. Describe the congruency concept.

5. Discuss the advantages and disadvantages of psychographics in consumer behaviour.

6. Why is it important to understand consumer motivation when thinking about personality?

Discussion questions

1. Visit the Online Resource Centre and follow the link to the website http:// www.teefury.com/ How can this brand/product best be understood in terms of personality and identity theory?

2. Why is an appreciation of negative symbolic consumption relevant for marketers? Finding your own examples, discuss what steps an organization or company might take to minimize the effects of negative symbolic consumption.

3. Search the internet to find your own examples of companies using personality and lifestyle approaches to segmenting consumers. Compare these approaches with the VALS™ system, and comment on the similarities and differences.

4. Consider the different levels of Maslow's hierarchy of needs. What products and services might be used to satisfy each level?

 Visit the Online Resource Centre to test your knowledge further and complete the Multiple Choice Questions for Chapter 7.

CASE STUDY 7

Using profiles to understand the Indian consumer

Examining lifestyles alongside demographics has been one way that business has used to get closer to understanding the lives and in some cases the personality and motivation of consumers around the world. This case examines some of the lifestyle issues relevant to Indian consumers.

In 10–15 years, the Indian economy could be as big as China's is today. India's one billion people (and counting) are getting richer but, unlike China's, India's population will remain relatively young for many years to come. India is culturally diverse with 1,500 dialects and many different faiths, ethnicities, customs, foods, and dress styles. India is also varied geographically, with some richer more literate areas around Mumbai and Bangalore contrasted with poorer, less well educated states found in the east of the country. This may be a problem for Indian development; in the state of Bihar, 67 per cent of women are illiterate, and while overall growth in India is impressive, about 400 million Indians are still living on less than $1.25 a day.

The western idea of self is about the individual and their personality, but the Indian self has a stronger social identity with the individual often subsumed by the social in a need to conform. This need to conform may in turn drive behaviour, although there is some evidence that the individual self is becoming more important under western influence. Prasad Narsimhan, Virgin Mobile's chief marketing officer, notes that the most important aspect of young Indians is that they like to network. They see networking as creating possibilities, and brands need to identify how to help them. This thinking has led to presenting the young in advertisements as very different from their parents' generation. The internet provider Bharti Airtel has used the idea of impatience in their advertising for Airtel Broadband. Their advertisements show a group of young people impatient to get on with their lives, download data, find new trends, and communicate with friends. This campaign, with the tagline 'Impatience is the New Life: Live it with Airtel Broadband', is aimed at attracting consumers aged under 25.

When thinking about the Indian's consumer's lifestyle one must consider a range of factors (family status, extended family, community and caste, peer group, and personal ability as well as personality). Many young Indians will undertake peer group benchmarking based on 'people like me' from similar geography and education. In India children do not leave home early, and so family status has a strong influence on how they see themselves. But the younger generation may be doing better financially than their elders, which may create particular tensions. A student from a top business school may be earning a salary way beyond what his father earns. When young Indians reach a goal in their career they are likely to celebrate with aspirational products such as premium car brands or expensive watches. Although similar to the aspirations of young successful people in other contexts, the symbolism attached has a resonance deeply connected to their family history. Being Indian is said to be an amalgamation of personality traits, ethnicities, and the melting pot aspect of living in India.

The McKinsey Global Institute (2007) identified five economic classes based primarily on disposable income (Table 7.4). These classes help companies understand their consumers, and they offer a sketch of a typical consumer for each. These descriptions provide a glimpse of the range of lifestyles of Indians today.

Economic class and description	Consumer sketch
Deprived—This is the poorest group, typically unskilled or low-skilled workers. They may well struggle to find employment throughout the year, settling for seasonal or part time employment.	Mangu (43) and his wife Basanti (35) live and work in a poor rural district in central India. They have five children and Mangu's mother lives with them. They do not have a regular income and life is a struggle. They rely on government-subsidized food and health care. Mangu is wondering whether to move to the city like many he knows have done. While he might find construction work and Basanti might work as a maid, they would have to live in a crowded slum with few amenities. They want their children to get a basic education as a means of getting out of poverty.
Aspirers—These are usually small-scale shopkeepers, farmers, or low-skilled industrial or service workers. Although they are not deprived, they still struggle and spend almost half their income on basic necessities.	Ramnath (43) graduated from high school and is an electrician. His wife Lakshmi is at home bringing up their three children and looking after her in-laws. They have some additional income from a small grocery shop run by Ramnath's father. They own an LPG stove, a small TV, and an iron, and use an electric rod for heating water. Most of their household articles are second-hand.
Seekers—These are varied in terms of employment, age, and attitudes. They range from young college graduates to traditional white-collar employees, mid-level government officials, and medium-scale traders and business people.	Suresh (35) is a commerce graduate who works as an accountant in a private company and his wife is a nursery teacher. They spend almost half their income on food and rent for their two-bedroom apartment. Educating their children is a priority, and they spend a large amount of their budget on sending their two children to private school. They live comfortably with a second-hard car, a colour TV, a music system, a mobile phone, a refrigerator, and some jewellery. Suresh is ambitious and aspires to luxuries and to own his own flat.
Strivers—People in this band and upwards are considered successful in Indian society. They work as business people in cities, professionals, senior government officials, and richer farmers in villages. They have stable sources of income and a reasonable wealth base.	Yash (32) and Radha (30) are college graduates from prosperous families. Yash works in a multinational bank and Radha is juggling a job as a marketing manager and a weekend course in interior design. They have bought a two-bedroom flat. They are brand conscious, with a Honda car and a Sony TV, air conditioners, and a washing machine. They holiday annually in India or neighbouring countries.
Global Indians—These are senior executives, large business owners, and top tier professionals. Recently, there are also increasingly upwardly mobile graduates who are commanding premium salaries from international companies and therefore may be young. They are global in their tastes and enjoy a high standard of living.	Rahul (40) is vice-president of a large IT company. He gained his MBA from the Indian Institute of Management. His wife is a senior executive in a leading ad agency. They have bought a four-bedroom apartment. They have a flat-screen TV and a Bose audio system alongside many other impressive lifestyle products. They have a full-time cook, maid, and chauffeur. They have two cars and regularly travel abroad to Europe and the USA.

Table 7.4   McKinsey's five Indian economic classes

Beyond these lifestyles based on economic differences, others have developed additional profiles of Indian consumers. These include the following

1. **Young and restless**—young people in all income segments who are influencing their parents' spending or spending their own money. Some have part- or full-time jobs which gives them scope for spending money without the responsibility of a family. The young and affluent among them will be eating out, going to movies, and clubbing. Dress is modern and they are looking for new fashions at affordable prices. Some work in IT or call centre type jobs; they are college-educated city dwellers, often working odd hours, and they want to be able to shop when they are off duty. Some will be married (both working) with children and will be looking to improve their lifestyles through appropriate services.

2. **The bold and the beautiful**—they have money or are getting it and want to show it. This group includes yeppies (young entrepreneurial professionals) and yippies (young international professionals). Truly self-made, they enjoy premium weekend getaways and travel outside India regularly, and their focus is on their career. The raffles (rural affluent farm folk) treat farming as a business.

3. **The golden folks in high spirits**—although India is a young nation, there are plenty of old people too. These are the wealthy retired. Typically, older Indians have remained close to their children, but that may change in the future as the lifestyles of the young themselves change.

It is difficult to make generalizations about how Indians respond to western brands. It appears they do not currently have the same preference for foreign brands that Chinese consumers have. Coca-Cola bought the leading Indian Cola, Thums Up, and wanted to kill the brand and let Coke take over, but local managers recognized that Indians preferred Thums Up, so it remained on the shelves next to Coke. Some believe that the social nature of identity in the country has led to greater assimilative and accommodative tendencies in terms of acceptable brands. This may have led to the adoption of multinational brands as Indian. Such brands include Lifebuoy, Dettol, Philips, Colgate, Cadbury's, Bata, and more recently Hyundai, Nokia, McDonald's, and Samsung. For example, Colgate is a brand which has long been part of the Indian household, despite the presence of many domestic brands such as Promise, Vicco, and Dabur and other multinationals such as Pepsodent. Above all, Colgate is not seen as a foreign brand and it cannot be outperformed on functionality. Brands such as this appear to receive a high degree of loyalty across the country, while a brand like Kellogg's had a tough time because Indians were loath to give up their calorie-rich breakfasts. Other premium brands have to compete in a more difficult market. While Nike, Adidas, and Reebok all have some loyal buyers, if a discount is offered they appear to become interchangeable. Why? Because from the Indian consumer's point of view they all have enough image value, and they prefer a premium brand at a bargain price rather than just sticking to one premium brand.

Questions

1. Consider the lifestyles presented above and think of products/brands that might appeal to the different profiles.

2. If the social self is important in Indian culture, what impact might this have on an individual's consumer behaviour? How might a marketing organization capitalize on the idea of the social self?

3. If you were marketing sport goods, how might you differentiate your brand to different segments of Indian consumers?

Sources: McKinsey Global Institute (2007); Prasad (2010); Subramanyeswar (2010); WARC News (2010); Dutta (nd).

 Visit the Online Resource Centre and follow the link to the authors' blog where you can keep up to date with the latest developments in consumer behaviour and further explore theories through additional articles and real-world examples.

References

Aaker, J.L. (1997), 'Dimensions of brand personality', *Journal of Market Research*, 34, 3, 347–356.

Aaker, J.L. (1999), 'The malleable self: the role of self-expression in persuasion', *Journal of Marketing Research*, 36, 1, 45–57.

Adams, J. and Nettle, D. (2009), 'Time perspective, personality and smoking, body mass, and physical activity: an empirical study', *British Journal of Health Psychology*, 14, 1, 83–105.

Ahuvia, A.C. (2005), 'Beyond the extended self: loved objects and consumers' identity narratives', *Journal of Consumer Research*, 32, 1, 171–184.

Arnould, E.J. and Thompson, C.J. (2005), 'Consumer culture theory (CCT): twenty years of research', *Journal of Consumer Research*, 31, 4, 868–882.

Axelsson, M., Brink, E, Lundgren, J., and Lötvall, J. (2011), 'The influence of personality traits on reported adherence to medication in individuals with chronic disease: an epidemiological study in West Sweden', *PLOS ONE*, 6, 3, e18241.

Baker, R. (2013), 'Cutting through the price clutter', *Marketing Week*, 27 June, http://www.marketingweek.co.uk/analysis/essential-reads/asda-creating-brand-personality/4007059.article (accessed 8 April 2014).

Banister, E.N. and Hogg, M.K. (2001), 'Mapping the negative self: from "so not me" … to "just not me" ', *Advances in Consumer Research*, 28, 1, 242–248.

Beckland, J. (2011), 'The end of demographics: how marketers are going deeper with personal data', *Mashable*, 30 June, http://mashable.com/2011/06/30/psychographics-marketing/ (accessed 8 April 2013).

Belk, R.W. (1988), 'Possessions and the extended self', *Journal of Consumer Research*, 15, 2, 139–168.

Bulik, B.S (2010), 'You Are What You Watch, Market Data Suggest', *Advertising Age*, 1 November, http://adage.com/article/news/research-links-personality-traits-tv-viewing-habits/146779/ (accessed 9 July 2012).

Chahal, M. (2013), 'Social media: this is what my stuff says about me', *Marketing Week* 11 April http://www.marketingweek.co.uk/trends/social-media-this-is-what-my-stuff-says-about-me/4006169.article (accessed 8 April 2014).

Coca-Cola Retailing Research Council (2012), 'Untangling the social web: insights for users, brands and retailers. Part 3: Social networking personas: a look at consumer and shopper mind-sets', http://www.gs1.ch/docs/default-source/prozesse-dokus/ccrrc-untangling-the-social-web_part4.pdf?sfvrsn=2 (accessed 1 August 2014).

Cross, S. and Markus, H. (1991), 'Possible selves across the life span', *Human Development*, 34, 4, 230–255.

Csikszentmihalyi, M. (2000), 'The costs and benefits of consuming', *Journal of Consumer Research*, 27, 2, 267–272.

Cuddeford-Jones, M. (2013), 'Designed for lives of customers', *Marketing Week*, 11 July, http://www.marketingweek.co.uk/analysis/marketing-tactics/design/designed-for-lives-of-customers/4007234.article (accessed 8 April 2014).

Donoghue, S. (2000), 'Projective techniques in consumer research', *Journal of Family Ecology and Consumer Sciences*, 28, 47–53.

du Gay, P., Hall, S., James, L., Mackay, H., and Negus, K. (1997), *Doing cultural studies: the story of the Sony Walkman*, London: SAGE.

Dutta, D. (nd), 'Indian consumers', http://thirdeyesight.in/articles/Indian_consumer_A_do-it-yourself_kit.pdf (accessed 1 August, 2014).

Elliott, R. and Wattanasuwan, K. (1998), 'Brands as symbolic resources for the construction of identity', *International Journal of Advertising*, 17, 2, 131–145.

Ericksen, M.K. and Sirgy, M.J. (1992), 'Employed females clothing preference, self-image congruence, and career anchorage', *Journal of Applied Social Psychology*, 22, 5, 408–422.

Foxall, G.R. and Goldsmith, R. (1988), 'Personality and consumer research: another look', *Journal of the Market Research Society*, 30, 2, 111–125.

Freud, S. (1923), *The ego and the id*, London: Hogarth Press

Goffman, E. (1959), *The presentation of self in everyday life*, New York: Anchor.

Goldsmith, R.E. and Hofacker, C.F. (1991), 'Measuring consumer innovativeness', *Journal of the Academy of Marketing Science*, 19, 3, 209–221.

Grubb, E. and Grathwohl, H. (1967), 'Consumer self-concept, symbolism and market behavior: a theoretical approach', *Journal of Marketing*, 1, 4, 22–27.

Haire, M. (2009), 'A brief history of the Walkman', *Time*, 1 July, http://content.time.com/time/nation/article/0,8599,1907884,00.html (accessed 1 August 2014).

Harris, E.G. and Fleming, D.E. (2005), 'Assessing the human element in service personality formation: personality congruency and the five factor model', *Journal of Services Marketing*, 19, 4, 187–198.

Haws, K.L., Bearden, W.O., and Nenkov, G.Y. (2012), 'Consumer spending self-control effectiveness and outcome elaboration prompts', *Journal of the Academy of Marketing Science*, 40, 5, 695–710.

Heine, P.J. (1971), *Personality in social theory*, Chicago, IL: Alpine.

Hollenbeck, C.R. and Kaikati, A.M. (2012), 'Consumers' use of brands to reflect their actual and ideal selves on Facebook', *International Journal of Research in Marketing*, 29, 4, 395–405.

Hughes, S.A. (2011), 'Mike "The Situation" Sorrentino sues Abercrombie & Fitch', *Washington Post*, 16 November, http://www.washingtonpost.com/blogs/celebritology/post/mike-the-situation-sorrentino-sues-abercrombie-and-fitch/2011/11/16/gIQAglmNRN_blog.html (accessed 8 October 2012).

Jansson-Boyd, C.V. (2010), *Consumer psychology*, Maidenhead: Open University Press.

Kassarjian, H.H. (1971), 'Personality and consumer behavior: a review', *Journal of Marketing Research*, 8, 4, 409–418.

Kassarjian, H.H. and Sheffet, M.J. (1981), 'Personality and consumer behavior: an update,' in H.H. Kassarjian, (ed.), *Perspectives in consumer behavior*, Glenview, IL: Scott Foresman, pp 160–180.

Kellner, D. (1992), 'Popular culture and the construction of postmodern identities', in S. Lash and J. Friedman (eds), *Modernity and identity*, Oxford: Blackwell, pp 140–156.

Kramer, T. and Yoon, S.-O. (2007), 'Approach-avoidance motivation and the use of affect as information', *Journal of Consumer Psychology*, 17, 2, 128–138.

Lastovicka, J.L., Bettencourt, L.A., Hughner, R.S., and Kuntze, R.J. (1999), 'Lifestyle of the tight and frugal: theory and measurement', *Journal of Consumer Research*, 26, 1, 85–98.

Lawler, R. (2011), 'SyncTweet will sync TV ads with your Twitter stream', http://gigaom.com/2011/08/26/synctweet/ (accessed 11 January 2012).

Lee, M., Motion, J., Conroy, D. (2009), 'Anti-consumption and brand avoidance', *Journal of Business Research*, 62, 2, 169–180.

Levy, S. (1999), 'Qualitative research', in D. Rook, (ed.), *Brands, consumers, symbols, and research: Sidney J. Levy on marketing*, Thousand Oaks, CA: SAGE.

Ligas, M. and Cotte, J. (1999), 'The process of negotiating brand meaning: a symbolic interactionist perspective', in E.J. Arnould and L.M. Scott(eds), *Advances in Consumer Research*, Vol. 26, Provo, UT: Association for Consumer Research, pp 609–614.

Lowe, M.R. and Butryn, M.L. (2007), 'Hedonic hunger: a new dimension of appetite?', *Psychology & Behaviour*, 91, 432–439.

McCrae, R.R. and Costa, P.T. (1990), *Personality in adulthood*, New York: Guilford Press.

McKinsey Global Institute (2007), 'The "bird of gold": the rise of India's consumer market', *McKinsey Report* http://www.mckinsey.com/insights/asia-pacific/the_bird_of_gold (accessed 11 April 2013).

Maslow, A. (1954), *Motivation and personality*, New York: Harper.

Maslow, A. (1971), *The farther reaches of human nature*, New York: Viking Press.

Mead, G.H. (1913), 'The social self', *Journal of Philosophy, Psychology and Scientific Methods*, 10, 14, 374–380.

Möller, J. and Herm, S. (2013), 'Shaping retail brand personality perceptions by bodily experiences', *Journal of Retailing*, 89, 4, 438–446.

Morgan, C.D. and Murray, H.A. (1935), 'A method for investigating fantasies: the thematic apperception test', *Archives of Neurology and Psychiatry*, 34, 2, 289–306.

Packard, V.O. (1957), *The hidden persuaders*, New York: McKay.

Park, J.K. and John, D.R. (2010), 'Got to get you into my life: do brand personalities rub off on consumers?', *Journal of Consumer Research*, 37, 4, 655–669

Prasad, S. (2010), 'Why some slumdogs feel like millionaires: the theory of multiple poverty lines', ESOMAR, Barcelona, www.warc.com

Richins, M.L. and Dawson, S. (1992), 'A consumer values orientation for materialism and its measurement: scale development and validation', *Journal of Consumer Research*, 19, 303–316.

Rokeach, M. (1974), 'Change and stability in American value systems, 1968–1971', *Public Opinion Quarterly*, 38, 2, 222–238.

Rook, D.W. and Levy, S.J. (1983), 'Psychosocial themes in consumer grooming rituals', *Advances in Consumer Research*, 10, 329–333.

Rosenberg, M. (1979), *Conceiving the self*, New York: Basic Books.

Shankar, A., Elliott, R., and Fitchett, J.A. (2009), 'Identity, consumption and narratives of socialization', *Marketing Theory*, 9, 1, 75–94.

Shimp, T.A. and Sharma, S. (1987), 'Consumer ethnocentrism: construction and validation of the CETSCALE', *Journal of Marketing Research*, 24, 8, 280–289.

Sirgy, M.J. (1982), 'Self-image/product-image congruity and advertising strategy', in V. Kothari (ed.), *Developments in Marketing Science*, Vol. 5, Marquette, MI: Academy of Marketing Science, pp 129–133.

Steinman, R.B. (2008), 'Projective techniques in consumer research', in J.B. Belloit and T.R. Johns (eds), *Northeast Association of Business, Economics, and Technology, Proceedings of the 30th Annual Meeting*, pp 253–261.

Stets, J.E., and Burke, P.J. (2003), 'A sociological approach to self and identity', in M. Leary and J. Tangney (eds), *Handbook of self and identity*, New York: Guilford Press, pp 128–152.

Strategic Business Insights (2013), 'The VALS™ survey', http://www.strategicbusinessinsights.com/vals/ustypes.shtml (accessed 25 July 2013).

Subramanyeswar, S. (2010), 'Brand loyalty: Indian consumers value substance over style', *Admap*, September, 32–34, http://www.warc.com/ (accessed 23 May 2014).

WARC News (2010), 'Brands target young Indian consumers', http://www.warc.com.ezproxye.bham.ac.uk/Content/News/N26363_Brands_target_young_Indian_consumers.content?CID=N26363&ID=5cdf82e1-bb70-4a8b-84b3-a2aabb5a2379&q=teenagers&qr= (accessed 8 May 2013).

Woodside, A.G. (2010), 'Brand-consumer storytelling theory and research', *Psychology & Marketing*, 27, 6, 531–540.

Zoepf, K. (2008), 'Saudi women find an unlikely role model: Oprah', *New York Times*, 18 September, http://www.nytimes.com/2008/09/19/world/middleeast/19oprah.html?_r=0 (accessed 22 July 2013).

PART 3

MACRO-VIEW OF CONSUMPTION

Where are we going?

**Future Trends in
Consumer Behaviour**

Macro-view

**Consumers in society and
the market: groups,
social processes, culture
and repeat purchasing
behaviour**

Micro-view

**The individual consumer:
Individual decision
making, learning,
perception, attitudes,
personality and
motivation**

How we arrived here

**Historical context and
contemporary
perspectives on
consumption**

8

GROUPS, SOCIAL PROCESSES, AND COMMUNICATIONS

Introduction

People do not consume in isolation. Who you are with, who you know, which groups you identify with, those you feel antipathy towards—all these and many more social states and processes affect how you consume. Companies make use of this knowledge to shape the ways they market to consumers. This chapter will focus on groups, and the processes within and across groups that may impact upon how people consume. We will also consider the ways that marketing uses this knowledge for the purposes of developing products and brands and communicating with different groups, or people within those groups. A particularly important group is the family, and the latter part of this chapter focuses on consumption within the family context.

LEARNING OBJECTIVES

Having read this chapter, you will be able to:

1. *Define the reference group concept* and describe the types of reference groups and how these influence consumers and their consumption behaviour.

2. Demonstrate understanding of the *processes of reference group influence*, including the mechanisms of group influence, the development of conformity within groups, and the concept of opinion leadership.

3. Explain the ***importance of social power and social connectedness***, and understand how we communicate within and across groups, both face-to-face and in electronic environments (word of mouth (WOM) and e-word of mouth (eWOM)).

4. Identify the role that reference groups such as the ***family*** have on consumption.

5. Discuss the ***importance of social class structures***, and how these impact on consumption behaviour.

Reference groups

Understanding the types of people we associate with or with whom we would prefer not to associate with is fundamental to marketing. Many products are purchased and consumed in a public setting, so we see what other people buy and often associate beliefs, attitudes, and behaviours with them. The Belgian-based company Ecover produces ecologically sound cleaning products, and its brand imagery is important for communicating those values to consumers. If we see a consumer buying Ecover cleaning products (Figure 8.1), we may assume that they are committed to environmental beliefs and attitudes.

Reference groups are *those groups that are used by a person as a basis for comparison and guidance when forming their beliefs, attitudes, and behaviours.* Reference groups were first defined by Hyman (1942) as reference points that individuals use to evaluate their situation. Park and Lessig (1977: 102) developed the concept to include 'an actual or imaginary institution, individual or group conceived as having significant relevance upon an individual's evaluations, aspirations or behaviour'. This broadens the idea of reference groups from an individual person to an institution (real or imaginary).

Types of reference group

Typically we describe reference groups across two dimensions—membership and attractiveness of the group. Membership groups are those to which we belong (termed contactual, identificational, or associative) and those which we may have been members of but no longer wish to be associated with (disclaimant). There are also groups that we may not be members of, but we aspire to belong to (aspirational) and others which we wish to avoid entirely (avoidance or dissociative). Table 8.1 shows the main types of reference group.

Contactual or associative groups are generally *close groups with which we interact regularly and where there is a degree of proximity.* This closeness may be through family or friendship ties

Figure 8.1   Ecover cleaning products   *Source*: Image courtesy of Ecover.

		Membership	
		Member	Non-member
Attractiveness	Positive	Contactual or associative	Aspirational
	Negative	Disclaimant	Avoidance or dissociative

Table 8.1   Group membership

Source: Adapted from Assael, H. (1998), *Consumer Behavior and Marketing Action* (6th edn), Mason, OH: South-Western College Publishing. Printed with kind permission from the author.

or through mutual interests such as work, a hobby, or a sporting interest. Carling's 'Belong' campaign, illustrated in Figure 8.2, emphasized the power of belonging represented by groups. Carling showed groups of friends in adverse situations, such as in outer space or in Arctic conditions standing up for one another, suggesting that Carling could suppport belonging to a group of like-minded young men.

A **disclaimant** group *is one that we currently belong to, or perhaps belonged to in the past, but no longer want to associate ourselves with.* At college a person may be part of a social goup that drinks alcohol, but if the group then experiments with soft drugs they may no longer join in with them (Figure 8.3). Disclaimant groups may be transitional groups from our past whom we are trying to move on from (e.g. school friends going in different paths), or typically are groups that we are part of, but know are stigmatized in some way by society (e.g. we may belong to a dieting club but prefer our other friends not to know).

Figure 8.2   Carling advertisement demonstrating the power of belonging

Source: Image courtesy of Beattie McGuinness Bungay.

Aspirational groups are composed *of people that the consumer can identify with or admire (often from afar), and aspires to be like in some way.* Often the aspirational group is actually an individual representing some state or position we aspire to be like. We may respect them for their skills (such as sports personalities) or for their style and glamour or their lifestyle (such as famous actors). We may try to emulate them through the consumption of certain products or brands. When Kate Middleton became engaged to Prince William, companies started to produce

Figure 8.3   Disclaimant groups, reflecting shifting interests among friends

Source: © iStock.com/sturti.

look-alike dresses to the one by Issa which she wore at her engagement announcement. A young woman knows that she will never be part of the British royal family, but can aspire to some aspects of their perceived life through emulating Kate Middleton's look. A number of sites have followed Kate through her marriage and, most recently, pregnancy with tips on how to get the Kate look (e.g. www.getwhatkatewore.com). Now there is even an app available for women seeking the Kate look (see Figure 8.4).

Dissociative or avoidance groups *are groups we have negative feelings towards and whom we avoid being associated with.* They differ from disclaimant groups in that we have never been members of such groups, and we associate negative feelings with them for their intrinsic qualities rather than because we or they have changed. We do not wish to emulate the way they look or behave and may associate certain products or brands with them that in turn we feel negative towards. Japan is well known for its different fashion groups among young people, many of which appear very extreme such that other young people avoid associating with them. One such group were Ganguro girls (see Figure 8.5) whose distinguishing features were their tanned skin, platform shoes, short dresses, and white lipstick. Ganguro girls suffered harassment and avoidance by others. Interestingly, as the trend died down, many tanning salons were closed.

If a brand becomes associated with a group that many others wish to dissociate themselves from, it can be damaged. Burberry, which had for years been associated with making raincoats for royalty and the rich and famous, was adopted by brand conscious football hooligans, and as a result the distinctive 'Burberry check' became something that many people in Britain no longer wanted to be seen in. In particular, the Burberry check became associated with so-called 'chavs', a derogatory term defined by the *Oxford English Dictionary* as 'a young lower-class person typified by brash and loutish

Figure 8.4   The Replikate Me app

Source: Image courtesy of Emma Poole.

Figure 8.5　Ganguro girls　*Source*: Image courtesy of Gozogomo (http://dozodomo.com/).

behaviour and the wearing of (real or imitation) designer clothes'. Burberry was a brand that had moved from being associated with aspirational groups to being associated with dissociative groups. However, Burberry skilfully repositioned itself away from the traditional check and back to a nostalgia-inspired, but still cutting-edge, fashion image. The company introduced a range of product lines that were quirky and difficult to emulate, with classically beautiful English models with an 'aristocratic' air, such as Stella Tennant and Emma Watson. Building such associations over a period of years has enabled Burberry to remove the 'chav' label and made it once again an aspirational brand.

Reference groups are also classified as formal or informal. A **formal group** is one that is *usually formed by some kind of outside structure, and is likely to have a formalized constitution and set of rules of conduct for members*. Examples of formal groups include being a member of a golf club and adhering to the strict dress codes associated with such a club. Formal groups can impact consumption when they exert power, often in terms of institutional expectations where individuals are required to conform. Many companies have 'dress-down days', where employees are expected to dress casually, but often the group exerts power such that there is a standardized approach to 'smart casual' in such contexts.

An **informal group** is formed by *a group of individuals who have some sort of commonality but no formal connection to each other*. They may get together because they have a mutual interest (such as gardening or singing), through common values (e.g. a boycotting group), or through friendship. Some formal and informal groups may be of more interest to marketers than others. A gardening group can be a target for particular products, but a boycotting group is unlikely to be so. Similarly, you may find informal groups within a formal group. Thus you may work within a large organization (formal group), but within that be part of an informal book group or five-a-side football team. While it is very useful for marketing to engage with such informal groups, it can be difficult to identify and reach them. However, it can be easier if they have some kind of mutual interest, such as reading or sport, as they are more likely to engage with relevant product information and then communicate within the informal group. Popular books now regularly include information about activities for book groups with suggestions for further reading. Similarly Facebook groups (whether initiated by a company or by enthusiasts) and the use of hashtags to identify and manage twitter conversations and promotions all make conversations on particular topics easier to identify and manage by companies.

In summary, there are many different ways of viewing the types of reference groups to which consumers belong or are influenced by, and these are summarized in Table 8.2.

Reference group influence

Mechanisms of reference group influence

Leigh (1989) recognized that reference group influence can be direct from the reference group to individual members, or indirect through an individual observing the behaviour of group members and altering his/her own behaviour because of it. The importance of reference groups for marketing is the influence that they can bring to bear on others, in particular in terms of which products or brands are bought and how different groups consume them. There are three main mechanisms of reference group influence: informational, utilitarian, and value-expressive (Park and Lessig, 1977).

- **Informational group influence** *is when a consumer uses the reference group to actively get information from opinion leaders or expert groups.* The person will attribute benefits to the product through its association with the group or individual, but does not necessarily have any personal interaction with them. We might purchase the same equipment as a celebrity cook or gardener, or we might follow the guidance of groups giving consumer advice, such as 'Which' for consumer goods or 'The Motley Fool' for financial products.

- **Utilitarian reference group influence** *is when a person is influenced in their choice of brand by the preferences of those with whom they socialize including family members and*

Reference group type	Definition
Associative or contractual	Close groups with which we interact regularly and where there is a degree of proximity
Disclaimant	A group that we currently belong to, or perhaps belonged to in the past, but no longer want to associate ourselves with
Aspirational	Composed of people that the consumer can identify or admire (often from afar), and aspires to be like them in some way
Dissociative or avoidance group	A group with which the individual wishes to avoid being associated and feels a sense of dis-identification
Formal	A formal group is usually formed by some kind of outside structure, and is likely to have a formalized constitution and set of rules of conduct for members
Informal	An informal group is formed by a group of individuals who have some sort of commonality; they may get together because they have a mutual interest or through friendship

Table 8.2   Types of reference group

work colleagues. The decision to purchase a brand will be influenced by the wish to satisfy the expectations others have, and in some cultures this utilitarian influence can be very strong. Research with second-generation Punjabis in Britain (Sekhon and Szmigin, 2011) found that family influence was very strong in terms of purchasing particular brands.

- **Value-expressive influence** *is when someone buys a particular brand to enhance their image and because they admire characteristics of people who use the brand.* Central to value-expressive influence is the idea that we want to be like others whom we admire or respect in society. Companies often develop ads which link their brand visually with an attractive model or character with a view to enhancing the image of their brand through this connection (see Figure 8.6).

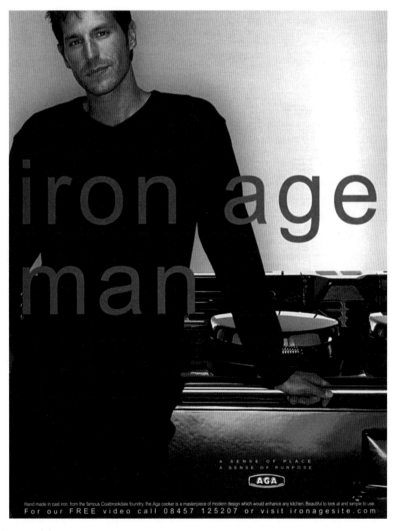

Figure 8.6   Aga model

Source: Image supplied by The Advertising Archives.

Public

Product / Brand	Weak reference group influence on product choice	Strong reference group influence on product choice
Strong reference group influence on brand choice	**Public necessities** Because it is a necessity, e.g. car, suit, or wristwatch, the influence for the product will be **weak**. But it will be seen by others, so the influence for the brand is **strong**.	**Public luxuries** Because it is a luxury, e.g. golf clubs, yacht, or skis, the influence for the product should be **strong**. Because it will be seen by others, the influence of the brand is also **strong**.
Weak reference group influence on brand choice	**Private necessities** This would be a product consumed out of public view but which almost everyone owns, such as a mattress or refrigerator. As a necessity, the product influence is **weak** and as it is not seen by others the influence for the brand also tends to be **weak**.	**Private luxuries** This would be a product that is not commonly owned and unlikely to be conspicuous, but would still convey meaning about the status of the owner, e.g. an ice-cream maker. As a luxury the influence of the product is **strong**, but as it is not seen by others the influence for the brand is **weak**.

Necessity — Luxury

Private

Figure 8.7   Model of reference group influence on consumption   *Source:* Adapted from Bearden and Etzel (1982).

Reference groups influencing public versus private consumption

Bearden and Etzel (1982) examined how reference group influence varied in relation to where consumption occurs (private versus public) and the extent to which it is considered a necessity or a luxury. Figure 8.7 gives an overview of the model, indicating the flows of influence we would expect to see for luxury and necessity products and brands consumed in public and privately.

How we decide which goods and services are a luxury or a necessity changes over time and across different cultures. In their original work, Bearden and Etzel classified mattresses, floor lamps, and refrigerators as public necessities with weak reference group influence. However, the kitchen has become a focal point for socializing for many in western countries, and the brands we own are more conspicuous and susceptible to reference group influence. Brands such as Smeg, Aga, or Jura are associated with aspirational reference groups, and coffee makers are often shown in a social setting or recommended by celebrities such as Roger Federer (Figure 8.8).

Development of conformity

For the concept of reference groups to be useful to marketers, there has to be some degree of conformity that results from group membership (see Research Insight 8.1). **Conformity** can be defined as *adoption of behaviour resulting from real or perceived pressure to comply with a person or group*. If you are with a group of friends and they all want to watch a football match, but you would prefer to go shopping, you may conform to their decision because their friendship is more important to you than going shopping.

Figure 8.8   Roger Federer and Jura coffee maker
Source: Image supplied by The Advertising Archives.

Mann (1969) identified four types of conformity: normative, informational, compliance, and internalization.

- **Normative conformity** applies *when a person wants to fit in with the group or is afraid of being rejected by them and will publicly accept the group's view even if privately they do not agree,* simply because standing out from the crowd can be uncomfortable.

- **Informational conformity** *occurs when someone actively looks for guidance from the group where they lack knowledge or are in an ambiguous situation.* Here the individual is also likely to internally accept the groups' view.

RESEARCH INSIGHT 8.1

Asch, S.E. (1955) 'Opinions and social pressure', *Scientific American*, 193, 5, 31–35

The classic study of the power of conformity in groups is found in Asch's work from the 1950s. Asch asked student participants, in a group setting, to estimate the length of a line (a form of a vision test). He manipulated the experimental setting such that all but one of the group were assistants of the experimenter and had been asked to provide the (same) wrong answer to the question. One member of the group was not in on the experiment, but he often also gave the wrong answer. In later experiments, when subjects wrote down their responses and thus kept them private, conformity dropped, suggesting the importance of public compliance.

 Visit the Online Resource Centre to read the abstract and access the full paper.

- **Compliance** *refers to publicly changing behaviour to fit in with the group but privately disagreeing, i.e. a behavioural shift without an attitudinal one.*

- However, **internalization** *involves both an attitudinal and behavioural change in favour of the group.*

If a person is using a neighbourhood recycling scheme, normative conformity may dominate in the early stages of recycling, when they sort and recycle packaging in order to fit into neighbourhood norms and expectations. They may then enter a period of informational conformity, where they chat to other neighbours and consult specialist websites to learn more about recycling. Compliance may occur if people recycle but perhaps disagree with and resent the time taken, but most likely a process of internalization will occur when they are recycling because they believe in the value and importance of this behaviour.

Of course, many people will not conform and this may be because of a difference of opinion and independence of decision-making, or because they are rejecting the group's norms. As we shall see later, individuals may also resist if they feel that the group is pressurizing them into conformity.

How group norms influence conformity

Venkatesan (1966) developed some of the early ideas on conformity in the context of consumer decision-making and concluded that in a group situation, and where it is difficult to assess the quality of the product, individuals will accept the information provided by others in the group. However, where group pressure appears to limit independent choice, people react to reassert their freedom to decide, a process known as reactance.

Reactance is *a motivational state which acts as a counterforce to threats to a person's freedom,* and can be a powerful force if groups of people feel that their freedom is compromised. In the realms of popular and consumer culture, Earls (2009) describes the social pressure to grieve for the death of Princess Diana (through the placing of floral tributes at her home in

Kensington Palace), and how the literary magazine *Granta* expressed reactance by calling the pressure to conform 'floral fascism'.

Social power and reference groups

Another important area to consider is social power. Understanding the role of power in group influence is largely derived from the work of French (1956), Raven (1993), and French and Raven (1959). Defining social power as potential influence, they examined the types of influence a person might draw on to exercise influence in various organizational and family settings, and developed six bases of social power: coercive, reward, legitimacy, expert, reference, and informational. Raven (1993) further developed the social power framework to provide a more elaborate understanding of how power influences people.

- **Reward power** *may be present when a person responds to the influence of the group and is rewarded in some way.*

- **Coercive power** *means that conformity to the group is brought about through the threat of punishment.*

- **Legitimate power** *is where the referent is seen to have authority by virtue of their position in the particular context,* often achieved in service businesses through the use of uniforms to show authority.

- **Expert power** *is when we are influenced to behave or purchase something by someone who we recognize has particular expertise, for example, a doctor or scientist.*

- **Referent power** is similar, *although the influence stems from our admiration of the qualities of a person, and how we try to imitate those qualities by copying their behaviour,* often evident in the way we consider celebrities.

- **Informational power** *is based on logical argument and knowledge which someone may have acquired from experience or through the nature of their job.* A person or group has informational power because they know something that others would like to know.

Raven highlighted the importance of recognizing how these forms of power can be personal or impersonal in character. Personal influences of reward and coercive power relate to the approval (or sanction) of those close to us. Personal approval from others in a friendship group of young people, say for having the 'right' MP3 player or mobile phone, can be as powerful as being ridiculed (and therefore punished) for wearing outdated sports gear. In advertising, legitimate power is sometimes attempted through the use of actors wearing white coats in ads for products such as dental hygiene or cosmetics.

Originally, expert and referent power were examined only in positive forms, but on some occasions we resist this power. Consider the celebrity chef Jamie Oliver who is an

RESEARCH INSIGHT 8.2

Thomas, T.C., Price, L.L., and Schau, H.J. (2013), 'When differences unite: resource dependence in heterogeneous consumption communities', *Journal of Consumer Research*, 39, 5, 1010–1033

While much of the theory around consumption groups and communities emphasizes the importance of similarity within groups, in this paper Thomas et al. (2013) adopt a different perspective—they consider how consumption communities or groups cope with heterogeneity (difference), and how this can be handled to ensure that the community sustains itself. Adopting a CCT perspective, the authors study the distance-running community, which has grown from a niche male-dominated group to a more mainstream community attracting all types of runners for all sorts of motives. They discuss how the community draws on and activates social and economic resources to overcome tensions and difficulties to develop a thriving community.

    Visit the Online Resource Centre to read the abstract and access the full paper.

expert in the world of cooking and food, and yet when he was involved in a campaign to introduce healthy meals into UK schools, many parents rejected his message, arguing that the school meals were expensive and were not particularly popular with their children, which led to many parents providing less healthy packed lunches for their children (Adams, 2012)

For informational power, Raven suggested that it may be effective if the information comes in an indirect form as a hint or suggestion. Personal hygiene products used to be sold in highly explicit ways with advertisements suggesting what brand to use if you suffered from 'BO' (body odour), but advertisers found more subtle ways of describing what their brands could achieve. Dove deodorants emphasize the skincare aspect of their deodorant products. Recently, however, Lynx have returned to the explicit presentation of such problems with ads showing men having relationship problems because of what they have termed 'premature perspiration'. These advertisements are clearly tongue in cheek and so engage the consumer in a more indirect manner than the early, more serious ones. However, social power remains an important influence and one that is recognized by companies in their communications, especially with regard to people's social fears of being rejected by groups (see also Research Insight 8.2).

Opinion leaders and opinion seekers

Rogers and Cartano (1962: 435) described **opinion leaders** as '*individuals who exert an unequal amount of influence on the decisions of others*'. Lazarsfeld et al. (1944), in their study of the 1940 US presidential election, found that the media had little direct influence on the public, but rather influence flowed from the media to opinion leaders who then passed on information to a broader public. This became known as the two-step flow of communication (Figure 8.9) and was further tested in consumer purchases (Katz and Lazarsfeld, 1955).

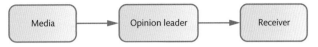

Figure 8.9   Two-step flow of communication

The idea that a small group of influential people can accelerate or stop the adoption of a product has become central to our idea of what an opinion leader is, which Gladwell (2001) calls 'The Law of the Few'. He identifies those who are well connected, knowledgeable, or persuasive as connectors, mavens, and salesmen. See also Consumer Insight 8.1 for more on types of opinion leaders.

- **Connectors** *are people who tend to know lots of other people, often from different subcultures to their own*, not necessarily very well but enough to pass on information to others.

- **Mavens** *are collectors and brokers of information but they use this information and want to start discussions with others or respond to requests.* They are the kind of people who have inside knowledge on what is going on in the marketplace. Market mavens (Feick and Price,1987) are very engaged with consumption and often pass on information about products they have not necessarily bought themselves (see Chapter 3).

- **Salesmen** *are the arch persuaders, people who will not accept 'no' for an answer and are always looking for an opportunity to get their message across to someone else.*

While opinion leaders are an important group to understand, so too are those on the receiving end of the communication. **Opinion seekers** *are people who seeks opinions and information to help their purchase decision.* Engel et al. (1990: 42) recognized the reciprocal nature of opinion seeking and leading, stating that 'When we actively seek advice from another, that person becomes an opinion leader'. Opinion seeking acts as a form of product information search; consumers seek opinions and information to make better purchase decisions, effectively a form of external information search (see Chapter 3).

CONSUMER INSIGHT 8.1

Hierarchies of opinion leadership

Examining how opinion leaders influence other consumers is a concern for many in business. Companies and organizations are keen to understand the hierarchy of influence, as demonstrated in a report by the Future Foundation (2010), which classified opinion leaders into three distinct types. Focusing on how they share information about brands, news, and personal experiences, this report revealed three distinct, but interrelated types of opinion leader.

1. Hub urbanites share information through social media and instant messaging services. They are highly motivated to start discussing stories in order to get a reaction and gain recognition.

2.   Email evangelists share ideas through email and other social media, aiming to reach more diverse networks than the hub urbanites, and motivated to share, educate, and inspire.

3.   Offline influencers are more likely to pass on information face to face or on the phone. They have small networks but often pass on online content to an offline audience. They want to help others, offer advice and guidance, and be helpful.

This study also found that the amount of international contacts in an opinion leader's network is higher in nations such as India, Hong Kong, and the UAE. These markets tend to have a high proportion of hub urbanites and email evangelists.

Another example is shown in the 2004 campaign by Glasgow City Marketing Bureau, who wanted to reposition the city as 'Glasgow: Scotland with Style'. They commissioned a media planning agency to undertake the research insight work that would feed into the advertising and marketing campaign. The agency proposed a repositioning based on Glasgow being recognized as stylish by opinion formers, and went on to identify four levels of opinion forming:

1.   exclusive style setters—working in fashion, journalism, and design;

2.   early style adopters—influenced by the exclusive style setters, they adopt stylish brands, are often Londoners, and influential journalists or celebrities;

3.   capital leaders—influenced by opinion formers 1 and 2, and go on to influence others;

4.   UK style followers—urban upmarket audiences to whom style is important.

The agency used media that they thought each level took their style cues from. For the exclusive style setters they targeted small circulation elite publications including *Icon*, *Next Level*, *Creative Review*, *Frieze*, and the *Architects' Journal* with a few ads and extensive PR. For the early style adopters they aimed at slightly broader titles including *Condé Nast Traveller*, *Dazed and Confused*, *How to Spend It*, and *Wallpaper**. The campaign helped to achieve the increase in occupancy and the city was voted 'Favourite City 2006' by *Condé Nast Traveller*.

Questions

1.   Think about your friends. If you had to categorize them in terms of opinion leadership, what would be their distinguishing features?

2.   How is information passed within your reference groups and who are the critical information providers?

3.   Think about the media you might use to promote a new band. What would you choose and why?

Sources: Future Foundation (2010); www.thedrum.com

   Visit the Online Resource Centre and follow the weblinks to learn more.

Opinion leaders or easily influenced individuals?

While the idea of opinion leaders has been widely accepted, some have suggested that the picture may be more complex. Watts and Dodds (2007) rejected the idea that some people are more influential than others and exert a disproportionate amount of influence on the community. Rather, they concluded that information flow does 'not succeed because of a few highly influential individuals influencing everyone else, but rather on account of a critical mass of easily influenced individuals influencing other easy-to-influence people' (Watts and Dodds, 2007: 454). Their model shows how influence can flow in both directions between leaders and followers, and that it can develop over a number of steps in a schematic network (Figure 8.10) The television in the centre represents the mass media where much of our information is gathered, and around this we see individuals receiving and passing on information, with some clearly more active than others.

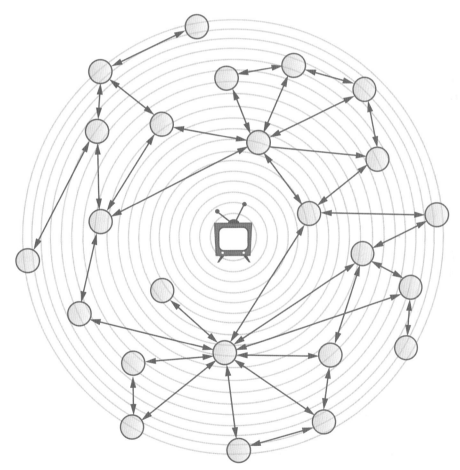

Figure 8.10   Schematic diagram of the network model of influence (Watts and Dodds, 2007)

Source: Reproduced with permission from University of Chicago Press.

Watts (2007) uses the example of the revival of Hush Puppies in the USA to say that just because a few fashionistas in New York began to wear them, the brand's subsequent revival may not have been solely caused by them. According to Watts, it is more likely that the success of this trend related to there being a critical mass of easily influenced people influencing other easy-to-influence people. He uses the terms 'accidental influentials' to capture the idea that getting a large number of ordinary people to reach out and influence other people is the best way to spread the message about a brand.

Expert influentials

Expert influentials are people who have real power to influence the marketplace. Sometimes this is because of the nature of the message, such as in the case of the article published in *The Lancet* medical journal in 1998 suggesting that regressive autism could be linked to the measles–mumps–rubella (MMR) jab. This story lead to a huge decline in immunization in children in the UK, and was linked to the spread of measles in Wales in 2013 (BBC News, 2013). We also need to consider whether the influence comes about because of the kinds of people that are communicating or because of how they communicate with others. Watts (2007) argues that the power of celebrities, such as Oprah Winfrey in the USA and Richard and Judy in the UK, to advocate a previously unknown book—which then becomes a bestseller—is more to do with their celebrity power through the mass media than word of mouth. But ordinary people can use the power of mass communication to influence public opinion dramatically. A notable example of this is Dave Caroll's YouTube video 'United Airlines breaks guitars'. Musician Dave Caroll composed a country and western style song (posted with a comic video on YouTube) which expressed his frustration with United Airlines, who he alleged had damaged his guitar and the subsequent poor customer service received.

At the time of writing, his video had nearly 13 million hits and his song became a bestseller on iTunes in Canada. Caroll himself has become a celebrity and has founded a website Gripevine (https://gripevine.com/) which aims to help consumers and companies handle and resolve customer complaints. Does this mean that anyone can influence the market if they have the right message? Doubtless Caroll benefited from the viral nature of his video, but it also struck a chord with many who have been frustrated by airlines' lack of care and above all his video was a highly professional communications tool.

The search for cool

For companies trying to discover influential people who can affect whether a brand or product will be successful, identifying trendsetters—those who set the agenda for what is worn, played with, eaten, watched, and listened to—is crucial. Marketers believe that where these 'cool' (usually young) people lead, the rest will follow. Nancarrow and Nancarrow (2007: 135) describe cool as 'an advanced form of knowledge about commodities and consumption practices'. These people have been termed urban pioneers, trendsetters, and alpha consumers, and those who follow them, seeking to identify what will become cool, have been termed 'coolhunters'. In the last twenty or so years an industry has been built on developing research methods, following young people and trying to engage with them in ways which will help to develop products and brands to appeal to a wider market. Techniques of coolhunting include ethnography, shop-alongs, and accompanied shopping trips. Coolhunters follow blogs and conversations on Facebook and Twitter. Commercially there are many problems with coolhunting. First, not all trends will have mass market appeal. Secondly, the techniques rely on interpretation by the coolhunters and companies as to how to turn a trend into a popular consumer product. Finally, and perhaps most importantly, once something that was cool becomes mass market, it loses its coolness. As the strategic planning director of one US advertising agency put it, 'By the time a celebrity had worn it, it had appeared in *InStyle* and then everybody wanted it right now … and then it was over in a few weeks' (Grossman, 2003: 4).

Social connectedness: the importance of word of mouth

Early studies of diffusion and mass communication revealed that it is rare for people to respond only to mass media information without transmission through personal ties as well (Katz and Lazarsfeld, 1955; Rogers, 1962). **Word of mouth (WOM)** is *an informal communication, either positive or negative, about goods, services, and sellers.* WOM occurs in both face-to-face contexts and in electronic contexts (mostly online), when it is often referred to as eWOM. This social contact between people is an important part of our social lives, as too are the social communications we share around consumption (e.g. telling one another about products, whether they work or not, where to buy them, how to get the best deal, and what to avoid). Understanding how such social connectedness works is important to marketers and is the focus of this section.

Firms want to effect useful word of mouth communication; they try to get consumers both to pass on information about their brand and to recommend it. **Endogenous WOM** is *when conversations happen among consumers as part of their natural communication and when they are just passing on information about their experiences with a product or brand.* **Exogenous WOM** occurs as a *direct result of the firm's marketing.* You can see how this work in practice in Consumer Insight 8.2. Firms may have a problem creating successful exogenous WOM

CONSUMER INSIGHT 8.2

Endogenous and exogenous WOM in action

When creating a buzz around a brand, product, or service, organizations recognize the power of WOM and make considerable effort to create positive WOM around their offering.

Endogenous WOM is considered the most authentic form of brand communication as it tends to be bottom-up, emerging through consumer-to-consumer interactions around the brand. There are a number of high profile examples of singers and bands becoming famous through the power of WOM. The Arctic Monkeys had two British number ones and a fastest-selling debut album and won many major wards without any commercial backing. They built a strong local following in Sheffield and gave away demos at their gigs. They encouraged their fans to upload their music on social networking sites and even banned record company scouts from their performances.

House Party is a word-of-mouth marketing firm which establishes a brand-dedicated website where consumers can interact and then recruits 1,000 fans to invite friends to a branded party. NBC recruited House Party to help launch the second season of the reality show *The Biggest Loser* and to assemble likely applicants. House Party's founder Parker Reilly commented: 'We find the biggest fans and get them to work for the brands that they love ... All the videos and pictures and blog comments they create are there for NBC to use and show as evidence of how much people love the show'.

A good example of a company successfully using both endogenous and exogenous WOM is provided by the Japanese fashion company Uniqlo when it launched in Singapore in 2009. Uniqlo had a relatively low awareness in Singapore, and advertising agency Tribal DDB was briefed to launch the first stores there (see Figure 8.11). The agency was surprised to find that only 16 per cent of the highly fashionable Singaporeans had heard of Uniqlo, and that most could not even pronounce the brand name. The agency found that Uniqlo actually had an established fan site on Facebook (endogenous WOM). The

Figure 8.11 Uniqlo store in Shinjuku Takashimaya, Japan

Source: Image courtesy of Uniqlo Stores.

agency worked with the fan, asking him to put up some information although most of it was his own. After just one week Uniqlo had 5,000 Facebook fans in Singapore.

Questions

1. Can you find other examples of these forms of WOM?

2. Do you think that consumers can detect or are sceptical of companies' attempts to create WOM?

3. What other suggestions would you have for companies to use these ideas to create positive WOM for their brands?

Sources: Lynskey (2005); O'Malley (2005); Thorniley (2011).

 Visit the Online Resource Centre and follow the weblinks to learn more about WOM and see further examples.

as consumers may identify ulterior motives and this could affect their WOM activity and their willingness to pass on information (Verlegh et al., 2004).

Whatever form it takes, WOM usually involves product seeding (Samson, 2010) whereby consumers can try out or experience the product in some way. It might be assumed that it is always the most loyal consumers that create useful WOM, but research by Samson (2010) and Godes and Mayzlin (2009) shows that it may be more useful for firms to target less loyal customers with WOM campaigns. This would appear to be particularly the case for a product or brand with relatively low awareness where the marketing communications objective is to spread information about the product.

The power of eWOM

Although a number of the examples in this chapter include eWOM, it is worth saying a little more about its power for consumer behaviour today. **eWOM** has been defined by Hennig-Thureau et al. (2004: 39) as *'any positive or negative statement made by potential, actual or former customers about a product or company, which is made available to a multitude of people and institutions via the internet'*. Many websites are developed by consumers and are primarily for the purpose of reviewing products and services; others are generated by marketers. Consumers appear to visit both if they are looking for advice and information. A national survey in the Netherlands examined information seeking by consumers planning holidays and found that 49 per cent visited a marketer-generated site and 36 per cent a consumer-generated site (Bronner and de Hoog, 2010).

There has been a growth in sites such as TripAdvisor where consumers share their own product experiences with others. eWOM is powerful because it is able to influence people on a global scale. Researchers have emphasized that people tend to trust others who are similar to themselves (Eccleston and Griser, 2008). Perhaps that is why many sites tend to specialize in a particular area, such as Mumsnet which supplies specialist knowledge and discussion for new and existing mothers, or Grannynet designed for grandparents who are helping to look after their grandchildren.

Many commercial sites, such as Hotels.com, encourage feedback that can help other consumers make decisions. Amazon asks customers for reviews of goods, which enable other customers to make decisions when choosing to buy online. There are many online communities, such as eFestivals.com where festival-goers can receive information and pass on their experiences of festival-going. There are also discussion forums and sites within sites, such as the ASOS.com Appreciation Society on Facebook, with thousands of members 'for those who love or are addicted to ASOS.com'. All of these are examples of companies attempting to manage eWOM and recognizing its importance and value. The importance of eWOM is recognized by market research companies such as Nielsen Research who in 2009 found that 70 per cent of respondents across fifty worldwide markets trusted online consumer posts.

From e-word of mouth to crowdsourcing and user-generated content

The internet provides somewhere for people to meet to share and explore ideas and creativity. Surowiecki (2004) identifies several examples where a solution to a problem results from a number of people working on that problem. Earls (2009) described this as comparable to the whiteboard in the movie *Good Will Hunting*, where mathematicians were invited to contribute solutions to posted problems. A number of people can help to provide a solution partly by building on one another's ideas; this is known as crowdsourcing. The term **crowdsourcing** was coined by Howe (2006) and described '*as the act of a company or institution taking a function once performed by employees and outsourcing it to an undefined (and generally large) network of people in the form of an open call*'. Wikipedia is a form of crowdsourcing as are many of the consumer online forums, but increasingly companies are looking to consumers and independent producers to crowdsource new ideas or business propositions. An issue with crowdsourcing is that the solution becomes the property of the company, rather than individuals being paid for their creative input, and as such, represents a form of internet exploitation (Postigo, 2003). Others have argued that the crowd gets to see the result of their creativity and this would not happen without an organization to put that creativity into action (Brabham, 2008). For example, the internet T-shirt company threadless.com invites people to send in their designs; members then vote on their favourite styles with the highest scoring designs printed and sold on the website.

Creators can make a living from taking part in crowdsourcing. iStockphoto sells royalty-free stock photography. Clients purchase credits to buy stock images and photographers receive 20 per cent of the purchase price every time their image is downloaded. Here we see how harnessing the power of the crowd can generate business in often different and better ways for producers and consumers. Earls (2009) suggests that crowdsourcing can lead to cheaper solutions for consumers; this is evident in iStockphoto where consumers no longer have to pay high royalty charges for images.

The role of social media

Much user-generated content has arisen through the growth of social media, blogs, Facebook, Flickr, and microblogs such as Twitter. All depend on people creating content and then sharing it amongst their friends. The numbers now using social media are phenomenal. In 2013, Facebook had over 1.06 billion users and Twitter 500 million total users, and more than 200 million active users. Such social media allows everyone to easily follow what others are doing and have instant conversations with a wide range of people. On Twitter, many users are interested in following celebrities—in 2012, the people with the most Twitter followers were Justin Bieber, Lady Gaga, Katy Perry, Rihanna, and Barack Obama—in that order! Twitter has also been highly influential in the rapid dissemination of information relating to disasters, political events, and requests for help from individuals in threatening or dangerous situations. Comm (2011) reports how the Red Cross use Twitter to update disaster information. Exactly how word of mouth works in social media is more difficult to identify. Bakshy et al. (2011) used a predictive model of influence to examine Twitter cascades, i.e. when a 'tweet' is sent on to others (retweeted) and they in turn send it on further. Large cascades are relatively rare; more common are the relatively small cascades, usually triggered by ordinary individuals.

The family

The family is an example of a specific reference group that exerts some of the most important social or group influences on individual consumption decisions. The family shapes consumption behaviour through acting as a source of informational, utilitarian, and value-expressive influence. Research shows that families play a particularly important role in providing information to their members, especially young adult consumers (Shim, 1996; Bravo et al., 2006). Families are especially important in terms of consumer socialization, representing one of the key influences on our consumption, because of the frequency of interactions and close relations between family members, at least during the early years. Increasingly, we hear about the influence children have on parents' consumption behaviour (Shoham and Dalakas, 2005).

Companies are recognizing the importance of getting into the mindset of children, and are using the full range of media available to communicate with children and parents to encourage buy-in and engagement. *The Lego Movie* positioned Lego as a lifestyle brand for children, with brand extensions in the form of clothing and video games to deepen this connection with the brand. While research with children is very important for companies, there are very tight regulations regarding what they can and cannot do, as is highlighted in Practitioner Insight 8 which looks at regulating children who act as brand ambassadors.

PRACTITIONER INSIGHT 8

Ian Douthwaite, Managing Director of Dubit Ltd.

Companies want to create more word of mouth and in this section Ian Douthwaite, Managing Director of Dubit Ltd, explains the commercial value of such word of mouth, and also the necessary regulations which govern marketing. Dubit Ltd is a kids digital entertainment and research business that also specializes in ethical marketing to children.

In *Consumer Kids*, Dr Agnes Nairn and Ed Mayo wrote that 'big business is grooming our children for profit' (Nairn and Mayo, 2009). They accused marketers of paying children to market products to their peers. The media furore that followed did little to ascertain the extent of this practice and the regulations in place to protect consumers of all ages. Both are still relatively unclear, so here I will explain how Dubit believes that the 'brand ambassador' could be used in the UK and how they are, in part, regulated.

A 'brand ambassador' is someone engaged by a brand or agency to promote or present a brand or product to others, sometimes their friends and family, and often for personal reward. The advertiser effectively employs the person as they would a traditional medium like TV or radio. The brand ambassador is the public face of the product, good, or service, such as Beyoncé Knowles for L'Oréal. More recently, this has extended to brand ambassadors being 'employees' of the company, such as Alicia Keys as Blackberry's Global Creative Director and Will.i.am's position as Intel Corp's Director of Creative Innovation. Red Bull is famous for its innovative marketing techniques and is known to indulge in similar practices, from having attractive staff conducting sampling activity at youth events, to not only sponsoring sports teams, but buying them too.

However, as the Advertising Association's 'Check' website (www.check.uk.com) points out, marketers cannot pay or give incentives to anyone to advertise a product without that person making it clear that they are giving a commercial message. This includes 'endorsements' made via social networking sites. The agent, on their part, must not hide that they are being employed to promote a product, and must state that fact in any conversation. In March 2011 enforcement action was taken against one 'group buying' website over illegitimate claims made on Facebook, where an employee of a company presented himself as an ordinary consumer and made positive comments about the company (Office of Fair Trading, 2011).

Regulations on the use of 'brand ambassadors' for commercial purposes are found in the Consumer Protection from Unfair Trading Regulations (2008), administered by the Office of Fair Trading. It is important to note that the output of any 'brand ambassadorship' activity is also regulated. For example, if Cheryl Cole used her 'ambassador' status online to market to children, her message would have to comply with advertising rules, such as the Committee of Advertising Practice (CAP) Code rules on inappropriate products or advertising content. The extension of the Advertising Standards Authority's digital remit, in March 2011, means that all online marketing communications must abide by the CAP Code wherever they appear, regardless of whether it is 'paid for' or not. Whilst the brand ambassador 'mechanism' and any output is regulated, there are currently no regulations about which age this can/cannot actually take place. In the recent

UK government review on the premature commercialization of children (Bailey, 2011), Reg Bailey recommended that the advertising industry takes steps to prohibit the use of brand ambassadors under 16 years old.

In response to the recommendations in the Bailey Review, over twenty leading organizations and trade associations, led by the Advertising Association, signed a Brand Ambassador Pledge. Dubit are signatories of the Brand Ambassador Pledge, and as such we recommend that brands do not conduct brand ambassador activity with children under 16 years of age. The Pledge states that: 'Young people under the age of 16 should not be employed and directly or indirectly paid or paid-in-kind to actively promote brands, products, goods, services, causes or ideas to their peers, associates or friends'. This initiative has been welcomed by the Prime Minister and the Government.

The review by CAP, which was due to end in December 2013, concluded that, though it could not ban the practice, the Advertising Code already applies to the use of children in peer-to-peer marketing and as brand ambassadors.

No figures are available on how many children in the UK are involved in brand ambassador activity. In a recent survey of 39 WOM practitioners, the UK Chapter of the Word of Mouth Marketing Association (WOMMA UK) found that 79 per cent of companies had never used under-18s as 'brand ambassadors', 21 per cent had used teenagers aged 16–17, and 6 per cent had used teenagers aged 13–15. None of the respondents had used children under 13.

WOMMA has a Code of Ethics and Standards of Conduct as a requirement of membership of the association, with the understanding that the Code and Standards reflect an attempt by industry members to 'do the right thing' by engaging in responsible self-regulatory efforts concerning their marketing practices. The fulcrum of the Code and Standards is the Guides Concerning Use of Endorsements and Testimonials in Advertising promulgated by the US Federal Trade Commission. The WOMMA code stipulates that children under 13 should not be used as the agent in any brand ambassador activity. It is unclear whether UK marketers did, or still do, work with child brand ambassadors en masse. It is cheaper, for example, to earn someone's endorsement through a 'share' or 'like' function in a social network or game.

At Dubit we recommend that brands do not conduct brand ambassador activity with children under 16, in order to keep in line with regulations.

Family structure and roles

The traditional view of families is based on the family unit as having two adults (mother and father), each undertaking clearly defined roles based on gender stereotypes and parent–child familial interactions, as shown in the recent advertisements for Argos (Figure 8.12). It has long been recognized that family decision-making is a joint (rather than individual) process, and that family members can occupy different buying roles depending on the nature of the product/service being consumed (see Research Insight 8.3). Typically, parents are the decision-makers and ultimate purchasers or buyers, but other family members also fulfil important roles, such as initiating purchases, influencing the purchasing process and as ultimate users of many purchases. This approach provides a useful description of the

Figure 8.12 Examples of the family unit in an advertisement for Argos
Source: Image supplied by Argos.

RESEARCH INSIGHT 8.3

Epp, A.M. and Price, L.L. (2008), 'Family identity: a framework of identity interplay in consumption practices', *Journal of Consumer Research*, 35, 1, 50–70.

In their CCT paper on family and identity, Epp and Price view family identity as mutually constructed, both internally among family members and externally in relation to the perceptions of outsiders based on observable family behaviour. 'Being a family' is a collective enterprise within which there are bundles of identities, including the overall family identity (e.g. what it means to be a member of the Smith family), but also smaller relational identities existing within family subgroups (e.g. mother–daughter, siblings, parent/couple).

 Visit the Online Resource Centre to read the abstract and access the full paper.

influences on family decisions, but it does not provide many insights into the complexity and variation of family decisions.

Research into family choices around holiday destinations has typically focused on roles and power relations, exploring the relative influence of each family member on the decision process. Wu et al. (2010) found that children were active participants in the decision process around holiday choices, but parents act as gatekeepers filtering out those attractions they judge inappropriate. So, although children are actively involved in making decisions, the range of options available maybe limited by the parents.

In relation to fashion and clothing purchases, Boden (2006) suggests that children are influencing parents' clothing consumption, and that this is welcomed by parents. Parents are relying on children to help them decide what is fashionable or trendy to wear, a form of reverse socialization whereby children are teaching parents.

Sociocultural trends and impact on family consumption

Recent sociocultural trends have resulted in a wider variety of modern living arrangements, challenging the notion of 'the family', with new family and household models where roles and responsibilities are more fluid and less clearly defined than previously. Children under 18 in Asia and the Middle East are still more likely to live in two-parent families than is the case in other parts of the world, and in these countries and South America extended families are often the norm. Adults are least likely to be married in North and South America, Europe, and Australia, with cohabitation becoming increasingly common. In Europe, significant social trends include the increase in lone- or single-parent families, delayed marriages, older parents, blended families, and postponed childbearing, but a woman in Nigeria is still likely to give birth to around five children (www.worldfamilymap.org).

Recent data from the UK indicates that single-parent families are on the increase. In 2009, around 23 per cent of families were headed by a lone parent, compared with a figure of around 8 per cent in 1971 (General Lifestyle Survey, 2011). This has numerous implications. Recent research shows that the involvement of children in consumption decisions is related to family type. Where children live with a single parent, they tend to be more involved in talking about and shopping for goods than children from two-parent or blended families (Tinson et al., 2008). The research attributes this to the complexity of the family arrangement (more complex family arrangements lead to less child involvement), but one-parent households may also expect greater participation of children in important decision-making.

Women in the UK are now older when they give birth for the first time. In 2010, the average age of mothers in the UK was 29.5 for all births and 27.8 years for first-time mothers (Office of National Statistics, www.statistics.gov.uk/). Italy has the highest rate of older births in Europe. The trend towards later parenting is partly fuelled by societal trends around women in the workplace, with many women now in professional occupations. Changing sex roles have led to a shift in how decision-making responsibility is allocated.

More equal distribution of family decision-making is evident, with children having more involvement where there is a less traditional approach to sex roles. However, despite advances in equality in division of labour within households, women still take most of the responsibility for household chores (Asher, 2011), which can impact on approaches to shopping and consumption.

Linked to the trend for late parenting is that such parents tend to have higher disposable incomes and are more likely to spend more money on their children, sometimes regarding children as extensions of themselves in terms of clothing and entertainment purchases. The launch of children's ranges by designers such as D&G, Gucci, and Stella McCartney, with the endorsement and patronage of celebrities (e.g. Jennifer Lopez for Gucci) in their marketing campaigns, captures this trend. A marked trend in recent years is the closure of the parent–child distance (see Consumer Insight 8.3). The proximity in tastes between parents and children is manifest in consumption of leisure activities (music, festivals, restaurants, games consoles), clothes (D&G, Stella McCartney, etc.), and even books (with the *Harry Potter* series being popular with both adults and children). The games console market demonstrates some interesting patterns of consumption as families spend leisure time together. Recent data indicates that 35 per cent of children are playing computer games with their parents (Handley, 2010), and consoles such as the Nintendo Wii, Sony Playstation, and Microsoft Xbox 360 are moving into the family living space.

Ekström et al. (1987) emphasized the importance of taking a reciprocal view of family decision-making and consumer socialization for a more realistic research perspective. In

CONSUMER INSIGHT 8.3

You never actually own a Patek Philippe

The luxury watch market is a lucrative business as watches have become increasingly associated with a person's image and identity. Watches can demonstrate your taste and aesthetic sense. The website bestwatchbrandsguide.com suggests that a high end luxury watch 'is indispensable when trying to advance yourself at your job, or even romantically'. High end watches are also valuable because they retain their value and can be sold for more than their original purchase price (Adams, 2013). The ongoing value of high end watches has been translated into an interesting marketing campaign by Swiss luxury watch manufacturer Patek Phillipe.

The Patek Phillippe brand is strongly identified with family subgroups, with advertisements based around mother–daughter relations and father–son relations. The campaign is called 'Generations' and its tagline is 'You never actually own a Patek Philippe. You merely look after it for the next generation'. The campaign focuses on the connections between parent and child over the life course, emphasizing how the brand is an important part of the development of the relationship. The brand is central to the developing mother–daughter relationship and identification, supporting the particular social dramas, rituals, and stories of that relationship. One advertisement focuses on mother and daughter

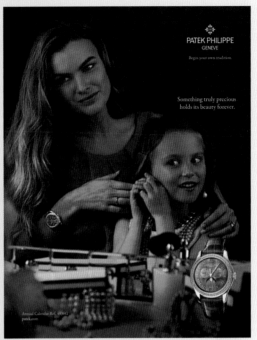

Figure 8.13   Patek Philippe 'Generations'   *Source:* Image courtesy of Leagas Delaney.

enjoying a range of grooming rituals associated with 'dressing up' (e.g. putting on jewellery, hair fixing), and another shows an older mother–daughter pairing, this time sharing a special moment which, although not explicitly stated, is most likely an important and defining occasion such as an engagement (see Figure 8.13). Another advertisement shows a father showing his son how to steer a speed boat. The ads link the rituals and dramas within these important relationships with the presence of the Patek Phillippe brand.

Questions

1. Identify two or three other brands that use a family relationship. What is the nature of the relationship and why do you think that the family context is suitable?

2. Look at some recent advertising for some other high end watch brands. How do they convey the value aspect of such watches addressed in this consumer insight. Can you link their communication approaches to any other theories in this chapter (e.g. word of mouth, opinion leaders)?

Sources: Adams (2013); www.bestwatchbrandsguide.com

  Visit the Online Resource Centre and follow the weblinks to learn more.

their paper they looked at the influence of parents on children and of children on parents in learning about consumption. They found evidence of **parental yielding**, *which is when a parental decision-maker is influenced by a child's request and 'surrenders'*, a range of tactics used by children (such as informing, persuasion, and reasoning strategies), and also the idea of **reverse socialization**, *which is where parents acquire consumer skills from their children*. This is evident in the area of technology (e.g. using the internet). Children also influence parents in relation to celebrity/popular culture, environmental issues, and ethical issues.

Social class structures and impact on consumption

As already suggested in this chapter, consumption behaviour and practices can play an important role in marking distinction and reflecting social position. Max Weber (1978) defined status groups as communities of people linked together on the basis of wealth, status, and power. Marketing is interested in how these communities share similar tastes and consumption practices. One area where this has been used extensively by marketers is in the categorization and classification of consumers based on social class position. These systems reflect divisions, or groups, of people based on a composite measure of income, occupation, and education. Two commonly used approaches in the UK are the Joint Indus- try Committee for National Readership Surveys (JICNARS) and that used by Office of National Statistics (ONS) where occupation alone is taken as an indicator of social class, but which reflects newer employment patterns.

The focus of these classification systems tends to be the resources available to people, with the emphasis on economic resources. Such classification systems are still commonly used in the UK for both policy/government and commercial purposes, in particular to identify appropriate products and services for particular groups and to target these differ- ent groups. According to Bourdieu (1984), people draw on three different types of resource (economic, social, and cultural capital) to compete for status, referred to as symbolic capi- tal (Holt, 1998). Economic capital relates to the financial resources available to the indi- vidual, while social capital covers the relationships and social networks that influence behaviour. Cultural capital, i.e. knowledge that is accumulated through upbringing and education(Bourdieu, 1984), consists of a set of 'socially rare and distinctive tastes, skills, knowledge and practices' (Holt, 1998: 3).

According to Bourdieu, people's tastes are predominantly a marker of class. Although an individual may have economic capital and consume brands and products that may confer social standing, without the necessary skills associated with high cultural capital, they will not occupy a higher social position. The role of class and status has been explored in a number of consumer behaviour studies, including research into the status consumption habits of upper-middle-class Turkish women (Üstüner and Holt, 2010), men's participation in DIY projects and how this links to identity (Moisio et al., 2013), and teenagers' use of brands as a form of social communication (Piacentini and Mailer, 2004).

There is a growing body of research looking at disadvantaged consumers, which examines how people living with severe resource constraints cope (e.g. Piacentini et al., 2013; Hamilton and Catterall, 2005; Baker et al., 2005). Where consumers are lacking in economic, physical, cultural, and social resources, they are less likely to fully access the consumer market and thus lose out in the marketplace. Many studies have established that those living on low incomes tend to rely more on cash rather than on bank accounts and often miss out as they do not qualify for discounts (e.g. through direct debit payment options). A recent report into broadband/internet usage (Consumer Focus, 2010) showed that the benefits associated with use of the internet, especially for price comparison purposes, were not viewed as particularly relevant for low income consumers, since many in this category do not have bank accounts or credit facilities to enable access to these deals. Socially responsible marketers need to ensure that they have channels whereby lower income consumers are not excluded in this way.

Conclusions

Our purpose in this chapter was to develop current thinking around the role of groups and social processes on consumption behaviour, and in so doing introduce the reader to some of the implications for marketing and brand communications.

We have **defined the reference group concept** and described the types of reference group which impact on consumption behaviour. We drew on a range of figures from contemporary consumer culture to show the different types of reference groups, including the Ganguro girls in Japan and Kate Middleton in the UK.

The **processes of reference group influence** were described, including the importance of informational, utilitarian, and value-expressive mechanisms of influence. Distinctions between goods consumed in public or in private were drawn, and related to luxury and necessity goods. In Research Insight 8.1 we described Asch's classic study of the development of conformity, an important mechanism for compliance within reference groups. Case Study 8 looks at gym membership, and the mechanisms of group and social influences on how young people use gyms.

We have looked at **social power and social connectedness** within and across groups. Marketers need to be aware of the importance that reference groups play in the lives of their customers and how people discuss issues and products among themselves. Increasingly the use of the internet and social media has meant that these discussions are faster, geographically spread, and can impact a company very quickly. Consumer Insight 8.2 explored how word-of-mouth communications work, focusing on the launch of Uniqlo in Singapore as an example of companies attempting to use social media to create buzz around their brand. While customers will spread good news about new products they have liked or advertisements they have found interesting or funny, they will also be quick to pass on negative information, as has been the case for companies such as Amazon, Google, and Starbucks when they were identified as possibly evading taxes (Barford and Holt, 2013). Within these discussions, some people will be followed more than others and therefore companies need to identify opinion leaders and other influential people and consider the best ways to communicate with them as well as the kind of information that they will be most interested in.

Finally, we paid attention to both **the family** and **social class** as important influences on consumers. One of the most important reference groups is the family, and understanding the changing role of families and family roles within the broader context of communities and social class structures is vitally important for marketing in terms of developing appropriate products and services and identifying different segments within the broader family grouping.

Review questions

1. List the main types of reference group relevant to consumer behaviour? Can you provide examples of each?

2. What are the main mechanisms of reference group influence? Can you provide examples of each in relation to grocery shopping?

3. What is conformity, and how is this relevant for consumer behaviour?

4. Define opinion leadership. Why is opinion leadership relevant for consumer behaviour?

5. What is WOM? How relevant is it for marketing/consumer behaviour today? How might companies manage eWOM?

6. Is family a relevant concept for marketing in the twenty-first century?

7. Why is the concept of social class relevant to consumer behaviour?

Discussion questions

1. If you were producing a matrix of 'reference group influence on product and brand decisions', what products that are important to you would you put into the four squares that reflect those reference groups. How do you think they might vary if your parents or friends were doing this?

2. Identify situations where conformity with the group might affect an individual's behaviour. How might the situation impact on the product, service, and/or brands purchased?

3. Visit a consumer-generated review website and a marketer-generated website. What differences do you notice between them? Examine some consumer comments on both and assess how a consumer might make a decision based on these comments. How would a consumer identify whether the reviewer was an expert or had a similar lifestyle to them.

4. Identify a crowdsourcing site. Make an assessment of what the site owner is getting out of crowdsourcing and what the producer/consumer does. Is this cheap labour or an avenue for creativity?

5. What recommendations would you give a company that is experiencing negative eWOM?

6. Identify one or two current trends in fashion, food, games, or music that you think a coolhunter might be interested in. Consider how they might be adapted for a larger market.

7. To what extent do you think there is variety in the ways that families approach consumption, and what are the key factors influencing this?

8. What do you think will be the impact of technology on the family and how it approaches consumption? What about the impact of children with high digital literacy?

 Visit the Online Resource Centre to test your knowledge further and complete the Multiple Choice Questions for Chapter 8.

CASE STUDY 8

Group and social influences on gym culture

This case focuses on the male gym market in the UK, looking at some of the key trends influencing this market and its growth in consumer terms. We consider gym users as an example of a consumption community, and present some insights into going to the gym from their point of view. The questions focus on (1) how the gym community can be analysed in terms of the key concepts from this chapter, and (2) how the community deals with tensions and difficulties within the community.

Trends in gym usage in the UK

Latest figures from the market research company Keynote indicate that just over a third (35.6 per cent) of all adults in the UK visited a leisure centre, gym, or health club in 2012. More detail is provided by the Leisure Database Company, which states that, in 2012, 12.1 per cent of the UK population were members of a health and fitness club (which includes both private and publicly owned clubs).

Working out in gyms is a popular activity for young people. In the UK, the most recent data tells us that 31 per cent of young adults (aged 16–25) are members of a sporting club or gym (Sport England, 2008), and that 46 per cent of gym users are under 35 years old (Leisure Data Base Company, 2008).

Gyms have become important spaces for people to work on their bodies and discipline their physical selves in the pursuit of improved physical condition and general well-being. Reasons for using a gym include building muscles, losing weight, toning up and looking better, keeping fit and healthy, and increasing performance in a particular sport (Muscle and Strength, 2006). The social aspect of the gym is also important, and friendship groups can be a powerful motivator in terms of both joining the gym and then working out together. The gym is a public space, and working out in the gym provides a place for consumers to scrutinize or 'check out' other users, to compare themselves with, and possibly learn technique from, others. In addition, media and popular culture can influence trends in gym usage, in terms of body ideals being influenced by the media and also in terms of practices. Since the 2012 Olympics, there has been a shift in perception among women regarding desired body shapes, with more young women aspiring to achieve an athletic body like Jessica Ennis. This shift is likely to lead to some women doing more resistance and weight training in their efforts to achieve that physique.

Another cultural shift is in how working out at gyms, and the practices associated with them, has shifted in the popular imagination as a result of featuring in the MTV shows *Jersey Shores* and *Geordie Shores*. Magazines such as *Men's Health* and *Men's Fitness* often feature articles based around the work-out habits of the stars of these shows (see Figure 8.14). Linked to this is a shift in perceptions of protein drinks, which are becoming mainstream and normalized among the gym-using public.

Figure 8.14 Example front cover of the magazine *Men's Fitness*

Source: Image courtesy of *Men's Fitness*, Dennis Publishing Ltd.

Group aspects of gym use

In interviews collected for this case, we investigated how gym users view themselves and other users, and what they think of shifts in the way that gyms are being used. There were a number of frustrations for those who viewed themselves as regular serious gym users compared with lighter users, who had different motives for going to the gym. This comes through in this interview with Michael, who considers himself to be 'a serious bodybuilder':

> *I get frustrated when people are in the gym, dressed in inappropriate clothing on their mobiles and just sitting on machines talking. I have an intense regime and I feel these people just slow down and ruin my experience in the gym.*

When discussing appropriate usage of the gym, for Michael there is a code of practice which includes what to wear and how to behave. This contrasts with some of the lighter users, who are more socially oriented in their motives. This is shown in the quote from Jon, a part-time social gym goer:

I would describe myself as a part time gym goer. For me it is more of a social reason; I like to go to the gym with my friends and then go out and party at night. I guess it's more of a 'yeah I go to the gym' thing.

Clearly, the social dimension is important for Jon, and he views the gym as something he does with friends and as a part of his evening going-out ritual. Going to the gym is a badge that signifies the kind of person he is ('I go to the gym'). Jon goes on to talk about the way that images and trends in popular culture impact his gym life, and it becomes clear that TV shows, such as *Jersey Shores*, do have an influence:

Personally I don't really watch these programmes [Jersey Shore and Geordie Shore], *but the people I socialize with certainly do. They constantly mention names such as Mike 'The Situation' and use the terms GTL—gym, tan, laundry. I go more for the social aspect but my mates like to emulate what they have watched on TV.*

Jon mentions one of the main characters from MTV's *Jersey Shore*, Mike 'The Situation' Sorrentino, who is looked up to and emulated by his friends. All the male characters from *Jersey Shore* are well known for their physiques, and are often shown displaying their 'ripped' bodies. These characters also have their own language and terminology based around going to the gym, which has filtered into the public discourse in gyms (as demonstrated in Jon's quote). GTL ('gym, tan, laundry') is a phrase coined by Sorrentino, and refers to the routine done on a daily basis to ensure that he (and people who want to be like him) look and feel good. According to Sorrentino, *'You gotta GTL every day to make sure you're looking your best bro. If your shirt looks bad it makes the whole product look bad'* (Urban Dictionary, 2010).

Similarly, there are gym users who are driven by more body-conscious motives, as shown by Rory, who works out to achieve a set goal and for a healthy lifestyle:

I really enjoy going to the gym and working out with some of the experienced bodybuilders. Myself, I want to get ripped, and talking to people who really understand nutrition and working out is a great help for me, especially as you can see that they know what they are on about.

A current trend in popular culture is towards men having a 'ripped' appearance, as mentioned by Rory, which means that there is a lot of muscle mass and low body fat—this is the look that features heavily in health magazines and manuals, such as *Men's Health*.

Rory also reveals that one of his motives for going to the gym relates to the guidance he seeks from other gym users, viewing the gym as a place to access expertise on both exercise and nutrition. It is not necessarily the gym staff who provide this support, but rather other gym users, experienced bodybuilders, emphasizing the strong social angle to his gym consumption.

Another aspect of their discussions around the gym relates to how the market has evolved to meet their changing needs and demands. This is seen in the access to protein-based products that are viewed as an important part of the serious bodybuilder's regime. As Michael says:

Looking at the community as a whole, I guess becoming more common we have seen benefits. I remember protein used to be really expensive, hard to come by but now companies seem to be offering various types of supplements helping me get my protein intake for the day—it's now a lot easier and more convenient than eating six chicken breasts and ten eggs!

Similarly, the growth in the market for supplements has changed gym user's perceptions of these products, probably due to increased familiarity with and awareness of them, and also de-stigmatization of their use. According to Rory:

> I have changed my opinion on supplements; I used to think it was unnatural but companies communicating with the market has really helped me understand that it's a great and effective way of getting into shape, keeping healthy quickly and conveniently which is a real added benefit in such busy day-to-day lifestyles. Having a shake stops me from choosing unhealthy take-away and fast food!

Gym users are seeing some benefits of the community becoming more popular and commercial. A few years ago, the protein community was avoided as something that is fake, unnatural, and illegal, and was surrounded by banned substances such as steroids for people who just wanted to get bigger. As mentioned already, the use of protein supplements and drinks has become mainstream, supported by popular culture reference points. In an interview in the magazine *Men's Fitness*, Sorrentino offered his fitness tips, which included: *'eat every few hours. Aim for small meals per day—three meals and three protein shakes* (*Men's Fitness*, 2010).

The gym and fitness market is evolving, and people are starting to see the benefits of working out, which leads them to have quite different goals from gym consumption. The sector is now more appealing and profitable for business investment, and consequently businesses are expanding markets and investing in research and development of new products and nutrition to help people achieve their goals. Drugs screening is being used on products to make them safer, natural, and normal. This is where the hard core community are now starting to see the benefits of a more mixed (or heterogeneous gym user)—because of the expanding market the core community has access to a wider variety of nutritional supplements that are cheaper, taste better, and are more readily available. With increased participation, what were once seen as 'freaks of nature' are now seen as 'wow that's really impressive' and 'role models', since there is a greater awareness and understanding of the effort and commitment needed for improved physical condition and well-being.

Questions

1. This case covers a range of issues around gym users. Analyse the gym community in terms of key concepts of reference group influences and motives for group membership.

2. From your analysis of the gym community, and your understanding of the material in Thomas et al. (2013), describe how the gym community draws on and activates social and economic resources to overcome tensions and difficulties within the community.

Sources: Muscle and Strength (2006); Sport England (2008); Leisure Data Base Company (2008); Men's Fitness (2010); *Urban Dictionary* (2010); Keynote (2013); Thomas et al. (2013); Stewart and Smith (2014).

Thank you to Lee Swinnerton (Lancaster University) for collecting the data for this case. All interviews were conducted in December 2012. All participants' names have been changed for this case work.

 Visit the Online Resource Centre and follow the link to the authors' blog where you can keep up to date with the latest developments in consumer behaviour and further explore theories through additional articles and real-world examples.

References

Adams, A. (2013), 'Wrist Watch Brands & Models of High Value' http://www.forbes.com/sites/arieladams/2013/01/10/wrist-watch-brands-models-of-high-value/ (accessed 8 July 2013).

Adams, S. (2012), ' "Jamie Oliver drove children away from school meals", says Prue Leith', *The Telegraph*, 10 June, http://www.telegraph.co.uk/health/healthnews/9322595/Jamie-Oliver-drove-children-away-from-school-meals-says-Prue-Leith.html (accessed 27 May 2014).

Asch, S.E. (1955), 'Opinions and social pressure', *Scientific American*, 193, 5, 31–35.

Asher, R. (2011), *Shattered: modern motherhood and the illusion of equality*, London: Harvill Secker.

Assael, H. (1998), *Consumer behavior and marketing action* (6th edn), Mason, OH: South-Western College Publishing.

Bailey, R. (2011), *Letting children be children*, www.gov.uk/government/uploads/system/uploads/attachment_data/file/175418/Bailey_Review.pdf (accessed 27 May 2014).

Baker, S.M., Gentry J.W., and Rittenburg, T.L. (2005), 'Building understanding of the domain of consumer vulnerability', *Journal of Macromarketing*, 25, 2, 128–139.

Bakshy, E., Hofman, J.M., Mason, W.A. and Watts, D.J (2011), 'Everyone's an influencer: quantifying influence on Twitter', http://misc.si.umich.edu/media/papers/wsdm333w-bakshy.pdf (accessed 9 March 2013).

Barford, V. and Holt, G. (2013), 'Google, Amazon, Starbucks: the rise of tax shaming', *BBC News Magazine*, 21 May, http://www.bbc.co.uk/news/magazine-20560359 (accessed 27 May 2014).

BBC News (2013), 'Measles in Wales: 2,500 given MMR jabs at clinics', 14 April, http://www.bbc.co.uk/news/uk-wales-22127237 (accessed 12 January 2014).

Bearden W.O. and Etzel, M.J. (1982), 'Reference group influence on product and brand purchase decisions', *Journal of Consumer Research*, 9, 332–341.

Boden, S. (2006), ' "Another day, another demand": how parents and children negotiate consumption matters', *Sociological Research Online*, 11, 2, http://www.socresonline.org.uk/11/2/boden.html (accessed 9 March 2013).

Bourdieu, P. (1984), *Distinction: a social critique of the judgement of taste* (transl. R. Nice), London: Routledge.

Brabham, D.C. (2008), 'Crowdsourcing as a model for problem solving', *International Journal of Research into New Media Technologies*, 14, 1, 75–90.

Bravo, R., Fraj, E., and Martínez, E. (2006), 'Differences and similarities in measuring family influences on young adult consumers: an integrative analysis', *European Advances in Consumer Research*, 7, 104–111.

Bronner, F. and de Hoog, R. (2010), 'Consumer-generated versus marketer-generated websites in consumer decision making', *International Journal of Market Research*, 52, 2, 231–248.

Comm, J. (2010), *Twitter power 2.0: how to dominate your market one tweet at a time*, Hoboken, NJ: John Wiley.

Consumer Focus Report (2010), 'Broadband minded?: Overcoming consumers' barriers to internet access', London: Consumer Focus, http://www.consumerfocus.org.uk/files/2010/10/Broadband-minded.pdf (accessed 21 February 2013).

Consumer Protection from Unfair Trading Regulations (2008), http://tinyurl.com/5rwnzjk (accessed 8 March 2013).

Earls, M. (2009), *Herd: how to change mass behaviour by harnessing our true nature*, Chichester: John Wiley.

Eccleston, D. and Griser, L. (2008), 'How does Web 2.0 stretch traditional influencing patterns?', *International Journal of Market Research*, 50, 5, 575–590.

Ekström, K.M., Tansuhaj, P.S., and Foxman, E.R. (1987), 'Children's influence in family decisions and consumer socialization: a reciprocal view', *Advances in Consumer Research*, 14, 1, 283–287.

Engel, J.F., Blackwell, R.D., and Miniard, P.W. (1990), *Consumer behavior* (6th edn), Chicago, IL: Dryden.

Epp, A.M. and Price, L.L. (2008), 'Family identity: a framework of identity interplay in consumption practices', *Journal of Consumer Research*, 35, 1, 50–70.

Feick, L.F. and Price L. L. (1987), 'The market maven: a diffuser of marketplace information', *Journal of Marketing*, 51, 83–97.

French, J.R.P. (1956), 'A formal theory of social power', *Psychological Review*, 63, 181–194.

French, J.R.P. and Raven, B. (1959), 'The basis of social power', in D. Cartwright (ed.), *Studies in social power*, Ann Arbor, MI: Institute for Social Research.

Future Foundation (2010), 'Global study for BBC Worldwide reveals power of word of mouth', www.future-foundation.net

General Lifestyle Survey (2011), http://www.ons.gov.uk/ons/rel/ghs/general-lifestyle-survey/2011/index.html (accessed 13 September 2013).

Gladwell, M. (2001), *The tipping point*, London: Abacus.

Godes, D. and Mayzlin, D. (2009), 'Firm-created word-of-mouth communication: evidence from a field test', *Marketing Science*, 28, 4, 721–739.

Grossman, L. (2003), 'The quest for cool', *Time*, 30 August, pp 2–6.

Hamilton, K.L. and Catterall, M. (2005), 'Towards a better understanding of the low income consumer', *Advances in Consumer Research*, 32, 1, 627–632.

Handley, L. (2010), 'Games console at hub of family entertainment', *Marketing Week*, http://www.marketingweek.co.uk/games-console-at-hub-of-family-entertainment/3014365.article (accessed 12 September 2013).

Hennig-Thurau, T., Gwinner, K., Walsh, G., and Gremler, D. (2004), 'Electronic word-of-mouth via consumer-opinion platforms: what motivates consumers to articulate themselves on the internet?', *Journal of Interactive Marketing*, 18, 1, 38–52.

Holt, D.B. (1998), 'Does cultural capital structure American consumption?', *Journal of Consumer Research*, 25, 1–25.

Howe, J. (2006), 'Crowdsourcing: a definition', http://crowdsourcing.typepad.com/cs/2006/06/crowdsourcing_a.html (accessed 8 January 2013).

Hyman, H. (1942), 'The psychology of status', *Archives of Psychology*, 269, 1–95.

Katz. E. and Lazarsfeld, P. (1955), *Personal influence*, New York: Free Press.

Keynote (2013), 'ABC1 consumer market report 2013', http://www.keynote.co.uk.ezproxye.bham.ac.uk/market-intelligence/view/product/10643/abc1-consumer (accessed 1 August 2014).

Lazarsfeld, P., Berelson, B.R., and Gaudet, H. (1944), *The people's choice*, New York: Duell, Sloan and Pearce.

Leigh, J.H. (1989), 'An extension of the Bourne typology of reference group influence on product-related decisions', *Journal of Business and Psychology*, 4, 1, 65–85.

Leisure Data Base Company (2008), 'Results of the Second National Audit of Fitness Consumers', http://www.theleisuredatabase.com/4/results-of-the-second-national-audit-of-fitness-consumers (accessed 29 March 2013).

Lynskey, D. (2005), 'Fast and furious' *The Guardian*, 30 September, http://www.guardian.co.uk/music/2005/sep/30/popandrock.arcticmonkeys (accessed 29 March 2013).

Mann, L. (1969), *Social psychology*, New York: John Wiley.

Men's Fitness (2010) 'The Situation: how to get my abs!', http://www.toofab.com/2010/11/03/the-situations-revealing-interview/ (accessed 28 February 2013).

Moisio, R., Arnould, E.J., and Gentry, J. (2013), 'Productive consumption in the class-mediated construction of domestic masculinity: do-it-yourself (DIY) home improvement in men's identity work', *Journal of Consumer Research*, 40, 2, 298–316.

Muscle and Strength (2006), ' Why do you go to the gym poll', http://www.muscleandstrength.com/forum/threads/106-Why-do-you-go-to-the-gym (accessed 13 March 2013).

Nairn, A. and Mayo, E. (2009), *Consumer kids*, London: Constable & Robertson.

Nancarrow, C. and Nancarrow, P. (2007), 'Hunting for cool tribes', *Consumer tribes*, B. Cova, R.V. Kozinets, and A. Shankar (eds), Oxford: Butterworth-Heinemann, pp 129–143.

Nielsen (2009), 'Trust, value and engagement in advertising: Nielsen Global Online Consumer Survey', July http://www.nielsen.com/content/dam/corporate/us/en/newswire/uploads/2009/07/trustinadvertising0709.pdf (accessed 27 May 2014).

Office of Fair Trading (2011), 'OFT takes action against group buying website for misleading iPhone sale', 10 March, http://webarchive.nationalarchives.gov.uk/20140402142426/http://www.oft.gov.uk/news-and-updates/press/2011/30-11 (accessed 1 August 2014).

O'Malley, G. (2005), 'NBC goes viral in effort to win with "Biggest Loser"', *MediaPost*, http://www.mediapost.com/publications/article/33866/nbc-goes-viral-in-effort-to-win-with-biggest-lose.html (accessed 1 August 2014).

Park, C.W. and Lessig, V.P. (1977), 'Students and housewives: differences in susceptibility to reference group influence', *Journal of Consumer Research*, 4, 2, 102–110.

Piacentini, M.G. and Mailer, G. (2004), 'Symbolic consumption in teenagers' clothing choices', *Journal of Consumer Behaviour Theory and Practice*, 3, 3, 251–262.

Piacentini, M.G., Hibbert, S.A., and Hogg, M.K. (2013), 'Consumer resource integration amongst vulnerable consumers: care leavers in transition to independent living', *Journal of Marketing Management*, 30, 1/2, 201–219.

Postigo, H. (2003) 'From Pong to Planet Quake: post-industrial transition from leisure to work', *Communication and Society*, 6, 4, 593–607.

Raven, B.H. (1993) 'The bases of power: origins and recent developments', *Journal of Social Issues*, 49, 4, 227–251.

Rogers, E. (1962) *Diffusion of innovations*, New York: Free Press.

Rogers, E.M. and Cartano, D.G. (1962) 'Methods of measuring opinion leadership', *Public Opinion Quarterly*, 26, 3, 435–441.

Samson, A. (2010), 'Product usage and firm-generated word of mouth: some results from FMCG product trials', *International Journal of Market Research*, 52, 4, 459–482.

Sekhon, Y. and Szmigin, I. (2011) 'Acculturation and identity: second generation Indian Punjabis', *Consumption Markets Culture*, 14, 1, 79–98.

Shim, S.Y. (1996) 'Adolescent consumer decision-making styles: the socialization perspective', *Psychology & Marketing*, 13, 6, 547–569.

Shoham, A. and Dalakas, V. (2005) 'He said, she said … they said: parents' and children's assessment of children's influence on family consumption decisions', *Journal of Consumer Marketing*, 22, 3, 152–160.

Sport England (2008) 'Active People Survey 2', http://archive.sportengland.org/research/active_people_survey/active_people_survey_2.aspx (accessed 1 August 2014).

Stewart, B. and Smith, A.C.T. (2014), 'The significance of critical incidents in explaining gym use amongst adult populations', *Qualitative Research in Sport, Exercise and Health*, 6, 1, 45–61.

Surowiecki, J. (2005), *The wisdom of crowds: why the many are smarter than the few*, New York: Anchor.

thedrum.com (2006), 'Glasgow: Scotland with style', *The Drum Modern Marketing and Media*, 6 April, http://www.thedrum.com/news/2006/04/06/glasgow-scotland-style (accessed 20 May 2012).

Thomas, T.C., Price, L.L., and Schau, H.J. (2013), 'When differences unite: resource dependence in heterogeneous consumption communities', *Journal of Consumer Research*, 39, 5, 1010–1033.

Thorniley, T. (2011), 'Uniqlo thrives on digital marketing', *Market Leader:* www.marketingsociety.com/the-library/uniqlo-thrives-digital-marketing (accessed 27 May 2014).

Tinson, J., Nancarrow, C., and Brace, I. (2008), 'Purchase decision making and the increasing significance of family types', *Journal of Consumer Marketing*, 25, 1, 45–56.

Urban Dictionary (2010), http://www.urbandictionary.com/define.php?term=GTL (accessed 18 June 2013).

Venkatesan, M. (1966), 'Experimental study of consumer behavior conformity and independence', *Journal of Marketing Research*, 3, 4, 384–387.

Üstüner, T. and Holt, D.B. (2010), 'Toward a theory of status consumption in less industrialized countries', *Journal of Consumer Research*, 37, 1, 37–56.

Verlegh, P.W.J., Verderk, C., Tuk, M.A., and Smidts, A. (2004), 'Customers or sellers? The role of persuasion knowledge in customer referral', *Advances in Consumer Research*, 31, 304–305.

Watts, D.J. (2007), 'Challenging the influentials hypothesis', *Word of Mouth Marketing Association*, 3, 201–211.

Watts, D.J. and Dodds, P.S. (2007), 'Influentials, networks, and public opinion formation', *Journal of Consumer Research*, 36, 441–457.

Weber, M. (1978), *Economy and Society*, Berkeley, CA: University of California Press.

WOMMA, 'Code of Conduct', http://www.womma.org/ethics/womma-code-of-ethics

Wu, K., Holmes, K., and Tribe, J. (2010), ' "Where do you want to go today?" An analysis of family group decisions to visit museums', *Journal of Marketing Management*, 26, 7/8, 706–726.

9

CULTURE

Introduction

Culture is often considered to be an important influence on how people behave. When we talk about culture, we are really talking about all the aspects of a society that distinguish members of that society, or group, from those of another. Culture is the shared understandings, meanings, and customs which together act as a 'blueprint' to guide behaviour and to help people live and function in ways that are appropriate and acceptable to others within that same culture. Culture shapes and guides everyday consumption behaviours, and more celebrated special events. Certain aspects of culture are stable and resistant to change, while others are malleable. In this chapter we focus on understanding culture in more depth, and on considering the relevance and impact on marketing practice.

LEARNING OBJECTIVES

Having read the chapter you will be able to:

1. **Define culture**, and appreciate the elements of culture and the varying perspectives on culture.

2. Examine the **elements of the cultural system**.

3. Understand how **cultures are classified** and consider the value of these classifications.

4. Appreciate the nature of **cultural myths and rituals** and the consumption of ritual artefacts.

> **5.** Consider the ways that culture is important for **marketing communications**.
>
> **6.** Understand the concepts of **subcultures** (demographic and consumption based), how these relate to culture, and the implications for consumer behaviour.

Defining culture

Culture *is the sum total of learned ideas, beliefs, values, knowledge and customs that regulate the behaviour of members of a particular society*. There are a number of aspects to this definition and each will be treated in turn.

Culture is learned or inherited

Culture is a learned process, and occurs through socialization. Socialization involves learning through social interactions, making observations, and actively processing this information to form impressions and understandings about everyday practices. The two main approaches to learning commonly discussed in relation to cultural learning are enculturation and acculturation.

Enculturation *refers to how an individual learns the traditional content of his/her native culture*. Cultural practices and values are assimilated through this process, which mostly takes place within family contexts. The development of food tastes provides a good illustration of enculturation in operation. Consumers are not born with likings and preferences for certain types of foods, but through observational learning children begin to mimic the choices of adults and their dietary choices are reinforced through overt social rewards (e.g. praise). Bitter gourd is a popular vegetable in South Asia which is used in curries and prized for its nutritional and medicinal qualities; it is also very bitter, and is definitely an acquired taste. However, various processes of learning come into play (e.g. habituation, learning to like the taste in your mouth; repeated exposure leading to instrumental learning (Chapter 4) reinforced via the praise from parents) which result in the child growing to enjoy (or at least endure!) the taste of gourd.

The approach to cultural learning is **acculturation** which relates *to the idea of movement between places or cultural contexts*. In Penaloza's study of the experiences of Mexican immigrants living in the USA, she defined **consumer acculturation** as '*the general process of movement and adaptation to the consumer cultural environment in one country by persons from another country*' (Penaloza, 1994: 33). The study was concerned with processes and conditions that shaped acculturation experiences and outcomes. The main outcomes were:

- *assimilation*, where the consumers entering the new culture abandon Mexican culture in favour of US culture;

- *maintenance*, where aspects of both cultures are maintained;

RESEARCH INSIGHT 9.1

Luedicke, M.K. (2011), 'Consumer acculturation theory: (crossing) conceptual boundaries', *Consumption, Markets & Culture*, 14, 3, 223–244

Luedicke traces the history of acculturation within the consumer behaviour literature, drawing together and classifying key acculturation studies. Luedicke describes the first wave of acculturation research, which covers studies that focused on migrants' consumption patterns, while the second wave of studies refers to those that explore consumer acculturation experiences. Drawing on empirical data from Germany and Austria, the author develops a model of mutual cultural adaptation, focusing on how both locals and migrants construct and adapt their identity in this new cultural context.

 Visit the Online Resource Centre to read the abstract and access the full paper.

- *resistance*, privileging Mexican culture over US culture and in so doing rejecting aspects of the new culture;

- *segregation*, where there is a separation of cultural needs.

Penaloza described how institutions of society (family, school, church) alongside marketing agents are important in the process of acculturation. An example of such marketing efforts is found in Unilever's Vive Mejor programme (Adweek, 2009). Vive Mejor takes the form of a website and social media presence, all in Spanish, providing helpful lifestyle, cooking, and beauty tips for 'Latina moms' in the USA. From an acculturation perspective, this programme enables Hispanics living in the USA to maintain their 'Spanishness' while living in another country. see also Research Insight 9.1.

Beliefs, values, knowledge, and customs

We refer to beliefs, values, knowledge, and customs in terms of their contribution to culture. As discussed in Chapter 6, **beliefs** are *the thoughts an individual holds about some object, idea or person*. **Values** *are the deep-rooted and enduring beliefs or ideals about what is good and desirable and what is not*. Values tend not to be situation specific; rather, they are more generally held, and act to guide and shape behaviour. The People for the Ethical Treatment of Animals (PETA) campaign in 2007, featuring the Indian film actress Shilpa Shetty, acted at the level of communicating *beliefs* about treatment of animals in circuses ('beaten, lonely and abused'), which spoke to more deeply held values about the ethical treatment of animals in society (Figure 9.1).

Knowledge refers to *the familiarity with people or things, which can include understandings, facts, information, and descriptions gained through experience and education*. Since culture comprises the prevailing norms, practices, beliefs, and values held by a particular group in society, then knowledge about these can be described as cultural knowledge.

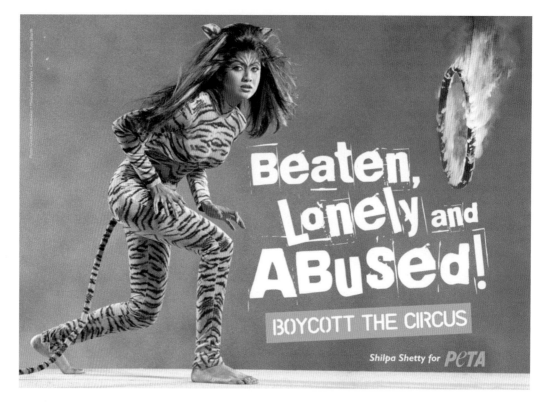

Figure 9.1   PETA campaign   *Source*: Image kindly supplied by PETA (http://www.peta.org.uk/).

Customs *are the norms of behaviour that have been passed from generation to generation.* These serve to control basic behaviour within a culture around the core facets of life, such as the division of labour within the home or how to celebrate rites of passage. It is customary in many cultures to leave a tip in service encounters—a gratuity for a service performed. The approach to tipping varies with culture and is influenced by local customs. In the USA, there is a strong tipping culture; in restaurant settings it is usual to leave 15–20 per cent as a tip (anything less suggests that you are unhappy with the restaurant service). In other countries, such as Japan, tipping is not the custom, and indeed to tip someone is viewed as rather insulting.

Culture regulates the behaviour of members of a particular society

Culture is communicated to members of society through a common language and commonly shared symbols. Because the human mind has the ability to absorb and process symbolic communication, marketers can promote intangible product concepts as well as tangible products. In the consumer world, advertising provides models for behaviour and also reinforces desired modes of behaviour and expectations. The promotional material for Cognation, an organization encouraging mountain bike and trail use in South Wales, UK, provides a good example of how cultural learning can shape consumer behaviour

Figure 9.2 Enculturation of family fun

Source: Image printed with kind permission from Cognation Mountain Biking Trails South Wales, Neath Port Talbot County Borough Council.

(Figure 9.2). This image shows a family out on their bikes, with the bold message 'Family Fun Day' labelled across the picture. A number of cultural messages are communicated here: the tagline 'Family Fun Day' emphasizes the point that this is a family activity; the way the family is dressed shows us the appropriate clothing and equipment needed for this type of activity; finally, the order of cycling (parents at the back, children at the front) conveys a message around the protective role of parents towards their children. All these together provide a clear example of how consumers are enculturated to practices that are developed and reinforced around cultural understanding of what constitutes 'family fun'.

The movement of cultural meaning

Another aspect of understanding learning within culture relates to how cultural meaning moves between the different aspects of society that make up culture (see Chapter 7). Figure 9.3 shows how meaning moves from the existing 'out there' in the wider cultural world to meaning for individual consumers which then shapes their consumer behaviour. According to McCracken (1986), cultural meaning is influenced by cultural categories (how the culture organizes time, space, nature, the sacred and society) and cultural principles—the values, ideals, norms, and beliefs that allow things to be grouped into cultural categories, ranked, and interrelated. McCracken's diagram can be used to demonstrate how the meaning associated with consumer goods transfers to consumers through cultural understanding of the world (e.g. catwalk parades of high fashion, worn by celebrities) and via consumption-related acts (e.g. fashion, grooming, and possession rituals). An analysis of the famous Alexander McQueen Armadillo shoe provides an illustration of this model in action.

In October 2009, the fashion designer Alexander McQueen launched his Armadillo shoe as part of his Spring/Summer 2010 collection (see Figure 9.4). This was a shoe like

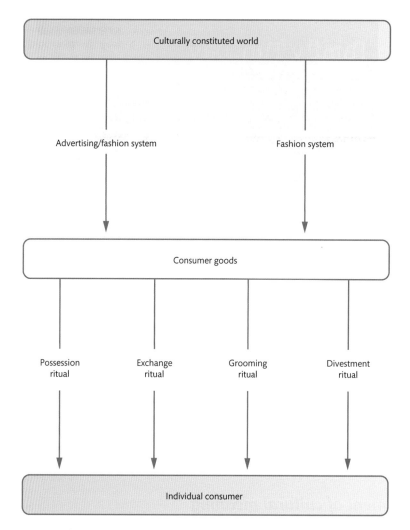

Figure 9.3 Movement of cultural meaning

Source: McCracken (1986). Printed with permission from University of Chicago Press.

no other—12 inches in total height, it was a completely new form of shoe which disrupted the consumer's idea of what a shoe could be. More suited to high fashion than everyday consumer lives, the shoe was initially a part of the *culturally constructed world* as shown at the top of McCracken's diagram. It was then famously worn by Lady Gaga in her video for *Bad Romance*, and subsequently by other celebrities (such as American singer–songwriter Kelis), moving the shoe from high fashion into mainstream consumer culture. Thus it became a *consumer good* as represented in the centre of Figure 9.3. The shoe then started to appear in mainstream fashion magazines and newspapers, and was worn by other celebrities; it then became a *form of possession and grooming ritual*, the final stage in the diagram, until it ultimately came to have greater familiarity for consumers and thus entered the worlds of

Figure 9.4   Left: the Armadillo shoe on the foot of Lady Gaga. Right: a ShoeTease T-Shirt signifying how iconic the shoe became, particularly after McQueen's death

Source: Left-hand image supplied by Getty; right-hand image courtesy of ShoeTease.

individual consumers. While the shoe probably had little impact on consumers in terms of purchases, it did so in terms of its role in popular culture.

The cultural system

A cultural system is comprised of three main elements, which together help to understand the culture: ecology, social structure, and ideology. Looking first at ecology, this refers to the physical geography of a place, and the way that a system has evolved and adapted to suit that environment. Ecology will shape culture, since it provides the conditions within which culture is played out. In warm climates, people wear light clothes, they participate in outdoor leisure pursuits, and air conditioning in buildings is common. Contrast this with colder climates, where warm clothes and jackets are worn, leisure activities are more indoor-based, and heating in buildings is important. Natural resources shape cultural practices, but so too do technological advancements. Japan is a population-dense country, where domestic space is scarce. Space-saving devices, such as the shopping bag which unfolds to produce an ironing board and the mobile compact kitchen (Figure 9.5) are useful and popular among Japanese consumers.

The second element, social structure, tells us about the way that orderly social life is maintained in a culture. This can apply not only to domestic life (including gender roles and parent–child relations) but also to political life. These ideas are often reflected in advertisements serving to reinforce stereotypes around the dominant social structure. A frequent narrative in the advertising of household goods involves the family and, within

Figure 9.5   Japanese mobile compact kitchen

Source: Image courtesy of Toshihiko Suzuki and Atelier Opa (http://www.atelier-opa.com/).

that, family roles. Figure 9.6 shows a recent advertisement that reflects dominant ideas about the social structure in the UK. Despite the increase in the number of women in the workplace, this advertisement (along with others) reflects the position that, in the UK, cleaning and household tasks are still largely considered to be women's work within families.

The final aspect of the cultural system relates to ideology, which reflects *the mental characteristics of a people*, building on the assumption that members of a society possess the same worldview, ethos, ideas, and principles. Hip-hop music is popular in Brazil, and is used by young marginalized people, living in the favelas (slums), to comment on and try to change their lives and Brazilian society as a whole (Pardue, 2005). More than acting as a form of musical expression, hip-hop music is an important way for young Brazilian men and women to express their ideology of social consciousness, truth-telling, and transformation.

Classification of cultures

Core societal values

We know that cultures emerge and form in relation to core societal values, which in turn shape behaviour and practices. While many authors have described the various dimensions of culture, one of the main ways that different cultures are discussed is in terms of their emphasis on collectivism versus individualism (Triandis, 1995). Although this is quite a blunt instrument for categorizing cultures, it does provide some insights into the key

Figure 9.6   Reflection of the family role in UK advertising

Source: Image supplied by The Advertising Archives.

concerns and values that influence people's behaviour in different cultures. Collectivist cultures, such as those of Portugal, Indonesia, Venezuela, and Japan (de Mooij and Hofstede, 2002; Bu et al., 2013), are characterized by a focus on collective well-being, and in these cultures people tend to prioritize the group's goals over personal goals. The 2009 Converse Japan advertising campaign recognizes the collectivistic influences in its society. The advertisement shows Japanese schoolgirls and schoolboys all in identical school uniform wearing various different Converse styles and coloured shoes. The advertisements are striking, as they contrast the traditional Japanese school uniforms with the colourful Converse shoes and thus show the schoolchildren expressing their individuality while retaining a strong sense of social connection to others.

In more individualistic cultures, such as the USA, UK, and Australia, people's behaviour is mainly determined by personal goals which may overlap with collective goals. In South Australia container deposit legislation allows people to collect a deposit for each drinks container they return to a recycling depot. This incentive encourages people to recycle at the individual level, but also leads to a wider societal and community benefit associated with greater levels of recycling behaviour and reduced littering.

Although it is helpful to see broad cultural differences, it would be wrong to assume that everyone in a certain culture is a collectivist or an individualist—rather, these provide a general way of understanding how society is shaped within a culture. This, in turn, is helpful to marketers in understanding the best way to communicate their brand message to each different culture.

Dimensions of cultural values

Core societal values are important in understanding cultures and underpin the various dimensions of culture which help us to understand how different people act and behave around the world. One of the most famous categorizations is the Dutch consumer behaviour researcher Geert Hofstede's dimensions of culture, which was developed from a work-based study of IBM employees (Hofstede, 1984, 2001). Hofstede identified the main dimensions of culture as individualism, masculinity, power distance, uncertainty avoidance, and long-term orientation. Although they have been criticized over the years (these criticisms will be discussed in the next section), these dimensions have been widely used. This approach does provide some useful insights for understanding consumption in different cultures. We will now look at each of Hofstede's dimensions.

Individualism *refers to the ways in which individual goals are balanced against collective or group goals, with individualistic cultures prioritizing the individual's goals over those of the collective (and vice versa).* This dimension refers to the strength of the ties people have with others within the community, with high individualism characterized by a lack of interpersonal connection and little sharing of responsibility, whereas low individualism is applicable in cultures where there is strong group cohesion. The German advertisement for Coca Cola Light emphasizes individuality in its strapline, 'Nur du, bist du', which translates as 'Only you are you'. According to Hofstede's framework, Germany is a highly individualistic culture, and this advertisement emphasizes the way that the drink resonates with and supports the maintenance of this particular dimension of German culture.

Masculinity *refers to motives which are classified as either achievement-oriented, with an emphasis in heroism, assertiveness, and material reward (labelled masculine in Hofstede's terms), or more consensus-oriented, where the emphasis is on cooperation, modesty, caring, and quality of life (labelled feminine in Hofstede's terms).* Sweden is often considered to be a feminine culture (de Mooij and Hofstede, 2002) where quality of life, caring, and cooperation are valued. A more masculine culture is one such as Slovakia (Sidle, 2009), and the digital campaign for Miele S8 vacuum cleaner provides an illustration of this (Figure 9.7). The agency behind the campaign used a billboard to turn a well-known tunnel in Slovakia into a vacuum cleaner pipe which sucked

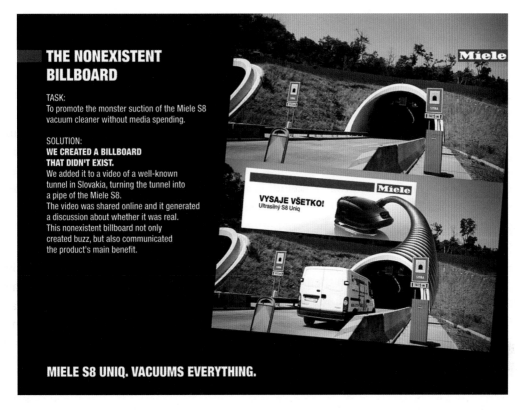

THE NONEXISTENT BILLBOARD

TASK:
To promote the monster suction of the Miele S8 vacuum cleaner without media spending.

SOLUTION:
WE CREATED A BILLBOARD THAT DIDN'T EXIST.
We added it to a video of a well-known tunnel in Slovakia, turning the tunnel into a pipe of the Miele S8.
The video was shared online and it generated a discussion about whether it was real.
This nonexistent billboard not only created buzz, but also communicated the product's main benefit.

VYSAJE VŠETKO!
Ultrasilný S8 Uniq

Miele

MIELE S8 UNIQ. VACUUMS EVERYTHING.

Figure 9.7   The Miele tunnel billboard

Source: Image printed and supplied with kind permission of Mayer/McCann Erickson, Slovakia, and Miele.

up everything—including cars and trucks going through the tunnel. The strong and powerful imagery of the advertisement suited this cultural context.

Power distance (PD) is about the relations between people, and the ways that interpersonal relationships form when power differences exist. Cultures with high PD tend towards a hierarchical structure, with an unequal distribution of power. In low PD cultures a flatter structure of relations exists, with power shared and well dispersed. Malaysia is considered to score highly on the PD dimension (de Mooij and Hofstede, 2002), implying a hierarchical structure, whereas as Austria, Israel, and Denmark have low PD scores (Aguinis, Joo and Gottfredon, 2012), suggesting a flatter structure.

Uncertainty avoidance (UA) *relates to how a cultural group feels about ambiguity, and the extent to which its members avoid or embrace uncertainty and risk.* It refers to the degree of anxiety members of the society feel when in uncertain or unknown situations. High UA cultures avoid ambiguous situations whenever possible, whereas low UA cultures enjoy novel events and value differences. Austria is a culture that scores reasonably highly on the UA scale, suggesting that Austrians tend to avoid ambiguity and reduce risks by relying on rules, laws, and regulations. China, on the other hand, is a country which scores relatively low on the UA dimension, implying that it is a culture that enjoys novelty and difference, as well as ambiguity (Aguinis et al., 2012).

Long-term orientation (LTO) This relates to the time orientation of the culture and its perspectives on time and tradition. Cultures with a long-term orientation tend to understand the importance of context and situation, and display characteristics associated with perseverance. These cultures are likely to save and invest, and exhibit thriftiness and perseverance in achieving results in the long term. In contrast, shorter-term cultures tend not to save for the future, but instead focus on achieving quick results. China is a country with a long-term orientation, and the China Construction Bank (Asia) ran a successful campaign in 2008 aimed at reinforcing the shared values that parents have for their children about the importance of education and building a successful career and future. The company adopted a multi-platform approach, including sponsorship of a family TV programme in the USA, *Are You Smarter Than a 5th Grader?*, in which children pitch their intelligence and wit against adults. Association with the programme made sense for the company. The show emphasized the importance of education and being smart for long-term gains, and this echoes the China Construction Bank's underpinning brand values. Of course, while some marketers want to capitalize on the particular cultural identities of countries, others can see an opportunity for undermining cultural characteristics, as was the case with the Norwegian soft drink Solo described in Consumer Insight 9.1

Critiques of Hofstede

It is important to note that much criticism has been levelled at Hofstede's work (McSweeney, 2002; Baskerville, 2003; Fang, 2010) (see Research Insight 9.2). This criticism includes issues around measurement and sampling. The original study was based on one organization only, it was undertaken at a time of political instability which may have influenced the dimensions, and there was a lack of inclusion of people from socialist and less affluent countries in the sample. Hofstede's assumptions about culture have also been criticized. For example the categorization assumes that national identity translates to cultural identity, and therefore ignores the variations within a culture/cultural group.

CONSUMER INSIGHT 9.1

How to be un-Norwegian

In their book *Cultural Strategy*, Holt and Cameron (2012) question cultural orthodoxy by stating that cultural innovations can undermine the status quo, just as changes in society create demand for new and different cultural innovations. This is what Solo, a soft drink from Norway, did through a combination of traditional and social media. Above all, the communications strategy built upon a cultural conundrum—Norwegians are both proud and frustrated by their modesty as a nation.

Solo is a soft drink, but for too long it was modest in its ambitions. Although it was drunk by Norwegians on special occasions, it had been losing market share to global brands such as Fanta. The strategy to rebuild the brand was constructed around the idea of making Norwegians proud of Solo by imbuing it with the same confidence as a global brand. Solo was aware that young people's perception was very important in the choice of soft drinks, both for themselves and in the family context, and they wanted to build an identity sympathetic to the young and also use them as a channel to talk to one another about Solo. Solo decided that its route to getting young people's attention was to challenge modesty and do something 'un-Norwegian' by sticking its neck out and advertising in the USA. The campaign began with a billboard on Sunset Boulevard in Los Angeles using lines such as 'Shocking but true—the world's best soft drink is yellow and Norwegian'. To enlist engagement, Norwegians were then able to upload their own billboards onto video screens on Sunset Boulevard with endorsements on Twitter from US celebrities such as Paris Hilton and Lindsay Lohan. This was followed by a competition where winners were able to get their pictures on a digital billboard with the line 'A Norwegian soft drink with an American Dream'. The line below the Solo brand name was always 'Soon to be world famous'—all modesty forgotten! The brand was not really trying to become world famous; what it wanted was to be noticed by Norwegians. Above all, the idea of a Norwegian brand acting in an un-Norwegian way appears to have resonated with young people who in turn shared their responses on Facebook and other social media—a true cultural innovation. By advertising in the USA Solo was not concerned about marketing to the USA, as the brand could not actually be bought there. It wanted its consumers at home to realize that it had big ambitions. Following this, Solo undertook an initiative with DHL allowing Norwegians to send a bottle of Solo to anyone in the world. Recipients sent photos of themselves with Solo from 130 countries using Facebook and other online initiatives.

The campaign was noticed by 80 per cent of the target group and sales increased by over 7 per cent.

Questions

1. If Norwegians are modest, what other national cultural stereotypes are you familiar with? Are they useful for marketing?

2. Solo used a national stereotype as the basis for their cultural innovation. What other characteristics might be used (e.g. gender, age, occupation) and how?

Sources: Michaelsen (2011); Ehrlich (2012); Holt and Cameron (2012); Larsen (2012).

 Visit the Online Resource Centre and follow the weblinks to learn more about Solo.

RESEARCH INSIGHT 9.2

McSweeney, B. (2002), 'Hofstede's model of national cultural differences and their consequences: a triumph of faith, a failure of analysis', *Human Relations*, 55, 1, 89–118

In this paper, the author critiques Hofstede's national culture research by challenging the assumptions made in the development of his model. The author questions the plausibility of analysing and explaining national culture in this way and drawing causal connections about culture.

 Visit the Online Resource Centre to read the abstract and access the full paper.

Culture norms and rules for behaviour

Within any culture there are norms of behaviour, which refer to the accepted main ways of behaving. These norms are shaped by the underpinning values or principles of a culture. Cultural norms are rule-bound, and in any culture there tends to be a fairly complex set of rules for behaviour. These norms can be either enacted (explicitly decided on) or crescive (meaning embedded in the culture). Crescive norms are often not formally noted—rather, learning about the culture takes place through experiences and interactions within that culture. Crescive norms can be further broken down into customs, mores, and conventions.

Customs *are the norms of behaviour that have been passed from generation to generation.* These serve to control basic behaviour within a culture, around the core facets of life. For example, in Japan it is the custom to always take your shoes off before entering someone's home. **Mores** *are particular forms of custom and have a strong moral overtone.* Mores often involve a taboo or forbidden behaviour, and violation of mores is met with strong censure from other members of a society. Some cultures strongly condemn people sleeping together before they are married. **Conventions** are also a specific form of custom, and relate to the norms for the conduct of everyday life. These are often subtle and not always easy for people outside a culture to learn. They may include conventions around how to behave at a dinner party, or the 'correct' way to dress within a specific cultural group. In the UK, 'going to the pub' is a fairly common cultural activity and viewed as a quintessential part of UK culture. Conventions might include routines for buying drinks, buying a round, and etiquette around buying a drink for the person working behind the bar. This knowledge of cultural norms is important for marketers, especially in terms of showing consumers how products might fit into their consumption patterns.

Making sense of culture: the role of myths and rituals

In addition to the norms of a culture, it is important for cultures to have stories and practices which help provide a collective sense of its values and what is important to the culture. Two key aspects of this are myths and rituals.

The **myth** *is a story that contains symbolic elements that express shared emotions and ideals of a culture.* Myths serve the function of emphasizing how things in a culture are interconnected; they maintain social order by authorizing a social code. According to Woodside et al. (2008: 98), 'a myth is a traditional story about heroes or supernatural beings', and often features a conflict between two opposing forces.

Myths provide psychological models for individual behaviour and identity. Effectively, these stories present cultural ideals and direction, and can provide consumers with guidelines about their world (see Consumer Insight 9.2). Archetypes are models of people, behaviours, or personalities (discussed in Chapter 7), and are central to myths.

CONSUMER INSIGHT 9.2

Consumer archetypes and myths

Stories are very powerful in people's lives as a way of communicating, and marketing companies strive to create brand myths, or stories, in order to produce powerful emotional connections with consumers. Sometimes marketers use the idea of myth creation to build or invent a myth around their brand. An interesting example is found in the clothing brand Jack Wills. According to the company's founders, 'Our registered trademark "Fabulously British" defines our inspiration: British heritage, style and culture. We interpret these traditional starting points in our contemporary way, playing off the tensions that are created between old and new, formal and casual. This eccentric, dandyish British style is the essence of our Fabulously British concept, and is reflected across our brand: from our product and store design to our graphical output and events' (www.jackwills.com). The company attempts to create an emotional connection with consumers, portraying itself as a heritage brand with a long history (named after the grandfather of one of the founders), with a key role to play in a particular form of British culture.

Questions:

1. Think of some archetypes that you are familiar with and consider how they are reflected commercially. You might start by considering how they are used in advertising and retailing, as well as in digital marketing contexts.

2. Visit the online resource centre and follow the weblink to Entreproducer to find out more about creating audience archetypes. For a product category of your choice, think about how you might develop a social media campaign based around one central archetype (e.g. the hero, the seductress, the friend/buddy).

Sources: Vernon (2012); Clark (2012); www.jackwills.com

 Visit the Online Resource Centre and follow the weblinks to learn more about Jack Wills, Entreproducer, and other organizations that make use of archetypes and myths.

Myths are often used in a nostalgic way in advertising, encouraging consumers to look back in time and remember the 'good old days' (often involving an element of re-imagining the past). Classic examples of this include the Ridley Scott advertisement for Hovis bread with the imagery of a boy cycling over cobbled streets to deliver bread, the voice-over of an old man yearning for the past, a brass band playing, and the overall implication of a more wholesome, better life. This is a very British advertisement, picking up on specific cultural cues, which would not translate to other cultures.

Rituals are very important in the transfer of meaning within cultures. The term **ritual** refers to a symbolic and expressive activity, often comprising multiple behaviours which occur in a fixed sequence and are repeated over time (Rook, 1985). There are many rituals in our lives: some can be viewed as sacred and relating to broad cultural or religious values (e.g. the ritual of removing shoes before entering a mosque), but others are considered more mundane, such as getting dressed in the morning. Within marketing, rituals have been applied to understand consumption, and six main types of ritual have been identified.

The main types of consumer ritual

Grooming rituals *are those private behaviours that consumers undertake to aid the transition from private to public self (and back again).* Rituals associated with getting ready for a night out (showering, putting on make-up, choosing outfit) prepares the consumer as they move from their private space to a more public and social space.

Possession rituals are *the rituals associated with transforming mass-produced products from the marketplace into more personal products for the home or workplace.* For example, home purification is a ritual favoured by new age practitioners which involves burning a sage smudge stick to 'cleanse and remove the residual or negative energy left behind by the previous occupants' (Allegheny, 2010). This product enables the new homeowners to make the house spiritually theirs.

Gift-giving rituals are *the rituals surrounding giving presents to others.* These rituals may be extensive, including obtaining/finding the gift, giving the gift, receiving the gift, and gift reciprocation. While gifts have an economic value, they also have a symbolic value which emphasizes the social connections between people.

Sanrio, owner of the Hello Kitty brand, lists its principal business as the 'sale of social communication gifts'. Japanese people have a deep gift-giving tradition, and Hello Kitty is a brand that plays on this cultural practice. According to the Sanrio Company website 'Giving someone a cute Hello Kitty letter set doesn't just say 'let's stay in touch'—it gives them a means to do so'. Figure 9.8 shows a range of Hello Kitty products.

Self-gifts are *a specific example of gift giving, where consumers purchase self-gifts as a way of regulating their behaviour.* We may buy a gift as a treat or a reward for some success, but also as a way to cheer ourselves up if we are having a bad day. Companies often encourage self-gifting; for example, an advertisement for the fashion company J. Crew, suggested 'Before you lavish your loved ones with gift upon gift this holiday season, take the time to treat yourself …'.

Holiday rituals are *the rituals associated with both tourism holidays and culturally bound holiday seasons (such as Christmas, Easter, and Eid).* Holidays are important rituals, and represent consumers suspending their everyday lives and performing particular ritualistic behaviours. Many of the main film companies schedule their major film releases to coincide with the holiday season (Easter, Summer, Christmas), tapping into family rituals around holidays and cinema-going.

Rites of passage rituals are *those rituals which mark a change in a person's social status.* Examples of such changes might include a child's first day at school, getting married, becoming a parent, and even getting divorced. In the USA, the baby shower party is a way of marking the beginning of a new chapter in people's lives, i.e. becoming a parent, and baby showers are also becoming popular in other cultures.

SANRIO / CHARACTERS LOGO   *Sanrio*

©'76, '13 SANRIO CO., LTD.

LO.01

© 1976, 2013 SANRIO CO., LTD.

Figure 9.8   Hello Kitty products and logo showing the range of characters

Source: Images courtesy of Sanrio.

Elements of the ritual

According to Rook (1985) there are a number of elements that are common to rituals. As with other aspects of culture, these are not formally noted down, but are learned through immersion in the culture. First there are **ritual artefacts**, *which are the objects and products that accompany or are consumed in a ritual setting.* These artefacts often communicate specific symbolic messages understood by ritual participants. There is also a **ritual script** which *guides the use of the ritual artefact—which artefacts to use, by whom, the sequence of use, and the types of comments that accompanies the ritual.* **Ritual performance roles** *are the roles occupied by people involved in the ritual as they perform according to the script.* Finally, there is a **ritual audience**, *who are the people who witness or are involved in the ritual in some way* beyond those involved in the particular performance roles.

Tea drinking is a ritual which can be analysed to reveal these elements. The ritual artefacts include the tea, the teapot, the milk, the crockery, and the cakes, but also the location or venue (e.g. Fortnum and Mason, London or the Victoria Room, Sydney) (see Figure 9.9). The script could include aspects such as the sequence of service within the tearoom, what additions are appropriate (milk, lemon, honey, sugar), and when it is appropriate to pour milk. In terms of performance roles, there will be roles around service within the tearoom, who pours the tea, and the appreciative recipient of the tea. Finally, the audience (other than those directly involved) may refer to other customers in the tearoom, as well as those whom you talk to about the tea (word of mouth). When you compare tea drinking around the world it can be seen that the elements may differ. Each culture has its own rituals, and these can be a very important aspect of that particular culture.

Rites of passage

Rites of passage *are a specific type of ritual that marks a change in a person's social status.* These rites can relate to changes that are a natural aspect of the consumer's life course, for example

Figure 9.9   Afternoon tea in The Victoria Room, Sydney

Source: Image courtesy of The Victoria Room, Sydney.

RESEARCH INSIGHT 9.3

Hogg, M., Folkman Curasi, C., and Maclaran, P. (2004), 'The (re)configuration of production and consumption in empty nest households/families', *Consumption, Markets & Culture*, 7, 3, 239–259

Hogg et al. (2004) conducted an in-depth study of female 'empty nesters' (mothers whose children have left home) in the UK, Ireland, and the USA. Their main findings were that this role status transition caused distress for mothers, forcing them to evaluate their mothering role and how this was enacted when their children no longer lived in the family home. Mothers talked of moving from production-led tasks (feeding, cleaning, laundry) to more consumption-based activities (meals out, phone calls, gifts for flats/halls of residence).

 Visit the Online Resource Centre to read the abstract and access the full paper.

moving from the world of the child to the world of the adult (such as becoming a teenager, moving out of the family home), but also to changes in people's lives which are more individual and specific in nature (e.g. being made redundant or facing a serious illness). However, in contemporary consumer society the markers of this transition (from child to adult) are not always obvious or clear-cut.

Such changes, or transitions, are marked by a time of uncertainty, and studies have shown that consumers rely on familiar products and brands to support them through uncertain times. Since rites of passage relate to times of change, it is clear that over the life course people go through many changes, and marketing has a role to play in providing consumers with the goods and services they need as they move through these stages (see Research Insight 9.3).

Culture and communication

It is important to understand culture in terms of giving meaning to objects, activities, and practices. Culture plays an important role in terms of the content and tone of advertising and marketing messages, and an understanding of the various aspects of culture informs communications (see Consumer Insight 9.3).

Apart from understanding cultural values and beliefs, it is important to appreciate the various customs and norms influencing the ways that people behave, which may impact on how they incorporate consumption into their daily lives. The Philips Augmented Reality Mugs Campaign worked in that context as a response to the cultural norms around male grooming.

In addition, an important aspect of understanding culture's impact on consumption lies with the idea of sacred and profane consumption, and how this exists in various cultural settings.

CONSUMER INSIGHT 9.3

Philips in Taiwan

The advertising campaign for Philips grooming products in Taiwan is a good illustration of a culturally informed campaign. Taiwanese men prefer a clean-shaven look, and the challenge for Philips was to interest them in facial hair and grooming in order to increase sales of shaving products. Philips created a campaign around 'Augmented Reality Mugs', clear glass mugs with facial hair stickers. The mugs were presented at selected salons in Taiwan, and drinking from one gave the consumer an indication of how he might look with facial hair (as shown in Figure 9.10). Interested customers were offered a coupon for 50 per cent off Philips' grooming kits.

Figure 9.10   Stills from the Augmented Reality Mugs Campaign

Source: Image courtesy of Philips, Taiwan.

Questions:

1.   Can you think of any other contexts where a culturally informed campaign has been used, or would be useful in your culture?

2.   Think of some specific cultural consumption contexts where this type of approach might be suitable?

Sources: Young (2012); Riley-Adams (2012).

  Visit the Online Resource Centre and follow the weblinks to learn more about this Philips, Taiwan campaign.

Sacred and profane consumption

In the consumer context, **sacred consumption** *is used to refer to objects and events that are 'set apart' from normal activities, and are treated with some degree of respect or awe.* In contrast, **profane consumption** *is the term used to capture those consumer objects and events that do not share the 'specialness' of sacred ones.* In the key article on sacred and profane consumption by

Belk et al. (1989), the authors describe the properties of the sacred aspects inherent to consumer behaviour and the processes by which consumers sacralize and de-sacralize dimensions of the experience described.

Sacred items are not necessarily associated with religion, but most religious items tend to be regarded as sacred. Sacred consumption can be applied to places, people, and events. The Vatican in Rome holds special religious significance for many Catholics around the world. The site of the Holy Thorn Tree on Wearyall Hill in Glastonbury, Somerset, is regarded as one of Britain's most important symbols of Christendom, and attracts visitors and pilgrims as a result. The tourism industry builds on the idea of creating sacred places in order to connect with tourists and to elevate holiday destinations to sacred and special places in consumers' minds. For example, the idyllic remote holiday island, a 'taste of paradise', is sold in this way as a special place that is set apart from the pressures of everyday life, representing a form of escape for consumers.

People can also have sacred status, mainly when they are idolized and set apart from others. This idea is easily applicable to religious figures (such as Mother Theresa or Ghandi), but it can also be applied to individuals who have achieved sacred status for other reasons, such as musical or sporting prowess. Elvis Presley is sacred in the eyes of his fans, many of whom go on a pilgrimage to his home Graceland (which is now a museum) to honour his memory.

Events such as football matches can also take on sacred status. Fans travel long distances to support their teams, and they often sing songs and chants particular to their team (or it can be their national anthem if it is an international game). The singing of *You'll Never Walk Alone* by Liverpool FC fans at the beginning and end of every match is highly ritualistic. Team colours are obviously symbolic. Particular players can have iconic significance for fans, receiving extra applause if they come on as a substitute, or they may occupy a more international cult status (e.g. David Beckham, who enjoys global status). The pitch itself can also be a sacred space, with fans going to stadiums when they close and digging up a piece of the pitch.

Appreciating the difference and symbolism associated with profane and sacred consumption is especially important from a marketing perspective in terms of ensuring that a company gets things right when they enter a market (see Research Insight 9.4). If an organization breaks the conventional norms and values in some way, it is important that they have a keen awareness and understanding of this and therefore what impact it may have on consumers' reactions to their communications (see also Consumer Insight 9.4 on language).

Sacralization and objectification

Attaching sacred meaning to profane consumption is often a challenge for marketers, but this is an important objective in terms of trying to imbue products and brands with distinctiveness and 'specialness' in the consumer's eyes. As sacralization is about giving special

RESEARCH INSIGHT 9.4

Jafari, A. and Suerdem, A. (2012), 'The sacred and the profane in Islamic consumption', *Advances in Consumer Research*, 39, 1, 427–429

The authors challenge the portrayal of Islam as a rigid ideological system and demonstrate that in their everyday life consumption activities (the profane), Moslems constantly (re)interpret religious guidelines of Islam (the sacred) as cultural codes rather than rigid rules. They show how Moslems interpret the sacred Islamic guidelines in multiple ways to shape their everyday consumption practices.

 Visit the Online Resource Centre to read the abstract and access the full paper.

CONSUMER INSIGHT 9.4

Lost in translation

Language is an important part of culture, but often words have meanings that are not so obvious from literal translations. The wider socio-political climate can influence how words are interpreted. There are numerous examples of marketing communication blunders due to a lack of understanding of wider cultural contexts.

- 'The future's bright ... the future's Orange' is the tagline of the telecommunications company Orange. However, it had to be changed for the Northern Ireland market because of the sectarian associations with the Orange Order. The implication of the message was that 'the future is bright, the future is Protestant, loyalist ...', which did not go down well with the Catholic Irish population (Tooher, 1996).

- Kraft foods relaunched its snack food company as Mondelez international. The name is pronounced as 'mohn-da-leez' meant to connote worldwide deliciousness ('monde' from 'world' in French, and 'delez' as a play on 'delish'). However, in Russian this pronunciation sounds like the Russian term for an oral sex act (MacArthur, 2012).

Questions

1. Can you find other examples of marketing blunders due to culturally inappropriate communications?

2. How do companies avoid this happening? What suggestions do you have for how such errors may be avoided?

Sources: Tooher (1996); MacArthur (2012).

 Visit the Online Resource Centre and follow the weblinks to see further examples of brand names that have also been lost in translation.

status to objects, marketing companies attempt to do this through the use of memorabilia associated with special places (e.g. a key ring from Graceland; a festival or concert T-shirt). This process is known as **objectification** *whereby sacred qualities are attributed to mundane items.* **Contamination** *is when objects associated with sacred events or people become sacred in their own right (e.g. items belonging to famous people).*

An associated process is that of **desacralization**, *which is when a sacred item or symbol is removed from its special place.* This can be seen in instances where an iconic object is mass produced—for example, souvenir reproductions of the Eiffel Tower or the use of religious symbols in mainstream jewellery. D&G attempted to make rosary beads a mainstream fashion item by putting models on catwalks wearing rosary beads as necklaces. This caused uproar and upset among Catholics and the Catholic media who considered it sacrilegious (Courier Mail, 2010). Similarly, the Christian cross has been used in mainstream fashion with a variety of designs available on the market, often bejewelled (Figure 9.11).

Figure 9.11 A man wearing rosary beads as a fashion item
Source: © iStock.com/korionov.

In this situation, the special aspect of the iconic object (the Christian cross) is eliminated, turning the objects into inauthentic commodities (no longer a prayer object, but now a fashion necklace). The central premise of desacralization is that objects and activities can move from one sphere to another, that some things that were formerly regarded as sacred have moved into the realm of the profane, and that some everyday phenomena are now regarded as sacred. Events can also undergo such a transformation from sacred to more profane (e.g. the commercialization of Christmas, the touristic exploitation of the sinking of the Titanic), although this is not without danger of criticism since this transformation is against the central values and beliefs of many people within a culture, and can never be accepted.

Subcultures

Within any culture, there exist subcultures (sometimes referred to as microcultures) which are important to marketing since these often capture meaningful links and connections between groups in society. Subcultures share similar values and tastes, and in many ways exhibit the same qualities and characteristics of a culture. The main distinction is that they are smaller in size. **Subcultures** can be defined in *terms of shared demographic characteristics (e.g. age, regionality, ethnicity) or in terms of shared consumption interests.*

RESEARCH INSIGHT 9.5

Hebdige, D. (1979), *Subculture: the meaning of style*, London: Methuen.

Dick Hebdige's 1979 book *Subculture: the meaning of style* provides a deep understanding of sub-cultures from a sociological and cultural studies perspective. In this book, Hebdige describes and discusses Britain's post-war youth subculture styles (such as Teddy boys, mods, and punks) as symbolic forms of resistance, with these groups setting themselves apart from the mainstream in terms of values, politics, and behaviour.

 Visit the Online Resource Centre to find out more about this book.

In marketing the term subculture is widely used to refer to any subgroup of consumption, although early usage implied some kind of subversive activity against mainstream society. Punks in the UK in the 1970s were concerned with individual freedom and being anti-establishment, and used their clothes, music, and behaviour to demonstrate their alternative views.

Subcultures may share demographic characteristics (e.g. in terms of age, race, gender, class), but there is usually a consumption dimension to membership in terms of the adoption of various symbols in the consumer world to signify membership of the group, identifiable ways of dressing (at least to the subcultural group), and shared interests and music styles. Both demographic characteristics and shared consumption interests can be useful for marketers when examining subcultures (see Research Insight 9.5).

Subcultures based on demographic characteristics

A number of criteria can be used to look at subcultures of society defined by demographic characteristics. Here we look at subcultures based on age, sex roles, region, ethnicity, and religion.

Age-based subcultures

Age is often used by marketers to define market segments, on the premise that people of a similar age share similar sets of experiences and can be engaged in a meaningful way through shared cultural reference points. There are many examples of age-based subcultures that are used in marketing (see Table 9.1 for some illustrations). Age-based subcultures can refer to groups of consumers at key stages in their life course (e.g. tweens, teenagers, pensioners). The other use of age-based subcultures is with reference to generationally based subcultures, groups of people who were born at certain key points in history (e.g. Baby Boomers, Generation X, and Millennials), and the marketing interest is in this group of people as they move through the life course.

Tweens
Definition Usually 8–12 years, although there is a slight variation in definitions (e.g. Mintel (2011) defines this group as aged between 10 and 12).
Main points of relevance • Consumers in training, first steps into independence in marketplace interactions. • A key characteristic of this group, making them attractive to marketers, is that they are beginning to make independent purchases. Tweenage girls tend to develop a keen interest in pop music, and are more likely than tweenage boys to listen to the radio and have MP3 players or similar in their bedroom. Tweens are like mini-teenagers, starting to exhibit similar emotional and symbolic aspects of purchasing and consumption. For an interesting application of marketing to this group, see Consumer Insight 9.5.
Teens
Definition Teens is the term used to refer to all youths in the 13–18 age group, although this is a wide-ranging age group, with the needs of young teens being different from those of older teens.
Main points of relevance • In commercial terms, teenagers represent a large and important market, with estimates suggesting that the US market is worth around $200 billion (Brafton, 2010). Teens are difficult for marketers to reach, since often just as marketers have worked out how to engage with young people using the latest communications tools, teenagers have moved on to something new (Roberts and Scott, 2009). • Teens are tech-savvy (often called digital natives), are heavy users of social media, and like interactive content. Many companies targeting this market include strong interactive elements to their campaigns. • Research into smartphone usage by teens shows that the rise in the number of low-priced Android-based phones on the market and the availability of free apps is popular among teens (Shields, 2011).
Generation X
Definition Varies as being born somewhere between 1962 and 1985.
Main points of relevance • Grew up under largely Conservative governments at a time of economic recession. Douglas Coupland's novel *Generation X*, about the lifestyles of young adults during the late 1980s, popularized the use of this term. • Although their needs are likely to be diverse and typical of anyone at this stage of life, it seems that that this cohort are more pessimistic about their financial future, they are used to cheap imports, they are suspicious of marketing, and they want straightforward talk and evidence to support claims.
Generation Y or Millennials
Definition Born between 1980 and 2000
Main points of relevance • Both in the west, often as children of Baby Boomers (also known as the Me generation), and in China (as a result of one child policy). Tend to have been brought up to be high in confidence and self-involved. • High rates of materialism and technology addiction. They are the generation that record everything through social media. • They have less civil engagement and involvement in politics than previous generations.

Table 9.1 Key age-based subcultures relevant for marketing (*Continued*)

Baby Boomers
Definition Those born between 1945 and 1964, sometimes regarded as Baby Boomer Cohort 1 (1946–1955) and Cohort 2 (1956–1964).
Main points of relevance • Baby boomers are those people born after the Second World War at a time marked by optimism and economic security. This group of people were the original 'teenagers', coming of age during the 1960s. • They have been the source and power behind many recent economic changes, but also played a key part in major social and cultural changes in the second half of the twentieth century. • Because of its sheer size, this is a substantial and important market, with high levels of savings and disposable income available. • The issues around the needs of the ageing consumer are considered in more depth in the Practitioner Insight 9.

Table 9.1 *(Continued)*

CONSUMER INSIGHT 9.5

Lollipop Bling for tweenage girls

An example of an age-based subculture are 'tweenagers', the term used to refer to children who are in the pre-teen age group. While various definitions exist, the general view is that this term applies to children aged 8–12 (Clarke 2003), clearly emphasizing their pre-teen status.

In 2010, the singer Mariah Carey launched a new fragrance called Lollipop Bling. Produced in collaboration with Elizabeth Arden and Bazooka Candy Brands, the brand is inspired by Carey's song *Candy Bling* and the story of her engagement ring being presented inside a lollipop package. The fragrance and its packaging are inspired by all things confectionery: sweet smelling, brightly packaged, and with a free gift of Ring Pop, an edible confectionery ring. The supporting website (http://www.lollipopbling.com/) plays the song on a continuous loop, and encourages extended consumer interactions through a game, a messaging service (Candy Gram), and news about future products (Gotta Have It! and Latest Goodies). This is a case of three major companies combining forces to target this age group very effectively.

Questions

1. Can you think of any ethical issues raised by this case?

2. What other product categories do you think are likely to be targeted to tweenagers?

3. Are there any lessons in this approach that can be used in social marketing campaigns aimed at this age group, say to encourage exercise or healthy eating?

Sources: Clarke (2003); Hawks (2010); *Marketing Week* (2010).

 Visit the Online Resource Centre and follow the weblinks to learn more about Lollipop Bling and other tweenage products.

However, marketers need to be careful about assuming that generations are comparable across national and cultural boundaries. In China, Japan, and South Korea, during the time span 1940–2000, there have been six, six, and four generational groups, respectively, all defined differently and with different names and birth periods. It would be a vast oversimplification to assume that Millennials in China are equivalent to Millennials in the USA, Germany, or South Korea, despite sharing some traits such as being highly connected via social networking sites.

Age cohorts are important to business, and the Baby Boomers in particular have drawn much attention from marketers as they have moved through their life course. Obviously, as people get older their needs change and they often become greater users of health and social services. We spoke to Roger Clough, Research Director of Age UK Lancashire, about some of the issues for older people as service users and customers.

PRACTITIONER INSIGHT 9

Roger Clough (Emeritus Professor), Research Director, Age UK Lancashire

For organizations such as Age UK, the UK's largest charity for older people, thinking about the words used to describe the relationship between the individual and the health and social care services is an important concern. Of course the same is true in wider society where, over the years, successive words have been adopted in an endeavour to capture different aspects of a relationship and then discarded as the word itself acquires unwanted overtones. 'Patient', it was thought, suggested too much passivity. Adults in contact with newly formed social services departments in the 1970s were called 'clients', with the hope that they would be seen to have the status of the individual instructing a lawyer. That word was discarded as 'clients' became stigmatized, and, more recently, in the search for a neutral phrase the term 'user' was adopted, although of course that term is now associated with taking illicit drugs. And so we have moved to viewing the individual in contact with social care as a *consumer*. Again, this word was chosen in part to convey normality—we are all seen as customers and consumers in our negotiations with the external world. Given that there had been weaknesses in the ways that some staff in organizations provided such care, one solution that was sought was to give the individual more authority, more negotiating strength. The mechanism was to be consumer choice; the market place was to provide the model.

There are dangers in looking too long and too hard at language and in trusting that new words will change perceptions towards individuals. There are parallel dangers in failing to recognize that changing the language used may be part of a wider shift in the construction of relationships between the worker and the older person who wants a service or activity.

Voluntary organizations like Age UK Lancashire have been working in this consumer framework. Any organization that provides services, support, and activity may find that staff and volunteers have presumed what is appropriate for others and offered limited choice. As voluntary organizations have become larger providers of services under contract to adult social care departments, they have recognized that they must show that they understand the implications of the current imperatives of consultation and choice in both establishing and evaluating their activities.

In *Linking Communities*, a three-year action research project funded by the Big Lottery, Age UK Lancashire has set out first to ask older people what gets in the way of their leading fuller lives and then to develop new activities to overcome the factors that inhibit take-up. As we move towards the end of the project we have become more aware that words like 'consultation', 'choice', 'engagement', and 'evaluation' too often become weasel words that have had the life sucked out of them; they are proclaimed too often without consequent action. Thus *consultation* may mean that people are asked for their views which are then tabulated. Older people, correctly, increasingly ask whether they wasted their time in stating their opinions and demand to know what account was taken of the consultation.

In this project we have attempted to involve older people in a number of ways: as researchers, following a seven-session training programme; as interviewees; as members of groups that have discussed findings, and re-examined themes; as volunteers who have supported activities; and as people who could participate in activities that were established. This short summary is not attempting to claim that this collection of methods is the solution to the involvement of older people in the development and provision of activities. What we are stating is that we aim to:

- involve older people more fully, so that they have greater potential to influence the life of the organization;

- develop styles of conversation where we take time not only to listen but to encourage people to reflect, so that there is greater understanding of their perspectives;

- further develop styles of feedback, providing participants with reports and inviting them to comment and help us to refine our ideas;

- clarify the different sorts of role that older people may take in research, perhaps administering questionnaires, helping others to complete questionnaires, or conducting qualitative interviews.

Our overarching point is that we are critical of the construction of older people as consumers and the limiting way that such construction is implemented. We want to challenge our own organization, as well as others, to think about what words mean, and then to examine how best to hold conversations (to listen, to reflect, to continue dialogue) and so to involve older people in ways that suit them. We have to create the means to ensure that older people's views—their opinions, knowledge, and wisdom—contribute to the goals and practice of Age UK.

Subcultures based on sex roles

Sex roles relate to society's expectations about the appropriate attitude, values, and behaviour of men and women. Examples of sex-role-based subcultures include Mumsnet, the web-based organization that connects mums and parents in the UK, and Fathers4Justice, the fathers' rights campaigning group. While sex roles are the point of connection, it is also useful to recognize that these groups can also unite in their resistance to stereotypical sex role norms that the subculture does not relate to or connect with, as mentioned already in this chapter. The 2012 Christmas advertisements for many of the large UK supermarkets portrayed the 'Family Christmas' in stereotypical ways, reinforcing the idea of sex roles within UK culture. The Asda advertisement focused on the harassed mother providing for everyone with the hapless father figure and helpless kids in the background. This campaign attracted many complaints by both Mumsnet and Fathers4Justice.

Regional, ethnic, and religious subcultures

We can feel a connection and affiliation with other people linked to our regional and ethnic identifications. Within the UK, there are regional subcultures based on county variations. The Yorkshire Tea brand, owned by Taylors of Harrogate (Figure 9.12), has a strong regional identity and is presented as the favoured tea brand of Yorkshire people, signifying their shared connection to the place. Ethnic subcultures, representing around 15 per cent of the UK population, are also important. Some companies serve specific ethnic groups. Boots sell the Mumtaz range of halal baby foods for Muslims. For companies marketing to ethnic groups there is the danger of appearing tokenist, and ending up with marketing communications that are based around stereotypical imagery of an ethnic group. In 2001 an advertisement for Chicken Tonight was taken off air after the Hindu community complained

Figure 9.12 Yorkshire Tea emphasizes regionality through its packaging by placing the product label against an idyllic backdrop reminiscent of the Yorkshire countryside.

Source: Image supplied by Bettys & Taylors of Harrogate Limited.

that the campaign ridiculed their religion by using a Hindu prayer to advertise the meat sauce when some sections of their faith forbid the eating of meat (Singh, 2004).

Religion represents one of the central institutions shaping consumer culture. It provides a point of affiliation for subcultures within a national culture, and these subcultures are based around the consumption of certain products which are symbolically and ritualistically associated with the celebration of religious ceremonies and holidays. Within the Catholic faith, the First Holy Communion is a ceremony that represents a person's first reception of the sacrament of communion. In Mediterranean Catholic countries, this is a major event in a child's life, particulary for girls. There are many shops that cater specifically for this market, and some even put on a First Holy Communion clothing fashion parade to show off the dresses and accessories. Other examples of religion-based subcultures impacting on consumer behaviour can be found in Jewish consumers following a kosher diet and celebrating a son's bar mitzvah, and Islamic consumers following a halal diet.

Subcultures based on consumption communities

Many companies have been keen to influence and nurture brand communities around their brands through creating branded social space. Starbucks set up the 'My Starbucks Idea' site (http://mystarbucksidea.force.com/) which aimed to develop a sense of community among its customers by encouraging them to share ideas and suggestions for new types of drink.

Community as a concept has a long history in sociology and anthropology, but its emergence in consumer behaviour research stems from the 1990s, with the publication of the paper by Schouten and McAlexander (1995) on subcultures of consumption, which focused on Harley-Davidson Owners, or HOGs (Harley Owners Group). Over the years, the focus has subtly changed from an interest in subcultures of consumption (Schouten and McAlexander, 1995) to consideration of brand communities (Muniz and O'Guinn, 2001) through to the current emphasis on consumer tribes (Cova and Cova, 2002). While there are some differences in meaning, they all represent forms of subcultural consumption, and as such share common features with cultures. Just like a cultural group, these subcultures share values, beliefs, and knowledge as well as customs and norms around ways of acting. We now consider subcultures of consumption, brand communities, and consumer tribes in more detail.

Subcultures of consumption

A **subculture of consumption** is defined as a group of consumers connected through a 'shared commitment to a particular product class, brand or consumption activity' (Schouten and McAlexander, 1995: 43). The Harley-Davidson community is the classic example of a subculture of consumption (see Research Insight 9.6). The defining characteristics of subcultures of consumption are an identifiable ethos underpinning the subculture, core values that are accepted to varying degrees by all adherents, and expression of these values in certain

RESEARCH INSIGHT 9.6

Schouten, J. and McAlexander, J.H. (1995), 'Subcultures of consumption: an ethnography of the New Bikers', *Journal of Consumer Research*, 22, 3, 43–61.

In their analysis of Harley-Davidson Owners, subcultures of consumption were characterized by having an identifiable ethos, by sharing core values that are accepted to varying degrees by all adherents, the expression of these values in certain products and their usage, and that members relate to other members through product and brand usage.

 Visit the Online Resource Centre to find out more about this book.

products and their usage. An interesting recent example of a brand that inspires a subculture of consumption is Fred Perry. This brand has a website (http://www.fredperrysubculture.com/) where it brings together and promotes the way that music, film, fashion, and other aspects of popular culture connect with the Fred Perry brand.

Brand communities

Brand community is a similar concept to subculture, but the focus is very much on the shared admiration of a brand. According to Muniz and O'Guinn (2001: 412), a **brand community** *'is a specialized, non-geographically bound community, based on a structured set of social relations among admirers of a brand'*. Muniz and O'Guinn defined brand community as sharing a consciousness of kind, rituals, and traditions, and also a moral responsibility to the brand. This was important, as it related to the idea of the brand community sustaining itself, and its members feeling a duty to ensure that the brand community thrives. BMW is an example of a brand that evokes strong brand community, with its own website (http://www.bimmerfest.com/) and events that promote the sense of brand community. There are three key aspects of brand community.

- *Consciousness of kind* is the recognizable connection to the brand and each other, the 'we-ness' of the brand community. Here the connection between people has great importance for understanding brand communities. For MacUsers, often cited as the seminal consumption community, the identification with the Apple Mackintosh brand, and the strong recognition with other users, implies a strong connection to the values and ethos of the company and brand.

- *Rituals and traditions* associated with the consumption community are those vital social processes by which meaning of the community is reproduced and transmitted within and beyond the community (e.g. shared consumption experiences with the brand). These rituals may involve storytelling and sharing of brand stories to create and maintain community around the brand, but also celebrate the history of the brand. Apple had a history of ritualistic unveiling of new products by the late Steve Jobs at company conferences, amid great media attention and consumer interest.

- *Moral responsibility* to the brand is a shared sense of duty to the community as a whole and individuals within, which involves looking out for and helping other members in their consumption of the brand. This is often about coalescing around the brand, in favour of this brand over others.

One final aspect of brand communities is the anti-brand community. As a backlash against capitalism, there is a growing resistance to corporate globalization, and there have been some recent high-profile examples of consumers who are actively opposing brands or companies, and in the process forming anti-brand communities around certain brands. Anti-brand communities, similar to brand communities, are non-geographically bound communities based on a structured set of social relationships (Hollenbeck and Zinkhan, 2006). In anti-brand communities, consumers form networks or communities in opposition to specific brands (e.g. Marlboro cigarettes) and/or in opposition to corporate brands (e.g. the anti-Starbuck's community http://www.ihatestarbucks.com/). Essentially, consumers take on social activist roles; anti-branding demonstrations are emerging as a new form of consumer activism. The damage that this can cause companies is considerable, and while the internet offers great opportunities, in cases of brand transgression there can be major negative implications for companies.

Consumer tribes

Consumer tribes are an extension of the brand community idea. **Consumer tribes** are *a group of people emotionally connected by similar consumption values and usage, who use the social 'linking value' (Cova, 1997: 297) of products and services to create a community and express identity*. The consumer tribes concept builds on ideas emerging from Maffesoli's work on neo-tribes (Maffesoli, 1988), taking them into the consumption context. Consumer tribes are similar to subcultures of consumption and brand communities in the sense that the collective is connected through their shared passion for a brand or consumption practice. The difference, however, is that consumption tribes recognize the multiple nature of consumption collectives and that consumers may belong to several collectives, or tribes, at the same time. Just as an individual has different aspects of their self, through membership of multiple tribes, consumers can express different aspects of their identity.

Cova and Cova (2002) emphasized the playful aspect of tribal consumption, and argued that one does not need to feel commitment or responsibility to the brand. Tribes are transient, in the sense that they emerge and grow, but they can also disappear as members of the tribe keep changing. Finally, tribes are entrepreneurial, as tribe members try and customize or produce market offerings to meet their needs. Unlike subcultures and brand community, tribal membership does not dominate consumers' lives, nor do members feel a strong moral obligation to the tribal collective. Tribes are prominent in consumer culture, as evidenced in the range of tribes discussed by Cova et al. (2007). They can emerge around consumption practices (e.g. surfers, clubbers); consumer brands (e.g. the Alfisti tribe who are committed to the Alfa Romeo brand); or in response to popular cultural trends (e.g. the Twilight Moms, a tribe sharing a passion for the Twilight series, its author. and its stars). Tribes are distinct from other ways of thinking about consumption collectives in that, from this perspective, they place less emphasis on the product or service, but instead focus on the linking value that connects consumers and hence is key to understanding (and supporting) consumer-to-consumer relations, and ultimately engendering affective based loyalty.

The form and nature of subcultures reflect major cultural and demographic trends within wider society, and clearly these tribes closely reflect popular cultural trends. Increasing cultural diversity and consumer affluence will impact on subcultures of consumption, as consumers are exposed to a wider range of influences (at a global level) and have resources available to participate in tribes. The relevance of understanding tribes is seen in the popularity of tribal marketing, with many companies embracing these ideas in their effort to understand their consumers better and to form greater connection to their brands. This is exemplified in the case of Oreo (Case Study 9) in their use of tribal marketing to celebrate 100 years of Oreo.

Conclusions

Culture is about where we come from, what we have grown up with, and basically 'our context'; as such, it represents an important aspect of, and influence on, our consumption behaviour and practices, and therefore is of importance to marketers. Our *definition of culture* has centred on the contents of culture, but has also given consideration to the role that culture serves as a blueprint for our lives. We examined the elements of culture in relation to a range of marketing examples, including Unilever's Vive Mejor campaign in the USA and PETA's campaign in India.

We considered the *elements of the cultural system*, explaining how ecology, social structure and ideology all shape culture. These ideas are often reflected in advertisements, serving to reinforce or challenge stereotypes around these elements.

Our section on the *classification of cultures* looked at core societal values which can shape behaviour and practices. We took a closer look at the dimensions of cultural values, drawing on Hofstede's classification. Consumer Insight 9.1 focuses on how the Norwegian brand Solo challenged the cultural characteristics associated with Norway as a way of drawing attention to itself.

We described the nature of *cultural myths and rituals* and the consumption of ritual artefacts. Consumer Insight 9.2 explored some consumer archetypes that are central to myths, and discussed the use of archetype by the Jack Wills brand. Consumption rituals were also explored in depth, drawing on a range of global marketing examples based around these rituals. Rites of passage were examined, and Research Insight 9.3 focused on this in relation to empty nesters adjusting to this life stage.

We examined a range of ways in which culture is important for **marketing communications**, including advertising tone and message, and in understanding sacred and profane consumption. Consumer Insight 9.3 provided a good example of a culturally informed campaign—Philips grooming products in Taiwan.

We have also discussed in detail the various **subcultural groups** that are important for marketing, linking them to our understanding of culture more generally. We focused on demographic-based and consumption-based subcultural groupings. Consumer Insight 9.5 highlighted how marketers target products and brands at tweenagers, while Practitioner Insight 9 discussed some of the issues around understanding older people as consumers. Research Insight 9.6 described the classic study of Harley-Davidson Owners (HOGs) as a subculture of consumption. When thinking of culture in these terms, it is important to remember that the cultural landscape has shifted and is shifting quite dramatically, and there are a number of trends that are affecting the way that culture influences consumption practices.

Review questions

1. How would you define culture?

2. What are the main perspectives on culture, and in what key ways do they differ?

3. Define the following terms in the context of culture: learning, knowledge, customs, and norms.

4. What are the key dimensions of culture as identified by Hofstede?

5. What are myths and why are they relevant for understanding culture?

6. What are the main rituals associated with consumer culture? Can you provide your own examples of each?

7. How does acculturation work? What are the main processes and why is this useful for marketers to know about?

8. What are the key issues around communication and culture?

9. What is the difference between demographic and consumption-based subcultures? Can you provide examples of such subcultures?

Discussion questions

1. Consider the material on the dimensions of culture. Read the paper by McSweeney (2002) (Research Insight 9.2) and, together with your understanding of culture, discuss what you think the main problems are with this approach.

2. Find an advertisement that you feel has a strong cultural dimension to it. Analyse this from the dimensions of both the culture perspective and the CCT perspective. Which offers greater insights and value for marketers?

3. Look for some advertisements that make use of archetypes in the brand narrative. Can you analyse these in terms of the classic archetypes? Do you think that archetypes have universal appeal? To what extent are these archetypes based on cultural and social context?

4. Can you think of key rituals in your life where consumption plays a significant role? Other than advertising, in what ways might marketing and social marketing use these ideas to influence consumer behaviour in some way?

5. Choose a consumer collective and analyse it in terms of the three main perspectives on consumption-based subcultures: subcultures of consumption, brand community. and consumer tribes. Which do you think is most useful for understanding these consumption-based subcultures?

 Visit the Online Resource Centre to test your knowledge further and complete the Multiple Choice Questions for Chapter 9.

CASE STUDY 9

Oreo's 100th birthday celebrations

This case focuses on the company Oreo and its 100th Anniversary Campaign (June 2012) as an illustration of the development of bonded loyalty created through the extensive use of social media, and on how to use social media to 'build brand love'. Oreo provides an interesting example of a company appropriating and applying the ideas of tribes of consumption, making extensive use of social media to facilitate and reinforce the sense of tribal connections around the brand.

Background to case

The Oreo biscuit was developed and first produced by the National Biscuit Company (now known as Nabisco, and owned by Kraft) in 1912. A chocolate sandwich cookie (or biscuit) with a creamy white filling, it has become an iconic symbol of US culture, and its 'twist, lick, dunk' ritual resonates with people all over the world. Oreo is the world's best-selling cookie, sold in more than 100 countries. To celebrate the 100th anniversary of the Oreo cookie, a global social media campaign was devised, based around the iconic 'twist, lick, dunk' ritual.

According to John Ghingo, senior director for Oreo Global, 'In today's hectic world, people have more responsibilities and pressures than ever before. Despite this, the simple act of enjoying an Oreo cookie and glass of milk continues to speak to a universal human truth: inside all of us ... there's a kid that deserves to be set free every once in a while'. This was the basis of the campaign, which aimed to inspire people to relive the magic of youth.

Social media as part of the Oreo campaign

Activities across social media platforms were critical to the success of this campaign, and there were a range of key activities driving the campaign. The central campaign was around the 100 consecutive 'Daily Twists', portraits created from straws, empty glasses, milk, and Oreo cookies. These were shared over Facebook, Tumblr, and Pinterest, and through the Daily Twist website (http://brands.nabisco. com/Oreo/dailytwist/). These reflected trending events, holidays, and major news events, and were not without controversy. To coincide with Gay Pride, Oreo posted an image of a multicoloured cookie with the message 'Proudly Support Love', which attracted a quarter of a million 'likes' on Facebook. However, this posting divided fans, drawing criticism from Christian groups.

Another key event was the Guinness World Record event which aimed to set the record for the most 'likes' on a Facebook post in 24 hours. This was promoted globally through their social media platforms and the Oreo website, and was also picked up by various online media outlets and local press. The Guinness event received 25,000 'likes' in the first 60 seconds of launching publicly and achieved a total of 114,619 'likes'.

A number of activities were organized over the anniversary year. According to the company, the 100th Anniversary Campaign connected 40 million people worldwide and attracted 8.5 million Facebook 'likes', and on Twitter the #OreoMoment hashtag became a trending topic, with birthday treats reaching nearly 15 million people.

Tribal marketing

For Sarah Hofstetter, President of 360i Foods (the digital agency that led the Oreo campaign), Kraft had to find out how to bring the campaign to centre stage as people were eating Oreos across the world but in different social settings: 'Brands today need to act as media companies and invite people to share content ... Social media is a conversation, not a one-night stand'. Taking a consumer tribes approach is a useful way for companies to think about how they create connections, and thus bonded loyalty, with consumers.

According to Cova et al. (2007:21), '... where once tribes were seen as transformative to their members, we are beginning to see how they are transformative to business and communicative practices and through them, to society itself'. The challenge for companies is to understand the dynamics of tribes and to support consumers' involvement with the tribe, and in so doing align marketing efforts with the tribe's values. Central to tribal marketing activities is the use of social media, since this presents a way for companies to connect with consumers. Figure 9.13 shows a framework for how firms can build bonding loyalty through supporting the tribe (Mitchell and Imrie, 2011).

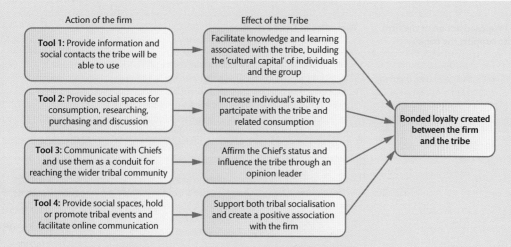

Figure 9.13   Building bonded loyalty through a firm's support of the tribe (Mitchell and Imrie, 2011)

Source: Reproduced with permission from Emerald Group Publishing Ltd.

Oreo as a consumption tribe

The tribal marketing approach to building loyalty can be used as a way of analysing Oreo's successful campaign (see Table 9.2)

Proposed action of the firm to support the tribe	Examples of Oreo activities
1. Company should provide information and social contacts that the tribe will be able to use, which can facilitate knowledge and learning associated with the tribe, building the cultural capital of individuals and the group.	• Daily Twists campaign, present across multiple platforms. Encouraged interest and engagement with the campaign across platforms. Built cultural capital through engagement with wider sociocultural events at the time. • Oreo set up a 100th Birthday Facebook page to provide a focal point for activities, and for information dissemination (http://www.facebook.com/oreo/app_192670807490788). According to company information, Oreo's Facebook community grew from 2 million to 60 million fans.
2. Provide social spaces for consumption, researching, purchasing, and discussion, increasing the individual's ability to participate with the tribe and related consumption.	• Active management of Facebook page, offering opportunities for consumers to connect; for example, a posting 'OREO cookies make every day a little more _____' attracted 7,749 comments. • Daily Twists postings reflect topical events, and their tongue-in-cheek graphics make them ideal for sharing on other platforms (Pinterest, Twitter, Facebook). Reflecting topics in the news and popular culture resonate with the interests and concerns of tribe members in a playful way. • Show participation and care of their tribe, for example through celebrating fans' birthdays (Fan Lisa T. was born in 1912—the same year Oreo cookies were introduced. Wish her a special happy birthday below!), and the creation (and posting on YouTube) of a short film showing 'Thousands of Oreo cookie Fans are celebrating the kid inside. Watch below to learn how you can join the movement!'

Table 9.2   Analysis of the Oreo campaign (*Continued*)

Proposed action of the firm to support the tribe	Examples of Oreo activities
3. The company communicates with chiefs and uses them as a conduit for reaching the wider tribal community. It affirms the chief's status and influences the tribe through an opinion leader.	• The main tribe 'chief' is the child at the centre of the campaign message 'Celebrate the kid inside'. The global reach of the campaign is demonstrated through a series of commercials, run in 15 countries, building on the Oreo 'twist, lick, dunk' ritual. The commercials bring the Oreo moments to life by transforming routine adult activities into something fun and playful—as the adults discover their inner children, the children hold up signs that say 'Next Stop: Childhood' and 'Recess for Everyone!' (http://www.youtube.com/watch?v=rJ8JZMtsqtk).
	• Award-winning advertising campaign to support engagement with the brand; the advertisement is titled 'Oreo Explanation' and in it a little girl introduces her father to the 'twist, lick, dunk' ritual during a play tea party. The winning advertisement is part of a Europe-wide campaign, with similar ads starring French and German children. (http://www.youtube.com/watch?v=QeA28L8Pt0U&fmt=18).
	• Live Daily Twist Finale—on the last day of the campaign (2 October) Oreo set up a virtual office in Times Square, New York City, to produce the final Daily Twist advertisement. In order to connect and include global fans, fans were able to submit ideas between 8 a.m. and 10 a.m. via Oreo's Twitter and Facebook pages.
4. Provide social spaces, hold or promote tribal events, and facilitate online communication, which can support both tribal socialization and create a positive association with the firm.	• Oreo devised the AmbassadOREO campaign, whereby Oreo (in consultation with fans) chooses an ambassador (an AmbassadOREO) to communicate with the tribe and promote their brand propositions and rituals.
	• Global AmbassadOREO Program—These brand evangelists gathered in New York City to share their childlike moment. They take an oath to help Oreo extend its movement to recapture and spread the wonder of youth and become part of the mission to 'celebrate the kid inside' when they return home.
	• According to Oreo, AmbassadOREO honorees were chosen in unique ways by each country. In the Philippines, a Facebook contest called on fans to submit family photos that creatively formed the number 100 with Oreo cookies. In Ecuador, lucky consumers who found a 'golden ticket' in their package of Oreo cookies were entered in a raffle for the chance to represent their country in New York as an AmbassadOREO. In China, AmbassadOREO honorees had to earn points by completing Oreo missions throughout the year. In the USA, millions of Oreo Facebook fans had the chance to vote for five national winners from video submissions of fans demonstrating their passion for the Oreo brand.

Questions

1. Oreo has been presented here as an example of a consumer tribe. Can you analyse this case material from (a) a brand communities perspectives, and (b) a subculture of consumption perspective? What similarities and contrasts can you make between the three perspectives (tribes, brand communities, subcultures of consumption) based on this analysis?

2. Can you analyse the Oreo case in terms of myths and rituals around consumption?

3. What next for Oreo? What do you suggest the company does next in order to sustain this successful social media campaign?

Sources: Cova et al. (2007); Shayon (2012); MacPherson (2012); Elliot (2012); *PR Newswire* (2012); Jacques (2012); http://brands.nabisco.com/Oreo/

 Visit the Online Resource Centre and follow the link to the authors' blog where you can keep up to date with the latest developments in consumer behaviour and further explore theories through additional articles and real-world examples.

References

Adweek (2009), 'Unilever expands Vive Mejor initiative', *Adweek*, 16 July, http://www.adweek.com/news/advertising-branding/unilever-expands-vivemejor-initiative-106120#1 (accessed 21 April 2013).

Aguinis, H., Joo, H., and Gottfredson, R.K. (2012), 'Performance management universals: think globally and act locally', *Business Horizons* 55, 4, 385–392.

Allegheny (2010), 'Home purification—how to do sage smudge ceremony', http://alleghenycandles.wordpress.com/2010/05/01/home-purification/ (accessed 30 November 2012).

Baskerville, R.F. (2003), 'Hofstede never studied culture', *Accounting, Organizations and Society*, 28, 1, 1–14.

Belk, R.W., Wallendorf, M., and Sherry Jr, J.F. (1989), 'The sacred and the profane in consumer behavior: theodicy on the Odyssey', *Journal of Consumer Research*, 16, 1, 1–38.

Brafton (2010), 'Marketers can tap into $200 billion marketing by targeting teens', http://www.brafton.com/news/marketers-can-tap-into-200-billion-market-by-targeting-teens-800014942 (accessed 9 November 2012).

Bu, K., Kim, D., and Son, J. (2013), 'Is the culture-emotion fit always important? Self-regulatory emotions in ethnic food consumption', *Journal of Business Research*, 66, 8, 983–988.

Clark, B. (2012), 'Three steps to creating audience archetypes for smarter content marketing', http://entreproducer.com/audience-archetypes/ (accessed 20 July 2013).

Clarke, B. (2003), 'The angst, anguish and ambitions of the teenage years', *Young Consumers: Insights and Ideas for Responsible Marketers*, 4, 3, 27–33.

Courier Mail (2010), 'Catholics angry as celebrities hijack rosary beads as a fashion statement', 11 July 2010, http://www.couriermail.com.au/lifestyle/catholics-angry-as-celebrities-hijack-rosary-beads-as-a-fashion-statement/story-e6frer4f-1225890174772 (accessed 8 November 2012).

Cova, B. (1997), 'Community and consumption: towards a definition of the "linking value" of product or services', *European Journal of Marketing*, 31, 3/4, 297–316.

Cova, B. and Cova, V. (2002), 'Tribal marketing: the tribalisation of society and its impact on the conduct of marketing', *European Journal of Marketing*, 36, 1–27.

Cova, B., Kozinets, R.V., and Shankar, F.A.C. (eds) (2007), *Consumer tribes*, London: Routledge.

de Mooij, M. and Hofstede, G. (2002), Convergence and divergence in consumer behavior: implications for international retailing, *Journal of Retailing*, 78, 1, 61–69.

Ehrlich, S. (2012), 'Solo make thousands of their fans famous', http://blog.contagiousagency.com.au/solo-makes-fans-famous/ (accessed 26 July 2013).

Elliot, S. (2012), 'The Oreo turns 100, with a nod to the past', *New York Times*, 27 February, http://www.nytimes.com/2012/02/28/business/media/the-oreo-turns-100-with-a-nod-to-the-past-advertising.html?_r=0 (accessed 13 July 2013).

Fang, T. (2010), 'Asian management research needs more self-confidence: reflection on Hofstede (2007) and beyond', *Asia Pacific Journal of Management*, 27, 1, 155–170.

Hawks, A. (2010), 'Mariah Carey launches "Lollipop Bling" perfume and ring pop candy', http://starcasm.net/archives/52913 (accessed 28 June 2012).

Hebdige, D. (1979), *Subculture: The Meaning of Style*, London: Routledge.

Hofstede, G. (1984), *Culture's consequences: international differences in work-related values* (abridged edn), London: SAGE.

Hofstede, G.H. (2001), *Culture's consequences: comparing values, behaviors, institutions and organizations across nations* (2nd edn), London: SAGE.

Hogg, M., Folkman Curasi, C., and Maclaran, P. (2004), 'The (re)configuration of production and consumption in empty nest housholds/families', *Consumption, Markets and Culture*, 7, 3, 239–259.

Hollenbeck, C.R. and Zinkhan, G.M., 2010, 'Anti-brand communities, negotiation of brand meaning, and the learning process: the case of Wal-Mart', *Consumption, Markets & Culture*, 13, 3, 325–345.

Holt, D. and Cameron, D. (2012), *Cultural strategy*, Oxford: Oxford University Press.

Jacques, A. (2012), '100 years of Oreo: how the iconic cookie brand is using social media', http://www.prsa.org/Intelligence/Tactics/Articles/view/9713/1046/100_years_of_Oreo_How_the_iconic_cookie_brand_is_u (accessed 3 March 2013).

Jafari, A. and Suerdem, A. (2012), 'The sacred and the profane in Islamic consumption', *Advances in Consumer Research*, 39, 1, 427–429.

Larsen, S. (2012), 'Solo: soon to be world-famous', *WARC* http://www.warc.com.ezproxye.bham.ac.uk/Content/ContentViewer.aspx?MasterContentRef=ef2da8ef-b06c-46a1-ad08-e613009a9181 (accessed 9 June 2013).

Luedicke, M.L. (2011), 'Consumer acculturation theory: (crossing) conceptual boundaries', *Consumption, Markets and Culture*, 14, 3, 223–44.

MacArthur, K. (2012), 'Kraft's new name sounds naughty in Russian', *Crain's Chicago Business*, http://www.chicagobusiness.com/article/20120322/NEWS07/120329920/krafts-new-name-sounds-naughty-in-russian (accessed 3 March 2013).

McCracken, G. (1986), 'Culture and consumption: a theoretical account of the structure and movement of the cultural meaning of consumer goods', *Journal of Consumer Research*, 13, 1, 71–84.

McPherson, R. (2012), 'Oreos mark 100 years of "twist, lick, dunk"', *ABS-CBN News*, https://ph.news.yahoo.com/oreos-mark-100-years-twist-lick-dunk-213454102.html (accessed 21 July 2014).

McSweeney, B. (2002), 'Hofstede's model of national cultural differences and their consequences: a triumph of faith, a failure of analysis', *Human Relations*, 55(1), 89–118.

Maffesoli, M. (1988), *Le temps des tribus: le déclin de l'individualisme dans les sociétés de masse*, Paris: Librairie des Méridiens.

Marketing Week (2010), 'Mariah Carey targets young with sweet-inspired fragrances', *Marketing Week*, 24 June, http://www.marketingweek.co.uk/mariah-carey-targets-young-with-sweet-inspired-fragrances/3015087.article (accessed 1 December 2012).

Michaelsen, E. (2011), 'Going Solo', http://press.emerson.edu/imc/2011/10/24/going-solo/ (accessed 9 May 2013).

Mintel (2011), 'Teens' and tweens' technology usage', *Mintel*, http://store.mintel.com/teens-and-tweens-technology-usage-uk-november-2011 (accessed 20 December 2012).

Mitchell, C. and Imrie, B.C. (2011), 'Consumer tribes: membership, consumption and building loyalty', *Asia Pacific Journal of Marketing and Logistics*, 23, 1, 39–56.

Muniz, A.M., Jr and O'Guinn, T.C. (2001), 'Brand community', *Journal of Consumer Research*, 27, 4, 412–432.

Pardue, D. (2005), 'Brazilian hip-hop material and ideology: a case of cultural design', *Image and Narrative*, 10, 23–31.

Penaloza, L. (1994), 'Atravesando fronteras/border crossings: a critical ethnographic exploration of the consumer acculturation of Mexican immigrants', *Journal of Consumer Research*, 21, 1, 32–54.

PR Newswire (2012), 'A cookie with a mission: oreo welcomes first "AmbassadOREO" honorees from around the globe to New York City,' *PR Newswire*, http://www.prnewswire.co.uk/news-releases/a-cookie-with-a-mission-oreo-welcomes-first-ambassadoreo-honorees-from-around-the-globe-to-new-york-city-170476916.html (accessed 13 July 2013).

Riley-Adams, E. (2012), 'Ogilvy Action Taiwan makes augmented reality mustaches', *Agency Spy*, http://www.mediabistro.com/agencyspy/ogilvyaction-taiwan-makes-augmented-reality-moustaches_b35190 (accessed 20 May 2013).

Roberts, J. and Scott, S. (2009), 'The teen commandments', *Marketing Week*, 20 May, http://www.marketingweek.co.uk/the-teen-commandments/2065514.article (accessed 8 April 2014).

Rook, D.W. (1985), 'The ritual dimension of consumer behavior', *Journal of Consumer Research*, 12, 3, 251–264.

Schouten, J. and McAlexander, J.H. (1995), 'Subcultures of consumption: an ethnography of the New Bikers', *Journal of Consumer Research*, 22, 3, 43–61.

Shayon, S. (2012), 'Oreo's Daily Twist finale goes live and crowdsourced from Times Square', *Brand Channel*, http://www.brandchannel.com/home/post/2012/09/28/Oreo-Daily-Twist-Finale-092812.aspx (accessed 13 July 2013).

Shields, R. (2011), 'HTC rivals BlackBerry's dominance of teen market', *Marketing Week*, 6 July, http://www.marketingweek.co.uk/sectors/telecoms-and-it/htc-rivals-blackberrys-dominance-of-teen-market/3028141.article (accessed 20 December 2012).

Sidle, S.D. (2009), 'Building a committed global workforce: does what employees want depend on culture?', *Academy of Management Perspectives*, 23, 1, 79–80.

Singh, S. (2004), 'Why ads don't reflect UK ethnic population', *Marketing Week*, 22 April, http://www.marketingweek.co.uk/why-ads-dont-reflect-uk-ethnic-population/2019104.article (accessed 31 July 2014).

Tooher, P. (1996), 'The future's not so bright as Orange gets the red light in Ulster', *Independent*, 13 July, http://www.independent.co.uk/news/the-futures-not-so-bright-as-orange-gets-the-red-light-in-ulster-1328424.html (accessed 8 April 2014).

Triandis, H.C. (1995), *Individualism and collectivism*, Boulder, CO: Westview Press.

Vernon, P. (2010), 'Jack Wills: the Sloane Ranger rides again', *Observer*, 9 May, http://www.guardian.co.uk/theobserver/2010/may/09/polly-vernon-jack-wills-preppy-fashion-teenagers-success (accessed 30 November 2012).

Woodside, A.G., Sood, S., and Miller, K.E. (2008), 'When consumers and brands talk: storytelling theory and research in psychology and marketing', *Psychology & Marketing*, 25, 2, 97–145.

Young, K. (2012), 'Philips "Augmented Reality Mugs" give hairless men faux facial hair', *Trendhunter*, 31 May, http://www.trendhunter.com/trends/augmented-reality-mugs (accessed 20 March 2013).

10

PATTERNS OF BUYER BEHAVIOUR

Introduction

So far in this book we have considered consumer behaviour from the perspective of the individual as part of a larger social group, or set within a specific microculture such as teenagers, or a broader cultural setting such as their country or ethnicity. In this chapter we take a different approach and consider consumers in light of research which has studied their actual purchasing behaviour. Consumer panel data, measuring the behaviour of thousands of consumers in different parts of the world, has been analysed by researchers to explain differences in purchasing behaviour. Such research is used in this chapter to draw implications to aid our understanding of consumer behaviour. Although the data does not tell us *why* people buy in the way they do, by showing *how* they buy the information can be used by marketing managers when considering their competitive strategy and to make decisions regarding whether to target new, existing, or both types of customer.

LEARNING OBJECTIVES

After you read this chapter, you will be able to:

1. Know what is meant by **repeat buying** and understand the implications for **brand loyalty** and market share.

2. Consider how people buy through looking at their actual *patterns of purchasing from consumer panel data*.

3. Explain the different ways of considering *brand loyalty*.

4. Recognize the importance of *light and heavy buyers* of a brand.

5. Understand the significance of what *patterns of buyer behaviour* tell us about segmentation and differentiation.

What are repeat buying and brand loyalty?

We begin by considering in detail what we mean by repeat buying. As consumers we are all subject to repeat buying. There may be some examples where we do not ever buy the same product or brand again—perhaps we dislike the taste or the texture, or perhaps we feel that it has not performed in the way advertised. For most goods and services, however, we are likely to be back in the market to purchase regularly, whether that is every few days, say in the case of bread or milk, or every week for foodstuffs such as meat and vegetables. Obviously some items may be stored for longer, such as frozen or tinned food, and some are used over a period of time, such as jars of instant coffee or bars of soap. Even these products may vary considerably in how long it is before we buy them again. Imagine, for example, a person who does not drink much coffee but keeps a jar of coffee in the house in case of visitors. The same person buys cereals once a week because they have children who eat them every day for breakfast. Although both products will be used over time, the different consumer needs and preferences of the household dictate when the product will be repeat purchased. There may even be products that we buy more than once a day—chocolate bars for example, although perhaps we should not! The point is that we all have a regularity to our purchase patterns, which is linked to consumer needs.

If we want to examine how people repeat buy we can use consumer panel data which records people's purchasing over extended periods (often, over a year or longer) so that we can see what brands are bought repeatedly and how often the consumer chooses alternative brands. Typically, panels are large representative samples of people. In Japan, for example, the consumer research company Sci-Personal has a panel of around 50,000 men and women across the country who use a portable terminal like that shown in Figure 10.1 to scan barcodes on products purchased. Often this data is then combined with attitudinal and demographic information.

Figure 10.1   Scanning a barcode for a consumer panel

Source: Image supplied and printed with kind permission from INTAGE Inc.

Purchasing patterns from consumer panel data

Repeat buying over time

Table 10.1 is a fictionalized and simplified table giving data about four people's purchasing habits over a nine-week period. Let us consider the different brands to be various types of coffee. A means they purchase coffee brand A, B means they purchase brand B, C means they purchase brand C, and 0 means that no purchase takes place. In this case, we see both the variety in the coffee purchased and the frequency in which it is purchased by four different people.

Person 1 seems to have a preference for brand A but then in week 5, after a gap of two weeks, switches to B. In week 8 they return to brand A again, but in week 9 buy brand B. It might be that they have discovered brand B and it has entered their repertoire of brands (perhaps because of taste), or that when brand A is not available they choose brand B as an alternative. Person 2 also has two weeks of buying brand A and then a gap followed by more brand A, then C, then B, and then C again. We cannot tell from this data the reason for their move from brand A or indeed whether in week 10 they might not return to brand A again. Person 3 switches from C to B, but purchases coffee at regular intervals—this may be because brand B was cheaper than brand C in week 7. The final person bought coffee only once in the nine-week period. This might be a person who buys instant coffee for guests but does not drink it herself.

Most brands are actually not bought that often, and when they are bought it is at irregular intervals. East et al. (2008) suggest that there are a number of reasons for this. First, most brands are just bought infrequently; East et al. suggest that a typical US household buys a particular coffee brand only about three times a year and the product category about nine times a year. Secondly, the intervals may vary as customers stockpile (e.g. when there is a price promotion) and at other times they may run out. Of course, there are exceptions to this; you may well have brands that you buy far more frequently; indeed if you are a 'coffee addict' you might buy coffee on regular basis.

Purchase frequency

The analysis of repeat-buying data is managed by considering the 'purchase occasion', i.e. the frequency of purchase. This is a useful approach as it recognizes that some purchase occasions may mean that more than one unit of the brand is bought on a particular

	Brands of coffee purchased each week								
Weeks	1	2	3	4	5	6	7	8	9
Person 1	A	A	0	0	B	0	0	A	B
Person 2	A	A	0	0	A	C	B	C	0
Person 3	C	0	0	C	0	0	B	0	0
Person 4	0	0	0	0	0	0	0	A	0

Table 10.1 Hypothetical repeat purchasing over nine weeks

occasion. When buying instant coffee it is most usual to buy a jar at a time, but when buying yoghurt it would be more usual for a family to buy this in bulk for consumption throughout the week. Fixed time periods (e.g. a month or a quarter) are followed to analyse repeat-purchasing behaviour, as this allows repeat buying for any brand to be presented using two variables:

1. **penetration**, i.e. the number of people who buy an item in a given time period

2. **purchase frequency**, i.e. the average number of times they buy in the time period.

This means that we can calculate sales for a brand by multiplying penetration (the number of buyers) by purchase frequency (how often they buy the brand). A brand may be big because it is bought very often by a few buyers or because it has lots of buyers who do not buy it so often. Having this data is important for companies as it means that they can see how their customer base is made up, i.e. lots of buyers, fewer buyers who buy the brand a lot, or a combination of both.

What has been found from the analysis of many product categories in many markets is that:

the penetration of brands may differ a lot but the average purchase frequency of any brand tends to be similar.

This is an important finding in terms of understanding how consumers' behaviour actually affects the market, and questions some assumptions about what brand loyalty really means.

To illustrate the importance of the difference between the penetration of brands and their average purchase frequency we show an example from an analysis of the instant coffee market in the USA (Table 10.2).

It is worth explaining that two important measures of market size discussed throughout this chapter are defined as follows:

$$\text{market share (\%)} = \frac{\text{total purchase of the brand}}{\text{total purchases of the category}}$$

$$\text{penetration (\%)} = \frac{\text{number buying the brand at least once}}{\text{total number of potential customers}}$$

Although the brands may be unfamiliar (this is an example from some time ago, but one which clearly illustrates the importance of penetration), what we can see is that the coffee market at the time was made up of eight players accounting for 87 per cent of the market share and a number of small brands which together held 13 per cent of the market. The penetration or percentage buying is the percentage of households that bought any coffee (67 per cent) and below this in the table is what percentage of this total figure was bought by each brand (e.g. 24 per cent for Maxwell House). If you add up the percentages for each brand you will see that it comes to over 100 and this is because many people buy more than one brand

Brand	Market share (%)	Penetration or percentage buying	Average purchase per buyer
Any instant coffee	100	67	6.7
Maxwell House	19	24	3.6
Sanka	15	21	3.3
Tasters Choice	14	22	2.8
High Point	13	22	2.6
Folgers	11	18	2.7
Nescafé	8	13	2.9
Brim	4	9	2.0
Maxim	4	9	2.0
Other brands	13	20	3.0
Average	11	17	2.8

Table 10.2   Penetration and purchase frequency for the US coffee market

Source: Ehrenberg and Scriven (1996).

of coffee. The average purchase rate is simply the number of times on average the brand was bought. This ranges from a low of 2.0 times to a high of 3.6 for the market leader.

Near-stationary markets

It is important at this point to note that the markets we are considering here are well established rather than new. An important feature of them is that they do not change much. This is known as a **near-stationary market** which *is an established mature market which appears stable over a period of several months or a year*. Of course some markets do change over longer periods, and this can be for all kinds of reasons including changing tastes and priorities, or the introduction of innovative technology. For example, the music industry has seen records replaced by tape recordings, then CDs, and most recently downloads; all these changes could be put down to innovative technology. An example of change in taste is the move away from beer drinking in Britain and an increase in lager and wine consumption, which can be explained by a behavioural change to lighter drinks and the environments in which people prefer to consume alcohol.

Looking at the numbers in Table 10.2 and in many different markets, the trends in the data are broadly similar, and Ehrenberg and Scriven (1996) noted the following important points about purchase behaviour.

- The market shares for the coffee brands differ up to six times and for penetration around four times, but the average purchase frequencies do not show such great differences. They are all broadly around the average of 2.8. This tells marketers that whether they are a big brand or a small brand they need to reach the market average purchase rate to succeed in that market.

- As market share declines, average purchase frequencies tend to go down. This is referred to as **double jeopardy** *which is the phenomenon whereby brands with smaller market share have fewer buyers and those fewer buyers buy the brand less often.* Again, this can act as a warning signal to brand owners; there are real advantages in being a bigger brand as you tend to have more buyers buying more often. Further information about double Jeopardy is provided in Consumer Insight 10.1

- Where there are discrepancies, they can usually be easily diagnosed and explained. Analysing the market in this way can give the brand owner the opportunity to find out if there is a problem and what it might be due to. In the coffee example, Brim had a slightly low average purchase frequency of 2.0. Checking the previous year's data showed that this was due to the one-off negative effect of a fire in a warehouse (Ehrenberg et al., 2004).

CONSUMER INSIGHT 10.1

Defection in the car market

Double jeopardy can affect the rate of brand switch. Defection from a brand will depend to some extent on its market share. Brands with a larger market share both win and lose more customers in a year than brands with a smaller market share, but their *relative* loss will be less. In other words, their size allows them to sustain customer defections and capitalize on repeat purchasing. The smaller you are the greater such losses are relative to your share of the market. Table 10.3 is an example of repeat purchasing of brands of cars in the Thai market.

Brand	Market share (%)	Market penetration (%)	Repeat purchase (%)
Toyota	46	61	56
Other	24	32	47
Honda	10	18	31
Nissan	8	15	33
BMW	7	9	30
Mitsubishi	5	10	29
Average	17	24	38

Table 10.3   Repeat purchasing in the Thai car market

Source: Bennett and Graham (2010).

The patterns that are seen here are also found in North America and Europe (Colombo et al., 2000; Bennett, 2005). However, defection rates from service industries are somewhat lower, at around 3–5 per cent (Sharp, 2010).

Questions

1. What do you notice about the biggest brand's repeat purchase rates?

2. What does this tell you about brand loyalty?

3. Why do you think defection rates from services might be lower?

Sources: Colombo et al. (2000); Bennet (2005); Bennet and Graham (2010); Sharp (2010).

 Visit the Online Resource Centre and follow the weblinks to learn more about the concept of double jeopardy and repeat purchase rates.

Brand loyalty: explaining how we buy

In Chapter 3 we considered the effect of having a lot of choice. Barry Schwartz (2004) described how his supermarket held 61 types of suntan lotion and 80 brands of pain relievers. Most of us are used to going into the supermarket and seeing shelves full of different types of shampoo or toothpaste. Currently, Colgate lists 23 types of toothpaste on its website (colegate.co.uk) including Total Advanced, Total Sensitive, Sensitive Whitening, Cavity Protection, and Deep Clean Whitening.

In the fast-moving consumer goods (FMCG) sector, having a wide range of product types under the same brand name is a worldwide phenomenon. Figure 10.2 shows a selection of toothpastes in a retail outlet in the UK. We know that the relative importance of FMCG purchases is low—buying toothpaste or suntan lotion is not like buying a house or a car. Choosing a brand that the consumer subsequently finds they do not like is not going to have a significant economic

Figure 10.2 Toothpaste choice

Source: Image courtesy of Frankie Roberto.

impact on most buyers. These are relatively low risk purchases. We may exhibit inertia, randomly choose brands, or engage in variety-seeking behaviour (see Chapter 3). For the most part, our shopping is frequently bought and in purchasing low priced goods where we encounter little risk, we 'develop *habits*, to simplify the repetitive choice-situation' (Ehrenberg, 1988: 5). However, while all brands are bought at roughly the same rate, a brand that has higher market penetration will have more customers buying it, and that is ultimately what makes the difference to market share.

What does repeat purchasing tell us about brand loyalty?

Understanding how consumers actually purchase over repeated occasions allows us to consider what brand loyalty really means. In particular, we can consider whether brand loyalty implies that you do not buy other brands, how often you have to buy the same brand to be considered brand loyal, and whether the brand loyalty that we see in consumer panel data might reveal nothing more than habit or inertia which might be broken with a sales promotion or discount on a competing brand (see Research Insight 10.1).

Ehrenberg defined **brand loyalty** as '*any tendency for people to buy the same brand again, whilst usually also buying other brands*' (Ehrenberg and Scriven, 1996: 3). Rather than consumers relentlessly switching from one brand to another, they shop from a repertoire of brands (see Chapter 3), all of which are acceptable to them, and from these they choose different brands at different times. Rather than being promiscuous, they could be described as polygamous or having split loyalties. So they are not switching from brand to brand without any apparent reason, but choosing from a selected group of brands, all of which are acceptable to them.

These alternative ways of considering what brand loyalty is has major implications for how companies manage their brands. Should a company try to improve brand loyalty or follow a different strategy such as trying to increase the penetration of the brand? It could be argued that if companies tried to make customers more satisfied, they would retain

RESEARCH INSIGHT 10.1

Brown, G.H. (1953), 'Brand loyalty—fact or fiction?', *Advertising Age*, 43, 251–258.

In 1953, Brown published a paper entitled 'Brand loyalty—fact or fiction?' which summarized analysis of consumer panel data for items such as margarine, toothpaste, and coffee over a year-long period. This seminal work was the starting point for research using consumer panel data to identify brand loyalty. Brown examined the purchasing habits of 100 members of the 610 families in the USA involved in the panel to identify whether there were differences in their purchase profiles. He identified four types of loyalty which he called undivided, divided, unstable, and no loyalty.

 Visit the Online Resource Centre to read the abstract and access the full paper.

more and increase their market share. So an important question for companies is whether they should aim to retain customers or acquire more?

Sharp (2010) argues that trying to increase brand loyalty is a waste of time. This is largely because of the nature of double jeopardy discussed in Consumer Insight 10.1. A large company will have more repeat buyers just because it has so many more buyers than a small company—the more customers you can get, the more likely you are that some of them will repeat buy, so being big really does make a difference. Of course, you will also lose customers but, as noted in Consumer Insight 10.1, this tends to be relatively fewer for a large company. Double jeopardy implies that it is not possible to change your defection rates without first drastically increasing your market share. Much defection occurs outside the company's control and is particularly troublesome for smaller companies. For example, if you are a small local delicatessen or dog-walking service operating in one locality, and your customer moves to another area, they will no longer be able to use your services and will have to find alternatives. There is little you can do about this unless you can open more branches throughout the country, perhaps by developing a franchise.

Light and heavy buyers—which matter most?

Of course, consumers have different tastes and make different choices. Examining consumer panel data for many different brands shows that most have a lot of light buyers who buy the brand only occasionally. Such people are often also light users of the product category and may buy from a wide repertoire of brands. These are people who do not buy much of the product category, and when they do they like to vary the brands they buy. There are also heavy users of a product category, but interestingly they are often seen to buy relatively few brands. Here we might suggest that as heavy users of the product category they have identified the brands they like best and stick to them. For example, consumer panel data from the UK shows that just 4 per cent of people who buy Coca-Cola once a week were responsible for a quarter of its sales volume (Sharp, 2010). If we were the marketing manager for Coca-Cola, we might think about targeting our marketing at these heavy buyers, since they have developed a relationship with Coca-Cola and will probably notice our marketing communications. But we would also have to consider whether such targeted advertising would be beneficial as they may have reached saturation point in terms of how much Coca-Cola they can drink. Also, if they are already heavy users, do we even need to communicate more with them as they know the brand well and clearly like it?

An alternative strategy would be to focus marketing effort on the infrequent buyers who, while they do not buy often in absolute terms, actually account for most of the brand's total customers. While it might be argued that they are more of a challenge, marketing to them could be an important defensive strategy as they may be prone to 'forget' the brand or readily switch to Pepsi or own-label brands as they do not appear to have any particular affiliation with Coca-Cola beyond occasionally buying the brand. As they account for a large number of Coca-Cola's buyers, they cannot be ignored and need reminding to buy the brand. This argument is in line with what we have learned about low involvement. We argued in Chapter 3 that marketers often want to increase involvement with their brand; to do so you may at the very least remind such occasional or low involved consumers that your brand is still there and to prompt them to buy it (if only now and again). These differences between a company's heavy and light buyers are examined further when we consider the Pareto Law.

The Pareto law

The Pareto law suggests that 80 per cent of your sales come from only 20 per cent of your customers. In practice, a company's heaviest customers may actually account for around 50 per cent of your sales in a year. This would mean that light and medium buyers are also accounting for 50 per cent, and so their importance cannot be overlooked. Table 10.4 provides information on the body spray and deodorant category from the USA and shows the Pareto law in action. Whether the brand has a 16 per cent or a 1 per cent market share, the percentage of heavy buyers in a 12 month period is around 50 per cent. See also Research Insight 10.2 for a method of evaluating a new brand.

The law of buyer moderation

When we look at the range of buyers for a brand, we are always looking over a particular time period—how many consumers buy in a month, six months, or a year. However, companies obviously need to plan over longer time periods to ensure that they have the appropriate marketing strategy. Do heavy and light buyers stay the same year after year? Anschuetz (2002) looked at the leading brand of ketchup in the USA using IRI panel data over two years. The brand had both high brand name recognition and large market share.

Brand	Market share (%)	Percentage volume accounted for by heaviest 20% of buyers in 12 months
Sure	16	53
Lynx	14	53
Impulse	8	55
Soft and Gentle	7	52
Rightguard	7	51
Dove	6	48
Mum	1	46

Table 10. 4   The Pareto law and the deodorant market
Source: Sharp (2010).

RESEARCH INSIGHT 10.2

Ehrenberg, A.S.C., Uncles, M.D., and Goodhardt, G.J. (2004), 'Understanding brand performance measures: using Dirichlet benchmarks', *Journal of Business Research*, 57, 12, 1307–1325

The Dirichlet model is a theoretical model that can be used to evaluate a new brand to see how it is fairing in the market place. This study takes an example taken from Campbell's who had launched a premium priced Tastes of the World soup in Britain. The brand had low loyalty-related measures compared with the bigger competitors in the market. It seemed that Tastes of the World would not succeed in this market until Campbell's was introduced to the double jeopardy effect by its marketing advisors. Using the Dirichlet model it was possible to see that in this case the impact of double jeopardy was that repeat-buying levels would be predictably lower for such a small brand. The brand's problem was not the level of repeat buying, but that it just needed more customers.

 Visit the Online Resource Centre to read the abstract and access the full paper.

Anschuetz first analysed only those customers who bought any ketchup in both years. Then he divided Year 1 consumers into groups that differed in terms of their volume contribution and value to the brand. He found, perhaps not surprisingly, that non-buyers of the brand were the largest group buying nothing in Year 1, while light buyers who bought only once contributed about 14 per cent of the brand's volume (see Table 10.5).

Those who bought two to four times were classified as medium buyers and contributed 43 per cent to volume, while the 9 per cent of customers who were heavy buyers (buying more than five times) also accounted for 43 per cent of volume. Anschuetz then compared Year 1 and Year 2 purchasing, looking at those who had purchased in both Year 1 and Year 2 and how often they had purchased. Interestingly, those who bought nothing in Year 1 contributed to 14 per cent of Year 2's volume and when combined with light buyers from Year 1 this rose to 29 per cent of Year 2's volume. Although still very important for the brand's

Buyer group	Percentage of sample (%)	Frequency in Year 1	Brand volume (%)	
			Year 1	Year 2
Non-buyers	45	0	0	14
Light	22	1	14	15
Medium	25	2–4	43	36
Heavy	9	5+	43	34
Total	100		100	100

Table 10.5 All buyers of ketchup across two years

Source: IRI Panel Data from Aschuetz, N. (2002), 'Why a brand's most valuable customer is the next one it adds', *Journal of Advertising Research*, January/February, 15–21.

volume, the medium and heavy buyers in Year 2 contributed less than in the previous year. This illustrates that just because non-buyers do not buy in one time period it does not mean they will not buy in the next, even if the period is as long as a year. Light, moderate, and even non-buyers in a particular year should not be ignored; while as individual units they deliver less profit for the brand, they deliver overall a large number of units sold which contributes to the revenue and profit of a brand selling to a mass market. This is termed the **law of buyer moderation** and is *the tendency for light buyers to become heavier and heavier buyers to become lighter* (Sharp, 2010).

Blips in a household's buying can arise for all sorts of reasons. One household may appear as a heavy buyer of breakfast cereal one year but not the next year, perhaps because a child who liked cereal has now left home or the family are going through a phase of different breakfast menus. Or maybe a household buys a lot of burgers in Year 1 but none the next year because they only cook burgers on the barbecue and the weather in Year 2 was not as good as in Year 1. While the reasons are manifold, for the marketer the main thing to bear in mind is that they occur and reveal the complexity of markets. Marketers must not assume that the patterns that occurred in one year will be replicated in the following year; the evidence reveals that markets really are dynamic and are often outside the control of the business.

Patterns of buyer behaviour and market segmentation

As noted in Chapter 3 we often buy a number of brands in a product category because the risk of trying different brands is low, we may seek variety, or it just does not matter enough to us which brand we buy. We may have some favourites that form our repertoire of brands, which inevitably means that each brand's customers are also another brand's customers. For example, in a given period in the UK 65 per cent or more of buyers of Diet Coke, Fanta, Lilt, and Pepsi also bought regular Coca-Cola (Sharp, 2010). Obviously Coca-Cola is a particularly large brand and so all soft drink brands have to compete with it. The **duplication of purchase analysis** explains this phenomenon and is described as '*the degree to which brands within a category share their buyers with each of the other brands*' (Sharp, 2010). Sharp considered a number of product categories and generally found that in most cases a brand will share its customers with others in that category. However, there is some deviation from this norm. For example, in the ice cream market Walls Carte D'Or is a strong market leader with whom all brands share customers, while the two brands Ben & Jerry's and Häagen Dazs share double the customers they share with other brands. In other words, if you are a buyer of Ben & Jerry's you are very likely to regularly buy Häagen Dazs. This has implications for segmenting consumers. In particular, it suggests that companies should be careful when assuming that their brand appeals to a very different segment of consumer than their competitors. Duplication of purchase analysis can be useful in helping a marketing manager see which other brands are also bought by their customers and whether, as in the ice-cream example, they have a particularly close competitor. It also shows that brands gain most new customers from the biggest brands, to whom they also lose most customers. Duplication of purchase analysis can provide a guide to the product category based on what consumers actually buy and perhaps also how they use brands. It may also give an insight into how companies go about segmenting their markets and how consumers respond to this.

For example, the UK cereal market used to be considered to be made up of two categories—hot (such as porridge) and cold (such as cornflakes)—but panel data showed that so-called cold breakfast cereals also sold well in the winter and investigations revealed that consumers were simply turning their cold cereal into hot by pouring warm milk on them (Sharp, 2010) (see Figure 10.3). Such data help managers to understand consumers better and to recognize that their segmentation categories may not always match up with how consumers actually use products.

How insights from research with consumer panel data can be used in practice is further explained by Tom Lloyd from Metametrics UK, in Practitioner Insight 10.

Figure 10.3 Consumers can defy situational segmentation

Source: © iStock.com/dulezidar.

PRACTITIONER INSIGHT 10

Tom Lloyd, Director, Metametrics UK

Metametrics is a company specializing in marketing analytics. Here, Tom Lloyd talks about the impact of the work done by Ehrenberg and his colleagues on practical marketing.

The work done by Ehrenberg and his colleagues has very significant practical implications for businesses today. In my experience there is no common, robust shared view amongst marketing practitioners as to 'how marketing works'.

But Ehrenberg's buyer behaviour principles provide a robust framework that we can use to make predictions and sensible decisions. Unlike many other marketing models, which are mainly theoretical, the buyer behaviour principles are empirical and can be very easily demonstrated and validated. The advantage of this is that the marketing manager does not have to 'believe' the model; he/she simply has to plot the data. For the brands in your market, does share correlate highly with penetration and less with loyalty/frequency? It is interesting to see how brands almost always follow the established pattern, and it is also interesting to look into any odd outliers that do not.

We can then give simple practical guidance to managers.

- All brands essentially work in the same way: there are almost no 'niche' brands or 'special'/ unusual brands in terms of buyer metrics (e.g. brands with a few customers who buy them very loyally). Brands are just large or small.

- Which key performance indicators (KPIs) are valuable? For example, traditional brand funnels that categorize consumers into those aware, trialists, occasional users, regular users, and loyal users are widely used but in reality provide little helpful insight—the buyer behaviour principles explain why all brand funnels within a category tend to be the same shape; they are just bigger or smaller depending on brand size.

- Setting sensible growth targets—if you want your 5 per cent share brand to be a 10 per cent share brand, it will need to look like a typical 10 per cent brand in terms of its buyer metrics. This provides very helpful insights into the marketing challenges in achieving that scale. What level of penetration will we need and how much will it cost us in advertising and trial activity to do that?

- Generating growth—to grow you almost always need to increase penetration. Frequency and loyalty strategies almost never work. This is a counter-intuitive leap for many marketers. They ask 'Surely it's easier to get existing buyers to buy more than to get new buyers?' The reality is that growing penetration does not mean attracting totally new buyers who have never bought you. It is mostly a case of reminding lapsed buyers to buy you again. The evidence for this can be easily seen by looking at the dynamics of the fastest growing successful brands. Even though they probably pursued different strategies, if they grow at all, they almost always do so by increasing the number of buyers they have.

- Learn from other brands. It is interesting how little analysis marketers undertake of the buyer metrics of successful growing brands even in their own categories. This is most likely because marketers believe that brands behave so differently that you cannot learn very much about one brand by looking at any others. By challenging this misconception there is actually a huge amount of insight to be gained from this type of analysis and this is a practice that should be encouraged.

Finally, we should not ignore the internal organizational and cultural issues involved in communicating buyer behaviour principles. It is a radical shift for a marketer to accept that growing their brand means attracting a lot of disloyal buyers who will buy their brand occasionally. Or that there are rules that dictate that most brands behave in the same way and that their brand is not 'special' or different in terms of its buyer metrics (although it will, of course, be unique in its creative positioning). Even though these principles are not 'models' but simple empirical observations that anyone can make, attempts to disseminate the learning within organizations have often failed simply because of the radical shift in understanding that is required and the perceived threat to marketing's role.

How duplication of purchase impacts segmentation

Consumer panel data also shows where there are real perceived differences in brands leading to different market segments. The market for flavoured milk in Australia includes brands with distinct attributes. One brand, Dairy Vale, is perceived as sweet and luxurious and is also considered as suitable for children. Max, is marketed to males and two other brands, Feel Good and Take Care, are 'healthy' brands targeted at women. Table 10.6 shows that most brands, following the law of duplication of purchase, shared about half their customers during the period examined with the largest brand, Farmer's Union, but note that the distinctly 'male' brand Max had no overlap of customers with the two 'healthy' female brands Feel Good and Take Care, revealing clear consumer preferences resulting from the brands' segmentation strategies. Indeed, segmentation by gender is an approach that has been used by other product categories as illustrated in Consumer Insight 10.2.

Do you need to differentiate your brand?

When buying a brand, to what extent does a consumer have to feel that there is something particularly different about it which motivates his/her purchase? If you were choosing between different brands of ice cream, for example, would you have to be struck by something very different to the other brands that would make you choose this brand? The reality is that there is not a great deal of difference between brands in any category. Imagine that each day you tried a different brand of shampoo but did not know which brand was which—would there really be that much variation in your experience or the performance of the brands? Of course, there would be slight differences in colour, perfume, and texture but how much would that matter to you? There are situational differences that can affect customers. You may choose Lynx shower gel because it is

Buyers of brand	Percentage of buyers who also bought brand				
	Farmers' Union	Dairy Vale	Take Care	Max	Feel Good
Farmers' Union	–	21	8	6	5
Dairy Vale	43	–	5	5	5
Take Care	52	16	–	0	20
Max	45	20	0	–	0
Feel Good	53	27	33	0	–
Average	48	21	12	3	8

Table 10.6 Duplication of purchase between flavoured milk brands
Source: Sharp (2010).

CONSUMER INSIGHT 10.2

Men are hungry, women deserve a treat

In a number of product categories you will see that companies have chosen to segment by gender. Carlsberg recently introduced a low alcohol spritzer drink named Eve, while Wrigley's 5 Gum (chewing gum) has flavours such as Cobalt, Pulse, and Flood, names that are reminiscent of aftershave fragrances, and the gum is presented in what has been described as a package designed to look like a box of condoms (Carter, 2010). But it is probably in chocolate that we can see the biggest gender divide. The Yorkie Bar began with a decidedly masculine trucker advertising the chocolate bar from Nestlé which some years later was followed by the line 'It's not for girls' (see Figure 10.4). Television advertisements showed women trying to buy Yorkie by wearing false beards or dressing up as builders. Snickers also has a masculine feel, most recently using the line 'You are not you when you are hungry'. In one advertisement the veteran actress Joan Collins is transformed back into a football player once she has eaten her Snickers bar.

In the past, brands like Flake and Galaxy have clearly been targeted at women with messages of indulgence and taking time away from the hurly burly of everyday life. The latest addition to the female chocolate line is diet chocolate Crispello. Cadbury launched the lower calorie Crispello after apparently identifying that women are becoming more health conscious and therefore buying fewer chocolate bars, with annual sales falling by over 6 per cent (Bartlett, 2012). The strap line for Crispello is 'A little treat for you'.

Figure 10.4 Yorkie, it's not for girls!

Source: Image printed with permission from Nestlé.

Questions

1. Given what you now know about duplication of purchase, how successful do you think such gender-based advertising would be?

2. Suggest some likely overlapping purchases in the chocolate bar sector?

3. In what other sectors might one find such overlapping purchase behaviour and why?

Sources: Carter (2010); Bartlett (2012).

  Visit the Online Resource Centre and follow the weblinks to see other examples of organizations that have chosen to segment by gender.

Brand	Different (%)	Unique (%)	Either (%)
Coca-Cola	8	13	19
Diet Coke	9	8	15
Pepsi-Cola	7	10	15
Fanta	8	5	12
Pepsi Max	9	10	19
Schweppes	6	9	13
Canada Dry	10	9	17
Average	9	9	16

Table 10.7 Brand user perceptions of differentiation in the soft drink category (UK)
Source: Sharp (2010).

stocked in your supermarket (where you happen to be buying other goods); you may actually really prefer Adidas shower gel, but it's not stocked in that store. When you go on holiday you may wish to take smaller packs of shampoo and conditioner and so choose from the brands that produce these holiday-sized packs. There is also differentiation by price, but within a competitive set customers of one brand will be similar to those of another. One might expect H&M customers to be broadly similar to Primark customers, and Gucci customers to be similar to Prada customers. Of course this does not preclude Primark or H&M customers from also visiting Gucci and Prada, and vice versa, but this will not be of great importance to the managers of Primark. Studies across products and services in different countries and using different methods reveal consistent patterns (Sharp, 2010: 123):

1. 'Buyers of a brand perceive very weak differentiation—yet this does not stop them loyally buying a particular brand.

2. A brand's level of perceived differentiation is very similar to their rivals'.

Table 10.7 illustrates that relatively few of a brand's regular buyers see it as either different or unique.

Similar patterns are found across different product categories unless there are exceptional functional differences. Therefore Aldi, a food retailer which does not stock national brands, was considered by 67 per cent as 'different' from other supermarkets, and Subway, a sandwich-based fast food brand, scored 50 per cent in comparison with McDonald's, Domino's, and KFC (Romaniuk et al., 2007) (see Figure 10.5). The message generally seems to be that consumers do not require differentiation in their brand to purchase it. See also Research Insight 10.3.

Figure 10.5   Subway and Aldi, perceived as different by consumers

Source: Subway © iStock.com/ivanastar; Aldi © iStock.com/ SeanPavonePhoto.

What matters to consumers?

As brands are continually looking to catch the consumer's attention, branding helps consumers to remain loyal while creative advertising reminds them about new and different brands. There is plenty of evidence to show that brand image impacts consumers' choice of brand, but even the leading brands in a market with strong brand images will, for most people, be just one brand in their repertoire. Therefore media strategies need to maximize reach and keep reminding customers of their presence (Sharp et al., 2012). However, does this mean that consumers have a different kind of relationship with the brands that they are more loyal to? The evidence from the research we have been discussing in this chapter would tend to suggest that this kind of loyalty is just a fact of life. It is a feature of habit, dependent on what is readily available, familiarity, and even a lack of really caring in some cases (Sharp, 2010), and does not reflect a deeper kind of connection. It may be that some of us do have different types of relationships with brands; we may feel strongly (positive or

RESEARCH INSIGHT 10.3

van Marrewijk, A. and Broos, M. (2012), 'Retail stores as brands: performances, theatre and space', *Consumption Markets and Culture*, 15, 4, 374–391

In this paper Van Marrewijk and Broos (2012) provide an interesting perspective on how retail stores develop brand distinctiveness from a consumer culture theory perspective. The authors explore how management and shop assistants in Oger, a Dutch fashion store, communicate and construct the brand to consumers. This in-depth ethnographic analysis of the Oger retail setting provides many insights into how organizations manage the spatial settings within the retail store to communicate differentiation in an effort to maximize consumer loyalty and relationships.

   Visit the Online Resource Centre to read the abstract and access the full paper.

negative) about some brands but that in itself does not mean we do not buy other brands. Brand communities (see Chapter 9) do exist and often people in such communities exhibit strong positive feelings about their chosen brand (Schau and Muniz, 2002; Casaló et al., 2008), but the question that Sharp and his colleagues address is whether this really matters in terms of the brand's market share and penetration. These 100 per cent loyal buyers tend to be light category buyers. Of course, many consumers are passionate about brands that are dear to them. The most often cited are Apple (Muniz and Schau, 2005) and Harley-Davidson (Schouten and Alexander, 1995), but if you explore other brand communities such as The Purse Blog you will find consumers passionate about many other brands—in this case premium handbag brands such as Louis Vuitton, Chanel, and Jimmy Choo. Even if you love Chanel bags it does not mean that that is the only brand you buy. Both Apple and Harley-Davidson have repeat purchasing levels that are broadly what would be expected in their categories; in the case of Apple it is higher, but there is also the fact that switching from Apple would require changing operating systems (Sharp, 2010).

While there may be some consumers who exhibit these kinds of highly loyal preferences, generally having a brand repertoire gives you more choice. By having a range of goods in mind the consumer has this choice but without the mental effort of constantly re-evaluating all the potential brands available, and this can be both convenient and reassuring. therefore it is important that marketing managers recognize that they need to be in the consumer's repertoire but not to expect total loyalty from them.

For the effect of seasonality on sales figures see Consumer Insight 10.3.

CONSUMER INSIGHT 10.3

Seasonality—do you sell more soup in the winter?

While stationary markets, if looked at over a period of time, seem fairly stable, there are some fluctuations throughout the year. The time of year and sales promotions are sure to have an effect on monthly sales figures. In the UK people buy mince pies at Christmas and chocolate eggs at Easter, and in Singapore and Malaysia Chinese New Year is celebrated with the consumption of pineapple pastries. In the northern hemisphere more soup is sold in the winter and more ice cream in the summer, while in countries such as Singapore, where the temperature varies very little, ice cream is sold all year round. Soup may be considered a seasonal product. Evidence shows that soup is bought at a higher rate in the winter than in the summer (Wellan and Ehrenberg, 1990). Research using the Dirichlet model (see Research Insight 10.2) revealed that the difference in sales was made up largely by people who only bought in the peak season. In other words, the seasonal effect in this case was due to those people who did not buy in the off season but bought during the winter months, while the rest retained a fairly steady rate of purchase throughout the year. This was an important finding, as the traditional view had been that those who bought all year round increased their purchases during the peak season. This knowledge helped decisions such as when to advertise and how to deal with the off-season dip with regard to production and cash flow issues

(Ehrenberg et al., 2004). By doing this type of analysis, companies can identify whether they have different types of segmented markets and can introduce appropriate marketing and internal organizational responses to help manage these differences.

Questions

1. With the knowledge from this consumer insight, if you were the marketing manager for a European soup company how would this impact your marketing communications?

2. Consider some other products that might be impacted by seasonality (e.g. sun cream, turkeys). How might you manage the seasonality of these products?

Sources: Wellan and Ehrenberg (1990); Ehrenberg et al. (2004).

 Visit the Online Resource Centre and follow the weblinks to see other examples of seasonal products.

Implications for marketing and advertising

If light, moderate, and even non-buyers are important for a brand, in terms of reach a company should consider media that are going to allow it to target more customers than it currently has—simply put, every non-buyer is a potential buyer. This may mean attention to distribution and sales force activity alongside marketing communications. Brands have to make the investment to reach more potential consumers. This is particularly difficult for a small brand as with a limited budget the temptation may be to focus only on the smaller segment of apparently more profitable consumers, but for the brand to grow it needs to be bought by as many consumers as possible.

Another important implication of this research is for marketing managers to understand the nature of loyalty among their customers. The goal of the 100 per cent loyal customer is not only unlikely but not necessarily worthwhile in terms of how much they actually buy. A large brand may have a relatively high number of 100 per cent loyal customers, although for a small brand this will be much less (the double jeopardy effect), but 100 per cent loyal users are generally light users of the category, purchasing fewer items than others, and so effectively they do not have much chance of being disloyal (Ehrenberg et al., 2004). As such, they may not be that useful to the brand.

There are also implications for the creative message. In particular, according to Anschuetz (2002), it is important that the brand's message connects inclusively across all types of user. A message, or indeed choice of media, that is too exclusive will not allow the brand to grow as it will not reach or appeal to a wide enough cross section of potential users.

Growing a brand's distribution into a previously unrepresented area is an important strategy because it reaches potential buyers who have not readily been able to gain access

Figure 10.6   Tesco Express and Tesco Extra   *Source*: Images printed with permission of Tesco Stores Ltd.

to the brand. Not only are light or non-buyers given access to the brand, but heavy buyers also have improved availability. This is a strategy that multiple retailers, such as Tesco, often pursue. In addition to Tesco Extra and superstores, often located on the outskirts of towns, Tesco has populated urban and inner-city areas with its Tesco Express stores, thus making the opportunity for consumers to buy from them that much greater (see Figure 10.6).

Ehrenberg and his colleagues have shown that a careful analysis of data often provides an explanation for why consumers are actually behaving in a way that is different to what is expected by marketers. For example, when Unilever ran a promotion that offered extra product with their leading UK laundry powder, they assumed that this would be particularly attractive to the brand's heavy buyers. However, analysis of the data showed the exact opposite; the extra product promotion appealed to recent non-buyers and light buyers (Ehrenberg, 1988). This illustrates that one does not have to have a complete change in attitude to brands to buy a different one; this is further explored in Consumer Insight 10.4.

CONSUMER INSIGHT 10.4

Do consumers always change their attitudes when they switch brands?

An area of contention in marketing is whether attitudes produce behaviour or behaviour influences attitudes—of course, both may occur in different situations (see Chapter 6). If we look at patterns of behaviour over time we can see that often even highly loyal buyers of a brand will buy other brands at some point. If we can switch easily between different brands, it seems to suggest that our attitudes to brands are not absolute in the sense that we prefer one above the other in every circumstance. Ehrenberg et al. (2004) argue that the nature of the polygamous consumer is the outcome of many years of past experience, and consumers do not change their beliefs and evaluations of brands in a way that constantly affects their brand choice. Therefore a consumer's behaviour, i.e. which brands they have bought in the past, is probably the best predictor of what they will do in the future. Indeed, rather than assuming that consumers have very different attitudes to different brands, it is far more likely that, within a product category, how someone feels about Brand A is not that different to how they feel about Brand B (Barwise and Ehrenberg, 1985).This suggests that a 'me-too' brand is quite viable if it can gain market penetration and share.

However, differentiation is seen by many marketers and business strategists as an important strategic option. For example, Michael Porter (1985) identified differentiation as one of three generic business strategies. A problem for differentiation is that it can usually be quite easily copied, especially in service businesses, and so any competitive advantage may be short-lived. The perceived need to differentiate has led to product innovation, which ultimately is a good thing for consumers, but it is rare for a brand in a product category to remain an innovator for long; most brands catch up fairly quickly.

Questions

1. Identify two or three 'me-too' brands in different product categories. Do you consider them to be successful and why?

2. Choose two or three differentiated brands in different product categories. How have they differentiated themselves? Have they been copied?

3. In your opinion, what are the pitfalls and opportunities of these two approaches?

Sources: Barwise and Ehrenberg (1985); Porter (1985); Ehrenberg et al. (2004).

 Visit the Online Resource Centre and follow the weblinks to learn more about consumers' attitudes when switching brands.

Price-related promotions may be entered into in the hope that they will appeal to potential customers of the brand, but this may not be the case. Ehrenberg et al. (1994) looked at 150 promotions in Britain, Germany, Japan, and the USA, and found that there were no before-to-after sales increases following the promotion and very few new buyers. In addition, repeat buying following the promotion was not affected. Their conclusion was that price promotions generally just brings the purchase occasion forward for existing customers.

Does your brand need to be distinctive?

We have discussed how differentiation does not appear to be that important to consumers; rather, their past purchasing history (their behaviour) seems to be a better indicator of which brands they will choose in the future. However, a brand needs to be distinctive; above all, customers need to be able to spot it and recognize it. As discussed already, distinctive elements might be colours, logos, or taglines, or they might be celebrities associated with the brand. Critical for the marketer is that the customer identifies the brand and that this builds awareness, or reminds or reinforces their memory of the brand and makes

Figure 10.7 Distinctiveness of the iPod   *Source*: Image supplied by The Advertising Archives.

it easier to choose. There are many examples of successful distinctiveness, but those discussed here are particularly well known. The Nike 'swoosh' logo alongside the powerful tagline 'Just do it' is distinctive and is used in all its advertising and point of sale material, and is even placed on many of its clothes as part of the design. Similarly, all people familiar with the Apple iPod recognize its white earphones (see Figure 10.7). To succeed in distinctiveness, the brand has to have something that is both unique and ubiquitous, i.e. when you choose your distinctiveness you need to stick with it and ensure that consumers can see it everywhere so that it acts as a trigger in their memories to identify the brand. This inevitably means a lot of investment in communicating to the consumer over time. It does not matter whether a logo or earphones of a particular colour is preferred by consumers; rather, what matters is that over time consumers connect such distinctiveness with that brand, such that a particular feature, such as the oil company Shell's distinctive red and yellow shell or the purple of Cadbury's Dairy Milk, can almost replace the brand name or other identifying feature.

An important message for companies advertising their brand to experienced consumers of the product class is that you can rarely imbue attributes that will differentiate it greatly from its competitors. Similarly, it will be difficult to increase customers' loyalty to the brand because, as previously discussed, these factors generally vary little from one brand to another. However, if a brand is publicized effectively, more people will be aware of it, interested in it, feel it may be worth trying, and so bring it into their consideration set. This does not preclude advertising that is aimed at informing the public, such as a price cut, a special promotion, or a new flavour, size, or package type.

Most of the time, however, marketers need to remind people that their brand is there. While copy and visuals need to be noticed and get into consumers' memories, this does

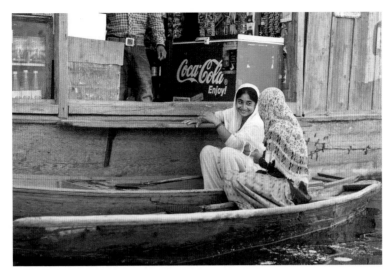

Figure 10.8   Coca-Cola ensures that its presence is everywhere   *Source*: © iStock.com/Pavliha.

not mean that a particular message is required or indeed that the advertising itself needs to be particularly outstanding (see Figure 10.8). What is necessary is that the brand is remembered. Perhaps counter-intuitively, the job may be easier for brands that are closer to and more substitutable by other brands. Why? Because the advertising does not have to try to change people's attitudes or behaviours around a particular product type, i.e. the functional differentiating factors. For example, if your preference for breakfast is Shredded Wheat, it may be much easier to convince you to try a new brand that is similarly constituted to Shredded Wheat than to get you to try a brand of muesli or even croissants as alternatives. Therefore Ehrenberg et al. (1997: 11) believe that the less difference between brands, the easier it may be for advertising to 'nudge choice behavior', but at the same time such brands must retain defensive reinforcement as they are potentially easily substitutable. So despite the rhetoric for differentiation and innovation, differentiation between brands is rarely sustainable for long and might not even be worthwhile as it is deliberately focusing on just part of a market.

Loyalty programmes and price promotions

The data presented in this chapter has major implications not only regarding *who* companies target but also *how* they do it. As we have seen, it is likely that inclusive advertising appeals will be more successful than those that are obscure or clearly exclude a large proportion of a potential market. Sharp (2010: 54) is particularly critical of loyalty programmes, saying they 'generate small or no shifts in market share'. Above all, he says, they are skewed, more than other marketing actions, towards heavier, more loyal brand buyers. This is because these buyers have a greater economic incentive to sign up, whereas many light buyers may not see the point of signing up. Sharp's argument is that this severely restricts the reach of such programmes. On the other hand, we know that some loyalty programmes have been very successful for companies despite being very expensive to run.

One of the most notable of these is Tesco who teamed up with the analysis agency dunnhumby to make sure that the loyalty programme they used, the Clubcard, yielded results beyond just being an incentive for customers. They use the information they received to target their customers more effectively. The amount and extent of the data they glean from their customers is so comprehensive that it acts as their own consumer panel. They carefully analyse the data to encourage heavy users of certain products to use more and non-users of other products to try them. For example, they might find that while a customer buys many of their toiletries from Tesco, they never buy shampoo, so vouchers for shampoo can be targeted to such customers. They might also find that someone else never buys meat from them, but in this case they would avoid offending what could be a vegetarian and instead offer more vegetable-based promotions. In this case the loyalty programme is built primarily on the information it provides Tesco rather than the incentive effect (East et al., 2008).

Conclusions

In this chapter, **repeat buying** habits and the implications for **brand loyalty** were explored with the conclusion that, on the whole, the repeat purchase rate of brands does not vary a great deal; the major differentiating factor is the size of the brand and how many customers it has. We also identified the importance for companies to have a range of loyalty profiles among their customers.

We have analysed **patterns of buying behaviour** through consumer panel data in order to shed light on explaining *how* consumers buy products and the ways in which this information can be used by marketing managers.

We have considered the phenomenon of double jeopardy and its impact on **brand loyalty and repeat purchasing** using defection in the car industry (Consumer Insight 10.1) as a good example of this. Of great importance to marketers is the argument that increasing brand loyalty can be a difficult task which may have very little effect on increasing a company's market share. In the FMCG sector, inertia or random choice sometimes dictates the purchasing decisions of consumers. In sum, a brand that has higher market penetration will have more customers who buy it, and that is ultimately what makes the difference to market share.

Data illustrating the Pareto law in action in the deodorant market (Table 10.4) highlighted the differences between **light and heavy buyers** of a brand and the **law of moderation**. Research Insight 10.2 also introduced the Dirichlet model as a method of evaluating the sales performance of a new brand. Overall, it is important for marketers to understand that light and heavy buyers may change their habits from one year to the next.

Market segmentation and differentiation were covered and their implication for marketers made clear through the phenomenon of **duplication of purchase**. Companies need to consider how to make their offering distinctive, but not so distinctive that they do not naturally fit into a repertoire of brands. Consumer Insight 10.4 presented an interesting debate around differentiation and buyer attitudes, noting that whilst differentiation is an important strategic option, being a 'me-too' brand is also a viable option if it can gain penetration and market share.

Practitioner Insight 10 supplemented these theories by showing how marketers use empirical buyer behaviour principles in everyday business decisions. We also learnt from the case of the Tesco Clubcard that there are other methods of collecting huge swathes of consumer behaviour information in a way tailored to your company's specific needs.

Review Questions

1. What does double jeopardy tell us about the difference between small and large brands in a market?

2. Explain what the Pareto law can tell us about heavy and light buyers of a brand.

3. Explain how understanding the law of buyer moderation might be useful to a company introducing a new brand into the market.

4. What is the difference between distinctiveness and differentiation?

5. Why is a company's penetration and coverage so vital to its success in the market?

Discussion Questions

1. Consider ways that brands of cosmetics and confectionery could increase their market penetration.

2. Ehrenberg distinguishes between promiscuous and polygamous consumers. Can you think of any situations or product purchases where you are more likely to be one than another? Why should this be?

3. Choose two product categories and list as many brands as you can within them. Consider which brands you think will be subject to duplication of purchase and which will not. What are the reasons for your choices?

 Visit the Online Resource Centre to test your knowledge further and complete the Multiple Choice Questions for Chapter 10.

CASE STUDY 10

Repertoire shopping in China

This case highlights a number of issues that have been discussed in this chapter, but in a particular cultural context. It shows that shopping habits are not that different wherever you look. But it also raises important questions for a brand entering a new market in terms of winning customers and managing its growth.

Do Chinese people shop any differently to the rest of the world? It is commonly believed that brands matter to Chinese shoppers. In studies by Bain & Company it is clear that the brand is an important factor in choice for both food and non-food categories, with more than 60 per cent of Chinese shoppers listing the brand as being among their top considerations in their decision-making process. What is interesting is that while the choice of brand is important, this does not mean that consumers stick to only one or two of their favourites. A series of studies by Bain & Company and Kantar WorldPanel show that, just like everywhere else, the Chinese consumer shops from a repertoire of brands.

Repertoire shopping

Bain and Kantar studied 26 of the top consumer goods categories across four areas: beverages, packaged food, personal care, and home care. This accounted for more than 80 per cent of the FMCG market. The research involved 40,000 households in urban China and barcode scanners were used to record purchases; 373 cities in 20 provinces and four major municipalities were represented. China's cities are ranked in five tiers. The large cities of Beijing, Shanghai, and Guangzhou Shenzen are in the first tier followed by a second tier of 20–30 cities, mostly developed provincial capitals. The third tier of about 20–30 cities includes less developed provincial capitals and comparably developed non-capital cities. There are over 200 cities in the fourth tier, while the fifth tier are county level cities. China's urban population exceeded its rural population for the first time in 2011, and increasingly Chinese workers are leaving rural regions to move to the city. There are now 160 cities with a population of a million or more.

Figure 10.9 Supermarket shopping in China

Source: © iStock.com/pengpeng.

Thus the survey represents a huge range of very different shopping options available in China from those in the modern urban Tier 1 cities, which include hypermarkets, supermarkets, and convenience stores, to the more traditional corner grocery stores, speciality stores, and department stores in the smaller cities (see Figure 10.9).

It was found that, in most cases, when consumers buy more times within a product category, they also buy more brands in that category. Bain and Kantar call this 'repertoire behaviour'. Their research showed that this repertoire purchasing is similar for heavy and average shoppers in a category. As consumers increase their purchasing within a particular product category, they are likely to try more different brands. For example, the Chinese are heavy purchasers of biscuits, with an average household buying 6.2 brands in 2012. Those that bought most frequently (the top 20 per cent) bought about 10.4 brands. Similarly, while average shoppers, who bought facial tissues 6.7 times in 2012, chose between three or four brands, the heavy shoppers, who bought facial tissues 14 times in the year, chose between five or six brands. Therefore the research concludes that a brand's heavy buyers are also likely to be heavy buyers of competing brands.

This repertoire behaviour appears to be consistent. It appears to exist whether the category is in the development stage or a more mature stage. For example, colour cosmetics (mascara, eye shadow, foundation, and lipstick) is an emerging product category in China compared with many other countries, as less than 40 per cent of households had bought in this category at the time of the research. Chinese women have not been using colour cosmetics on a daily basis, as is the case in other Asian countries, and they spend much less money on them, but as they begin to buy this product category more frequently, they purchase a wider range of brands. For example, women who purchase these products more than three times a year buy on average 2.86 brands, and when they purchase them more than five times over two years the average number of brands increases to 4.1.

Loyalist shoppers

There do appear to be some product categories where currently Chinese consumers are more loyal, buying the same brand repeatedly. Labelled as loyalist behaviour, the categories this covers include baby formula, nappies, beer, milk, carbonated soft drinks, and chewing gum. For these products, an increase in buying frequency has not translated into buying more brands. Bain and Kantar suggest two reasons for such loyalist behaviour. First, in these product categories there may be more limited brand choices, and secondly they suggest that in some cases buying the particular brand has become a habit. However, it should still be noted that these loyalists are a small group, accounting for only 10 per cent of total brand sales in these categories.

The research identified that leading brands in all the repertoire categories had one thing in common—they all had relatively high rates of penetration. For example, in toothpaste Crest had 57 per cent penetration compared with an average of 15 per cent for other top 20 brands, even though its repeat purchase is not very different from these brands. It is also the category leader, with a 15 per cent market share. Similarly, Oreo has a penetration of 46 per cent which is about three times the national average for the top 30 brands. Oreo also has the highest rate of repurchasing frequency at 3.3 times per household in 2011. Even for the leading brands in a category, more than 40 per cent of shoppers are only buying the brand once a year.

The findings from the research show a number of other important factors.

1. There appears to be no difference in repertoire and loyalist behaviour in terms of whether the brand is foreign or locally owned. The Chinese consumer is looking for brands they consider to be safe and trustworthy, whether they are home grown or from abroad. They will not necessarily take note at the point of sale as to whether they are buying a foreign or a local brand.

2. Where shoppers live appears to impact on repertoire behaviour. Shoppers living in Tier 1 or Tier 2 cities buy more brands in a category than those living in Tier 3–5 cities. For example, in 2011 the average family in Beijing, Shanghai, and Guangzho made 22 purchases of biscuits and bought nine different brands, while those in a Tier 5 city bought four brands, on

average 11 times. However, in loyalist categories such as milk and beer there does not seem to be a great difference among cities.

3. Repertoire behaviour does not vary by a person's stage in their life cycle. Some may think that young shoppers are less brand loyal, while the older shoppers like to stick to tried and tested brands. This does not appear to be the case; the only difference found was that young families bought more biscuits, sweets, and yogurt brands, but that may well be because they are at a stage where they are just consuming more of that product category.

Questions

1. Explain the reasons for brand loyalty in different tiers of city.

2. Would you expect to see repertoire behaviour increase in Tier 3–5 cities and if so why?

3. What does the case tell us about penetration versus brand loyalty?

4. What recommendations would you make to a foreign FMCG brand entering China for the first time?

5. Would you expect the loyalist brands to change? How and why?

Sources: Bain & Company and Kantar WorldPanel (2012); Bolger (2012); Yu and Lannes (2013); www.chinanormal.com

 Visit the Online Resource Centre and follow the link to the authors' blog where you can keep up to date with the latest developments in consumer behaviour and further explore theories through additional articles and real-world examples.

References

Anschuetz, N. (2002), 'Why a brand's most valuable customer is the next one it adds', *Journal of Advertising Research*, January/February, 15–21.

Bain & Company and Kantar World Panel (2012), 'What Chinese shoppers really do but will never tell you', http://www.bain.com/Images/BAIN_REPORT_What_Chinese_shoppers_really_do_but_will_never_tell_you_.pdf (accessed 3 June 2014).

Bartlett, E. (2012), 'Why Cadbury's Crispello bar 'for women' leaves a nasty taste', *The Telegraph*, 3 October, http://www.telegraph.co.uk/women/womens-life/9581866/Why-Cadburys-chocolate-for-women-leaves-a-nasty-taste.html (accessed 14 August 2013).

Barwise, P.T. and Ehrenberg, A.S.C. (1985), 'Consumer beliefs and brand usage', *Journal of the Market Research Society*, 27, 81–93.

Bennett, D. (2005), 'What car will they buy next?', *Report 19*, Ehrenberg-Bass Institute for Marketing Science, Adelaide.

Bennett, D. and Graham, C. (2010), 'Is loyalty driving growth for the brand in front? A two-purchase analysis of car category dynamics in Thailand', *Journal of Strategic Marketing*, 18, 7, 573–585.

Bolger, M. (2012) 'China's cities', www.edc.ca.

Brown, G.H. (1953), 'Brand loyalty—fact or fiction? *Advertising Age*, 43, 251–258.

Carter, M. (2010), 'Men buy Mars, women prefer Galaxy: gender targeting is advertising industry's secret weapon', *The Independent*, 18 March, http://www.independent.co.uk/life-style/food-and-drink/features/men-buy-mars-women-prefer-galaxy-gender-targeting-is-advertising-industrys-secret-weapon-1922941.html (accessed 12 March 2013).

Casaló, L.V., Flavián, C., and Guinalíua, M. (2008), 'Promoting consumer's participation in virtual brand communities: a new paradigm in branding strategy', *Journal of Marketing Communication*, 14, 1, 19–36.

Colombo, R., Ehrenberg, A.S.C., and Sabavala, D. (2000), 'Diversity in analyzing brand-switching tables: the car challenge', *Canadian Journal of Marketing Research*, 19, 22–36.

East, R., Wright, M., and Vanhuele, M. (2008), *Consumer behaviour: applications in marketing*, London: SAGE.

Ehrenberg, A.S.C. (1988), *Repeat buying* (2nd edn), Oxford: Oxford University Press.

Ehrenberg, A. and Scriven, J. (1996), 'Brand loyalty under the microscope' unpublished paper.

Ehrenberg, A.S.C., Hammond, K., and Goodhardt, G.J. (1994), 'The after-effects of price related consumer promotions', *Journal of Advertising Research*, 34, 4, 11–21.

Ehrenberg, A., Barnard, N., and Scriven, J. (1997), 'Differentiation or salience', *Journal of Advertising Research*, 37, 6, 7–14.

Ehrenberg, A.S.C., Uncles, M.D., and Goodhardt, G.J. (2004), 'Understanding brand performance measures: using Dirichlet benchmarks', *Journal of Business Research*, 57, 1307–1325.

Muniz, A.M., Jr, and Schau, H.J. (2005), 'Religiosity in the abandoned Apple Newton brand community', *Journal of Consumer Research*, 31, 737–747.

Porter, M. E. (1985), *Competitive advantage: creating and sustaining superior performance*, New York: Free Press.

Romaniuk, J., Sharp, B., and Ehrenberg, A.S.C. (2007), 'Evidence concerning the importance of perceived brand diffferentiation', *Australasian Marketing Journal*, 15, 42–54.

Schau, H.J. and Muniz, A.M., Jr (2002), 'Brand communites and personal identities: negotiations in cyberspace', *Advances in Consumer Research*, 29, 344–349.

Schouten, J. and McAlexander, J.H. (1995), 'Subcultures of consumption: an ethnography of the new bikers', *Journal of Consumer Research*, 22, 3, 43–61.

Schwartz, B. (2004), *The paradox of choice: why more is less*, New York: HarperCollins.

Sharp, B. (2010) *How brands grow*, Oxford: Oxford University Press.

Sharp, B., Wright, M., Dawes, J.L. et al. (2012), 'It's a Dirichlet world: modeling individuals' loyalties reveals how brands compete, grow and decline', *Journal of Advertising Research*, 52, 2, 1–10.

van Marrewijk, A. and Broos, M. (2012), 'Retail stores as brands: performances, theatre and space', *Consumption, Markets and Culture*, 15, 4, 374–391.

Wellan, D.M. and Ehrenberg, A.S.C. (1990), 'A case of seasonal segmentation', *Market Research Society*, 30, 1, 35–44.

Yu, J. and Lannes, B. (2013), 'Chinese shopping behaviour: China's repertoire shopping', *Admap*, 48, 1, 36–38.

PART 4

WHERE ARE WE GOING?

Chapter 11 **Future trends in consumer behaviour**

11

FUTURE TRENDS IN CONSUMER BEHAVIOUR

Introduction

So far in this book we have shown how consumer behaviour has developed into a coherent and systematic academic perspective. While there are diverse ways of considering how the consumer behaves, a key element has been the development of a set of tools and analytical approaches drawn from psychology, economics, sociology, cultural studies, and anthropology that help improve our understanding of the complexity of consumption in the modern world. We have also shown something of this complexity, considering the different perspectives on consumption and examples from a range of contexts.

However, consumers change, and so do the contexts in which they consume, as shown by the ongoing recession in many countries. Where does consumer behaviour go next? What developments in consumer behaviour are we likely to see? And what are the theories, frameworks, tools, and methods that will help understand these changes? We suggest three main areas where consumer behaviour may be susceptible to change. The first is the domain of technology-induced change. This is a thread that runs through this chapter, but we examine it specifically in terms of technology, sociocultural contexts, and its manifestations in virtuality and the move away from ownership. The second thread is around sustainability, not only environmental sustainability but also economic sustainability and a wider perception that the western economic model of growth may be under threat from a variety of directions. Third, recent recessionary pressures at a global level remind us that consumers do not always live in times of abundance and opportunity, and it is important to consider constraints on behaviour and the impact this has on consumers and the organizations serving those consumers. Issues around consumer misbehaviour are also covered in this chapter, and we discuss such concerns in relation to the wider social and cultural context of consumer behaviour. Finally, we look at ways that consumer researchers are trying to understand consumer well-being through the theme of transformative consumer research.

LEARNING OBJECTIVES

After reading this chapter you will be able to:

1. Describe **technological trends and developments** and their relevance for consumer behaviour, including understanding how neuromarketing can help marketers explain how consumers behave.

2. Appreciate why issues around **sustainability and sustainable consumption** are important and the impact these will have on consumers of the future.

3. Understand how **global recessionary pressures** impact consumer behaviour.

4. Discuss **consumer misbehaviour** and recognize marketing's role in this and its impact on society.

5. Consider the relevance of **transformative consumer research** for dealing with issues around consumer well-being.

Technology trends on the horizon

Monitoring consumer trends around the world is important, especially given that technology and environments change at an incredible pace. Organizations such as trendwatching.com and futurefoundation.net specialize in identifying global consumer trends and business ideas. The importance of digital and social media in consumers' daily lives in terms of providing useful information and advice is clear, but in the coming years there is likely to be an increase in popularity for products, apps, and services that work for consumers by reminding them to behave 'better'. This trend has been labelled the **quantified self** (Wolf, 2010), and refers *to the idea that tracking metrics can lead to self-improvement in some way*. Examples include the Nike+ Fuelband, which uses an accelerometer to track all daily activity and calorie intake, and can monitor its wearer's efforts against preset goals. The trend towards wearable technology is illustrated in the development of a working 'smart watch', a device that communicates with a modem wireless headset or other devices. The smart watch may include features such as a camera, a compass, a mobile phone, and GPS navigation (see Figure 11.1). Some are currently available (e.g. the Sony SmartWatch and the Pebble SmartWatch), but the market is in its infancy. Recent media reports suggest that both Apple and Google are developing products (Titlow, 2013; Graziano, 2013).

Digital technologies such as apps are being used by doctors and physicians to improve health outcomes. For example, the Antibiotics Reminder app, which reminds patients to take their prescribed medicines, has been

Figure 11.1   Woman wearing a SmartWatch
Source: © Robnroll/Shutterstock.com.

launched in Australia. In July 2011, an augmented reality (AR) app called Lungs was launched in the USA to show smokers the damage caused by cigarettes. Users enter the number of cigarettes smoked per day and for how long, and the app provides a visual representation of the damage they will have suffered and a 'time taken for lungs to recover' statistic. The app has been used to promote anti-smoking messages and raise disease awareness.

Self-monitoring technology has already had an impact on companies in the health and fitness sector (see Figure 11.2). Gym companies can offer their clients portable monitors to provide data on performance, including heart rate, distances run, and weights lifted. Companies can work together to offer tailored benefits to consumers based on performance data. The health insurer Pru Health, for example, offers a reduced gym membership fee for Virgin Active where policy holders' gym use is monitored and rewarded with points that can be redeemed through its various Vitality Partners (including cinema and holiday companies).

Responsibility for health may soon devolve more towards the individual and less towards the state as these new systems, techniques, and technologies enable people to monitor their own health performance. With such information, consumers may be considered accountable for their own health choices. Issues also emerge in relation to ownership of data; this information is valuable to the business customers of the companies providing the tracking tools for targeting their marketing to individuals and identifying market trends.

Another technological trend is evident in how consumers share their interests, likes, and experiences from the real world through social media platforms. Posting images and messages on Facebook and Twitter has become a key part of many people's lives and of their

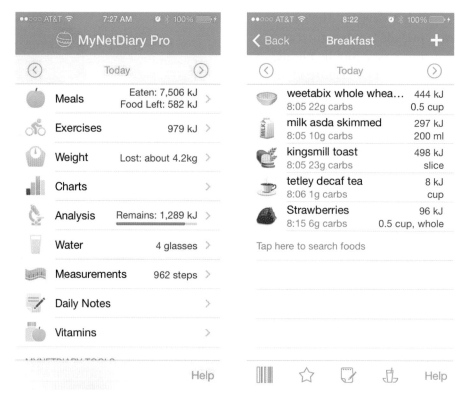

Figure 11.2 Example of self-monitoring technology an app from MyNetDiary called Calorie Counter Pro
Source: Image courtesy of MyNetDiary Inc.

consumer experiences. For example, the theme park Luna Park in Australia has introduced radiofrequency identification (RFID) wristbands that let visitors update their Facebook status while in the park. Swiping their wrists over sensors as they go on rides allows consumers to connect with their Facebook pages and 'Like' features, notify friends of their activities, and have their pictures captured and tagged. Figure 11.3 shows examples of RFID wristbands used at music festivals around the UK.

Marketing activities and campaigns are sometimes facilitated by the use of **QR (quick response) codes**, which are *optical machine-readable barcodes that record and store information related to items* (Dean, 2013). QR codes offer a method of effectively adding web-based content (a URL) to real-world messages, objects, or locations. A QR code looks similar to a bar code, but is scanned from a QR reader on a smartphone or tablet to connect to web content. QR codes can be placed on packaging, advertisements, websites, carrier bags, key rings, newspapers, banner ads, T-shirts, invoices—any place where the target consumer is able to access these codes and where they have the means to scan them.

Companies use QR codes in various ways. In Chapter 1, we described how Tesco used QR codes with Korean shoppers in virtual stores based in subways and metro stations (Consumer Insight 1.3). Shoppers browsed lifelike images of supermarket shelves with

Figure 11.3   Examples of RFID wristbands used at festivals around the UK
Source: Image courtesy of ID&C Ltd (www.idcband.co.uk).

their smartphones and scanned the QR codes on products to add them to their shopping carts to be delivered to their homes. Another application of QR codes is to provide more detailed consumer information on products. For example, the Haidian district of Beijing has thousands of restaurants that allow customers to check food safety information, including information on additives and breaches of food safety regulations, through QR codes.

It is worth noting that QR codes are particularly effective in situations that can provide consumers with real-time updates, especially where there is a constant flow of information such as train stations, bus stops, restaurant specials, or airline bookings. Deutsche Bahn's NFC system is a QR-based system which allows users to simply scan a QR code to check in and out of the train station.

The use of QR codes in marketing has resulted in more experientially based marketing, where the consumer feels that they are interacting directly with the company. Many cases discussed in this book (such as the Jimmy Choo example in Chapter 2) are based on QR technology and other social media. Consumer Insight 11.1 describes how social media has been used in the context of the reopening of the Rijksmuseum in Amsterdam and asks you to consider how QR codes might be used in the museum or art gallery context.

The trend towards self-monitoring and the explosion in consumer sharing are driven by technological advancements, facilitated by the dominance of social media and enhanced through the use of sensors to provide detailed information and awareness of various aspects of everyday life and performance. These new tools change our sense of self in the world, acting not only as mirrors for self-improvement, discovery, and

CONSUMER INSIGHT 11.1

Using social media in museum marketing

The Rijksmuseum in Amsterdam reopened in April 2013, to much fanfare, after a decade-long renovation process. This museum is famous for hosting artworks by Dutch masters such as Rembrandt, van Gogh, and Mondrian. One of the most famous pieces held in this gallery is Rembrandt's *The Night Watch*, which became the focus of a social media campaign to mark the reopening of the museum (see Figure 11.4).

Figure 11.4 The flash mob re-creation of Rembrandt's *The Night Watch*

Source: Image courtesy of ING Nederland.

A flashmob event was staged in a local shopping mall, dramatically recreating the *The Night Watch*. A film of the event was posted on YouTube (visit the Online Resource Centre for the link) and via social media, such as Twitter and Facebook, it attracted viewers from around the world. Within a couple of weeks of being launched, the flashmob clip had been viewed 926,479 times (now over 4.5 million times). This use of social media to draw worldwide attention to the reopening of this famous museum was very effective, and the same interest would not have been achieved if it had just been reported through the press and similar sources.

Many museums are embracing social media as a way of opening dialogue with visitors and widening accessibility. Other interesting examples of social media use include the Facebook postings by the Museum of the City of New York—each week they post a piece of artwork on Facebook, with a clue to its location, inviting visitors to identify the unknown location and to prove their response with evidence. Facebook enables the organization to have greater engagement with and involvement of users. The challenge aspect acts as a way of motivating people to (re)visit and increase footfall to the museum. Additionally, consumer-to-consumer interactions are encouraged, further enhancing the connection that visitors feel towards the museum.

Questions

1. Can you find any examples where social media has been used by arts organizations in ways that you feel are not effective? Can you explain why?

2. What do you think are the ingredients for effective social media campaigns?

3. How might you develop a marketing activity for museums or art galleries using QR codes?

Sources: Fowler (2013); Macleod (2013); Museum of the City of New York (2013).

 Visit the Online Resource Centre and follow the weblinks to learn more.

knowledge, but also in how we engage with other people (see Research Insight 11.1). For marketers, they offer opportunities to develop greater connectivity and conversations with consumers.

Neuromarketing

We have seen that people often make choices at a subconscious level and that choices do not always appear to be rational. In some cases people may not know why they choose a particular product or brand. Traditionally, market researchers have used either direct

RESEARCH INSIGHT 11.1

Giesler, M. (2012), 'How doppelgänger brand images influence the market creation process: longitudinal insights from the rise of Botox cosmetic', *Journal of Marketing*, 76, 6, 55–68

Giesler's paper is about how consumers and the market for Botox have evolved since 2002–2003. In this CCT paper, he discusses the historical context of the American consumer's relationship with technology, recognizing the ambivalence in consumer positions ranging from 'technology as salvation' (the answer to all our problems and ills) to 'technology as damnation' (it is destructive and harmful). Botox is precisely this kind of innovation, representing a contradiction between those consumers who are seeking technological solutions to the problem of ageing set against consumers with a preference for natural ageing processes.

 Visit the Online Resource Centre to read the abstract and access the full paper.

questions to ask people which brands they prefer, or motivational techniques such as those suggested by Ernst Dichter (see Chapters 1 and 7). The problem with direct questioning is that we find out what people *think* but not necessarily what they *do*. There is also the problem that respondents may give answers that reflect favourably on them or which they think are acceptable to the researcher, as in the case of the 'light' or 'regular' beer example described in Chapter 1. People are often asked to report on things that have happened in their past, and sometimes they find it difficult to reconstruct and interpret past actions, thoughts, and emotions in retrospect (Bagozzi, 1991). Neuromarketing is a new field of marketing research which uses brain-imaging techniques such as fMRI (functional magnetic resonance imaging) to identify brain activity through changes in blood flow. It directly examines how the brain works and the choices it makes without requiring the consumer to participate consciously (Morin, 2011). In other words, it identifies the choices the brain is making without the social, rationalizing, or other activities that can get in the way. **Neuromarketing** is '*the application of neuroscientific methods to analyze and understand human behaviour in relation to market and marketing exchanges*' (Lee et al., 2007: 200).

The relationship between the brain and our social and cultural environments and preferences is complex. Consider the following description of a restaurant meal devised by McClure et al. (2004: 379):

> A salad of perfectly grilled woodsy-flavored calamari paired with subtly bitter pale green leaves of curly endive and succulent petals of tomato flesh in a deep, rich balsamic dressing. Delicate slices of pan-roasted duck breast saturated with an assertive, tart-sweet tamarind-infused marinade.

For many, this lush description triggers appealing memories of food experiences, although if you were a vegetarian or disliked calamari your response might be different. Nevertheless such a description can fire our imagination so that we can almost taste the imaginary meal. McClure and his colleagues took this knowledge of the importance of social and cultural cues to recreate a neuromarketing version of the Pepsi Challenge. From 1975, Pepsi instigated a blind taste test in shopping malls as part of a promotional campaign directly attacking their chief competitor Coca-Cola. Shoppers would be faced with two unmarked cups, one containing Pepsi and the other Coca-Cola, and were invited to taste both and select the one they preferred. Their brand preference was then revealed. The results showed a general preference for the taste of Pepsi even though Coca-Cola had the larger market share.

The problem with the Pepsi Challenge is that while it may be testing people's *taste* preference, it is not testing their *brand* preference. Flavour is in fact a composite sensory perception which is made up of taste and experience. In the experiment performed by McClure et al. (2004), people's brains were scanned to uncover their neural responses not only to the taste of carbonated drinks but also to the brand image. They found that when there was no brand information, i.e. the participants did not know whether they were drinking Pepsi or Coke, there was little difference in their neural responses. However, when those who described themselves as preferring Coke were cued that the drink they were tasting was Coke, there was significant activity in key areas of the brain. A possible explanation is that the brand effectively has a life of its own in people's minds, recognizing that preference is more than just taste (Ariely and Berns, 2010) or, perhaps more controversially, that the idea of the brand itself actually tastes like something (Montague, 2006).

Such research tells us that it is virtually impossible to find a purely objective response to brands. We cannot experience a brand purely in terms of its physical qualities because our brains also process the imagery that has been built up around it. Consider, for example, the impact that knowing the price of an object may have on our interpretation of its taste. In one study neural responses were measured when people sipped wine. Particular neural responses were heightened when the participants were told that the wine was expensive versus inexpensive. Indeed, the responses correlated with self-report preferences, i.e. the participants preferred the expensive wine even though it was the same as the inexpensive one (Plassmann et al., 2008).

Marketers are interested in such research as they hope to access people's hidden desires and preferences, just as Ernst Dichter did nearly 100 years ago. Thus one might consider showing subjects pictures of new product designs or concept advertising and measure their brain activity to see which looked likely to be most favourable (see Research Insight 11.2). Various foods have been tested using the MRI scanner, and different perceptions of taste, smell, texture, and even sound have been mapped onto areas of the brain to identify their contribution to the overall experience. For example, using chocolate as a reward and a motivation to continue eating, researchers identified different brain areas for reward and punishment (Small et al., 2001). Companies could use such techniques to design more appealing food products. Such developments have a downside; companies could create foods so carefully linked to neural responses that individuals over-eat (Ariely and Berns, 2010).

Another technique used by neuromarketing companies is EEG (electroencephalography) which identifies brain activity from electrodes placed on a person's scalp. This method gives real-time information, but an EEG cannot locate exactly where the activity in the brain's reward or emotional centres is coming from. However, from a consumer behaviour and

RESEARCH INSIGHT 11.2

Erk, S., Spitzer, M., Wunderlich, A.P., Galley, L., and Walter, H. (2002), 'Cultural objects modulate reward circuitry', *NeuroReport*, 13, 18, 2499–2503

Susan Erk and colleagues hypothesized that sports cars have become symbols of value because of their relation to social status. Twelve male subjects were studied with fMRI while being shown pictures of different classes of car. The results revealed that, for these male brains, the sports cars engaged reward circuitry more than other types of car. In other words (and probably something many would intuitively believe), men like sports cars!

 Visit the Online Resource Centre to read the abstract and access the full paper.

marketing context this may not be necessary, as the following example explains. An international cosmetics company pre-tested two versions of an advertisement for a skincare product. They differed only in that in one version the model looked passively at the camera and in the other the model briefly touched her cheek with the back of her hand. Viewers preferred the version where the model touched her cheek. It appeared that this gesture enhanced the effectiveness of the advertisement even though focus group participants were unable to articulate why. The researchers used EEG to monitor skin conductance and registered significant changes in neurophysiological reactions in the scene with the gesture. What this meant was that the simple gesture brought about a brief but powerful emotional impact in this version of the commercial; consumers' brains can show different reactions to marketing stimuli even if they are not able to identify this at a conscious level (Ohme et al., 2009). Such research offers the possibility for companies to diagnose in the pre-campaign stage whether new advertisements can produce the kinds of response they are looking for (see Figure 11.5).

Figure 11.5 Two people watching a Blu-Ray disc whilst researchers monitor their neurophysical responses

Source: Image courtesy of Pocket-lint.com.

This research indicates that neuromarketing will be used extensively in key areas of business and marketing such as product design, the development of advertising, brand image, pricing, and other applied areas such as the optimum store layout. As the Practitioner Insight outlines, a new technology such as neuroimaging can even show that old methods of marketing still work well.

PRACTITIONER INSIGHT 11

Simon Harrop, BRANDsense

Simon Harrop talks about how Royal Mail used neuroimaging to assess consumers' responses to marketing material.

Royal Mail wanted to discover the different ways in which consumers responded to a piece of marketing information, presented with exactly the same layout, whether it was delivered on paper or digitally. To do this they used neuroimaging techniques to identify consumers' brain responses to the two forms of communication. What was found was that those areas in the brain which highlight emotional responses were more active when presented with the stimulus in paper than in digital form. It appears that there is something about reading a message on paper that is associated with a physical locality that gives an object a place in space and time which resonates with people. Research such as this also reveals what is termed 'super-additivity'. Here, the emotional response is non-linear. So if you have a document and add texture to it and then smell, the increased emotional response may be greater than each element's contribution i.e. rather than 1+1 equalling 2, it produces 3. What seems to happen is that additional emotional response is created by the synergy of the elements.

Rory Sutherland from Royal Mail describes physical post as producing high attention processing (HAP). Although direct mail will be thrown away by some, if people open it, they look at it, and may file it and look at it again; unlike digital forms of communication, you do not often look at it while doing something else or flicking through different web pages. Now BRANDsense is working with Royal Mail to develop SensationalMail where direct mail communications include other sensory elements such as fragrance and sound.

Sustainable worlds, sustainable consumption

Contemporary consumer culture is dominated by ideas around abundance and excess. Much of marketing is aimed at selling goods and services that enhance people's sense of self; the underlying premise is that the 'self' is a never-ending project, to be worked on and developed, and that products and brands are available to satisfy potentially end-less needs. However, a number of ethical issues are raised by this. First, the focus on materialism raises questions about the role of goods in people's lives. Why are material goods so desired? What happens if we try and step out of that system, consume less, and have a lifestyle less focused on buying things? Further, resource shortages, the increased economic power of countries outside the western bloc, and climate change together are likely to lead to a reappraisal of both individual and social attitudes to consumption. What are the implications of this for our understanding of consumption and consumer behaviour?

The emergence of the voluntary simplicity (VS) movement in the 1970s, as a simpler way of living, provided one route for consumers to opt out of some of the demands of consumer and marketplace cultures. There is also now the distinct possibility that con-straints on consumption will be necessary rather than voluntary. At the moment austerity is a political concept that largely focuses on cuts in government spending, but in future we may be facing a kind of austerity that has more in common with the rationing that Second World War populations in Britain and Europe experienced. It is too soon, and possibly too gloomy, to say that this is necessarily the case, but one consequence of this may be what might be called 'mindful consumption', where consumers are motivated to be more careful and aware of their consumption. The trend towards less ownership may be partly analysed in terms of sustainable consumption. These ideas are developed in the following sections.

RESEARCH INSIGHT 11.3

Black, I.R. and Cherrier, H. (2010), 'Anti-consumption as part of living a sustainable lifestyle: daily practices, contextual motivations and subjective values', *Journal of Consumer Behaviour*, 9, 6, 437–453.

In this qualitative study, the authors interviewed 16 women about the practices surrounding sustainable living. Their research offers some interesting insights into how people manage the day-to-day demands of a sustainable lifestyle while still engaging with consumer culture. One of their conclusions is that sustainable living is informed and transformed within their daily lives by using whatever is available to them, which can include consumer goods and services.

 Visit the Online Resource Centre to read the abstract and access the full paper.

Voluntary simplicity

Voluntary simplicity refers to a lifestyle choice where people opt to limit material consumption and free up resources, such as time and money, which they believe will raise the quality of their life (Huneke, 2005). Voluntary simplicity can involve a wide spectrum and variety of practices and values. Shaw and Newholm (2002) describe this spectrum as ranging from consumers who fully embrace the ideas around reducing consumption, driven by ethical concerns to own and use fewer goods (see Research Insight 11.3), through to those consumers who simply 'refine' their consumption towards ethical standards (e.g. buying Fairtrade coffee in their supermarket), enabling them to continue to have similar levels of consumption, but to consume differently and in line with their ethical concerns (see Consumer Insight 11.3). Similarly, Huneke (2005: 546) distinguishes between 'highly committed simplifiers' and 'less committed simplifiers' who change their behaviour, but not in highly disruptive way.

Mindful consumption

The global outlook, particularly in western cultures, towards environmental and ethical concerns (Huneke, 2005) has changed, and so has the attitude to voluntary simplification. While this concept was regarded as radical 30 years ago, it is now more relevant to society (Elgin, 2009). Many commentators argue that contemporary consumer culture cannot be maintained for long, with the threats of climate change and peak oil (the point when oil supplies decline after reaching the highest rates of extraction) resulting in a situation where consumers must be mindful of their own consumption activities. Millward Brown reported that following the world financial crisis, Japanese consumers, traditionally willing to pay a premium for convenience, were increasingly likely to be spending more time to save money. There are signs as well that following the earthquake and tsunami of 2011, and the subsequent nuclear crisis, the Japanese are becoming more concerned about mindful consumption. The *danshari* movement, derived from the Japanese for throwing away and letting go, has resulted in many books and television programmes focused on reducing conspicuous consumption and identifying low cost alternatives. This increased awareness of the issues around sustainable living, such as composting and recycling, are now becoming increasingly encouraged by governments and therefore normalized by some countries such as Germany and the UK (DEFRA, 2009).

Following the global recession of 2008–2009, there has been an increase in self-reliance among consumers, with more people moving from consumption to production (Burch, 2012). For example, the increasing popularity of allotments in the UK is a shift towards more self-sufficient consumers and contributes to a rise in the barter economy, where people trade goods and skills (Yarrow, 2012). Car boot sales and online auction sites, such as eBay, have meant that consumers can trade or sell their unwanted possessions to others instead of throwing them out. There are also numerous websites (such as freecycle.org) dedicated solely to giving away unwanted items free, thus reducing waste which could otherwise end up in landfill sites. Consumer Insight 11.2 describes some of the ways in which consumers are demonstrating and celebrating acts of mindful consumption.

CONSUMER INSIGHT 11.2

Celebrating mindfulness

There are various movements that encourage and support consumers to be more mindful of their consumption. The Adbusters Media Foundation is a not-for profit anti-consumerist movement which produces a magazine devoted to challenging consumerism. Adbusters also promotes the international event 'Buy Nothing Day', which encourages consumers to lessen consumption during one day in the run-up to Christmas (see Figure 11.6). This event is taking hold on the international stage in countries as diverse as Japan, the UK, and Germany (Corner, 2011).

International Frugal Fun Day is celebrated every year on the first Saturday in October. Created by Shel Horowitz, the event promotes the idea of doing fun things that cost $5 or less and encourages individuals to be creative about what constitutes fun and enjoyment. Increasingly individuals are blogging their own frugal ideas, which often contain recommendations regarding what foods to buy and where to buy them, and also information on how to make meals rather than use convenience foods.

Figure 11.6 'Keep calm and don't shop' poster: an example of Buy Nothing Day anti-consumption promotional material

Source: Image courtesy of Buy Nothing Day, UK (www.buynothingday.co.uk).

Questions

1. Why is Buy Nothing Day relevant for marketers?

2. Can you think of ways that companies can build on this concept to their advantage?

Sources: Storify (2012); IndyMedia (2013); theyearoflivingunofficially.com www.thefrugalgirl.com

 Visit the Online Resource Centre and follow the weblinks to learn more about mindfulness in consumption.

Shift towards an ownerless economy?

Consumer practices are also shifting in relation to ownership, with people considering what they can live without and alternative ways of accessing goods and services. For many of these consumers, owning goods and services is not critical, but rather it is the experiences and solutions that are valued and required. Many commentators have discussed how important it is for consumers to share their experiences via social media, such as Twitter and Facebook. Importantly, this sharing and the associated social media updates are acting as status symbols for consumers in the way that possessions have in previous times (Malnight and Keys, 2013). Posting your holiday photos on Facebook is driven by a need to share the experience, but for many, the number of 'likes' is also important. In this context, ownership is becoming less valued. The example of Vélib in Paris and Barclays Cycle Hire in London (Figure 11.7), services that provide access to a fleet of bicycles parked across these city centres, illustrates

Figure 11.7 Barclays Cycle Hire in London

Source: Image courtesy of Transport for London and Copyright James O. Jenkins, 2010, Moral Rights Asserted. This work may not be reproduced without the permission of James O. Jenkins.

RESEARCH INSIGHT 11.4

Bardhi, F. and Eckhardt, G.M. (2012), 'Access-based consumption: the case of car sharing', *Journal of Consumer Research*, 39, 4, 881–898

This CCT research interviewed Zipcar users to investigate the connections they felt to the car and the brand. They found that consumers do not have or want an emotional connection to the brand, and do not feel any psychological sense of ownership of Zipcar. Given that the company is trying to develop brand community, these findings represent a major hurdle for Zipcar.

 Visit the Online Resource Centre to read the abstract and access the full paper.

the appeal of this mode of consumption access. Once registered with the service, you receive a smart key that unlocks the bike from its docking station; you then make your journey and return the bike to any of the docking stations dotted around the capital. The pricing scheme is devised to encourage short trips. Apart from removing the burden and responsibility of ownership, this mode also removes the fear of theft and the lack of safe parking.

Other companies benefiting from this trend towards access rather than ownership modes of consumption include Fashion Hire (luxury handbags, where you can rent a Chanel handbag for £130 per month), Zipcar (car sharing), and Netflix (film and media rental) (see Research Insight 11.4). The term 'asset-light generation' has been used to describe the behaviour of young people who are part of a growing trend towards storing and streaming music and documents digitally in a move away from physically owning books, CDs, magazines, and TV (Fitzgerald, 2012). Companies such as Netflix and Spotify can offer the consumer access to a wide range of goods or services rather than having to buy or own a particular film or CD. Of course, borrowing is nothing new; in the past most people obtained their books from libraries.

Recession and consumption

At times of recession, people often change their consumer behaviour in response to the constraints on their economic budget. Sometimes these changes happen in unexpected ways. For example, cosmetic sales often increase as they are viewed as an affordable indulgence, somehow more essential than other luxuries that women may give up (such as designer clothes and shoes). Leonard Lauder, chairman of Estée Lauder, coined the term 'lipstick index' to encapsulate this rise in cosmetic sales (Rigby, 2009).

Some consumers tighten their belts and avoid taking on debt, which can have a major impact on business. During recessions, higher end, more expensive categories tend to do badly (e.g. cars, kitchens), as consumers are fearful of taking on new debts when jobs and future incomes are not guaranteed. Companies in these product categories have to allay these fears when promoting their products. In 2009, Hyundai developed a finance package whereby they offered an assurance to all customers that if in the year following purchase of a Hyundai car they lost their income, they could return the car. This assurance was an attempt to offer some safety to consumers in uncertain times, and of the million vehicles sold since the agreement began only 350 cars were returned based on the agreement. Many hailed this as a very effective marketing campaign, and the approach was copied by General Motors and Ford (Anon., 2011a). In 2011, Hyundai stopped this assurance programme, declaring that it was no longer needed since America was coming out of the recession.

The recession has an impact on leisure activities outside the home, and evidence from Keynote (2010) shows how eating out and going to the cinema tend to decline during a recession. Anything to do with home entertainment usually does well, as people spend more time indoors and cheer themselves up through greater expenditure on broadband and satellite TV packages (Easier Finance, 2008).

In terms of more essential purchases, such as food and energy, consumer spending patterns show less variation, mainly because there is less scope to cut down on these items. Consumer volatility is a characteristic of recessions—people re-assess their expenditure. At times of recession, consumer 'savviness' tends to go up, as does usage of websites offering money saving advice, such as moneysavingexpert.com. Recent reports suggest that almost all shoppers, across all socio-economic groups and all age groups, now use coupons (PitneyBowes, 2013).

A major trend in the retail sector is the increasing popularity of smartphone digitally based discount vouchers, fuelled by changes in mobile technology but also a response to recessionary pressures on consumers. This implies that marketers should be investing particularly where consumers are considering changes in expenditure, and are also willing to invest time looking for and collecting coupons and discount vouchers. However, this is the reverse of what many companies do during a recession, and it is often marketing budgets that are the first to be hit. In Consumer Insight 11.3 we discuss how the trend towards renting, rather than owning, occurs in the luxury market.

CONSUMER INSIGHT 11.3

Living a life of borrowed luxury

A recent consumer trend taking hold in a number of countries is the growth in rental culture, where consumers are renting, rather than owning, cars and properties in their bid to save money during the recession. As people's confidence in this new consumption mode increases, we are witnessing consumers with slightly more discretionary income going further in their rentals, and renting designer gowns, shoes, and handbags for short periods of time (anything from a few days to a month or so). This is what is coming to be known as 'borrowed luxury'.

Rental companies are found in many categories, including designer dresses (Rent the Runway, Wish Want Wear, Girl Meets Dress); handbags (Bag Borrow or Steal), watches (Borrow Time Watches), and luxury cars (Dream Car Hire, Elite Rent).

The attraction of this approach is that it assuages any guilt consumers may feel about such expenditure—they can have a small amount of luxury without the negative feelings that may accompany extravagant spending. It also removes the hassle and cost associated with the maintenance and insurance of expensive items. The Borrowed Time Watches club offers luxury watch rentals for men, with different levels of membership reflecting the needs and passions of its members, from 'executive' for enthusiasts who want an all-year membership through to 'basic' which suits the occasional wearer. In Milan, the Circle Club emerged as a way of enabling people who are already fairly wealthy to access designer jewels, luxury cars, and customized watches in order to convey greater wealth than they perhaps have. Its members pay about $26,000 to join, and this entitles them to a number of points. These points are then used to 'pay' for use of a range of luxury items (including boats, helicopters, and small planes!). When members' points run out, they pay the fee again. Another attraction of renting is that consumers can keep 'refreshing' their wardrobe, while keeping costs down.

Questions

1. What factors do you think will influence the wider uptake of this trend?

2. Try and think about different types of consumers (different age groups; income bands; different country contexts) and consider the issues for them in terms of considering renting rather than owning.

Sources: Castonguay (2006); Wilkinson (2007); Hevrdejs (2011); Scharf (2012); http://borrowedtime-watches.com/ http://www.bagborroworsteal.com/ http://www.dreamcarhire.com/ http://www.eliterent.com/ http://www.girlmeetsdress.com/ http://www.renttherunway.com/

 Visit the Online Resource Centre and follow the weblinks to learn more about the growth in rental culture.

Consumer misbehaviour

Much of this book has focused on attempting to explain and explore the ways that consumers behave, assuming that the consumer is acting according to the socially agreed norms of the marketplace. If you stop and think about a recent shopping experience, you may consider that you knew the way to behave in the store, how to interact with sales staff and other customers, and generally how to navigate the various aspects of the retail encounter. Many organizations are focused on customer satisfaction ratings, and have the philosophy that the customer is always right.

However, some types of consumer behaviour are definitely not what we would expect—some consumers can be deviant and dysfunctional in the way they act (Daunt and Harris, 2012). While some dysfunctional behaviours may occur in marketplace contexts and are linked to the acquisition of goods and services (e.g. compulsive buying, in-store abuse of staff, theft), others can be linked to product misuse (such as addictive or compulsive buying/consuming of food, drugs, or alcohol). **Consumer misbehaviour** is the term used to capture these types of behaviours, and is defined as *'behavioral acts by consumers, which violate the generally accepted norms of conduct in consumption situations, and thus disrupt the consumption order. It represents the dark, negative side of the consumer'* (Fullerton and Punj, 2004: 1239).

When we discuss the dark side of consumption, we are talking mainly about consumer misbehaviour, although a range of terms are used including deviant customer behaviour (Moschis and Cox, 1989), jay customers (Lovelock, 1994), and dysfunctional customer behaviour (Harris and Reynolds, 2003). All the definitions share a common focus on consumer behaviour that violates social norms of the exchange encounter. As we discussed in Chapter 9, social norms tend to be formed through customs, rules, laws, and values of a cultural context. Underlying the deviant nature of the consumer misbehaviour definition is the assumption that consumers know the 'accepted' norms of the encounter. Further, discussions of the dark side of consumer behaviour encompass issues in terms of disruption for other consumers and for the environment and society at large. It is also important when considering the darker aspects of consumption to question the broader ramifications of marketing practices, and the negative consequences associated with excess in contemporary consumer culture.

Deviant acquisition behaviour

The term deviant acquisition behaviour refers to consumer misbehaviour in acquiring goods. Black Friday, the day after Thanksgiving in the USA, is regarded as the start of the holiday shopping season when shops offer sales and special offers. In recent years, most major retailers have opened extremely early and offered promotional sales to kick off this important shopping period. There have been stories from the USA of consumers behaving badly during the Black Friday sales (Figure 11.8), with one report stating that customers rushing towards early morning (5 a.m.) deals in Wal-Mart pushed employees against stacks of merchandise (Barbaro, 2006). There have been reports of injuries and deaths associated with Black Friday sales (http://blackfridaydeathcount.com/). Although this is an extreme example, behaviour such as this is expected at sales time and has almost become part of the retail mythology around major sales events.

Other problematic behaviour include skipping payments, late payments, breaking rental agreements, and aggressive behaviour towards staff or other customers. Such behaviours are a pervasive part of everyday customer behaviour (Fullerton and Punj, 2004) and are sometimes deliberate or a result of thoughtlessness, but can also result when a customer does not have control over the situation or lacks knowledge or experience of roles and responsibilities. Marketers can ease such situations by providing clear guidance and information on how to behave in certain situations, such as queuing guidelines in banks or posters alerting customers how to behave in their interactions with staff. Two particularly

Figure 11.8   Typical scenes from Black Friday sale in the USA   *Source*: Image courtesy of Martin Thuresson.

problematic forms of consumer misbehaviour are found in compulsive shopping and theft—the negative consequences of each can be far-reaching.

Compulsive buying

Compulsive buying is *an unusual obsession with shopping such that it significantly affects the person afflicted*. It is considered to be a form of deviant acquisition behaviour. Those people who buy in a compulsive way have a strong preoccupation with shopping, often characterized as uncontrolled, which has significant negative consequences. Most often these consequences are financial (since many buy excessive amounts that cannot be afforded), but there can also be serious personal and emotional consequences, such as stress and broken relationships. For compulsive buyers, it is the experience of shopping and the accompanying emotions, that drive their behaviour. Various estimates of this phenomenon in the USA suggest that it affects 3–6 per cent of the population (Koran et al., 2006; Rose and Segrist, 2012). A number of causes have been suggested, ranging from a psychological basis (such as low self-esteem, low mood, as a way of coping with stress and anxiety, and as a form of fantasy) through to a more socially oriented basis, including a form of materialistic value endorsement, dissatisfaction with identity, or as a way of exercising power and control in relationships (O'Guinn and Faber, 1989; Elliott et al., 1996; Dittmar, 2005). Contemporary consumer culture, which emphasizes materialism, can heighten the problem for compulsive buyers, and those with low self-esteem or self-worth are particularly vulnerable. It is important for companies to be aware of the potential (unintended) consequences of their marketing messages. However, we should also consider the prevalence of store cards which are frequently offered with an immediate discount at the point of sale; these may impact compulsive shoppers in terms of how much they are able to spend if they amass a number of such cards.

Theft

In marketplace contexts, consumers have a sense of what they think is honest and acceptable behaviour, which is informed by cultural and societal values and beliefs. As discussed already, people generally know how to behave in shops and how to interact with sales staff. A real problem for companies, and society, is consumer theft. When talking about theft it is important to appreciate the spectrum of dishonest behaviours that may fall under that heading. Many people shopping in supermarkets think it is acceptable to try grapes, as if they are a free sample, yet there is no sign saying 'help yourself to grapes'. However, many consumers rationalize this as acceptable and not even dishonest, since the act is considered to be so insignificant compared with the profits that the supermarkets make. At the other end of the spectrum are organized gangs of shoplifters stealing to order. In this section we are referring to the more significant acts where the thief (acting on their own or in a gang) leaves the store with goods that have not been paid for. Although shoplifting is criminal behaviour, and hence primarily the domain of criminologists, it is also consumer behaviour (albeit deviant behaviour), since it is 'part of people's conduct in their role as consumers' (Fullerton and Punj, 1997: 336). Clearly, this is a problem that represents a cost for many companies, and so it is important for businesses to have strategies for handling consumer theft.

Consumer theft *refers to the desire to steal as a way of acquisition of consumer objects,* and is a significant phenomenon affecting the experience of all consumers. It is costly for businesses and ultimately for consumers. One recent study from the USA suggests that one in every eleven people who walk into a shop will leave with at least one item that has not been paid for (National Association for Shoplifting Prevention, 2011), and in recent years there have been well-publicized cases of celebrities being caught shoplifting (e.g. Anthony Worrall Thompson in the UK, and Winona Ryder and Lindsay Lohan in the USA).

The recent rise in more middle-class shoplifters has been explained in terms of their stealing goods to maintain a standard of living, rather than to sell them on to make money. The Centre for Retail Research in Nottingham, UK, tracks projected losses from retail crime in the Christmas season. Their research covers 19 countries and the data provides an interesting snapshot of how retail crime is viewed in different countries. Retail crime comprises shoplifting, staff theft, and supply chain fraud. In nearly all countries (except the USA) shoplifting is the single most significant form of retail theft. The countries worst hit by shoplifting are the USA (£23.7bn), followed by the UK (£5.2bn), Germany (£4.6bn), France (£4.3bn), and Italy (£3.4bn) (Bamfield, 2012).

The most popular items for consumer theft are those that are CRAVED—Concealable, Removable, Available, Valued, Enjoyed, and Disposable (Barkham, 2012). Items that are in high demand, easily disposed of (i.e. sold or passed on), and in small mobile formats are popular items. Reports of the 'most popular items stolen' emerge annually in the UK and the USA, and these often includes expensive cuts of meat, cheese, alcohol, small electrical items such as toothbrushes and DIY tools, electronic gadgets such as video games, smartphones, and laptops, razor blades, and designer clothing and shoes (Faw, 2012; Barkham, 2012). Although specific data is not available for all countries, Barkham (2012) reports that cheese is the most popular item stolen across the world!

Product factors influencing whether or not people steal are linked to the CRAVED aspect of the product, but also the product may be one that is embarrassing (e.g. condoms) or illegal (e.g. cigarettes or alcohol to youths). Environmental factors are also relevant, which may emanate from the marketing context, particularly the way that products are presented to make them look attractive and enticing. Merchandising of goods may also make it seem easy for thieves to steal goods or switch tags. Some consumers seek the thrill and excitement of thieving (which may be a contributory factor in adolescent and youth thefts). Another important consumer factor may relate to attitudes towards the store and big business in general. Consumers may justify their theft by suggesting that the environment encourages it and the company somehow deserves it and can absorb the cost, and so it is a victimless crime. Finally, the moral development of consumers may be a factor influencing their views on stealing, and they may not see stealing as wrong. Linked to this are their beliefs around the extent to which thieves think they can get away with stealing.

Finally, it is worth noting the increase in other forms of retail crime, as reported in the British Retail Crime Survey (BRCS), linked to advances in technology and practices around shopping and accessing goods. With the increase in e-business and card transactions online there has been a rise in e-crime and fraud in retail contexts. E-crime, which is made up of identification-related frauds, card and card-not-present frauds, and refund frauds, accounts for 37 per cent of the total cost of retail crime. The other major component of retail crime is fraud, accounting for 26 per cent of the total cost of retail crime in 2011–2012 (BRCS, 2012).

The main challenge for marketers is to discourage shoplifting. Measures in place include making access to expensive goods difficult, often by locking them away (e.g. perfumes and jewellery) or by having them available behind a counter (e.g. sales of razor blades and spirits in convenience stores). While these strategies may not be ideal in terms of consumer experience, they are adopted to reduce shoplifting opportunities. Other theft-reducing devices include the use of security tags on merchandise that are deactivated or removed for reuse at the cash register. The costs of these thefts need to be covered somehow, and often consumers pay the price for lost merchandise and the costs of security systems through higher prices.

Deviant usage behaviour: excessive consumption

Some of the problems associated with excessive consumption have been mentioned in our discussion of the issues around sustainability and consumption. When we talk of excessive consumption, we are referring not only to the problems associated with levels of consumption that are unsustainable for the planet's resources, but also those that pose health problems for consumers. In a global context, two significant problematic areas of excessive consumption relate to food and alcohol.

The obesity crisis

A global obesity epidemic was first identified by the World Health Organization (WHO) in the 1990s (WHO, 2012). Although initially considered a problem associated with developed countries, records show that rates are rising worldwide, and most dramatically in urban settings.

Obesity levels have more than doubled around the world between 1980 and 2008 (WHO, 2012). In the UK the latest figures state that 26 per cent of adults and 16 per cent of children are obese. The picture in the USA is similar, with 35.7 per cent of adults and 16.9 per cent of children and adolescents reported as obese in 2012 (Food Research & Action Center, 2012). Reports from other countries suggest that rising obesity levels are a problem. In Brazil, 48.5 per cent of the population are overweight and 15.8 per cent are obese (BBC, 2012). The number of overweight people in China is also on the rise, with one adult in four reported to be overweight or obese, and this figure is higher in urban areas (Howard, 2012). This increase is partly related to the vast change in lifestyles oriented towards greater use of processed food and supermarkets, and a drop in physical activity as a result of huge economic expansion (Bristow, 2010).

Paradoxically, many developing countries (such as India) are facing the dual challenge of suffering from both under- and over-nutrition. In Mexico, where the tap water is unreliable, soft drinks are a popular alternative; in the Middle East, the increasing wealth of Bedouins and their tradition of feasting has led to overeating in a climate where exercise is not favoured.

The data on the relationship between income level and obesity is mixed. In the UK, there appears to be a pattern of greater obesity among the most deprived in society (National Obesity Observatory, 2012). In the USA, the disparities between high and low income consumers and obesity levels are weakening. However, the Food Research & Action Centre (FRAC) reports that those living on low incomes are more vulnerable to becoming obese for reasons including limited access to quality healthy fresh produce, greater reliance on cheaply produced processed foods, and greater exposure to marketing of obesity-promoting foods (e.g. fast food restaurants, TV advertisements).

When discussing the problem of global obesity, many commentators point to the role of the global food industry in producing more processed cheaper foods, high in fat and sugar, which leads to 'passive overconsumption' of energy and ultimately results in higher levels of obesity (Swinburn et al., 2011). The term 'obesogenic environment' has been used to describe the role of environmental factors in influencing food consumption and activity levels (Jones et al., 2007), and the marketing environment is implicated here in determining the availability and consumption of different foodstuffs. In the UK, the Academy of Medical Royal Colleges (AMRC) has published a set of recommendations to deal with the obesity problem, calling for action by government, the National Health Service, local councils, and food firms, as well as changes in parental behaviour (AMRC, 2013).

Excessive and irresponsible alcohol consumption

Excessive alcohol consumption is another major global problem. The WHO conducts an annual survey, the Global Information System on Alcohol and Health, and the most recent data shows the developed world as having the highest alcohol consumption levels.

Many Eastern European countries have high consumption, risky patterns of drinking, and, accordingly, high levels of alcohol-related deaths and disabilities. The global pattern among young people is towards higher levels of alcohol use and binge drinking (WHO, 2011), and there are 320,000 deaths annually from alcohol-related causes among young people aged 15–29 years, which results in 9 per cent of all deaths in that age group (WHO, 2011). In the UK, the levels of alcohol consumption among the 16–24 age group remain high (Robinson and Harris, 2011), but there is also a trend towards abstinence among young people and this appears to be on the increase (Robinson and Harris, 2011; Measham 2008).

Researchers from a range of disciplines, including public health, criminology, psychology, and social marketing, have focused on the issues around alcohol consumption, seeking to understand the drivers of excessive alcohol consumption. A number of studies have highlighted the central role that drinking and drunkenness play in many young people's social lives (Griffin et al., 2009; Smith and Foxcroft, 2009). Reasons for drinking alcohol are diverse, and include the social function that alcohol plays in young people's lives (Szmigin et al., 2008), the importance of alcohol for how young people act out the gender roles associated with being young (Measham, 2002; Abel and Plumridge 2004), and the hedonistic appeal of the deliberate and determined drunkenness that characterizes contemporary youth culture. The marketing and retailing practices around alcohol and the UK drinking culture are important considerations. Over the last 10 years, the alcohol industry has changed the way that alcohol is marketed in a number of ways, such as developing new alcohol products that encourage new ways of drinking (e.g. new higher strength alcohol products to be consumed as 'shots', which are discussed in more detail in Consumer Insight 11.4). The industry has also engaged in greater use of price promotions and point-of-sale materials in bars and retail environments which encourages higher consumption.

CONSUMER INSIGHT 11.4

Does the marketing of alcohol influence consumption?

The role of the alcohol industry in promoting alcohol consumption has been the focus of much government and media attention in the UK in recent years. In 2009, The Showbar Club in Warrington, UK, was in trouble for encouraging irresponsible drinking through its 'Two Bob Tuesdays' promotional event (see Figure 11.9). Entry to the event was £5 and, following that, all drinks were sold for 10 pence (colloquially, 'two bob'). The company defended this promotion as follows: 'They will only be allowed to have one drink at a time. It's not irresponsible. Other places have had promotions of drink at 1p a time—now that is irresponsible." (Jenny Keep, Manager of Showbar, quoted in Verge Magazine (2011)). Other nightclubs, such as the Tokyo Club in Oldham, Greater Manchester, have been criticized for offering all-inclusive drinks promotions (BBC, 2009).

Figure 11.9 Alcohol promotion for 'Happy Hour'   *Source*: © iStock.com/ManuelVelasco.

Novel approaches to alcohol packaging, often reflecting consumer trends, have emerged in recent years, and some have argued that these have contributed to excessive alcohol consumption. 'Suck & Blow' jelly shooters are a case in point—these plastic shot cups are sold to individual and corporate clients as 'The most fun way to do a party shot ever!'. The idea is that consumption is accomplished through the combined effort of two people—one blowing and the other sucking—leading to very quick consumption of the alcoholic jelly.

Cell Drinks, who make pre-packaged spirit (PPS) drinks sold in flexible packaging via unique vending machines, ran into problems with their advertising. One of the main appeals of this drink is that consumers can hold the drink while dancing, and it will not spill. The no-spill aspect of its packaging was emphasized in its advertising campaign of 2011, where it showed young people in various scenarios (a free-runner running and jumping over buildings while holding the drink; a girl raver dancing frantically while holding the drink) who were not spilling the drink. The Advertising Standards Authority found that the advertisements appealed to under-18s and ruled that they should be withdrawn.

Questions

1. To what extent do you think marketing and the alcohol industry contribute to excessive alcohol consumption among young people?

2. Can you think of ways in which marketing could be used to dissuade young people from drinking so much?

Sources: Measham (2008); Anon. (2011b); ASA (2011); Verge Magazine, 2011; www.suckandblow.com

 Visit the Online Resource Centre and follow the weblinks to learn more about the marketing of alcohol.

Transformative consumer research

Transformative consumer research (TCR) *refers to a stream of research that focuses on benefit-ing consumer welfare and quality of life across the world.* While high quality and rigorous research has been a central plank of much consumer welfare research over the years, what distin-guishes TCR work is that it emphasizes the dissemination and sharing of valuable findings (Mick et al., 2011), in ways that are geared towards having effective and impactful outcomes. A key aspect of TCR work is the recognition that in order to develop effective consumer welfare solutions to real consumer problems it is important to include all stakeholders in the research from early on, and for these stakeholders to be involved throughout the whole pro-ject. The TCR perspective lends itself to problems and contexts where there is a consumer welfare implication. The global problems around food well-being are important and have been the focus of TCR work (Block et al., 2011), as has addiction (Martin et al., 2012), poverty (Blocker et al., 2013), and risky consumption behaviour among youths (Mason et al., 2013).

A typical TCR approach to a consumer well-being issue would aim to inform interven-tions to address the problematic behaviour by including relevant stakeholders in all aspects of the intervention, from research through to design of campaign materials and evaluation of impact of the campaign. For example, research for Alcohol Research UK reports that there has been a steady increase in the amount of alcohol consumed by older age groups in recent years, and that a growing number of older people are at risk of alcohol-related harm (Wadd et al., 2011). However, alcohol problems are often difficult to detect in older people because of complex physical and social problems, including a lack of awareness amongst health profes-sionals in recognizing alcohol misuse, or barriers for older people seeking to access help. From a TCR perspective, health and social care workers would be included to inform the health and social care perspective, community-based public service workers (such as community police and the fire service) might be included, since they often interact with and see the consequences of the effects of alcohol consumption and may have something to contribute, and substance misuse practitioners might also be included. The approach might be closer to action research, with the focus on the impact of the research to bring about social change. This is an impor-tant theme in current consumer research as it goes beyond understanding how and why con-sumers purchase and use products to identifying problems in consumption and helping to improve consumers' lives in a holistic way. It is possible that TCR will become an important stream in consumer research which can also inform welfare policy.

Conclusions

When the certainties of the growth economy are removed and the economic and finan-cial parameters are shifting it becomes imperative to understand how consumer behaviour responds to these new conditions. In this chapter we have addressed a range of issues that are likely to have a major impact on consumer behaviour.

We discussed some of the **technological trends and developments** in marketing, and Practitioner Insight 11 from the Royal Mail provided a further set of insights into how commercial organizations are using neuroimaging in the assessment of consumer responses to marketing materials.

Issues around **sustainability and sustainable consumption** were discussed in this chapter, and in Consumer Insight 11.2 we focused on Buy Nothing Day as an example of an international voluntary simplicity initiative.

Another important theme in this chapter related to how **consumers are responding to global recessionary pressures**. Consumer Insight 11.3 looked at how consumers are changing the ways that they access goods, with a greater move towards rental and hiring.

We also looked in detail at **consumer misbehaviour** and recognized marketing's role in this and its impact on society, with Consumer Insight 11.4 focusing on the issues around the marketing and consumption of alcohol.

,Finally we considered the relevance of **transformative consumer research** for dealing with issues around consumer well-being.

In terms of marketing's future, there are important points to consider, not least the role that marketing and business has played in creating the conditions that have led to some of the problems discussed here (e.g. advertising foods high in fat/sugar to children, and developing alcoholic products that encourage swift consumption of high alcohol content short drinks). Questions are raised as to whether marketers should be involved in advising people on 'life choices'. Controversially in the UK, the Conservative–Liberal Democrat coalition government has launched the Public Health Responsibility Deal, which aims to work collaboratively with business and the voluntary sector to develop a set of pledges or actions that will contribute to improved public health. Some have argued that the companies involved (which include Coca-Cola, McDonald's, Greggs, Bacardi, Asda, Diageo, and Burger King) are driven by commercial imperatives rather than concerns for consumer well-being, and therefore there is a tension at the heart of this approach. The underlying hope with this broad collective approach involving industry is that it will create and improve the conditions for access to information and environments that are more conducive to healthy living (Jebbs, 2012).

Further, marketers need to think about consumer trust and cynicism. Chylinski and Chu (2010) comment that consumer cynicism is commonly related to suspicion, mistrust, scepticism, and distrust of an agent's or organization's motives, and can lead to reactions such as dissatisfaction, alienation, resistance, and hostility towards the organization. However, they point out that this is a fairly under-researched area, and it is difficult to say what the consequences of consumer cynicism are. Some consumers may engage in consumer activism (similar to the Buy Nothing Day discussed in Consumer Insight 11.2), others may boycott particular stores and brands, and voluntary simplicity and more mindful consumption may also result.

To close this book, it is useful to consider the argument developed by Kevin Roberts and Brian Sheehan in their book *Loveworks*. They argue that in contemporary marketplaces where consumers keep changing, power is moving away from manufacturers and retailers towards consumers, who are armed with information, choice, and connectivity (Roberts and Sheehan, 2013). Knowing those consumers, engaging in dialogue, and forming emotional connections with them is central to successful consumer relationships.

Review Questions

1. Outline and discuss two main technological developments which are impacting on consumer behaviour.

2. Explain what neuroimaging can tell the marketing manager that other research methods cannot.

3. What is the difference between voluntary simplicity and mindful consumption?

4. What are the reasons behind the trend away from ownership towards borrowing and renting?

5. How does compulsive consumption differ from excessive consumption? Can you identify the factors leading to each type of compulsive consumption?

6. What are the key characteristics of consumer crime?

7. What does CRAVED stand for?

8. What is transformative consumer research, and why is it relevant to the study of consumption?

Discussion Questions

1. What apps do you have? How do you use them? Discuss with your classmates which are most popular and why? Do you think that they lead to more consumption?

2. Why might neuromarketing techniques be superior to traditional market research techniques?

3. If you had to reduce your consumption, how would you do it? What changes to your lifestyle would you make and how do you think it would affect you?

4. Consider different products or services you might borrow rather than buy. What are the advantages and disadvantages?

5. Discuss what you consider to be consumer theft. Are some types of theft worse than others and if so why?

6. What do you consider are the main drivers for young people to drink excessively?

 Visit the Online Resource Centre to test your knowledge further and complete the Multiple Choice Questions for Chapter 11.

CASE STUDY 11

Are you a virgin consumer?

In this case we examine the idea of the virgin consumer. The fast pace of innovation and changes in contemporary society mean that in many consumer contexts everyone is at times a virgin consumer, unfamiliar with the brands, services, apps, and experiences they come across on a daily basis. In this Case Study, we discuss this in more depth, and offer some suggestions for connecting with virgin consumers.

The website trendwatching.com identifies a recent trend in consumer behaviour which they describe as the 'virgin consumer'. The reason for this term is more to do with the constant innovation and development of new and unfamiliar products, services, brands, and experiences that become available every day than the nature of the consumers themselves; indeed, such virgin consumers are usually highly experienced. Trendwatching.com say that virgin consumers want new things, they look for them and lust after them, and they want to experiment and have fun. In the twenty-first century, not only are there lots of new things for consumers to experience but the choice is overwhelming and there is much more on the way, with China alone granting millions of new patents.

In the past new brands might take a long time to become popular as consumers were wary and preferred to stick with tried and trusted brands. Today new brands may become trusted quickly for a number of reasons. Why? People are less concerned about the value of the old 'trusted' brand; indeed choosing new unknown brands can offer novelty, authenticity, and a feeling of discovery, and the risk associated with trying new brands is much lower because consumers are easily able to share information. Consumers discover new products and services through their social networks. They receive recommendations and reviews and ask friends and followers to improve and validate their buying decision. The actual sharing of information can become a business in itself; the coupon site Groupon has used referrals from friends and colleagues to drive sales of 40 million since its launch in 2008. Trendwatching.com has recently published some facts regarding social connections and the impact they have on brands:

- three-quarters of Facebook users have 'liked' a brand

- over 50 million users 'like' brands every day

- Juicy Couture found that their product purchase conversion rate increased by 160 per cent after installing social sharing features

- Incipio Technologies, a gadget accessory retailer, found that referrals from Facebook had a conversion rate double the average.

It is important to remember that different cultures may be looking for different experiences. Although social media is a worldwide phenomenon, it is going to be used in many different ways. China's largest food and drinks company built the success of its new product, an organic juice called Loahs, on the Farmville mania gripping China in 2009 by encouraging social media game players to plant organic products in their virtual gardens, produce organic juice, and then share it with their friends. Therefore the campaign raised awareness, which led to 130 million virtual bottles being shared with friends. Sales jumped by 30 per cent.

Trendwatching.com suggest three important approaches for engaging with consumer virgins.

1. Cast off industry convention—this means thinking about how your consumers live now and what they want, rather than developing existing products (see Chapter 2 on discontinuous innovations). The product also needs to be intuitive to use—no messing about with instruction manuals. Thermostats may seem like an unlikely product to be developed in a new way to meet consumer needs. Nest has achieved this and produced a product that looks good and is not overly technical (see Figure 11.10). The company posts that three out of four people can install it within 30 minutes. Nest learns people's schedules and is programmed to save energy. They also provide an app so that if you are coming home early you can turn up your heating so your home is warm when you arrive (see www.nest.com).

Figure 11.10   Left, the Nest Thermostat UK app for an iPhone; right, a Nest thermostat
Source: Image courtesy of Nest Labs Inc. © 2012 Dwight Eschliman.

2. Explain your brand—a virgin brand is going to be new to consumers so it has to be explained, and one way that new brands are doing this is telling stories about their brand and then finding ways to keep the story in the consumers' minds. When you go on the Welsh jeans manufacturer Hiut it has a section entitled 'Story'. Here they tell you that the jeans are made in Cardigan in Wales which used to have Britain's biggest jeans factory producing 35,000 pairs a week for decades. When the factory closed down, people lost their jobs but not their skills. Hiut, although a small company, wants to offer the opportunity for some of those people to use their skills again. To stimulate consumer demand, and also to engage more effectively with its consumer base, Hiut created the History Tag. The History Tag harnesses the potential for storytelling through objects by creating a mechanism (the History Tag) allowing consumers to develop and track their personal history with the

company's jeans. Each pair of jeans is issued with a unique number, which the consumer registers (and activates) on the company website. They are then encouraged to upload photographs of themselves wearing the jeans as a way of preserving memories associated with wearing the jeans (see Figure 11.11). The message on the website also encourages consumers to think about how they preserve these memories, and reinforces the point that their jeans are made to a high standard and are built to last: 'And that's the genius of making a product to last. It will give our objects more meaning. It will mean we throw things away less. Because it attaches the stories to the objects that we love' (hiutdenim.co.uk).

Figure 11.11 Hiut advertising campaign   *Source*: Image courtesy of Hiut Denim Co. (http://hiutdenim.co.uk).

3. Finally, trendwatching.com warns companies not to expect commitment from their consumers. Rather than expecting a long-term relationship, companies need to embrace the fact that consumers may want variety, so alternatives such as streaming or renting products rather than selling them may be the best solution. What is clear is that renting can work for any kind of product, not just films and music—now you can even rent your clothes (see thesixosix.com). As this site notes, many people want clothes not a closet.

Questions

1. What new products, brands, or experiences do you think will appeal to virgin consumers? Try to think about ways that a brand is delivered, not just what it is?

2. What new ideas or brands have you recently adopted? What do you like about them and why?

3. Write a history for a new brand/experience/service of your choice. Think about what you would emphasize, e.g. history, sustainability, novelty, exclusivity.

Sources: Yu and Lannes (2013); trendwatching.com www.hiutdenim.co.uk www.nest.com

 Visit the Online Resource Centre and follow the link to the authors' blog where you can keep up to date with the latest developments in consumer behaviour and further explore theories through additional articles and real-world examples.

References

Abel, G.M. and Plumridge, E.W. (2004), 'Network "norms" or "styles" of "drunken deportment"?', *Health Education Research Theory and Practice*, 19, 5, 492–500.

AMRC (2013), 'Measuring up: the medical profession's prescription for the nation's obesity crisis', Academy of Medical Royal Colleges, http://www.aomrc.org.uk/doc_view/9673-measuring-up (accessed 4 June 2014).

Anon. (2011a), 'Research review: technology adoption depends on customer relationships', *Teller Vision*, 1407, 3–4.

Anon. (2011b), 'Cell Drinks escapes censure from the Portman Group', *The Drum*, 25 August http://www.thedrum.com/news/2011/08/25/cell-drinks-escapes-censure-portman-group (accessed 8 May 2013).

Advertising Standards Association (nd), 'Adjudication on Cell Drinks', http://www.asa.org.uk/Rulings/Adjudications/2011/8/Cell-Drinks/SHP_ADJ_164359.aspx (accessed 21 November 2012).

Ariely, D. and Berns, G.S. (2010), 'Neuromarketing: the hope and hype of neuroimaging in business', *Nature Reviews Neuroscience*, 11, 4, 284–292.

Bagozzi, R.P. (1991), 'The role of psychophysiology in consumer research', in T.S. Robertson and H.H. Kassarjian (eds), *Handbook of consumer behavior*, Englewood Cliffs, NJ: Prentice Hall, pp 124–161.

Bamfield, J.A.N. (2012), 'Shoplifting for Christmas 2012: how criminals profit from the festive season', Centre for Retail Research, http://securityadvancement.com/wp-content/uploads/2012/12/Shoplifting+for+Christmas+2012+Study+US+3.pdf (accessed 5 June 2014).

Barbaro, M. (2006), 'Attention, holiday shoppers: we have fisticuffs in aisle 2', *New York Times*, 25 November, http://www.nytimes.com/2006/11/25/business/25shop.html?_r%C2%BC1&pagewanted%C2%BC2&ei%C2%BC5087%%200A&em&en%C2%BCe8b3e335cf3fa05c&ex%C2%BC1164603600&oref%C2%BCslogin&_r=0 (accessed 25 January 2013).

Bardhi, F. and Eckhardt, G.M. (2012), 'Access-based consumption: the case of car sharing', *Journal of Consumer Research*, 39, 4, 881–898.

Barkham, P. (2012), 'Why is cheese the most shoplifted food item in the world?', *Guardian*, 10 January, http://www.guardian.co.uk/lifeandstyle/shortcuts/2012/jan/10/cheese-most-shoplifted-food-item (accessed 2 July 2013).

BBC (2009), 'MP blasts club's drink promotion', 27 January, http://news.bbc.co.uk/1/hi/england/manchester/7853882.stm (accessed 24 February 2013).

BBC (2012), 'Brazil health study shows growing weight problem', 11 April, http://www.bbc.co.uk/news/world-latin-america-17671253 (accessed 24 February 2013).

Black, I.R. and Cherrier, H. (2010), 'Anti-consumption as part of living a sustainable lifestyle: daily practices, contextual motivations and subjective values', *Journal of Consumer Behaviour*, 9, 6, 437–453.

Block, L.G., Grier, S.A., Childers, T.L., et al. (2011), 'From nutrients to nurturance: a conceptual introduction to food well-being', *Journal of Public Policy & Marketing*, 30, 1, 5–13.

Blocker, C.P., Ruth, J.A., Sridharan, S., et al. (2013), 'Understanding poverty and promoting poverty alleviation through transformative consumer research', *Journal of Business Research*, 66, 1195–1202.

Bristow, M. (2010), 'China faces obesity explosion', BBC, http://www.bbc.co.uk/news/world-asia-pacific-11368027 (accessed 23 December 2013).

BRCS (2012), British Retail Consortium, http://www.brc.org.uk/downloads/BRC_Retail_Crime_Survey_2012.pdf (accessed 24 February 2013).

Burch, M.A. (2012), 'Educating for simple living', Simplicity Institute, http://simplicitycollective.com/wp-content/uploads/2012/08/EducatingforSimpleLivingSimplicityInstitute1.pdf (accessed 8 June 2013).

Castonguay, G. (2006), 'The rich are choosing to live on borrowed luxury', *International Herald Tribune*, 7 November, http://www.nytimes.com/2006/12/07/business/worldbusiness/07iht-auto.3822935.html (accessed 21 December 2012).

Chylinski, M. and Chu, A. (2010), 'Consumer cynicism: antecedents and consequences', *European Journal of Marketing*, 44, 6, 796–837.

Corner, L. (2011), 'Buy Nothing Day: Adbusters' role in the global Occupy movement', *The Independent*, 20 November, http://www.independent.co.uk/news/world/politics/buy-nothing-day-adbusters-role-in-the-global-occupy-movement-6263205.html (accessed 8 April 2014).

Daunt, K.L and Harris, L.C. (2012), 'Exploring the forms of dysfunctional customer behaviour: a study of differences in servicescape and customer disaffection with service', *Journal of Marketing Management*, 28, 1/2, 129–153.

Dean, D.H. (2013), 'Anticipating consumer reaction to RFID-enabled grocery checkout', *Services Marketing Quarterly*, 34, 1, 86–101.

DEFRA (2009), *Waste Strategy: Annual Progress Report*, London: Department for Environment, Food and Rural Affairs.

Dittmar, H. (2005), 'Compulsive buying-a growing concern? An examination of gender, age, and endorsement of materialistic values as predictors', *British Journal of Psychology*, 96, 4, 467–491.

Easier Finance (2008), 'Economic recession impacts broadband ISP migration', http://www.easier.com/17403-economic-recession-impacts-broadband-isp-migration.html (accessed 23 March 2012).

Elgin, D. (2009), *The Living universe. Where are we? Who are we? Where are we going?*, San Francisco, CA: Berrett-Koehler.

Elliott, R., Eccles, S., and Gournay, K. (1996), 'Revenge, existential choice, and addictive consumption', *Psychology & Marketing*, 13, 8, 753–768.

Erk, S., Spitzer, M., Wunderlich, A.P., Galley, L., and Walter, H. (2002), 'Cultural objects modulate reward circuitry', *NeuroReport*, 13, 18, 2499–2503.

Faw, L. (2012), 'Why do people steal meat from grocery stores?', *Forbes*, 24 December, http://www.forbes.com/sites/larissafaw/2012/12/24/why-do-people-steal-meat-from-grocery-stores/ (accessed 8 April 2014).

Fitzgerald, E. (2012), 'An ever-connected generation is going asset-light', *Eamonn Fitzgerald's Rainy Day Blog*, http://www.eamonn.com/2012/12/05/an-ever-connected-generation-is-going-asset-light/ (accessed 23 June 2013).

Food Research &Action Center (2012), 'Overweight and obesity in the US', http://frac.org/initiatives/hunger-and-obesity/obesity-in-the-us/ (accessed 5 June 2014).

Fowler, R. (2013), 'The Rijksmuseum in Amsterdam performs an amazing PR stunt', *Trendhunter World*, 4. April, http://www.trendhunter.com/trends/flash-mob (accessed 27 June 2013).

Fullerton, R.A. and Punj, G. (1997), 'What is consumer misbehavior?', *Advances in Consumer Research*, 24, 336–339.

Fullerton, R.A. and Punj, G. (2004), 'Repercussions of promoting an ideology of consumption: consumer misbehavior', *Journal of Business Research*, 57, 11, 1239–1249.

Giesler, M. (2012), 'How döppelganger brand images influence the market creation process: longitudinal insights from the rise of Botox cosmetic', *Journal of Marketing*, 76, 6, 55–68.

Graziano, D. (2013), 'Google reportedly 'actively exploring' the smartwatch market', http://bgr.com/2013/01/24/google-smartwatch-rumor-305233/ (accessed 13 July 2013).

Griffin, C., Bengry-Howell, A., Hackley, C., et al. (2009), 'Every time I do it I absolutely annihilate myself': loss of (self-)consciousness and loss of memory in young people's drinking narratives', *Sociology*, 43, 3, 457–476.

Harris, L.C. and Reynolds, K.L. (2003), 'The consequences of dysfunctional customer behavior', *Journal of Service Research*, 6, 2, 144–161.

Hevrdejs, J. (2011), 'A frock on the clock?', *Chicago Tribune*, 28 January, http://articles.chicagotribune.com/2011-01-28/news/sc-cons-0127-save-savvy-renter-20110128_1_rental-cars-frock-late-fees (accessed 24 February 2012).

Howard, C. (2012), 'The big picture', *Economist*, 15 December, http://www.economist.com/news/special-report/21568065-world-getting-wider-says-charlotte-howard-what-can-be-done-about-it-big (accessed 24 February 2013).

Huneke, M. E. (2005), 'The face of the un-consumer: an empirical examination of the practice of voluntary simplicity in the United States', *Psychology & Marketing*, 22, 7, 527–550.

IndyMedia UK (2003), 'Santa Parade, Buy Nothing Day, Birmingham', 30 November, http://www.indymedia.org.uk/en/2003/11/282245.html (accessed 23 February 2013).

Jebbs, S. (2012), 'On our way to 5-a-day', https://responsibilitydeal.dh.gov.uk/dr-susan-jebb-on-our-way-to-5-a-day/ (accessed 21 May 2013).

Jones, A., Bentham, G., Foster, C., et al. (2007), 'Tackling obesities: future choices—obesogenic environments—evidence review', Foresight Government Office for Science, http://www.bis.gov.uk/assets/foresight/docs/obesity/03.pdf (accessed 8 July 2012).

Keynote (2010), 'Leisure outside the home market review 2010: Keynote Market Review Report', http://www.keynote.co.uk/market-intelligence/view/product/10374/leisure-outside-the-home?utm_source=kn.reports.browse# (accessed 8 June 2012).

Koran, L.M., Faber, R.J., Aboujaoude, E., et al. (2006), 'Estimated prevalence of compulsive buying behavior in the United States', American Journal of Psychiatry, 163, 1806–1812.

Lee, N., Broderick, A.J., and Chamberlain, L. (2007), 'What is neuromarketing? A discussion and agenda for future research', International Journal of Psychophysiology, 63, 7, 199–204.

Lovelock, C, (1994), Product plus, New York: McGraw-Hill.

Macleod, I. (2013), 'Rijksmuseum and ING promote museum exhibit with flash mob', The Drum, 5 April, http://www.thedrum.com/stuff/2013/04/05/rijksmuseum-and-ing-promote-museum-exhibit-flash-mob (accessed 27 July 2013).

McClure, S., Li, J., Tomlin, D., et al. (2004), 'Neural correlates of behavioral preference for culturally familiar drinks', Neuron, 44, 379–387.

Malnight, T.W. and Keys, T.S. (2013), 'A top ten for business leaders', Economist, http://www.economist.com/blogs/theworldin2013/2012/11/global-trends-2013 (accessed 24 June 2013).

Martin, I.M., Kamins, M.A., Pirouz, D.M., et al. (2012), 'On the road to addiction: the facilitative and preventive roles of marketing cues', Journal of Business Research, 66, 8, 1219–1226.

Mason, M.J., Tanner, J.F., Piacentini, M., et al. (2013), 'Advancing a youth-centred approach for risk behavior: foundations, distinctions, and research directions', Journal of Business Research, 66, 1235–1241.

Measham, F. (2002), ' "Doing gender"—"doing drugs": conceptualising the gendering of drugs cultures', Contemporary Drug Problems, 29, 2, 335–373.

Measham, F. (2008), 'The turning tides of intoxication: young people's drinking in Britain in the 2000s'. Health Education, 108, 3, 207–222.

Mick, D.G., Pettigrew, S., Pechmann, C.C., and Ozanne, J.L. (eds) (2011), Transformative consumer research for personal and collective well-being, New York: Routledge Academic.

Montague, R. (2006), Why choose this book?', New York: Dutton.

Morin, C. (2011), 'Neuromarketing: the new science of consumer behavior', Society, 48, 2, 131–135.

Moschis, G.P. and Cox, D. (1989), 'Deviant consumer behavior', Advances in Consumer Research, 16, 1, 732-737.

Museum of the City of New York (2013), https://www.facebook.com/MuseumofCityofNY (accessed 27 June 2013).

National Association for Shoplifting Prevention (2011), The shoplifting problem in the nation, http://www.shopliftingprevention.org/TheIssue.htm (accessed 24 February 2013).

National Obesity Observatory (2012), 'Adult obesity and socioeconomic status', NOO Data Factsheet, http://www.noo.org.uk/uploads/doc/vid_16966_AdultSocioeconSep2012.pdf (accessed 1 December 2012).

O'Guinn, T.C., and Faber, R.J. (1989), 'Compulsive buying: a phenomenological exploration', Journal of Consumer Research, 16, 2, 147–157.

Ohme, R., Reykowska, D., Wiener, D., and Choromanska, A., (2009), 'Analysis of neurophysiological reactions to advertising stimuli by means of EEG and galvanic skin response measures', Journal of Neuroscience, Psychology, and Economics, 2, 1, 21–31.

PitneyBowes (2013), 'The coupon renaissance', http://pressroom.pitneybowes.co.uk/the-coupon-renaissance/ (accessed 5 June 2014).

Plassman, H.O'Doherty, J., Shiv, B., and Rangel, A. (2008), 'Marketing actions can modulate neural representations of experienced pleasantness'. *Proceedings of the National Academy of Sciences of the USA*, 105, 1050–1054.

Rigby, E. (2009), ' "Lipstick index" smeared by recession', *Financial Times*, 10 April, http://www.ft.com/cms/s/0/443d639e-25f4-11de-be57-00144feabdc0.html#axzz2sdI6tD14 (accessed 8 April 2014).

Roberts, K. and Sheehan, B. (2013), *Loveworks: how the world's top marketers make emotional connections to win in the marketplace*. Brooklyn, NY: Powerhouse Books.

Robinson, S. and Harris, H. (2011), 'Smoking and drinking among adults, 2009: a report on the 2009 General Lifestyle Survey', Office of National Statistics, http://doc.ukdataservice.ac.uk/doc/6737/mrdoc/pdf/6737report.pdf (accessed 5 June 2014).

Rose, P. and Segrist, D.J. (2012), 'Difficulty identifying feelings, distress tolerance and compulsive buying: analyzing the associations to inform therapeutic strategies', *International Journal of Mental Health and Addiction*, 10, 927–935.

Scharf, C. (2012), 'Accessible excess: how luxury marketing is changing' *TrendReports.Com*, 14 November, http://www.trendreports.com/article/luxury-marketing (accessed 27 June 2013).

Shaw, D. and Newholm, T. (2002), 'Voluntary simplicity and the ethics of consumption'. *Psychology & Marketing*, 19, 2, 167–185.

Small, D.M., Zatorre, R.J., Dagher, A., et al. (2001), 'Changes in brain activity related to eating chocolate: from pleasure to aversion', *Brain*, 124, 1720–1733.

Smith, L. and Foxcroft, D. (2009), 'Drinking in the UK: an exploration of trends', *Joseph Rowntree Foundation Report*, http://www.jrf.org.uk/publications/drinking-in-the-uk (accessed 20 June 2013).

Storify (2012), '#OccupyXmas starts with Buy Nothing Day', http://storify.com/adbusters/occupy-black-friday (accessed 9 May 2013).

Swinburn, B.A., Sacks, G., Hall, K.D., et al. (2011), 'The global obesity pandemic: shaped by global drivers and local environments', *Lancet*, 378, 9793, 804–814.

Szmigin, I., Griffin, C., Hackley, C., et al. (2008) *'Reframing "binge drinking" as calculated hedonism, empirical evidence from the UK'*, *International Journal of Drug Policy*, 19, 5, 359–366.

Titlow, J.P. (2013), 'Apple's iWatch concept is real—and here's how it might work', *Readwrite Mobile*, http://readwrite.com/2013/02/22/apple-smartwatch-patent (accessed 9 July 2013).

Verge Magazine (2011), 'Warrington club comes under fire for 10p drinks student night', 27 September http://www.vergemagazine.co.uk/girls/2011/09/warrington-club-fire-10p-drinks-student-night/ (accessed 24 February 2013).

Wadd, S., Lapworth, K., Sullivan, M., et al. (2011), 'Working with older drinkers', *Report for Alcohol Research*, http://alcoholresearchuk.org/downloads/finalReports/FinalReport_0085 (accessed 5 June 2014).

WHO (2011), *Global status report on alcohol and health 2011*, Geneva: World health Organization.

WHO (2012), 'Obesity and overweight fact sheet 311', May, http://www.who.int/mediacentre/factsheets/fs311/en/ (accessed 24 February 2013).

Wilkinson, T (2007), 'Italy's rich pay to look richer', *Los Angeles Times*, 18 February, http://articles.latimes.com/2007/feb/18/world/fg-bella18 (accessed 20 June 2013).

Wolf, G. (2010), 'The quantified self', http://www.ted.com/talks/gary_wolf_the_quantified_self.html (accessed 20 February 2013).

Yarrow, J. (2012), 'Tips for recession-busting bartering', *Beyond Green Living*, http://www.wildernesswood.co.uk/blog-post/tips-recession-busting-bartering (accessed 20 June 2013).

Yu, J. and Lannes, B. (2013), 'Chinese shopping behaviour: China's repertoire shopping'. *Admap*, 48, 1, 36–38.

GLOSSARY

Absolute threshold is the smallest amount of stimulation that can be picked up by any of our senses.

Acceptance/rejection when the consumer considers existing choice criteria and elaborates the message received to reach a point of acceptance or rejection of the information.

Acculturation relates to the idea of movement between places or cultural contexts.

Active learning involves the acquisition of knowledge before purchase, and therefore extensive information search.

Actual self refers to the core sense of self, that sense of self which is enduring and stable across situations.

Adaptation is the extent to which people's awareness of a stimulus diminishes over a period of time.

Affective component (of attitudes) relates to the emotional connection the consumer has with the target object about which an attitude is formed.

Aggregation is where the person becomes used to a new role and transforms within that role.

Anchoring is over-reliance on one piece of often irrelevant information to make a decision.

Approach-approach conflict is when you have to choose between two or more equally attractive alternatives.

Approach-avoidance conflict is when a desired goal also has negative consequences.

Archetypes are models of people, behaviours, or personalities.

Aspirational groups are composed of people that the consumer can identify with or admire (often from afar), and aspires to be like in some way.

Attention is the mental activity given to a stimulus.

Attitude is a learned predisposition to respond in a consistently favourable or unfavourable manner in relation to some object.

Attitude object/act is the thing about which the attitude is held, and can include brands, services, ideas, people, and behaviours.

Attributes are the characteristics or features of the attitude object/act.

Attributions relate to the process whereby a person explains the causes of a behaviour. In consumer terms this is the extent to which the product/service lives up to consumer expectations, and the reasons behind this.

Automatic mode is used to describe a human being operating in a routine mode with little effort and no feeling of voluntarily being in control, such as jumping when you hear a loud noise.

Availability heuristic refers to a situation where people judge the likelihood or frequency of something happening in the future by how easy it is to remember similar events.

Avoidance-avoidance conflict is when the choices available all have some apparent negative consequences.

Behavioural component (of attitudes) refers to the action or behaviours associated with the attitude object.

Behavioural intention is an intention to act in some way.

Behavioural learning is concerned with learning as a response to changes in our environment.

Beliefs are the thoughts an individual holds about some object, idea, or person.

Biogenic needs or innate needs enable us to survive and include the need for food, water, and shelter.

Brand community refers to a non-geographically bound community, who are connected through brand admiration, with a structured set of social relations.

Brand loyalty is the inclination to make repeat purchases of the same brand.

Brand personality scale describes the underlying brand dimensions of sincerity, excitement, competence, sophistication, and ruggedness.

Choice architecture describes how the way a choice is presented influences the choice made.

Choice heuristics is a process which allows people to reduce the number of attributes to be considered for possible alternative choices.

Chunking is the grouping together of similar or meaningful pieces of information.

Closure is the tendency for people to fill in the 'missing' elements of an incomplete picture.

Coercive power is when conformity to the group is brought about through the threat of punishment.

Cognitive component (of attitudes) refers to the beliefs and thoughts the individual has in relation to the target attitude object, its character, and its relations to other things.

Cognitive dissonance is the state of having inconsistent beliefs and attitudes.

Cognitive learning theories focus on learning through internal mental processes and conscious thought.

Collective unconscious stores hidden memory traces inherited from the human ancestral past.

Compensatory models are made up of a number of beliefs and use a scoring system to derive a final score. Attributes are averaged such that a low score on one attribute can be compensated by a higher score on another attribute.

Compliance refers to publicly changing behaviour to fit in with the group but privately disagreeing, i.e. a behavioural shift without an attitudinal one.

Compliance heuristics are those heuristics built around the likelihood of choosing something based on complying with a request.

Comprehension is where the consumer searches (and identifies) meaning.

Compulsive buying is an unusual obsession with shopping such that it significantly affects the life of the person afflicted.

Conformity is the adoption of behaviour resulting from real or perceived pressure to comply with a person or group.

Conjunctive decision rule is when a consumer chooses a brand based on minimum levels for each of any key evaluative attributes.

Connectors are people who tend to know lots of other people, often from different subcultures to their own.

Consideration set refers to those brands consumers might actually consider buying.

Consumer acculturation refers to the process by which people moving from one country to another adapt to the consumer cultural environment.

Consumer ethnocentrism is based on the idea that ethnocentric individuals view their group (or culture) as superior to others, and therefore that in consumer terms there is a strong preference towards buying domestic, rather than foreign-produced, goods.

Consumer innovativeness is defined as a generalized tendency toward innovative behaviour applicable across product classes.

Consumer misbehaviour is a behavioural act by a consumer which violates accepted norms of consumption conduct.

Consumer theft refers to the desire to steal as a way of acquisition of consumer objects.

Consumer tribes are groups of people who are emotionally connected by similar consumption values and usage and who use the social linking value of products and services to create a community and express identity.

Consumption function maps the relationship between disposable income and level of wages.

Contamination is when objects associated with sacred events or people become sacred in their own right, for example, items belonging to famous people.

Contactual or associative groups are generally close groups with which we interact regularly and where there is a degree of proximity.

Contexts of decisions are the environments within which consumption choices take place.

Continuous innovations are innovations that tend to create little change in consumption patterns and generally involve the introduction of a modified product rather than a totally new one.

Conventions are a specific form of custom, and relate to the norms for the conduct of everyday life.

Crowdsourcing occurs when a company or institution takes a function once performed by employees and outsources it to an undefined (and generally large) network of people in the form of an open call.

Culture is the sum total of learned ideas, beliefs, values, knowledge, and customs that together regulate the behaviour of members of a particular society.

Customs are the norms of behaviour that have been passed from generation to generation.

Decision rules are used by consumers to identify what is the best choice for them.

Declarative memory is specifically about knowing things. It is made up of two different types of memory systems, episodic memory and semantic memory, which remember different types of event.

Default is a preselected option without active choice.

Desacralization is when a sacred item or symbol is removed from its special place.

Differential threshold is the point at which we notice a difference between two stimuli.

Direct influence by a reference group refers to direct, often face-to-face, contact between members of a group.

Disclaimant group is one that we currently belong to, or perhaps belonged to in the past, but no longer want to associate ourselves with.

Disconfirmation paradigm is the difference between a consumer's pre-purchase expectations of the product's performance and their post-purchase experience.

Discontinuous innovation has a disruptive effect, and will require the establishment of new behavioural patterns by consumers.

Dissociative or avoidance groups are groups we have negative feelings towards and whom we avoid being associated with.

Double jeopardy is where brands with smaller market share have fewer buyers and those fewer buyers buy the brand less often.

Duplication of purchase analysis states that all brands within a category share their customer base in relation to the size of the other brands' market penetrations.

Dynamically continuous innovations create some change in behavioural patterns, but the magnitude of change is not very great.

Ego represents the interests of the individual, ensuring the necessary arbitration between the demands of the id and constraints of the superego.

Ego-defensive function (of attitudes) refers to the idea that attitudes can have the function of defending our self-image.

Ego involvement is when consumers perceive his/her self-esteem, interests and needs to be closely connected to a product or brand.

Elaboration continuum describes the amount of thought given to an advertising message/communication.

Elimination-by-aspects decision rule ranks evaluative aspects by importance and establishes a minimum cut-off point for each attribute.

Encoding refers to how information enters the memory.

Enculturation refers to the way that an individual learns the traditional content of his/her native culture.

Endogenous WOM is when conversations happen among consumers as part of their natural communication and when they are just passing on information about their experiences with a product or brand.

Endowment effect describes how highly we value what we already have, and it shows that people assign specific values to a thing relative to their situation.

Enduring involvement can be described as a long term interest in a product, brand or service.

Engrams are neural networks connecting new memories with old ones.

Episodic memory refers to our memories of specific events and experiences which have formed our autobiographical time line.

Evaluation refers to the process of determining how valuable, or important, something is to us.

Evaluative criteria are the factors we use to compare alternative offerings.

Evoked set includes the possible brands already known to the consumer from which they choose.

eWOM is any positive or negative statement made by potential, actual, or former customers about a product or company, which is made available to a multitude of people and institutions via the Internet.

Exchange value can be said to represent what the value of a good is to the consumer and therefore what it could be exchanged for, usually its price.

Exogenous WOM is word of mouth that occurs as a direct result of the firm's marketing efforts.

Expectancy-value model suggests that people form attitudes towards objects (e.g. brands) based on their expectations and evaluations of the attributes that make up the brand.

Expert power is when we are influenced to behave or purchase something by someone who we recognize has particular expertise, for example a doctor or scientist.

Explicit memory is the conscious recollection of an experience.

Exposure ensures that the stimulus is in the appropriate place for consumers to have access to it.

Extended self refers to the idea that our possessions and belongings form such a close connection to us and our past that they come to represent us in some way.

Extinction is the decrease in the conditioned response which occurs when the unconditioned stimulus is removed from the conditioned stimulus.

Extrinsic need requires some return or goal from the external environment.

Fetishism of commodities refers to the domination of objects or things in the market, and relates to the idea of masking the human activity that is critical to, and lies behind, the production of consumer goods and services.

Financial risk is the perception of a likely financial loss.

First-order conditioning occurs when a conditioned stimulus acquires motivational importance by being paired with an unconditioned stimulus which is intrinsically aversive or rewarding.

Fixed interval schedule is when reinforcement is provided after a specific known period of time.

Fixed ratio schedule applies reinforcement after a specific number of responses.

Formal groups are formed by some kind of outside structure and are likely to have a formalized constitution and set of rules of conduct for members.

Framing refers to how we make a decision through the context in which a choice is presented to us.

Gestalt means 'whole' and refers to how people look for meaning and patterns in the stimuli in the environment as a whole rather than in terms of the individual parts.

Gift-giving rituals are the rituals surrounding giving presents to others.

Grooming rituals are those private behaviours that consumers undertake to aid the transition from private to public self (and back again).

Heuristics are methods to aid decision making to arrive at satisfactory solutions by simplifying the complexity of assessing the probability and prediction of value in a choice situation.

Higher-order conditioning is the pairing of two conditioned stimuli.

Holiday rituals refer to the rituals associated with both tourism holidays and culturally bound holiday seasons.

Hyperbolic discounting refers to many people's inability to prefer future gains over current losses and where they place more emphasis on immediate pleasures and pains.

Id corresponds to primary needs, focused on immediate gratification, directing a person's psychic energy towards pleasurable acts without regard to the consequences.

Ideal or idealized self relates to the self we aspire to be like.

Ideal congruity refers to the extent to which the product image matches the ideal self-image.

Ideal social self-image is how consumers would like to be seen by significant others.

Identity schema represents one's understanding of oneself with respect to a particular role and is thus both personalized and often realistic.

Identity-ideal schema corresponds to how the person would like to become as one who enacts that role.

Implicit memory is remembering without conscious awareness.

Impulse purchasing is a sudden powerful urge to buy a product with little regard to the consequences of what we are buying.

Indirect influence occurs through an individual observing group members' behaviour and altering his/her own because of it.

Individualism refers to the ways in which individual goals are balanced against collective or group goals, with individualistic cultures prioritizing the individual's goals over those of the collective (and vice versa).

Inept set are those brands that the consumer may have come across during their search or from previous experience but would not consider for this particular decision.

Inert set includes those brands not under consideration at all.

Informal groups are formed by a group of individuals who have some sort of commonality but no formal connection to each other.

Information search is the process by which we identify appropriate information to help aid our choice in a decision-making situation.

Informational conformity occurs when someone actively looks for guidance from the group where they lack knowledge or are in an ambiguous situation.

Informational group influence is when a consumer uses the reference group to actively get information from opinion leaders or experts in the group.

Informational power is based on logical argument and knowledge which someone may have acquired from experience or through the nature of their job.

Internalization involves both an attitudinal and behavioural change in favour of the group.

Interpretivist perspective stresses the subjective meaning of the consumer's individual experience and the idea that any behaviour is subject to multiple interpretations rather than one single explanation.

Intrinsic need is an internal motivation.

Involvement is the perceived relevance of a purchase to the consumer.

Just noticeable difference (JND) is the smallest change in a stimulus to be noticed by the majority of people.

Knowledge refers to the familiarity with people or things, which can include understanding, facts, information, and descriptions gained through experience and education.

Knowledge function (of attitudes) relates to the human need to have a meaningful, stable, and organized view of the world.

Law of buyer moderation is the tendency for light buyers to become heavier, and heavier buyers to become lighter.

Learning is the activity or process of acquiring knowledge or skill by studying, practicing, or experiencing something.

Legitimate power is where the referent is seen to have authority by virtue of their position in the particular context.

Lexicographic decision rule is when the customer ranks the evaluative attributes by their importance.

Liminality is the period when a person is moving between roles in his/her life, and is consequently often unsure of him/herself.

Long-term orientation (LTO) relates to the time orientation of a culture, and refers to a society's search for virtue and hence its perspectives on time and tradition.

Loss aversion describes the fact that most people dislike losses more than gains of an equivalent amount.

Malleable self refers to the idea that people will act differently according to the situation, influenced by social roles, cues, and the need for self-presentation.

Masculinity refers to one of the key dimensions of culture, the other end of which is femininity. Masculinity captures the motives driving people within a culture, which are classified as either achievement-oriented, with an emphasis on heroism, assertiveness, and material reward (labelled masculine in Hofstede's terms), or more consensus-oriented, where the emphasis is on cooperation, modesty, caring, and quality of life (labelled feminine in Hofstede's terms).

Materialism is a trait that captures the degree to which a consumer is overly concerned with physical objects and material goods.

Mavens are collectors and brokers of information but they use this information and want to start discussions with others or respond to requests.

Memory is both a system and a process whereby information is received, sorted, organized, stored, and retrieved over time.

Mental accounting is when individuals allocate assets into separate non-transferable groupings to which they may assign different levels of utility.

Message-response involvement reflects the consumer's interest in marketing communications.

Microcultures are subgroupings within a culture, where people are classified based on shared demographic characteristics (e.g. age, regionality, ethnicity) or in terms of shared consumption interests.

Monomorphic opinion leaders are experts in a limited field.

Mores are particular forms of custom and have a strong moral overtone.

Motivation describes the processes that cause people to behave in a particular way.

Motivation to comply (MC) is the extent to which the consumer wishes to comply with or conform to the preferences of significant others.

Multi-trait approach (to personality) is where researchers are concerned with a number of personality traits taken together and how they combine to effect consumption.

Myth is a story that contains symbolic elements that express shared emotions and ideals of a culture.

Narrative approach (to identity) is where consumers are viewed as identity seekers and makers using marketplace resources to construct and express both individual and collective identities.

Needs are the result of the difference between the actual and desired states.

Near-stationary markets are established mature markets which appear stable over a period of several months or a year.

Negative self refers to the person you are not, and do not want to become.

Neuromarketing uses neuroscientific methods to analyse and understand human behaviour and decision-making in the marketing context.

Neutral operants are responses from the environment that neither increase nor decrease the probability of a behaviour being repeated.

Non-compensatory models are where some overriding factors or attributes are dominant in the choice process.

Normative beliefs (NBs) are the individual's perception about relevant or important others' beliefs that the individual should engage in a behaviour or not.

Normative conformity applies when a person wants to fit in with the group or is afraid of being rejected by them and will publicly accept the group's view even if privately they do not agree.

Norms are informal rules that govern behaviour.

Novelty refers to the quality of being new, original, or unusual, and in marketing it can include new or unfamiliar products, services, brands, ideas, people, or experiences.

Objectification is the process whereby sacred qualities are attributed to mundane items.

Operant conditioning is the changing of behaviour through reinforcement following a desired response.

Opinion leaders are those people who have great influence on the decisions and choices of others.

Opinion seekers are people who seek opinions and information to help their purchase decision.

Parental yielding is when a parental decision-maker is influenced by a child's request and 'surrenders'.

Passing off is the marketing of a good in a way that enables it to be mistaken for another brand. It relies on the phenomenon of stimulus generalization.

Passive learning is the acquisition of knowledge without active learning.

Penetration is the proportion of people who buy an item in a given time period.

Perceived behavioural control is the person's perception of how easy or difficult it is likely to be for them to perform a particular behaviour.

Perception is the process through which information in the form of stimuli in the environment is selected, organized, and interpreted through the sense organs.

Perceptual defence is when a consumer inhibits perception of potentially threatening or unpleasant stimuli.

Perceptual vigilance is when a consumer consciously or unconsciously filters stimuli for relevance.

Performance or functional risk is the perception of how well the product will perform its expected task.

Personal unconscious is a Jungian term that refers to anything which is not presently conscious but can be, holding previously conscious experiences and memories that have been repressed, forgotten, suppressed, or ignored.

Personality is the combination of the characteristic patterns of thoughts, feelings, and behaviours that make up an individual's distinctive character.

Persuasion heuristics refer to how consumers take short cuts when processing advertisers' messages.

Physical risk is the perception of harm that a product or service might have.

Polymorphic opinion leaders are experts in a number of areas, although generally within a particular category such as sport, fashion, food, or technology.

Positivist approach emphasizes the objectivity of science and the consumer as a rational decision-maker.

Possession rituals are the rituals associated with moving products from the marketplace to the home or workplace.

Possible selves are personalized representations of one's self in future states.

Power distance (PD) is about the relations between people and the ways that interpersonal relationships form when power differences exist.

Prediction heuristics are where the consumer is trying to predict an outcome such as 'If I buy a new mobile phone now, when will I need to update it?'

Priming is the alteration of people's behaviour outside their conscious awareness as a result of their first being exposed to certain sights, words, sensations, or activities.

Principle of proximity states that things we see close together are perceived to be more related than things that are seen as farther apart.

Problem recognition is a realization that a problem needs to be solved through purchase.

Procedural memory is memory involved with knowing how to do things.

Product involvement is the perceived personal relevance of the product, based on needs, values or interest.

Profane consumption is the term used to capture those consumer objects and events that do not share the 'specialness' of sacred ones.

Psychogenic needs are socially acquired needs and include the need for status, affiliation, self-esteem, and prestige.

Psychographics is based on building a picture (sometimes literally) based on demographics, alongside activities, interests, and opinion variables.

Psychological risk is the risk which reflects the individual's perception of themselves.

Purchase frequency is the average number of times consumers purchase a brand in a given time period.

Quantified self refers to the idea that tracking metrics can lead to self-improvement in some way.

QR (quick response) codes are optical machine-readable barcodes that record and store information related to items.

Reactance is a motivational state which acts as a counterforce to threats to a person's freedom.

Recognition requires the memory to retrieve information by experiencing it again.

Recollection is when we reconstruct memory through a range of different narratives and bits of memory.

Reference groups are those groups that are used by a person as a basis for comparison and guidance when forming their beliefs, attitudes, and behaviours.

Referent power is influence that stems from our admiration of the qualities of a person, and how we try to imitate those qualities by copying their behaviour.

Reflective mode is used to describe when a person gives effortful attention to a mental activity, and this is often associated with considered choice and concentration.

Relearning is when you relearn something that you had previously learned, and the process of relearning helps you to remember and retrieve.

Representativeness heuristic is when we judge something on the basis of how similar it is to something else.

Retention: learning has to be retained in the memory for future use.

Retrieval is the process whereby we remember and access our stored memories.

Reverse socialization is where parents acquire consumer skills from their children.

Reward power may be present when a person responds to the influence of the group and is rewarded in some way.

Rites of passage rituals are those rituals which mark a change in a person's social status.

Ritual refers to a symbolic and expressive activity, often comprising multiple behaviours which occur in a fixed sequence and are repeated over time.

Ritual artefacts are the objects and products that accompany or are consumed in a ritual setting.

Ritual audience are the people who are witness of or are involved in a ritual in some way.

Ritual performance roles refer to the way roles occupied by the various people involved in the ritual are performed according to a script.

Ritual script guides the use of the ritual artefacts—which artefacts to use, by whom, the sequence of use, and the types of comment that accompany the ritual.

Role schema contains shared representations, such as norms and cultural stereotypes about 'doing' a particular social role.

Sacred consumption is used to refer to objects and events that are set apart from normal activities, and are treated with some degree of respect or awe.

Salesmen (relating to opinion leaders) are the arch persuaders, who will not accept 'no' for an answer and are always looking for an opportunity to get their message across to someone else.

Salient beliefs are those beliefs that are most important to consumers.

Schemas are cognitive frameworks which are used to organize and interpret information.

Scientific approach in consumer behaviour emphasizes the objectivity of science and the consumer as a rational decision-maker.

Selective exposure is the active seeking and avoidance of stimuli.

Self-concept refers to the beliefs that a person holds about his/her attributes and how he/she evaluates those qualities.

Self-congruity refers to the extent to which a product image matches a consumer's self-image.

Self-gifts are a specific example of gift giving, where consumers purchase self-gifts as a way of regulating their behaviour.

Self-schema are thoughts and feelings you have about yourself, based on past experiences, especially those resulting from your own experience and the feedback you receive.

Semantic memory involves the structuring of specific records, facts, concepts, and knowledge about the world we live in.

Semiotics is concerned with exploring the links between signs and symbols and the meanings they signify and convey.

Separation is the point of detachment or separation from the original group or status held by the individual.

Sign or symbolic value is the symbolic meaning consumers attach to goods to construct and participate in the social world.

Similarity refers to how things that are similar to one another are perceived to be more related that those that are dissimilar.

Single-trait approach (to personality) is where the focus is on isolating the key trait of interest and how this impacts on consumption.

Situational involvement is involvement with a product class or brand dependent on some other event.

Situational self recognizes the self-concept as a dynamic entity, where different aspects of self are activated depending on the different situations the consumer is in.

Social power is the degree of influence an individual or organization has among their peers and within society as a whole.

Social risk is the personal and social risk that may arise from a purchase.

Social self sometimes referred to as the 'looking glass self', is how consumers believe they are seen by significant others.

Stimulus generalization occurs when a stimulus similar to a conditioned stimulus (CS) elicits a similar conditioned response.

Storage is how the encoded information is retained in the memory.

Subcultures are defined in terms of shared demographic characteristics (e.g. age, regionality, ethnicity) or in terms of shared consumption interests.

Subculture of consumption is defined as a group of consumers connected through a shared consumption activity.

Subjective norm construct represents a person's perceptions of specific significant others' preferences as to whether the person should or should not engage in the behaviour.

Sumptuary laws are laws that attempt to control and regulate permitted consumption activities.

Superego reflects the rules, values, and norms imposed by society, and serves as the person's conscience working to prevent the id from seeking selfish gratification.

Symbolic consumption is the tendency of consumers to rely and focus on the meanings attached to goods, beyond their physical properties.

Symbolic interactionism states that relationships with other people play a large part in forming the self.

Terminal values are our desired end states in life and preferred paths to achieving them, constituting the purposes and goals for which we believe human life should be lived.

Theory of cognitive dissonance is based on the belief that people need consistency or consonance between their behaviour and their attitudes.

Time risk is the risk embodied in the uncertainty regarding the time required to buy or learn to use the product.

Trait-based approach (to personality) regards personality as being the sum of a set of traits or qualities about a person, and these can be used to predict or explain consumption behaviour.

Transformative consumer research (TCR) refers to a stream of research that focuses on benefiting consumer welfare and quality of life across the world.

Uncertainty avoidance (UA) relates to the way that a cultural group feels about ambiguity, and the extent to which members of a culture avoid uncertainty (and accordingly avoid risk), or embrace risk (and uncertainty).

Use value is the value of a good to the consumer in terms of the satisfaction it provides.

Utilitarian function (of attitudes) stems from the idea that consumers seek maximum utility and value from their consumption.

Utilitarian reference group influence is when a person complies with perceived expectations of those with whom they socialize including family members and work colleagues.

VALS™ (acronym for Values and Lifestyle) is a trade-marked segmentation system, based on US adult consumers, where subjects are grouped into eight segments using the VALS™ questionnaire, which consists of questions around primary motivations and resources.

Value-expressive function (of attitudes) is concerned with the drive to express important aspects of the self, and linked to this, of the self that one aspires to be.

Value-expressive influence is when someone buys a particular brand to enhance their image and because they admire characteristics of people who use the brand.

Values are the deep-rooted and enduring beliefs or ideals about what is good and desirable and what is not.

Variable interval is when the reinforcement occurs at some unknown but consistent rate.

Variable schedules are where reinforcement is provided on an irregular basis.

Volitional control is a state where there are no internal or external factors preventing performance of the behaviour.

Wants are specific manifestations of motives and are linked to a specific goal object.

Weak ties act as a bridge between other different but strong social networks.

Weber's law suggests that the stronger the initial stimulus, the more difference would be required for a change to be noticed.

Weights are the levels of importance attached to object attributes.

Word of mouth (WOM) is an informal communication, either positive or negative, about goods, services, and sellers.

INDEX